BOOKS BY ALVIN MOSCOW

Collision Course:
 The Andrea Doria and the Stockholm

Tiger on a Leash

City at Sea

Merchants of Heroin

The Rockefeller Inheritance

The
Rockefeller Inheritance

The
Rockefeller Inheritance

ALVIN MOSCOW

1977
DOUBLEDAY & COMPANY, INC.
Garden City, New York

Library of Congress Cataloging in Publication Data

Moscow, Alvin
The Rockefeller inheritance.

Bibliography: p. 441
Includes index.
1. Rockefeller family   2. Capitalists and
financiers—United States—Biography. I. Title.
HG172.A2M67   322′.092′2 [B]
ISBN: 0-385-08087-5
Library of Congress Catalog Card Number 73-81445

*To the children—
theirs, mine, and yours*

PREFACE

This book is not authorized, subsidized, controlled, financed or backed in any way by the Rockefeller family or any organization with which they are associated.

This disclaimer seems necessary because so many people who have crossed my path in the years I have been working on this book have assumed that the Rockefellers, "with all their money," would be paying to have a biography written of them. Some expressed disbelief that any book could be written about the Rockefellers which they would not control—either by "buying" the writer, or by buying the publishing firm. Such opinions overestimate the authority of the Rockefellers and reveal a common misconception of their thinking and their way of life.

As long ago as 1932, Ivy Lee, then public relations adviser to the Rockefeller family, discussed, with a well-known and highly respected author, the writing of a definitive biography of John D. Rockefeller, Sr., "as that of a gigantic figure moving across the stage of modern life." The author expressed interest, but stipulated that he would require a guaranteed advance of $250,000 from the Rockefellers.

Ivy Lee set forth the project in a letter to John D. Rockefeller, Jr., who replied immediately: "To make any guarantee to a writer would subject us to criticism and him as well—us on the ground that we had sought to influence his findings, and him on the ground that he had allowed himself to be influenced in his interpretation of his subject by our views." Then he added: "A guarantee of the size proposed would leave no slightest question in the public mind that both the author and the family were guilty on the above grounds."

Ivy Lee relayed those sentiments to the author and received in reply:

16th April 1932.

Dear Mr. Ivy Lee,

Many thanks for your letter of
April 1st. I quite understand
the position and I am sure there
is no way out of it.

> With many thanks,
> Believe me,

> (s) Winston S. Churchill

The idea for this book was solely mine. Its financing came from the publisher as an advance against expected royalties and from the *Reader's Digest* for an option on the magazine serialization rights to the book. The idea originated in a one-paragraph story in the New York *Times* in the summer of 1967, reporting that the Rockefeller Brothers Fund, representing the five Rockefeller brothers, had made philanthropic contributions totaling $6,669,940 in 1966.

In my years as a news reporter in New York City, I had learned much of the many and widespread activities of the five Rockefeller brothers. Since those years, I had written a book on the disastrous and mystifying collision of two ocean liners and another on the agony encountered in the crash of an airliner. When I read the item in the *Times,* I was working on a book about the skulduggery involved in the illicit traffic in drugs around the world. I was determined that the book after that would not be about tragedy or crime; I was searching for a likely subject in a positive facet of American life. The paragraph in the New York *Times* struck a chord. The lives of the Rockefeller brothers, grandsons of perhaps the greatest of all the nineteenth-century business titans, and sons of perhaps the greatest individual philanthropist in America, might be my subject.

It was the time of the "flower children"—those young people who, questioning American values in the 1960s, chose not to work for a living, not to have families, not to take part in society. They were not poor, deprived or wronged youngsters demanding their civil, social and economic rights. They were, for the most part, the children of the affluent who had been educated, fed, sheltered and clothed better than perhaps any others in the world.

Affluence gave them a choice in how to lead their lives and they chose to find, somehow, their own way. They found drugs, communes, free love, the open road, violence, flowers, ecology—and more questions than answers.

In this context, a study of the lives of the Rockefeller family seemed apropos. Weren't they the most affluent of the affluent? Didn't each of the five brothers have the freest of choices in leading his life? Long before the advent of the "flower children," wasteful and dilettante progeny of successful fathers had become so common in American history that they were stereotypes. What made the Rockefeller brothers different? Had the Rockefeller parents—again, the most affluent of the affluent—faced the same problems in bringing up their children that other wealthy parents did, and that the affluent today do? How did they cope?

If the answers lay somewhere within the Protestant Ethic, which dominated American social mores for so long and which was now under attack by the young, then the Protestant Ethic as practiced by the Rockefellers deserved to be examined and described as significant for our times. If the Rockefeller brothers represented the Establishment, then the story of the Establishment, or at least their part in it, their aims, their activities, their accomplishments and their failures, deserved to be told.

These ideas I committed to paper and several months later, when I was free to start work on another book, I approached Steven David, public relations adviser to the Rockefeller family, with a proposal for a biography on the five brothers. The only way I could do the kind of biography I had in mind, I said, was with the cooperation of the five brothers. I wanted not only to describe what they were like and what they did, I wanted to know and to explain why they did what they did. I wanted to write a biography from within the subjects rather than a history of events involving them. So I would have to interview each of the brothers in depth, and as many of their associates as would see me. If I achieved my goal, the reader would come to know each of the Rockefeller brothers as an individual rather than as a name.

Mr. David approved the idea and suggested that I submit a brief memorandum which he would circulate among the five brothers. He warned me that while the idea might be good, the brothers preferred privacy to public display, and each of them was so busy that he might not be able to give me the time I would need. One thing was certain, however: only if all five brothers agreed to cooperate would I get a go-ahead. Any one of them could veto the project and the others would abide by the veto. That was my first lesson in how the family operated.

I sent the memorandum in February 1968, outlining the project and stipulating the minimum time I would need with each brother. Five affirmative replies were received by late March. My work began. The Rockefellers' cooperation was generous: their archives were open to me, their associates and friends ready to answer my questions and they themselves available and patient with my probing, although they were under no obligation to answer all of my questions. Their doubters and critics I found on my own. The pages which follow represent eight years of my researching, interviewing, writing, rewriting and thinking on the Rockefellers; and I found, at the end, this was not enough time and these are not enough pages to include all that could be said about the Rockefellers. They are very active and controversial men. Nevertheless, the selection of data, the organization of this book, the words, the interpretations and conclusions are wholly my own, for better or worse.

Alvin Moscow

CONTENTS

PREFACE   ix

PART ONE

1   A New Beginning
    "Isn't this all impressive?"   3

2   John D. Rockefeller, Jr.
    "I want you to do what you think is right."   18

3   Raising Affluent Children
    "To have given the world one clean, honest,
    God-fearing son . . ."   34

4   Growing up
    "Nelson took his punishment in his usual
    philosophical way . . ."   46

5   John D. Rockefeller
    "The business is yours!"   62

6   The Standard Oil Company
    "It's the figures that count."   72

7   Philanthropy
    "What a delightful habit you are forming!"   83

8   Stewardship
    "An extra 5 per cent . . ."   99

9   The Rockefeller Brothers
    "I have my fingers crossed . . ."   109

10 The Rockefeller Credo
    "There are certain fundamental and
    underlying things which do not change."   123

PART TWO

11 John 3rd
    "The man everyone would like to be as
    rich as."   137

12 *Nelson*
    "Looking back is a waste of time."   152

13 *Laurance*
    "What can I prove I am, besides having
    lots of money?"   176

14 *Winthrop*
    "Carefree, pleasant and meaningless days."   197

15 *David*
    "I sometimes think he's got electricity
    in his head."   213

PART THREE

16 *David*
    "The social responsibility of the
    capitalistic system . . ."   235

17 *Winthrop*
    "A victory even in defeat . . ."   267

18 *Laurance*
    "The people of the United States want
    a better environment and . . . they are
    ready to work for it."   299

19 *Nelson*
    "I am not standby equipment."   326

20 *John 3rd*
    "This is an exciting time to be alive."   377

21 *Rockefeller Power*
    "The blanket of happiness seems too short."   407

ACKNOWLEDGMENTS   438

BIBLIOGRAPHY   441

INDEX   443

ILLUSTRATIONS

1. *John D. Rockefeller*   Following page 54

2. *John D. Rockefeller, Jr.*   Following page 102

3. *John D. Rockefeller, Jr., later*   Following page 150

4. *John D. Rockefeller 3rd*   Following page 198

5. *Nelson A. Rockefeller*   Following page 246

6. *Laurance S. Rockefeller*   Following page 294

7. *Winthrop Rockefeller*   Following page 342

8. *David Rockefeller*   Following page 390

ILLUSTRATION ACKNOWLEDGMENTS

All photographs not otherwise credited below are courtesy of the Rockefeller Family Archives.

Grateful acknowledgment is made to the following for illustrations provided:

32: Rockefeller Center, Inc.
48, 86: Wide World Photos
51: NYT Pictures
57, 69, 70: Official White House Photographs
61: Courtesy of the National Broadcasting Company, Inc.
98, 105, 106, 109, 111, 112: Arthur Lavine, courtesy Chase Manhattan Bank
100: Chase Manhattan Corporation Archives
104, 107: Raymond Juschkus, courtesy Chase Manhattan Bank
113: CBS News Photo

"*I believe that every right implies a responsibility; every opportunity, an obligation; every possession, a duty.*"

John D. Rockefeller, Jr.

Part One

1

A New Beginning

"Isn't this all impressive?"

In the beginning, of course, there was John D. Rockefeller, who was in the right place at the right time while an industrial revolution swept a still-young nation. Building a single enterprise which he called the Standard Oil Company to the peak of capitalistic success, he achieved monopolistic control of a national resource and amassed the largest personal fortune in the history of the country. America's first billionaire, he became the very symbol of the relatively few men who controlled American industrial empires, and as the richest of them, he soon became, not surprisingly, the most hated of them all.

His only son focused his talents in another direction, toward what he realized were the needs of his own time. At the turn of the century John D. Rockefeller, Jr., turned away largely from business affairs deliberately to devote his life to philanthropy and what he liked to call "the well-being of mankind." He developed a skill at giving away money that rivaled his father's at making it, and he established persisting standards for the prudent disbursement of personal and corporate wealth. He left an imprint on American life as deep, if not so visible, as his father had a generation before him.

For the third generation—five sons and a daughter—the Rockefeller inheritance constituted more than wealth and fame. With the name came a bloodline that promised health, stamina and longevity. It also provided a set of values that included a missionary zeal for the conduct of one's life. For the third generation of Rockefellers, the bare-knuckle business competitiveness of their grandfather's day was now prohibited by law; the social and medical needs of the people, as seen by their father, had been recognized as the responsibility, at least in part, of the government. Still, there was no dearth of old problems and new dilemmas, and the third generation of Rockefellers took them as personal challenges. Each of the sons of John D. Rockefeller, Jr., became an activist in his own fashion, but despite their impact and influence, not one person in a hundred today can name all five brothers. Not one in a thousand knows of the existence of their sister. Not one in ten thousand, despite television, would recognize more than one, or possibly two, of them in an elevator. The reason is simple: the Rockefeller style of life—when political or economic pressures do not obtrude.

They have lived well for three generations, but without ever flaunting their wealth, privilege or position. Unostentation is the family style. The five brothers and their sister have spread out to houses, hotels, ranches, farms and urban duplexes that they own from Maine to the Caribbean. Yet the true family homestead has always remained the place their grandfather and father called home, and where they grew up. It is a 3,487-acre estate—a six-square-mile principality—overlooking the Hudson River in the unincorporated village of Pocantico Hills, some thirty miles north of New York City. Despite its size, it is so cleverly hidden from view that the ordinary passer-by would never realize it was there.

The family's "place of business" is equally hidden in the anonymity of a seventy-story office tower in New York City. It is referred to merely as Room 5600. The name Rockefeller does not appear on its doors or its letterheads. The office stationery simply states: Room 5600, 30 Rockefeller Plaza, New York, New York. You know that Room 5600 in the RCA Building is the office of the Rockefeller family or you don't. Room 5600 encompasses all of the fifty-sixth and the fifty-fifth floors and more than half of the fifty-fourth floor of the seventy-story RCA Building. The Rockefellers do not rent the space. They own it, as they own the entire building and the entire complex of buildings—the largest of its kind in the world—known as Rockefeller Center. (The land itself, however, belongs to Columbia University.)

It was to Room 5600 that the five grandsons of the founder of the Standard Oil Company returned in late 1945 and early 1946. They were in the prime of their lives. They had served their country in time of war and like other veterans—of whom they were the richest and most powerful— they were eager to resume their careers. It was a turning point for the Rockefellers, as it was for the nation, which entered the postwar era as the richest, most powerful country in the world.

Of the great wealth amid which the five brothers had grown up, their father had explained late in life: "I was born into it and there was nothing I could do about it. It was there like air or food or any other element. The only question with wealth is what you do with it. It can be used for evil purposes or it can be an instrumentality for constructive social living." John D. Rockefeller, Jr., according to his biographer, Raymond B. Fosdick, had suffered—particularly during his early years—from "a stifling kind of wealth." Fosdick wrote: "When he went to college he was tagged the son of the richest man in the world. Entering his father's office, he was greeted with the public skepticism reserved for those whose success, if any, is unrelated to observable talent. He learned the bitter taste of sycophancy and the disillusionment of friendships based on selfish expectation. He was subjected to the hollow deference paid to wealth and the obsequiousness of timid minds. He was isolated from many of the contacts which often bring balance and perspective."

From that, John D. Rockefeller, Jr., tried to protect his children. He was only partly successful. As Rockefellers, the five grandsons of John D. would have to live their lives in a fishbowl: they were different and set apart from other men—until the Second World War freed them, at least for a time, from the ubiquitous protection of their family name, wealth and power. Each of them recognized the opportunity and enlisted in governmental service—military or civilian—to prove to himself as much as to others his own value as a man. For the first time in his life, each could go it alone. They enjoyed the taste of individual challenge and achievement, and on their return home they intended to continue savoring it. David Rockefeller, who had only completed his schooling before his wartime service, wanted to discover who David was and what he could do. Winthrop needed to assert the Winthrop in him. Laurance, older, had some fairly definite ideas about the life he wanted to pursue. Nelson already had made a beginning on several careers and was impetuously eager to pursue all of them. John 3rd, perhaps because of his name, suffered the greatest identity crisis of all of them.

In 1946, John 3rd was forty years old, six-foot-two, slender and slightly stooped, courteous and even courtly, but painfully shy, earnest and modest about his attributes. Married for eight years and father of a son and three daughters, he looked most like his grandfather, but was closest in character to his father. He was the eldest of the brothers and on his shoulders and psyche the responsibilities and obligations of the family lay most heavily. More than any of his brothers, he was expected to succeed his father in directing the family endeavors toward the "well-being of mankind throughout the world"—the charter purpose of the Rockefeller Foundation. But at age forty, he had never done anything totally on his own. He had served as an apprentice among men of his father's age, heir apparent always subject to suspicion by some and indulgence by others. Returned from the Navy a lieutenant commander, after three years' service in the Naval Military Government division of the Office of the Chief of Naval Operations, John 3rd wanted desperately to free himself from some of the obligations which had burdened him before the war.

As much as any of his brothers, John 3rd was strong-willed and eager to make his own mark. But his ascetic demeanor concealed from all but those who knew him well his inner strength, determination—and ego. He had been indoctrinated as a boy to conceal such qualities.

Nelson Aldrich Rockefeller was the shortest of the brothers, standing five-foot-ten, but he was stocky and strong, and the most aggressive. At thirty-eight, with an open, square face and broad unlined forehead, he resembled his father more than did the others. But he seemed to have inherited the dominant genes of his maternal grandfather, Nelson W. Aldrich, a dynamic, free-swinging man who had risen from farm boy to wealth and to power as the U.S. senator from Rhode Island and Republican leader of the Senate. Nelson, the antithesis of brother John, was an exuberant optimist, convinced from the time he was seven years old that anything he set his mind to, he could accomplish quickly. In a family dedicated to caution, Nelson was the plunger: after college, marriage and a honeymoon around the world, he had pitched avidly into New York real estate, undaunted by an economic depression. He had hastened into the world of art. He had discovered the wants of Latin America, and at thirty-two, he had dived into the wartime maelstrom of Washington bureaucracy as Coordinator of Inter-American Affairs, answerable only to the President. At the war's end, Nelson returned home in more of a hurry to get things done than he had been before he left.

Laurance Spelman Rockefeller, two years younger and two inches taller than Nelson, was philosophically, as well as chronologically, the middle brother; he had become the centerboard of the third generation, the stabilizing influence to whom the others turned in need. He had been named for his grandmother, Laura Spelman Rockefeller, but, lean and wiry, with a long thin face, he closely resembled in appearance and mentality his paternal grandfather. His long silences, his demeanor, his flashes of wry humor and the plain common sense of his decisions reminded oldsters around Room 5600 of stories about old John D. He was the business mind, methodical, exploratory and adventuresome: he had bought, back in 1937, old John D.'s seat on the New York Stock Exchange. A mystique always hovered about him. He showed a poker face to outsiders and explained nothing: he was difficult to appraise and even today, despite his nationwide activities, he is probably the least-known, the least recognizable of the Rockefeller brothers.

Winthrop was the family's maverick. Named for an Aldrich uncle, he was a giant of a man at thirty-four—six-foot-three, big-boned and close to two hundred pounds, open, gregarious. The only unmarried brother, he wore his heart on his sleeve. Consequently, he was the most vulnerable. He had labored in Texas oil fields as a roustabout, had enlisted in the Army as a private ten months before Pearl Harbor, had become a sergeant, then a lieutenant. He had led infantrymen in jungle combat at Guam,

Leyte and Okinawa. He returned to the Rockefeller fold a lieutenant colonel with a Purple Heart and two Oak Leaf Clusters to his Bronze Star.

David, at thirty-one, almost ten years younger than his brother John,
had been brought up with all the advantages and the disadvantages of the
baby in the family. Roly-poly and non-athletic as a child, too young to
compete with his brothers, but competitive nonetheless, David had turned
to books and the study of beetles and just about everything else he encountered—which led him to Harvard, the London School of Economics
and a doctorate in economics at the University of Chicago. Still considering himself untested, he had enlisted in the Army as a private and had
served in the O.S.S. in North Africa and in France. Returning home a captain, he was determined to find his own place in the postwar Rockefeller
firmament—baby of the family or not.

It is hardly surprising that the arrival of five such dynamic, headstrong, eager young men, each with his own ideas and visions, would dis-
compose the sedate routine established by their father. They shocked the
old-timers in Room 5600 with their pace, their questions, their demands,
their needs. Where the staff had had to answer to one man before, it now
had to answer to six. "They descended on the office like an avalanche,"
mused a senior adviser long afterward. "It was chaos by Rockefeller standards."

The offices were much as the young Rockefellers had left them.
Black-skinned Howard Douglas, who had been with their father as long as
any of them could remember, was still sitting at the reception desk reading the Bible when they returned. The center corridor running the length
of the fifty-sixth floor still was carpeted in red, the walls were an institutional beige and green, the leather chairs and couches deep red or black.
Opening on the center corridor, large offices for the senior staff and
smaller ones for secretaries and assistants—all were furnished plainly,
heavily and serviceably, like a bank of the thirties. Austerity prevailed over
luxury.

Their father's office at the southwest corner of the fifty-sixth floor
reflected the inner man as much as the fourteen-building complex of
Rockefeller Center itself represented his most spectacular achievement. As
the Center's sole sponsor, who had invested more than $125 million dur-
ing the depths of the depression, John D., Jr., had closely supervised the
design, the architecture and the construction of the complex, and the result reflected what he had wanted. The clean lines of the buildings and
the open spaces between them, with center mall and gardens in the heart
of a crowded city, were not to the 1930s taste for the Gothic and the baroque. As it was being built, the Center was criticized by architects as bar-
ren, and by economists as uneconomical. Rockefeller Jr. went on building
to his own taste. In time, others saw what he had seen, and the simple,
functional, eye-pleasing appearance of Rockefeller Center soon set a style

for business architecture throughout the United States. But his own office, where he worked and thought and planned long hours every day, and which few other people ever saw, was of another era. It might have been the chamber of an abbot in a royally favored seventeenth-century monastery.

It had been his wife, as usual, who had induced him to do something for himself in keeping with his station in life. His office in the old Standard Oil Building at 26 Broadway had been his father's and was in 1923 still furnished with a rolltop desk, a plain table and a few leather-upholstered wood chairs, and the radiators were coverless. "This is a terrible office and there's no comfortable place to sit down," Mrs. Rockefeller told him when he was fifty years old. "Really, John, you are a Rockefeller and you should have a better office than this," she said.

Rockefeller, who devoted his spare hours to beautiful things, but demanded only utility of a place to work, allowed his wife to lead him to Charles of London, an antique dealer. There he found carefully preserved dark oak paneling from an old English manor house. A large Jacobean refectory table, intricately carved and inscribed 1632, when James I was King of England, would make the centerpiece of his office. A smaller Elizabethan table, seven by three feet, would serve as his desk at one end of the room. A carved oak mantelpiece, an overmantel and a working fireplace would cover the opposite wall. Two Charles I chaise longues, six Charles II straight-back chairs and a couple of Cromwellian chairs would provide more than enough seating for any meeting. A Charles I oak credence, which had held the bread and wine for communions in the 1640s, now would hold a small glass-enclosed bookcase.

That had been his office at 26 Broadway after his wife had had her say, and he had moved it intact to the RCA Building when it opened in 1933. Charles of London merely supplied some more antique oak paneling for a small waiting room outside the office.

The inner sanctum was always monastically quiet and as dim as three o'clock of a gray winter afternoon—severe and perfect for a self-disciplined man who wished to gain perspective from the past, contemplate the future and seek within himself the answers to the present problems of the outside world.

The power of the Rockefeller fortune abided in one man, answerable only to himself and his conscience. In the fifty years since his college days, John D. Rockefeller, Jr.—first as an aide to his father and then on his own —had disbursed more than $822 million for the betterment, as he saw it, of his fellow men. At age seventy-two, when his five sons returned from the war, he was still at it. "Giving is the secret of a healthy life," he once said, "not necessarily money, but whatever a man has of encouragement and sympathy and understanding." Since he had inherited, rather than earned, his fortune, and because it was so much greater than he or any other man could possibly consume, he considered himself its steward, rather than its owner.

Of moderate height and slight stature, his silvery white hair carefully parted just off center, his silver-rimmed, old-fashioned spectacles high on the bridge of his nose, John D. Rockefeller, Jr., appeared a nice, genial and gracious old man. Age had thinned and elongated his face, and people now could discern a resemblance to his father. But his hands retained the strength of his younger days and outdoor life: they were thick and muscular as a lumberjack's.

He was not a simple man. Shy, modest, retiring, soft-spoken, he was gracious to all with whom he came in contact. People in all stations in life stood in awe of him and their awe embarrassed him. Beneath this exterior, however, he was a stern, self-disciplined Baptist who took his ethics directly from the Bible, viewed alternatives as black or white and strove constantly to "do the right thing." He was a perfectionist. His mind could encompass vast projects and broad spectra, as it did in so many of his undertakings, and yet his perfectionism demanded painstaking attention to minor details. He thought incisively but worked slowly, methodically and carefully toward decisions. His commitments, philanthropic and economic, were long-ranging, carefully investigated from the start and followed through to the finish. In the Rockefeller offices there were no day-to-day crises, no panic buttons. Calm, reserve and dignity prevailed in Room 5600.

The staff numbered no more than forty, and each one of them knew he or she was there to serve the boss. When he walked through the office, secretaries straightened up at their typewriters. Word preceded him when he went from one place to another. No one had to be told what to do.

Rockefeller Jr.'s method of operation was based on what he had learned from his father, and perfected. He made no secret of the Rockefeller formula for success: in fact, he liked to spread the word.

"The secret of sensible living, of the sane solution of all problems, whether personal or group problems, is simplicity," he told more than one interviewer. "That is the secret of success: avoidance of waste in effort, motion, money."

On his desk, he kept a six-slot leather letter rack. All he had to do, he once explained with straight face, but tongue in cheek, was to go through all the papers and problems which reached his desk and put them in one of the six slots for one of his six associates to handle.

There was no formal organization to his staff. Aside from outside consultants hired for particular projects, he needed no more than six senior advisers for his multitudinous projects. Advisers were considered and called associates, not assistants, and all were theoretically equal in their personal relationships to Mr. Rockefeller. Some, though, were more equal than others. Thomas M. Debevoise, an attorney and personal friend of

Rockefeller Jr.'s since their college days, served as his legal counsel for more than thirty years. His advice was sought on virtually every undertaking. He was the only one in the office who addressed Mr. Rockefeller as John. In the office, he was addressed as T.M.D., but out of earshot he was referred to as "the Prime Minister."

The Rockefeller banking, investment and business affairs were directed by two men: Bertram P. Cutler, who had entered the office as a stenographer with a high school education; and Barton P. Turnbull, an investment specialist, somewhat Mr. Cutler's junior in years and experience. Their vast fiscal responsibilities were centralized in the Chase National Bank, the Merchants Fire Assurance Company and no more than five categories of blue chip stocks, with U. S. Steel and Standard Oil high on the list, of course. Rockefeller Jr.'s policy of conserving and using his fortune to the best advantage, rather than expanding it, made their jobs relatively easy. Thus, while they kept close watch on the stock and bond markets, the two men were not involved in daily trading; and it took little of their time to provide the boss with pertinent information on the range and state of his investments. In any case, business affairs were secondary to his philanthropic and cultural interests. Though most of the world believed he and his family still owned the various Standard Oil companies, he himself had taken care to limit his investments in them to minority interests: he was not represented on the board of directors or in the administration of any of the Standard Oil companies. But his prestige did surpass that of other stockholders: as each New Year's Eve rolled around, the chairman of the board of Standard Oil of New Jersey would pay a call on the son of the founder.

"Mr. Rockefeller, how are you?"

"Just fine, and you?"

"I want to wish you and your family a very happy New Year, sir."

"Thank you. And a very happy New Year to you and your family. Please do give my warmest regards to your associates at Standard."

"Thank you, Mr. Rockefeller."

The accounting and tax problems of the Rockefellers were entrusted to Philip F. Keebler, whose office and small staff were tucked away at the opposite end of the floor from Rockefeller's office.

Close by Mr. Rockefeller's office was that of Arthur Packard, overseer of and adviser on all of Rockefeller Jr.'s philanthropic interests, except the Rockefeller Foundation, which operated independently and with its own staff, but in Room 5600.

Kenneth Chorley, the only associate with true girth to his figure and the mirth to match it, was the outdoor man of the office, the expert on Mr. Rockefeller's extensive conservation interests, including the restoration of Colonial Williamsburg and the historical landmarks of the lower Hudson Valley.

"Never come in just to report to me," Mr. Rockefeller instructed one new man at the start of what proved to be a thirty-year stint in the office. "If you need my help, let me know, by all means, but I will assume everything is going along satisfactorily unless you tell me to the contrary."

Mr. Rockefeller seldom instructed his associates. He went over a project or a problem with them at the beginning and, in consultation, decided what should be done. Then he left it to his associate to do it—and backed the man's decisions. If he ever lost faith in the man's judgment or ability, the man would be eased out of the establishment.

Rockefeller Jr.'s last secretary, Miss Janet Warfield (few in the office were aware of her married name), worked in the small waiting room attached to the inner sanctum. She took his dictation, typed his letters, posted his schedules and appointments and zealously guarded his privacy. She served as "Mother Superior" to the office staff. In the office, she was known as the watchdog.

Another watchdog, whose seniority matched that of Rockefeller himself, was Robert Gumbel: a small, birdlike man, still quick and tireless in his seventies, he seemed to handle everything that the others did not—travel arrangements, personnel at the Pocantico Hills estate, personal insurance matters, personal loans, church affairs. Most offices would rank him as executive assistant, but Bob Gumbel insisted he still was what he had been hired as: the office boy. He had joined Mr. Rockefeller when both were in their twenties doing church work and had devoted his life to his employer. Facts, figures and folklore of Rockefeller's activities were stored for instant recall in Mr. Gumbel's head or in his giant rolltop desk.

Each new employee was taken into Mr. Gumbel's office for indoctrination. His methods were so old-fashioned that they bemused postwar newcomers. One young investment counselor who accepted Mr. Gumbel's invitation to tea was astonished to see the old man take out from the rolltop desk a pad of asbestos, a hot plate, a teakettle, cups and saucers and two cookies. The "tea" filled the better part of an hour.

The sedate decorum of the Rockefeller offices, exemplified by Bob Gumbel's tea, tended to subdue even the biggest men to enter them. But one man who came unawed and impatient, and remained so, was Nelson A. Rockefeller. He arrived from Washington with a platoon of his own associates that included Frank Jamieson, Martha Dalrymple, Victor Borella, Lawrence Levy and Louise Boyer. He wanted to "get organized" for the battles he foresaw he would have to fight to accomplish for Latin America as a private citizen (but a Rockefeller) what he could not do as U. S. Coordinator of Inter-American Affairs or as Assistant Secretary of State. He was ready to take over as the chief executive officer of Rockefeller Center. He was eager to return to the Museum of Modern Art, where from the start he had been a significant influence. He was interested in war relief work. There were the problems of money management and personal investments. There were the postwar problems of New York City, the United States, the United Nations, the whole world. Nelson Rockefeller was gleefully ready to take them all on.

His brothers, too, returned with their associates, their problems, their interests.

"Let's get organized" became Nelson's familiar battle cry at 5600 as the five brothers sought to readjust to civilian life.

There was also an immediate personal problem. The small offices which had been theirs before the war had long since been taken over by others. A shifting of personnel, desks and files scattered them in temporary quarters, unsatisfactory to them and to those they had displaced. Even the "Prime Minister" had to change offices to make room for John D. 3rd near his father. The Rockefeller Foundation staff was obliged to move from the fifty-sixth to the fifty-fifth floor to accommodate Nelson, Laurance, Winthrop and David. The brothers would need space for their own staffs, their files, their books. Which brought up the question: should the brothers centralize and share their facilities and staff or should each work separately? The answer, of course, depended upon what each of them decided to do in the years ahead. How should they handle their investment portfolios? Hundreds, and often thousands, of personal appeals for help flowed into the office to each of the brothers—particularly when any of their names appeared in the newspapers. How should they be handled—by each one individually or by the family as a group?

The overriding issue, simplified to be sure, was: what did each of them really want to do with the rest of his life? Each of them seemingly had as free a choice as any man in America, and perhaps the world. Trust funds had made them millionaires, and they possessed more money than they could use up in a lifetime, so they did not have to work. But their father had told them, "I can conceive of nothing so unpleasant as a life devoted to pleasure," and each had agreed.

Yet even if they wanted to, they could not amass as great a fortune as their grandfather had, or dominate a national industry. That era had passed. Neither could they establish and endow such mammoth philanthropic enterprises as their father had devised: they did not have that much money and that era, too, had passed.

"Anyway, we never wanted to walk with little steps in the big footprints of those two generations," Laurance explained. "I believe that all of us have felt since we were in college that there was something we could do to help meet the challenge of our own time. One way or another, all of us have worked at that idea."

Each of them had worked at that challenge individually, for if no one wanted to walk in the big footprints of his father or grandfather, he certainly did not want to follow in the shadow of a mere brother. The Rockefeller brothers had always been highly competitive, perhaps genetically so. But they had also been instructed since childhood not to take unfair advantage of others less fortunately endowed than themselves. So they could compete, no holds barred, only against each other. In deciding what they wanted to do in the future, each had to consider: how will it affect the family and the family name? And will it conflict with what one of my brothers plans to do?

To those who worked with them or for them at 5600, "it was not an easy time."

The five men thrashed out the problems at what came to be called "Brothers' Meetings."

These Brothers' Meetings, as distinguished from ordinary conferences with or without others, were inviolable. Their sister, Abby, attended when her interests were involved in a specific issue. No one else ever. Here the brothers could speak their minds, test ideas, ask for help, take one another to task, demand and give explanations and, finally, reach decisions—all without any of it going beyond the doors of the room. Because he was the youngest, David kept the written minutes. For the same reason, he spoke first in discussion. The brothers ranked themselves in order of seniority, like Supreme Court justices in conference. However, there was no Chief Brother.

John, the eldest, did not want the title or the authority; and Nelson, although the most family-conscious, did not dare to claim leadership. Unlike the Supreme Court, the majority did not rule among the brothers. Each was a free agent. No one had to go along with what his brothers thought. To the outside world they would reveal only a united front, but it was only with unanimity that all five would speak or act in public in the family name. Consequently, the process of reaching unanimous decisions most often involved a great deal of verbal, moral and quid pro quo suasion. Conflicts arose at virtually every meeting, for each brother had a strong ego and said what he thought—loud and clear. (When their voices resounded through the closed door, it was a point of honor among the office staff to keep moving and not stop to listen.)

One subject of long discussion was: should they go it alone as individuals or act in concert as the third generation of the Rockefeller family? Could they do both? Each had his own aims and ambitions. By virtue of the income from trusts that their father had established as far back as 1934, each brother, in effect, was the head of a small financial empire, although they did not think in those terms. But the vast family empire, whose purse strings were held by their father, dwarfed their own individual wealth. As princes of that empire—although, again, they did not think in those terms—they felt an obligation to act and operate as part of the whole. If they tried both to go it alone—to a point—and to act as a family, then what would happen in the event of a conflict of interest? Should the family have veto power over the personal desires or ambitions or projects of any one of them? How could they avoid conflicts of interest among themselves? In any given situation, what is fair, what is just, what is right?

The decisions most often came about gradually after a number of meetings and arguments. Many of the agreements were informal and tacit; for, despite the heat of their discussions, the brothers never, it appears, reached the point of acrimony, and a common concern for each other settled many a conflict.

Some of the decisions that would affect their lives and careers were hammered out one stroke at a time over a number of years. John D. Rockefeller, Jr., avoided taking part in the process. He had told his sons, as they matured, that each must choose for himself what college to attend, what career to pursue, what style of life to adopt. But—and it was an awesome but—he also had told them that he expected each of them to lead a decent and useful life, and that only to the extent that each proved himself would he be entrusted with the family wealth.

The brothers had heard him expound again and again on the responsibility of wealth and the even greater responsibility of inherited wealth. He had even voiced his opinion publicly—a rare occurrence—when he told an interviewer: "I say to them with perfect frankness that wealth will go only to those of them who show fitness and ability to handle it wisely; that neither their father nor grandfather will leave them money unless they give evidence that they know how to lead decent, useful lives, and that they will make good use of any property."

Now that his sons were back from the war, John D. Rockefeller, Jr., began his own review of his assets and commitments. He was past seventy and he considered it appropriate to begin easing his heavy workload. He expected his sons to take over the key philanthropic enterprises to which he had devoted so much of his life.

At the same time, he began revising his will—a document which would fill fifty-nine pages. But more important was the distribution before anticipation of death, as the Internal Revenue Service puts it, to minimize estate taxes. For that, he had to review meticulously his philanthropic commitments—and he was currently supporting close to one hundred causes. Senior associates provided information and advice, but he himself made the judgments—comparing organizations on the bases of the financial help already bestowed, their purposes and the sums they needed currently and would need in the future to fulfill those purposes; and then, finally, his moral commitment to each.

Aside from the trust funds he had established in 1934, which were controlled by trustees at the Chase National Bank, John D., Jr., had not yet released any capital to any of his sons. They got only the income from those trusts and the income, substantial as it was, did not really give them the financial clout associated with the Rockefeller name. The brothers were all too aware of the disparity between their reputed power and the reality.

Each brother, for instance, had been appointed by their father to the board of directors of Rockefeller Center, Inc., the corporation that nominally owned the complex of buildings: Nelson, president before the war, had been made chairman of the board and chief executive officer in 1945. Nevertheless, they had to ask their father's permission to redesign a portion of the fifty-sixth floor to provide office space for themselves. There was no misunderstanding, despite their titles, about who actually owned Rockefeller Center. The corporation, which had run the complex at a loss during the depression years, was just about breaking even operationally in the postwar business upswing. However, breaking even did not include payment on $74 million in notes—representing loans to help cover the $125 million building costs—held by John D. Rockefeller, Jr.

It was Nelson who presented to John D., Jr., the brothers' proposal to model the east wing of the fifty-sixth floor to provide office space for four of them and their staffs. John 3rd, who was working closely with his father on philanthropic activities, preferred an office near his father's in the west wing. Nelson then submitted preliminary plans and cost estimates prepared by Wallace K. Harrison, who had been one of the three chief architects to design Rockefeller Center and who had become a close friend and confidant of Nelson's.

With his father's approval, Nelson swung into action gustily. The offices would be modern, streamlined and functional, and furnished in Scandinavian modern: similar in design and size, the offices would be made individually distinctive by their artwork.

Nelson supervised the transformation with delight and pride. As plans were changed and costs rose above estimates he wrote notes of apology to his father, confident that the result would justify the time, effort and money.

The furious activity of the five young Rockefellers hit the staid offices like a shot of Adrenalin. The ringing of telephones, the stream of visitors, the clacking of typewriters, the influx of new office help multiplied by far more than five times.

Then the brothers were stricken by the word that their father had decided to give away Rockefeller Center. His decision was still a secret. He had not even informed his sons of it, and they learned of it piecemeal from one of his advisers. There seemed little they could do about it. Laurance thought it would have been presumptuous of them to remonstrate. They knew their father made his decisions after much deliberation and that, once reached, they were seldom, if ever, changed.

Their father had decided, the brothers learned, to give the $74 million in notes the corporation owed him to the Rockefeller Institute for Medical Research. It would provide the Institute with income and capital to continue its work in perpetuity. The Institute, established in 1901–3, had been the first of the philanthropic institutions endowed by their grandfather. Their father, the Institute's first president and first chairman of the board, considered it the most significant and important of all the family-founded philanthropies. That the brothers knew. But still, they had always assumed that their father would leave Rockefeller Center to them. It was their place of business, as well as their father's most visible achievement.

It was Nelson, after recovering from the initial shock, who decided to approach his father on the subject. His carefully chosen words expressed his brothers' and his own bewilderment at the decision.

John D. Rockefeller, Jr., listened patiently and said: "I'll think about it, Nelson."

In thinking about it, and about the whole "final disposition" of his estate, he no doubt recalled the advice his first mentor had given to his own father. When John D., Jr., had just emerged from Brown University, his father had engaged Frederick T. Gates, a Baptist minister, as an adviser on philanthropic activities. John Jr. had served his own apprenticeship in philanthropy under Gates. He would have good reason to remember Gates's advice to John D., Sr., given after Gates had been permitted to go over the books and records of the richest man in the world. Gates had said: "Your fortune is rolling up, rolling up like an avalanche—you must distribute it faster than it grows! If you do not, it will crush you and your children and your children's children."

It was with a bemused air that John Jr. allowed Nelson to lead him around his sons' brand-new offices in the east wing of 5600: he had refused to enter the east wing until the remodeling had been completed. Two corridors, slightly curved rather than straight, ran from the central elevators to a walnut-paneled waiting room at the east end. Machinery serving the floor had been walled in out of sight in the center, and the office suites off the outside walls were hidden by doors flush with the walls. The institutional colors of the old offices had vanished: instead, the interior walls were covered with warm brown pebbled vinyl, and the exterior walls paneled in textured off white—highlighted with modern prints of modest size, but vivid lines.

The brothers' offices were identical in size, twenty by sixteen feet. Nelson's, at the northeast corner of the building, had a view of Central Park and the East River; Laurance's, at the southeast corner, a vista of the Empire State Building in the foreground and—on a clear day—the towers of Wall Street. Winthrop's office was farther along on the north side, near the middle of the corridor, and David's was opposite on the south side of the east wing. Each of the brothers had adjoining offices for his senior staff and a small, rather cramped space for secretaries.

Nelson turned to his father at the end of the guided tour, which he had conducted with his characteristic enthusiasm, and asked, "Gee, Pa, isn't this all impressive?"

His father looked at him quizzically for a moment, and then softly replied, "Nelson, whom are we trying to impress?"

2

John D. Rockefeller, Jr.

"I want you to do what you think is right."

John D. Rockefeller, Jr., was a profoundly serious and religious man with a deep sense of humility and obligation. Of the vast Rockefeller fortune, he considered himself merely the custodian or the steward. Born to that fortune through no merit or fault of his own, he thought of himself as merely the vessel through which the fortune would pass as it was employed for the greatest good possible for the greatest number of people it could serve.

The idea of doing anything to impress anyone was anathema to him. An inner-directed man, he searched his conscience, his ethics and his reading of the Bible daily to find the best answer to that relentless question: "What is the right thing to do?" Once that was determined, the next question was simply: "What is the best way to do it?"

His apprenticeship in life, in business and in philanthropy was served under two great masters: his father and his father's chief aide of his later years, Frederick T. Gates, who not only advised on philanthropic matters but also adroitly handled some of the elder Rockefeller's investment ventures outside the oil industry. Upon graduating from Brown University in 1897, John Jr. went to work in his father's office at 26 Broadway, the headquarters for Standard Oil in New York City, where at twenty-three years of age and at a salary of $10,000 a year he told his father he thought he was being overpaid. His position was assistant to his father. Actually, he worked under the tutelage of Gates. His father had "retired" from Standard Oil, in the sense that he had stopped coming into the office daily, three years earlier at the age of fifty-five. He worked from their home in Pocantico Hills, devoting his attention to his outside investments. The principal one of these was his purchase of various parcels of land in the Mesabi iron ore range in Minnesota.

Upon Gates's advice, the oil magnate had chosen to invest heavily in the ore range, rather than pull out entirely. At the time the Mesabi iron ore was considered practically worthless, being too fine a grade for use in making steel, too far from the steel mills of Pittsburgh and without the necessary transportation needed to bring it to market. John Jr. joined Gates in overseeing this investment. As for Rockefeller Sr., he passed final judgment on the investment and philanthropic advice given to him by Frederick Gates, abetted by John Jr. But that left him plenty of time to tend to his landscaping and to perfect his golf game on the nine-hole course he had developed behind the main house.

In 1901, when J. P. Morgan, the renowned financier, and his associates had bought out Andrew Carnegie's vast steel plant as part of his plan to amalgamate the largest steel companies in the country into one giant, the United States Steel Corporation, Morgan then turned his eye on the Rockefeller holdings. By then the Mesabi range was recognized for what it truly was, the greatest source of iron, the raw material of steel, in the nation. Rockefeller Sr., then sixty-one, wanted to sell. He had bought his Mesabi shares, built a fleet of ore boats, established his ore market, all to protect his original investment. But what Morgan and his associates feared, as Carnegie had before him, was that John D. Rockefeller, with his ten to fifteen millions of dollars in annual income from the oil business, might decide himself to go into the steel manufacturing business.

Early negotiations were carried on through intermediaries because, to put it simply, the two men did not like each other. As historian Allan Nevins explained: "By nature, he [Morgan] was arrogant and imperious, anxious always to play a dominating role, and unwilling to admit the equality of any contemporary figure," and "For his part, Rockefeller, austere, self contained, and coldly averse to public gaze, disliked Morgan's ways: his regal pose, his huge expenditures on his yacht, art treasures, and private library, his versatile interests, his lordly glittering magnificence. It was the Puritan against the Medicean prince, each incapable of understanding the other."

Mr. Rockefeller had met Morgan on only one occasion before the Mesabi negotiations and he described the meeting himself: "We had a few pleasant words. But I could see that Mr. Morgan was very much . . . well, like Mr. Morgan; very haughty, very much inclined to look down on other men. *I looked at him.* For my part, I have never been able to see why any man should have such a high and mighty feeling about himself."

When the mogul of finance called upon the mogul of oil to discuss Mesabi iron ore, Rockefeller informed Morgan that John Jr. and Frederick Gates were in charge of his investments and he would have to see them.

This set the stage for a business exchange which delighted the elder Rockefeller as a father.

John D. Rockefeller, Jr., at age twenty-seven, was ushered into the office of John Pierpont Morgan, elderly, stern and domineering. Morgan at first took no notice, went on talking with an associate, and then, when the polite introduction was made, Morgan glared at the young, frail-looking Rockefeller and thundered, "Well, what's your price?"

Young Rockefeller stared back. "Mr. Morgan," he replied, "I think there must be some mistake. I did not come here to sell. I understood you wished to buy."

Silence ensued. A moment, two moments passed, and then Morgan changed his tone, whereupon John Jr. suggested, "If you are really interested in buying the properties, isn't it wise to find some man competent to advise you on their value?"

It was agreed finally that Henry C. Frick, a close associate of Andrew Carnegie's, would act as a neutral adviser on setting the sale price. When John Jr. described the meeting in a letter to his parents, then visiting Cleveland, his mother wrote back: "When Father read your letter aloud, he exclaimed, 'Great Caesar, but John is a trump!' . . . Are we a bit proud, as parents, of our boy!"

Five million dollars separated the parties, but in the end Morgan acceded to the sales price set by the Rockefellers: $80 million for the Mesabi properties, half of it in preferred and half in common stock of the new United States Steel Corporation, plus $8.5 million in cash for the ore-carrying fleet of barges. In one swoop, the Rockefellers became major stockholders in the largest single company in the United States, valued at its inception at $1,402,000,000. The net profit on that particular Rockefeller deal was more than $50 million.

Nevertheless, John Jr. just did not have the flair for business that his father had had. Despite all the training, coaching and help of his father's associates and advisers, John Jr. could not engross himself in the details of business affairs as he could with his father's philanthropies. Making money held no fascination for him and as he learned more and more about the inner workings of large corporations, he developed more and more misgivings. In 1902, he resigned as a director of the National City Bank, then a family-connected institution, because, as he explained in a letter to his father, in any large business, bank or corporation, it was "practically impossible for the directors to know anything about the business or to have any voice in its management, while at the same time they stood to the public as guarantors for the conduct of the business." For John Jr., it was a matter of conscience.

The same thing held true in his relationship with the Standard Oil Company. First as a director and then as a vice-president, he discovered he was being used largely for window dressing because of his famous name and that he really had no voice in the management. He was particularly disturbed when he learned of the secret political contributions being made by Standard Oil, under the presidency of his father's successor, John D. Archbold. But there were many other aspects of big business that disturbed him just as profoundly and, being as young as he was, there was nothing he could do about it. So, in 1910, after much agonizing, he decided to resign as a vice-president and director of Standard Oil. "I made up my mind," he explained later, "that I could not become responsible for the acts of other people. I was willing to face any criticism for things that I had done myself, but I could not keep still and accept criticism for actions in the determination of which I had had no part whatever."

Archbold was vehemently opposed to John Jr.'s resigning. It would hurt the company, particularly at a time when it was under attack in 1910. John Jr. was much more concerned, however, with hurting the feelings of his father, who had poured most of his life into Standard Oil. However, the elder Rockefeller responded with his usual levelheadedness.

"John," he said slowly, "I want you to do what you think is right."

John Jr. quit Standard Oil at the age of thirty-six. He also resigned as a director of the United States Steel Corporation in that year.

Ironically, he failed to follow through on a much smaller company in the family portfolio, of which he had become a director as his father's representative, the Colorado Fuel and Iron Company, located in a tiny mining town called Ludlow.

This Rockefeller company, however, was the largest of twenty mining companies struck by some nine thousand miners in southern Colorado in September 1913. It soon became the focal point of one of the nastiest, bloodiest strikes in labor history. A month later, after shots had been exchanged between the state militia and miners living with their families in tents outside the mining camps, John Jr. was called to testify at a congressional investigation. There he had to admit that although he was a director of the company and a major stockholder, he had never attended a directors' or stockholders' meeting. He did not have firsthand knowledge of conditions in the mines or in the mining towns where all the homes, stores, hospitals and politics were owned or controlled by the mining companies. He had never been there. Instead, he declared his faith in the management of his company and in its reports to him that the vast majority the miners were satisfied with their working and living conditions and that they did not want to be forced to join the United Mine Workers of America.

Public reaction to his testimony was split, although his father commended his "splendid effort at Washington before the Committee" with a gift of ten thousand more shares of common stock of the Colorado Fuel and Iron Company. John Jr. had certainly been enunciating the opinions held by company management and his advisers in his father's office. L. M.

Bowers, the chairman of the company, had characterized the leaders of the strike as "disreputable agitators, socialists and anarchists." In a characteristic letter to John Jr., he had written: "When such men as these together with the cheap college professors and still cheaper writers in muckraking magazines, supplemented by a lot of milk and water preachers with little or no religion and less common sense, are permitted to assault the business men who have built up the great industries and have done more to make this country what it is than all other agencies combined, it is time that vigorous measures are taken to put a stop to these vicious teachings which are being broadcast throughout the country."

Two weeks after his testimony, however, on April 20, and seven months after the strike had begun, another pitched battle broke out between the miners and a small contingent of the Colorado State Militia. Who fired the first shot was never determined. But in the end the militia rode through the tent colony firing rifles. The tents were set afire late that night. The next morning it was discovered that in seeking refuge from the gunfire, eleven children and two women had suffocated in the bottom of a cave. It was promptly labeled for all time "the Ludlow massacre."

The full wrath of public and press opinion descended upon John Jr., reminiscent of the opprobrium attached to his father in his day. He was mocked and scorned at mass meetings. Angry pickets marched in front of his home at West Fifty-fourth Street and at his office on lower Broadway. A contingent of the Industrial Workers of the World (IWW) threatened to storm the locked gates of the Pocantico Hills estate and were driven away by the townspeople. More than one speaker urged mobs to "shoot him down like a dog," and four members of the IWW were killed when a bomb they were presumably preparing for him exploded prematurely. John Jr.'s immediate response was to support the officers of the Colorado Fuel and Iron Company, refusing to negotiate with the United Mine Workers so long as they remained on strike and insisted on a closed shop or enforced unionization of all the miners. The strike finally ended in December 1914, fifteen months after it began, when the miners capitulated and voted to return to work.

Before the strike had ended, however, John Jr. began quietly to entertain some doubts about the company management's position and the reports he had relied upon describing conditions in the mines. As a result, he sent Ivy Lee, the family's public relations adviser, to Ludlow for an on-hand inspection, and then, based upon his report, he engaged an expert in labor relations to investigate the causes behind the strike and to recommend how future labor strife could be avoided. The man he found for the job was W. L. Mackenzie King, who had years of experience in labor relations and had been Canada's first Minister of Labor under the Liberal Party there. With his party's defeat at the polls, Mackenzie King had been hired to head a division of economic research for the Rockefeller

Foundation and was available for the assignment. Later, during World War II, Mackenzie King would become Prime Minister of Canada, but in 1914 he became the mentor of John D. Rockefeller, Jr., in labor relations, an association that lasted more than ten years. It was also the start of a warm and close friendship that continued for almost fifty years.

Mackenzie King proposed and John Jr. championed a plan for a joint labor-management board at the Colorado Fuel and Iron Company to mediate all workers' grievances on wages, hours and working conditions. When Bowers, the chairman of the board, refused to go along with the plan, John Jr., with 40 per cent of the company stock, insisted upon his resignation. In September of 1915, nine months after the strike had ended, John Jr. went on a two-week personal tour of the mines, listened to the miners' complaints, wielded a pickax himself, surveyed living conditions and scored a public relations coup when, after a labor-management meeting, he danced with the wives of miners attending a social function. All the fears of his own advisers back in New York, excepting King, did not materialize. There was no violence, no attempted assassination. The miners accepted this Rockefeller, whom before they had pilloried, as an honest man. At the end of his visit, they voted overwhelmingly to accept his plan for a grievance board and vastly improved living conditions. In sponsoring this plan, which was a far cry from full unionization, John Jr. was far, far in advance of current management thinking on unions and labor relations.

In the years that followed, John Jr. worked tirelessly to persuade other companies and the American public to bring labor and management closer together in a spirit of cooperation. At an industrial conference in Washington, called by President Wilson in 1919, the public was treated to a Rockefeller championing the right of labor to represent workers in collective bargaining. He went on to condemn company paternalism and to come out unequivocally against the prevalent twelve-hour day and seven-day work week. When Judge Elbert Gary, the arch-conservative head of U. S. Steel, refused to negotiate the twelve-hour-day issue in 1920, John Jr. announced he no longer wanted to be a stockholder in such a company. He sold all his stock in U. S. Steel that same year.

"The Colorado strike was one of the most important things that ever happened to the Rockefeller family," John Jr. said many years later. It was a turning point in his life, a veering away and a churning ahead from the thinking of his own father and the opinions of the older men in the Rockefeller establishment. As the whole country began to recognize facets of economic democracy, the son of the founder of Standard Oil was in the forefront of liberal and social-conscious thinking in regard to the working man. John Jr. never ceased to work in the cause. What he had learned from Mackenzie King, his own children and grandchildren would learn from him; they would adopt for themselves what John D. Rockefeller, Jr., had discovered, the concept he liked to call "the kinship of humanity."

Kinship of humanity implied responsibilities of the individual toward the society in which he lived. Having recognized and defined his responsibilities as a director of a company, John Jr. had no trouble in facing up to his responsibility as a stockholder. So, when in 1925 the chairman of the board of directors of Standard Oil of Indiana, Colonel Robert W. Stewart, came under attack in a congressional investigation for allegedly taking part in a shady deal, John D. Rockefeller, Jr., as a minority stockholder of the company, called upon him to testify and answer any and all criticism directed at him. Colonel Stewart was out of the country. On business, he said. For three years, he avoided the investigation, steadily declaring his innocence.

The investigation, an aftermath of the infamous Teapot Dome scandal, revealed that a phantom company named the Continental Trading Company had negotiated a contract to buy some 33 million barrels of oil from a Texas producer for $1.50 a barrel and to sell it to Standard Oil of Indiana, its wholly owned subsidiary Midwest Refining Company, and to the Prairie Oil and Gas Company, owned by H. F. Sinclair, for $1.75 a barrel. The congressional investigating committee wanted to know what happened to the profits, amounting to some $3 million over an eighteen-month period, all for performing no more services than being an intermediary between buyer and seller at $.25 a barrel.

When Colonel Stewart finally appeared before the committee, on February 2, 1928, he was evasive in answering questions about the Continental Trading Company. He would say only that he personally had never made a dollar out of the transaction. John Jr. called upon him to answer more forthrightly. He himself spoke out publicly on the issue and appeared before the committee, supporting the investigation on the grounds that the whole oil industry was affected by doubts cast upon the integrity or honesty of business management.

The case broke open when the heads of the other two oil companies admitted that they and Colonel Stewart had negotiated the contract themselves in a New York hotel room in 1921 and that the profits of the Continental Trading Company, which had been formed two days before the contract, had been invested in Liberty bonds and distributed to the four principals involved, themselves, Colonel Stewart and the lawyer who drew up the deal and served as president of Continental.

Colonel Stewart was called back to testify in April of that year. By this time, the committee had discovered that Colonel Stewart had deposited Liberty bonds worth $750,000 in a Chicago bank and they were of the same issue as bought by the Continental Company. Colonel Stewart, in a most embarrassing position on the witness stand, blithely swore that he had been keeping the bonds in trust for his company, Standard

Oil of Indiana. The trust agreement in his safe-deposit box with the bonds was written in pencil.

John D. Rockefeller, Jr., called upon him to resign. He refused. "I cannot recognize Mr. Rockefeller's right to speak for all the 58,000 stockholders," he said in a letter to stockholders. "It was never my intention . . . to make him the sole arbiter of my future or of the future welfare of the company."

John Jr. called upon the board of directors of Standard Oil of Indiana to ask for Colonel Stewart's resignation. It refused. He asked for a special stockholders' meeting on the subject. The board refused. It said it was standing behind its chairman.

There it was—the nitty-gritty of bald conflict. What could a stockholder, do, even a Rockefeller, against an entrenched head of a corporation whose honesty and, therefore, management of the company was, to say the least, in question? At the time, John Jr. owned only 4.5 per cent of the stock of the company, another 5 per cent was held in trust for two of his sisters, and the Rockefeller Foundation owned another 5 per cent.

The son of the founder of the company led a proxy fight to oust Colonel Stewart. He formed a committee to solicit proxies from the stockholders and hired Charles Evans Hughes, the eminent attorney, to serve as counsel to the committee. Public opinion was on his side. The press noted that this was the first time a stockholder had called an officer of a company to account on the issue of integrity, personal integrity, as it affected the company. On Stewart's side were most business and banking leaders along with the more conservative stockholders who argued that his dismissal would hurt the company, and that he had been convicted of no wrongdoing. Indicted first for contempt of the Senate committee, he was acquitted. Indicted then for perjury, again he was acquitted.

In the midst of the proxy fight, Stewart undoubtedly helped his cause by having the company declare a 50 per cent dividend, paying out some $116 million to the stockholders who would be voting shortly thereafter. Predictions were that John D. Rockefeller, Jr., would lose his proxy fight. At the highly dramatic meeting of stockholders on March 7, 1929, in Whiting, Indiana, the proxies from both sides arrived under armed guard. Of the 8,446,120 shares of stock represented at the meeting, John Jr.'s committee won 5,519,210. Colonel Stewart was fired by his stockholders.

"The action taken requires no comment," John Jr. told the press after the meeting. "It makes clear, however, that the thoughtful investor estimates the permanent and underlying value of an investment not alone in terms of dividends, essential as they are, but quite as much in terms of the unquestioned integrity and singleness of purpose of management. The action is significant because it emphasizes the conviction that the highest ethical standards are as vital in business as they are in other relations of life."

In one of those other relations, John Jr. made what for him at the time was the most momentous decision of his personal life. He decided to propose to the girl he loved. That decision, in 1901, was reached only after four years of deliberations, indecision and soul-searching. She was Abby Aldrich, one of the most outgoing, cheerful and popular debutantes of Providence, Rhode Island, daughter of Senator Nelson Aldrich, a millionaire in his own right and one of the most powerful Republican leaders in the U. S. Senate. Their courtship had started while John Jr. had been a student at Brown University in Providence and continued on an even keel for four more years after he had graduated. Yet, somehow, John Jr. found it most difficult to reach a decision. Perhaps it was fear that this gay, popular girl would reject him or that his own inhibited personality would not mesh well with hers. Finally, though, after consulting with his mother, John journeyed to Providence and did propose, and he was accepted. Overjoyed, he sat down to write of his feelings to his mother:

" 'Tis long before breakfast but I can't wait to tell you that my fond wish of all these years has at length come true, and the only woman whom I have ever cared to make my wife and whom I have loved for so long, although not daring to believe it was a deeper feeling than the truest and deepest friendship, has given me her love in return for my love, my life and my name . . . I could bring you no daughter, Mother, whom you would love and yearn over and be more proud of than Abby. She will add new brightness and honor to the name which I am so proud, so very proud, to give her."

The wedding in 1901 was a huge affair with more than a thousand guests at the Aldrich summer home in Warwick, Rhode Island; the honeymoon was a quiet one in near isolation at the Rockefeller estate in Pocantico Hills.

The young Rockefellers—they were both twenty-seven at the time of their marriage—established themselves in a separate house on the Pocantico estate, but lived with his parents in their city home on Fifty-fourth Street off Fifth Avenue after the honeymoon until a nine-story home on the same street became available.

"Why do you need so large a house?" a friend asked.

"Why, to fill it with children, of course," replied Mrs. Abby Aldrich Rockefeller.

In the summer of the following year, 1902, the old Wentworth house, where Rockefeller Sr. lived in Pocantico Hills, caught fire and burned to the ground, obliging him to move into another house on the grounds. It was smaller and did not have the broad view of the Wentworth house, but the elder Rockefeller seemed to settle in there just as comfortably. He put off his son's suggestion that he build a more suitable home for himself and his family. The house he lived in was just not as important to John D. Rockefeller as were the grounds around it.

In anticipation of his retirement, he had bought the land—seventeen parcels on a ridge between the Saw Mill River and the Hudson River, located in a small unincorporated village called Pocantico Hills (a political subdivision of Tarrytown), about thirty miles due north of New York City. The price was $168,705. Then in 1893 he had moved into the main house, a rambling wooden structure, two stories high with an attic on top, which had once belonged to a man named Wentworth. Its appeal to Rockefeller Sr. was its wide porches and verandas and the view they afforded him of the flowing Hudson, the cliffs of the New Jersey Palisades and the verdant landscape of the Saw Mill River Valley. The memory of those first years long remained with him and he described them fondly in a gem of a little book, called *Random Reminiscences of Men and Events.*

"At Pocantico Hills, New York, where I have spent portions of my time for many years in an old house where the fine views invite the soul and where we can live simply and quietly, I have spent many delightful hours, studying the beautiful views, the trees, and the fine landscape effects of that very interesting section of the Hudson River . . ."

As small parcels or large tracts of land came up for sale, he bought them. By the end of the century, the estate spread over some sixteen hundred acres. Buildings were demolished, wooden fences torn down, houses moved from one place to another, boulders were blasted to make fill for new lawns and roads. Trees, large and small, were dug up, moved and replanted where the oil magnate thought they should be. Pitching in with manual labor along with his workmen, Rockefeller delighted in becoming a knowledgeable landscape architect. Old stone walls on the property, which had divided fields and pastures since the time of the early Dutch settlers, were left untouched, but then he had new stone walls added to extend the old ones.

This was the age of great homes, palaces and chateaux, filled with marble, crystal and antiques, built with millions of dollars by millionaires like Vanderbilt, Whitney, Carnegie and Frick in New York, Newport, Tuxedo Park and on Long Island. But John D. Rockefeller much preferred Benjamin Franklin's idea of the simple life and of taking "our bowl of porridge on a table without any table cloth." And his son realized that.

John Jr. had an architectural firm draw plans for a home large enough to accommodate the Rockefeller family and the expected grandchildren, with some rooms for guests. His father nodded his approval of the plans but he never gave the go-ahead to start construction. It took a while for John Jr. to realize why his father, usually so decisive, was avoiding this decision. "The reason he did nothing," his son explained later, "was because he hesitated to build so large a house, with the additional care which its operation would involve, but on the other hand was too generous to suggest a smaller house, which would not adequately accommodate children and grandchildren. I therefore suggested that the plans be redrawn to provide a house that would fully meet his needs and Mother's, and provide for such guests as they might want to have but go no further in size. This met with Father's immediate approval and seemed a great relief to him."

John Jr. took upon himself at age twenty-eight the entire responsibility of supervising the planning and construction of the new house. He had a vision of what he wanted, a home to serve his father, and after his father, himself, and after himself, his children and their children, with, of course, all their families.

John Jr. worked closely with the architects and later with the decorators of the house. He hired advisers on specifics as he needed them. He found a slim four-foot folding ruler which he used to check measurements on the blueprints of the house. He came to like that folding ruler so much that he carried it in his back pocket for years afterward. He used it on Rockefeller Center, Colonial Williamsburg, the Riverside Church and countless other building projects. Those acquainted personally with John D. Rockefeller, Jr., during his long adult life knew of that four-foot ruler and his affection for it. It became for many a symbol of the man, much as the shiny dimes did for his father.

In working out the design of the house, the size of the rooms, the placement of the windows, even the type of moldings used on the walls, John Jr. held fast to the ideal he wanted: "a residence so outwardly simple that friends visiting his father, and coming from no matter how humble an environment, would be impressed by the homelikeness and simplicity of the house; while those who appreciated fine design and were familiar with beautiful furnishings would say, 'How exquisite.'"

While Rockefeller Sr. was content to allow his son to go ahead with the architects on the house itself, he could not resist taking a hand in the landscaping of the home. As he himself described it with such evident pleasure in his *Reminiscences:* "The problem was, just where to put the new home at Pocantico Hills . . . . I thought I had the advantage of knowing every foot of the land, all the old big trees were personal friends of mine, and with views of any given point I was perfectly familiar—I had studied them hundreds of times; and after this great landscape architect had laid out his plans and had driven his line of stakes, I asked if I might see what I could do with the job.

"In a few days I had worked out a plan so devised that the roads caught just the best views at just the angles where in driving up the hill you came upon impressive outlooks, and at the ending was the final burst of river, hill, cloud and great sweep of country to crown the whole; and here I fixed my stakes to show where I suggested that the road should run, and finally the exact place where the house should be.

"'Look it all over,' I said, 'and decide which plan is best.' It was a proud moment when this real authority accepted my suggestions as bringing out the most favored spots for views and agreed upon the site of the house. How many miles of roads I have laid out in my time, I can hardly compute, but I have often kept at it until I was exhausted."

Once the final plans were drawn and approved, Rockefeller Sr. did not go near the project until the time arrived for him and his wife to move into a completed home. He was long a firm believer in delegating authority, finding the right man to do the job (in this case, his son) and then allowing that man to do the job his own way. John Jr. was never far from that job, and Abby joined him in choosing the furniture, the draperies, silver and tableware for the house.

The new house was placed on the broad top of Kykuit Hill overlooking the Hudson with a view of fifty miles. To the north, the eye can see as far as West Point; to the south, at the time, the Singer Building and the old Metropolitan Tower could be seen in New York City. Later, of course, the skyscrapers would rise into view, including the seventy-story shaft of the RCA Building of Rockefeller Center—but that view would be the Rockefellers' only on a clear day.

The house was built of weatherstained stone quarried on the estate or borrowed from some of the old stone walls which had been redesigned. Each stone was carefully selected for form and color and laid out in patterns before being mortared into place. The immense roof was of green slate, blending with the treetops but still discernible to the keen eye on the New Jersey side of the Hudson.

The weatherstained stone gave it the appearance of a home which had withstood the vicissitudes of time and inclemency of the weather even on the day it was completed. The trees, shrubs, lawns and the contours of the land look as though nature had placed them perfectly where you see them today. Only specialized knowledge or perhaps intuition about the Rockefeller family would lead one to the truth: that the trees had been moved from one place to another, that thousands of tons of land fill, bolstered in places by retaining walls, had been used to improve on nature, that sixty tons of fertilizer are still used every year to make two hundred acres of manicured lawn a lush, primitive green, that some three hundred men were employed on the grounds in Rockefeller Sr.'s day and more than one hundred tend the grounds full time for his grandchildren and great-grandchildren. But that is the way Rockefeller Sr. and Rockefeller Jr. wanted it. Mr. Sr. wanted simplicity; Mr. Jr. wanted simplicity and perfection. John Jr. was a stickler all of his life on detail. "It's the last 5 per cent of effort that counts," he would tell his five sons years afterward. He himself always put in that extra effort on seemingly minor details, to satisfy demands he imposed upon himself. The time and effort he put into the family house were an excellent illustration of his methods. While he did not stint on the amount of work or money he expended, he did not want either the effort or the money to show. Unless a visitor stopped to look closely and think about what he was seeing, he would likely not notice the parts which made the whole effect so pleasing to the eye. Although his sons were not yet born when the project was undertaken, they lived and learned with the final product all of their lives. "Unostentatious luxury" was the most common description of the final result. Nothing stands out starkly; everything blends, the trees with the contour of the land, the house with the rise of the hill, the Chinese porcelains with the nineteenth-century paintings. By design, almost everything appears smaller than it actually is.

The main entrance to the estate was tucked away in a small side street of Pocantico Hills, difficult to find unless one is directed where to look. From the main gate, ten feet high, a long narrow road leads to the wrought-iron gates, decorated with oxidized copper leaves, standing eighteen feet high before the main house. Resplendent in their craftsmanship, they remind the old-timers on the estate today of the days of Mr. Sr. They remember the original gates, once rusted, had been replaced by Mr. Jr. with simple, smaller bronze ones, and those, in turn, had been replaced by Mr. Nelson, who traced the grandson of the original ironmonger so that the new gates could be made from the same drawings as those in his grandfather's day.

On the terraced balcony just beyond the gates stands the Fountain Oceanis, a huge bowl thirty-two feet in diameter standing on a pedestal, the largest of its kind in the world, and yet dwarfed in proportion to the surrounding rolling hills. Up a broad footpath from the fountain stands the main house. It appears small, only forty-odd feet across, brownish gray stone, three stories high and yet seemingly shorter because of the great sloping slate roof. The depth of the house runs closer to ninety feet, but neither its depth nor the grandeur of the broad terrace and elaborate rose garden in the rear or west side of the house can be seen from the front approach. And that, too, is the Rockefeller design: there is more there than immediately meets the eye.

The front terrace is bare except for one marble sculptured figure of a young girl, slim, beautiful and not more than four feet high, which one cannot quite place as old, very old or modern. But then one is not likely to recognize the simple sculpture because there are only three or four in existence in the world. The host today would have to inform you that it is one of his lifelong favorite pieces of sculpture, a sixth-century Chinese bodhisattva, the figure of a young Buddha neophyte. This particular piece, chosen by his mother, had stood for years in the vestibule of their city home on West Fifty-fourth Street and Nelson, long ago, had asked his mother to leave it to him in her will.

The most important room in the house for the occupants was the first one off the front hall on the left, a dark-oak-paneled study with a small fireplace on one wall, sometimes called the den, the library, but most often known as "the office," furnished in the period of William and Mary with simple solid types of late-seventeenth-century furniture. The room remains today much the same as it was when Nelson's grandfather and father used it. A portable typewriter sits open, ready for use, on a small desk in one corner. An old Morris chair with adjustable back faces the hearth.

To the right of the hall was the delicate and feminine drawing room of his mother and grandmother in the Adam style of the eighteenth century, unchanged to this day. This was the arrangement the Rockefellers preferred in all of their homes, at Pocantico Hills, at Fifty-fourth Street and in Seal Harbor, Maine: off the front hall, the room on the left was "Father's office," where weekly allowances and punishments were meted out and where the family gathered for morning prayers; the room on the right was "Mother's drawing room," where the children could find milk and cookies at teatime and a sympathetic ear.

The music room in the very center of the house seems even more spacious than its actual dimensions because of the cupola which extends through the second floor, making the room seem ceilingless. The eye travels to a height of almost thirty feet. In the days of Mr. Sr., when hymn singing was an integral part of home life, an organ dominated the room, with the organ pipes covering most of one wall. But the organ has been replaced by a grand piano which occupies only a minor portion of the room amid the couches, upholstered chairs and sideboards.

Beyond the music room, along the western side of the house, are the dining room and living room, separated by an alcove sitting room half their size, each of them furnished in eighteenth-century English-style Chippendale, Hepplewhite and Sheraton, producing a remarkable unity of the period in all three rooms. The most spectacular aspect of these rooms is the view from each of them of the broad, flowing Hudson River, sparkling when the sun shines. The entire western wall seems to be glass— glass doors and windows, leading out to a broad open terrace where, with the hill falling away to the Hudson, two miles away, the broad river seems within inches of arm's reach.

On the floors above are eleven master bedrooms and ten servants' rooms. Beneath the main floor are a ground floor and basement, the first of which accommodates utility rooms and a hotel-size kitchen, tiled in white ceramic and outfitted with two enormous gas ranges, walk-in refrigerators and freezers, all of ancient vintage. The prepared food is sent by electric dumbwaiter to a pantry on the main floor where it is then arranged on heirloom dinnerware and served to the family and their guests.

The house is terraced on all four sides, leading to the beautiful lawns which slope away down the hill on all sides, ending in wooded borders so that, standing on any one of the terraces, one has no sense of boundaries. The broadest terrace, twice the width of the others, is, of course, the western one with the view of the Hudson. It leads to the formal garden, English in style, bounded by stone walls waist-high, with a maze of privet hedge in the center and Hawthorne roses hung from a bronze trellis on either side. Since the family did not plan to live there in the summer months, the garden was designed primarily as a spring and fall garden with a variety of walks and places to sit and enjoy the views under constantly changing weather conditions.

The principal walks are of white and gray marble and the low-cut stone walls are inlaid with a pattern of mica and granite. A stone teahouse, perched atop a pattern of rocks, which was a popular innovation in the era of Rockefeller Sr., has been converted by his grandson Nelson into a soda fountain family room where his great-grandchildren gather for Sunday festivities to this day.

The house and estate accommodate themselves remarkably well to modern living. The changes made over the years by Rockefeller Jr. and later by Nelson have improved details on an excellent and well-thought-out design. Loving care, more than mere money, went into making this house a home. The original construction and landscaping consumed seven years and it was 1909 before Rockefeller Sr. was able to move into his new home. He was delighted with it. By that time, public curiosity was at a new peak concerning John D. Rockefeller as the richest man in the country, the head of the biggest monopoly in the world. What kind of mansion was he building for himself beyond the gaze of the public? Newspaper stories in that era of explosive journalism ran the gamut of speculations. The Rockefellers barred their home to the press during construction, as they would, as a general principle, years after its completion. However, when the house was first completed, during a sense of euphoria that had settled upon the family, the architects, construction men, landscape designers and decorators, Mr. Rockefeller invited the editor of *House Beautiful* to tour the home. His impressions are interesting not because of what the magazine editor thought of the house, but rather because of the standards of home building of that era:

"It is not exaggeration to estimate that nine-tenths of those who have built houses during the past twenty years have said to themselves, 'We cannot afford this or that—we are not Rockefellers, and we must curtail expenses.' And so nine-tenths of those who have homes are interested in knowing what kind of residence Mr. John D. Rockefeller has built for himself. But when they see the pictures of the house that accompany this article, and read a description of the place, there will come a curious feeling of surprise. Just what kind of a house the American public thinks Mr. Rockefeller should have built cannot be known, but there are many who will look for something different from the reality, and be disappointed. For those who expected the palace of a Croesus, the house will be a failure; there are no columns of porphyry, no elaborate French decorations. In fact the house is not a palace at all. It is just the kind of country place that you or I or any other sane person would have built, provided we had the necessary taste and money.

"The house was designed for comfort rather than show, and as such is eminently successful. In addition to comfort, there is refinement and reserve, qualities sometimes absent in the homes of American millionaires."

Actually, the Rockefellers being Rockefellers, both father and son went to considerable pains to curtail expenses as much as possible in building their home.

Some of John Jr.'s economies did not work out well. The original dormer rooms for guests on the third floor were found to be too small and too dark. Also, the entrance side of the house was thought to have an inadequate view of the grounds. His father particularly objected to the noise at the service entrance to the house when deliveries were made. So Rockefeller Sr. moved out of the main house while major changes were made. The house was taken down to the second story and a full third story with a mansard fourth story was added, all with matching weather-stained stone. Then the approach to the house was extended some five hundred feet by adding thousands and thousands of tons of dirt fill, brought in by caravans of horse-drawn wagons. A huge retaining wall was built to support the fill. To overcome the noise at the service entrance, a tunnel some five hundred feet long was bored through rock and earth, at considerable expense, so that deliveries could be made underground to a subbasement without bothersome noise to those on the upper floors.

It was 1913 before the rebuilt house was once again ready for occupancy and John D. Rockefeller, Sr., moved into it again.

From the outset in 1902 to the final completion of the house, many other endeavors occupied the time of the Rockefellers, father and son. There were the increasing philanthropic ventures, the sundry court fights culminating in the 1911 decision of the Supreme Court of the United States that the Standard Oil Company which John D. Rockefeller had built was indeed a monopoly and trust in violation of the Sherman Antitrust Act and must be dissolved into its component parts. On a personal side, John Jr. and his wife, Abby, during the years of work on Kykuit, brought their own family into the world. Their first, Abby, was born in 1903, John 3rd arrived three years later, Nelson was born in 1908, Laurance in 1910 and Winthrop in 1912. Only David, the baby of the family, born in 1915, postdated the completion of the main house at Kykuit in Pocantico Hills, New York, the family home for generations.

3

Raising Affluent Children

"To have given the world one clean, honest,
God-fearing son . . ."

The upbringing of the Rockefeller children—all six of them born between the years 1903–15—is a study in the expertise of child rearing. Not that it was perfect. But the parents involved had the wherewithal—the money, the time, the intelligence, diligence and purpose—to try to raise their children in the best manner possible.

"To have given the world one clean, honest, God-fearing son, with an active sense of his obligations, is about as large a contribution to our day as any father can hope to make," John D. Rockefeller, Jr., told a group of fathers of Princeton students in 1927, when Johnny, his eldest son, was a sophomore there. "Even in this machine age, there are certain things so important that they demand personal attention," he explained almost a lifetime ago. "Many try to transfer it, but we cannot be relieved of this responsibility and privilege . . . We cannot live one thing and advocate another to them. We must be their example. To do so may at times cramp our style, but there is no alternative."

A deeply introspective and conscientious man, he regarded his role as a father precisely as a God-given duty and privilege. The duty was clearcut, but the privilege of child rearing was more subtle: it put him on equal grounds with other fathers. In fact, he was convinced that the "proper rearing of children" was more difficult for the very rich than for more moderately circumstanced parents. Affluent children were always open to greater temptations, more pleasurable pursuits, more paths of least resistance than the less affluent. They were freed of the necessity of having to earn their own livelihoods. The personal problems of the affluent have almost always been based upon their affluency.

"Anyone with your money and five sons," an acquaintance once warned him, "has a right to expect at least four black sheep in the family."

Mr. Jr. was aware of the problem. Hardly a day went by, he himself admitted, that he and Mrs. Rockefeller did not worry about how their children were shaping up. After all, they were third-generation Rockefellers and the popular aphorism of the day, attributed to no less than Andrew Carnegie, predicted "from shirtsleeves to shirtsleeves in three generations."

In another sense, he felt it was a true proving ground of his abilities. As the son of the wealthiest man in the world, John Jr. was plagued with the rich man's curse of doubting his own accomplishments: never being certain whether what he did, the praise he received or the friends he made were due to his own merit or to his father's money. In the rearing of his children, particularly his five sons, the result would more than anything else he did be based upon his role as a father, aided and abetted, of course, by his loving wife, Abby.

The lodestar by which John Jr. charted the course of his own life, by which he fixed his own values, was the Bible. Raised as a good Baptist, church, Sunday school hymnals, missionaries and meetings all had been part of his family life. Religion was an integral part of his father's being. His mother was a fundamentalist, with a literal interpretation of the Bible, including hell, damnation and salvation. While John Jr. had become more liberal in his own interpretation of the Scriptures, he was as religious as his parents, abiding with the Baptist bans on bodily pleasures, such as drinking, smoking, breaking the Sabbath. Fresh out of college, at the height of public attention focused upon his father, John Jr. had taught a men's class of Sunday school at the Fifth Avenue Church, which, open to the public, had drawn relentless newspaper reporters who, each Sunday, demanded that a Rockefeller comment on the New Testament's warning that a rich man had as much chance of going to heaven as a camel through the eye of a needle. He had quoted biblical verses back at them week after week, refusing to be daunted by the stories, cartoons and editorials mocking his sincerity. He was steadfast in his beliefs. With the birth of his children, he was equally determined to make the Bible their guidebook of personal ethics.

A sense of religion permeated the daily atmosphere of the Rockefeller home. Whether they were staying on West Fifty-fourth Street in New York or at Pocantico Hills on weekends and holidays, or up in Maine for the summer, there were the morning prayers, the saying of grace at the table, Sunday school and church on Sundays and hymn singing in the evening. The Sabbath was observed as a day of rest and communion for everyone, parents, children and household help. Not until Nelson reached his teens did his father relax the rule which had forbidden sports, particularly tennis, on Sundays. Smoking, drinking and all the other sins prohibited by the Baptist Church were strictly forbidden in the Rockefeller household.

The Holy Bible became part of the boys' lives from the time they learned to understand the spoken word. It was translated daily into the ethics, morals and values they were taught as governing their everyday activities. Their mother and father both were wise enough to know, long before psychology formalized child rearing, that you cannot teach children merely by lecturing them. You have to demonstrate by your own actions and attitudes the behavior you intend your children to exemplify.

As for the children themselves, not until they were grown would they recognize the *design* of their own upbringing, the design which would carve out the manner of men they would become. From the tenderest ages, they were obliged to fall into the regular routine of their family's life. If that included coming to meals at a precise time, properly washed and attired, bringing along one's best manners for the occasion, then that is what the children did. Nothing less, they knew, would be tolerated. If it included religious training, extra tutoring, reading and being read to, then that is what they accepted. That was the only kind of life they knew at home. There were the special favorite verses from the Bible which they were called upon each day to recite from memory. To aid them, Mrs. Rockefeller wrote out an appropriate verse on a five-by-eight-inch index card so that brother John or Nelson or Winthrop could memorize his verse during the week. These verses, of course, were carefully chosen for the instruction they would implant. And at times the children enjoyed the competitions of a round robin of all the biblical verses each, in turn, could remember.

The children were never in doubt that their father loved them. The Bible instructed them that "For whom the Lord loveth, He correcteth; even as a father the son in whom he delighteth." Hardly a day went by that their father did not have occasion to "correcteth" them. A glance down the long length of the dining room table, a sharp calling of the name, was usually enough to stop an offender. But, above all, a reprimand from Father was something to remember, something to fear and something to respect far beyond the physical pain of a spanking. And yet they knew that they could count on their father to support them in their troubles, to sit patiently by the side of their bed, rubbing the back of a child brought down with the flu until the alcohol cooled the fever. Mr. Rockefeller saw his role as that of a father who spends as much time with his children as possible, instructing them, reading to them, correcting them, but always as a father, never as a co-equal or as a pal.

The children growing up observed the obvious: their father was a very busy man, indeed, dedicated to work. They heard their mother often comment in his absence that he was "out saving the world somewhere." They saw him return from the office fatigued, bothered with a migraine, and take to his bed for an hour's rest before the evening meal. When sickness kept him from the office, he worked on his papers in bed. He was driven by work to be done and as he himself remarked, "I can think of nothing less pleasurable than a life devoted to pleasure."

He was involved, active, and not wont to waste the precious hours of his lifetime. He was busy learning the oil business at Standard, he was being guided in the intricacies of stock investments, he was his father's seeing-eye in the new giant philanthropies, he was deeply involved with church work and missionary movements, and then there were the community social programs. Weekends, in addition to work taken home from the city, were devoted to managing the sprawling and ever changing estate at Pocantico Hills.

In the city, breakfast was the one meal at which the children could be assured of seeing their father. Work kept him from lunch at home. Dinners most often were formal affairs at which the parents entertained various eminent guests who were involved in either the business, church or philanthropic affairs of the Rockefellers. The children then ate separately with the governesses or tutors living in the house.

The nine-story town house on West Fifty-fourth Street with its infirmary, gymnasium, art gallery, two living rooms and multitude of bedrooms was nevertheless a formal and somber domicile, laden with heavy carved Victorian furniture, dark and thick mahogany stairways and moldings of the period, and fairly crowded with butlers, footmen, maids, governesses, tutors and visiting Baptist clergymen. Manners and attire were equally proper and correct, the small boys raised in Eton suits, velvets and short pants, their father in Edwardian-cut clothes with top silk hat for out of doors, and their mother attired in long silk dresses down to her ankles. School and homework consumed most of the day for the boys and for those too young for school there were tutors and private lessons.

But "at home" in Pocantico Hills, it was different. Father wore one or another of his old favorite baggy suits, in which he was often mistaken for a workman or foreman on the estate. The boys wore plain play clothes much like those of the children of the hired hands. They were *meant* to have a certain amount of free time on the weekends, time to play at games of their own devising. In the early days of their childhood they enjoyed none of the accouterments of the super rich, no swimming pool, no tennis courts, no baseball field. Those would come later, out of sheer necessity, but the boys were never raised to expect them. They played simple games, like follow-the-leader. Nelson, more often than not, pre-empted the lead. To be sure, there were tricycles and then two-wheelers, and later, ponies and still later, horses. Their father, an excellent horseman, taught the boys to ride as he taught them to swim, to hike, to camp out, to chop wood, to gather sap from the maple trees on the property.

Being "free and easy" in the Rockefeller syndrome, however, was only relative. Most of the children's activities were supervised by governesses or tutors. The day's activities were parceled out, usually, in hourly sections— an hour for tennis, an hour for study, an hour for horseback riding. That still left time for the boys to play among themselves and to wander about, poking into the various carpenter and craft shops on the estate, making friends along the way with the men who worked there and at times, with their children.

The estate in those days was virtually self-sufficient. There was a dairy farm on the grounds, and chickens, and vegetable gardens large enough to feed not only the Rockefellers but the employees, too. The men were paid on an hourly basis and in cash. On the fifteenth of each month, they would line up at two of three windows in the basement of the coach house and each would present a round metal check with his employee number on it. Each man's pay, computed precisely on the hours he worked, would be given to him in an envelope containing another metal disk for his next month's pay. Then he would move on to the third window, where he would pay his bill for the eggs and chickens he had purchased during the previous month. Surplus fruit and vegetables were distributed free on a first-come-first-served basis. It was not until John 3rd reached manhood and relieved his father's management that the system was changed, the pay windows boarded up and the workmen paid on a weekly salary. It was not until after the Second World War, when the five sons *bought* the estate at its assessed valuation, that a much more sophisticated arrangement was devised: the five brothers capitalized a separate corporation, Greenrock, to run the estate as a private enterprise, albeit wholly owned by John, Nelson, Laurance, Winthrop and David.

But in those early days, Pocantico was wholly run by their father, who imposed his own image upon the setting. John D., Sr., was seen as a friendly, benign old gentleman who visited all parts of the operation at least once a week, his only object seeming to be to look around and to chat amiably with the men at work. No great or memorable words tumbled out of this enormously rich and powerful man, nothing more than might be expected from the deacon of the village church. But he was a good listener, looking the speaker straight in the eye, nodding his understanding of what was being explained to him.

Outside of the Pocantico gates he was being condemned in the muckraking press as the most evil man in America, fleecer of widows, skillful manipulator of men and businesses. Within the gates, Mr. Sr. went about his business of living in retirement (which did not preclude an active interest in the stock market and in real estate), calm, benign, patient, confident, his passion for golf unabated.

Golf was a simple, solid game by which he could measure himself against perfection and at the same time get the exercise so important to his good health. He had applied himself to learning golf as he had once focused his attention on the oil business—with concentration, hard work and imagination. To learn the game he had hired the best of professional teachers; to correct his stance, he had someone drive croquet wickets over his golf shoes to staple himself in the proper position; to improve his swing he had motion pictures taken so that he could study what he had been doing wrong.

When his wife died in 1915, fifty years of married life came to an end. But he went on living in the big main house alone and his routine continued. He would start the day with a tour of the kitchen, greeting the cook and the other help, eat a light breakfast and then make his way from the golf room on the ground floor of Kykuit to the first tee. His valet would accompany him with an umbrella, rubbers and a supply of paper vests in deference to rain, snow or the early morning chill and dew. Most often he played by himself, primarily for the exercise, driving five or six balls off each tee and then playing the ball in the best position. He worked a little each day, going over the stock market quotations, rested after lunch, went for an auto ride in the afternoon, usually had guests for dinner, and lived a calm, contemplative life of retirement.

In contrast, Rockefeller Jr. was remembered by the old-timers of Pocantico Hills as having been quite different. Where his father in his old age was genial, John Jr. as a young man was generally shy, and yet quite firm in his demands upon the help. In the management of the estate, he was exact and exacting. He could and often did astound a superintendent or a foreman with his memory of orders or requests made months before.

"I know you are a busy man," he told one superintendent, "but you have had a year to finish this job. Now tell me why it hasn't been done." And he would wait silently for an answer. Such an encounter leaves a mark on a man, and word of it gets around.

One night watchman never forgot when "Mr. Jr." once asked him at what time a particularly violent thunderstorm had started the previous night.

"About one o'clock," he replied.

"About one o'clock?" Mr. Jr. shot back. "Don't you know?" And thereafter that watchman, and every other one to whom he repeated this encounter, made a note of what was expected of them.

John Jr. seldom stopped to chat with workmen on the estate. More often than not he passed his orders to them through the various foremen and superintendents. Perhaps his reticence was due to his age—he was younger than most of the men working on the estate; perhaps it was his own natural introversion. Nevertheless, there was no question who was the boss. John Jr. did not like dogs around and so there were no dogs in the

"Park" section of the estate—not during his lifetime. Everyone working there *knew* that waste in any form, no matter how minute, incurred Mr. Jr.'s annoyance. They could see him going from room to room turning off lights not needed. They could see him bending over to pick up scraps of litter from the grounds, or moving the smallest object found out of place. They knew that machinery was repaired and repaired before it was replaced. They knew that any bill submitted was scrupulously checked, no matter how small, by Mr. Jr. himself. Those charged with buying anything for the Rockefellers were expected to pay the going price and no more. Food, fertilizer, fuel were bought in wholesale lots and paid for at wholesale prices. It was not a question of miserliness; the Rockefellers were generous when it came to giving money. It was a moral matter: money, like everything else, was not to be wasted.

Deploring waste on the one hand, Mr. Jr. was equally demanding of a high rate of excellence in the performance of everyone's duties, including his own. He expected that each one working for him on the estate, as well as in the office in the city, give the utmost of his ability. As long as a man tried, Mr. Jr. could and would forgive a mistake. But he would not condone negligence or laziness; it seemed that he simply could not understand it. In those days prior to the First World War, he was undoubtedly in tune with his times. Men were expected to work to the limit of their abilities and to be paid a living wage (but little more) in return for it. On the Rockefeller premises, a man took pride in his work for its own sake, whether he was painting a barn or administering a multi-million-dollar organization.

None of this was lost upon his children. They could see that their father did not spare himself in investing that "last 5 per cent" of time and effort on any project. They could see the demands he made upon himself and upon others, the integrity that became part of every decision, the striving for self-perfection as a way of life. The standards he set, all in all, became a considerable burden upon the children as they were growing up. At the same time, they learned, because they had to, how to carry a burden, even at a tender age.

At seven or eight, depending on degree of maturity, each of the children was introduced to the subject of money. Allowances. Money of your own. To do with as you wished. But money was not meant only to be spent right away. If you wanted something special which cost more than one week's allowance, you had to save until you had enough to buy that something special. So you were obliged to save at least some of the allowance. And then there were those who needed that money more than you did, and the Bible says that a good Christian helps his fellow man in need. So you must give also.

The Rockefeller allowance at the start was $.30 a week. Out of that each child was given to understand that he or she was expected "to save and to give, as well as to spend." How much? It was suggested, although not made obligatory, that $.10 to be saved, $.10 for church and $.10 for spending for that week.

And there was another proviso. Since money really was only a tool which could be used for many things and used properly or improperly, like any tool, Father would check every week to see how Babs, or John, or Nelson was handling his or her money. So each child, upon being given an allowance, was also handed a small account book in which he or she was to record how he or she was handling the allowance. Every penny had to be accounted for and dated, each expenditure explained or defended, and if the ledgers were well kept then one could expect his or her allowance to be increased.

Grandfather had kept such a personal ledger all of his working life from age sixteen onward, and Father also kept one because it was the only way a person could know how he was using his money, the only way a person could plan ahead on how he intended to use his money. If one did not keep a record then most likely money would slip through one's fingers and not be there when wanted. And that was a waste of a valuable tool.

As the years went by the allowances were increased: about $1.00 at age eleven or twelve, around $2.00 at age fifteen. At the $1.00 mark, however, Father expected each child to be accountable for his or her handling of the allowance. So rewards and demerits were instituted. If the account book was correct and the money handled well, the allowance for the following week went up to $1.05 and $.05 more for each succeeding week. If not, the allowance dropped correspondingly, $.95, then $.90, then $.85. Every Saturday morning after breakfast, each child, one by one—Babs, Johnny, Nelson, Laurance, Winthrop and David—would file into Father's office and there would ensue a strict accounting of the ledgers and the doling out of the next week's earned allowance. Allowances and account books went hand in hand with one another beyond childhood and into the days of college away from home and, in fact, right up to the time when each of the Rockefeller children went to work and earned his own income. But as long as they were receiving money *given* to them by their father, they had to account for the use of that money. The allowance grew, of course, to include clothes, living expenses at college and the purchase of pleasures beyond candy. Nelson, for instance, was given a generous wedding gift of an extended trip around the world, but he had to take with him not only his new bride, but also one little black account book.

The Rockefeller children, of necessity, learned the value of money. From the start, their allowances were always less than they themselves felt they needed at the time. By design, they were kept under economic pressure. They soon learned that they could not get more money from their father merely by asking for it. Allowances were as inflexible as the need for keeping accurate accounts. The only way to fulfill the need for more money was by earning it. There were always chores, plenty of things to be done around the estate at Pocantico Hills or up in Maine: flies to be caught on the porch at $.10 a hundred, mice to be trapped in the attic at $.05 a mouse, firewood to be carried and stacked, weeds to be plucked at so much an hour. Chores were never forced upon them. Economic pressure worked well enough. Nelson and Laurance, at nine and seven respectively, were delighted to take on the shoeshining concession at the household, rising at 6 A.M. in order to do their work before morning prayers: $.05 per pair of shoes, $.10 for boots. At that age and in that time $.10 went a long way at the penny candy counter of the DeMichele general store across the road from the estate gate.

Rockefeller Jr. positively delighted in seeing his children doing things that had to be done, from chores to money-making schemes. Such activities indicated that his children were developing a sense of self-sufficiency. He particularly wanted them to do things that they did not like to do. He believed fervently that that helped train one's will and determination to cope with problems that would surely come later in life. This attitude at times did not particularly endear him to his children and he knew it, but he considered his insistence his "duty" as a father in raising five sons and a daughter. He once commented: "The tendency with many children of today is to follow the easiest way, the line of least resistance. Of course, we all do best the things we like doing. But life cannot be lived wholly that way. How can a child later learn how to avoid the things he should not do? A disorderly mind is an untrained one." He believed that with all his soul.

When America's entry into the First World War brought about shortages and rationing, the Rockefeller household converted to a wartime economy. Mrs. Rockefeller organized a Red Cross bandage unit in the basement of John D., Sr.'s home at 4 West Fifty-fourth Street. All five boys were assigned to carrying bandages from a table where they were made by women in the neighborhood to other tables where they were being packed. Dressed in white uniforms for the task, they got a feeling of participating in the Great War, as well as an inkling of the serious realities behind the parades which they liked so much.

All of the boys would long remember the row of glasses in the kitchen, carefully labeled with each one's name, containing his or her ration of sugar for the week. When a cake or pie was to be baked for the boys, an equal measure of sugar from each of their glasses was taken for the joint venture. Their parents were very strict about rationing: a nation's limitations had to be shared by all the people. To a small boy who had used up his sugar allotment by Thursday, it was personally sacrificial to have to wait until the following Monday for his next sugar allotment. One of the boys' companions at Seal Harbor, Wallace Worthley, in a letter home to his own parents, described the scene in the summer of 1918:

"The R's are doing everything that [Herbert] Hoover wishes the people of the U.S. to do. No sugar, except for the coffee or tea, is used. The boys don't eat any sugar on their cereal in the morning. We have bacon only twice a week and I have not had a bite of beef at the R's house since I've been here. Speaks pretty well for them, don't it? Also only twice since I've been here have I seen white bread."

In Pocantico Hills that year the boys started their Victory gardens of lettuce, cucumbers, squash, pumpkins. They worked hard planting, hoeing and weeding before experiencing the pleasures of greens popping forth from the earth. David still was too small to take part, but the other boys enjoyed most the selling of their produce. Mr. Jr. paid Winthrop, age six, the going price for his pumpkins, but the three older boys carted their produce to market in their play wagons and sold it at the local grocery store.

For two years the Victory gardens continued, and then Nelson and Laurance branched out into a more profitable venture of raising rabbits. They bought "mother and father" rabbits from the Rockefeller Institute for Medical Research and sold the progeny back to the Institute for what they considered was a "neat profit." At age eleven and twelve, Nelson considered himself to be in the business, in partnership with brother Laurance. He denied allegations that the rabbits did all the work. There were the care and feeding and cleaning up and the hiring of boys to care for the rabbits in the owners' absence.

The boys were also introduced into the culinary arts and the logistics of feeding a large family. It was arranged that one of the housekeepers at their summer home in Seal Harbor would teach the boys to cook and soon afterward their mother and father "agreed" to eat the meal the boys "prepared" for them each Wednesday night. Preparing a meal meant more than merely cooking it. The boys had to plan the meal, order all the ingredients, set the table, cook and bake, serve and then clean up afterward. Winthrop and David, at the bottom of the totem pole, drew KP duty; if very good they were allowed to peel potatoes and cut the salad. The older boys did the cooking and serving. John often tried his hand at baking. Nelson and Laurance years later won the plaudits of the crew of an expedition ship voyaging in Arctic waters when they served as ship's cooks. When they were boys, however, their Wednesday night "feasts" gave them an understanding of (as their parents pointed out) and consequently a respect for those who regularly prepared meals for the large Rockefeller family.

Self-sufficiency was the goal of their parents' training. When they learned how to do something for themselves, then and only then could they appreciate the work and service being done for them by others. Each was taught how to pack a suitcase for a trip, how to fold trousers and coats so that they would emerge unwrinkled. The boys were taught to sew, and by their father, so that they would grow up believing that such things as cooking and sewing were not necessarily women's work. These precepts would stay with them. Almost a half century later, running for President of the United States, Nelson would astound his staff aboard his 1968 campaign plane when the back seam of his trousers split. Without asking for help or suggestion, the multi-millionaire candidate for the Republican nomination for President took off his trousers, found needle and thread in a travel sewing kit and then sat down and sewed them up himself. It was, in the words of one staffer aboard that plane, a sight to behold.

A deep and abiding love of nature, the need to preserve it, comingled with a religious view that trees, mountains, streams and flowers, along with the changing seasons, revealed the hand of God upon the earth—all were parts of the tenets of faith in Rockefeller Jr.'s life which as a father he sought to imbue in his own children. There were the regular Sunday afternoon hikes in the woods of Pocantico Hills and on Mount Desert Island in Maine. The boys, particularly when young, were not overly enthusiastic about six- and seven-mile treks. They often refused such suggestion from one of their companions or tutors. They preferred their bikes or their ponies. But with their father there never seemed to be the option to refuse. Father sweetened the venture with a promise of chocolate or sugar maple candy at the farthest point of the hike. Besides, there was little else allowed them on the Sabbath. Each Sunday the boys hiked with their father. He would point out the aesthetic beauty of a vista or a particular clump of trees or bushes or the budding of an early spring flower.

When the boys became old enough to handle cameras, their father struck a bargain with them: for every good photograph each took he would pay for the film and the cost of developing. Discovering that their father preferred and paid for landscapes, the boys set up and took their pictures in the woods and learned perspective as revealed in nature. Their father explained how he had gone about laying out the walking, riding and driving trails at Pocantico Hills, and up on the property at Seal Harbor. The objective always was to preserve the natural beauty of the environment, to change God's design as little as possible, to set a trail or a road where it would give the viewer the very best perspective on his surroundings. Later, when he came to build the extensive roads in the wilderness of the miles of woodlands he owned at Seal Harbor, he would talk fascinatingly about the difficulties and complexities of the engineering involved in making the woodlands into a park accessible to many people without destroying the beauty of the land. Much of this land on Mount Desert Island was later to be given by Rockefeller Jr. to the federal government as Acadia National Park.

Still later, as the boys grew older, the simple hikes expanded to overnight pack trips deep into virgin forests out west, lasting three, four or five days and nights at a stretch. The boys learned the skills of camping and self-preservation. More than that, they came to absorb their father's deep

and abiding love of nature and conservation. Nature for their father was
the great equalizer. Hiking or riding horseback in the woods seemed to
give him a mellowing pleasure, a sense of time and space. Away from the
city and its people and its problems, it gave him what he liked to call a
good perspective on life.

Well into his eighties, retired from the cares of the organizations,
board meetings and causes to which he had devoted his life, Rockefeller
Jr. still spent part of each year at his JY Ranch at the foot of the Grand
Tetons in Wyoming, and part of each day there on horseback. One morning, while riding on a narrow mountain trail thousands of feet above the
foot of the valley, with "Red" Matthews, the resident cowboy of the
ranch, leading, and Lindsley F. Kimball, a vice-president of the Rockefeller Foundation, on horseback behind him, John Jr. stopped short and
sat upright and quiet in his saddle. Red continued on a bit until he noticed his elderly employer was no longer behind him. "Anything wrong,
Mr. Rockefeller?" he shouted back. "No, Red," answered the philanthropist with a wave of his hand toward the imposing vista. "I was just
thinking. God made all this and he made me and I was just getting things
in perspective."

The passing years, as they do to most men, had mellowed the personality of John D. Rockefeller, Jr. He had been sixty-three years old when his
own father died and most people remember him as he was in the years
after 1937, a slender white-haired man of medium height, wearing round
silver-rimmed spectacles, speaking in a soft modulated voice, personally
humble and gracious in his manners toward all others. But in his younger
years he had been albeit personally humble and shy, almost pure perfectionist with a wide puritanical streak, and color-blind to shades of gray between right and wrong. Even in the years of rearing his own children, the
years between the oldest children, Babs and John, and the youngest ones,
Winthrop and David, there was a perceptible leavening in his strictness.
Perhaps it was a change in the times and the mood of the country entering
into the Roaring Twenties; perhaps it was merely that he himself was
older. Years later, when Babs herself was a grandmother, she would
describe the difference: "Oh, Father was much more strict with us older
children when we were growing up than with Win or David. When he
found that Nelson was left-handed, for instance, he tried and tried for
months to change him over, but when Win and David also favored their
left hands, why, he just let them be."

David, of course, had the benefit of an experienced father who had
raised five children before him. Nevertheless, it was David, looking back to
when he himself was chairman of the Chase Manhattan Bank, who would
say: "If we had been raised by Father alone with his too puritanical background, there would have been much more rebellion from us, I think, but
then we also had Mother."

4

Growing Up

---

*"Nelson took his punishment in his usual
philosophical way . . ."*

Their mother brought to them a whole other side of life and way of living
without once contradicting their father or his indoctrination. More than
anything else, it was her personality and manner of conducting herself
which came through to them. Children do learn from watching and seeing. In contrast to her husband, Abby Aldrich Rockefeller, in the words of
one of her sons, was always "relaxedly human." She enjoyed doing things,
she liked people, she adored parties, she drew her strength from plunging
into large gatherings, she preferred to take part in worthwhile activities
without having to run them on her own. She also liked to have fun just
for the sake of having fun, to treat the children to an expensive restaurant
when no special occasion called for it, to experiment with an exotic dish
only because she had never tried it before. Her children loved her for it.

Perhaps the best description, in summary, of the relationship between
their mother and father was given by Mary Ellen Chase in her small and
personal biography of Abby Aldrich Rockefeller: "Perhaps, indeed, no two
partners in marriage could have been less innately similar than they. He
was serious, thoughtful, reserved, and inclined to be cautious and slow in
his judgments and decisions; she was gay, outgoing, confident and quick in
all her reactions. He was perhaps over-scrupulous in his adherence to
moral and religious precepts and principles; her spiritual nature, sensitive
yet sure, was less disciplined than it was intuitive. He was logical in his approach to most matters, seeing cause and effect, thinking things through;
she was often illogical. Her imagination was more volatile than his, her humor more ready, her fancy more rich . . . He was precise and exact in his

attention to particulars and details; she was likely to throw details to the winds, since she could go straight to the heart of the matter without them and, moreover, could gather them together later, disguised and more attractive than mere items. He preferred, whenever possible, to avoid large social groups, to shun casual and time-consuming conversation; she was in her element in the midst of many people and could elicit confidence and confidences from almost anyone . . .

"Yet in spite of fundamental differences they posed equally fundamental similarities. They shared a profound sense of the responsibility which one human being bears for the welfare of another, and a genuine desire to fulfill that obligation; they respected the minds of others; they held tenaciously to what they believed to be right in human behavior; and although in many ways their cultural tastes were dissimilar and remained so, each cared deeply for whatever was best and highest in the nurture of the human spirit. They held in common a hatred of disloyalty in any form toward a person or a principle, believing it to be of all offenses the most difficult to forgive. They never lost a consuming pride in each other . . . And perhaps the strongest single tie which bound them together and was to be the primary and supreme influence upon them both was the sincere conviction that life is neither made nor judged by mere possessions."

Abby Aldrich Rockefeller very definitely had a mind of her own and her husband learned of it soon enough. On their honeymoon in 1901, spent at the Rockefeller estate at Pocantico Hills, John Jr. suggested, in outlining her future duties, that she keep a weekly expense account. She replied succinctly, "I won't," and never did. When he ventured to ask what she had done or intended to do with the rather large sum of money he had given her as a wedding gift, presumably to buy something of lasting value, she informed him that she no longer had it. "You see," she said, "I gave it away."*

Rockefeller Jr. was captivated by her from the start and throughout the fifty years of their marriage. Whenever he was away traveling, he would each night write to her a letter of admiration or outright passion. It was as though in a letter he could express thoughts he was too inhibited to say aloud. "What you might say next I never could tell," he wrote her a few years after their marriage, "but I always knew that I should probably like it better than what you had said last, however captivating that might have been."

Mrs. Rockefeller also had a room of her own in each of the family houses, a frilly, delicate sitting room most often located to the right of the front door, opposite her husband's office. There, at 5 to 6 P.M. every school day, she took her tea and was available to her children when they returned home. She never told them they had to report in. But it was the only

* To the YWCA of Providence, Rhode Island, of which she was a director.

place in the house where they could get cookies with their milk. The result was, of course, a family habit of "having tea with Mother" and discussing the events of the day, the night's homework, or sibling disputes and grievances.

She counseled them on how to respond with a laugh when schoolmates called one or the other "Mr. Moneybags" or "Mr. Rockedollar," or asked how many yachts they owned or how much money they had in the bank. She explained her belief that every person, no matter how nasty he or she may seem or act, had some good in him, and that it was up to each of them to seek out the good, not the bad, and to benefit by it. She urged them to be kind to those of their friends who seemed to be lonely, to help those in need of help, to seek out those who seemed to be superior to themselves and to learn from them. The Rockefeller children were well aware of the virtues spelled out in the Bible, but it was their mother who, even more than their father, personalized those virtues for them. She always understood their individual shortcomings and she empathized with any one of them who stumbled on the path to perfection. She did it all, more often than not, with a smile. One of her favorite ploys was to explain away such shortcomings with "Perhaps there is a little bit too much Aldrich in us and not enough Rockefeller!"

As they grew up, Mrs. Rockefeller liked to remind her children that they had Aldrich blood flowing through them as well as Rockefeller. The mixture was different in each of them, she would say, pointing out that one son had a Rockefeller nose, Aldrich eyes and a Rockefeller chin, while another had the Rockefeller eyes and an Aldrich forehead and ears just like those of Uncle So-and-So. She lived with the children every day, much more than did their father. The rearing of the children was her concern and responsibility. She was there. While their father set the standards of conduct high, quite high, their mother enveloped the Rockefeller standards with the warmth and good cheer of the Aldrich family. This was exemplified best perhaps by her personally favorite verse from the Bible, the one she most often quoted to her children: "And what doth the Lord require of thee, but to do justly, and to love mercy, and to walk humbly with thy God?" (Micah 6:8)

The heritage of the third generation of Rockefellers, it would seem, was munificent in more ways than money. In their mother and father, the five brothers and their sister had what future psychologists would postulate as ideal parents: an authoritarian father figure who said, in effect, you must live up to my demands and earn my love, and an all-encompassing mother who assured them of her love no matter what they did. And yet, no matter how carefully their parents apportioned their love and care, the six Rockefeller children grew up individually different from one another. Their heredity and environment might have seemed the same, but the permutations of inherited genes and chromosomes ensured a difference, and home life for each of them was subtly different because of the normal changes brought on by the passage of time and events.

Abby, the first-born, named for her mother but called "Babs" by her brothers, was an only child for three years before John 3rd was born in 1906. Not only did she suffer new and inexperienced parents, she also remained the only girl as one after another of the new additions to the family turned out to be a brother. There was the loneliness of being the only girl in a male-oriented family. More than that, she was aware of all the added years of rules and regulations and religion and parental expectations. She knelt in prayer every morning five years more than her brother, Nelson. Maturing earlier than her brothers, she bridled silently, having to listen to her father recite verses from the Bible which she had heard him do so often before; as a young lady she resented having to rise at 7 A.M. to accompany her younger brothers to church on Sunday morning, particularly when she had been out late the night before. She rebelled against having to do chores for extra pin money. "I can always get a dollar from Grandpa," she would tell her brothers. Nor did she think the war effort in 1918 needed her particular Victory garden. She had a mind of her own and, once past the tomboy days of her childhood, she was stubborn.

Before her father got around to offering a $2,500 reward to any of the children who refrained from smoking cigarettes until twenty-one, Abby was smoking them and liking them. She started at age fifteen, alone in the privacy of the rowboat in the middle of a lake where no one could see her. By the time her father discovered one of her cigarette butts in the house and confronted her, she had decided that she liked smoking well enough to defy her parents. Her father lectured her on her health. She had forfeited the $2,500 bonus for not smoking, but he offered her a much needed increase in her allowance in exchange for a promise to give up cigarettes until she was twenty-one. She refused.

She scandalized the Rockefeller name by making headlines in the 1925 tabloid press for a summons she received for speeding on Riverside Drive—at twenty-seven miles per hour.

Her brothers had each other to play with, but she found only one friend during the years of her childhood, Ellen Milton, whose family lived near the Rockefellers in Pocantico Hills. Abby married Ellen's brother, David, the "only boy on the block," soon after he got his law degree. She left with him to live in a New York City apartment rather than stay in Pocantico Hills. Only eleven years later, when she was thirty-five and the mother of two, would she return to Westchester and build her own home, Hudson Pines.

In retrospect, she could look back on those childhood years and recall that although her father had never said so in so many words she, Babs, was probably his favorite child. Perhaps it was because she was the only girl among so many brothers, perhaps because she was the most rebellious.

She never doubted that he loved her deeply. But she was never able as a child to return that love: she was scared to death of him. She felt she could never live up to his high standards. She could not get over the implicit criticism when she came back from school with poor grades. She could never find the right answer when he asked her at the week's review of her grades and accounts, "What have you accomplished this week?" Her father went to great pains to be kind to her. He would treat her to a trip to see her grandfather in Florida and then spoil it on the way with the discovery that she forgot to pack her comb. He would take her to a jewelry store to buy her something personal and no matter how small the item, it had to be perfect of its kind. He gave her his time and she understood with a child's awe the "wonderful things" he was doing for mankind in his own work. But, "He was so serious, so God-fearing, he never developed the knack of seeing the lighter side of life," she would recall.

John 3rd and Nelson were as unlike one another as the reverse sides of a coin. Tall, thin, sensitive and introverted, John 3rd strove to emulate his father. Naturally an obedient child, he accepted without question the good sense, wisdom and advice of his parents. He seemed to gather his pleasure from doing what he knew was right. The allowances and account books made sense to him; he found he would rather save his money than waste it for the momentary pleasure of sweets. Nelson would rush off to the candy store after receiving his allowance and he was without spending money by the middle of the week, if not sooner. Long before he became aware of the family wealth and position, John 3rd sensed the importance of bearing the name of his father and his grandfather. He understood almost from the very start his father's concept of obligation inherent in money not earned. It was therefore perfectly reasonable to his young mind that he should apply himself to the best of his ability in all of his undertakings. He had to work hard to earn acceptable grades at the classical prep school he attended, and he worked equally hard at Princeton.

While John 3rd was so serious, Nelson was carefree, the complete extrovert and optimist, full of energy and indefatigable, ready to plunge into anything which seemed new and challenging. He defied the Rockefeller credo of caution and good sense. A bright and happy boy, he seemed incapable or unwilling to apply himself as he should. Of all the boys, Nelson was the one undaunted by his father's chastisements, unconcerned with the outside taunts about the family name, unabashed by the responsibilities and obligations of being a Rockefeller. He was what some people would call a "little devil" with the family rules, all boy, rambunctious and just full of joy. His mother secretly delighted in his pranks, or at least in some of them. She recognized that Nelson had a zest for life.

At age seven, he went without dessert one day for having emptied his paint powders over Winthrop's head. As the children's governess, Florence Scales, reported to Mrs. Rockefeller, "Nelson took his punishment in his usual philosophical way and got a bit of gristle from his beefsteak and chewed on it all the time we were eating our dessert."

A year later, she wrote Mrs. Rockefeller about the difficulty in teaching an eight-year-old Nelson to recite his poetry. "Nelson is as gay as possible and I am having a struggle with him over his poetry. He will fool away his time, apparently not paying a bit of attention to what I am trying to teach him, then all of a sudden, when I get stern with him I find that he knows it perfectly and what is more, he remembers it."

Only Nelson would have the nerve to put a baby rabbit in his mother's muff on the solemn way to church. He trusted that his mother would sit through the service with the rabbit without reporting him to his father. Only Nelson would dare to flip food at a brother across the sedate Rockefeller table when his father was not looking. Time and time again he was sent away from the table in the middle of the meal. Nevertheless, he took great joy in flicking a piece of cookie or of bread from the fingers of the one sitting next to him just as his sister or a brother was about to put the morsel in his or her mouth. The trick was to flick the food without Father catching on and then to enjoy the snicker or giggle which invariably came from the butler or a footman who had observed the action. At the family hymn singing on Sunday night, only Nelson could sing ever so slightly off key so that his father could never be sure if it were deliberate, but the others knew. His pranks were of such good nature that no one could be angry with him for long.

Being so temperamentally different from his older brother, Nelson gravitated to his younger one, Laurance. At ages eight and six, they became "best friends," sharing the same room in the West Fifty-fourth Street house, sharing toys, chores and boyhood secrets. Laurance, thin and wiry, quick-witted and mature for his age, could keep up with his exuberant, stocky brother, match him in wrestling, daredevil bike riding and in ideas. They formed a "business partnership" in shoeshining, raising rabbits, pulling weeds and running errands. They played "pretend" games in which they were big-game hunters in Africa or explorers in the Arctic. It was to Laurance that Nelson, at age seven, confided that when he grew up he was going to be President of the United States.

"We led a delightful happy life together," Nelson commented years afterward. "He could always put the rapier right through me with a twist. but he was amusing about it and I loved it."

The essence of their relationship was preserved in a letter from a governess to Mrs. Rockefeller: "When the boys were ill they played chess for hours. At first Laurance could beat Nelson pretty badly and I rebuked Nellie for letting him. The next day he called me and said, 'Now I can beat him about half the time. I made up my mind to think hard and move slowly and find that was the thing I needed.' Many of his mistakes are only carelessness."

That was what his father had been telling Nelson all along and would go on telling him past his college years: "You have great admiration for your Grandfather Rockefeller," he wrote Nelson in one of his parental letters. "Remember that one of the qualities that made him great and that not infrequently made him successful over other people was his ability to wait and to be patient to a degree that was almost superhuman. Waiting is often hard work, much harder than working and doing, but not infrequently it is the quickest and most effective way to accomplish the desired end and it is the goal that the wise man keeps his eye on."

Laurance seemed to have inherited that ability "to wait and be patient." As introspective and shy perhaps as his brother John, he often preferred to go off by himself on a bicycle or pony and think things out, but, unlike John, he was not inhibited by that introspection. He could participate in roughhouse as well as his brother Nelson and, unlike him, Laurance seemed to be able to do almost all things well without undue effort. He reminded observers at an early age of his grandfather.

Laurance, named for his grandmother, Laura Spelman Rockefeller, considered his name sissyish. Nelson disliked his own given name just as much. What boy at age eight liked to be called Nell or Nellie? So the brothers decided to change their names. Laurance chose Bill, and the nickname stuck. Nelson chose Dick. Long before one Dick Nixon came into his life, Dick Rockefeller just did not take hold, and Nelson remained Nelson.

Poor Winthrop; he was too young to keep up with his older brothers and too old to want to play with David. Three years younger than Laurance and three years older than David, Winthrop suffered all the pangs, or at least he thought so, of being a middle child. From the time he could walk and run, he was big for his age and overweight and awkward. Babs and Johnny lived in a different world. Nelson and Laurance rebuffed Win's overtures as intrusions upon their own friendship. David, at the early stages, was too young to be much fun. So Winthrop tried to force his way into the world of Nelson and Laurance and found himself, time and time again, the butt of their pranks, their teasing and downright cruelty.

The Rockefeller boys, so carefully instructed not to take advantage of those less fortunate than themselves, felt perfectly free to compete fiercely among themselves. They matched wits, physical strength, endurance, skills and whatever for the sheer joy of competing. Winthrop took a continuing beating. Nelson and Laurance considered it good clean fun and convinced themselves that Win liked to be tripped up or have his chair pulled from under him or, when playing cowboys and Indians, tied to a tree and left there.

Winthrop developed a fierce temper and that encouraged Nelson and Laurance to goad him more, until he would lose control and attack one of his tormentors, usually Nelson, only to find that when he caught Nelson, Laurance would join in. Two against one. It would invariably end with Winthrop on the ground, flat on his back, raging and impotent, with Nelson sitting on his head, and Laurance sitting on his feet, waiting for him to cool off.

Nelson called him "Wissy-Wissy" and he hated it. When in the presence of either parent, Nelson and Laurance had a private code for teasing him. They would allude obliquely to a black birthmark he had on his thigh. When they learned that he suffered from a semi-chronic kidney condition (which cleared up in his twelfth year), Nelson and Laurance would remind him that his cousin Winthrop Aldrich had died of a kidney ailment at the age of three. "You were cousins, you both had the same name and the same disease, and it killed him," one would say, and the other would ask, "How are you feeling today?" After a while, all either of them had to do was ask, "How are you feeling today, Win?" and he would get the reference.

Winthrop was a sucker for the old seesaw trick. Nelson would get him up in the air, jump off and leave him to crash to the ground. Then he would reassure his younger brother that he would not do that any more. Up would go Win, only to be disillusioned again. The down trip would be swift and painful. One Sunday morning, before church, having crashed three times, Win grabbed a pitchfork and took after Nelson. Somehow, for it was a rare occasion when he did, Win caught him and jabbed Nelson in the knee.

The incident had to be reported to their father because Nelson required first aid. It was long understood in the Rockefeller household that it was proper and courageous to report any wrongdoing oneself before anyone else did. Their father listened quietly and then advised the boys that both would get a spanking after church. What they could not know beforehand was the severity of the spanking. The anticipation was worse than the punishment, for the boys had to endure the long, long walk to church, a sermon they could not concentrate on and the long walk home. The spanking was administered impartially, without passion, but thoroughly.

Despite all the peccadilloes, Winthrop (in his own mind) grew up resenting his younger brother David more than he did Nelson or Laurance. He himself dates that resentment to the summer of 1920 when his mother took Babs on a trip to Paris, his father took John, Nelson and Laurance on an extended camping trip out West, and he, Winthrop, at age eight, was left at home with David and the governess because his parents did not think it would be fair to leave David alone. It was about this time, when Winthrop was seven going on eight, that he came to the conclusion his parents were keeping him prisoner in his room at the West Fifty-fourth Street house in New York. His room had bars on the window.

His brothers had none. The conclusion was obvious: the bars were to keep him from running away. He did not dare confront his mother or father with this outrage. If he had, of course, he would have learned that the bars were there because *his* window led to a fire escape; they were there to keep would-be kidnappers out rather than to keep Winthrop in. A simple latch opened the bars from the inside. Nevertheless, those bars on the window troubled him for years and his parents never knew because he never told them.

Winthrop did gain some measure of revenge for the beatings he took from Nelson by teasing and socking David. But Winthrop was so much bigger and older than David that there just was not quite that much fun in taking advantage of him.

Mrs. Rockefeller, the peacemaker in the family, often urged her boys to try to be more considerate of one another. When Winthrop was ten, she wrote to Nelson and Laurance, who were away at camp: "I hope, when you boys come home, you will do nothing to disturb David's present friendly feelings with Winthrop. It seems cruel to me that you big boys should make Winthrop the goat all the time. I realize that he is often trying, but you know very well that the only way to help him is by being kind to him. Abuse only makes him angry and much worse, while for love and kind treatment he will do anything. Also, remember how young David is, take time to play with him, and be good to him."

David took his lumps from brother Win, but he was spared the sibling competition of his older brothers because he was so young. He was a rather fat, roly-poly youngster, not athletically inclined. He enjoyed just watching the others, reading books and collecting things. As the "baby" of the family, he seemed in constant favor. He was, in fact, bright, cheerful and lovable. Governesses and tutors gushed over him. Descriptions in letters to his parents paint this picture: At age seven "his face just shone. Whatever David does he does with all his heart." At age nine "David seems to take after his father in his thoughtfulness, for when he took a trip to Providence he bought a present for each member of the family here . . . he bought nothing for himself but for friends. David has the spirit of thrift." At age ten he was making apple jelly and baking chocolate cakes, and when his governess explained how Russia had gone "Bolshevik," he said, "Well, if America did too, he knew he could make his own living cooking." At age fourteen, "David is doing his schoolwork faithfully though his heart is in his bugs."

David began collecting bugs at age eight in the summer of 1923 at Seal Harbor. His tutor, a science teacher named Mr. Sperry, sparked his interest with explorations of the swamps on Mount Desert Island. Setting up his "lab" in a closet off the playroom, David lined up his preserved specimens in bottles of formaldehyde, neatly labeled. He had bugs with long tails and bees with short ones, and a fine collection of beetles, all of

Richford, N.Y., 1839: the birthplace of John Davison Rockefeller.

William Avery and Eliza Davison Rockefeller and their children.

John, Mary Ann, Lucy, Frank and William.

John D. Rockefeller. *Laura Spelman Rockefeller.*

At age fifty, when Standard Oil was at the height of its power.

The two homes in
Cleveland, Ohio:
Forest Hill and
Euclid Avenue.

The children: Edith,
Bessie, Alta and John Jr.

PARTNERS IN STANDARD OIL

Henry Flagler.

John D. Archbold.

PHILANTHROPY

The Reverend Frederick T. Gates.

JOHN D. ROCKEFELLER

At eighty.

At ninety.

At ninety.

At ninety-five.

Father and son striding up Fifth Avenue, New York, 1925.

which led his governess to write his mother, "There won't be a bug on the island when David is finished with all of his specimen collecting." Winthrop derided the whole idea, calling the lab "Mrs. Candage's pillow closet," but David said it was his lab and he kept it locked at all times.

The next summer David went on collecting bugs and beetles and seaweed and shells, and the following summer he joined various neighbors, including Henry Ford II, in a children's class in nature study on the island, where a marvelous teacher, Mrs. Herbert Neal, wife of a professor of sociology at Tufts, inspired David with the wonders of entomology. At twelve David discovered Dr. Frank E. Lutz, curator of the Museum of Natural History in New York City, and he would stop off at the museum one afternoon a week on the way home from school to study the identification and classification of families of beetles. By this time, with a sizable collection of his own, David had narrowed his field of interest down to beetles. They fascinated him. Of all forms of life, he discovered, there are more species of beetles than any other. Recognizing the family and genus of a given beetle revealed the order of nature, evolution and environment. Undoubtedly David fascinated Dr. Lutz, who was one of the foremost entomologists in the United States. He invited the boy to spend the next two summers at his insect farm in Tuxedo Park, New York, and made an entomologist out of him.

David continued collecting through his teen years, and studying beetles with Dr. Lutz, so that when he entered Harvard he was granted special permission to take a graduate course in entomology. He got an A, his only one as an undergraduate at Harvard. The summer following his sophomore year, he joined Dr. Lutz's expedition studying insect life in the Grand Canyon, which yielded a range of insects one would find from south Mexico to Alaska.

While at Harvard, David taught nature study at a settlement house, where he found a youngster who, like himself years before, was fascinated by beetles and willing to work at it. David took him on as an assistant, and for years afterward his protégé, who went to work at the Chase Manhattan Bank, came to David's home in Pocantico Hills on weekends to sort, mount and classify David's collection of some thirty thousand beetles. On his worldwide travels for the bank, David carried with him several glass bottles, cotton and formaldehyde, and he collected beetles wherever possible.

Why beetles? What is the fascination to warrant a lifelong concern with beetles? David today would shrug and say, "Anything you study in depth becomes interesting and grows in importance." His hobby has given him a certain understanding and feeling for nature and for the outdoors in general which he might not have had otherwise. But the importance of his beetle collection for him personally is the inner satisfaction he derives from having a knowledge in depth of a specific subject.

David's childhood was a relatively lonely one. At the beginning, he was too young to join in the camaraderie of his brothers, and by the time he was twelve, the older boys were away in college and Winthrop had transferred to a boarding school in Connecticut. So David, from the age of twelve, was alone, an only child with four brothers and a sister.

The Rockefellers, Mr. and Mrs., were concerned with the effects of the rarefied isolation in which their children were growing up. Try as they might, there seemed to be no easy way to give their children the well-rounded experience of other children in the neighborhood. Security and precaution necessitated the bars on the windows of the house on Fifty-fourth Street and the ten-foot-high stone wall with the barbed-wire fences around the Pocantico estate. At Seal Harbor there were neighborhood children for part of July and August, to be sure, but they were all of one class: super rich, with the same problems and more. So it was, at least in part, that John D. Rockefeller, Jr., and his wife leaped at the idea of an experimental school in progressive education where children, naturally inquisitive, coming from all walks and levels of society, would learn from their peers, learn from each other, learn by doing, develop their own individual personalities, concentrate on what interested them most, and pick up the formal reading, writing and 'rithmetic at their own speed and their own inclination. This was the concept of a new educational theory, which John Dewey, the eminent teacher-philosopher at Columbia University, proposed to the Rockefeller Foundation. What Dewey wanted was the money to establish an experimental school to put his theories into practice.

The Rockefeller Foundation in 1917, with the blessing of its chairman, granted $3 million for the new school to be run by the Teachers College of Columbia University, and the Rockefeller children who were of age—Nelson, Laurance and Winthrop—were enrolled there as charter students. John 3rd continued at the Browning School, a traditional day school just around the corner from their Fifty-fourth Street home, and David, when he was old enough, followed his brothers to the new experimental progressive school. The Lincoln School was to influence all of their lives, as it would education throughout the United States for years and years to come.

Unlike private schools of its time, Lincoln was co-educational and non-segregated. The Rockefeller boys mixed with children from all walks of life. In the early grades there were no tests, no marks, no emphasis at all on the competitive aspects of learning. Students laid out their own rules of conduct, wrote their own class constitutions, chose their own courses of study within a certain framework, learned to express themselves in class and in public speaking before an entire school assembly. Boys studied sewing and cooking with the girls, and the girls took shop courses with the boys. Reading, writing and arithmetic were introduced only when a child was ready and eager to learn. He was expected to pick up these fundamentals out of a natural curiosity and desire to learn. The emphasis at Lincoln was aimed at developing the individual personality, preparing a child emotionally to fulfill his potential by working at what he enjoyed doing, and finally, learning through daily experience how to get along with all kinds of people.

There was a conflict, to be sure, between the Lincoln School's philosophy of "doing your own thing" and their father's belief that children should be made to do things they don't enjoy as a preparation for the unpleasantries which crop up in life. The Rockefeller boys seemed to be able to bridge that gap. Nelson never did learn to spell or master his numbers adequately, and his report cards left a good deal to be desired. The school principal wrote home at the end of the eleventh grade that "Nelson should work harder," and his father agreed. Approaching graduation, Nelson found himself short on school credits because of the courses he had chosen, and he had to get private tutoring in his senior year. Laurance did somewhat better, but he, too, encountered trouble with his three R's. However, he did make Princeton, where, in his freshman year, facing written examinations for the first time, he almost flunked out. Winthrop had the most trouble. He floundered in the freedom and lack of discipline at Lincoln and in the tenth grade he was transferred to the Loomis School, a more formal prep boarding school which his brother John had attended at Windsor, Connecticut. The transition was tough on Winthrop. Unprepared for the higher scholastic standards of Loomis, at the first marking period, where D was the lowest passing mark, Win earned two E's and three F's. But he liked Loomis and was saved there by his high marks for effort. The chores imposed upon the boarding students—cleaning your room, sweeping the halls, waiting on tables—came easy to a Rockefeller boy, and he excelled in as many extracurricular activities as were permitted him. He led a student campaign to raise funds for a new athletic field, four new tennis courts and a new wing on the gymnasium. He played rather poor second-string baseball, was fairly good at the hammer throw in field events, but his academic studies plagued him through his high school years. In order to stay in Loomis, he had to take extra tutoring at night and on weekends.

David, on the other hand, breezed through the laissez-faire atmosphere of Lincoln School, a model student whose personality and self-sufficiency developed progressively with the maturity of years, and he had no trouble at all with the three R's, just as Professor John Dewey theorized. Harvard was happy to have him.

The four brothers, Winthrop included, looked back afterward with great favor upon the years spent at the Lincoln School. They credited the school, along with the training by their father, for their outlook on life, for teaching them the role of the activist who welcomes new problems and challenges and is eager to become involved, to make a decision and to take action. Lincoln School gave them in the 1920s the freedom and independence in education which many students a half century later would still be seeking. Brother John missed something by not having attended Lincoln.

While their father was a strict disciplinarian in one sense, he permitted them all a great latitude of freedom so long as those activities led to a development of self-sufficiency. He did not want his offspring to grow up to be dilettantes, snobs or overdependent, overprotected children. The Rockefellers encouraged their boys at an early age to take overnight camping trips, allowed them to use axes and saws in land-clearing projects, permitted them to go off canoeing or sailing by themselves, despite their own parental fears. They gave the boys the best instruction available and then let them find out for themselves the dangers involved in various ventures. Laurance, at nine, broke his arm just above the elbow falling off a pony. Nelson, at twelve, shot himself in the foot with an air gun. Winthrop, at six, fell headfirst off a ten-foot-high retaining wall and missed by inches cracking his head open on a graveled road.

The boys also took on several projects of their own choosing. The manufacture of maple sugar candy at Pocantico was a favorite activity. Each would tap a number of maple trees assigned to him as his own. The syrup would then be boiled in huge caldrons for hours and hours until it was reduced to the fudge-like consistency of maple candy. The Rockefellers lost at least one cook because even their hotel-sized kitchen stove could not accommodate the maple sugar and dinner, too. When a second cook threatened to quit, the boys switched to the old Vermont method of boiling the syrup outdoors with the caldrons set upon a slab of iron about eight feet long and three feet wide over open wood-burning fires.

Another project each would long remember with a special intensity was the building of a secret log cabin in the woods of Mount Desert Island in the summer of 1921. The idea was conceived by John and Nelson from the remembrance of the family trip the previous summer in which they had watched logging operations in the state of Washington. Now, in Maine, the two boys undertook to build a cabin just as the pioneers had done years before. Sneaking away in their free hours, John and Nelson cleared a site, chopped down balsam trees, used two Shetland ponies and yokes to drag the logs and proceeded to build their own cabin, ten feet long and eight feet wide. It was hard but wondrous work, with perhaps the first intimations of the Rockefeller family urge to build. Halfway through the summer, Laurance began to complain that he was never allowed to accompany his two older brothers. But that, they insisted, was half the fun: it was a secret cabin because no one knew where it was. Finally, through their mother, eleven-year-old Laurance negotiated his way as an apprentice into the union. The cabin walls grew to shoulder height and a pitched roof was built over that, the windows were cut out and a door finished off the job. Neither their mother nor father, nor any tutor, was allowed to see the secret cabin. Winthrop could not wrangle his way into the project and was bitter about it. David, at age six, could not have cared less and was spared the pangs of ostracism. The cabin was embellished with an outdoor fireplace, where the boys cooked their "pioneer" meals for several of the following summers. Remnants of their first building venture remain hidden in those woods to this day. In the summer of 1970, Nelson and Laurance, both grandfathers, rediscovered that campsite.

Their grandfather played an integral and subtler part in their growing up, a steady presence they all felt profoundly, and an influence on all of their lives. He was an old, old man, thin with parchment-like skin when they were rosy-cheeked youngsters, sixty-nine on the day that Nelson was born in 1908. But he retained his strength, his wit and his sharp mind. The popular press may have pictured him as a cadaverous old pirate with an ulcerous stomach who subsisted on crackers and milk, cackling over his crafty schemes to mulct widows, but his young grandchildren, knowing nothing of all this, positively adored him. He was more fun to be with than their own father. Prayers in his house were always shorter than in their own. He could smile and put up with the rambunctious tricks of energetic young boys far better than their father. In the very early days he would walk the quarter mile from the "Big House" to theirs for a game of blindman's buff. He delighted in chasing them, blindfolded, with arms outstretched, shouting out that he was a blind man seeking his fellow man. Later, when they were old enough, they went to his house for lunch or dinner on one or the other day of the weekend. Meals at Kykuit were always long, seldom under two hours, and most enjoyable for the youngsters. Their grandfather to them was the greatest storyteller alive, better than the popular Will Rogers. He would eat everything served his guests, but the portions on his plate were minute. He would eat slowly, masticating his food well as his doctor advised, and then over dessert, he might launch into one of his stories. The children usually knew what was coming and stifled their giggles until the end. But a first-time guest at the Rockefeller table might well be in some doubt whether the story being told was truth or fiction because the famous old man often interjected himself into the story. They were shaggy dog stories without any particular point or moral lesson to them, and for that the children were thankful. The point was in the telling of the story. A favorite was the tale of the character with a heart of gold who perhaps liked his liquor too much, and one dark night stumbled into a water trough in the town square, thrashing the water and screaming for help. (Standing at the head of the table, his napkin dangling from his fingers, Mr. Rockefeller would wave his arms in the air, cry "Help, help," as he described the man's plight.) Finally the town's policeman would arrive on the scene and reach out to rescue the drowning man, whereupon the town drunk would cry out, "No, no, save the women and children first!"

Or the story of the time Mr. Rockefeller's friend toured an insane asylum, guided by an inmate he was assured was harmless. After a long tour in which the inmate quite lucidly described the institution and each of its inmates, the visitor thanked him, commented upon his obvious sanity and asked, "Is there anything I can do for you?" "Yes," replied the inmate. "Do you happen to have a dry piece of toast in your pocket? You see, I'm a poached egg."

Young Winthrop once tried that story at the dinner table to his grandfather's obvious pleasure. But when he gave the punch line, "Do you happen to have a piece of toast in your pocket because, you see, I'm a poached egg," his grandfather corrected him. "Dry toast, brother, dry toast."

John D. Rockefeller, Sr., was exact and meticulous. There was an established time for meals, naps, walks, car rides, golf, work on stock market investments. Each of his grandchildren was impressed as time went by with his imperturbability, his patience, his common sense and the aura of self-confidence that hung about him. Unlike their own father, he liked to talk to people, and he almost always had guests join him in meals, auto rides or golf. He was famous, of course, for giving away dimes to people he met on the street. Only his intimates knew that giving away dimes served not so much as a public relations stunt to soften his public image, but rather as a wedge to open a conversation. He would often say as he gave someone a dime, "As long as you have this dime, you'll never be broke." And those who received such dimes remembered the occasion and kept those dimes.

Despite advice to the contrary, the old man insisted upon picking up hitchhikers during his daily auto rides. He liked to talk with new and strange people. Actually he preferred to listen more than to talk. At home, his grandchildren came to realize that he seldom, if ever, talked of the past. He never mentioned the Standard Oil Company. But he was passionately interested in what was going on in the present and what was likely to happen in the future. The Rockefellers like to think of it as a family trait: never to worry about the past.

His golf game was characteristic of him, imperturbable, accurate and steady. His shots would go down the fairway for about a hundred yards, never much more and never much less, but always right in the middle of the fairway. The boys when teen-agers, each got their chance to play against their grandfather and they recall that while they had more power they also had more slices and hooks. Their grandfather was not above using the prerogative of age when calculating his score. When a shot displeased him, he would say to his caddy, "Augustino, I think we'll take that shot over." No one dared to count the faulty shot.

As he grew older, into his eighties and then into his nineties, he continued the same round of activities, except that each of them became of shorter duration. Golf was cut from nine holes to six and then to four, the daily walks were curtailed, the social gatherings were shortened so as not to tire him, he spent more and more time having to rest. But he never complained. He faced reality, understood it and accepted it with a fine measure of common sense. To brother Laurance he once explained, "I'm like your bike when you're coasting downhill. I can coast just so far and nothing much can be done about it."

5

John D. Rockefeller

"The business is yours!"

A bronze bust, smaller than life size, of John D. Rockefeller stands today on a pedestal off to one side of the reception desk of the family offices on the fifty-sixth floor of the RCA Building. It portrays the founder of the family fortune in his old age, thin and wrinkled, serious, but with a trace of a wry smile and a bit of a twinkle in his eyes. It is as if he were silently content now in his background niche, the course of his long life run, slyly amused to see the foibles of men following in his wake. Even in bronze replica, if you look closely enough, he seems somehow just a bit smarter than the next fellow. But perhaps that is only hindsight. He certainly was not born a business genius, a robber baron or a millionaire. In fact, few, if any, recognized any particular attributes about him as a child that presaged what he would become.

Born in a small town in upstate New York in 1839, a mere life span away from the birth of a new nation, he was raised by a God-fearing, Baptist mother who believed what the Bible said literally, and taught the practical ways of the world by an unpious, flamboyant father, "Big Bill" Rockefeller, who sold quick and quack cures for cancer and other ailments from a covered wagon in the wilds of the West. Financially the family had its ups and downs. Big Bill was often on the road for long periods of time and not until the children were grown did they learn of the estrangement of their mother and father. At sixteen years of age, the oldest boy of five children, then living near Cleveland, John D. went out to fulfill his own potential in the world of business.

He quit high school shortly before he was due to graduate when he decided not to go on to college. In high school his classmates called him

"Deacon" because he was so religious, a regular churchgoer. His high school teacher years later would recall him as "just an ordinary, well-behaved boy plodding along with his lessons," adding that "there was nothing about him to make anybody speculate about his future." In preparation for finding a job, he did attend Folsom's Commercial College in Cleveland for a four-month course in accounting and bookkeeping.

Then, in time-honored fashion, he pounded the pavements of Cleveland, walking door to door, seeking his first job. After three weeks of searching, he found it, but only on a trial basis, which he dutifully noted in his personal account ledger, purchased his first week on the job: "September 26, 1855,—Commenced business as a book keeper for Hewitt & Tuttle, Cleveland, Ohio."

He worked without pay for three months and only then was he officially hired, paid $50 for these three months and put on a salary of $25 a month. "January 1, 1856—Arrangements made to stay with Hewitt & Tuttle one year for the sum of $300."

Across America in 1856, with the seeds of a great civil war being sown over the issue of slavery, most homes were lighted with candles, the economy was agricultural, people went to bed soon after the sun went down. Only the well-to-do could afford whale oil or a newly discovered and rather explosive kind of kerosene (a coal distillate) for their lamps. There was no petroleum oil, at least not aboveground. It had not yet been discovered. Cleveland at the time was a new and rapidly expanding city, a shipping center between East and West, and Hewitt & Tuttle was one of several commission merchants and produce shippers flourishing in Cleveland. The teen-age bookkeeper's task there was to audit bills and inventories, to check on items bought and sold on consignment and to see that Hewitt & Tuttle received its proper commissions. He soon developed a good auditor's eye for figures. There was a satisfaction in catching discrepancies in bills presented to the firm, most of which meant money found for Hewitt & Tuttle. He worked in the front office with the two partners, observing at first hand all facets of the business and developing for himself a philosophy of good business policy: integrity, character, attention to detail.

He worked diligently at his job, but his interests went beyond mere bookkeeping. He had an innate feel for the world of business. In May of his first year at work he made his first investment in real estate, "One share of land in the Settler's New Home Association situated in the Southwestern corner of the county of Franklin, Iowa." And before the year was out, he was lending money to his own employers, at 10 per cent interest. "September 3, 1856—I have this day loaned Hewitt & Tuttle $1,000 (received of my father September 1st) and received their note September 3rd at 10% per annum."

That first full year at work in which he earned $300, every nickel and dime he spent was noted in his personal account ledger under heading of Donations, Board, Washing, Horse Account, Sundry Expenses and others. That year John D. Rockefeller lived beyond his means. "Excess of Expenses above Sallary [sic]—$23.26," he wrote with some dubious spelling, but impeccable arithmetic, in his ledger. But it was the only such year.

Two years later, while still working for Hewitt & Tuttle, he turned entrepreneur, borrowing money from his father, from his mother and from his younger brother, William, all to speculate in pork and lard. In Ledger B, still preserved in the Rockefeller Family Archives in the RCA Building, he duly noticed that from April to December 1858, on his "Pork Account" he paid interest of $27.24 to his father, $6.59 to his mother and $8.70 to William while he himself made a profit of $159.35.

The next year he came to a parting of the ways with Hewitt & Tuttle over his annual salary. John D. Rockefeller wanted $800 a year and his employers thought he was worth no more than $700.

So, looking around again for the right opportunity, he went into business for himself with a partner, Maurice Clark, an English immigrant ten years his senior, who worked for a competing commission firm in Cleveland. Their business was the same, buying and selling farm produce and supplies on consignment for a commission. However, to start as full partner, Rockefeller had to come up with $2,000 to match Clark's capital investment. To augment his own savings he asked his father for a loan of $1,000. His father agreed, saying, "But John, the rate is ten."

It was to be the first of many large loans from father to son, but always at the prevailing rate of interest. His father took particular delight in calling his loans at unexpected intervals just to see if John would come up with the money. Then he would lend him money again. In later years John D. would credit his father with teaching him the "practical ways" of business. And Big Bill Rockefeller would boast about his son's success in business, saying, "I cheat my boys every time I get a chance. I want to make them sharp. I trade with the boys and skin them and just beat them every time I can." John D., when an old, old man, told his grandson Nelson that his own earlier training was very much different from Nelson's. When he, John D., was a little boy, his father had taught him to jump full out from his high chair into the arms of his father. Then one time his father took his arms away, John D. crashed to the floor and his father told him sternly, "Remember, never trust anyone completely, not even me."

On the other hand, John D. came to believe that integrity was the underlying commodity a businessman sold in any transaction and throughout his life he went to great pains that his word would be trusted. This might well have been a distinct reaction to how he knew his father had conducted his business, for in 1905, when he himself was sixty-six years old, he wrote a touching letter to the superintendent of his estate at Forest Hill in Cleveland on the subject. The problem then at hand was that a group of small orphan boys was to revisit the estate and one of them had written John D. reminding him of his promise the previous year that the boys would get to eat one of the pigs being raised on the estate this year. But the pigs had been sold. John D. wrote his estate manager at length that he wanted him to explain the situation to the boys so they would not think the matter had been forgotten or overlooked, adding: "I want simply an explanation, so that they will understand the matter and feel happy about it. If they do not, we must see what we can do. I leave it to you. I remember to this day that my father promised me a Shetland pony, near sixty years ago, and I never got the pony."

Clark & Rockefeller, commission merchants, opened for business March 18, 1859, at 32 River Street, Cleveland. John D. was nineteen and a half years old. Clark was the "outside man," dealing with customers and consignments, while John D. remained "inside" most of the time, tending to the facts, figures and financing of the business. As Clark described him in those days, "He was methodical to an extreme, careful as to details and exacting to a fraction. If there was a cent due us, he wanted it. If there was a cent due a customer, he wanted him to have it."

The firm of Clark & Rockefeller worked hard and well and prospered from the start. John D. never had a bad year ever after. At the end of the first year of business, John D. netted $2,200 as his share of the profits, three times as much as he would have earned at Hewitt & Tuttle. At the end of the second year, 1861, his share came to $6,000 and the Civil War had begun. Business boomed.

Even as a young man, John D. was much more than a persnickety bookkeeper. While exacting in auditing the pennies, he was also out borrowing dollars by the thousands in order to expand the business. In his first year as a businessman, he convinced a local bank to lend him $2,000 on the basis of the firm's books alone. It made quite an impression upon him. "As I left that bank, my elation can hardly be imagined," he wrote years later in his memoirs *Random Reminiscences;* "I held up my head— think of it, a bank had trusted me for $2,000! I felt that I was now a man of importance in the community." He was then not yet twenty.

Meanwhile oil had been discovered. Five months after Clark & Rockefeller opened the doors of their business, Edwin L. Drake, a man whose mission in life was to drill into the earth and bring up oil, brought in the first oil well ever drilled, in the desolate farm town of Titusville, Pennsylvania, less than 150 miles from Cleveland. He died broke, but others made millions. Farmers became rich merely by leasing their land for drilling. The oil rush was on in 1859, just like the gold rush of ten years earlier. Thousands flocked into western Pennsylvania to prospect for oil. They were followed by the speculators and con men looking for a quick killing, followed, in turn by those who would make money from those who had it, the supply merchants, the gamblers, the saloonkeepers and, of course, the camp followers. But oil flowed and men became rich. Storage facilities overflowed. Oil lay about in large pools aboveground. Statistically production grew from 650,000 barrels in 1860 to 900,000 in 1861, to more than 3 million in 1862.

Oil refineries, large and small, sprang up almost every day to convert this crude petroleum into kerosene for lamps across America, as well as for sundry by-products. Oil pollution flowed from the refineries into the rivers nearby and in Cleveland the smell of oil was carried by the Cuyahoga River through the city.

One group of Cleveland businessmen, deciding to investigate the profit possibilities in this new bonanza, chose that up-and-coming young businessman, John D. Rockefeller, to make a personal inspection tour of the Pennsylvania oil fields and to report back to them. The reaction of this good Baptist and devout puritan to what he saw in Titusville was horror. He reported back chaos and pandemonium, and recommended that no sane businessman would want to invest in oil production. He allowed as that there might well be some profit in refining oil, but even that was of high risk and not advisable.

There is nothing on record to indicate that Rockefeller at that time or even in the immediate years afterward thought further about going into the oil business.

However, three years later his partner, Maurice Clark, was approached by another Englishman who had come to Cleveland, Sam Andrews, who was then working in a refinery making oil from coal. Andrews told Clark that he had discovered a better way to refine petroleum into kerosene by using sulfuric acid. But he needed money to start up a refinery of his own. As a result, the firm of Clark & Rockefeller, enjoying an excess of profits, invested $4,000 for a half interest in a refinery to be operated by Sam Andrews. Rockefeller did not deign even to put his name on the new firm, Andrews, Clark & Company. As the new company grew—for indeed Sam Andrews did have a superior method for refining oil —Clark & Rockefeller was called upon to supply more and more capital for expansion. John D. Rockefeller went out borrowing again.

During the next year, however, Maurice Clark and John Rockefeller came to an amicable parting of the ways. Their disagreements on business policy had become irreconcilable. Clark objected to his younger partner's rigidity against extending credit to customers while at the same time borrowing tens of thousands of dollars to expand the oil business at considerable risk to the parent firm. It was apparent to both of them that the oil business had far more potential value, however risky, than the handling of farm produce. So in 1865 the partners decided to separate the two, along with their partnership, and to auction off between them the firm's share in Andrews, Clark & Company: the highest bidder would get the oil business and the other would keep the commission firm as his own plus the money pledged by the highest bid.

The auction started at $500. John D. raised every bid of his old partner without hesitation. "I had made up my mind that I wanted to go into the oil trade, not as a special partner, but actively on a larger scale," he commented in his *Reminiscences*. When the bidding reached $50,000 both partners realized that they were well beyond the actual value of the oil firm.

As Rockefeller himself described that scene: "Finally it advanced to $60,000, and by slow stages to $70,000, and I almost feared for my ability to buy the business and have money to pay for it. At last the other side bid $72,000. Without hesitation I said $72,500.

"Mr. Clark then said: 'I'll go no higher, John; the business is yours.'"

John D. Rockefeller, age twenty-six, was in the oil trade. A year earlier he had courted and won the hand of Laura Celestia Spelman, the daughter of a prosperous businessman in Cleveland. She was well educated, a teacher, an ardent abolitionist and a deeply religious congregationalist. The courtship and marriage was duly noted in John D.'s account book, Ledger B, which ran from 1856 to 1872. An accountant at heart, he kept no journal or diary but he did make note in Ledger B in 1864 of each flower bouquet he bought, one for $.60, another for $.50 and undoubtedly the most impressive one for $1.50. On April 8, 1864, he purchased the diamond engagement ring. That cost $118. The marriage ceremony on September 8 of that year is down for $20; the marriage certificate was $1.10. The honeymooners' view of Niagara Falls cost $.75 and a cushion for his bride cost him another $.75. Nor did postage for $.03 escape the ledger.

John D's preoccupation with the oil business can be inferred easily from the penalties he imposed upon himself in the early years of his marriage, all duly noted in Ledger B: "Laura, for late meals $2.00 . . . late for meals 25¢ . . . 75¢ . . . 25¢ . . ."

The new firm of Rockefeller & Andrews immediately began expanding. Sam's brother, John, became the new purchasing agent. John D.'s brother, William, was taken to build a second refinery. Sam continued as the production genius of the firm, refining more and more products from crude petroleum with less and less waste. John D. applied himself to watching those "little details" such as the cost of barrels, storage facilities, transportation and, of course, finance and marketing.

The trouble in the oil trade at the time was obvious: overproduction, oversupply, chaotic competition, price wars and falling prices. There were fifty-five refineries in Cleveland alone and many more in Philadelphia, Pittsburgh, Baltimore, New York and New Jersey.

"The cleansing of crude petroleum was a simple and easy process, and at first the profits were very large," Rockefeller explained in *Reminis-*

cences. "Naturally all sorts of people went into it: the butcher, the baker and the candlestick maker began to refine oil, and it was only a short time before more of the finished product was put on the market than could possibly be consumed."

The plight of the producers—the men who brought the oil up from the earth—was even worse. Their market was absolutely glutted. Crude oil, which sold at the start in 1859 at an *average* price of $20 a barrel, fell to $9.60 a barrel in 1860 and then plunged to an *average* of $.52 a barrel in 1861. At its low, crude oil in 1860 and 1861 sold at $.10 a barrel. Attempts to form alliances and associations to stabilize prices all failed. This was an era of free competition, laissez-faire capitalism and belief in survival of the fittest. Bankruptcy in the oil trade was common.

Rockefeller, with his logical and analytical mind, set out to meet all competition by selling a better product, expanding his market and, above all, cutting costs so he could safely reduce his prices. He borrowed money from banks to enlarge Sam Andrews' old refinery, the Excelsior, and then to build a new and better refinery in Cleveland which he called the Standard. The name was based on the product John D. wanted to market, a standard quality of oil which the consumer could rely on as opposed to most of the kerosene then on the market. In those early days if you bought two barrels of oil from the same refinery you might find one so purified that it would flare instead of burn, and another one which produced more smoke than light. Rockefeller instituted from the very start quality control.

He also opened an office in New York City, headed by his brother William, from which to sell Standard's oil on the East Coast and abroad. He wanted an international market. He spent money to cut costs wherever possible. Standard began to make their own oil barrels and saved $1.00 on a barrel; it bought out a firm in order to produce its own sulfuric acid for refining; it poured profits back into building huge storage tanks so it could purchase crude oil when most advantageous. Rockefeller spared no expense in research to improve his product. As the years went on he invested in buying Standard's own oil containers for railroad shipment, barges and tankers for shipping oil via the Great Lakes, and then pipelines to avoid the cost of railroad shipments.

What John D. Rockefeller sought and accomplished, in short, would one day be recognized as the *vertical integration* of the Standard Oil Company, a practice which would become the goal of sophisticated companies of the twentieth century. He wanted to make Standard as self-sufficient as practicable, paying no one a profit on an item which Standard itself could produce.

With a genius for finance, he recognized early on that sufficient money and credit were as essential for the success of Standard as any other ingredient which went into refining and marketing oil. He solved Standard's financial problems two years after going into business with Sam

Andrews. He took in two new partners. One had been a grain commission merchant like himself, the son of a Presbyterian minister, a man with a head for business. This kindred spirit was Henry Flagler, nine years older than Rockefeller. He became the new "outside man" for the firm, a bold and enterprising entrepreneur who would become second only to John D. in the hierarchy of the company. But Flagler's primary contribution to the firm at the start was to bring into it as a silent, limited-liability partner his brother-in-law, one of the richest men in Cleveland, Stephen V. Harkness, who had made a fortune in whiskey. Harkness gave the firm not only needed cash but, more important, a solid credit rating with all the banks in Cleveland.

Three years later the partners reached the conclusion that the firm had outgrown its efficiency as a limited partnership and on January 10, 1870, they changed it legally to a corporation, to be known as the Standard Oil Company. Its capitalization was $1 million, consisting of ten thousand shares of stock, par value $100 each. Sam Andrews, Flagler and William Rockefeller were given 1,333 shares of each; Harkness got 1,334 shares, other top executives split 2,000 shares and John D. Rockefeller, as founder, president and chief executive officer of the company, received 2,667 shares, or just over one-quarter ownership of the company. He was thirty years old at the time.

In an era of fierce competition as the start of an industrial revolution swept not only the "oil trade" but almost all facets of the national economy, the Standard Oil Company prospered. It met the competition in lower prices, in quality of product and in expanding its markets. Those who could not compete fell by the wayside. Of the fifty-five oil refineries in Cleveland when John D. first went into oil in 1865, only twenty-six survived by 1870 when the Standard Oil Company was incorporated. Before the end of 1872, Standard controlled twenty-one of those twenty-six.

Rockefeller, with his penchant for efficiency, abhorred the waste of effort, costs and profits inherent in the unbridled competition of the times. The practice then was to reduce prices until you drove your competition out of business and then you could raise your prices again. Rockefeller saw beyond this. It was so wasteful. Instead, he would call in the heads of a competing refinery and offer to buy them out, to merge the companies rather than compete for the prize of winner-take-all. He was a pioneer in recognizing the value of mergers. By merging competing firms, Standard Oil would avoid the waste of duplication of plant, labor force and sales effort over the same market. He was one of the first to compute the unit cost of a barrel of oil and to see that a large refinery working at full capacity for a ready market was many times more efficient than several smaller competing ones. He offered his competitors cash or stock in Standard in exchange for ownership or control of their refineries. The alternative, stated or not, was further competition and the risk of bankruptcy.

Most chose to sell out to Standard and most of them chose cash in hand, rather than shares in Standard. They lived to rue that decision. There were some who took cash and, contrary to their agreement with Standard, started new refineries and instituted particularly virulent price wars with the suspected purpose of forcing Standard to buy them out again if only for their nuisance value. Nevertheless, Standard Oil forged ahead. In cases where Rockefeller or his associates admired the work of a competitor, he was invited to continue to operate his refinery as an executive of Standard. Competent men at whatever level in the rival firms were invited to join the Standard "family," because, as Rockefeller explained, he needed them. Such men as Oliver H. Payne, Charles Pratt, Henry H. Rogers, John D. Archbold—empire builders in their own right—sold their companies to Standard, joined the "family" and rose through the years to positions of considerable power, wealth and fame.

Standard Oil continued to grow, and in 1872 it increased its capitalization to $2.5 million and then to $3.5 million in 1875. Profits were reinvested in the growth of the company itself because Standard Oil was *owned* almost entirely by only seven men. As the company grew rich, they grew rich. It was one of the few large companies in America which did not need to go public to raise money. While many, if not most, other companies sold stock, a good proportion of it watered, to the public, to raise needed capital, Standard Oil remained considerably undercapitalized; that is, its stock was worth more than its ostensible market value in relation to the actual assets of the Standard Oil Company.

With growth, of course, came power and economic clout. Standard Oil used its clout with the railroads, demanding and getting bigger and bigger rebates from the railroads which connected Cleveland with its sources of oil in western Pennsylvania and with its eastern and overseas markets in New York City. Rebates were legal and not uncommon in those days as a form of reduced freight rates for large shippers. Flagler, as Standard's "outside man," negotiated most of these rebates, which were based on a guaranteed amount of oil to be shipped on that line over a given year. Later Standard guaranteed whole trainloads of oil shipments, built and provided its own huge tanks which could be placed, like uniform containers, on railroad flatcars, then still later built its own storage tanks and warehouses at sidings and then insured its own shipments against fire —all in return for larger and larger rebates on the published freight fares.

Competing refineries cried unfair competition. Transportation always had been one of the largest costs in marketing oil. Without doubt, these rebates gave Standard a tremendous advantage in underselling its competition. But Rockefeller and the railroads defended the practice as moral as well as legal. Didn't everything sell more cheaply wholesale then retail? Weren't the rates really the same for any company which could guarantee to ship so many millions of barrels of oil per year on one railroad and was it his fault if only Standard could meet that specification? Could you blame the Standard Oil Company or a railroad if the railroad preferred to do business with one large company, with a guaranteed amount of business per year, rather than twenty-three small and unreliable customers who wanted to ship their oil?

From the very earliest days of the 1870s, as it grew larger and larger and more and more powerful, Standard became the focal point in the oil industry of envy, resentment, outrage and downright hatred. As the good times of high prices and easy fortunes of the 1860s slipped in the business recessions and "panics" of the 1870s, more and more refineries went bankrupt or were forced to sell out, competitors of Standard complained of unfair competition and sought legal redress from state legislatures. They blamed Standard for their troubles. "If someone slipped on a banana peel in those days he blamed Standard," one wag said. The oil producers were in an even worse economic situation than most refiners. Crude oil still was in overabundant supply, the competition was fierce, and in line with the economic law of supply and demand it had always been the refiners who could pretty much set the price they would pay for crude oil. The producers were dependent upon them. As John D. Rockefeller's company gained dominance among the refiners he did indeed enjoy a stranglehold on the producers. In this sense he was like the robber barons of medieval Germany who extracted tolls from all ships navigating the Rhine because they, the barons, controlled the strategic narrow points along the river.

John D. Rockefeller became the man to hate in the oil industry because he was indeed the "mastermind" of the Standard Oil Company. He himself could not understand the resentment held against him. He thought he had been more than fair in buying out his competitors, as opposed to crushing them. He felt he paid a fair price for the crude oil Standard bought. But above that he saw that he and his company were riding the wave of the future in America. The day of the small entrepreneur was over. An industry composed of hundreds of small, uneconomical, clashing units could not satisfy a vast country's need for oil. An industrial revolution was sweeping the country to provide the needs of the people. Only large-scale manufacturing and marketing could bring economic stability to the oil industry and bring kerosene and other oil products to the American consumer at the cheapest costs.

John D. went on buying up refineries all over the country, and by the end of 1879, just nine years after it came into being as a legal entity, more than 90 per cent of all the refined oil sold in America was controlled by the Standard Oil Company, John D. Rockefeller, president.

6

The Standard Oil Company

"It's the figures that count."

At forty years of age, John D. Rockefeller was a handsome man, straight-backed, six feet tall, with regular features, thick wavy brown hair, a bristle guardsman mustache beneath the dominating feature of his face—a long, straight, severe nose. He was happily married, father of four children, owner of a large home on Millionaires' Row in Cleveland, Euclid Avenue, and a large estate in the suburbs. A multi-millionaire astride the oil industry, controlling a nation's natural resource, he was one of the wealthiest men in America and still virtually unknown to the public at large. He preferred it that way, eschewing ostentation or conspicuous waste long before Thorstein Veblen studied the affluent. Money itself had never been his aim, nor power per se. He never flaunted either of them. He did not enter Cleveland society or take part in the city's social or civic events. Politics did not entice him. Books, theater, the arts evoked none of his interest. He bought no yachts, joined no country club, searched for no antiques. He devoted his time, his interest and his efforts to the Standard Oil Company, the Rockefeller family and the Baptist Church. In that sense he was a narrow man. Or you might call him single-minded, his energies concentrated, a monomaniac of a sort.

A friend tells a revealing story of riding with John D. along a country road as they passed a boy driving a horse-drawn sled loaded with barrels. Both observed the happy boy whistling and cavorting on a beautiful day, whereupon Rockefeller commented wryly, "That young man will never be a success in life." The nonplused friend asked why, and Rockefeller readily replied, "Because he is not thinking of driving his horse, and that is his business." His grandson, Nelson, in a college thesis on the Standard Oil

Company, told another illustrative story of his grandfather: being called out to a fire which was obviously destroying a Standard refinery, John D. did not go about shouting orders nor did he even help try to put the fire out. Instead, he stood there, pencil and paper in hand, drawing plans for a new refinery to replace the one still on fire.

He obviously tended to his own business. His mind and will were so disciplined that he wasted little time or effort or money or anything in the course of his affairs. Waste was sinful. His personal life was never complex. He lived by the Bible, a devoted husband to the same wife for more than fifty years, a responsible father to his children, and there is no evidence that he was ever perplexed or troubled with his role in life. He was a practical man with an abundance of common sense, an activist and a doer, rather than a thinker.

The result was a kind of personal equilibrium, a quiet confidence, a patience which comes from a sense of time, place and person. They were rather subtle qualities of personality which only those around him seemed to recognize at that time and which allowed him to escape the pitfalls of other empire builders. He suffered no illusions of grandeur, no fears of failure, no paranoia of usurpation. He did not try to run Standard Oil alone. His word was not law in the board room. Nor did he surround himself with lackeys or yes men. The men around him were his "associates" and they were powerful, dynamic men, each in his own right. And yet there were few of the conflicts, personal feuds or bitter rivalry which marked other business empires. Standard Oil needed capable independent men for its swift rise among its competitors. Rockefeller himself explained: "We had a group of strong men from the outset. There were Flagler, Harkness, Colonel Payne, Andrews, my brother, and later, others. Our general rule was to take no important action until all of us were convinced of its wisdom. We made sure that we were right, and had planned for every contingency before we went ahead." John D., of course, was an exemplary leader, an administrator, a solver of problems who never had need to pound on the table or to browbeat a subordinate. In his *Reminiscences* he drew a picture of how the men who ran Standard Oil worked together: "It is not always the easiest of tasks to induce strong, forceful men to agree. It has always been our policy to hear patiently and discuss frankly until the last shred of evidence is on the table before trying to reach a conclusion and to decide finally upon a course of action. It is always, I presume, a question in every business just how fast it is wise to go, and we went pretty rapidly in those days, building and expanding in all directions. We were being confronted with fresh emergencies constantly. But we had with us a group of courageous men who recognized the great principle that a business cannot be a great success that does not fully and efficiently accept and take advantage of its opportunities. How often we discussed those trying questions! Some of us wanted to jump at once into big expenditures, and others to keep to more moderate ones. It was usually a compromise, but one at a time we took these matters up and settled them, never going as fast as the most progressive ones wished, nor quite so carefully as the conservatives desired, but we always made the vote unanimous in the end."

So the question arises: Did John D. Rockefeller "control" Standard Oil? Did he "control" these forceful and independent men on Standard's executive committee? These questions have been asked of Rockefellers down through the generations. Do they control everything they touch? And if so, how do they do it?

It would seem in the case of old John D. that his word carried considerable weight among his associates because they realized he was so often right. At times he bowed to the opinion of others. But what happened when differences were irreconcilable and there was no way to compromise? A case in point, perhaps, was the problem in the 1880s of whether or not to buy newly discovered crude oil from the Lima field in northwestern Ohio and eastern Indiana. It was called "sour crude" because the sulphur content was so high the oil smelled like rotten eggs, and no one had found a way to refine it profitably. Its quality was so poor it sold for $.15 a barrel, but there was plenty of it. Rockefeller bought the "sour crude" and stored it and then proposed that for the first time Standard ought to buy the oil fields themselves in anticipation of someday discovering a new method of refining out the high sulphur content. Archbold was against it, Pratt was against it, Rogers was against it, the majority of the executive committee was adamantly against it. "Very well, gentlemen," said Rockefeller at last, "at my own personal risk I will put up the money to care for this product —two million, three million, if necessary."

Faced with that alternative the executive committee agreed. Standard Oil, for the first time, began buying oil-producing fields at an eventual cost of $8 million. At the same time Rockefeller hired Herman Frasch, a German immigrant who was considered the outstanding chemist in oil refining, and sent him to Lima. For two years, in experiment after experiment, he failed. Standard poured more than $200,000 into his research. The argument went on in Standard's executive committee whether or not to abandon the seemingly hopeless project. But in 1888, the German chemist finally reported success. Lima oil rose from $.15 a barrel to $1.00. Standard Oil built the world's largest refinery to handle what was called "one of the greatest bonanzas ever struck," profits soared into the hundreds of millions and the Standard Oil Company of Indiana was born just seventeen miles from the metropolis of Chicago. Archbold, one of the doubters at first, readily admitted that John D. indeed had greater foresight than any of the other leaders of Standard. "Yes, John Rockefeller can see farther ahead than any of us—and then he sees around the corner," said Archbold.

The 1880s saw the further expansion of Standard Oil to the overseas markets of western Europe and China—to such an extent that for most of those years Standard sold more oil abroad than in this country, to the great benefit of the United States' balance of trade. Competing against the Rothschilds, the Nobel brothers, the vast oil resources of the Russians in the Baku region, Standard Oil won a major portion of the kerosene market through most of Europe without, it should be noted, any railroad rebates. American technology had made Standard's product better than the Europeans', but to win out in the price competition, Standard built up one of the first worldwide marketing systems of American enterprise. Rather than shipping barrels of oil to Europe as was usual, for instance, Rockefeller and his fellow accountants found it much cheaper to ship bulk oil in huge fireproof oil tankers, to barrel the oil in Europe and then to market it there on a regional basis. In Latin America there was no worthy competition to Standard's inroads. In China Standard created a wholly new market for itself. It gave away millions of cheap lamps so that the Chinese would buy and burn Standard's kerosene. These were the Lamps for the Light of Asia, and Standard started out with a self-made monopoly. This was creative marketing. The Rockefeller answer to the problem of overproduction was to extend the market for U.S. refined oil and all its products from Cleveland and the Midwest to all of America and then to all of the world.

So great had the overseas market become that Rockefeller moved the home base of Standard in 1884 from Cleveland to New York, and he made the move with it. Standard's worldwide headquarters was established in one of the first "skyscrapers" in the Wall Street area at 26 Broadway, fourteen stories tall. It soon became one of the most famous addresses of its day in New York. After living in a hotel for a number of years while in New York, Rockefeller bought a twenty-year-old home, a four-story brownstone, for his family at 4 West Fifty-fourth Street, just off Fifth Avenue, for $600,000. For a man of his means it was a simple house indeed, dominated in decor with heavy dark mahogany so popular in that period. Sliding doors between the main rooms on the first floor allowed the Rockefellers to hold Bible class meetings and hymn singing there on Sundays. At home Rockefeller was gay and relaxed, enjoying singing and telling stories, ice skating in his back yard, entertaining his fellow Baptists without aid of drink, smoking or card playing.

In his office, however, he was austere, deliberately eschewing friendships lest they mar the efficient chain of command. Despite the growth and well-being of the company, he never let up. As the company grew, he grew with it; as it turned from a single corporation to an amalgam of companies to a monopoly, and then to an international trust, John D. Rockefeller became a genius at industrial organization. That was another essential ingredient in the success of Standard. The worldwide empire of Standard Oil reported to one place—26 Broadway. Every month each division of the company sent in the facts and figures of its work to the appropriate committee at 26 Broadway, the Manufactures Committee, the Lubricating Committee, the Production Committee, the Export Committee and so on; and each of these committees reported with its recommendations to the executive committee, of which the chairman was John D. Rockefeller. Standard Oil was one of the very first large industrial enterprises in the United States to be so centrally controlled. Rockefeller, who had been baptized in business as a bookkeeper, could and did check on each and every division of the company by readings of its figures on costs and expenditures, sales, and profits and losses. He was a pioneer in statistical analysis, cost accounting and unit pricing, a keystone of big business today. "It's the figures that count," he would say time and time again. The cost of refining a gallon of crude oil was figured out to the third decimal, to the one thousandth of a cent. Selling kerosene to the consumer was basically a penny business.

This kind of accounting and cost control enabled Rockefeller to write the manager of one western refinery in 1879 the prodding inquiry: why did it cost him 1.820 cents to refine a gallon of kerosene when an eastern refinery did the same job for 0.910 cents per gallon? He wrote thousands of such letters. Perhaps the best-known of these was a letter to a Standard refiner concerning bungs which were used as stoppers in barrels and cost a fraction of a penny each: "Last month you reported on hand 1,119 bungs. Ten thousand were sent you at the beginning of this month. You have used 9,527 this month. You report 1,012 on hand. What has happened to the other 580?"

Many of Rockefeller's letters in the 1880s and 1890s reflected his concern that some Standard people might overlook the basic policy of the company. "I am most gratified," he wrote to the Manufactures Committee on its report of a new reduction in the cost of manufacturing kerosene in 1885. "Let the good work go on. We must ever remember we are refining oil for the poor man and he must have it cheap and good." To his chief lieutenant, John Archbold, concerning pricing, he wrote the following year: "I think the lesson we should draw is to continue making the best goods, so far as possible reduce the cost of manufacture, be content with a small profit, and continue wisely seeking for orders." Other letters reflect the reason behind such policy. It was not pure altruism. As technology reduced the cost of refining crude oil Rockefeller's policy was to decrease the price of the refined products to the consumer. That not only helped sales but a low *margin* of profit served to keep would-be competitors out of the oil trade. Thus he would write one of his partners in 1886: "Our returns for the first six months are coming very satisfactorily indeed. Indeed, I think we have made more money than we ought, and that the margin of profit is unduly stimulating to our competitors, notably in the oil regions. We are not free from the annoyance and trouble incident to this smooth-running business, but it seems to me we have every reason to be grateful when we compare it with any other."

Business was so "smooth-running" that Standard in the late 1880s no longer fought off an increase in competition so long as it did not upset the order and efficiency Rockefeller had brought to the industry. Over the next ten years or so independent refiners' share of the market grew from a low of 5 to 10 per cent to a figure of 18 to 20 per cent at the turn of the century. In 1888, for instance, when Standard was negotiating merging with several independent refiners in Cleveland, Rockefeller wrote Standard's man on the scene: "We want to be exceeding [sic] careful in reference to the gentlemen referred to or any others who at any time may be considering with us the question of adjusting their relations . . . Let nothing be said or done to unjustly or unfairly influence their minds. I believe you fully appreciate the importance of this and will see to it, that this spirit is carefully observed by all men representing Standard Oil Co. of Ohio in any negotiations, but I send this message from extra precaution feeling it very important."

By 1890, with the business running so smoothly, Rockefeller began thinking of his own retirement. He had turned fifty, the age he had set arbitrarily some time before as appropriate for his retirement. After all, he had been working every day, except the Sabbath, since the age of sixteen. But perhaps that was more easily said than done. He worked on at Standard until two years later; his excellent health and staunch constitution failed him for the first time. He suffered a rather severe digestive ailment that laid him low for a time. In 1893 he quietly purchased the first parcels of land near Tarrytown, New York, for what he planned as his home in retirement. In 1896 he quietly packed up his belongings at 26 Broadway and moved to Pocantico Hills. No public announcement was made. No business associates outside of 26 Broadway were informed. The actual running of the business was taken over by John Archbold, one of the vice-presidents, perhaps because the more senior partners, like Flagler, William Rockefeller and Henry H. Rogers, also wanted to turn their attention elsewhere. In all the years that followed, according to the Rockefeller Family Archives, John D. signed only one company document. Occasionally he visited the office and no doubt his advice was sought on some matters, and he still retained some staff there to handle his personal business and investments. But for all practical purposes, John D. in 1896 considered himself retired and removed from the daily affairs of the company he had founded twenty-six years before. He was fifty-seven years old, well aware of the forty-one work years behind him. But little could he realize that he had forty-one more years ahead of him.

There were good business reasons for not announcing his retirement publicly. Standard Oil was under ever increasing attacks in the courts and in the daily press. For the good of the company, as Archbold insisted,

Rockefeller agreed to lend the prestige of his name to the continued well-being of the company. The decade of the 1890s saw the flowering of business under the umbrella of the industrial revolution in the United States. Corruption in politics, in business, in the stock market reached new highs in the bare-knuckles competition of free enterprise. The 1890s also gave rise to a new era of public unrest, demands for the rights of labor, a wave of populism among farmers in the Midwest and what Theodore Roosevelt would label for all time as muckraking journalism.

John D. Rockefeller, for all his business acumen, grossly underestimated the power of the press and the force of public opinion. Through the years of Standard's growth, he understood the antagonism of the oil producers, the men who drilled for oil; Standard did indeed, to a large extent, control the price paid to those producers. Nor did John D. expect competing oil refiners to love him in those early days when the least efficient were driven out of business by the refiners who could undersell them. That was the nature of free enterprise under the economic rules of Adam Smith. Competition was designed supposedly to drive the least efficient out of business. Certainly many oil producers and refiners were hurt in the process of building up an industry which could efficiently serve the public as it needed to be served. It was the public—the consumers—who benefited by lower prices and a better quality of oil sold by Standard as it developed one of the greatest natural resources of the country for the benefit of its people. John D. Rockefeller believed this with all his heart. He sincerely believed he should have been praised for buying out, at whatever the price, the less efficient competitors when he could just as easily have driven them into the ground. He thought Standard should be praised for reinvesting its profits in order to increase the volume of its business so that oil and all its by-products could be brought to the public everywhere. He believed that Standard Oil, under his reign, had been thoroughly honest and responsible in all its business affairs, paying the best wages in the industry to its workers, instituting pensions and side benefits to its long-time employees and, in general, serving the public good.

What he could not comprehend is why the general public so readily believed the muckrakers who published stories about Standard, garnered entirely from Standard's competitors and enemies in the oil fields.

The first great blast which shook Standard Oil, proving the power of the pen, was the publication of *Wealth Against Commonwealth* in 1894, a polemic by Henry Demarest Lloyd, which did not mention John D. Rockefeller by name, but alluded to the "President of the Light of the World." Highly exaggerated and distorted in interpretation, rejected by four publishers before a fifth accepted the book, *Wealth Against Commonwealth* was read and acclaimed around the world. It was the first case history of alleged social abuse wrought in the name of free enterprise. It told of big-business men, greedy for wealth and power, swindling widows, driving small-business men to ruin and suicide, and blowing up the facto-ries of competitors.

Magazines and the penny press took up the cry and their circulation soared with each new exposé. Lincoln Steffens, Henry Adams, Frank Norris, Upton Sinclair and others won everlasting fame as they wrote of corruption, venality and unfair competition in industry after industry, in the railroads, the meat-packing yards, the mines, the banks, the stock market and, of course, in oil.

To make matters worse, in the years immediately following John D.'s retirement in 1896, just as the muckraking exposés began to gain a head of steam, John D.'s successor, John Archbold, launched Standard on a much more aggressive program of competition, driving even more competitors out of business, increasing the price on domestic oil to compensate for price reductions overseas where the competition was greater. All of this was reported in the daily press. Archbold also plunged Standard into poli-tics and lobbying to an extent never indulged in by Rockefeller. The daily press in excoriating such doings roundly blamed John D. Rockefeller as well as Standard. During the same period two of Standard's senior part-ners, perhaps bored with the smoothly running company, and freed from the baleful eye of John D., launched themselves with apparent glee into the whirlwind of stock market manipulations, proxy fights, mergers and blatant take-overs of companies in need of money. The two were John D.'s brother, William, and Henry H. Rogers, each of them self-admitted plungers and gamblers in the game of high finance. Again John D., who had no part in their activities, received a major part of the blame for their escapades, which were reported almost always as those of "the Standard crowd." William Rockefeller and Rogers, to be sure, plunged into outside activities with their own money, dividends from Standard Oil profits which ran into the millions, but the press, particularly Pulitzer's World, castigated "Standard Oil" and "the Standard crowd" almost daily. A fea-ture article in the World in 1897 proclaimed "Standard Oil to Swallow All" and went on to say: "From hounding and driving prosperous busi-nessmen to beggary and suicide, to holding up and plundering widows and orphans, the little deal in the country and the crippled peddler on the highway—all this has entered into the exploits of this organized band of commercial cutthroats."

John D. Rockefeller would respond to none of these attacks. He was unmoved by what other men might think or say of him. He felt no guilt. He thought his accusers mistaken and trusted that future writers and his-torians would correct the false impressions portrayed in the daily press or by the men who wished to make political capital by their attacks. He went about his business in retirement, moving and replanting trees on his Pocantico estate, contemplating how best to give away his excess money, how to save souls among his fellow Christians, while the world outside made him the symbol of all that was wrong with the free enterprise system.

To top it all came the most spectacular success of muckraking journalism, a 550-page book called *The History of Standard Oil* by Ida Tarbell, published in 1904, based on articles she wrote for *McClure's Magazine* beginning in 1902. In contrast to *Wealth Against Commonwealth*, Miss Tarbell's book was sober in tone, well documented and serious in intent. Crediting Rockefeller and his associates for organized efficiency, she charged that the Standard empire had been built on fraud, coercion, special privilege or sharp dealing, and she cited chapter and verse. She disarmed her own critics by admitting at the outset that she was biased: she was the daughter of an oil producer in the west Pennsylvania regions who had been hurt, if not ruined, by Standard's early rise to power. There is without doubt, as Allan Nevins, the historian, says, a bias that runs through Miss Tarbell's *History*, and many of her accusations have been refuted. Nevertheless the impact of her book was like thunder across the land. Standard Oil had been hurt and officers of the company appealed to John D. to refute the charges. But he stood fast in his own sense of righteousness. "Not a word! Not a word about that misguided woman," he insisted.

Miss Tarbell went on to write more articles for *McClure's*, picturing John D. Rockefeller personally in the mind of the public as a cruel, crafty old hypocrite who played golf in his old age so that he could "live longer in order to make more money." Others took to the attack. Yet Rockefeller remained quiet in the face of the attacks, at peace with his Maker and his own conscience, confident that history, once the true facts were known, would vindicate him. He failed, however, to read the message between the lines in the vast outpouring of news stories, magazine articles and books about corruption, unfair advantage and unprincipled competition in business and industry at the turn of the century. There were answers to the accusations against Standard Oil and himself, right or wrong, but behind the immediate accusations was a larger, more momentous charge: that Adam Smith's theory of laissez-faire capitalism, based upon enlightened self-interest and the fundamental pressures of supply and demand in the market place—upon which the economy of the country was based—did not in reality work very well for the benefit of the people as a whole. That message, somewhat veiled, was taken up in the political arena and the populist movement spread across the land.

The populist movement rallied under the banner "The people against the tycoons," which translated a half century later with the same appeal to "more power to the people." The industrial revolution no sooner succeeded in the 1890s than the people demanded protection from the economic stranglehold of big business. Standard Oil was only one out of many. There were trusts and monopolies in almost all of major industry.

The protection demanded by the people came politically from the government, as an arbitrator of what constituted free enterprise. The government
intervened. It outlawed monopolies, trusts and all combinations in restraint
of trade. It set up regulatory agencies to define the limits and boundaries of
free enterprise—all for greater good of the greatest number of people. To
this day that struggle continues between the concept of free enterprise and
the need for government regulation of business, all the way down the economic line to wages and prices. The struggle today remains as it was in
John D. Rockefeller's day: where to draw the line on who should control
the economy of the United States.

So far as John D. Rockefeller's Standard Oil Company was concerned, the decision was handed down on May 15, 1911, by the Supreme
Court of the United States: "Seven men and a corporate machine have
conspired against their fellow citizens. For the safety of the Republic we
now decree that this dangerous conspiracy must be ended by November
15th."

Standard Oil was found guilty of being a combination and a conspiracy in restraint of trade and in violation of the Sherman Antitrust Act of
1890. The trust had been established, the first of its kind in the country,
back in 1879, when the state of Ohio passed a law forbidding any corporation of Ohio from owning stock in a company located in another state. In
response, as a practical means of continuing to do business as before,
Rockefeller had the company counsel draw up a new legal instrument by
which the majority of stockholders gave their stock "in trust" to three individuals, who then legally could own controlling stock in companies in
various states. The number of trustees later was increased to nine and still
later, when Ohio and other states outlawed such trusts, Standard joined
several hundred other companies in moving their corporations to the state
of New Jersey, which welcomed the businesses and taxes they brought in
by specifically allowing New Jersey corporations to hold stock in out-of-
state businesses. Later, Standard Oil of New Jersey changed its legal form
from a trust to a holding company, but the practical effect was the same.

The Supreme Court ordered Standard Oil of New Jersey to divest itself of all its subsidiaries, not to operate any longer as a combination or a
single enterprise and to transfer back to the stockholders of the original
subsidiaries all the stock they had exchanged for shares in Standard of
New Jersey. The action was directed against the corporation, not its stockholders.

The decision was hailed throughout the land. It became a legal prece-
dent and landmark case in the business world, governing the extent to
which other giant corporations could grow before their very size would be
deemed in restraint of trade. Nevertheless, considering what the trust
busters, the populists and the popular press set out to do, the results of
that landmark decision were ironical. For one thing, it certainly helped

make John D. Rockefeller a far richer man than he had been before. Where he once owned one fourth of the Stock in Standard Oil of New Jersey, after the decision he became the owner of one fourth of the outstanding shares in thirty-three different oil companies. Then for the first time these oil companies went public. The value of their shares, which had been deliberately undercapitalized for so long, now soared skyward. In the first *month* of 1912, Standard of New Jersey stock almost doubled; Standard of New York more than doubled; Atlantic Refining tripled. Standard of Indiana went from $3,500 a share in January to $9,500 in October. John D. Rockefeller's estimated wealth rose from $200 million in 1901 to more than $900 million in 1913!

Nor did prices go down. They went up, along with the new demands for gasoline, thanks to Henry Ford's Model T, the first mass-produced automobile which the common man could afford. Dividends went up, way up, in the first year, and they stayed up. Nor did the dissolution bring about much more competition between the thirty-three new companies. Their management remained the same as before, men trained in Rockefeller methods. They obviously saw the advantages in not invading the territorial domain of others. Today, sixty years later, those companies are individual behemoths of American industry, comprising approximately 50 per cent of the oil industry in the United States, and the extent of their competition, cooperation and enlightened self-interest is still debatable. John D. Rockefeller's legacy of organization, efficiency and order lives on.

However, at the time of the dissolution of Standard Oil, John D. Rockefeller had become a whipping boy, a symbol of the hardhearted mogul of big business. Ida Tarbell's portrait of John D. was taken up and enlarged upon in the political arena. Theodore Roosevelt denounced him as a lawbreaker. William Jennings Bryan stumped the country demanding that he be put in jail. Leo Tolstoy cried out that no honest man should work with him. He was called a pirate, a buccaneer and a robber baron. A Congregationalist minister denounced a $100,000 gift from Rockefeller as "tainted money" and unwanted. The pundits of the country debated in the press whether or not it was right to accept such money. The minister, of course, did not know that his Church had spent two years pleading for that gift. Nor did John D. divulge that fact. It was not long before someone described John D. Rockefeller as the most hated man in America, and the public believed that, too. All of his philanthropies—the greatest example of giving of a private fortune in the history of America, totaling more than $500 million—were suspect. People believed and said aloud at the time that he was giving only in atonement for his sins and a sense of guilt. Some believe that to this day. His son and his five grandsons would suffer the same suspicion of all their endeavors in the years ahead. Yet the truth is that old John D. and his children and his children's children after him felt no guilt, no need for atonement at all.

7

Philanthropy

"What a delightful habit you are forming!"

"I am sure it is a mistake to assume that the possession of money in great abundance necessarily brings happiness," John D. Rockefeller wrote in his *Reminiscences*. "The very rich are just like all the rest of us; and if they get pleasure from the possession of money it comes from the ability to do things which give satisfaction to someone besides themselves."

This was a distillation of many years of thought and experience, written in 1909. By then he had been an abundantly wealthy man for a long, long time. In 1872, just two years after the incorporation of Standard Oil, for instance, he had written his wife, Laura, apropos another subject, "You know we are independently rich outside investments in oil—but I believe my oil stock the very best . . ." He recognized, as have others, that there is only so much one can spend on oneself before the mere expenditure of money for things "soon palls upon one." After all, how much more can one eat than the next man? How many clothes, how many houses, how many "things" can a man buy before such possessions cease to give him pleasure? "As I study wealthy men," concluded Rockefeller, "I can see but one way in which they can secure a real equivalent for money spent, and that is to cultivate a taste for giving where the money may produce an effect which will be a lasting gratification."

Getting and giving were an integral part of his everyday life. It was the ethic he lived by; the Protestant Ethic. At first, when he started to work, he gave nickels and dimes to various causes espoused by his own Church. Year after year his ledgers show as his income grew he gave more and more money to more and more causes, cutting across denominational, ethnic and color lines.

In the early 1890s, when his annual contributions for the first time topped $1 million, Rockefeller turned his mind to some of the complexities of giving money away. Paradoxically, at the same time that he was being portrayed as the ogre of oil, but a rich one, thousands of personal letters poured in from everywhere, appealing for his help or his money, or both. He set up a staff at 26 Broadway to go over these letters. Most were easily disposed of. "Four fifths of these letters are requests for money for personal use, with no other title to consideration than that the writer would be gratified to have it," he noted.

However, the other one fifth were worthwhile pleas, coming from local and nationwide charities, from religious and civic organizations, and from other institutions and individuals. To distinguish the more worthwhile from the less so required time, effort and study. It also occurred to Rockefeller that he was giving only to the worthy causes requesting his aid, but there might well be causes even more worthy of which he knew nothing. He began to apply his logical, methodical mind to the problem of giving. He wanted to find a system, a set of governing principles, an organized and efficient way of giving so that he could do the greatest good with the means at his disposal. He wanted to make an efficient business, stripped of emotion, the means to the end.

Looking about him, Rockefeller came to the conclusion that Americans were kindhearted and generous (perhaps to a fault) whenever disaster struck. They responded to emotional appeals—that of the orphan, of the hungry, of the crippled man, of the victims of floods and fires. But he recognized that if he gave his money to all victims he would be stripped of money long before the world was depleted of victims. Logically he decided to concentrate his giving upon the causes of despair and the conditions which made victims.

His first major benefaction was in education, and he entered into major philanthropy with characteristic research, deliberation and caution. It took him three years to decide upon the proper course in funding a new and needed university of Baptist persuasion. In a long and fierce controversy between the fundamentalists and liberals of the Baptist Church, Rockefeller, who was more of a fundamentalist himself, put his money with the liberals, who wanted to build an all-purpose university in the West rather than in New York. It was one man, Frederick T. Gates of Minneapolis, the general secretary of the newly created Baptist Education Society, who swung Rockefeller's decision to the West. Gates's clear and businesslike report proved to Rockefeller that there was a greater *need* for a university in the West, where half the Baptists in the United States lived, than in the East, where there were already several reputable Baptist institutions of learning. In 1889 Rockefeller made his first contribution—$600,000 for the founding of a new University of Chicago, on the proviso that the people of Chicago would raise another $400,000.

With that gift it was understood that Rockefeller had committed himself to supporting the university to a much greater extent—anywhere from $10 million to $20 million. The amount was not fixed. But Rockefeller did establish the principle of matching funds. "We frequently make our gifts conditioned on the giving of others," he explained, "not because we wish to force people to do their duty, but because we wish in this way to root the institution in the affections of as many people as possible who, as contributors, become personally concerned, and thereafter may be counted on to give to the institution their watchful interest and cooperation." He helped bring in the best men available to set up and run the university, and he told them firmly that they must make the university an integral part of the community and not count entirely upon his gifts. It was their university, not his. He did not intend to control it. Nor did he want his name attached to the enterprise, nor did he want to serve on its board of trustees. He promised his support for ten years and then, he said, the university must be self-sustaining because he would give no more. And he stuck to his word. Twice and only twice did he ever visit the campus, and only after his death was one building on campus named for him, the Rockefeller Memorial Chapel. His contribution in money, not to mention effort and advice, to the University of Chicago, now one of the great institutions of learning in the country, totaled $34,708,375 over those ten years.

A by-product of Rockefeller's first venture into the million-dollar class of philanthropy, as significant perhaps to him as the founding of the University of Chicago itself, was his discovery of a new associate, the man who was to become as close and as important to him as any of his associates in oil: Frederick T. Gates. For three years, from the day in 1888 when Gates submitted his report on Baptist education in America, Rockefeller had looked the man over carefully as Gates advised him on Chicago University. He came to see Gates as a man he could admire, a man of humble beginnings who had worked in a bank and in business before becoming an ordained minister and general secretary of the Baptist Education Society. He was independent, self-confident, energetic and dynamic.

"Sit down, Mr. Gates," Rockefeller told him one day in 1891 at 26 Broadway, after a conference on the affairs of the University of Chicago. The thirty-eight-year-old minister sat down.

"I am in trouble, Mr. Gates," said the magnate of Standard Oil. "The pressure of these appeals for gifts has become too great for endurance. I haven't the time or strength, with all my heavy business responsibilities, to deal with these demands properly. I am so constituted as to be unable to give away money with any satisfaction until I have made the most careful inquiry as to the worthiness of the cause. These investigations are now taking more of my time and energy than the Standard Oil itself. Either I must shift part of the burden or stop giving entirely. And I cannot do the latter."

"Indeed you cannot, Mr. Rockefeller," replied Gates, as he noted in his private journal.

"Well, I must have a helper," said Rockefeller. "I have been watching you. I think you are the man. I want you to come to New York and open an office here. You can aid me in my benefactions by making interviews and inquiries, and reporting the results for action. What do you say?"

Frederick T. Gates said yes. He opened an office in the financial district and only later moved into John D.'s office at 26 Broadway. Gates took on more and more work for Rockefeller, who steadfastly believed in delegating as much authority as an associate could handle. All requests for donations were routed to Gates, who reported directly to Rockefeller. They held innumerable discussions on the philosophy and tactics of giving wisely; they sounded each other out and explored ideas together; each came to know the other's mind. Rockefeller, who was so secretive in his business dealings, trusted his new subordinate to such an extent that he opened his "ledgers" to him and it was the perusal of these account books which prompted Gates one day to say: "Mr. Rockefeller, your fortune is rolling up, rolling up like an avalanche. You must distribute it faster than it grows. If you do not it will crush you and your children and your children's children." Rockefeller agreed and in turn told his lieutenant that what he wanted to do with his money was to seek the "finalities" —to strike at "the causes of evil" and thus alleviate as best he could the woes of his fellow man.

It was a book, and more precisely, what the book did not say, which sparked the conception of a way to attack at least some of the "finalities." On a vacation at Lake George in upstate New York in 1897, Gates read William Osler's classic textbook, *Principles and Practice of Medicine,* and was struck that Osler's book told how to diagnose more than a hundred different diseases but in very few cases did it tell how to treat a disease. Indeed Gates, whose grandfather was a doctor, concluded that in only one case of a hundred could a doctor actually treat a patient with a known cure. In the other ninety-nine he did little more than make the patient comfortable and allow nature to take its course. Rockefeller himself was treated by a homeopathic doctor. The United States had no medical research centers at all—nothing like the Pasteur Institute in France or the Koch Institute in Berlin. Here then was a new field of endeavor which, as such, would appeal to the entrepreneur in John D. Rockefeller, or so Gates believed. He returned from vacation to dictate a memorandum immediately to Rockefeller, who was vacationing in Cleveland. Gates was right, of course—John D. Rockefeller was interested.

Another principle of good business was recognized almost immediately. The undertaking was so new and so vast that Gates realized he himself could not devote the time that was needed. So he enlisted "an associate" to do the detail work—a young lawyer of Montclair, New Jersey, named Starr J. Murphy. Neither of them was expert in medical affairs. But they knew the way to proceed. Murphy enlisted seven eminent doctors who, contrary to most, believed in medical research, and it was this group of doctors who met and planned what was to become and would remain to this day the world-renowned and foremost medical research center in the United States. The Rockefeller Institute for Medical Research was incorporated in 1901 with a modest gift of $200,000 from Rockefeller. One of the original group, Dr. Simon Flexner, Professor of Pathology at the University of Pennsylvania, was chosen as director. The country was scouted for outstanding competent men in the various medical sciences, and by 1904 their work began in a rented building. Rockefeller and Gates, by this time aided by John D. Rockefeller, Jr., confined their activities to providing money for worthwhile causes. Gates or young Rockefeller would come to the medical board and ask: if you had such and such money, what would you do with it?

The organization of the Institute was so far ahead of its time that it would be and is considered among the avant-garde in medical circles even today. The Institute was organized around the scientists who worked there and was not directed to any specific disease or program or goal. Its scientists were chosen because of their ability, freed of financial care and trusted to run their own programs and to control their own expenditures. Rockefeller provided the money for medical research and then he kept his hands off. As Dr. Flexner explained the guidelines of the Institute as conceived in 1901: "The Institute . . . has been expected to explore, to dream. Our founders and his advisers have said to us again and again, in effect: 'Don't be in a hurry to produce anything. Don't worry about making good. We have faith that you will make good, and if you don't the next fellow will. It is faith—not mere hope—that this or that man will make the best use of his opportunities. Don't you worry. This thing may go on for generations; then suddenly somebody will give us a practical result.'"

This faith in men over programs paid off handsomely without having to wait on future generations. Within a year, Dr. Flexner himself broke through on his own research on epidemic meningitis. His single discovery brought under control a ravaging disease that killed four of every five of its young victims. The virus causing infantile paralysis was isolated. The whole field of bacteriology was opened for the world at the Institute. Dr. Hideyo Noguchi became world-famous with his work there on yellow fever, paresis, rabies and syphilis. Dr. Alexis Carrel pioneered in surgical methods still used today, leading the way to open-heart surgery. Over the years Institute scientists won twelve Nobel prizes for their work, more than were collected at any other single institution. The Rockefeller Institute for Medical Research, within ten years, became the foremost institution of its kind. It also soon became the very best-equipped research facility in the world. Rockefeller provided money as needed, a million for the first building of laboratories, then several million for the first hospital-laboratory complex, then several million more as the work of the Institute expanded. John D. Rockefeller, still treated personally by an old homeopathic physician who wrote tirades against the research center, gave some $60 million to the Institute before he turned the financial responsibility over to his son.

The Institute was John D. Rockefeller, Jr.'s first major venture into philanthropy and it remained for all his life his personal favorite, his first-born. Emerging from college in 1897 and going to work for his father, he was intimately involved in the details of establishing the Institute for Medical Research, even to the choosing and acquiring of its site along the East River in New York. He became a member of its first board of trustees in 1910 and later its chairman. He retained that post until he reached the age of seventy-four in 1950, although as a matter of policy he had resigned from all other institutions at sixty-five.

It was Junior, or Mr. John, as he was sometimes called then, who at the age of twenty-seven initiated the second great Rockefeller philanthropy, one which would represent a giant leap forward in the means, method and amount of giving, even for the Rockefellers. Its task was nothing less than "the promotion of education within the United States without distinction of race, sex or creed." Its focus was the South, where educational facilities and standards were abysmal. Its real purpose, which could not be stated publicly in those days, was to help elevate the education of Negroes below the Mason-Dixon line.

Rockefeller Sr. had given handsomely to Negro causes over the years, particularly to Baptist-run schools and colleges in the South. For this reason, most probably, Junior was invited in 1901 to join fifty prominent and wealthy citizens on a tour of southern schools as a guest of Robert C. Ogden, a merchant long associated with John Wanamaker, the department store magnate. The trip was by chartered train, derisively called in the South "the Millionaires' Special," but Ogden, who paid the fare, was most serious in wanting to focus attention on education as a means of kindling an industrial awakening of the Deep South.

The most prescient advice to those Northerners came from Henry St. George Tucker, the president of Washington and Lee University, near the end of the trip. "If it is your idea to educate the Negro you must have the white of the South with you," he told the group. "If the poor white sees the son of a Negro neighbor enjoying through your munificence benefits denied to his boy, it raises in him a feeling that will render futile all your work. You must lift up the poor white and the Negro together if you would ever approach success."

Junior returned from the trip with a sense of mission. Here was a true opportunity to help one's fellow man in a fundamental way. It was a project much needed to which no one could object so long as southern sensibilities were not aggravated. Junior reported his findings and discussed the possibilities of the situation with his father, with Gates, and then he enlisted the support of several others, including Dr. Wallace Buttrick, secretary of the Baptist Home Mission Society. In January 1902 the three of them met with six prominent members of "the Millionaires' Special." They decided to go ahead with the project. A month later at a second meeting Junior was able to pledge, on behalf of his father, financing of $1 million. A year later, 1903, Junior's father-in-law, Senator Nelson W. Aldrich, steered through Congress the incorporation of the project as the General Education Board. Dr. Buttrick was named executive secretary, or chief operating officer, and Gates was named to the board of trustees along with John Jr. and other originators of the cause. They set about their task in their usual businesslike fashion with a detailed survey of educational conditions in the South and of all the varied alternatives proposed for "the promotion of education . . . without distinction of race, sex or creed."

Several obvious truths soon rose to the surface: elementary school education in the South was substandard because the teachers were insufficiently trained; most children quit with eight or fewer years of schooling because of the lack of high schools in many locations; that the Board itself could never raise enough money to build the needed schools or to train teachers throughout the South; furthermore, the federal government would not and the state governments were disinclined to spend money for those purposes.

The Board, led in this aspect by Gates and John Jr., arrived at a solution which encompassed a new principle of philanthropy and appealed greatly to the business orientation of Rockefeller Sr. Leverage was the answer. The idea was for the Board to pay the salaries of professors of education, selected by the state universities involved in the South, and the professors themselves would go about their own states selecting sites for needed high schools, enlisting the support of citizens for local governmental support and, at the same time, instituting a training program where needed for teachers.

Even such a scheme, with all its leverage, would have required millions upon millions of dollars. The project was vast, new and untried, a kind of Point IV program under private auspices. Gates, whose vision went even beyond the immediate needs of education in the South, proposed the underwriting of the General Education Board to Rockefeller Sr. as part of an over-all philosophy on the handling of his snowballing fortune. On June 3, 1905, after consultations with John Jr., Gates wrote his most significant letter of advice on philanthropy to the elder Rockefeller:

"Two courses are open to you. One is that you and your children while living should make final disposition of this great fortune in the form of permanent corporate philanthropies for the good of mankind . . . or at the close of a few lives now in being it must simply pass into the unknown, like some other great fortunes, with unmeasured and perhaps sinister possibilities.

"These funds (or foundations) should be so large that to become a trustee of one of them would be to make a man at once a public character. They should be so large that their administration would be as much a matter of public concern and public inquiry and public criticism as any of the functions of the government are now. They should be so large as to attract the attention of the entire civilized world, their administration become the subject of the most intelligent criticism of the world, and to their administration should be addressed both directly and indirectly the highest talent in those particular spheres of every generation through which the fund would go . . ."

The Gates letter was long and detailed, envisioning separate and distinct foundations for medical research, for the arts, for the promotion of scientific agriculture, for the promotion of "intelligent citizenship and civic virtue in the United States." John Jr., the heir apparent, supported the proposal wholeheartedly with a letter of his own to his father: "Mr. Gates' letter to you seems to me a powerful and unanswerable argument . . . a most comprehensive treatment of the subject . . . I very much hope it may seem wise to carry out this plan."

Within two weeks John D. Rockefeller gave $10 million to the General Education Board. Eighteen months later he gave $32 million more! The Board moved forward with care and tact. In time all of the southern states, without exception, provided professors of secondary education for the project. Civic leaders in town after town joined the crusade for more schools and over the next fifteen years more than sixteen hundred new high schools were built for black and for white students throughout the South at a cost of some $46 million, all raised by local taxation. The impact and reverberations of these new schools stimulated the whole educational system of the South, particularly in the poverty areas. New high schools brought increased enrollment to colleges and universities, and a new awareness to the first eight grades of schooling.

The General Education Board also recognized poverty as an educational problem in the rural South: poverty kept farm children away from all schooling. Without flinching at the size and scope of the problem, the Board enlarged its program to a study of how to help the cotton farmer, whose average income was as low as $150 a year, learn the new scientific methods of farming for his own economic good. The immediate need, the

study showed, was somehow to convince the farmer that new exciting
scientific methods of farming were better than those he had learned from
his own father. Rejecting the simple idea of trying to teach farming in the
schools, the Board after a full year of investigation hired Seaman A.
Knapp, a remarkable expert in demonstration farming, and he went from
town to town in the South showing the most influential farmers in each
area how Knapp's methods could double or even triple the amount of cotton raised per acre. When the next cotton crop proved Knapp's point,
other farmers in the area were invited over to judge the results. Again the
policy of self-help on a local basis became a phenomenal success, a true beginning for scientific farming in America.

The General Education Board then went on to finance the expanding
enrollment and curriculum of colleges and universities beyond the South,
and on to the West, but with the double proviso: that each institution so
helped improve its planning and financial administration and that it also
enlist the support of others in the community. The Board doled out more
than $20 million to 134 colleges and universities, while they in turn raised
$76.5 million more. That done, Rockefeller gave another $50 million to
the Board in 1919, of which $40 million was distributed among some 170
colleges and universities in the following five years, matched by about $83
million raised locally, solely for the much-needed purpose of raising
teachers' salaries.

In all, John D. Rockefeller gave in excess of $129 million to the Gen-
eral Education Board and its work. He seemed particularly delighted to do
so because his gifts induced others to give along with him. The way he put
it was: "If a combination to do business is effective in saving waste and in
getting better results, why is not combination far more important in philanthropic work?"

A chance remark at a railroad station in the Deep South led to another Rockefeller venture into philanthropy, a remarkable one in that
cause and effect could be seen so clearly and so quickly: "See that man
over there?" said one man to another, pointing to a miserable, misshapen
figure with distended stomach. "That man is a 'dirt eater'! His condition
is due to hookworm infection. He can be cured at a cost of about fifty
cents in drugs and in a few weeks' time he can be turned into a useful
man."

The remark came from one who knew his subject, Dr. Charles Wardell Stiles of the U. S. Public Health Service, who had been working on
hookworm infection for years, but no one would heed his cries. The man
listening was Walter Hines Page, a magazine editor and one of the origi-
nators of the General Education Board. Page was intensely involved in
trying to raise living standards in the South. "You can make a healthy
man of that wreck?" replied Page. "Good God, Stiles, are you in earnest?"

Stiles explained that the hookworm, only a third of an inch long, entered a man's body usually through his feet when he walked barefoot in dirt, lodged in his small intestine, hatched thousands of eggs and debilitated the man with its poisons. The cure was simple: a few doses of thymol to loosen the hookworm and Epsom salts to eject it in a bowel movement.

Page brought the good doctor to Dr. Buttrick, executive secretary of the General Education Board. Buttrick listened to his story and brought Stiles to Gates. Gates called in Dr. Flexner of the Rockefeller Institute and when Stiles' data checked out, Gates went to John D. Rockefeller. Rockefeller forthwith gave $1 million and the Rockefeller Sanitary Commission was born in 1909. It was greeted initially with derision in the South. But by 1913 some 900,000 people had been examined and 500,000 had been treated for infections and the work went on. By 1927 almost 7 million people had been treated and cured: hookworm disease ceased to be either an epidemic or dangerous disease in the United States.

The culminating Rockefeller venture into major philanthropy evolved out of what had preceded it: the Institute for Medical Research, the General Education Board, the Sanitary Commission and the Reverend Gates's concept in 1905 of a permanent independent philanthropy with an endowment so large that any man appointed to help run it would automatically become a national figure. Gates worked with John Jr. on the intricacies involved. The concept envisioned a giant foundation, unlimited in scope, worldwide in extent, designed—as its first statement of principles later set forth—to endow and promote activities "which go to the root of individual or social wellbeing, illbeing or misery." By March 1908 the plans were drawn and John Jr. once again wrote to his father-in-law, Senator Aldrich, this time to sponsor in Congress a federal charter for the Rockefeller Foundation to be launched with $100 million. Unlike the swift approval of the Education Board in 1903, this time the federal government was in the midst of its antitrust suit against Rockefeller and Standard Oil. Attorney General George Wickersham, fighting the antitrust suit, bitterly opposed a Rockefeller Foundation as "an indefinite scheme for perpetuating vast wealth." He argued that the federal government could not very well seek to break up Rockefeller's source of wealth in the courts and then, through Congress, act to perpetuate that wealth through "a small body of men, in absolute control of an income of $100 million or more." President Taft agreed with his attorney general.

Counterexplanations that Rockefeller was *giving away* his money rather than controlling it were to no avail in the heat of that time. Feelings in 1908 were violently anti-Rockefeller. The bill to incorporate the Foundation was pigeonholed in one session of Congress after another until in 1913 the bill was withdrawn. The Rockefeller Foundation, with the same charter "to promote the wellbeing of mankind throughout the world" was incorporated in May 1913 by the state of New York without any trouble or public outcry. John Jr. served as its first president for four years and then became chairman of the board for the following twenty-three years, focusing his own work on the financial underpinnings of the Foundation. Succeeding presidents who were the chief operating officers proved Gates's vision of outstanding national figures. Two of them went on from the Rockefeller Foundation to become Secretaries of State—John Foster Dulles and Dean Rusk. As the work of the Sanitary Commission and the Laura Spelman Rockefeller Foundation (a fund named for Mrs. Rockefeller, Sr., in 1918, specializing in the humanities) were absorbed by the Rockefeller Foundation, John D., Sr., added another $83 million to the original $100 million endowment of the Foundation.

It should be noted that the elder Rockefeller did not give cash. He gave stocks and securities which grew in value with the ever increasing prosperity of the nation in general and of the old Standard Oil companies in particular. There were no strings attached to the gifts. All of the Rockefeller philanthropic institutions were staffed with knowledgeable money managers and securities specialists, and it became a matter of policy to live off the income of the securities as much as possible, dipping into capital only when the need absolutely warranted it. Thus the Rockefeller Foundation, for instance, with an endowment of $182,851,000 in securities, has dispersed over the years more than $1 billion and it is still today third only to the Ford Foundation and the Johnson Foundation in total assets.

The scope, breadth and implications of the Rockefeller Foundation's benefactions from 1913 to date, enough to fill volumes, give the impression of a wise and beneficial para-government at work. In fact much of the U.S. government's involvement in health, education and welfare in the latter half of the twentieth century seems to have been pioneered by the Rockefeller Foundation in the first half of the century. Concentrating first on disease, "the common enemy of all mankind," the Foundation financed doctors and medical researchers in the fight against disease: hookworm in fifty-two countries on six continents, malaria in all tropical and subtropical regions of the world, yellow fever in South America and in Africa. The work of these scientists and doctors is credited with relieving the scourge of those diseases to modern man. From the realm of health and disease, the Foundation focused on the problems of hunger and food supply around the world. Brilliant scientists, financed by the Foundation, developed new strains of corn, wheat and rice which immeasurably helped the economy and well-being of underdeveloped nations throughout the world. It went on to finance pioneering efforts in science technology—the world's largest celestial telescope at Mount Palomar in California, and the 184-inch cyclotron at the University of California, which helped split the atom. J. Robert Oppenheimer, Enrico Fermi, Arthur Compton, Henry Smyth and others were among the more than sixteen thousand

Rockefeller fellows whose pioneering work was underwritten by the Foundation.*

None of these gigantic far-reaching ventures were born full-grown. That was not the Rockefeller way of business. The Rockefeller Foundation, when chartered, began with two men, John D. Rockefeller, Jr., as president, and Jerome D. Greene as secretary, with a four-drawer file in a cubbyhole office at 26 Broadway. The primary task in each case was to find the competent men, experts in their fields, to direct the philanthropic efforts desired by the Rockefellers. The principle of gradual, step-by-step growth, based upon care, study and experience, which governed the affairs of Rockefeller businesses and philanthropic ventures was applied equally to the training of his only son. From the time John Jr. entered the Rockefeller offices to the end of his father's life, the son took on more and more responsibilities in the varied affairs of his predecessor. His father wanted him to learn by experience, and he backed him all the way. He never gave him any power of attorney and yet his son knew that he was expected to sign his father's name with his own initials underneath, without consultation, to business transactions large and small. "Do what you think is right, John," was his father's most frequent response to questions posed by his son. When asked he would give advice but he would never direct his son to do this or not to do that. When John Jr. was humiliated in one of his first ventures on Wall Street, being swindled out of about $1 million on a margin account in 1898 by a man who became known as the "Wolf of Wall Street," his father listened to every detail of his son's explanation of the fiasco and then said simply, "All right, John, don't worry. I will see you through." And that was that. No word of reproach over the past, no warnings as to the future. And the son never forgot how his father had handled that situation.

Over the years there developed between the two men a deep sense of mutual trust, admiration and devotion. Quite consciously the son tried to pattern his life, his habits of work, his turn of mind on the qualities he admired in his father. The elder Rockefeller in turn responded over and over again with gratitude. One such letter, from father to son in 1918, was typical: "What a Providence that your life should have been spared to take over the responsibilities as I lay them down. I could not have anticipated in earlier years that they would have been so great, nor could I have dreamed that you have come so promptly and satisfactorily to meet them, and to go beyond, in the contemplation of our right attitude to the world in the discharge of these obligations. I appreciate, I am grateful, beyond all I can tell you."

With the major Rockefeller philanthropies launched and on their

---

* See *The Rockefeller Foundation* by Raymond B. Fosdick, Harper & Brothers, Publishers, 1952.

way—the Rockefeller Foundation, the Institute for Medical Research, the
Sanitary Commission and the General Education Board—the elder Rockefeller turned his attention to the next logical step. The time had come to
begin transferring the Rockefeller fortune and its obligations to his son.
John Jr. had demonstrated during the years that he had worked in his
father's office that he was well equipped and fully inclined to carry on the
family's work. Starting in the year 1917 and continuing over the next five
years, the elder Rockefeller handed over his fortune to his only son and
heir with no strings attached. He did not do it all at once. His method
paralleled all his other giving. The recipient first had to prove himself
worthy and then the money was given in stages. Yet it was all done quite
simply and quite directly. The elder Rockefeller, in 1917, was seventy-
eight years old, his son forty-three, and he was ready to cast off the responsibilities he felt in the handling of his fortune and the demands, often
quite conflicting, made upon him for his financial help. Approaching his
eightieth year he wanted to simplify his own life, to play more golf, to in-
dulge himself in the relaxing pleasures of old age, to swap jokes with old
friends who were not after his money, to meet new people by giving away
new shiny dimes, to pick up hitchhikers on his afternoon automobile rides
so that he could learn of worlds other than his own and, of course, to landscape new homes and build new verandas.

So in 1917 he set up ample trust funds to provide for his two surviving daughters, Edith Rockefeller McCormick and Alta Rockefeller Prentice, and their families, and then he began to give the rest to John Jr. in
cash and dividend checks, in stocks and bonds and in real estate. He did it
with an easy heart and no doubts. As he explained, "The gifts which I
have made to John during my lifetime and in my will have been prompted
by my desire to have my fortune used, as he has used it and as I know that
he will continue to use it, for the benefit of mankind." Each gift was announced in a short and simple letter with far less fanfare than another father might use in sending his college son a monthly allowance.

A typical letter of the period was one dated March 13, 1917:

Dear Son,
I am giving you 20,000 shares of the stock of the Standard Oil Company
of Indiana, of the capitalization of $30,000,000. I think it is best to have
the transfer made as soon as possible.

                                                        Affectionately,
                                                        Father

Three days later the son replied:

Dear Father,
To my previous letter I can only add that I thank you from the bottom of
my heart and that I am deeply appreciative of the tremendous magnitude of the gift, of the responsibility which it places upon me and of the

opportunities which it sets before me. To the full extent of my ability I shall strive to use this money in a way that will make it of the greatest possible blessing.

> Affectionately,
> John

The son never took his father's gifts for granted. Each one came to him if not as a surprise then as a reminder of his father's continuing faith in him. There appeared to be no particular pattern to the giving. It would seem that as the elder Rockefeller reviewed his portfolio of stocks, bonds, dividends and real estate from time to time, he would send to his son that of which he wanted to divest himself. The largesses arrived one at a time with no promise of another to follow. However, the gifts flowed with the rush of a fast-moving spring stream.

> October 22, 1920

Dear Son:
I am giving you a check for $500,000. It will be available for use on Monday next.

> Affectionately,
> Father

> October 23, 1920

Dear Son:
I am giving you a check for $500,000. It will be available for use on Tuesday next.

> Affectionately,
> Father

> October 25, 1920

Dear Father:
Hardly had the ink dried on my letter of thanks for your splendid gift of Saturday before another letter was received, announcing a second gift of equal size.

Again I thank you most truly and most sincerely. There was never so loving and so thoughtful a father as you are.

> Affectionately,
> John

> October 28, 1920

Dear Son:
I am today giving you a check for $500,000. It will be available for use at once.

> Affectionately,
> Father

October 28, 1920

Dear Father:

What a delightful habit you are forming! This third gift, of which your letter of October 28th advises me, is as acceptable as was the first.

Again I would express my truest thanks. How can I ever make clear to you how much I appreciate your wonderful generosity!

Affectionately,
John

The letters continued through the month of November, $700,000 the first week, $1 million a week later, another $1 million three days later, and then $500,000, and then another $500,000. The following month, the father sent his son bonds of the state of New York and corporate stock of the city of New York with a par value of $20,688,000. Two months later came 111,135 shares of the Consolidation Coal Company worth more than $9 million.

By the end of 1922, in a period of five to six years' time, John D. Rockefeller, founder of the Standard Oil Company, now aged eighty-three, had turned over to his son properties and securities at the then current market value of something in excess of $400 million.

As far as anyone knows, these gifts and the manner of their giving were seldom if ever discussed between father and son. Their personal relations were, if not formal, reserved. Certainly they loved and cared for one another, but they were not the kind of men to broach these emotional subjects face to face. The gentle art of letter writing served in that age as a means to exchange vows which would have embarrassed either of them to say aloud.

Thus, while sailing to the Orient with his wife, Abby, in 1921, the son took the time to write his father of their last visit together: "The quiet visit with you at dinner the night before we left was for me the happiest event connected with our departure. Your simple, loving and tender words of benediction will ever be treasured in my memory, but you will never know how profound an influence on my life your daily life has ever been, so kindly, modest, unself [sic] and generous, and at the same time so strong, so courageous and so tolerant. As I came away from Pocantico the other night, I reflected as I never have before that it is not what you have said to me by way of advice or admonition, for both have been singularly infrequent, but rather your own example has been so powerful an influence in my life."

Everyone who visited with John D. Rockefeller in his eighties and then in his nineties came away with a sense of awe over his composure, his patience, his simpleness. His quiet assured self-confidence was unimpaired. He seemed to see life plain, enjoying the simple pleasures of old age, spending more time of the year in the warm climate of Ormond Beach, Florida, talking with people at church and on the street, living there simply as "Neighbor John," accepting the gradual and inevitable curtailments forced upon him by advancing age, accepting the deaths of all those of his age whom he held dear, his wife, his brother William, his old partners at Standard Oil. He never liked to look back, to relive or begrudge the past. At sixty-two he had bought a relatively modest old clubhouse and seventy-five acres in Lakewood, New Jersey, so that he could enjoy golf more months of the year. At seventy-nine he bought The Casements, in Ormond, Florida, an unpretentious home with gray-shingled walls and many large windows, and there he spent the years of his old age, landscaping and building new verandas and terraces as he did years before at Pocantico, so that he could enjoy the splendid view of the Halifax River instead of the Hudson. However, he kept the seat on the New York Stock Exchange which he had bought when he was forty-four, so that he could buy and sell stocks through his own organizations. Every day of his life he kept his hand in business, never losing his feel for the figures that count.

8

Stewardship

"An extra 5 per cent . . ."

"His heart just gradually stopped beating and his pulse became weak and irregular, his breathing became fainter and fainter, and finally ceased at 4:05 o'clock." With these words, Dr. Harry L. Merryday, his personal physician, present at the bedside, described to reporters in Ormond Beach the passing of John D. Rockefeller, founder of the Standard Oil Company. He had died peacefully, without pain and unaware, on the morning of May 23, 1937, a Sunday, at the age of ninety-seven years, ten months and fifteen days.

Despite his age his death had been unexpected. He had been frail, weighing less than a hundred pounds, and confined to a wheelchair most of the day, not because he was incapacitated, but just to conserve his strength. He had gone to his dentist for a routine semi-annual checkup just a week before and had received friends and visitors all that week at The Casements. Three days before, Dr. Merryday had examined him and found no need to worry, which he reported by phone to Rockefeller Jr. in Pocantico Hills. His father's condition, the doctor said, was "as good as usual," he was "bright and cheerful, attended to his daily correspondence, manifested a keen interest in news and events of the day and took a long automobile ride daily." On that final Saturday he had basked in the sun in his garden and chatted with Lucille Frasca, the eight-year-old daughter of his chauffeur, assuring her, "I'll see you tomorrow." But that night he admitted to his secretary, Ward Madison, "I am very tired." Shortly after midnight he slipped from sleep into a light coma, rising only once at 2 A.M. to ask John Yordi, his personal valet, to "raise the bed [a hospital bed] a little higher." By the time the doctor arrived, there was nothing he could do.

At his bedside in the large, sparsely furnished bedroom, equipped with oxygen and hospital supplies, were his doctor, a male night nurse, his personal valet and Mrs. Fanny Evans, a distant cousin who had served him cheerfully as housekeeper, companion and hostess for the sixteen years since his sister Lucy died in 1915. In the sense that his immediate family was not there, he died alone.

The official cause of death was sclerotic myocarditis—hardening of the heart muscle, or simply, old age. On the death certificate Mrs. Evans gave his occupation as "Member of the Stock Exchange," his business as "Buying and selling stocks and bonds," and for the date upon which the deceased last worked at his occupation, Mrs. Evans said, "Until death."

At Pocantico Hills the news was received with equanimity. His son decided upon simple and private services at home in the main house, Kykuit, and sent word to his six children to return home for the funeral. Four of them were in the New York area. Nelson was reached in Panama and Winthrop, who had been with him on a tour of South America, received the news garbled in Dallas, Texas. Alighting from a plane he was told, "Telephone home right away, your father has died." John Jr. sent identical cablegrams to his two sisters, one in London, the other in Switzerland: "After only a few hours' weakness Grandfather passed away early this morning. He died as he lived, peacefuly and happily . . . John."

At The Casements the twenty-three men and women employees plus several close friends gathered for brief services and then the body, in a simple wood coffin, was transferred to a private Pullman car which was attached to the scheduled 5 P.M. train to New York on May 24.

Two days later in the early evening it arrived at a little-used railroad siding about one hundred yards south of the Tarrytown station. The family and a small group of neighbors stood waiting in the tall grass and weeds as the casket was taken from the train and loaded on a hearse for the three-mile drive back to the estate.

The fourteen-foot-high Italian scroll gates of the estate were closed and locked to the public and press. There, the next day, in the great center hall of the main house, the family and some three hundred employees attended another brief and simple funeral service at eleven in the morning. The Reverend Harry Emerson Fosdick of the Riverside Church in New York City, an interdenominational church endowed by the Rockefellers, read from the Scriptures and Harold Milligan, the church organist, played some of Rockefeller Sr.'s favorite hymns upon his favorite leatherpipe organ in the great hall. At the same time, 11 A.M., in all the offices, refineries and satellite companies around the world which had once made up the Standard empire, work ceased for five minutes in tribute to the man who had "created" the oil trade as we know it today.

The next day, with the immediate family in attendance, the body of John D. Rockefeller was interred alongside the grave of his wife, Laura, in the wooded slopes of Lakeview Cemetery in Cleveland, the city where the founder of Standard Oil had had his beginning. His grave was marked by a simple headstone, twenty-eight inches long and fourteen inches high.

Ever efficient and farsighted in the handling of money, the book-keeper who became America's first billionaire left a taxable estate of only $26,410,837.10 for probate. Federal and state taxes duly took 60 per cent of that amount, some $16 million. All the rest of the great fortune had been given away long before his death, in trust funds for most of his surviving relatives, for philanthropic causes close to his heart, and to his son, so that he could carry on the work of the latter half of his life. Even the house he died in he did not own. Title was in the name of his son. Most of the estate was in U. S. Treasury notes. The stock market in 1937 was at one of its lowest ebbs in history. Of all his Standard Oil stock John D. Rockefeller had kept only one share for himself—Certificate No. 1 of Standard of California—presumably for sentimental reasons, although he never mentioned it during his lifetime. His death, of course, was headline news in the newspapers, magazines and journals of the day. The obituaries, noting the highlights of his life, filled whole pages of the leading newspapers. But the stock market showed no reaction; it tumbled no further. The oil companies of the nation did not tremble; they went on producing, refining and marketing U.S. oil throughout the world. The surviving Rockefellers carried on.

John D. Rockefeller, Jr., at the time of his father's death was in firm control of the family fortune and power. He had been so for fifteen years, by which time his father had transferred to him the bulk of his fortune, $465 million. With that fortune came the responsibilities of wealth, power and the family name. Before, John Jr. had done the legwork and consulted with his father on all family enterprises, business and philanthropic, but from 1922 onward, he, John Jr., made the ultimate decisions and dispensed the necessary cash. While continuing to superintend the vast family philanthropies like the Rockefeller Foundation, the Medical Research Institute and the General Education Board, John Jr. branched out on his own to one of the abiding fascinations of his life: conservation. He loved the outdoors with a religious fervor. Nature provided him with a sense of proportion, the sensation that he, despite all his wealth, was but one of God's creatures. He never ceased to marvel at the grandeur of mountains, the serenity of lakes, the openness of green fields. With that enjoyment came the realization that what he enjoyed others deserved to enjoy also. As early as 1910, when he bought a summer home at Seal Harbor on Mount Desert Island off the coast of Maine, he had come to realize that the rugged beauty of the island as he knew it would eventually be destroyed by the parceling of land by private ownership. To preserve the scenic island he joined others in buying up some thirty thousand acres of unimproved land, extending from Frenchman Bay on the north to the Atlantic Ocean on the south side of the island. Then he envisioned a road which would follow the perimeter of the island so that visitors could enjoy the scenic view without interruption. To realize that vision required many years of labor, but it was a labor of love, for he himself designed the roadways and bridges and supervised the construction of the scenic ocean drive. He followed a principle in conservation which would grow through the years: it was not enough merely to preserve the land as wilderness, the land must also be used so that *people* could enjoy the natural beauty being preserved. The thirty thousand acres, made accessible by roadways to accommodate at first horse and carriages and then automobiles, was later presented to the government as a gift and became Acadia National Park, the first national park east of the Mississippi.

In 1924 John Jr. went on an extensive tour of the national parks in the West, Grand Canyon in Arizona, Bandelier National Monument in New Mexico, Mesa Verde in southern Colorado and Yellowstone in Wyoming. He took his three oldest boys with him, John 3rd, Nelson and Laurance, and they traveled through the parks on horseback and on foot with packs on their backs. John D. Rockefeller, Jr.'s commitment to conservation dates from that 1924 trip. At Mesa Verde, where he and the boys viewed the ruins of prehistoric Indian civilization and had the intricate cliff palaces explained to them by Jesse Nusbaum, the park superintendent, John Jr. decided to finance the building of a park museum or information center there so that future visitors could also have the sights explained to them. That pilot project worked so well that all national parks today and most of the large state parks in the United States have information centers or nature museums for the benefit of park visitors. At Yellowstone John Jr. was appalled at the sight of fallen trees, brush and debris left on the side of roads being built through the park. Congress had refused to appropriate funds for clearing roadsides, it was explained. So at a cost of a mere $50,000 John Jr. financed the clearing and landscaping of separate roads as a visible demonstration of what could and should be done. Five years later clearing roadsides in all the national parks became a government policy for all time.

On his next trip out West in 1926 with his wife and three of their sons, John Jr. traveled through the redwoods of California, Yellowstone National Park and then, just to the south of Yellowstone, to the Grand Tetons, which he described as "quite the grandest and most spectacular mountains I have ever seen . . . a picture of ever-changing beauty which is to me beyond compare." Here again, it was explained, a group of concerned conservationists had been struggling for years to convince the federal government to preserve this marvelous area as a national park. The problem was that one fifth of the land, the very best part of the valley

The Rockefeller homes on West Fifty-fourth Street, New York City, 1913, with John Jr.'s nine-story home in the background, John Sr.'s smaller house in the middle and the carriage house in the foreground. All were torn down in 1938 to make way for the Museum of Modern Art.

John D. Rockefeller, Jr.

Abby Aldrich Rockefeller.

John D. Rockefeller's Spartan office at the Standard Oil Company, 26 Broadway, New York City, also used by John Jr.

John D. Rockefeller, Jr.'s new office, his inner sanctum at Rockefeller Center.

Above left,
*at Ludlow, Colorado, 1915, with
Mackenzie King.* Above right, *at the U.S.
Industrial Relations Investigation, following
the Ludlow strike, 1915.* Right, *playing
squash at the Whitehall Club, N.Y.C., 1923.*

POCANTICO HILLS, N.Y.

Kykuit.

Abeyton Lodge.

Abby (Babs), John 3rd, Nelson, Laurance, Winthrop, David, 1916.

Laurance, Babs, John 3rd, Mrs. Rockefeller with David, Winthrop, Mr. Rockefeller and Nelson, at Seal Harbor, Maine, 1920.

which lay between the mountain ranges and afforded the best view of the towering thirteen-thousand-foot Grand Teton, was spotted with abandoned farmhouses, ramshackle buildings, billboards and the like, all privately owned. This spectacular valley, known as Jackson Hole, being privately owned, was highly unlikely to be included in plans to make the Teton mountain range into a national park. John Jr. decided to do what the government would not: buy out all the private owners, involving more than 33,000 acres, and turn over Jackson Hole in its entirety as a gift to the public.

These decisions, being Rockefeller decisions, were not made lightly; they involved time, effort and study. To John D. Rockefeller, Jr.'s mind, once he made a commitment to a cause, he considered it an ongoing pledge without end, unless for good and sufficient reason. If a cause were worthwhile, he intended to see it through and he wanted to do it the right way. In the complex field of conservation involving the purchase of land for public use, there was considerable opposition from private owners, ranchers, farmers, lumbering men and, at times, politicians. Conservation causes, seen as so worthwhile today, involved years of negotiations and millions of dollars to accomplish. Thus more than $3 million of Rockefeller money went into the making of Acadia National Park in Maine; almost $6 million was the cost of buying up the land and giving Fort Tryon Park to New York City; to save the Palisades cliffs along the Hudson River for New York State cost more than $10 million. He contributed $2 million to the "Save the Redwoods" League in California; another $1,646,000 to Yosemite National Park; $164,000 to the Shenandoah National Park; and for the Jackson Hole Preserve at the Grand Tetons, a major undertaking, John Jr. spent $17,497,000 to convert a mountainous wilderness into a recreational area enjoyed by well over a million visitors every year. All of these projects were undertaken by John Jr. in tandem with the outstanding conservationists of the day, men like Fairfield Osborn and Horace Marden Albright.

His boldest conservation venture, which consumed more of his personal interest, involvement and, in fact, money than any other single undertaking, was the restoration and reconstruction of a whole colonial city. That was Williamsburg, the colonial capital of Virginia, where the American colonists decided to strike out for independence, where Patrick Henry in the House of Burgesses had cried out, "Give me liberty or give me death." The city had come upon bad times over the years, its heritage largely neglected, its beauty marred by haphazard growth and a World War I boom in defense building and a postwar recession. Restoring Colonial Wiliamsburg to its eighteenth-century beauty had long been the dream of the rector of Bruton Parish there, William A. R. Goodwin. He approached several men of wealth, J. P. Morgan, Henry Ford and others, but not until 1926, when he conducted John D. Rockefeller, Jr., on a tour of the town, explaining what had stood on each street 150 years before when Thomas Jefferson, James Madison, Patrick Henry and others had walked there, did the concept take hold. Gradually, step by step, John Jr. became more and more involved in the restoration, reconstruction and conservation of this priceless American heritage.

Conceptual plans were drawn. Individual pieces of property were purchased—anonymously, to keep prices within reason—until the heart of the city was owned by "David's father," as John Jr. chose to be known during the negotiations. Then one of the largest-scaled archaeological digs in America was begun to locate the foundations of the old colonial buildings and to find thousands of artifacts which would help re-create the city as it had been. Researchers combed libraries, archives and courthouse files to locate maps, plans, journals, news accounts and to find architectural details of the old city. Kenneth Chorley, John Jr.'s aide in the undertaking, who later became president of Colonial Williamsburg, described it this way: "No Sherlock Holmes seeking to deduce the character of a man from a cigar ash ever pursued more thoroughly and relentlessly all of the evidence which would reveal the character of the restored and reconstructed area of Colonial Williamsburg." In reconstructing the governor's mansion, for instance, architects used three hundred pages of research, including a detailed floor plan drawn by Governor Thomas Jefferson.

John Jr., who involved himself personally, according to his associates, in every building that was restored or reconstructed, authorized the adherence to the utmost authenticity, whatever the cost in time, money or effort. "I wasn't trying to re-create a lovely city nor was I interested in a collection of old houses," he once explained. "I was trying to re-create Williamsburg as it stood in the eighteenth century."

It became, among all others, his pet project, one which he considered a true challenge to his love of nature, landscaping, planning and building combined. He moved into one of Williamsburg's reconstructed colonial homes, Bassett Hall, and used it as his home two months of the year, one month in the spring and one in the autumn, so that he could personally be on hand for the project, which he knew would span the rest of his life. What had first been envisioned as a $5 million venture expanded for the benefit of millions of Americans to a Rockefeller expenditure of $52.6 million. In all, 81 original colonial buildings were restored, 413 colonial buildings were reconstructed from plans, 731 non-colonial buildings were moved or torn down, eighty-three acres of gardens and greens were re-established, and 45 other buildings, including three hotels, were built to serve the visiting public.

As if all this were not enough for one man, with Colonial Williamsburg and various conservation projects to occupy him, on top of the ongoing family enterprises, John Jr. could not resist, in early 1928, the worthy proposal of a group of New York community leaders, headed by Otto

Kahn, to help develop a new opera house for the Metropolitan Opera, which had outlived its 1883 building. The idea was to make the new opera house the focal point of a public square for New York, perhaps as part of a small park to be donated to the city at Fiftieth Street and Fifth Avenue. The entire site, twelve acres running from Forty-eighth to Fifty-first streets and from Fifth to Sixth avenues, was owned by Columbia University. After due consultations and caution, John Jr. signed his name to a twenty-four-year lease with options to renew at a rental of $3.3 million a year. That was in September of 1928. Demolition began on 228 old brownstone houses and the stores on the property. Plans for the new opera house were commissioned. Then came the shock of October 29, 1929. The stock market crashed. The Metropolitan Opera lost all hope of selling its existing property to make any move, the backers of the new opera house faded fast away and John D. Rockefeller, Jr., was left holding the bill for $3.3-million-a-year rent on property which produced only $300,000 income in the midst of America's worst economic depression.

Over the next several months, as economic conditions steadily worsened, John Jr. agonized over the decision he alone had to make: to abandon the project and cut his losses or to go ahead solely on his own with an alternate project. In December of 1929, measuring his faith in the future of American business against the bleak prognostications of those sounding the death knell of the capitalistic system, he decided to go it alone, to build an entertainment-business complex of modern buildings.

Soon he was "living knee-deep in blueprints," as one associate described those days for John Jr., with his four-foot ruler in hand, quiet but firm as the final arbiter on plans and proposals submitted by three different architectural firms hired to design what would become a new heartland to the city of New York, a mecca for millions of tourists from around the world and a new standard for office buildings in America.

This was an enormous, challenging venture, even for a Rockefeller. Aside from the money involved it was the first time several skyscrapers were planned and built as an integral group. In all there were to be fourteen buildings, the pivotal one being the seventy-story RCA Building. The design was to be modern and functional, a radical departure from the baroque and Gothic styles predominating in New York. As a conscious attempt at making "a contribution" to the architectural development of modern cities, John Jr. deliberately provided for 15 per cent of the land to be left open, or "wasted," in order to design adequate air space around his buildings. That too was a first of its kind. Real estate experts promptly labeled the whole project as "Rockefeller's Folly." It was inconceivable to them that anyone could hope for a profit under such liberal plans for open space around office buildings.

However, John Jr. went ahead from plans to models to the start of construction. He told his architects he wanted "a commercial center as beautiful as possible consistent with the maximum income that could be developed." When final plans were submitted, he went even further. He asked his architects to go over the plans once again and to add "an extra 5 per cent" to all building estimates to ensure excellence and beauty. That extra 5 per cent, he told them, would raise their best efforts over and above what they could ordinarily do. It was his credo.

In building Rockefeller Center, John Jr. wanted the project to be functional, serving the people who would work inside the buildings, but he also wanted it to be aesthetically satisfying, as beautiful as possible. While the stock market continued to tumble, businesses folded, other building projects were abandoned and while unemployment brought ugly protestations and the whole economic system of capitalism came under attack, John Jr. never wavered in his purpose with Rockefeller Center. He paid extra for vast underground garages and supply-loading facilities long before traffic congestion warranted them. He went ahead with landscaping, roof gardens and the best in artwork to decorate the project. He recognized fully and counted it as a plus that this vast project, the largest ever undertaken by a private individual, was providing employment directly for more than 75,000 men, and indirectly for 225,000 others who supplied the construction material that went into the building of Rockefeller Center.

The total cost, which came in very close to original estimates, was in the neighborhood of $125 million, one third of which was secured by a mortgage from the Metropolitan Life Insurance Company. Two thirds was paid for with Rockefeller cash. John Jr. sold his blue-chip stocks to pay the bills as they came in. When asked by Raymond Fosdick, his long-time associate and biographer, if it hadn't taken courage to undertake the building of Rockefeller Center in the midst of the depression, John Jr. gave a classic response to matters of courage: "I don't know whether it is courage or not. Often a man gets into a situation where there is just one thing to do. There is no alternative. He wants to run, but there is no place to run to. So he goes ahead on the only course that's open, and people call it courage."

The scope of this man's activities in his maturity, even for a Rockefeller, was remarkable, for not only was he immersed in building a modern "city within a city" in New York, he was also involved in restoring and reconstructing a colonial city in Virginia, and in purchasing virgin forests for preservation as wilderness or as recreational areas open to the public. Nor did his lifelong interest flag in trying to bring together the diverse denominations of the Protestant Church. During these same years he was instrumental in building Riverside Church, an edifice magnificent in beauty, near Columbia University, which would thereafter serve as New York City's most prominent interdenominational church.

The theme underlying all of these activities was that his wealth should be spent wisely to promote the well-being of his fellow men. John D. Rockefeller, Jr., never lost sight of that purpose. He looked upon it quite consciously as his duty. It was something he felt he had to do. He expected no praise for his good work. He wanted no plaques commemorating his deeds and said he did "not want his name plastered" on Rockefeller Center, which he had preferred to name Radio City. There was little publicity and certainly no fanfare in announcing his numerous bequests, gifts or building plans. He much preferred to work behind the scenes and on a basis of equality with the experts he hired to achieve his purposes. Experience over the years made him an "expert" in land development, architecture, construction and, above all, the management of money. In his own mind—and he expressed it time and time again—he considered himself the "steward" or the "custodian" of the Rockefeller wealth, after his father, and it was his "duty" in life to use that money wisely and effectively, not to make more money, but to produce an effect for the common good. In all the years after his father's retirement, when he worked on alone, he arranged for the credit to go to his father rather than to himself. He never forgot, nor did he allow others to forget, that his own money, influence and power were derived from his father. He liked to say that his proudest title would always be "my father's representative."

When Senior died in May 1937, ten of the originally planned fourteen buildings of Rockefeller Center had been completed, and John Jr. was sixty-three years of age. Much of his own life's work had been accomplished and although he tore down his father's town house on West Fifty-fourth Street as well as his own to make room for the Museum of Modern Art, he and his wife moved into his father's home, Kykuit, at Pocantico Hills. Still he refused to drop the "Jr." from his own name. He would never be John D. Rockefeller, he explained, because there could only be one John D. Rockefeller.

He was not only content, but happy and proud, to be "my father's representative." As he had carried on his father's work, so he wanted his five sons to continue and to enlarge upon his own enterprises. He knew he could not force this upon his sons. His father had instructed him by example and similarly John Jr. wished to lead his sons into living useful lives.

Years later, when he himself was on the verge of full or almost full retirement, and the third generation of Rockefellers was established each in his own line of activities, John Jr. explained in a memorable speech before the Chamber of Commerce of the state of New York his relationship with his father. There had been no generation gap. Over the forty years he worked with his father, he said, from the day he entered his office "until the day of his death my one desire was to help him in every way in my power.

"I was always as glad to black his shoes, to pack his bag, to act as the courier of family travels at home or abroad, and on such trips to write his letters, to decipher his business cables, to handle his mail and callers, as I was later to represent him in various of his interests, business and philanthropic, and to help initiate and carry on the several foundations and other eleemosynary organizations which he brought into being and heavily endowed.

"Neither before I went into his office nor any time thereafter did my father ever tell me, either directly or through his associates, what I was to do. Left entirely on my own I sought, as rapidly as possible, to familiarize myself with his various interests and to be helpful wherever I saw the opportunity. He never gave me any authority, any power of attorney, or any title. For years, however, in helping to carry out his plans I signed his name 'by John D. Rockefeller, Jr.' to countless agreements committing him to large sums of money. He could at any time have challenged my legal right to do so. He never did, for from the outset he trusted me, knowing that I shared fully his high ideals of business integrity and social responsibility. As my experience grew, his confidence in my judgment increased. Of that fact he gave abundant proof in the large gifts which he made me from time to time and which have enabled me with the passing years to continue in my own way the work for humanity throughout the world which he initiated and of which his own life and deeds were ever my example and inspiration."

In retrospect that speech describes the course John Jr. set for the third generation of Rockefellers as, one by one, his sons entered his office.

9

The Rockefeller Brothers

"I have my fingers crossed . . ."

At the age of sixty, with the nation in the midst of deep depression, the future uncertain, John D. Rockefeller, Jr., knew he was well advised to make some financial arrangements for the future well-being of his own children. The problem was how to do it wisely and, more precisely, how much money to give his daughter and five sons.

The third generation of Rockefellers by 1934 were all grown and to a degree launched upon their separate individual lives, although well within the Rockefeller family orbit. Babs, married for nine years, was living a quiet life at thirty as a wife and mother of two girls. John 3rd, at twenty-eight, married but childless as yet, had come from college to work at his father's philanthropic ventures. Nelson, at twenty-five with two children, had followed into the office, energetically plunging into the sundry problems of Rockefeller Center. Laurance, twenty-three and just married, had only that year come to work at 5600, ready to carry his share of the family work load. Winthrop was off in Texas learning the oil business. David, at nineteen, was still at college but showing much promise.

One would imagine that parents of six such children would be highly pleased and satisfied indeed. There was not a "black sheep" among them. Even Winthrop, whom one might consider the problem child of the family, had followed a Rockefeller tradition of avoiding waste. He had told his father that he had decided to drop out of Yale rather than be left back a year because of poor grades. "I felt I was just not getting enough out of school for the time I was putting in," said Winthrop. He had gone directly to work for Socony-Vacuum, an offshoot of the old Standard Oil empire. Nevertheless when the question came up in one interview in 1938,

John Jr. agreed that his sons indeed were measuring up to Rockefeller standards of competence and responsibility. But he was wary.

"I have my fingers crossed," he said, "and not a day passes but Mrs. Rockefeller and I don't pray that they will continue to do so." To his way of thinking, so cautious and careful, his daughter may well be settled down to a private, quiet life as Mrs. David Milton, but his five sons were still very much in their formative years.

In deciding, John Jr. did not want to hand over too large an amount of money to his children and certainly not in the midst of a depression when dollars loomed so large. He did not want to risk upsetting the fine equilibrium he had established with them over the years in regard to wealth and responsibility. They were not ready, he thought, at least not all of them. Nor did he want to differentiate between them at this stage of their lives by giving more to one than to another. Yet the time had arrived to provide for their financial welfare beyond the allowances he regularly gave them, supplemented from time to time with gifts.

As a result of this thinking he set up in 1934 identical trusts of $20 million for each of his children, stipulating that only the *income* of each trust should be paid to each of them, while the principal would be distributed in equal shares to their offspring sometime in the future. In another $20 million trust for his wife, he named as beneficiaries his three oldest sons, John 3rd, Nelson and Laurance.

These were living, generation-skipping, irrevocable trusts. The $140 million in seven trusts, once given, was then forever more beyond his control. But he went even further. He put the trusts beyond his children's control. They were set up at the Chase Bank in New York and placed entirely under the direction of a committee of advisers there, men whose financial acumen John Jr. knew he could rely upon. Rather than tie the money up absolutely for a generation, he gave the trust advisers considerable flexibility. (This, too, was in accord with Rockefeller principles in giving money away under certain conditions, carefully looked into at the time, but thereafter with no strings attached.) The trust executors have full power of discretion to give his children all, part, or none of the principal when and if they request capital funds, but only if their reasons are worthy and warranted. The children can and do confer with the trustees on the trust investments, their needs and wishes, but the trust executors are under no obligation to follow their wishes. In fact the law imposes strict obligations and responsibilities upon the trustees to preserve the trusts for the ultimate beneficiaries, the future generations of Rockefellers.

The trusts will come to an end and all the money in them distributed to the beneficiaries upon the death of the last of John Jr.'s descendants living at the time the trusts were made. When that will occur no one knows. The youngest of those descendants alive in 1934 were Babs's two young daughters, Abby and Marilyn, and Nelson's first two children, Rodman and Ann. Upon their deaths the money will come out of the trusts, tax-free, and be distributed equally to all the then living descendants of John Jr., namely the children and grandchildren of Babs, John 3rd, Nelson, Laurance, Winthrop and David. Upon their deaths the fortunes will be fully subject to inheritance taxes.

As John Jr. had foreseen, over the ensuing years some of the third generation of Rockefellers have dipped into the principals of the trusts as individual needs arose. However, the withdrawals have not been substantial.

However prescient, their father could not foresee what the stock market would do thirty and forty years hence. At the time, however, it was understood that these trusts were a beginning, providing a vehicle into which John Jr. could add more money as time and events warranted. He told each of them time and again that he would leave real Rockefeller wealth only to those of them who proved themselves fully capable and competent to handle such wealth wisely and well. The proof was in the living of a useful and fruitful life.

Other men of wealth have used similar generation-skipping trusts to escape inheritance taxes: the trusts name grandchildren as the beneficiaries, but give the children control and use of the funds during their lifetimes so that what is left of the principal is taxed only once when distributed to the grandchildren. But John Jr.'s primary motive in those days of low taxes was to keep a tight rein on those millions, however much he loved and trusted his daughter and five sons. If he were to err, he preferred to give them too little rather than too much.

For his sons, indeed, it was a very tight rein. Through the 1930s when each of them was starting out, the income of his trust yielded less than $1 million a year, a princely sum to the average or above-average man, but hardly enough to enable a third-generation Rockefeller to go about saving the world in his own modern fashion. Well provided for, yes, but they themselves hardly felt rich, not by Rockefeller standards. Moreover they knew their father was watching them all the time. He still expected them to keep their personal daily account books. He expected them to know the value of the penny. He was in no visible hurry to give them more money. After all, he had been forty-three years old before *his* father, who also trusted him implicitly, gave him substantial control over the family wealth.

Through their college years the five boys, as well as their sister, were shackled financially, materially and morally. There was no letup in church-going, in dinner-table lessons, in everyday parental expectations or in allowances. Each of the boys was allotted only $1,500 a year while away at college. Requests for extra money required explanations as detailed as an application for a Rockefeller Foundation grant. Each of them had to learn to live under "economic pressure." Quite deliberately their father allotted them just a bit less money than he thought they needed. John 3rd was the only one trusted with more money than he needed because, their father said, John 3rd was the only one who could be counted upon to save some portion of his allowance.

Of all the boys it was John 3rd who seemed to fit most perfectly into the Rockefeller mold cast by his father. By nature he was less competitive, less venturesome than his brothers, more willing to do what was expected of him. He was shy, gentle, tall, thin and gawky, rather reticent, happy in doing things by himself, wandering off alone at times. His aloofness was something respected by his brothers. They seemed to understand that John 3rd just did not want to enter into the competitive rough-and-tumble sibling rivalry of the others. He was liked by all of them as he was by his friends at school and play. He gave offense to no one. A sweet disposition, one might say. His course through adolescence into manhood was smooth, his childhood completely normal. He attended the Browning School in New York, where his father had gone before him, and on to Loomis, a top-notch prep school in Windsor, Connecticut, and then to Princeton, where he won honors in economics. But he was not a brilliant student. He found that he had to study arduously to keep up the grades he knew were expected of him. While the 1920s were "roaring" around him, with prohibition, whiskey, flappers and the jazz age in full swing, John D. Rockefeller 3rd spent most of his extracurricular hours working at the YMCA, teaching English to immigrants in the area and working as a counselor in a summer camp for tenement boys in New Jersey.

A moral dilemma which confronted John 3rd at Princeton is quite revealing of his personality at that time. Elected to Cap and Gown, one of the more exclusive social clubs at Princeton, he learned that during his initiation he would be expected to sip wine from a goblet passed around. These were prohibition days, drinking was against the law; furthermore, John 3rd was a teetotaler, drinking was against his religion. What should he do? Refuse the cup? Raise it to his lips and fake it? Or take a sip? So seriously did he consider all of this that he wrote his father for advice. His father acknowledged the problem and, as might be expected, told his son that he would have to resolve it himself. And he never asked John 3rd what he had done. What John 3rd did when the time came was to raise the goblet to his lips "in a symbolic gesture," but he did not drink.

The most significant event of John 3rd's college career occurred unexpectedly in 1928 during the summer vacation of his junior year when he worked as a clerk in the information section of the League of Nations in Geneva. He saw at first hand and close up the men who were considered the leaders of the world as they struggled to alleviate international problems. John 3rd had, of course, sat through not unsimilar discussions at his father's dinner table back home, but in Geneva, more or less on his own at the age of twenty-two, the affairs and problems of the world seemed to swim within the grasp of his own work potential. Perhaps it was merely growing up, but whatever it was, part of this new awareness was due to the realization that the name "Rockefeller" meant something special to men of importance. Ministers like Aristide Briand of France did not mind stopping to chat with a serious-minded young man named John D. Rockefeller 3rd.

The following year, upon graduation from Princeton, he was selected as one of four junior secretaries to attend an international conference in Kyoto, Japan, sponsored by the Institute of Pacific Relations, which was followed by a trip across Russia on the trans-Siberian railroad and a tour of some twelve Asian countries. Again he saw people and problems at first hand, he saw how primitive these Asian countries were, he saw the contrast between discussions in the abstract and reality. "That trip showed me the world," he commented long afterward. "I knew then that only by visiting a country could you understand its problems. It is like the difference between seeing an accident and reading about it in the newspapers."

Upon his return he went to work at his father's office, then at the old Standard Oil Company Building, 26 Broadway. Twenty newspapermen showed up the first day for the event: the first third-generation Rockefeller at Standard Oil. "For the present I don't know just what my duties around here will be," he told the press. "I intend to prowl around under Father's supervision, trying to familiarize myself with at least the most obvious parts of the business, and attempt to find the thing I am best at. Of course I don't know where that will take me. I would be interested in going to the oil fields or to the coal fields, but I don't know whether that will be in the apprenticeship or not."

His father told the newsmen he did not intend to plan his son's career for him. "I want him to do what he is most interested in. I believe that in this way a man may realize his own possibilities. I don't propose to make John's career for him. He must do that himself."

Neither the oil fields nor Standard Oil was to be in John 3rd's apprenticeship. Where he was needed most to help his overinvolved father was in the broad spectrum of philanthropy. Family investments were explained to him and he served as his father's assistant in running the family estate at Pocantico, but the main thrust of his work, which he seemed to prefer himself, was helping his father with the detail work involved in philanthropy. He soon became a trustee of the Rockefeller Foundation, the Rockefeller Institute for Medical Research, the General Education Board, the Spelman Fund, the China Medical Board, Colonial Williamsburg and a host of others. As the youngest trustee on these boards among men far older, wiser and more experienced than he, John 3rd sat through long meetings, quiet and observant. It was well understood he was serving his apprenticeship for the future.

Those were busy and yet confining days for John 3rd. He was not of the nature to step out beyond his assigned or supposed position to grasp at power. In a matter of three or so years he found himself serving on thirty-three different philanthropic boards, confined to the role of a young apprentice, the heir apparent of his father, whose soft voice and mien of politeness struck awe among men of power. Nor was John 3rd unaware of the situation. Questioned for jury duty one day during this period, he gave his occupation as "a clerk."

Gradually John 3rd's interests began to focus, growing out of his college trip to Geneva and his post-graduate journey, upon Japan and the Far East. He discovered a certain affinity with the Far East and the non-aggressive oriental mind. He took an active part in the development of the Peking (Peiping) Medical College, the outstanding training center for doctors in China, supported by his father personally and by the Rockefeller Foundation. His concern for Asian affairs led him to the problem which afflicted the economic, social and cultural well-being of all the Asian countries: overpopulation. Here was a fundamental worldwide problem receiving too little attention in the 1930s to which he, John 3rd, could apply himself and his energies. He went on record—something of which he would be proud for all of his life—as early as March 17, 1934, when he wrote his father, urging his financial support of several birth control efforts in the United States, including the American Birth Control League, the National Committee on Maternal Health and Margaret Sanger and her birth control Clinical Research Bureau. "I take the liberty of making this suggestion to you because of my great interest in birth control and related questions . . ." he wrote. "I have come pretty definitely to the conclusion that it is the field in which I will be interested, for the present at least, to concentrate my own giving, as I feel that it is so fundamental and underlying."

Birth control in the 1930s was so sensitive a subject it was not talked about in polite society; the dispensing of contraceptive devices was illegal in many states; it was, in short, as unpopular and unfashionable a cause as anyone could espouse in the United States. Nevertheless John 3rd became the primary donor to Margaret Sanger's Research Bureau, which trained more than 36,000 doctors and nurses in contraceptive techniques. Her Birth Control Clinic on West Sixteenth Street in New York was the largest and best-known of its kind throughout the country.

At the same time John 3rd also became a prime mover and contributor of a little-known organization called the National Committee on Maternal Health. Behind that innocuous, nice-sounding name was a private agency, the only one of its kind in character and scope in the 1930s, which was sponsoring basic scientific research on human sexuality, fertility and contraceptives. It conducted the earliest surveys on sex education, birth control clinics, marriage advice centers, and it published its findings in books and manuals of particular interest to doctors. An important part of its work in those early days was merely enlisting doctors to join the committee in order to give respectability to the study of sex.

John 3rd moved cautiously, of course. His early contributions in this field were given anonymously and only in the latter 1930s, early still for those times, did he allow his name to appear in connection with the work he did behind the scenes. Nevertheless his interest remained at a peak as the years rolled on. Each time he undertook a trip to the Orient in connection with his other work he came away with the conviction that population control was at the root of the economic ills of the underdeveloped nations of Asia.

Philanthropy paid John 3rd an early dividend: at a charity drive he met a tall, slender, dark-haired girl named Blanchette Ferry Hooker, who was to become, when he mustered up the nerve to ask her, his wife, mother of his four children and the single most influential individual in his life. A descendant of Charles Ferry, who settled in Massachusetts in the seventeenth century, the youngest daughter of Elon Hunting Hooker, one of the foremost chemical engineers of his time, Blanchette came from a family only slightly less renowned in society than the Rockefellers. A graduate of Vassar, a member of the Junior League, the shiest of the four beautiful and ebullient Hooker sisters, well known in the "cafe society" circles of the time, she was very much like John 3rd in upbringing and outlook. She was retiring, reticent and serious-minded, interested in politics, economics and the future of the League of Nations. "They were meant for each other," was the word around town by the society gossips: they were expected to get married. They were married November 11, 1932, at the Riverside Church, with a reception which followed for 2,500 guests at the Colony Club on Park Avenue. No champagne was served; the Hookers were every bit as teetotaling as the Rockefellers. However serious-minded, the twenty-seven-year-old John D. Rockefeller 3rd was not without a sense of humor. Upon their return from a month-long honeymoon in Bermuda, the ship-news press demanded to know what was the most interesting part of his trip. "Why, the honeymooning part, I guess," he replied.

By the time John 3rd had taken a bride at twenty-seven, Nelson, two years his junior, had been married for more than two years and was the vociferously proud father of the first Rockefeller boy of the fourth generation. He did not name him John D. IV out of deference to his older brother. As a young man, Nelson was stocky, robust, competitive, dynamic and intuitive, even impetuous. Those who knew him well in his formative years remarked more than once that Nelson was a chip off the maternal block of his heredity. He may have looked like his father but he acted like his mother and his maternal grandfather, his namesake, Senator Nelson Aldrich of Rhode Island.

Much more than any of the other boys, even Winthrop, Nelson

seemed at odds with his father's way of doing things. There was no lack of love between them; Nelson agreed with all the lessons and advice. It was just that he seemed incapable of doing things his father's way. As a boy he had always been too boisterous for his father's taste, but no amount of discipline or reprimand seemed to curb his enthusiasm for cutting up. The progressive Lincoln School suited Nelson. He excelled in getting along with his peers, in extracurricular work, in becoming a "whole person," in his handling of life's problems—all important aspects of the John Dewey philosophy of education—but somehow his grades were terrible. In the eleventh grade it was discovered his marks in mathematics and French could not be certified for college. "Nelson should work harder," his principal wrote home. Nelson promised. His grades did not improve. So his father analyzed Nelson's study habits as he would any Rockefeller project, and he wrote his son: "You go at things with too much of a rush and a dash. You're careless about the way you study, but any time you want to put your mind to it you can do much better work without spending any more time at study than you do now." Nelson put his mind to it, took special tutoring, improved in French and mathematics and began to flunk Spanish in his senior year. In the end he decided to drop Spanish and his hope of following John to Princeton. Instead he chose Dartmouth, a smaller, less prestigious college with lower entrance requirements. His parents approved of Dartmouth for Nelson: it was far off in New Hampshire, away from the parties and social activities of New York which were so distracting. Nelson had discovered girls in his senior year at high school and the girls had discovered a Rockefeller who liked parties, dancing and things.

While his parents allowed Nelson to select his own college his mother artfully suggested a suitable room-mate. She introduced Nelson to John French, the son of one of her very good friends in YWCA work, Mrs. Mary M. Billings French. The two young freshmen hit it off well together and as Nelson said years later, "He was a tremendous influence. He was brilliant but I was damned if I was going to let him take me. So I worked."

At Dartmouth, away from home for the first time, Nelson was able to shrug off more than ever before the aura of being a Rockefeller. He just took no notice of it. According to one classmate, he was one of the boys: "His normal appearance—crew cut, dirty corduroy pants and a green sweater—was as sloppy, if not more so, than the college average . . . He was always so outgoing and cheerful it was impossible not to like him . . ." For most of his first two years, Nelson pursued extracurricular activities as much as the college curriculum. He made the soccer team, joined the photography club, a social club, and seemed never to miss a campus free-for-all fight, so popular in those days. He apologized profusely to his parents when the Boston newspapers picked up one story of his exploits:

"JOHN D. JR. SON MAULED IN FIGHT . . . Plays Heroic Part as Freshmen Best Sophomores at Dartmouth." Sophomore Nelson Rockefeller, it seemed, had held off a group of freshmen storming the sophomore dormitory by turning a fire hose upon them.

Yet beneath this exterior there was that Rockefeller upbringing in Nelson. Without fanfare he volunteered to take over Sunday school classes for twelve-year-old girls at the local church, and he stuck to it throughout his college years. He stayed on campus when his pals went downtown to the local beer parlor. Nelson did not swear, drink or smoke, but that did not stop him from having a good time. Somewhere along in his sophomore year Nelson did begin to concentrate more on his studies. John French remembers that while he was not a brilliant student, he had an inquiring mind and that once he set to a task he could work conscientiously at it. The C's in his report card rose to A's and B's, and in his junior year he did honors work in economics, his major. His thesis for that class was a forty-five-page study of the Standard Oil Company, of which he admittedly knew little before he began. As an aid, his father sent him an unpublished manuscript on the life of John D., Sr., written by a former employee and based upon long interviews with the founder of Standard Oil. It had quite an effect upon Nelson who wrote home: "For the first time I felt that I really knew Grandfather a little—got a glimpse into the power and grandeur of his life . . . Among other things it brought out the importance and value of money. And I was able to see as never before the reason and true significance of keeping accounts as you have always asked us to do." Nelson admitted to his father that in his own accounts "I have up to now merely been obeying the letter of the law, as it were, and not the spirit, and that I have been missing the whole point." And so, said Nelson, he was returning his father's $100 bonus for keeping his expense accounts in good order. "I don't feel I can accept it—at least not until I have attained the real goal and not merely an artificial one." The truth was that Nelson at times had balanced his accounts from memory and as often as not, by borrowing from friends.

Nelson settled down—relatively, for Nelson—during his last two years at college, dropping many of his extracurricular activities, concentrating on his studies and winning an honors fellowship in his senior year. The fellowship freed him from routine classroom work and allowed him to pursue an elective study course of his own. He then focused his attention upon the arts. One of his achievements at college was, according to a professor there, making art "socially accepted" at Dartmouth. Nelson started a music recordings library where students could come and listen. He inaugurated a program of bringing guest writers, clergymen and poets to lecture at Dartmouth. All this was part of an extracurricular organization known as The Arts at Dartmouth. Nelson summed it up in a long article written in 1930 for the *Dartmouth Alumni Magazine* in which he urged college men studying for a life in business or the professions also to plan for their use of leisure time by devoting part of their college studies to the arts and culture. "To my mind colleges in the future will have to lay greater stress on training students how to use freedom, for it isn't something that can be picked up after graduation." Nelson also reached a traditional Rockefeller value judgment: "I have been working for the personal joy and satisfaction derived from it," he wrote at the age of twenty-two.

Letters flowed regularly between Nelson and his parents, usually one a week, sometimes more, and aside from the news of the day they followed a pattern: apologies and promises to do better from Nelson and words of wisdom and advice from Mother and Father on conduct, values, relationships with others and keeping oneself physically and mentally fit. Such letters went to all the boys at one time or another. But to Nelson in particular, his father, time and time again, reminded him not to rush headlong into things. "You have great admiration for your Grandfather Rockefeller," his father wrote. "Remember that one of the qualities that made him great and that not infrequently made him successful over other people was his ability to wait and to be patient to a degree that was almost superhuman. Waiting is often hard work, much harder than working and doing, but not infrequently it is the quickest and most effective way to accomplish the desired end and it is the goal that the wise man keeps his eye on."

Patience, the art of waiting, the faculty of deliberately doing nothing, however, were virtues which Nelson Aldrich Rockefeller found impossible to grasp and to retain. He understood the principle but the practice seemed to elude him. In contemplating a future career, he could not decide just what he wanted to do. He knew he did not relish the idea, suggested by his father, of going into business. "There is nothing very appealing, challenging about it," he wrote his father from Dartmouth. "Just to work my way up in a business that another man has built, stepping from the shoes of one to those of another, making a few minor changes here and there and then finally, perhaps at the age of sixty, getting to the top where I would have real control for a few years. No, that isn't my idea of living a real life . . ." He thought he might like to become an architect, but his mother dissuaded him from that on the grounds that architecture hardly offered him a sufficient scope of activities. His father advised more patience. "Time helps to solve so many problems and make clear so many paths," his father wrote him, adding, "Fortunately there is no [need for] haste . . . as the days and months go by you will get added light."

As his college days and months went by, however, Nelson's thoughts turned to love and his interests narrowed down to one girl in particular, an old and true friend from his teen-age days on Mount Desert Island in Maine, where she and her family spent summer vacations not far from the Rockefellers: Mary Todhunter Clark, of Philadelphia. The Clarks were one of the largest, oldest, wealthiest and most socially prominent families in Philadelphia, if not in all of Pennsylvania. In the social register, at least by Philadelphia standards, the Rockefellers were definitely Johnny-come-latelies in comparison. Mary Todhunter Clark was a tall, thin, plain-looking but highly intelligent young woman with a quick wit and caustic tongue, a year older than Nelson, with a concern over social affairs at least equal to that of the Dartmouth graduate. Her grandfather had been the president of the Pennsylvania Railroad, her father an investment banker, and she had been raised along with six brothers on a huge estate outside Philadelphia in an aura of happy well-being not unlike that of the Rockefellers. In the summer after his sophomore year Nelson had gone on a bicycle trip through Europe with his brother John. The following summer, after his junior year, he went to the Arctic with Laurance as crew members aboard a sailing ship (where they ended up serving as cooks) as part of the Sir Wilfred T. Grenfell mission to bring medical care to the Eskimos. The long boring nights at sea gave Nelson time to think and on his twenty-first birthday he wrote his mother: "You know, I am beginning to think that I really am in love with Tod, whatever being in love means . . . She is the only girl that I know who measures up anywhere nearly to the standards set by you, Mum. But don't get worried. I am not going to run into anything in a headstrong way . . ."

Of course not. Two months later, back at Dartmouth, he wrote that now he was "really and truly desperately in love" and despite pleas from his family that he wait, Nelson proposed. Nelson and Tod Clark were engaged that fall. The objection was not directed toward Miss Clark. She was a friend of the family's and much admired by both Mr. and Mrs. Rockefeller. John Jr. was particularly upset. Nelson had not consulted his parents and he was too young, too precipitous to take such a serious step. However, in time, Mrs. Rockefeller brought her husband around and he gave the young couple his blessing. The couple then journeyed to Ormond Beach in Florida, where Miss Clark played a round of golf with John D. Rockefeller, Sr., and received his blessings. They were married a week after Nelson graduated from Dartmouth, on June 23, 1930, at Bala-Cynwyd, a fashionable suburb of Philadelphia. The wedding was attended by 1,500 invited guests. The story that made the rounds—apocryphal or not —which Nelson cherished for years, concerned a crusty old Philadelphia socialite who asked at the wedding: "Who is this fellow Nelson Rockefeller who is marrying into the Clark family?"

For a wedding gift the Rockefellers gave the young couple a medium sized colonial home on the Pocantico Hills estate and a honeymoon trip around the world.

Nelson clashed with his father over the furnishing of the house. His father offered to furnish it for them if Nelson would choose the pieces from a catalogue of colonial reproductions which he himself had used to furnish his home on the estate. Nelson wanted original pieces in his home. But his father insisted that would be wasteful; reproductions were every bit as good as antiques as far as colonial furniture was concerned. Nelson, unable to convince his father, finally went through the catalogue, listing each piece with its price that he would need for the house, and then he asked his father to give him the total cost in a lump sum and let him spend just that much on the furnishings. To that his father agreed and Nelson, along with Mary, scrounged the backwoods of New Hampshire, going from house to farm, searching out attics, and much to their delight, came home with a houseful of colonial originals at below the cost of reproductions, including two rare and unlisted pine grandfather clocks, bought for $8 and $10.

Their honeymoon trip was scheduled in the style of a foreign mission abroad. After a brief stay in Maine alone, they set out for the Far East, armed with letters of introduction and a heavy schedule of meetings with foreign representatives of the Standard Oil Company, the Chase National Bank, the Rockefeller Foundation, heads of state, subheads of state and friends of the various and sundry Rockefeller interests around the world. Nelson also carried with him, at his father's request, his little account book in which to note expenditures. The idea was to expose Nelson to the multiplicity of family interests in the hope that something or someone would catch his interest and point the way to choosing a career. Japan, China, Korea, Sumatra, Indo-China, Burma, Siam, India and points west, the honeymoon lasted almost a year, from July 1930 to May 1931. Nelson collected primitive art, was fascinated by political leaders he met, disappointed in the outlook of businessmen he met, spent hours and days thinking over what he should do with the rest of his life and wrote his father, "As yet I've come to no conclusions."

Returning to New York, Nelson reported to work at 26 Broadway and soon became interested in the architectural and building problems of Rockefeller Center and Colonial Williamsburg. He was there to help his father in any way he could and by tacit agreement not to overlap the activities of his brother John. But he was not particularly happy in the role of an apprentice. He wanted to do things, not to sit on a board of directors or to nod his head in unison with the older men serving his father. So Nelson and two of his young friends launched a business of their own as middlemen in real estate ventures and after a year Nelson bought his partners out and devoted the firm to renting space in Rockefeller Center on a commission basis. He soon became involved in a rather public and bitter lawsuit when August Heckscher sued him and the entire board of directors of Rockefeller Center for $10 million on the grounds that Nelson had employed unfair business practices in buying up unexpired leases of Heckscher's tenants as a means of inducing them to move to the Center.

His defense was that what he did was legal, ethical and customary in the rental business and the suit was dropped before coming to trial.

Nelson spent a good deal of his time as the "front man" for his father, making those brief and innocuous speeches so necessary for opening a new building, garden or exhibit at Rockefeller Center. He was quite good at it, too, smiling affably, sincere in his optimism over the future, eager to shake hands and meet new people. He joined in the campaign to raise $2 million for a new home for the Museum of Modern Art, a project close to his mother's heart, as she was one of the founders of the Museum in 1929. He also accepted the post of trustee of the Metropolitan Museum of Art, defying his father's advice that he was too young, too busy and too undecided upon his own future for such a responsibility. But Nelson liked to be busy, he liked to expose himself to challenging responsibilities. He also was instrumental in bringing the Mexican artist Diego Rivera, one of the most famous and gifted muralists in the world, to Rockefeller Center to paint in his vivid colors a fresco on the central wall facing the entrance to 30 Rockefeller Plaza. That resulted in a fiasco of major proportions, headlined around the world. Rivera, as renowned a Marxist as he was a painter, submitted a sketch portraying Lincoln and Washington and then went ahead to paint the head of Lenin, the flag of the Soviet Union, happy Communists dancing in the streets, contrasted to scenes of warfare, police brutality, germ warfare and capitalists with social diseases in the United States. Nelson pleaded with him to change his painting in wet plaster. Rivera went on painting. The newspapers picked up the story. There were demonstrations, picketing and protests far beyond the importance of one painting. When Rivera absolutely refused to change his painting the Rockefeller Center management covered the huge fresco, sixty-three feet long and seventeen feet high, with canvas, paid him in full and dismissed him. Communists and left-wingers screamed that the work of an artist of the people was being destroyed. The conflict, in a microcosm, seemed to symbolize the struggle for men's loyalties rampant in the 1930s, socialism versus capitalism, and E. B. White, the humorist of the *New Yorker* magazine, immortalized the scene in a memorable poem in which Diego Rivera insists, "I paint what I see," and John D. Rockefeller's grandson, Nelson, says, "But, after all, it is my wall," to which Rivera has the last word: "We'll see about that."

Restless and not entirely happy working under the domination of his father in the sedate family offices and still in search of a career he could call his own, in 1934 Nelson went to work for his uncle, Winthrop Aldrich, president of the Chase National Bank. He made a cross-country tour of branch offices and major customers with his uncle, and then he tried the London and the Paris offices of the bank. He learned something about banking, to be sure, but he also learned that he was not cut out to a banker.

The man who sent young Nelson upon the right path and on his way was Bertram Cutler, a brilliant and intuitive investment specialist who worked closely with John Jr. on the Rockefeller investments and stock portfolio. One of John Jr.'s closest associates in the office, Cutler understood people as well as he did the stock market. When Nelson's trust fund provided him with more than $1 million in income in 1935, Cutler advised the young Rockefeller to invest in a new exploratory oil company, a subsidiary of the Standard Oil Company of New Jersey, named the Creole Petroleum Company, of Venezuela. The company had not yet brought in a single oil well and so Nelson's investment would guarantee that he would become a director of a young, risky enterprise with a great future potential. Nelson liked the idea and plunged right in.

When Nelson made his first trip down to Venezuela two years later as a director of Creole, his father and others in the office hoped that he would discover a personal interest in the oil business. But Nelson, being Nelson, discovered much more, he discovered Venezuela and all of Latin America. Here was a challenge, indeed, a whole continent rich in natural resources with an underdeveloped economy, waiting for someone with modern know-how to lead the way as no one had before.

As a young man with substantial wealth, excellent health and stamina, a good education, with, in short, everything going for him, Nelson Rockefeller followed his own personal open-door policy: *he* was open to opportunities, ready to walk through any open door to see what was on the other side, to follow whatever path in life looked most interesting. In South America the vista to Nelson seemed nothing short of wide open.

10

The Rockefeller Credo

"There are certain fundamental and
underlying things which do not change."

The least-known publicly of the Rockefeller brothers, Laurance, more
than any of the others, brings to mind for outsiders what his grandfather
must have been like in his day. Within the family it was Laurance who
seemed always to hold the "swing vote." He was the fulcrum, the youngest
of his two older brothers and the oldest of the two younger ones. By nature he was perhaps the most objective of all of them. He had the faculty
of stepping outside himself, putting his own emotions and personal interests aside and seeing a situation plain. It was Laurance whom the other
brothers most often sought out for advice and help when in trouble. It
was in Laurance's apartment that his brother Nelson would seek refuge
when he separated from his first wife, and it was in his home at Pocantico
that he would be married quietly to Margaretta Fitler.

To those close to him, his family, his associates and his friends, he
was a concerned, sympathetic, giving man with a highly developed sense
of social consciousness. He was ruled however by a sharp intellect and a
caustic wit which seldom allowed him to relax with outsiders. The visitor
who sat across a business desk from Laurance would see the stern, narrow
face of the Rockefeller side of the family with the beak nose, thin lips and
the look of a cold, cool business executive. That was Laurance Spelman
Rockefeller unsmiling. But when he smiled a different, fuller face
emerged, another part of the iceberg came into view, and the visitor, if observant, could glimpse the complexity of the man who was saying, in
effect, "Do not try to understand me too easily." At the same time he also
would give the unsettling impression that he knew what you were think-

ing about him and that he was not about to tell you in any way whether you were right or wrong.

Beneath that exterior, however, there was a shy, reserved, inhibiting streak in Laurance which he concealed so well from the outside world. In his formative years he was very much like his brother John, and yet he spent most of his time keeping up with his brother Nelson's exuberant range of activities. His twelve years at the progressive Lincoln School, from the first grade through high school, were most significant in his development. Mixing with students of different nationalities and races from all economic strata, Laurance learned how to force himself, to an extent, out of his own insulated shell.

The Lincoln School taught Laurance and his brothers how to be practical, how to take one step at a time in attacking long-range problems. The concept of being practical became a part of Laurance's life, as it did with Nelson and David, and in their opinion, served them well through the years. "One has his ideals but also at the same time a sense of what you can do here and now," Laurance believed, "and that gives you the confidence in what you are doing today for the ideals of tomorrow." He also learned at the Lincoln School for the first time that there were ways to view life other than what he had been taught at home and at his Baptist Sunday school. Not that he could reconcile the two so readily, but he became aware of the chasm.

Even so, Princeton in 1928, when the twenties were in full swing, came as a distinct shock to Laurance at eighteen years of age. The prohibition drinking, flappers and high living which he saw almost every day overwhelmed him with an adolescent sense of conflict. He was at the time, as he recalled years later, "frustrated, inhibited and concerned."

So he decided quite deliberately to try to find an answer to this conflict. From an interest at the Lincoln School in the pre-engineering sciences, Laurance at Princeton turned to philosophy. He wanted to understand people. He wanted to understand life. He wanted to know what to do with the rest of his own life. With characteristic Rockefeller thoroughness Laurance took philosophy course after philosophy course until there were no more to take. By the time he graduated in 1932 he had set some sort of record at Princeton, having taken every single one of the philosophy classes offered.

Then, as a practical consideration, Laurance went on to Harvard Law School, thinking that there he would learn how to employ the social values and philosophy he had garnered at Princeton in a useful activist career. He did not intend to become a practicing attorney, but he wanted the tools of the law for furthering social causes. At Harvard he discovered that that was not a good enough reason for studying law. He found also that he was temperamentally unsuited for the law, which was based so arbitrarily on precedents set by old court cases. His two years there, however, did help cure him of a certain intellectual fuzziness inherent in abstract philosophy. But all in all, Laurance, at twenty-four, decided he had had enough of law school for his own purposes and that he was quite ready to start applying himself to social causes in his father's office, where there were certainly enough such concerns available to him. Besides, he had fallen in love with Mary Billings French, a demure, sensitive, lovely girl, a friend of the family's whom Laurance had known for years. Her brother, John French, had been Nelson's room-mate at Dartmouth. Her mother was a close friend of Laurance's mother's and her religious, upper-class childhood had not been much different from that of Laurance. Proximity played its role; Mary had moved to Cambridge to study sculpture when Laurance was in his first year at Harvard Law School. They saw more and more of each other and, as Laurance put it, "an old friendship matured into a courtship."

As with his brothers before him, Laurance moved into a home on the Pocantico estate and an office at Rockefeller Center. At the time, Laurance was described by someone very close to him as "a serious young man, solemn and stooped over, carrying the problems of the world upon his shoulders." Once in his father's domain, he was left to find his own way. Laurance gravitated to two of his father's major interests not yet taken up by his older brothers: conservation and cancer research. He divided his time between the Bronx Zoo and Memorial Hospital in New York, and soon afterward branched out to the hotel operation at Colonial Williamsburg. Nothing was forced upon him. His father firmly believed that everyone worked best at whatever he himself chose as his own personal interest. Laurance had the benefit, as did his other brothers, of consulting with his father's associates, older men who were knowledgeable, capable and experienced in the specialties in which they served his father. They, in turn, were delighted to help a young Rockefeller find himself.

These associates were much more available to the Rockefeller boys in the office than was their own father. The boys did not feel free just to drop in on their father in his inner sanctum, for it was well understood by all that he was very, very busy. They could send him memos. They could request an audience on a particular problem and, of course, it would be granted, but it was also understood that one did not abuse such a privilege. It was assumed, rather than spelled out, that each of them would follow in his father's footsteps, taking on the responsibilities and causes to which he had devoted his life. He had done as much for his own father. In fact, as the only son he had devoted his entire life to fulfilling the various philanthropic roles started by John D., Sr. Now the time was at hand when each of John Jr.'s five sons, when of age, would lend his helping hand. However, as young men all over have found, it was not enough, not sufficiently fulfilling, merely to go into your father's business and to carry on along a well-paved road. Laurance felt the obligation of helping his fa-

ther, but he also wanted to strike out on his own, to do something original, to make his own personal contribution to society. Strangely enough, it
was Laurance, the philosophy major, rather than Nelson or John 3rd, who
became fascinated with economics, finance and investments in his father's
office. All of the boys were exposed in turn to that side of the Rockefeller
operations, but it was Laurance who bought the seat on the stock exchange held in his grandfather's name. It was Laurance who discovered
the fascination of investing money at great risk in new businesses, in men
or small groups of men, innovating a new service or a new product and in
need of the launching fuel known as venture capital.

There was, for instance, a new line of modern furniture from Scandinavia which Laurance bought for his own home and liked so much that
he started a successful import business which lasted until World War II
cut off supplies. Then there was Captain Eddie Rickenbacker, the famous
World War I flying ace, a flamboyant hero who was much more admired
by the public than by the conservative banking community in the 1930s.
Rickenbacker first approached Nelson, who was much better-known than
any of his brothers, even in those days in 1938, for financial help to enable
him to exercise his option to buy Eastern Air Lines for $3.5 million from
General Motors, which was under court order to divest itself of the airline
subsidiary. Nelson was not interested but said, "I have a brother who
might like the idea." And with that he brought Rickenbacker and his supporters across the hall and into Laurance's office. Laurance, who had a
flair for the technology that went into modern machines, radio and photography, agreed wholeheartedly with Rickenbacker's vision of the future
in commercial aviation. He committed himself to an initial investment of
$250,000 in Eastern Air Lines and that opened the floodgates of the bank-
ing and investment community. Eastern Air Lines, with Captain Eddie
Rickenbacker as president, and Laurance Rockefeller as a member of the
board of directors, was born anew. Laurance continued to invest in Eastern, which was on its way to becoming one of the largest, most important
airlines in the nation at a turning point in the history of air transportation, while Laurance himself was on the way to making a small fortune.

As the war clouds gathered over Europe, Laurance delved ever more
deeply into the military aspects of airplanes and aviation. That same year
Laurance joined with his brother Winthrop in organizing the Air Youth
of America to train young men and women in aeronautics. He also supported the Inter-American Escadrille to promote interest in private flying,
became a trustee of an international quarterly known as *Air Affairs* and
became a member of the Institute of Aeronautical Sciences and of the
New York City Airport Authority. By 1939 Laurance was quite receptive
to new ideas in aviation, and he listened intently to a wildly enthusiastic
young Scotsman named J. S. McDonnell, Jr., who had walked into his

office with a briefcase full of blueprints for a new pursuit plane he wanted
to build for the U. S. Army Air Force. His plane would outperform any
existing aircraft of its kind, said McDonnell as he explained his project. Of
course, he had no orders for the plane from the government. He had no
money, could not find financial backing and his entire plant consisted of a
small workshop in a garage in St. Louis. McDonnell left Laurance's office
a few hours later with a check for $10,000 and a promise of cooperation.
Laurance found he was able to provide precisely what McDonnell, an engineering prodigy, lacked: financial backing, managerial skill and organizational know-how. Laurance invested more than a quarter of a million
dollars, the limit of his remaining fortune at the time, and then he appealed to his brothers for more, receiving from the more adventurous of
them another $200,000. Thus Laurance, at the age of twenty-seven, had
made his own personal plunge, at considerable risk, in a realm of activity
far removed from previous family interests. His father did not trust
airplanes, had never been up in one and would never do so for all the
years of his life. But Laurance had faith in his own instincts. His investment of money, time and reputation was based primarily upon those instincts. In a mere two years he had undertaken two full-time jobs. He had
become a major stockholder and director of Eastern Air Lines and of the
McDonnell Aircraft Corporation.

Winthrop, born and bred a Rockefeller every bit as much as his
brothers, nevertheless seemed to march to a different drummer. He had
had a rough boyhood and could not reconcile the need to study with the
easygoing open permissiveness of the Lincoln School. When his parents
transferred him to the Loomis School in Windsor, Connecticut, a classic
and strict prep academy, his schoolwork was disastrous. On his first report
card he failed every subject. Money troubles stalked him at Loomis. Absolutely unable to keep his account book up to date, he would run weeks
behind and then forget how he had spent his money. As a result, his father cut his allowance again and again. Accounting for his money became
most painful for Winthrop, the bane of his adolescence. He became un-
comfortable in his father's presence, especially when alone with him: he
was always afraid his father would bring up that unpleasant subject of
money. Years later Winthrop would recall "two or three occasions when
the discrepancies in my accounts reached such an acute state that I
thought about stealing money to balance my books. Once, at least, I actually worked out a plan to steal what I needed . . . but an eleventh-hour
bit of common sense stopped me." It was better to face up to a reprimand
from Father than actually to steal, he decided. One gets the impression,
however, it was a close decision. Later, at Yale, he once got so far behind
in his accounts that he begged a loan from his sister in order to avoid a crisis with his father, a loan he only finished paying off years later when he
was in the Army. By the time he came into money of his own, Winthrop

had developed a great sympathy for anyone in financial difficulties. He became the "softest touch" among the Rockefellers.

Winthrop was in and out of trouble at Loomis, but with the aid of a summer's tutoring after his final year there he managed to get into Yale. He enrolled, however, without enthusiasm or purpose. Yale, of course, was much tougher than prep school, and Winthrop soon concluded he was not suited at all for the academic life. He didn't have the desire, temperament or ability to get through. Also, out on his own, he discovered the pleasures of smoking, drinking, card playing and girls. There just did not seem to be enough time left over for studying. The days were "carefree, pleasant and meaningless," but he knew they could not last. Either he would quit Yale or flunk out. He didn't know which would come first.

He spent his first summer as a camp counselor in Maine and for his second summer, he went to work as a trainee for Standard Oil of New Jersey in 1932. A strapping, husky young man of twenty, slightly taller than six foot three, and over two hundred pounds, he was welcomed enthusiastically at Standard of New Jersey. After all, he was the first Rockefeller to go on the payroll of the company since his grandfather. To get a feel of the business, he started in industrial relations at the Bayonne, New Jersey, refinery, living at the YMCA and spending his spare time at the nearby Bayway Community House which his mother had started thirty years before in order to help teach wives of immigrant workers the newest ways of cooking, sewing and baby care. Winthrop then worked briefly in sales for the Beacon Oil Company of Massachusetts. He then went into the producing end of the business with the Humble Oil and Refining Company in Houston, Texas. There he found what interested and excited him: men working with their hands and their minds, producing something real, something of value.

He started as a roustabout, at the bottom of the ladder, with the day laborers, digging ditches, carrying tools, helping the drillers, doing what he was told, sweating in the 100° summer heat. Winthrop loved it. He found he could prove himself as good as the next man and be taken for what he was, judged on the quality of his work. At the end of that summer he returned to Yale, reluctantly. He stayed there only a few months, long enough to convince himself that college studies were not giving him what he wanted. So he quit, announcing to his father he wanted to go into the oil business, and with his father's mixed blessings, Winthrop returned to his life as a roustabout in Texas, as tough a backbreaking job as any man could find in the 1930s for $.75 cents an hour. He lived in a boarding house for $4.50 a week, drank beer with his new buddies, visited their homes and families, worked in the oil fields and learned the business. He graduated from roustabout to a "boll weevil," an apprentice driller, and learned to handle fourteen-pound sledge hammers and twenty-five-pound wrenches. Then he learned how to explore for oil with a geophysics crew, detonating dynamite beneath the ground. Winthrop spent three years in Texas, learning oil production, working with his hands under the open sky, feeling free, making friends with tough, proud, independent men, all the while finding out about himself. He considered these, at the time, the happiest years of his life.

Upon his return to New York City he went to work as trainee in the Chase National Bank. That lasted one year. Then he tried the foreign trade department of the Socony-Vacuum Oil Company. But office work in a large institution appealed to Winthrop no more than it had to his brother Nelson. He felt "bored to death." In 1938 he took a leave of absence to devote full time to the Greater New York Fund, the first united philanthropic movement of its kind. Winthrop, as vice-chairman, helped set up the administration and organization of the drive, which was so successful and established a pattern for united charitable drives for years ahead.

In the summer of 1940, aware that American involvement in the war raging in Europe was inevitable, Winthrop joined an Army basic training program for businessmen in Plattsburg, New York, which was part of a government effort to popularize American preparedness and the draft. One of his fellow recruits at the training camp was Robert Patterson, who was pulled off KP duty to become Undersecretary of War, and later became the Secretary of War. Winthrop, young, single and in the best of health, found he liked Army life better than life in a bank. Despite his very low number in the draft, he decided to join up. But in the manner of the third generation of Rockefellers, he thought he would needle his brothers first. At a brothers' meeting, he solemnly lectured his brothers that the menace of Nazi victory in Europe threatened the well-being of the United States, that the nation had indeed been kind to the Rockefeller family, that the family had as much to lose as anyone and that, therefore, one of them should, as an example to all Americans, enlist in the Army. John, Nelson and Laurance were married at the time and David, at age twenty-five, was engaged. Winthrop threw the proposal open for discussion and sat back to enjoy himself. David drew the brunt of the ploy. As the youngest it was his place to speak first. Citing the reasons he could not enlist, not at this time, David spoke his piece. Then Winthrop announced he was enlisting in the U. S. Army as a private.

David had been fourteen years old when Winthrop transferred to a boarding school. He was then alone at home and at school. Babs was married and the older boys were away at college. More and more David became a self-contained, self-possessed loner, an only child. He had no trouble at all accepting the Rockefeller family precepts, the sanctity of work, thrift, the keeping of accounts, the injunctions of the Bible, the avoidance of waste and ostentation, the routine of healthful everyday living. It helped, no doubt, that his sister and brothers had smoothed that route before him. Unlike his brothers Nelson, Laurance and Winthrop, David also had no trouble at the Lincoln School. He thrived on the modern techniques of education, for David was able to grasp his reading, writing and 'rithmetic on his own, while learning to live with and react to his classroom peers in everyday-learning life situations. His ingrained Rockefeller competitiveness came forth in his schoolwork and his grades were at or near the top throughout his years at Lincoln.

As a freshman at Harvard in 1932, because of his beetle hobby, David received special permission to do graduate-level work in entomology, and he got an A in that course, the only one he received as an undergraduate. His major was economics. Highly organized, David had no trouble with his studies. He taught a course in nature study at a Boston settlement house, spent his summers further investigating the world of beetles and kept his account books straight. One classmate remembers traveling with David on a train from Boston to New York and being amazed to see the young Rockefeller nonchalantly mark down the cost of each item of a lunch in his little black account book, and later accepting a free taxicab ride to his home on Fifty-fourth street. David himself was proud of being able to live on a modest allowance while classmates outspent him with ease. Another Harvard classmate, the son of a self-made millionaire, was given everything he wanted even before he asked for it: a large allowance, a new car, clothes, phonograph records, and he became, in David's words, "the unhappiest man I ever knew, a man who later married three times, changed jobs even more often, and never could find himself."

Graduating from Harvard in 1936, David took another year of postgraduate courses at Harvard and then, for contrast, went to the London School of Economics, where he studied under the socialist-economist Harold Laski. He went on to earn his doctorate in economics at the University of Chicago, proud that he was the only one of his brothers to earn an advanced diploma.

A subject close to the heart of his father and grandfather—waste—was the central theme of David's doctoral thesis: *Unused Resources and Economic Waste.* A scholarly work, published in book form in 1941, it did contain some personal family intimations, such as: "From our earliest days we are told not to leave food on our plates, not to allow electric lights to remain burning when we are not using them, and not to squander our money thoughtlessly because these things are wasteful . . . Of all forms of waste, however, that which is most abhorrent is idleness. There is a moral stigma attached to unnecessary and involuntary idleness which is deeply imbedded in our conscience."

After Chicago, David went to work as a "political intern" for New York's Mayor Fiorello La Guardia in the spring of 1940. Having tried banking by working a few hours a week for the Chase Bank branch office in London while at the School of Economics there, David tested his hand at government under La Guardia, handling special assignments. The idea was to expose himself to various career experiences and then to see which one, if any of them, grabbed his interest.

That year, however, before selecting a career, David, at twenty-five, chose a wife—Margaret McGrath, a vivacious, outspoken, fun-loving girl his own age. They had met at a dance seven years earlier when she had been a student at the Chapin School and he a freshman at Harvard. The daughter of a successful attorney, Peggy McGrath had grown up in Mount Kisco, a Westchester suburb of New York City which had given her the advantage of growing up unsheltered among a wide variety of neighborhood friends. Her relaxed, informal manner and her ease in getting along with people appealed enormously to David, who, in those years, knew he still had to learn how to enjoy himself for the mere sake of enjoyment.

As for choosing a career, David did not get the chance to make a decision right away. World War II engulfed the United States and gobbled him up as it did the other Rockefeller brothers. David Rockefeller, Ph.D. in economics, enlisted in the U. S. Army as a buck private.

In 1941, the year that would culminate with that December "day of infamy," concerned Americans across the land were searching their souls over the implications of a very possible Nazi victory in World War II. The Axis powers had conquered the European mainland from Scandinavia to the Mediterranean. Hitler's armies were blitzkrieging the Soviet Union from Leningrad to Moscow to Stalingrad. England was standing alone. The realization that Great Britain, too, might fall, soon after the expected defeat of the Soviet Union, caused many Americans to re-examine their traditional isolationism. Those who could look ahead envisioned the inevitability of the United States entering the conflict. They could not conceive of permitting the world to be ruled by the brand of national socialism espoused by Adolf Hitler. Others with equal sincerity, disillusioned with the failure of the 1914–18 war to end all wars, clung to the belief that America should steer clear of the European conflict. National opinion was divided. Franklin Delano Roosevelt had been elected in 1940 to an unprecedented third term in office on the promise to keep American boys out of the war.

After much soul-searching, John Jr. was one of those who overcame his lifelong antipathy to war to join the ranks of those who believed America could not stand aside while European democracies went down to defeat. Despite a personal reluctance to call attention to himself, he wrote a public letter to the New York *Times* in April 1941, summing up the attitude of millions of Americans across the land:

"Let me say at the outset that, like most people, I hate war. All my life I have hated it. I have always preferred the ways of peace and have followed them whenever possible. But when all peaceful methods have failed and the issue was worth standing for at any price, even if it meant a fight, I have never hesitated to see it through on that basis.

"That is my position regarding the present conflict. It is my firm conviction, arrived at in anguish of spirit, that the people of the United States and of all the Americas should see this conflict through; that we should stand by the British Empire to the limit and at any cost . . .

"I am convinced that force can never be permanently subdued by force, that hate cannot annihilate hate nor evil drive out evil. Nevertheless, for myself, and I say it deliberately, I would rather die fighting the brutal, barbarous, inhuman force represented by Hitlerism than live in a world which is dominated by that force."

The war, casting its shadow of death, brought out into the open some fundamental soul-searching: what should one live for, what should one be willing to die for? Eminent Americans began putting down on paper their creeds and philosophies of life. John Jr. had been at this task for many years, long before the war. As a religious, introspective man of great wealth and power, he questioned the fundamentals of almost everything he did, he sought precepts which he could live by. As early as 1937 he began to formulate, organize and make concise his own personal feelings on what he believed was universally true and unchanging. He wrote and rewrote. He tested each concept with one or more of his sons time and again. This became his personal credo. An early version was tried out for the first time on November 19, 1937, in a speech at International House in New York City, which the Rockefellers had built for foreign students near Columbia University. The country was in its darkest days of economic depression and uncertainty, and John D. Rockefeller, Jr., gave then, in one of his most eloquent speeches, the reasons behind his writing a personal credo:

"Wherein, then, lies the hope of the future?" he asked. "In this day of changing standards, is anything stable and enduring? What is the answer to the fears and insecurity and bitterness that dominate the world today? Frankly, I do not know the answer. Moreover, I do not believe *anybody* knows the answer. Mankind is wandering in heartbreaking perplexity, bewildered by many false prophets and discouraged by many false hopes. But there is an antidote to fear, and that is faith . . .

"This creed is based, first, upon the conviction that there are certain fundamental and underlying things which do not change. Look at the mountains and the valleys; they do not change. Turn your eyes to the heavens; the sun still shines upon mankind by day and the moon by night, nor is there a star missing from its accustomed place. As surely as the fall winds strip the leaves from the trees which the snows of winter cover as with a shroud, will the miracle of the spring bring them back to life and clothe them anew with verdure. The tender and sacrificial quality of a mother's love does not change. The Good Samaritan still binds up the wounds of the man who has fallen among thieves. Do we not continue to witness the transcendent beauty of the sunset and to hear the happy voices of innocent children . . ."

Thus, in one speech he combined his faith in God and in nature to explain the fundamental, unchanging values he sought to live by.

Four years later, on May 3, 1941, during the most bleak and discouraging days of World War II, he made public his completed ten-point personal credo in a speech he gave at Fisk University. This speech was covered by the press and it drew such a response that he repeated it in a nationwide radio address on July 8 of that year for the United Service Organizations (USO), which he had helped organize to provide recreational clubs for American servicemen through the cooperative efforts of Protestant, Catholic and Jewish welfare organizations. Since then it has been widely reprinted in newspapers, magazines and books. On a personal level, it was a legacy for his sons and grandchildren and all the Rockefellers who would ever follow in his footsteps. When he died, his sons decided that the most fitting memorial they could provide for him was his own personal credo, carved in polished granite at the entrance to the skating rink of Rockefeller Center for millions of Americans each year to gaze and reflect upon:

I believe in the supreme worth of the individual and in his right to life, liberty, and the pursuit of happiness.

I believe that every right implies a responsibility; every opportunity, an obligation; every possession, a duty.

I believe that the law was made for man and not man for the law; that government is the servant of the people and not their master.

I believe in the dignity of labor, whether with head or hand; that the world owes no man a living but that it owes every man an opportunity to make a living.

I believe that thrift is essential to well ordered living and that economy is a prime requisite of sound financial structure, whether in government, business, or personal affairs.

I believe that truth and justice are fundamental to an enduring social order.

I believe in the sacredness of a promise, that a man's word should be as good as his bond; that character—not wealth or power or position—is of supreme worth.

I believe that the rendering of useful service is the common duty of mankind and that only in the purifying fire of sacrifice is the dross of selfishness consumed and the greatness of the human soul set free.

I believe in an all-wise and all-loving God, named by whatever

name, and that the individual's highest fulfillment, greatest happi-
ness, and widest usefulness are to be found in living in harmony
with His will.

I believe that love is the greatest thing in the world; that it
alone can overcome hate; that right can and will triumph over
might.

Part Two

"One of the most widespread superstitions is that every man has his special, definite, qualities: That a man is kind, cruel, wise, stupid, energetic, apathetic, etc.

"Men are not like that . . . men are like rivers . . . every river narrows here, is more rapid there, here slower, there broader, now clear, now cold, now dull, now warm.

"It is the same with men. Every man creates in himself the germs of every human quality and sometimes one manifests itself, sometimes another, and the man often becomes unlike himself, while still remaining the same man."

Tolstoy

11

John 3rd

"The man everyone would like to be as
rich as."

The end of the all-encompassing Second World War clearly marked a new beginning for the nation and its 11 million returning veterans. For the five Rockefeller brothers the vistas of opportunity seemed virtually limitless. Eager to cope with this brave new world, each of the brothers returned to the family offices in Rockefeller Center with his own plans for the future—some fixed in mind, some still open to scrutiny. Once back in civilian life, however, they found, as most men did, that there were indeed limits to their long-awaited freedom. What to do, how to do it and what were the priorities involved concerned each of them individually, John 3rd, Nelson, Laurance, Winthrop and David. But their equations were complicated by the obvious factor that they were not ordinary, anonymous men; they were Rockefellers. How much did they owe to that name? To what extent should individual desires be curbed when in conflict or even possible conflict with the family's reputation? What of conflicting interests among themselves—how would they be resolved?

These were difficult, amorphous, far-reaching questions. The brothers could try to look into the future and anticipate, but they could not be certain what they could see there. So the answers to the questions evolved in a consensus among them. They did not decide or vote as much as they talked each problem over and over again, sounding out each other's opinions and gradually coming to an understanding among themselves of what was right and appropriate. Their first allegiance, they agreed, they owed to themselves and to their own families. But they also agreed that no one among them should undertake on his own any action which might reflect adversely upon the others or upon the good name of the family.

They held countless Brothers' Meetings, some of them formal gatherings of a sort of board of directors of the family, but most of them informal discussions of how to coordinate their activities and their needs in the family office. Of course, it was easier to decide what *not* to do than what they should do. They agreed as a matter of good family policy to follow their father's resolution to stay out of the world of communications—it was too open to controversy, too liable to bring charges that the Rockefellers were attempting to exercise control over public opinion. They agreed not to invest in any undertaking which might leave them open to charges of profiteering upon the ills of their fellow men. Pharmaceuticals was a case in point. On the other hand, knowing they lacked the financial resources of their father, they agreed that they would venture forth publicly in behalf of the causes they supported—but judiciously and with discretion. Any action taken by one, which might affect the reputation of the others, would first be discussed among them all. They drew the line on veto power, however. They just left it unsaid but tacitly understood that no one of them would put his own personal interests above those of the family. Common sense would prevail. Each would be free to pursue his own career and his own interests but as gentlemen and brothers they would undertake nothing which would embarrass their father, the Rockefeller name or each other.

In the event that the interests or plans of one brother conflicted with those of another, the one who held the previous claim would have precedence. In short, they agreed not to compete with one another in public, nor in business, career or philanthropy. Nothing could tear open the fabric of family unity more easily than personal career conflicts. On the other hand, they agreed that no one among them would be asked to sacrifice his own career for the benefit of another. That would be asking too much of a man in the cause of family unity. Each of them would go forward on his own as an individual and, at the same time, as an integral member of the Rockefeller family. To the public, they would present a united front. No one brother would speak for the others or as a spokesman for the whole family, not without the prior consent of each and every one of them.

The third John D. Rockefeller, like his father and his grandfather before him, knew full well that in America he was regarded as an institution, a symbol, "the man everyone would like to be as rich as." He was labeled by his name. Try as he might, he could not avoid that familiar reaction: people who meet him see the name first and then the man himself. His ascetic appearance, tall and lean and so graciously mannered, conjured up the image of his famous grandfather. Despite the humble cocking of his head to one side, a characteristic gesture, despite the bashful smile and soft voice, he still evoked the image of wealth, of power and of influence, which was his by birth.

No signs of material wealth or position show on his person. The cut of his suit or the length of his shirt collar are no indications of the latest styles or custom tailoring. He might be taken on sight as one of thousands of middle-level executives. Few would recognize the man as he walks briskly crosstown from his apartment on exclusive Beekman Place to the hub of New York City at Rockefeller Plaza. He goes unnoticed on the crowded Forty-ninth or Fiftieth Street crosstown bus. He takes his chances on catching a taxicab in getting around New York rather than have a limousine waiting for him. His everyday life is relatively simple, not unlike that of a great many other men. He lives in the same apartment he has occupied since his marriage, has worked five days a week in the same medium-sized office for the past forty years, spends his weekends in a not too large home in suburban North Tarrytown and allows himself a two- to three-week summer vacation in a summer cottage at North Haven, Maine. He has bought no mansions, no yachts, no private airplanes, no fleet of automobiles and no wardrobe that ever entitled him to be called one of the best-dressed men of America. He lives, as he prefers, in comfort rather than in luxury.

Nevertheless, John D. Rockefeller 3rd has few peers, few men who relate to him as equals. So many people he meets socially or in philanthropic ventures seem to become afflicted with "Rockefelleritis" that John 3rd, the man, is left somewhat wistful upon his pinnacle of fame. Outside of his own family and small circle of long-time associates, there are precious few men and women with whom John 3rd can unwind, drink a cold beer, say without caution what is on his mind, or with whom he can feel complete rapport. "What a heavy burden is a name that has too soon become famous," bemoaned Voltaire of his own early fame. John D. Rockefeller 3rd has borne that burden all of his life. Even among his own brothers, with the familiarity of family, he has felt that extra edge of responsibility—the oldest of the five brothers, the bearer of the name, the titular head of the third generation of Rockefellers.

The pattern was set early and John 3rd accepted without demurrer the philosophy and way of life of his father. There never was any question, as far as he was concerned, of his not carrying on the worthwhile work started by his father and his grandfather. It never came up. When he returned from the war at the age of forty, he no longer was "a clerk" in his father's office; he was a philanthropist working with John D. Rockefeller, Jr. The wealth and power were there and he, John 3rd, became a custodian and steward of that wealth and power, one who had learned over the years how to use it wisely and well for the greatest good possible. To do that well was a career in itself, one for which he had been trained since college. Nor was it as easy as it might seem. To squander money or influence on a whim or an emotion could do far more harm than good. Nor could one simply dispense cash to all the needy; even the Rockefellers did not have enough for that. Nor had it ever been proved that money alone could solve the problems of the world. Philanthropy had come a long way in sophistication since the turn of the century. John's father had been instrumental in putting corporate management practices into large-scale philanthropy, administered independently by competent and knowledgeable experts.

So it was that John 3rd in the 1940s was in no position to preside at the Rockefeller coffers, dispensing money like a King Solomon or even as the son of a King Solomon. Instead, he began as one of a number of trustees on a number of boards of directors of a number of selected philanthropic corporations designed to alleviate a selected number of the ills of the world.

Even after he had shuffled off some of these trusteeships, passing the responsibility to some of his brothers, it was still John 3rd who retained most of the positions on philanthropic boards established by his father. He was the heir apparent of the Rockefeller philanthropic ventures. He was "the philanthropist of the Rockefeller family." It seemed only natural. He was the oldest. He was John D. Rockefeller 3rd.

Everything he said or did in public, he felt, would have reverberations beyond those of an ordinary man. It followed logically that he must exercise great care in everything he did or said. If people seemed to hang on his every word, then it seemed right to be even more cautious before giving that word. He adopted his father's policy of examining every problem from all angles and in excruciating detail. A Rockefeller opinion was not to be given lightly. A Rockefeller opinion once formed, by dint of studious examination, took the form of a principle, one which could stand for a long time to come. So while the name Rockefeller opened many doors and gave many privileges, it also closed vistas that could be explored by another man not burdened with the deep, inbred sense of obligations, responsibilities and duties borne by John 3rd.

By nature and training a patient yet persistent man, John 3rd proceeded in the years after the end of the Second World War with caution and care as to where and to what he would commit himself. He wanted desperately to strike out on his own beyond the foundations, organizations and boards of directors established by his father. However, he knew he should not rush himself. It was just as easy, if not easier, for a rich man to make a fool of himself as a poor man. He recognized this time as a period of transition, a change-over from his prewar apprenticeship in philanthropy to something new, although he did not yet know what that something new would turn out to be. But the whole world was in a period of transition, too. Every thinking man, every organization devoted to benevolence or business, every government was re-examining the road ahead, dividing time into the prewar and postwar years.

As part of this reappraisal, the Rockefeller Foundation sponsored a trip to war-torn Europe in 1946 by two of its trustees, John 3rd and Dean William I. Myers of the School of Agriculture of Cornell University. For six weeks, the two men visited England, France, Germany and Austria, conferring with knowledgeable men in and out of those governments on what the Rockefeller Foundation could do, within the scope of its activities, to help in the transition from war and destruction to peace and prosperity. The Rockefeller Foundation, dedicated in its charter to the "well-being of mankind throughout the world," was nevertheless a hard-nosed, businesslike corporation whose directors believed in on-the-spot investigations, rather than book knowledge, as an essential to formulating policy on grants and disbursements. Since all policy of the Rockefeller Foundation was in the hands of its twenty-one-member board of trustees, the report of John 3rd and Dean Myers upon their return was considered crucial in the future directions of the Foundation.

In his personal diary on this trip John 3rd noted the overwhelming need of raising the standards of living in all the countries of Europe. Yet he saw in his talks with men in England that the greatest needs in raising standards of living was not in Europe but in India and the Middle East. While the world's attention seemed focused on Europe's recovery from the war, it was in India and Egypt and throughout the Middle East that the standard of living would decline rather than rise in the postwar years. The reasons were apparent: overpopulation, soil erosion, outmoded traditions of land tenure and decreasing productivity in agriculture as well as industry.

In France the most obvious problems noted by John 3rd were a declining population and a moral decline because of the war and the postwar fear of Germany and the Soviet Union. In Germany, beaten into submission, there was the need to rebuild democracy, which he thought could be best accomplished by introducing educational and cultural programs to help the Germans understand the workings of democracy in the United States. In Austria, John 3rd thought, the Rockefeller Foundation could become active in various health, education and agricultural programs being considered by Austrian officials.

The following year, 1947, John 3rd at his own expense made a three-month trip to Asia, touring China, Japan and Korea, accompanied by his father's key adviser on philanthropic affairs, Arthur W. Packard, who had served John as a teacher, mentor and guardian in his own philanthropic career. Once again the purpose of the trip was to help obtain a better understanding on the spot of postwar conditions in Asia so that John could be more effective as a trustee to the Rockefeller Foundation. And it was here in Asia, visiting Shanghai, Canton, Hongkong, Peking, Tokyo, Fuku-

oka, Hiroshima, Kyoto and Seoul that John 3rd became genuinely fascinated with the opportunities to help in the reconstruction of a major
part of the world. It was apparent to him, as to others, that the focus of
American foreign policy was upon the Western world, specifically Europe,
and that not nearly enough attention was being paid by the United States
government to the problems and affairs of the Asian continent. The role
of private philanthropy and of the willing private individual was to render
aid where it was most needed, where governments were neglecting needs
because of political necessities, where private means could venture beyond
shallow waters, affording to err where governments and bureaucracy could
not. This John 3rd had always believed. Despite the war in the Pacific,
Asia still remained an unknown mass of land to most Americans in 1947.
But on the spot, John 3rd could see most clearly that Japan, China and
the underdeveloped nations of Asia would loom larger and larger as an important and significant part of the world in the postwar years ahead. The
whole continent—with the exception of industrialized Japan and the uncertain future of mainland China, then undergoing a fierce civil war between the nationalist rulers and the rebellious Communists—was generations behind the quality of life known in the Western world. To bring the
Asian continent into modern times, with all of its political, economic and
social ramifications, seemed of utmost importance to John D. Rockefeller
3rd. Here was something to which he could devote his time, his effort and
his money. Here was something he could urge the Rockefeller Foundation
to focus upon. Here was a real need of private philanthropy. On the personal side, he liked the people he met in Asia. He was struck with their
genuine openness, their turn of mind, their willingness to accept help
from the West.

John 3rd's particular orientation, running parallel to that of the
Rockefeller Foundation, centered on medicine, public health and more
recently upon food supply, each of them considered of paramount
significance in the well-being of man. As he studied these matters in
Japan, in China and in Korea, speaking with men there about conditions
in the southeastern Asian countries, he became more and more aware of a
rather simple dilemma: as medical care and public health programs improved in Asian countries, the high death rate was being reduced significantly, and as the death rate fell, the population grew proportionately,
creating more severe problems of overcrowding in urban areas, more and
more demand on existing facilities and, most important, a seemingly insatiable demand upon the food supply in these countries. The good work
of the Rockefeller Foundation, at this stage of development, seemed perhaps to be running in a veritable squirrel cage. The more it succeeded
in saving lives through medicine and public health, the more people
there were to cry out for needs to sustain even a minimum quality of
life. The other side of the coin, obviously, was somehow to reduce that

population growth so that there would be fewer people making demands upon the resources of these underdeveloped nations. The paradox was simple to understand but intricately difficult to solve. Yet it was fundamental to and underlying all the good work done in trying to help the nations of Asia. Or so John D. Rockefeller 3rd thought at the time. It would be fair to say that he caught a glimpse of the problem. In those early days just after the end of the world war there was no great body of knowledge to fall back on for support. There were no reliable statistics on the population of Japan, China, Korea or any of the other Asian nations, and certainly no charts on the rate of population growth. Nevertheless, the mass of people were there to be seen on the streets, the traditional need of having a large family to run a farm was known by everyone. Birth control was not only a forbidden subject, it was largely an unknown one in the hinterlands of the Asian continent.

John 3rd returned to America in October 1947 with more than an inkling of the cause to which he could envision himself devoting his energies in the years to come. Perhaps, he thought, this was what he had himself personally been looking for. Yet he was not the kind of man to rush headlong into a cause, any cause. Naturally, he brought it up at his meetings with the president and chief executive officer of the Rockefeller Foundation and he talked over the problem with the various heads of departments at the Foundation. He did not push his cause, he merely brought it up, sounding out men who were sincere and eminently expert in their fields: spelling out the theories he had come up with, he asked wouldn't it be in line with the Foundation's work toward the well-being of man to make population stabilization an area of major focus for the Foundation. To his chagrin, the answer came back: no, what you say is of interest, of course, and of importance, and yet, it would seem that the time is not yet right for an effort in this direction. There were, of course, political implications, and moral aspects to family planning particularly in Catholic countries, and so little known even about the size and scope of the problem, and so much need particularly in these postwar years for increasing health services and food supplies that there would hardly be enough funds to support a major effort in this field. In short, the various officers of the Foundation did not believe that the problem of overpopulation in Asia or around the world measured up to other needs in those areas to warrant the Rockefeller Foundation's diverting funds for a major attack on the question. Of course, these experts were specialists in medical research, public health, agriculture and the social sciences. Population or demography, the study of population trends, was not their field and, as is well known, every man believes his own work, his own field of endeavor, is more important than the next man's.

While John 3rd failed to convince them, it must be said they did not dissuade him from his own "deep belief" that the population explosion was one of the major problems facing the world, underlying so many other problems, and that there were too few people concerned with the population problem. As a trustee of the Foundation, John 3rd could have submitted his proposal to the full twenty-one-member board of trustees at one of the semi-annual trustee meetings. But that was not the way it was done. The Rockefeller Foundation had a long tradition of allowing the competent experts on the staff to suggest carefully worked-up plans of activities for the Foundation. While the trustees had the responsibility for deciding policy on what the Foundation would do and not do, there was nevertheless a fine but firm line of respect between the trustees and officers and staff of the Foundation. The trustees, who were not experts, followed a wise course of never dictating what the expert staff should do. They would never have kept the staff of experts if they had. Instead, trustees were free to suggest lines of study to the staff, but it was the staff who first would investigate any and all proposals and then report its findings to the board of trustees. John D. Rockefeller 3rd, as a trustee, considered himself in a particularly delicate position on making suggestions to the Foundation. At all costs he wished to avoid even the semblance of a Rockefeller dictating policy to a foundation established by his grandfather and run for so many years by his father as an independent philanthropic corporation of outstanding, competent and independent experts.

On the other hand, since he was John D. Rockefeller 3rd, there were other ways to attack the problem. Rather than merely try to press his opinion further upon the Foundation, John sought further facts and figures by which to make his case. He made his low-key approach to Harold Willis Dodds, president of Princeton University, explaining the problem and his concern and finally suggesting that at his own expense he would like to sponsor personally a demographer and a public health man together on a three-month trip through the Far East. Their task would be to think about the interrelationship of their fields as it might apply to the Asian countries and, of course, to report back. In other words, what was the rate of population growth in the Far East and what were the chances of successfully instituting some program of population stabilization through public health measures? Yes, John 3rd had a demographer in mind, Frank W. Notestein, director of the Office of Population Research at Princeton, a man he had met as far back as 1937. The president of Princeton made the call and Dr. Notestein said yes, he would be happy to undertake such a trip. John 3rd then returned to the Rockefeller Foundation and presented his proposal to the president of the Foundation, Chester Barnard, and he agreed. He suggested two men from the Foundation, Dr. Marshall Balfour, director of the Foundation's public health activities in the Far East, and Roger Evans, assistant director of the Social Sciences Division of the Foundation. Princeton thereupon balanced the team with its own expert on the Far East, Dr. Irene Taeuber. At this stage, Mr. Barnard suggested that it might be more appropriate for the Foundation to sponsor the research group as its own undertaking and John 3rd agreed, for it was understood that the trip was to be in the nature of a preliminary look-see and nothing more than that.

The four experts toured urban and rural areas in Japan, Korea, Indonesia, the Philippine Islands, Taiwan and the China mainland (just before the Bamboo Curtain fell), inspecting facilities, conferring with government and academic people in the fields of public health and population problems, seeing living and working conditions in each of the countries, and then returned home to write a 125-page erudite report, which said, in essence, that of all the health and social problems in the Far East "those of the reduction of human fertility are at once the most difficult and important."

The importance was obvious: more than one half of the world's population lived in the Far East—1 billion people and more—and they lived in poverty and poor health. Only the high mortality rate—one third of those born would never live to see their fifteenth birthday—prevented a threefold population explosion in the next hundred years. Poverty, poor health and population were held in the grip of a vicious circle. The more public health measures decreased infant mortalities and epidemics, the more people would live to increase demands upon any hoped-for rise in farm or industrial productivity.

Reducing the birth rate alone would not solve all the problems of the Far East, the study noted, but without that all other improvements in health, food production and social services stood little chance, if any, of success.

However, the difficult part was how to go about reducing the fertility of peasant populations. The study divided the problem into two parts: motives and means. Both were critically important, both amenable to attack and neither receiving the attention it deserved. One demanded a broad educational effort to change social custom and tradition from a desire for large families to an interest in small healthy ones. That would require a careful study of a wide variety of rural populations before any reeducation program could be undertaken. But even if you could change people's motives, the study warned, someone in the West would have to provide the means for birth control and it would have to be cheap, simple, safe and effective. And as of that date in 1950, there just was not any such contraceptive method in existence or on the horizon. That problem, however, the study said, could be attacked immediately and in the West. "We doubt that any other work offers a better opportunity for contributing to Asia's and the world's fundamental problems of human welfare," said the report.

If that report, so clear-cut and well done, backed with the advocacy of no less a power than John D. Rockefeller 3rd, had led the Rockefeller

Foundation, as great an organization as any of its kind, to undertake the study of population stabilization in the Far East as a program of major focus, then this would be a very simple world indeed. But this is not a simple linear world we live in.

While the research team was still out in the Far East, the leaders of the Rockefeller Foundation sounded out opinion on population control back at home. Chester Barnard, the president, invited Francis Cardinal Spellman, Archbishop of the Catholic Archdiocese of New York, to lunch at the Foundation. The cardinal, wise to the ways of the world, once he had learned the subject to be discussed, insisted that the Foundation people come to lunch at the archdiocese. He wanted the battle on his own home ground. There he offered his considered opinion that under no circumstances would the Catholic Church in America, the Far East or anywhere else in the world look with favor upon any kind of program involving birth control.

Within the Foundation, there was a split in opinion among the senior staff. A majority were opposed to any major program involving family planning. The public health experts, pre-eminent on the senior staff, simply did not believe population control was as important as their own work in the health fields. Furthermore, they warned of the risk involved: the animosity toward birth control they could expect of the strongly Catholic countries in which they were already operating in the Far East. The agricultural experts believed increasing food supplies would be easier to accomplish and of greater benefit to underdeveloped countries than any improbable program involving sexual behavior. Then, of course, there was always the problem of the budget. Even in the Rockefeller Foundation, money spent on population problems would mean money taken away from other efforts.

However, there was a split in opinion and out of deference to Dr. Balfour, the Foundation's chief expert on Far Eastern activities, who wrote the report, and to Dr. Alan Gregg, director of the foundation's Division of Medical Sciences and the senior director on the staff, who favored the proposal, the staff did agree on a very modest project. Demography and human ecology in Ceylon was proposed to the board of trustees. But even that proposal, which carefully avoided mention of birth control, was recognized for what it was at the trustees' meeting. It met the vehement opposition of John Foster Dulles, newly elected chairman of the board. A staunch Presbyterian and puritan moralist, Dulles argued most forcibly that the Foundation had absolutely no business butting into the religious and social customs of another people. Trustee Henry Van Dusen, president of the Union Theological Seminary, added his opposition, and the Ceylon project was voted down by the trustees. A negative vote by the trustees on a project proposed by the Foundation staff was a rare event in itself. The message was clear. Family planning, birth control and contra-

ceptives were not to be areas of study or activity by the prestigious Rockefeller Foundation.

The rejection came neither as a surprise nor as a shock to John 3rd.
As well as anyone, he understood his fellow trustees. They were all accomplished, independent and powerful men who had made their mark in the
world and they did not choose to sit unsalaried on the Rockefeller Foundation board in order to rubber-stamp the projects of the Rockefeller family.

The original concept of the Foundation was that of an independent
professional charitable institution with such prestige that its trustees could
extend their influence for the good of the world by banding together in
common cause. Yet, internally, the trustees felt the Foundation was still
in a state of transition from the dominance of John 3rd's father. He had
served as the Foundation's first president back in 1913 and then as chairman of the board of trustees from 1917 to 1939, when he had retired at
sixty-five. Even after that, his presence was felt through the efforts of his
close associate Raymond B. Fosdick, who served as president of the
Foundation from 1936 to 1948. With all due deference to the skill and
sensibilities of John D. Rockefeller, Jr., the Rockefeller Foundation had
been a "founder's foundation." However theoretically independent, the
Foundation's driving force through the years had been mostly Rockefeller:
Rockefeller money, Rockefeller time and effort, Rockefeller appointees
and Rockefeller staff. Although this delicate area was not discussed—at
least not openly—it was a matter of concern among some of the trustees
and senior staff. John Jr., upon his retirement, was well aware of it, as was
John 3rd, and it was in furtherance of directing the Foundation toward
real independence that John 3rd was passed over when Walter W. Stewart was elected chairman of the board to succeed John Jr. and then again
in 1950 when John Foster Dulles succeeded Stewart.

Then, of course, in the background, there was the Kinsey Report.
One of the most controversial series of grants ever made by the Rockefeller Foundation was the $400,000 given to Dr. Alfred C. Kinsey of Indi-
ana University between 1941 and 1946 for his case studies of human sexual behavior. When his first book, Sexual Behavior in the Human Male,
was published in 1948, the unexpected wide popularity and dissemination
of the data aroused a national debate on the subject of sexual mores. The
august Rockefeller Foundation was drawn into the controversy. Dr. Kinsey
spared no effort to publicize the imprimatur of the Rockefeller Foundation upon his work as a much needed scientific study of human behavior.
In addition to that, Dr. Alan Gregg, head of the Foundation's Division of
Medical Sciences, believed so fervently in Kinsey's work that on his own,
and contrary to Foundation policy of staying in the background, he wrote
a glowing introduction to the book, asserting that the Kinsey survey would
break "a conspiracy of silence" about sex. Although Dr. Gregg had the

vital backing of John D. Rockefeller, Jr., he incurred the distinct dis-
pleasure of the more conservative trustees. The controversy raged beyond
the board of trustees and included theologians, socialists and civic leaders
across the nation. The Foundation's support of the Kinsey study subsequently was questioned severely in a congressional investigation of various
foundations conducted by the Reece Committee in 1954, by which time
the Rockefeller Foundation had given some $899,000 to Kinsey's research.
Ironically enough, when the Foundation ended its support in 1954, after
publication of *Sexual Behavior in the Human Female*, it incurred the
wrath of Kinsey himself, who charged the Foundation had succumbed to
public and congressional pressure. The Foundation's answer to that was a
vehement denial. The Rockefeller Foundation, as a matter of policy, does
not support any organization or cause in perpetuity and it had supported
Dr. Kinsey's research longer than any other single individual's, over thirteen years with a total of almost $900,000 in annual grants. However, the
fundamental criticism of the Rockefeller's Foundation was not so much
over the content of Dr. Kinsey's sex study, but rather over the Foundation's responsibility for the cultural effect and impact of the Kinsey Report. What right does a tax-free private foundation have to finance activities to change or even to influence the cultural customs of a nation? The
question has survived unanswered to this day. Thus, to the extent one believes that the Kinsey surveys did affect and change the sexual mores in
America—for better or worse—the Rockefeller Foundation deserves its
share of the credit or blame.

Such were the fundamental questions being pondered within the
structure of the Rockefeller Foundation when John 3rd sponsored his
pilot project of demography, leading to the study of sexual behavior and
family planning in the Far East, and was rejected by the board of trustees.
It must have occurred to John 3rd at the time that the trustees were predominantly old and conservative men, but, of course, he was too much of
a gentleman to say so. He took his defeat with his familiar wisp of a smile
and kept his thoughts to himself.

John 3rd's interest in the Far East was not lost upon John Foster
Dulles, an international corporate lawyer and an authority on foreign
affairs. When Dulles was appointed by President Truman to serve as his
special representative in negotiating a permanent peace treaty with Japan,
Dulles asked John 3rd to accompany him as a special consultant on cultural affairs. John 3rd was immediately intrigued with the task. Dulles explained that United States policy was to draw Japan back into the society
of nations and to establish a positive relationship between the United
States and Japan to help ensure peace in the Far East. The treaty
itself was not to be punitive, like the Versailles Treaty which ended
World War I and sowed the seeds of World War II. Instead it was designed to help Japan establish a democratic, up-to-date nation which

would take its place as a power in the free world. However, the treaty itself was nothing more than a piece of paper, a business contract, its value dependent upon the will and intent of both the Japanese and American people and their leaders. Hence, said Dulles, an honest and open cultural exchange between the two nations would be as important in their future relationship as the treaty itself. Establishing the foundation of that cultural relationship would be the mission of John D. 3rd and a small staff assigned to him, working more or less independently from the official U. S. Mission.

Plunging into his new assignment, John 3rd made three separate trips to Japan during 1951 and following a heavy schedule of conferences large and small, he met with more than a thousand Japanese leaders from all walks of life and from all parts of the country. Out of those meetings several working groups were formed, totaling about one hundred Japanese leaders, to hammer out a plan for a cultural exchange between the two countries. For John D. Rockefeller 3rd it was an education in itself, a fascinating experience, an exposure to a new part of the world and a new culture. As did the thousands of American servicemen in the Occupation forces before him, he discovered with delight the friendliness and the sympathetic give-and-take of the Japanese. In turn, he talked of the ramifications of the American democratic system to a people who still believed in the divinity of their emperor. The response he received from Japanese eager to learn of America was indeed, in his word, "gratifying."

The gentle, self-effacing personality of John 3rd meshed beautifully with the oriental tradition of Taoism, decorum and protocol he discovered in the Japanese. What he called "the Rockefeller factor," the oversolicitude of others toward him, seemed to play no part in the relationship of the Japanese to him. He was accepted as the man he was, rather than as a name, and in turn he was only too ready to listen to others, to learn what they had to offer. It just was not in his nature to act the role of the autocrat. All of his life, he had wanted to deal with people on "a man-to-man basis" and here in Japan just that was happening for the very first time. Nor did it escape his attention that assignment as cultural adviser to the State Department on future Japanese-American relations was the first major policy-making role entrusted to him, himself, not as an apprentice to his father.

John 3rd's eighty-page report on his cultural mission, particularly the recommendations for future government and private activities, laid the groundwork of what was in fact accomplished in the years ahead to make Japan the strongest ally of the United States in the Far East. Some would call it "the Americanization of Japan." In reality it was a two-way street. Americans were to become more and more cognizant and accepting of Japanese art and literature, automobiles and electronics, Japanese philosophy and values. In all of this, John D. 3rd played a significant part. Out of his 1951 recommendations came an exchange of intellectuals and teachers between the two countries, a program to teach English as the second language in Japanese schools, programs to bring Japanese art and music to the United States and vice versa, and the building of an International House of Japan in Tokyo as a meeting place for Japanese, American and other intellectuals from all parts of the world.

John 3rd, of course, was in the unique position of being able to implement many of his own recommendations of what the private sector of society could do to foster better Japanese-American relations. It was his grant of money to Columbia University which made possible the exchange of U.S. and Japanese intellectual leaders, among them Mrs. Eleanor Roosevelt, Harvard sociologist David Riesman and theologian Dr. Paul Tillich, as well as the presidents of Hiroshima University and Japan's Women's University.

The International House of Japan, fashioned after the International Houses built by John 3rd's father in New York, Chicago, Berkeley (California) and Paris where students from foreign lands could live together while attending college under the Houses' theme *That Brotherhood May Prevail*, was financed partially by a substantial grant from the Rockefeller Foundation, sponsored by John 3rd. His hand was behind the arrangements for the year-long tour of the United States of Japanese art treasures and of the full-sized Japanese house which stood for two summers in the garden of New York's Museum of Modern Art.

With today's hindsight, of course, it is perfectly easy to see that these measures helped enormously in dispelling the wartime psychology of hatred urged upon Americans following the "day of infamy" at Pearl Harbor. But in those early postwar years, it was no foregone conclusion. The first indication that the cultural exchange between the two wartime enemies was indeed working was the dinner hosted in 1952 by John D. Rockefeller 3rd as president of the Japan Society for Eikichi Araki, the first Japanese ambassador posted to the United States after the war. For the first time since the war, the rising-sun flag of Japan flew over the Plaza Hotel in New York, and in the streets no one rioted, no one demonstrated.

John 3rd's involvement with Japanese culture was not conducted in a vacuum; it naturally extended beyond cultural activities and beyond Japan itself. The future of Japan could be studied only in terms of the entire Far East and only in relation to all the other factors affecting its culture and society: industry, agriculture, food supply, trade, customs and mores. And underlying all these factors in the well-being of man in Japan as well as in Sumatra, Indo-China, Korea and down the Asian continent was population. From the poorest underdeveloped nation to the most industrial, as John 3rd viewed it, every country in the Far East faced one seemingly inescapable and unsurmountable problem: overpopulation.

The theme became a litany in John 3rd's private talks with leaders in

Rockefeller Center today, expanded through the years.

Above, *the founder placing the last rivet in the original Rockefeller Center, November 1, 1939.* Right, *in his office at Rockefeller Center.*

Above,
*four generations of Rockefellers
at Pocantico Hills.
Rodman, the first great-grandson,
in his father's arms, 1936.
Right, Father, Mother, Laurance,
Grandfather, Winthrop, Babs,
Nelson at Pocantico Hills, 1936.*

The five brothers and their father at the Tarrytown, N.Y., railroad station, awaiting the train bearing the body of John D. Rockefeller, who died in Florida, May 25, 1937.

John D., Jr., and his sons at the gates to their Pocantico Hills estate.

Four of the brothers at the family office in Rockefeller Center, shortly after their return from World War II. David apparently away at the Chase Bank.

Mr. and Mrs. John D., Jr., with servicemen at the opening of the USO at Colonial Williamsburg, Va., in May 1943.

In their favorite electric car at Pocantico Hills, 1943.

John D. Rockefeller, Jr., at eighty-one.

The Credo in granite, a memorial to John D., Jr., at Rockefeller Center.

government, philanthropy and the academic world. The future of Asia seemed to depend upon breaking the vicious circle of ever increasing populations consuming the gains in food supplies and industrial production and the advances in public health which decreased the death rate in the Far East only to add to the problem of overpopulation. John 3rd was convinced he knew what to do about that underlying problem, at least where to start, and yet no one he approached would heed him. Then, only after the most diligent search for outside help, he came to the realization: he would have to do this himself.

12

Nelson

"Looking back is a waste of time."

Nelson Rockefeller, upon returning to the family offices in New York in late 1945 after five of the most dynamic, stimulating and educational years of his life in wartime Washington, plunged right back into Rockefeller activities and before he himself realized it, he was once again working around the clock. He did not stop to look back, Washington was behind him. He knew he had risen on merit to the position of Assistant Secretary of State for American Republic Affairs and had been instrumental in developing some key provisions in the charter of the United Nations. His career in government had been firmly launched, he had become known in Washington as Mr. Latin America, and then, abruptly with a changing of the guard at the White House and at the State Department, he had been fired. He did not blame President Truman, whom he would serve again, later on, in an important capacity, nor did he harbor any resentment against the new Secretary of State, James F. Byrnes, who, he realized, wanted his own man in the job. He was shocked and chastened, however, as time went on that not one phone call for advice came to him from any of his successors. But he took it all with a philosophic shrug of his heavy shoulders. "Looking back is a waste of time," he would say to those who asked. "My real interest is always, always, looking ahead."

At thirty-seven, he was a dynamo of energy and action, ever on the move, the unabashed extrovert and persistent optimist. He liked people and he liked physical contact, the hearty handshake, the slap on the back, the arm around the shoulder. New situations intrigued him. In comparison, his brothers suffered from what might be called an embarrassment of riches. Each of them in his own way was shy and painfully aware of the Rockefeller name and position, as Nelson was not, and they learned to proceed ever so slowly and carefully, lest they embarrass the Rockefeller name through an error in judgment or action. Nelson moved by intuition as much as by any other propelling force and he moved usually at breakneck speed toward any and all objectives which he took to heart. He disdained concern over the possibilities of anyone taking advantage of him; he shrugged off the burden of notoriety, the living of one's life in a fishbowl of fame, the doubts of caring whether people loved him for himself or for his money. He made jokes about his wealth and he went about his own business as he saw fit.

As chairman and chief executive officer of Rockefeller Center, Nelson took the lead in plans for extending, refurbishing and updating the complex of office buildings his father had built before the war. He resumed his position as a director of the Rockefeller Brothers Fund, which combined the brothers' philanthropic endeavors. He plunged into reorganizing the family office staff and the handling of his investments, taking it upon himself to brace his father on the most delicate and pressing problem facing the third generation: the transition of the Rockefeller family commitments—financial, philanthropic and personal—from his aging father to the third generation of Rockefellers. He owed time and concern also to his wife and five children, whom he had neglected during his busy days in Washington. And, on top of all this, he keenly felt a personal commitment to Latin America. Yes, to all of Latin America—he wanted to carry forth a program he had conceived in government for improved relations among the nations of the Western Hemisphere. To anyone else, all this might have seemed overreaching, too much for a single plate. But not to Nelson Aldrich Rockefeller. He had grown (literally) accustomed to global thinking. Hadn't he grown up absorbing stories of how his grandfather and then his father had dealt with problems all over the world—wiping out hookworm in the South, promoting education for the American Negro on a grand scale, reducing malaria and yellow fever worldwide, creating personally three major national parks? With a fierce pride in the accomplishments of his two predecessors, Nelson personally intended to carry on.

For as long as he could remember, in the back of his mind, was the conviction that someday he would become President of the United States. He confided his personal destiny to his brother Laurance when he was seven years old. No doubt thousands of other red-blooded American boys shared similar impossible dreams, but with Nelson Rockefeller it was something more than a dream, it was a measure of his own self-confidence and an integral part of his life. "I always took it for granted [that he would be President] . . . It was always there, in the back of my head," he told this writer in a moment of congenial candor.

That is not to say that he planned or plotted any specific route to the

Oval Office, at least not at the time he left his first government service at the end of the Second World War. He was not that kind of man. He believed that specific projects, policies and activities should be planned carefully in advance, wherever possible. But on the personal level, he had faith in what he called "happenstance." That his life, as are all others, was ruled by chance opportunities. "People show specific aptitudes, a door opens and something develops . . . Such things happen by happenstance," was the way he put it. His life up to then already demonstrated that for him.

Ten years earlier, at twenty-seven and literally having more money than he knew what to do with, he had sought the advice of Bertram Cutler, an astute, warm and experienced old man who had served as Nelson's grandfather's secretary and had learned enough to become financial adviser to his father and then to the five brothers. Cutler advised Nelson to invest in a new oil company by the name of Creole, a subsidiary of Standard Oil of New Jersey, which at the time was exploring in Venezuela and had not yet struck oil. A reasonably sized investment at this stage would put Nelson on the board of directors at a point when he could influence that company's policies. Nelson made his investment in 1935. His first trip to Venezuela in 1937 as a Creole director led to his personal discovery of South America, its needs and its challenges. It gave new direction to his life.

Two years later, another happenstance changed the course of his life. In preparation for the formal opening of the Museum of Modern Art in New York, of which his mother was one of the founders, Nelson as the Museum's new president was delegated to ask *the* President, Franklin D. Roosevelt, if he would please agree to speak at the opening ceremonies. Nelson, then thirty-one, sallied forth with an array of facts about the cultural value of this new museum. He also had found the clincher: the President, famous for his fireside chats to the American people, had never addressed the nation on culture. When the President agreed to tape a fifteen-minute radio talk, Nelson remarked that while war clouds gathered over Europe, no one in the United States seemed to be paying attention to the vulnerability of South America. Speaking rapidly and earnestly, his genuine enthusiasm for the subject apparently touched the President. When Nelson's allotted time was up, the President said, "Please, write me a memo on it."

Nelson had been appalled at North and South American relations during the two years he traveled through the continent. It all seemed typified to him by one woman he had met at a luncheon party, the wife of the manager of a large U.S. company, who explained innocently to Nelson that although she had lived in South America for twenty years she did not speak Spanish because, as she quaintly put it, "Who would I talk to in Spanish?"

American personnel of U.S. companies lived in segregated compounds surrounded and protected by high barbed wire fences. They did not mix or socialize with the "natives." It was no wonder that most Latin Americans felt they were being exploited by the *norteamericanos*. No wonder the people there were bitter. No wonder the Communists were making such headway in their appeals to labor unionists and university students. Nelson had traveled from country to country, talking with national leaders, presidents, university professors, labor leaders, and he had returned home eager to enlighten his fellow countrymen, who knew as little of South America as the South Americans knew about us. He made it his business to attend a meeting of Standard Oil of New Jersey and to address its executives from all over the world. That speech, in 1937, was far ahead of its time. "In the last analysis," Nelson told the oil executives, "the only justification for ownership is that it serves the broad interest of the people. We must recognize the social responsibilities of corporations and the corporation must use its ownership of assets to reflect the best interests of the people. If we don't, they will take away our ownership." The Standard Oil people didn't exactly laugh at this young Rockefeller. But neither did they heed him.

Over the next two years, Nelson had met regularly with a small group of friends who thought as he did about Latin America, including Beardsley Ruml, the economist; Wally Harrison, one of the architects of Rockefeller Center; Jay Crane, of Standard Oil; and Joseph Rovensky, of the Chase Bank. He had this group of men to turn to when he returned from Washington to write his memo on what the United States should do in relation to South America during World War II.

Nelson took that memo, drafted by the entire group, back to Washington and presented it to the President's right-hand man, Harry L. Hopkins. It was only three pages long, but it was as broad in its implications as it was concise and specific in its recommendations. In order to protect this country's hemispheric position vis-à-vis South America, regardless of the outcome of World War II, it recommended emergency measures to absorb Latin American commodities and products: eliminate tariffs, encourage private investments in Latin America, increase government personnel south of the border and appoint a small but separate interdepartmental government committee to administer the program under an executive assistant to the President. It also proposed a program to improve cultural, scientific and educational relations in the Americas.

Three weeks later, on his thirty-second birthday, Nelson was summoned back to Washington. The President had considered the Rockefeller memorandum, had presented it to his Cabinet and had approved it, Nelson was told by the new administrative assistant for inter-American affairs, James Forrestal. Nelson was invited to work with Forrestal to implement his own recommended program. Two weeks later, after checking with his father and with Wendell Willkie, who was running against FDR for the presidency, Nelson accepted the offer. Then he was told that Forrestal had been shifted to the Navy Department as Under Secretary (he was later to become the nation's first Secretary of Defense) and now the President wanted Nelson to head the program himself.

"Are you sure you want me for this job in view of my family's connections with the oil companies in Latin America and the fact that I'm Republican?" Nelson asked in the Oval Office.

"I'm not worried about that, if you're not," the President replied with a wave of his cigarette holder. "You'll have an absolutely free hand," he assured Nelson in response to his other question. "There'll be no political interference."

Thus, the first Rockefeller went to work for the federal government and for a Democrat in the White House at that. To be sure, the salary was only $1.00 a year. But under ordinary circumstances it would never have happened. Since the turn of the century, the Rockefeller family had been financial mainstays of the Republican Party, always working behind the scenes, never out in front. Not even the antitrust actions of such Republicans as Theodore Roosevelt or William Howard Taft could turn the Rockefellers away from their faith in the Republican Party. The family would support Wendell Willkie in 1940 and Thomas E. Dewey in 1944 and not even Nelson would contribute a thin dime to the campaigns of Franklin Delano Roosevelt. But in 1940 the circumstances were extraordinary. Holland, Belgium and France had fallen to the Nazi blitzkrieg. Only England stood in the way of German domination of Europe and perhaps the world. The United States was barely waking up to the ominous significance of its own isolationist policies of the past. Only a minority of Americans, Nelson Rockefeller included, could see that the war clouds were spreading across the Atlantic. No one seemed concerned at all over the influence of the German colonies of expatriates from World War I who had ingrained themselves in the business, political, cultural and family life of South America.

The Office of the Coordinator of Commercial and Cultural Relations Between the American Republics was established by executive order. Its first budget of $35 million came out of the President's emergency funds. Nelson, as Coordinator for Inter-American Affairs, was told he would have to fight for his future budgets on his own. It was the start of Nelson Rockefeller's education in government. At one budget hearing, for instance, Nelson was embarrassingly raked over the coals on the fine detail in the budget submitted for his office to the Senate Appropriations Committee. He was unprepared and Senator Kenneth D. McKellar, the testy Neanderthal and segregationist from Tennessee, was very well prepared indeed. Nelson learned and vowed never again to underestimate a member of Congress or to appear at a public hearing unprepared.

He also learned that the State Department had opposed the creation of his office in the first place as an encroachment upon its proper domain in conducting foreign affairs. Secretary of State Cordell Hull referred to him as "that young whippersnapper" and Under Secretary of State Sumner Welles treated him with equal coldness and disdain, although the latter warmed up to him as time went on. But there were several attempts to dismantle his whole operation. Early on, his office was severely embarrassed by a massive propaganda campaign launched in South America extolling the virtues of the United States in ads in the leading newspapers of Argentina, disguised as tourist advertisements. It turned out that the leading newspapers were Nazi-owned and -operated—so, in effect, Nelson Rockefeller was pouring hundreds of thousands of American dollars into Nazi operations. Besides, with the German blockade of shipping, tourist trade was highly unlikely. The United States became the butt of a good joke in Argentina. The State Department complained that Nelson had not obtained its approval of the operation. Nelson received a chastising letter from the President, written, it turned out, by Sumner Welles. After that, every operation of Nelson's office was proposed first by memo to the State Department and only after it was properly initialed there was the operation launched. Nelson Rockefeller learned to dot his i's and cross his t's.

Nelson himself was grossly underestimated by a great number of men in Washington. Even men in high places think in stereotypes. Nelson, at least at first, was regarded widely as another of FDR's young millionaires who merely wanted a job in Washington. But he was a far cry from a dilettante. Learning as he went along, he was a hard worker, a fighter for what he believed in, and he sincerely believed in the importance of what he was doing. He brought his own top staff with him to the capital and for a time they lived with him in a rambling white-frame home he leased and later bought on Foxhall Road in high-society Washington. His office was set up in a wing of one floor of the Commerce Department in downtown Washington. He left for his office at 8 A.M., worked through to 6:30 P.M. and held evening conferences at home. Weekends, he held open house to Latin American officials for combined social-business gatherings. He was a "morning man," working best in the early hours of the day and winding down at nine or ten at night, not infrequently nodding off among his guests. Later, he would take up 7 A.M. tennis with such men as Vice-President Henry A. Wallace or Senator William Smathers or this or that Congressman. It was a social game, but it never hurt bureaucratically to know such men socially in Washington. Nelson was learning all the time.

In the office of the Coordinator itself, there was no question who was boss. Nelson, at thirty-two, was a take-charge man. He asked for and he took advice but it was he who made the decisions. Some of the men on his staff, senior in years to him, thought him too precipitous at times, too eager to rush into a quagmire of complexities—but then Nelson's father had told him that long before. Nelson had, in fact, spent years observing his own father in action, and while by nature he could not be patient as his forebear, he did believe in method and good business practices in attempting to solve problems. His method was to survey a situation in sufficient depth to define a problem at hand, to analyze the alternative actions, to resolve upon a line of attack, and then, with dispatch, to travel in the straight and shortest line to the solution of that problem. He thought of himself as a catalyst. He could also take a recommendation of his staff and then run with it.

Unbeknown to his own staff or to anyone else for that matter, Nelson had a private tutor on how to find his way through the labyrinth of governmental bureaucracy in Washington. Late every Friday afternoon, usually at the end of the business day, he would go upstairs in the Commerce Building for a private chat with Jesse Jones, a crusty old conservative banker from Houston, Texas, who was Secretary of Commerce and had been Director of the federal Reconstruction Finance Corporation from 1933 to 1939. Jones knew his way around all of Washington as well as any man alive. Having met young Nelson Rockefeller at a social gathering and having taken a liking to him, Jones had agreed to give the young man any advice he needed, strictly on a personal, social level. His help proved invaluable. Jones instructed Nelson on the personalities of everyone he was likely to deal with in Washington, who were the important men at the second level of administration, how to get to the President directly, how to handle a given problem. He taught him specific tactics, too. "Never, never go to the President with a problem, unless you can also give him your recommended solution to that problem," Jones advised him. "The President always has lots of problems," he explained. "What he is looking for are the answers." "Once you have the President's approval for a project," Jones also advised, "then you must whip out a memo on the subject and have him initial it. In that way, you have proof of the President's action and even he can never conveniently deny that approval."

Nelson made a friend, for instance, of General Edwin M. (Pa) Watson, the President's appointments secretary, and thereafter enjoyed relatively easy access to FDR. This Rockefeller and this Roosevelt hit it off well together without embarrassment, perhaps because they had similar backgrounds and personalities and a mutual personal interest in Latin America. On several occasions the President invited Nelson to private dinners and stag get-togethers, a sure sign in Washington of his acceptance. Despite rumors to the contrary, personal politics were never discussed.

On two occasions after Pearl Harbor, Nelson, who was then thirty-three, offered to enlist in the armed forces. Washington was flooded with men in uniform. But the President told him he was serving best where he was and to stay put. He recollected for the young Rockefeller that he too had made the same offer to Woodrow Wilson during the First World

War when he, Roosevelt, had been an Assistant Secretary of the Navy, and President Wilson had told him, too, at the time, to stay put. The implication was not lost upon the young Coordinator for Inter-American Affairs.

The CIAA, as the office was popularly known, was a small agency in a vast federal bureaucracy but it had a wide mandate from the President of the United States, a charter which Nelson Rockefeller interpreted broadly and enthusiastically. To coordinate all government activities vis-à-vis South America, with particular emphasis on commercial and cultural affairs, Nelson and his small loyal staff sailed forth, often against the wind and into uncharted waters. Much of the publicity in the news media covered the "cultural" half of his job. That included sending U.S. movies, news columns, cartoons to Latin America. But to Nelson's mind, the more important work involved the trade agreements, the decision to buy all strategic materials available so as to deny them to the Axis powers, and the specific economic agreements which would tie the welfare of specific South American nations to the interests of the United States. Underlying it all, of course, was the task of persuading Latin American countries that the United States cared, truly cared, about their welfare, and was willing, war or no war, to help these developing nations solve their own pressing problems in an atmosphere of mutual self-interest. It was neither simple nor easy. Most Latin American nations were suspicious of "Big Brother" up north.

Then there were the special assignments. How many German nationals were working for American firms in Latin America? How dangerous were they potentially? The CIAA conducted a survey, secretly, and with the help of the Federal Bureau of Investigation. The findings were alarming and Harry Hopkins asked Nelson Rockefeller to do something about it, discreetly; the United States was still ostensibly a neutral, not yet at war. The project was marked "top secret." Nelson approached the heads of the twelve largest U.S. corporations with extensive Latin American interest. Eleven of them were persuaded without too much trouble that in the event of war it would be best if these corporations had no agents, distributors or representatives in South America with Nazi sympathies. The twelfth corporation refused. Its vice-president insisted that his company did business around the world, was non-political, and that the nineteen suspected agents on the CIAA list were employees of long standing and loyal to the company. Nelson Rockefeller cajoled, argued and pleaded. When that failed, he threatened. He would make the whole affair public. The company vice-president gave in and the nineteen suspected employees were fired. By the time the United States entered the war, thousands of business accounts had been taken away from suspected Axis agents: 85 per cent of the CIAA suspect list had been eased out. The remainder was then easily blacklisted after Pearl Harbor.

In a reverse situation, Nelson went to Harry Hopkins to report that the CIAA had discovered the German airline Lufthansa controlled several airfields in South America within striking distance of the Panama Canal. A few strings were pulled and with considerable discretion, because this was before America's entry into the war, a government loan was arranged for a United States firm to buy the airline's holdings in Latin America for $8 million and that potential danger was eliminated.

When the United States entered the Second World War, the pace increased, but the CIAA mission was essentially the same. Nelson Rockefeller thrived on the sense of urgency, the need to "get things done." In the four years that Nelson ran his office, the CIAA spent $140 million, built up a domestic staff of 1,100 and had 300 specialists working in Latin America. He had experts in everything from economics, agriculture, industrial planning to newsmen, photographers and folk dancers. More than that, the CIAA initiated programs which it turned over to other departments and it handled a varied assortment of wartime projects assigned to it from other governmental agencies. Of them all, Nelson was personally most proud of the CIAA's Institute of Inter-American Affairs, which he proposed to Harry Hopkins in 1942. The most ambitious of all his projects, it was designed to help Latin American countries combat malnutrition, disease and illiteracy. It was humanitarian in design and also served as a means of proving the good faith, interest and concern of the United States. Rather than giving money outright or through a lend-lease program, rather than offering charity, rather than approaching a reluctant Congress for appropriations each year, Nelson's innovation was to set up independent corporations, under the aegis of the IIAA, which would provide financial aid, skilled technical assistance and whatever else was needed—all on a sliding scale and with a five-year cut-off date. Thus, the United States would provide 80 per cent of funds needed the first year, 60 the next and so on, until the recipient country in 20 per cent increments would take over the continuing program by the end of five years. Each project would stand or fall on its merits. Another significant innovation called for each project to be run locally. Harry Hopkins so liked the idea that immediately upon hearing Nelson out, he carried Nelson's charts and statistics into the next office—the Oval Office—and ten minutes later returned with FDR's approval and authorization for an initial allocation of $25 million from the President's emergency funds to start the program rolling. It was eminently successful. By the end of the war, eighteen Latin American countries were involved, matching funds with $40 million spent by the United States. It continued beyond the war's end to 1948, when it merged into a larger program. By that time, more than two thousand individual projects had been launched, training more than ten thousand Latin Americans for all kinds of skills from midwife to sanitary engineer, and in all kinds of work from farming to rubber plantations, to education, health services and housing. It became the forerunner and pilot project for President Truman's later Point Four program.

That program was a high point of Nelson's accomplishments as Coordinator of Inter-American Affairs. It epitomized him in many ways. It was bold in concept, massive in scope and practical in operation. It was also humanitarian. Nelson himself characterizes it as a fine example of "creative capitalism," solving age-old problems with a new, innovative approach, worthy perhaps (although he wouldn't say so) of his grandfather's acumen.

Nelson harbored a profound respect, admiration and love for John D., Sr., who served in many ways as his lodestar, although he shied away from speaking publicly of this feeling. Years later, he would succeed his father as the owner and occupant of Kykuit, his grandfather's home on the Rockefeller estate, and he would preserve much of it in what he called its "authentic 1913 style," even to the extent of duplicating the intricately scrolled iron gate to the main house which his own father had replaced with a simpler, plainer one. Although he did not go about quoting his grandfather, neither would he let pass the slightest slur upon his name. At a congressional hearing on FDR's reciprocal trade policy, Nelson was attacked as "just another New Deal bureaucrat" by a Massachusetts Republican, who remarked in passing, "You seem to have got religion. You seem to believe—and yet your grandfather was known as a shrewd and ruthless trader."

"You may say what you please about me," Nelson shot back, "but I resent what you say about my grandfather. He was a great man. I accept your first adjective in describing him but I reject the second." His father, after reading an account of that exchange in the newspapers, wrote him the next day: "Your quick reply was, I think, perfect . . . how proud both of your grandfathers would have been at the way you handled yourself."

Nelson seemed to have a way about him, a natural touch in all kinds of situations and with all kinds of people. It may very well have been inherited from his mother, who was an outgoing woman. He simply liked people, men and women from all walks of life. He was good at making friends and he cultivated a loyalty in many men with whom he was to be associated for many, many years. But equally, he enjoyed doing battle, matching wits and strategy, with those who opposed him. In the inner sanctums of government bureaucracy, he frequently was involved in power struggles and personal conflicts. Twice he fought off attempts to pare down the jurisdiction of his Coordinator's office and on numerous occasions he became involved in fiery disputes with U.S. ambassadors in South America or with various officials of the State Department. But where he thought he was in the right, he fought furiously for what he believed in, even to the extent of putting his job on the line. He found that he enjoyed it all, especially the winning. Some labeled him arrogant; others considered him a man of vision and absolute integrity. Nelson himself never stopped to analyze; he was always in so much of a hurry to do what he thought had to be done. Some attributed his independence of action to his family position, his name and his wealth. He himself never thought in those terms. Nelson undoubtedly would have been as fiercely Nelson Rockefeller and just as independent with relatively few dollars behind him, or even none at all.

In November 1944, when Edward R. Stettinius, Jr., succeeded the frail Cordell Hull as Secretary of State, Nelson Rockefeller was promoted to Assistant Secretary of State for American Republics Affairs. The promotion came, as Nelson was later to learn, not from the new Secretary but from the President. That backing and support were essential because Nelson did not get along particularly well with the new Secretary. He found, too, that he had more enemies than friends in the State Department, most of them long-term career officers who did not often agree with his views on Latin American problems, did not like his direct, even brash manner of operating and did not particularly like him personally. But the inside battles now were on a level higher than tactics, with the grand strategies of national policy, and Nelson, with his four years of experience as Coordinator behind him, was every bit as good an infighter as any other man in government. By this time, he had earned the respect and personal trust of the leaders of most of the countries of Latin America. In the nine months he held the job, he initiated and guided one of the most important international conferences on Western Hemisphere unity, helped structure the organization of the United Nations, limited the power of the veto in the UN and made for himself a niche in history which would endure even if his career had carried him no further.

As the war drew to its end and the upper structure of the State Department was involved in preparing for the organization of the United Nations, Nelson persuaded President Roosevelt to approve the calling of a conference of all Latin American nations in Mexico City to coordinate and unify all their efforts and actions "on problems of war and peace." The conference was opposed within the State Department itself on the grounds it would detract from the UN meeting, but Nelson Rockefeller, the new Assistant Secretary, had the President's initials on his memorandum outlining the conference. The immediate pragmatic purpose of the conference was to force the pro-Nazi regime of Juan Perón in Argentina to declare war on Germany and to reinstitute a democratic government, including elections, in Argentina. To allay the fears of the nations bordering on Argentina, it also called for a mutual defense agreement, which became known as the Act of Chapultepec, guaranteeing the borders of all the Latin American nations by declaring that an attack on one was an attack on all, requiring joint action against the aggressor. The conference was a resounding success as it established the framework for the future development of economic, social and defense cooperation in the Western Hemisphere. It succeeded also in forcing Argentina to declare war on Germany and to seize all Nazi assets in Argentina, although by that time the war was almost over. Nelson Rockefeller, as the ranking U.S. delegate, cooperated closely with the Latin American delegates but ran roughshod over the dissensions of the more conservative State Department officials under him. Secretary Stettinius, returning from the Yalta Conference, appeared only to sign for the United States.

When the time came, however, for the charter meeting of the United Nations in San Francisco, Stettinius, rather coldly, told his eager assistant for Latin American affairs that he was being left behind: the men of the International Division of the State Department wanted as free a hand in San Francisco as Nelson Rockefeller had wielded in Mexico City.

But later when the State Department men realized that the Soviet Union was lining up a majority of nations to vote along with it on crucial issues, the votes of the Latin American countries suddenly loomed large and important. Now Nelson Rockefeller was invited to San Francisco "for a few days" to talk up the U.S. position among his Latin friends. He arrived at the conference late but in style, in his own chartered plane. Characteristically, he plunged right into the fray.

The foreign policy experts were split ideologically on how best to get along with the Russians, reflecting divided opinion across the country. One faction advocated bending over backward to prove our friendship to the suspicious Russians and thereby winning their cooperation for a peaceful postwar world. The other side held out for a hard *quid pro quo* arrangement, lest the United States give up too much to a nation founded on the principle of spreading communism throughout the world.

Nelson became involved in the top-level policy fight over seating the Perón government of Argentina. Within the inner council deliberations, he insisted that the United States' pledge at Mexico City be honored in the face of the Soviet Union's violent objections. The fear was that the Soviet Union might walk out and destroy the hopes of a world deliberative organization. The United States did hold firm, Argentina was admitted to the UN and the Russians did not walk out.

The next conflict was far more serious. The Big Powers had already agreed to twenty-seven amendments to the Charter, one of which permitted military alliances only against former enemy states, which, in effect, would allow the Soviet Union to form alliances against Germany or Japan, but would have subjected any Latin American alliance to a Big Power (particularly the Soviet Union) veto. Nelson argued against that amendment, which already had been agreed to, among his equals on the U.S. delegation. He tried to get to see Secretary Stettinius. When that failed, he embarked on his own course—going right over the Secretary's head.

With considerable aplomb for an Assistant Secretary, Nelson invited Senator Arthur Vandenberg to his hotel suite for a private dinner. The venerable Michigan senator, a Republican prewar isolationist who had become a supporter of the UN concept, was the most politically powerful member of the U.S. delegation. Vandenberg would lead the Republicans of the U. S. Senate in ratifying or rejecting American participation in the United Nations. Nelson outlined his position on the necessity for regional agreements beyond the control of the UN and found that Vandenberg agreed with him entirely. The result was a letter written that night to Stettinius that led to an uproar within the U.S. delegation over what young Nelson Rockefeller had wrought. In the end, Vandenberg prevailed. The U.S. position was changed and a new Article 51 of the UN Charter was hammered out among the Big Powers, providing that "nothing in this Charter shall impair the inherent right of individual or collective self-defense if an armed attack occurs against a member of the United Nations." Years later the full significance of Article 51 was realized when the so-called Iron Curtain descended and the cold war necessitated the forming of the North Atlantic Treaty Organization as a protection against the Soviet Union. Only then did the State Department acknowledge with appreciation that Nelson Rockefeller's part in protecting the Act of Chapultepec permitted similar regional defense pacts to be made under the UN Charter.

When the conference ended in June 1945, amid the cheers and hopes of the people for future world peace and unity, the U.S. delegation returned to Washington to discover that Stettinius had been fired, replaced as Secretary of State by James F. Byrnes, former senator from South Carolina and a close friend of the new President's, and that Secretary Byrnes, a forthright politician, wanted no part of Nelson Rockefeller in his organization. He told him so forthrightly. Nelson took his case to President Truman. He did not want to resign, not when there was still so much to do to cement relations with Latin America. "Harry was very decent about it," Nelson reminisced in later years. "He told me I'd done a good job. But he fired me."

So Nelson Rockefeller went home to New York and before long set out to do himself what the government of the United States would not let him do on its behalf. Barely a month before his thirty-seventh birthday, he returned from a different war and a character-molding experience different from that of any of his four brothers. They had left the protected solidarity and privacy of the family, as he had, but for the confines of the hierarchy and regimentation of the armed forces. Nelson had enjoyed the full intoxication, truly for the first time, of personal power in his own right, meeting and dealing with men at the upper and uppermost levels of government, men who were directing the course of conduct of the United States of America. It had been heady stuff. And he, Nelson Rockefeller, had come away from it fully satisfied that he was as qualified and equipped as any man he had encountered, short perhaps of the men who occupied the Oval Office in the White House. Some may call this hubris, but it is the stuff of which dreams are made.

To be sure, he had garnered enough sophistication over his five years in Washington to avoid flaunting or advertising his inner convictions. Nor did he entertain much speculation on his specific future. He had learned the theory of "the open doors of opportunity." Some door would open sometime in the future and all he had to do was to be prepared and qualified to walk through that door. He had already turned down an offer to run for mayor of New York. That was not the door which appealed to him. His real interests lay in foreign affairs, he thought, particularly in North and South American relations and by extension in East and West relations. There had been some hints in Washington that if he would consider switching his political allegiance, a new place might be found for him within the Truman administration. That door would always remain closed for Nelson, despite his liberal position on the political spectrum. His prime allegiance was to the Rockefeller family, and the good name of the Rockefellers had always been traditionally associated with the Republican Party.

Having clashed, conflicted and negotiated with three different Secretaries of State during a world war, Nelson did not flinch from facing up to the one man he held in awe: his father. Upon his return home, he became the chairman of the board and chief executive officer of Rockefeller Center; his brothers were directors; but there was no mistaking the real boss. John D. Rockefeller, Jr., still owned the place. Nelson threw himself wholeheartedly into the postwar modernization needed in the thirteen buildings of the Center, erected from 1933 to the beginning of the war. Central air conditioning was to be installed for the first time. Plans were under way for the new Esso Building, stretching from Fifty-first to Fifty-second Street, and there were conferences on the wisdom of expanding Rockefeller Center still farther on Sixth Avenue, or, as it was to be known, the Avenue of the Americas, reflecting Nelson's continuing interest in Latin America. Behind the scenes, a more intense drama than all the building and renovation activity was being played out in a slow, tortuous and low-key crescendo: what was to become of Rockefeller Center in relation to the third generation of Rockefellers?

While his brothers were too decorous—since they themselves stood to benefit financially—to suggest to their father how he dispose of the greatest piece of real estate in New York City, Nelson harbored no such restraints. He felt very strongly that the unity of the family in the third generation was irrevocably tied emotionally and by heritage to two prime Rockefeller entities—Rockefeller Center and the family home at Pocantico Hills—and he told this to his father repeatedly.

John D., Jr., wanted to give the Center to the Rockefeller Institute for Medical Research, later to become the Rockefeller University, so that it would be financially well endowed for as far into the future as any man could plan. The Institute was the first and favorite of his philanthropic institutions. Nelson objected strenuously. He had already devoted some nine years of his life to Rockefeller Center, being involved in the architecture of the buildings, the organization of management, financing, renting offices in the depths of the Great Depression, and finally helping to take the operation out of the red and into the black.

"If you give the Center to Rockefeller Institute," he told his father, "I'm out—forget it. I'll step out of the management, because I'm not going to spend my time and energy on something symbolic and I'm not going to work for a philanthropy that already has all the endowment it needs. I'll have nothing further to do with it."

Characteristically, John D., Jr., came to no immediate decision. Years elapsed before he finally accepted a plan devised by Nelson whereby he sold Rockefeller Center to his five sons at its appraised net value of $2,210,000. What he actually sold were the shares of stock in Rockefeller Center, Incorporated. The appraised value was so low because the corporation still owed him some $58 million on mortgage notes he held for money he spent in building the Center. The mortgage notes of $58 million he gave as a gift to the Rockefeller Brothers Fund. The RBF was a philanthropic organization incorporated by the five brothers in 1940 as a means of coordinating their charitable gifts to worthy institutional causes. The gift of $58 million, in one swoop, lifted the RBF from a small, family convenience to one of the wealthiest foundations in the nation. In fact, by 1974 the charitable gifts of the Rockefeller Brothers Fund totaled nearly $150 million.

The family estate at Pocantico Hills was sold to the five brothers at its appraised value in much the same manner—again by a plan devised by Nelson, and again after protracted negotiations with his father, lasting this time some seven or eight years. Their father, of course, retained a lifetime occupancy of all the property, including Kykuit, and it was understood that his five sons would make no changes without his permission during his lifetime.

Under Nelson's plan, a corporation was set up to own the property, pay taxes on it and provide for its upkeep. As in the purchase of Rockefeller Center, Nelson took the lead in pushing this plan through. He offered to buy up the share of any brother who did not wish to participate. But they all went along with the plan, investing enough capital so that the corporation could acquire other assets which would provide income to cover all expenses in the operation of its properties. (The corporation was dissolved in late 1969 as the brothers themselves prepared to dispose of the greater part of the estate, which they held as tenants in common, as a donation for public use after their death.)

The proceeds of Mrs. Abby Aldrich Rockefeller's trust fund, upon her death, were distributed as provided for to her three eldest children. Reviewing this in 1952, Mr. Rockefeller Jr. decided to equalize that distribution by providing similar second trusts (of about $12 million each) for his three youngest children.

But true to his word of old, John D., Jr., did not include his daughter Abby in his transference of Rockefeller Center. Nor did he provide for her in his will. He had told his children, each of them separately, years before that the Rockefeller fortune, of which he considered himself more the steward and guiding hand than the owner, would be passed on only to those of his children who proved to him that they intended to use that wealth wisely and well for the good of others. Abby, or Babs as she was called, preferred to live her life privately and for her own family and not particularly for the well-being of mankind. She made no secret of it at all. She understood her father's position and concurred in his ultimate assessment. However, her brothers thought better of it. After waiting an appropriate period following their father's gift of the Rockefeller Center notes, they elected their sister Abby as an equal trustee in 1934. Babs, in her maturity, attended RBF meetings and dabbled slightly in philanthropic matters, but she deliberately took a minor role in RBF decisions, pleased and proud to see her younger brothers at work giving away Rockefeller money.

The RBF was run by an expert professional staff headed by Dana Creel, and as the years rolled on its disbursements reflected more and more the special interests of the five brothers: population studies, ecology, education medical research, the arts, Asia and, of course, Latin America.

Nelson was not a bit shy in tapping all family resources for help in his determination to carry on what he so firmly believed had to be done to bring Latin America into the modern world and as a friend of the United States. Upon returning from Washington, he began daily morning meetings in his office at 5600 with his old top crew from the Coordinator's office—John Lockwood, the family counsel, Wally Harrison, Frank Jamieson, Lawrence Levy and others. He knew Latin America and he knew what the Latin Americans feared: that now that the war was over, the big rich capitalists up north would forget about their neighbors to the south. Nelson wanted to reach two main goals: to help upgrade the standard of living in Latin America, which involved improving health, sanitary conditions, education and the like; second, he wanted to broaden the economic base of those countries by starting new industries and bringing modern methods into the old. What came out of all the planning at 5600 was the resolution that two organizations were needed rather than one.

These were vast undertakings, to say the least, and it demonstrated that Nelson Rockefeller was not afraid to "think big." It also proved to those around him that Nelson possessed that Rockefeller family trait: when a Rockefeller became interested and involved in something, he stuck with it. Nelson fought without stint for what he believed in. He pressed his brothers, he accosted his friends and he talked social responsibility to the heads of the major oil companies doing business in South America.

In July 1946, the American International Association for Economic and Social Development (AIA) was incorporated as a philanthropic agency to help ameliorate problems of health, sanitation and education, and to help in raising living standards of rural people in Latin America. The design, similar to the one Nelson inaugurated as Latin American Co-ordinator, established separate non-profit corporations to bring U.S. methods to new programs in South America, financed on a sliding scale by which the individual country ultimately took full responsibility for carrying on the programs established.

Six months later, in January 1947, the International Basic Economy Corporation was set up as a profit-making business "to promote the economic development of various parts of the world, to increase the production and availability of goods, things and services useful to the lives or livelihoods of their people and thus to better their standards of living." The underlying pragmatic purpose of IBEC was to *demonstrate* that American business could take its technological and industrial know-how to underdeveloped nations, help those nations develop and at the same time make a profit. In short, a Rockefeller wanted to show that the capitalistic system works, that it can offer underdeveloped nations and their people more than the Communist system can.

Into this ultra-high-risk capital venture, Nelson and his brothers laid out $4 million to make a beginning. Then Nelson cajoled another $12 million out of the oil companies over a five-year period, and then he talked the governments of Venezuela and Brazil into investing in IBEC. His real coup, however, was persuading the oil companies to buy only preferred, non-voting stock, so that for their $12 million they had absolutely no say in the operation of IBEC. In fact, they even agreed to apportion one third of that money into AIA, whose charter stated that "No profits will ever be realized by subscribers to the Association."

AIA fared well over its life span of twenty-two years, bringing medical teams, sanitation experts, agricultural scientists to South America, following tried and true paths. But IBEC struggled and stumbled along in virgin territory during its early years of operation. The usual mistakes of a new company all were made. American heavy farm equipment sank in soft, marshy and unfamiliar ground. Motorized fishing boats were used more for smuggling than fishing. Incompetents were incompetent, and on a purely personal basis messed up otherwise good programs. But Nelson Rockefeller stuck with it. The Rockefellers poured in more money, some $16 million, to keep the company solvent. And, in ten years of ups and downs, the company finally turned a profit. After the company gained the necessary experience and local acceptance, profits began to grow, attracting more and more local investors. To speak of it as one company is perhaps misleading. IBEC ultimately operated through 119 subsidiaries on a worldwide scale in twenty-five countries. Each subsidiary was a separate company. There were farming companies, milk companies, fishing companies, a grain storage company, a food marketing company, supermarkets, crop dusting, farm machinery, fishing, egg production, low-cost housing (which constructed more than ten thousand homes) and even a mutual fund company to stimulate capital investments by wage earners in Latin America.

The two private enterprises, AIA and IBEC, held a favorite place in Nelson's heart. Through them he had kept his faith in the original idea behind both ventures and he had kept his word with the many leaders of the Latin American world he had encountered in his very first undertaking. as Coordinator of Inter-American Affairs. AIA, after twenty-two years and more than sixty separate operating activities, was phased out of existence, its job done, in 1968. Upon the occasion, Nelson described its work as having created "a quiet revolution" in providing the Latin American countries with the "tools" of education, health and opportunity for achieving a higher standard of living. IBEC still prospers today as a $300 million capitalistic enterprise with head offices still on the fifty-fifth floor of the RCA Building, its president and chief operating officer being Nelson's first-born son, Rodman, who held his first job as a teen-ager in an IBEC supermarket in Caracas.

Nelson's idealism and enthusiasm for IBEC and AIA was tempered, however, by a pragmatic sense of the realistic, an old Rockefeller trait. He realized that IBEC and AIA, however successful, were at best pioneering efforts. They might help point the way, but by themselves they were a small, private effort. Neither Nelson nor all the Rockefellers combined had the financial resources to solve national problems, not even in the smallest country of South America. The Rockefellers might deal in millions of dollars but only the government had the national resources of billions to provide the needed economic help for Latin America. The same held true in almost all other fields of need. Private enterprise can venture into philanthropy, plant seed money and technical know-how, but only a national government can carry through on the enormous programs needed to help solve people's problems. Nelson wanted in on those problems. To do so, he realized, he had to get back into government and into public affairs and public policy making.

With the election of Dwight D. Eisenhower in 1952, the first Republican President in twenty years, Nelson Rockefeller moved with alacrity. During the campaign, Nelson had, in addition to his generous financial contributions, supplied the candidate with suggested economic policy speeches, and when the campaign was won, he had shot off an immediate memo recommending that the new administration seize the opportunity of restructuring the Executive Branch in order to meet the vastly changed problems facing the United States. Before November was over, the President-elect appointed his ardent supporter Nelson Rockefeller to head a three-member President's Advisory Committee on Government Organization. It was a select committee with carte blanche, free to do what it wished—at least as far as *recommendations* went. The other two members were the President's brother, Milton, and Dr. Arthur Fleming, a noted social scientist who later was to become Secretary of Health, Education and Welfare. Once again, it was a heady assignment for Nelson Rockefeller. But this time, at the age of forty-four, he was no longer a neophyte in the bureaucratic alleyways of government: he had experience behind him. He enjoyed a wide acquaintance with men in the Executive Branch and he had learned, he thought, how the government worked. There was the feeling now, too, that he was part of a team, a Republican team, a team of practical men who could get things done, and that was what Nelson Rockefeller liked to do best. With unabated enthusiasm, Nelson set to work. He had many ideas, most of them on the grand scale. Over the Eisenhower years, that small, select President's Advisory Committee, abetted with skilled staffs, recommended thirteen major reorganization plans, all of which the President approved and sent to the Congress, ten of which were sustained.

The first and foremost among them, a lasting achievement of the Eisenhower administration, led to the creation of the Department of Health, Education and Welfare, which consolidated for the first time all the related governmental programs scattered throughout the bureaucracy. It was a masterful accomplishment in itself, weaning pet political and patronage programs away from their traditional bureaucratic keepers. No sooner was that done than Nelson presided over a thorny reorganization of the Defense Department, which would curtail the powers of the military, strengthen the powers of the civilian heads of the Army, Navy and Marine Corps and cut through at least some of the inter-service rivalries. When Congress approved the establishment of the Department of Health, Education and Welfare in April 1953, President Eisenhower appointed Oveta Culp Hobby, a Texas newspaper owner and former commander of the Women's Army Auxiliary Corps (WACS) as the first Secretary of HEW. On her recommendation, he appointed Nelson Rockefeller as her Under Secretary. His job, as she described it, was to be the "general manager" of the huge new department with its 35,000 employees, its annual budget of $2 billion and its distribution of more than $4 billion a year in Social Security benefits.

Nelson plunged into his new job with even more than his own customary gusto. What an opportunity! What a challenge! So it seemed to him. For here, with the health, education and general welfare of the American people at the receiving end of what he and others in the new department could devise, was a scope of humanitarianism far greater than even his father and his grandfather enjoyed in their lifetimes. And what an opportunity for the Republican Party, he thought. This was a great chance to demonstrate the humanitarian instincts of the Republican Party, which had suffered so long under the label of the party of big business and Wall Street. He spent almost two years at HEW, working hard as an administrator and policy maker, getting the new department set up to function well under new guidelines, revamping old programs and innovating new ones. Oveta Culp Hobby was out front as the Secretary; Nelson worked behind the scenes, finding key personnel to head various programs, promulgating research and studies, putting together new programs and then trying to steer those new programs through the Eisenhower administration and through a sometimes skeptical Congress. He thoroughly enjoyed it all, the search and discovery of new ways to accomplish what could not be done before, the finding of "the right way" and the right political support and the right tactics to put together a program of social benefits and then to see it through the legislative process. He worked long hours, eating a sandwich lunch at his desk, taking home briefcases full of reports and papers, and he prospered as an administrator and problem solver. His family name, his famous wealth, his reputed influence played little part in his effectiveness as an Under Secretary of HEW. During those two years, he steered through a program of substantially increased Social Security benefits, extending those benefits to almost 10 million more workers; expanding federal aid to vocational rehabilitation programs, and for hospital and school construction. He was a good ten years ahead of his time in proposing federal aid to education and to health care for the aged, which failed to pass Congress at the time.

With easy access to the Oval Office in the White House and a good working relationship with the man behind the desk there, Nelson moved laterally at the end of 1954 from HEW to the White House itself. Eisenhower appointed him as his Special Assistant for Foreign Affairs.* (Nelson asked for the job because of his keen interest in foreign affairs and it was given.) Specifically, his task was to advise the President on the psychological aspects of foreign policy, particularly as it pertained to the ensuing cold war with the Soviet bloc of nations. As Special Assistant, Nelson attended meetings of the Cabinet, the National Security Council, the Council on Foreign Economic Policy and the Operations Coordinating Board. He had virtual free reign at the highest level of policy making within the Administration. He was involved, in short, in planning and development.

* This was the same title and position given to Henry Kissinger under President Richard M. Nixon. But the times were different, the job was different, and certainly the President and Secretary of State in office were different.

But he was without Cabinet rank. The final decisions were not his to make.

Almost of necessity, Nelson, being Nelson and brimming with innovative ideas and the zest to make things happen, found himself stepping into the domains and upon the toes of some of the most powerful men in the Eisenhower administration: John Foster Dulles, the domineering and intractable Secretary of State; Herbert Hoover, Jr., son of the former President, who was Under Secretary of State; George Humphrey, the powerful and ultra-conservative Secretary of the Treasury; or Rowland Hughes, the equally conservative Director of the Budget. It was enough, for instance, for Eisenhower to pick up the telephone and say to his Secretary of State, "Foster, listen to this, Nelson has an idea," for that idea to be quashed, forgotten or amended beyond recognition. In the highest sanctum of government, Nelson learned the extent to which egos and personalities played a heavy role in the decision-making process. President Eisenhower encouraged innovative proposals, entertained new and even wild ideas, but in the end he almost always chose the safest, most conservative alternative offered as a solution to a given problem. With his military background, Eisenhower believed in the chain-of-command structure of organization. Ideas were processed up through the hierarchy of his Administration and Nelson, in that chain of command, ranked beneath the department heads in the Cabinet. It was frequently very frustrating.

One of the few occasions on which the Assistant to the President for Foreign Affairs actually succeeded in pushing a wholly new concept through to the President, over the objections of John Foster Dulles, occurred at the 1955 summit conference in Geneva, which had been billed as a peace conference for the raging cold war of the period. In preparation for the conference, Nelson Rockefeller, on behalf of the President, conducted a five-day seminar of intellectuals from academia and the so-called "think tanks." Meeting in closed sessions at the Marine Corps School at Quantico, Virginia, Nelson posed the essential problem: what was the true assessment of the cold war? Was the U.S.S.R. winning the war for men's minds as the true promoter of peace in the world? What, if anything, could the United States do at the summit conference to convince the uncommitted nations of the world that this country wanted disarmament and peace?

The scholarly minds did very well in surveying and diagnosing the questions posed, but only one member of the panel came forth with a realistic, pragmatic proposal as to what President Eisenhower might do at the Geneva conference to capture the imagination of the free world in the quest for peace. That man was a young, obscure Harvard history professor who spoke ever so slowly with a thick German accent. His name was Henry Kissinger. His idea, so simple and direct, immediately won the admiration of Nelson Rockefeller: to counter the Russians' unacceptable proposal for the immediate destruction of all nuclear armaments in both countries, the United States should propose to the Soviets an exchange of military blueprints, to be followed by an open skies aerial inspection of each other's territories. That would reduce the risk of surprise attacks; negotiations on general disarmament would then follow. The entire panel worked out the details of the proposal. Nelson Rockefeller and Henry Kissinger hit it off so well working together that they then and there started a friendship which would endure for years and years. In Kissinger, Nelson Rockefeller discovered a cohort who was extremely imaginative as well as knowledgeable, a man who could combine conceptual thinking with pragmatic savvy. In Rockefeller, Henry Kissinger found a man eager to put broad conceptual ideas to work on immediate practical problems. Nelson, for instance, lost no time in presenting the "open skies" proposal to the President, and Eisenhower reacted positively to the idea. But, almost as Nelson had come to expect, Dulles dismissed the proposal as a "public relations stunt." The President and his Secretary of State went to Geneva in July; Nelson Rockefeller was told to stand by in Paris, from where he could be summoned if needed. There, together with Harold Stassen, Special Assistant to the President on Disarmament, and with several top military officials of the Joint Chiefs of Staff, the open skies proposal was further refined and cabled anew to Geneva. At the last minute, the Paris group was invited to Geneva for hasty consultations and Eisenhower carried the open skies proposal on a separate sheet of paper to the podium of the summit conference. Then, departing from his prepared (State Department) text, he surprised the conference and won the admiration of the world with his challenge to the Soviets for an exchange of military blueprints and open skies inspections. "I propose that we take a practical step," he announced dramatically, "that we begin an arrangement very quickly as between ourselves—immediately!" It produced a lessening of international tensions known as "the spirit of Geneva," which lasted for a time, until the U-2 American spy plane was shot down over the Soviet Union in 1959. But by that time, Nelson Rockefeller had long been out of the Eisenhower administration.

After Geneva, Nelson Rockefeller won some more skirmishes in the battles that went on behind the closed doors of government, but they were tactical, short-range victories; he lost out on the major strategic policy debates. He succeeded in convening another Quantico seminar of experts, including the Harvard professor named Henry Kissinger, which produced a report on long-range aspects, with predictions and recommendations on the future of the cold war and Soviet intentions. It warned of the likelihood of smaller brush wars, the need for military preparedness and more. But its major recommendation was for a broad policy of keeping the public informed of what to expect in the future. That last recommendation was rejected by the President and his advisers and the whole report was confined to circulation among those within government with a need to know.

For all his activity and zest, Nelson Rockefeller found himself stymied by a Republican administration much more conservative than himself: Dulles resented his intrusion into foreign policy; Humphrey thought his recommendations too expensive, and their views were backed by the Director of the Budget and by others with at least equal if not more power within the Eisenhower administration. Nelson of course had his friends and admirers within the Administration, particularly Sherman Adams, the chief of staff to the President, and Charles Wilson, the Secretary of Defense. He did, however, often find himself on the same side of important issues with the Vice-President, Richard M. Nixon. At one point, not long after the Geneva conference, Defense Secretary Wilson offered Nelson the job of Under Secretary of Defense, with the understanding that in a short time Nelson could expect to succeed him as Defense Secretary. The new job was cleared with Sherman Adams and with the President. Nelson was delighted. He would have a department of his own, a place in which to show what he could do. But euphoria lasted only a short time. Wilson was obliged to withdraw his offer because, as it turned out, there were objections from Humphrey, Herbert Hoover, Jr., and Budget Director Hughes, and, finally, the President had changed his mind.

Disillusionment replaced his natural optimism. Nelson took stock of his position in the Eisenhower administration and came to the realistic conclusion that it was time for him to go.

He had the opportunity to see close up or at first hand the inner workings of the Executive Branch of the federal government and he had to admit, despite his long-held admiration for Dwight D. Eisenhower, that what he had observed was not the way he, Nelson Rockefeller, would run the government. There was virtually no long-range policy planning, not of the kind Nelson's father employed in his philanthropic work or his grandfather had used to build up Standard Oil or that any good, well-run business relied upon for success. The government seemed to go from crisis to crisis on an *ad hoc* basis, treating each problem as if it were separate from all others, standing alone in time and space. He was genuinely and deeply concerned over the problems facing the United States and he came to the realization that he as an individual was not and most likely could not greatly influence the momentous decisions being made. It led him—optimist and activist that he was—to the self-realization that he personally was as well equipped as any to sit in the Oval Office and to preside over the solving of the problems of this country. In short, he decided he wanted to become President of the United States. This was quite different in quality from his boyhood dream of becoming President one day. This was the beginning of what is known in Washington as "presidentitis," that chronic disease which afflicts men and which can be cured only by election to that office. Nelson Rockefeller also reached another conclusion, derived from his nine years in Washington under three Presidents: the currency of politics is votes. If he wanted real power in this democracy, he would have to return to Washington not as an appointee but as an official elected by the people. With that in mind, but not spoken, he submitted his resignation and left Washington on the last day of 1955. He was not quitting, not in the sense of giving up; he was merely changing course. Nelson Rockefeller had no doubt as to what he wanted to do with his life: he wanted to serve some bigger purpose than mere personal aggrandizement; he wanted to take on some of the big challenges in the world and to make a difference. He had learned that as a private citizen he just did not have enough money or enough power or enough influence to make much of a difference in world affairs. Only the government had the money and power for that. And only the elected officials of government had the true power to influence United States policy for the betterment of mankind.

These were big ideas. But Nelson Rockefeller at age forty-seven had grown accustomed to thinking big ideas. His conclusion was simply that he would have to someday, some way, return to Washington as an elected official. Preferably as President of the United States. Just how he would do that, he did not know. But he was still an optimist. The opportunity would present itself. Of that he was confident. All he had to do was to seize the opportunity.

13

Laurance

"What can I prove I am, besides having
lots of money?"

Laurance Spelman Rockefeller, lean and sinewy with a new glint in his
pale blue eyes at age thirty-five, returned home from World War II with a
self-confidence and sense of maturity he had never possessed before. His
close to four years in the United States Navy had freed him from the
ubiquitous protection and isolation of being a Rockefeller. Trouble-
shooting aircraft production problems from coast to coast had taught him
as much about himself and the world outside the family as it had about
aircraft procurement for the Navy. He even walked straighter than he ever
had before, as though the worries of the world had somehow and to some
extent slipped off his sloped, rounded shoulders.

A seemingly slight shift in attitude effected the change, which for
him was momentous. Reared "with a Bible in one hand" and an awesome
sense of the need as a Rockefeller to help solve the problems of the world,
he had felt almost overwhelmed. But the war years had taught him that
there were no simple answers to the complex problems of the world. Nor
were there any simple problems either. A bit of study in any subject
revealed the complexities involved. For Laurance Rockefeller personally
that meant he could relax, put things in proper prospective, and be
satisfied with doing the best of which he was capable: he could take one
step at a time in the general direction of a desired goal and not expect immediate results. He could lend his best efforts to helping others with similar aims and since he could not do it all himself, he could stop worrying as
he had before. He adopted the pragmatic philosophy that a good begin-

ning deserved a good finish, even if one could not envision the goal line when starting out.

He changed his father's strict concept of "duty" to his own idea of "opportunity." A product of the Protestant Ethic, his father had lived his life and taught his children their responsibilities under a heavy rod of "duty." Not out of a sense of repenting past sins but rather because of one's God-given sense of responsibility, John D. Rockefeller, Jr., felt it his "duty" to use his inherited wealth and position to help his fellow man, to serve society at all levels. Laurance had grown up observing how hard his father worked, how seriously he devoted himself to self-assigned tasks, how he shouldered the burden cast upon him even at the expense of his health. It was assumed, although not enunciated, that his sons would carry on that burden of self-imposed responsibility. Laurance had carried in his mind the knowledge of what his father expected throughout his young life. It had weighed him down. His father had rarely taken time out from that sense of duty. Seldom had he ever seemed to enjoy himself. It was the free-swinging style of life during the war which had opened Laurance up to the point where he could view the responsibilities incumbent upon the third generation of Rockefellers more in the sense of "opportunities" than "duties." In solving some of the detail problems in the production of Navy aircraft, Laurance had derived a sense of enjoyment in a job well done. He valued that in contrast to working under the oppressive stigma of doing one's duty. And he wanted more of it. All this might have seemed a mere matter of semantics: what is a duty and what is an opportunity and what is the difference? To Laurance Rockefeller, the difference was enormous. It changed his outlook on life. It helped him choose the line of work he would follow on his own, beyond the influence of his father.

Laurance viewed the postwar years ahead of him with a new sense of eagerness. Every day would present him with new opportunities to learn and to do things. While other young men upon their return to civilian life ordered new business cards for themselves, Laurance Rockefeller had his new philosophy tastefully printed on a two-by-three-inch card, which he carried with him as a daily reminder and inspiration. One side of the card bore verses from Walter Malone's poem "Opportunity."

> They do me wrong who say I come no more
> When once I knock and fail to find you in;
> For every day I stand outside your door
> And bid you wake, and rise to fight and win.
> Wail not for precious chances passed away!
> Weep not for golden ages on the wane!
> Each night I burn the records of the day—
> At sunrise every soul is born again!

On the other side of the card was his mother's favorite point of philosophy from the Old Testament, slightly amended and modernized:

"What doth God require of thee but to do justly, and to love kindness and to walk humbly with thy God."

MICAH 6:8

Laurance took a wry pleasure from handing out his personal philosophy cards.

These fundamental changes in personality and outlook were internal. To outsiders Laurance still appeared to be the shy, self-effacing young man who had been taught it was better to listen and learn than to speak out upon subjects upon which his father and his father's senior office advisers were more experienced. Nevertheless, he knew what he wanted to do in the years ahead. As if to maximize "opportunities" in his daily life, he had decided to go into a new field called venture capital. That was the investing of capital funds into highly speculative new businesses, new products or new technologies. The impetus of war needs had nurtured a host of experiments on new products and new technologies and they fascinated Laurance Rockefeller, particularly those which, if successful, would significantly change the way people lived in the postwar world. He had come to believe the United States was on the threshold of a new era. The agricultural revolution of the eighteenth century and the industrial revolution of the nineteenth would now be followed by the scientific revolution of the twentieth century. The implications of the atom bomb, nuclear energy, the new strides in aviation, computers, radar, communications, all of the new technology pioneered during the war held a special fascination for Laurance Rockefeller. With an educated glimpse into the future he could see the potentialities of a new world and he was eager to play his part in it.

When the war had ended in Europe, Laurance had gone to Europe to examine the latest British experiments with jet propulsion for military aircraft. He looked into the technology of the German rockets used in the blitz of London and he came back to New York convinced that just as the automobile had outmoded the horse and buggy and changed the world, some day jet propulsion and rockets would replace the old piston airplanes. Back in 1938 he had invested in Eastern Air Lines with Eddie Rickenbacker because he had then recognized the significance of air travel. Now he recognized the qualitative jump in speed of jet propulsion, rockets and the like. It would shrink the size of the civilized world; it would bring people together; it was something worth doing.

When he voiced these ideas in the family offices, his brothers were fascinated and they explored the legalities involved in their pooling their money for joint ventures into new enterprises which would be found by Laurance and the small staff he had gathered from among his wartime

Navy friends. The senior financial advisers in the office, who had counseled the Rockefeller brothers before the war, shuddered at the ideas proposed by Laurance. His father kept his own counsel, declining to advise his son. But it became known anyway that they were all deeply concerned for Laurence's welfare. Recognizing the philosophic and idealistic streak in the young man, they feared that Laurance was not temperamentally equipped to succeed in the fierce world of highly speculative investments. It one thing to believe in the need for research and development of new products on the frontier of scientific knowledge; it was another to pick and choose the one out of ten companies which would not fail. Venture capital might be glamorous, exciting and attractive as investments for rich young men in a dilettantish sort of way. But to the conservative men in the Rockefeller offices versed in blue-chip stocks, venture capital investments were akin to sheer speculation on the market and outright gambling in untried infant companies—heresy by old Rockefeller standards—and an invitation to financial disaster. They fully expected young Laurance to lose a good deal of money. But it was his own money to lose. When they found they could not dissuade him, they hoped he would go through this new experience in short order, losing not *too* much money, and learning enough to come out of it a wiser man.

But they underestimated him. Laurance, being a Rockefeller, was in no way a dabbling dilettante. He thought long and hard before he took an action of one kind or another, although more often than not, his final decisions were based upon his first affirmative instincts. Venture capital appealed to him intuitively and rationally. He believed in science and technology and had spent a major portion of his adult life fascinated with the concept of how science and technology had changed man's relationship to nature and his environment. His first ride in an old Ford trimotor plane in 1934 from Tulsa to Oklahoma City and the spectacle of ground sweeping away beneath him had convinced him of the future of air travel. Thus he had been prepared psychologically for his first meeting with Eddie Rickenbacker in 1938, at which he had been asked to back the World War I flying ace in salvaging a small company named Eastern Air Lines from the remains of an old subsidiary cast off by General Motors. More had gone into Laurance's decision than mere intuition. Captain Eddie's personality appealed to him. Flamboyant, egocentric and difficult, Rickenbacker was regarded by most bankers and potential backers as an extremely high risk as a businessman. But Laurance could recognize beneath that exterior Rickenbacker's extraordinary drive to succeed, his utter faith in the work ethic, his complete integrity as a man. And behind Captain Eddie had been a young investment banker named William Barclay Harding, who had the facts and figures showing the potential of an airline with the high traffic routes along the East Coast from New York to Washington and to Florida, along with a cost-analysis system set up by General Motors which no other airline of that day possessed. While most airlines were catch-as-catch-can, run by seat-of-the-pants bush pilots, this new airline would be run as a business by a hard-nosed chief executive, Captain Eddie Ricken-backer, who knew as much about flying airplanes as any man in the United States. Laurance had invested $125,000 at first and then gradually increased his investment to some $550,000 which convinced the dubious investment banking house of Smith, Barney & Co. to float the bonds which would inaugurate the new airline with a capitalization of $3 million. Laurance had held onto that investment through the war so that in 1946 Eastern Air Lines, as one of the very few airlines to show a profit that year, was on the threshold of a vast expansion in business. Laurance's investment in Eastern had grown to $850,000.

Laurance also retained his early faith in that feisty Scotsman named James S. McDonnell, Mac to his friends, whom he had backed on the eve of the war in the the designing of a military pursuit plane. It had been an ultra-high-risk venture, starting with a mere $10,000 and then growing into the hundreds of thousands. At the time, McDonnell had only the preliminary blueprints for the plane he had in mind and a record of failure behind him. Accidents had plagued the first plane he had built, a low-cost monoplane called the Doodlebug, a short-takeoff-and-landing craft which was designed to be everyman's airplane, and his company had been wiped out in the 1929 economic crash. With an excellent educational background and a reputation as an innovative aeronautical engineer, he had worked for other companies but was yearning once again to go into business for himself. With Laurance's backing, McDonnell had completed his design and in 1941 won an Army contract of $14 million to build his fighter plane. But that plane too had crashed and the Army had canceled the contract. Laurance, believing in the man, had poured more money into the McDonnell Aircraft Corporation, which then turned to subcontracting aviation parts during World War II. But by that time, Laurance had joined the Navy and to avoid a possible conflict of interest sold out his interest in the McDonnell company.

When the war ended, McDonnell found himself in the enviable position of being free of any production contracts and ready to design a jet-powered fighter plane. Laurance reinvested some $300,000 in McDonnell and resumed his seat on the board of directors, and the Phantom jet was born soon after the war, the first all-jet plane to land on the deck of an aircraft carrier. McDonnell Aircraft was on its way to $90 million a year in contracts and more, toward the fulfillment and success Mac McDonnell had dreamed of in the 1930s. He remained the same provocative innovator in his success years of the 1950s that he had been in the 1930s when Laurance Rockefeller had shared his dream of building a better, faster, modern fighter plane for the U.S. government. McDonnell possessed more than technical brilliance in his field. His personality loomed larger than

life, a man with a dream of doing something himself, a man with a practical, iconoclastic turn of mind, who insisted that the best way to judge a
man for a position in his company was to take him swimming, stripped of
clothes, and then listen to his ideas on life.

Laurance had lost money in Platt le Page, a company which pioneered in helicopters before the war and had gone bankrupt. The military
brass in World War II had scoffed at the helicopter as "a machine designed to destroy itself." But Laurance never lost faith in that concept.
When Frank Piasecki, the son of a Polish tailor in Philadelphia, discovered that the Le Page helicopter flew better sideways than forward, he
launched his own company and built a helicopter with two rotors, instead
of one, which gave it the stability and maneuverability it never had before.
Laurance invested in the company at its start in the early days of 1946, envisioning the day when helicopters would be used for air taxi service
within every major city of the United States. Neither he nor anyone else
could foresee that helicopters would become the short-range work horses
of a new type of warfare, called police actions, in Korea and later in South
Vietnam, making fortunes for manufacturers of the whirlybirds.

His prewar investments had been made at considerable personal risk,
representing at times from half to two thirds of all the capital at his disposal. Even after the war, his father kept a tight hand on the purse strings.
Laurance felt wary and the need to move with care on his high-risk investments, lest his father consider him frivolous and cut him off from future
funds. At the time, his father had not yet decided how to disburse the
Rockefeller wealth among his children and his favorite philanthropies.
Laurance's 1934 trust in the 1940s yielded him an income of about $1 mil-
lion a year. But with taxes, the cost of living and his own philanthropic
commitments, it left him (to his mind) precious little capital to risk in
new and untried businesses. Nevertheless, he was driven "to risking everything as soon as I got it."

In 1946, he settled down to formalizing his venture capital enterprise
with assets of about $1.3 million, most of it in Eastern Air Lines, McDon-
nell Aircraft and Piasecki Helicopters. While he had made his prewar investments on his own, seeking outside counsel when needed, now he
brought in a small staff of personal advisers: Harper Woodward, a calm,
pipe-smoking, astute lawyer, a former secretary to the president of Harvard
University; Randolph B. Marston, a financial expert who had been with
the Chase Bank, and T. F. (Ted) Walkowicz, a former research and development officer in the Air Force. Their first order of business was to help
formulate a general policy to govern all Laurance's future venture capital
investments. But Laurance set the policy. Their job afterward was to help
him carry it out, to guard him against going off on tangents.

"What can I prove I am, besides having a lot of money?" Laurance
asked his new associates. He explained that he did not intend to live a use-

less life on inherited wealth. He did not want to leave his money in Standard Oil and watch it grow. Nor did he have any desire to gain control over any one company and spend his life at that. (He could never equal the accomplishment of his grandfather, nor did he feel the need to try.) He wanted to corner no market, amass no new or greater fortune for its own sake.

He viewed his own role, as he explained to his new associates in venture capital, as that of a catalyst, the agent which could bring together and meld the various elements necessary to transform a worthwhile concept or a new technology into a needed and marketable product. There were many ingenious men in postwar America who had started up small research and development companies and who needed not only financing but also competent managerial and marketing know-how to make an economic success of their small companies. They were often the genius type of men, fiercely independent and impractical and usually egocentric, men who refused to work for the large, staid companies which maintained research and development departments. But they also were too risky and unproven to be able to win support from the usually conservative banks and investment underwriters. These were the men Laurance wanted to help.

But his support, in financing, recruiting and managerial advice, was in no way to be thought of as eleemosynary. For all his future investments, Laurance set forth two major critera:

(1) First and foremost, the nature of the project, if successfully developed, must be socially significant, making a real contribution to the national security, welfare or economy. He was not looking for mere moneymakers.

(2) The project must have the capacity for great expansion, if successfully developed.

By the very nature of venture capital, his every investment would entail considerable risk of loss as well as a decent chance of gain. To reduce the risk, Laurance preferred to support a company which already had demonstrated competent management, rather than a single man with a good idea. He also preferred a company large enough to require an investment of not less than $250,000 or $300,000 to launch its project. He did not want to spread himself too thin, not at the start, or to take on the headaches of starting up an entirely new company. Later, however, he would amend that condition. The general criteria were set at the start but most of the policies on investment were refined and polished as experience warranted. One other rule was generaly adhered to: a company would be given five to ten years to prove itself or to fail, and in either event Laurance would withdraw his investment and put his money and, hopefully, profits into a new and needy venture capital enterprise. The idea was to be a catalyst, to make a change and then to move on.

An embarrassing difficulty at the start was how to offer his venture capital opportunities to his brothers. One of his first investments was shared equally by all of them and it went broke. Laurance felt terrible about it. On the next venture, he tested the situation himself and made an enormous profit alone before he could open it again to his brothers. He was equally chagrined. So, it was decided, and all the brothers agreed, Laurance would take the lead and the major share of each new venture, but at the start, when he invested, he would explain and offer shares in the new venture to all the brothers and their sister and each would invest according to his or her own judgment.

Laurance did not limit his investment search strictly to aviation and related fields. At the very outset, two great opportunities came to his attention and captured his and his brothers' fascination: food and housing. Postwar America was in dire need of millions of units of new housing for the returning veterans and their families. Harmon Goldstone, one of Laurance's best friends in the Lincoln School, who had become an architect associated with Wally Harrison, Nelson's best friend, had discovered a German architect's original and unique design for a low-cost, prefabricated home. It was a great concept: an aluminum structured house, precut at the factory and put up quickly over a concrete slab poured at the site. Given the existing housing shortage, the low cost of the prefab home and the massive federal government underwriting for veteran home mortgages, this seemed to be a guaranteed no-loss situation. It also fulfilled the Rockefeller criteria of being socially beneficial and capable of vast expansion. The brothers invested in excess of $250,000 to launch Harmon Houses. It turned out to be a disaster, a total loss.

Producing the prefabricated houses was no problem; putting them up was something else again. The German design was so precise that if the concrete floor slab was more than one quarter of an inch off specifications, the prefabricated aluminum beams did not fit as designed. Worse than that, the Rockefellers had underestimated the tangle of local building codes, the ferocity of opposition from construction unions and the high cost of land. Afterward, with hindsight, the Rockefellers could see that while the concept of prefabricated homes had great merit and a place within the housing industry, the timing of their venture had been wrong: they had been too far ahead of their time.

However, the time did seem right to "harvest the oceans" to satisfy the worldwide need of food following the end of the war. A group of investors, led by the Rockefeller brothers, financed a two-year study of the world's oceans and the means to catch enough fish to feed the peoples of the underdeveloped nations of the world. A great deal of research, involving scientists and business school experts, went into the concept of where and how to tap the food resources beneath the seven seas of the globe. This concept was so grand, if not grandiose, that its future potential titillated even the Rockefeller brothers. Their investment in the idea grew to more than $500,000 and some twenty other investors put up another $1 million to set up Island Packers, Inc., which employed the natives of the Fiji Islands to catch tuna, which would be processed and canned in a new factory by the natives of American Samoa, thereby bolstering the economy of both underdeveloped areas. The experts hired for the project even had worked out an ingenious plan for catching fish quickly by chumming and using a barbless hook. Once a tuna was hooked, the fisherman could sling it over his shoulder and the fish would slip off the hook and onto the boat. The concept was great. What they neglected to do was to consult with any local fisherman about how good or bad the fishing was. Great schools of tuna could be observed from airplanes in the area. But from airplanes, one can see only the fish near the surface of the water, not to any great depth. At any rate, the fish just did not bite to the extent expected. Then the Rockefellers consulted with a French Sardinian fishing company to no avail. To save the project they turned to a Japanese fishing executive, a former admiral in the Nippon fleet, who tried to catch tuna with nets off Vancouver for the Rockefellers. That too failed dismally and the entire project collapsed, a total loss. The Rockefeller prowess obviously did not extend to fishing. Laurance later commented, "It taught me a lesson about going too far afield where my contacts with conditions and people were not firsthand."

Laurance's firsthand knowledge at the time was primarily in the new aviation and military technology. And that was where the money was—at least potentially. With the advent of the cold war and the Soviet-American race for military and arms superiority, the government appropriated billions of dollars for research and development in atomic energy, electronics, jet propulsion and missiles. The catch-22 of winning a government contract, however, was that first there had to be a research and development company with proven capabilites of researching and developing a product to government specifications. That required private capital and at the time there were a handful of companies or individuals set up or willing to invest in such high-risk ventures. Thus, in 1947, it was the Navy who first approached Laurance to invest in a new, small company out in Denville, New Jersey. It was one of only two companies in the nation which was working on liquid fuel rockets and without new capital it would go broke. When its founder, Lovell Lawrence, showed up at the Rockefeller offices, he pounded on a desk and insisted he needed Rockefeller money to survive and he needed it within the hour—or else he would sell out to his lone competitor. He did not get his answer within the hour. He had to wait a month, while Laurance's staff investigated the situation and the man. Then he got his financing, Rockefeller backing and a start into a fabulous future. For the company was Reaction Motors, which in time produced the first liquid-fuel rocket, known as the Viking, followed by a rocket engine for the Bell X-1, the experimental plane which broke the sound barrier for the first time in 1947, and then an auxiliary rocket engine for the Douglas Skyrocket jet which enabled it in 1953 to fly faster and higher than any plane ever built before. Reaction Motors stock soared along with its successful products.

With the boom in the general economy, the whole stock market did some high flying too in the 1950s. The Dow Jones averages climbed steadily from 200 to 700. With such good economic times and easy money, Wall Street investors turned to the more speculative stocks which had been privately financed before. Laurance and his associates naturally were delighted. The infant companies he had invested in always needed more financing once they reached the production stage of what they had researched and developed. Money in big chunks, known as capital, was the protein necessary for healthy growth of adolescent research and development companies.

Laurance, with his focus on aviation, invested in Airborne Instruments Laboratories, a small outfit in Mineola, Long Island, trying to develop new and improved navigation and flight instruments. Aircraft Radio Corporation of New Jersey also joined his portfolio, as did Stavid Engineering of New Jersey, and others. Horizons, Inc., was still another company, on the threshold of developing a cheaper method of producing a titanium alloy which would have the lightness of aluminum and the strength of steel. Wallace Aviation pioneered in a new cold metal process of making jet engine compressors. Marquardt Aircraft of Los Angeles was engineering the then new ramjet engine, which promised to revolutionize air travel by combining the best attributes of the jet engine and the rocket for swift long-distance flights.

In these investments and others, it was the concept of new products and new technologies which attracted Laurance Rockefeller. With his penchant for philosophy and the significance of life-changing forces, he was particularly adept at recognizing the potential of a new idea. More than most others, he could quickly grasp the technological concepts and problems and where and how to size up a man in short time, and where it came to a choice of investing in a more glamorous idea or a more worthy man, he invariably invested in the man.

For Laurance personally, the Rockefeller reputation or stereotype hovered over everything he did, with its advantages and its disadvantages. There was no escaping it. Fledgling companies needing financial backing welcomed Rockefeller money, because with it came the Rockefeller name and reputation which attracted other investors. A project, however risky, always seemed more secure with a Rockefeller behind it. While Laurance usually limited the Rockefeller investment in any new company to around $300,000, either he, his staff or the company's management would seek several times that amount when necessary from other investors. At the same time, however, the man who welcomed Rockefeller's investment in his firm often retained a deep, abiding suspicion that a Rockefeller meant to gain control over his precious infant company. In policy decision battles, time and again the Rockefeller men sought to convince company management that Laurance was not interested in controlling the company but only in what was best for the health and welfare of the company itself.

Laurance soon evolved a policy of a "three-legged-stool ownership" of new, budding companies: one third of the stock to be held by the active management, one third by himself and his associates, and the final third by outside investors, each third represented equally on the board of directors. Thus, no one interest would control the company. It would guard against any one segment of ownership going off on a tangent. It would prevent deadlocks on policy decisions. It would demonstrate once and for all that Laurance did not want to control the company. Over the years, this policy worked well. His opinions were sometimes overruled or ignored on the board of directors, but only once in thirty years did he ever become involved in a proxy fight over the direction of a company in which he was the largest single investor, although a minority stockholder.

From the very beginning, Laurance decided that he had better not sit on the boards of directors of these new, finicky companies. The problem he anticipated was that if he became a director of one company, how could he refuse to be a director of another one? With all his commitments, he could not possibly serve as a director in all of them. There was not enough time. To represent his interest, he had his closest business associate, Harper Woodward, replace him on most of the boards while his other associates sat in on the boards of other companies. They served as his alter egos or as regents. There was no mistaking that when one of them voiced an opinion, it reflected the opinion of Laurance Rockefeller.

Eastern Air Lines, however, was a special case. It was not properly one of Laurance's venture capital new companies. As a founding director of the airline in 1938, Laurance had been an active member of the board and a close friend of its president, Eddie Rickenbacker. Nevertheless, to be fair to the other companies, Laurance with some trepidation announced to Captain Eddie that he had decided to resign from Eastern and hoped Harper Woodward would be elected to the board to replace him. Fearing the wrath of the outspoken Rickenbacker, Laurance assured him he was not at all deserting the airline. To Laurance's surprise, Rickenbacker grinned and fairly shouted across the luncheon table: "Damn glad to hear it, Laurance. You've always been a terrible handicap to me on the board. Specially when I go out and try to raise some money. Now, Harper here would be great: no one's ever heard of him!"

With Woodward on the board, in the place of the airline's largest individual stockholder, Laurance continued his keen interest in and association with Eastern Air Lines down through the years. It had been his first major investment and his first commitment to the field of aviation. Eddie Rickenbacker and most of the old-timers on the Eastern board of directors had become long-time good friends, sharing in the spectacular success of the airline. But business is business. When Eddie Rickenbacker, who had been the airline's one-man management, ruling like a tyrant, had outlived his usefulness, the board of directors voted his retirement as chief executive officer in 1959. As he approached the age of seventy, he had become too domineering and irascible even for his friends. He had insisted that an airline's job was only to provide the best transportation at the cheapest price possible, refusing to match the frills, public relations and extra services of competing airlines.

With McDonnell Aircraft, Laurance reached another decision. Not only would he resign from its board of directors, he would sell out. By 1949, ten years had passed since he had plunked down the first $10,000 on the blueprints and faith of James McDonnell. Since the war's end, McDonnell had produced the fabulously successful Phantom jet and the more advanced Banshee jet fighter, and had become one of the foremost builders of military aircraft. With $90 million worth of backlog orders, a huge production plant near St. Louis and six thousand employees, it was hardly a venture capital enterprise any more. It was now a very good investment. Its future success was virtually assured. In fact, it would continue to grow and prosper, capping Mac McDonnell's dream of merging his company with that of the other successful Scotsman in the business, Donald Douglas, to become McDonnell-Douglas Aircraft. But in 1949, Laurance was more interested in further explorations than in piling up profits. So over the next few years, he gradually disposed of his McDonnell shares. When it was done, the Rockefeller bookkeepers found that Laurance's investment in McDonnell Aircraft had amounted to $550,000. When sold in the early 1950s, it brought in $1.5 million, almost tripling his original investment.

As Laurance's reputation in the field grew, an increasing number of new business proposals flowed into his office at Rockefeller Center. He and his associates could pick and choose. Of course, there were mistakes made, as well as errors in judgment. They were to be expected. But the ones that hurt most were those good ones that got away. Laurance was offered, for instance, a 15 per cent share of a new company, called Haloid, which had developed an office copier or duplicating machine said to be better than others already on the market. But a young staff member turned in a negative recommendation on the grounds that there was not much of a market for such duplicating machines. So Laurance did not invest in Xerox, one of the most successful companies in the postwar world. The young man who gave the negative recommendation sought employment elsewhere. Nevertheless, most of the companies he did invest in were growing healthily, producing worthwhile products and finding acceptance in the market place.

As a multi-millionaire in both earned and unearned income, Laurance maintained a decidedly low profile in public. In New York City, he lived on a scale not much above that of an executive of a medium-sized corporation. Five days a week he lived in an apartment barely large enough for his wife, himself and their four children. It was the same apartment he had occupied with his wife before the war and neither saw any reason to change. When the children came along, they rented the next apartment and connected the two. The dining room accommodated eight guests, cramped, and no more. But they preferred intimate dinner parties and never gave large ones. At Pocantico Hills, they had added rooms as needed to the original prefabricated U. S. Steel home they had built after their marriage in 1935. Most of the furnishings had been given to them by their parents. To be sure, these hand-me-downs were Shaker, early American and otherwise fine furniture or china, silver, oriental rugs, all of them family heirlooms, sensible, practical and comfortable. They had Mary's family home in Woodstock, Vermont, which had come to her by inheritance, fully furnished and stocked and beautiful, and his father's ranch in the Grand Tetons of Wyoming. Away from New York City, Laurance was perfectly happy dressed in old clothes, chopping wood, riding a horse or walking along trails in a forest. They were not collectors, not in the sense of collecting for acquisition. They bought things they needed to use and they used them. Laurance kept a fine string of riding horses and his stables and corrals as well as his horses at Pocantico Hills were superb. But they all were for use, not for show. Laurance delighted in driving good, fast automobiles, but he did not collect them. He disdained the use of a chauffeur, at least until quite late in life.

His one indulgence as a man of wealth after the war was to have designed and built for himself an aluminum-hulled, sixty-five-foot motor cruiser, fashioned on the lines of a PT boat and powered by twin Packard engines. It was more of a utilitarian vessel than a luxury yacht. Laurance loved to commute from Pocantico to work at Rockefeller Center every morning in season, chugging down the Hudson River in fifty minutes, which was as fast or faster than the trip by local commuter train. Over the next twenty-odd years, *The Dauntless* would become a familiar sight on the Hudson, beeping greetings by horn to other river travelers.

As a student of philosophy, consciously greeting each day as a new beginning, Laurance sought the simple life. He tried to concentrate upon one thing at a time, to cut away the extraneous, to delegate as much as possible, to free himself to think, to act and to be. As a Rockefeller, however, he soon learned that the simple life was difficult to attain. There was a limit to how much he could really delegate. The more he passed out, the more came in to fill his time. The scope of his venture capital interests, enough to fill most men's entire working time, was only one of a great many equally important commitments Laurance had made as a Rockefeller and as a son of his father.

He represented the family's interest—really his father's—in the Chase National Bank, taking his seat on the board in 1947. He served there for ten years, until brother David, then a vice-president working at the bank, succeeded him. The following year he gave up his seat on the N. Y. Stock Exchange, which he had held for twenty years as much for the family as for himself. As a third-generation Rockefeller, he had joined his brothers as a director of Rockefeller Center in 1936, when the Center was only half completed. With his business background, he remained close to daily operations of the Center, taking over from Nelson as chairman of the board in 1953 when Nelson left New York to join the Eisenhower administration and life in Washington. As a director of the Rockefeller Brothers Fund, the philanthropic arm of the third generation, Laurance was frequently on call primarily because he often was the only brother around the office. John 3rd was often away on trips to the Far East, Nelson was in Washington, David was at the Chase Bank and Winthrop hardly ever came to the office before he quit New York City entirely.

In line with the brothers' decision to take over and carry on the major interests of their father's life, Laurance joined the board of managers of Memorial Hospital for Cancer and Allied Diseases in 1947. The step for Laurance was a lifetime commitment to a cause. Memorial had maintained a pre-eminent position as a cancer specialty hospital since 1884. At the turn of the century, Laurance's father had convinced his father to make anonymous gifts to the hospital and then in 1927, Rockefeller Jr. had pledged $300,000 to support research, clinical developments and six new clinical fellowships at the hospital for five years. In those days, $60,000 a year would go a long way. When the hospital had outgrown its original plant, Laurance's father had been instrumental in moving Memorial Hospital to York Avenue and Sixty-eighth Street in New York, for proximity with New York Hospital and Cornell Medical School, with which it was already affiliated, and with the Rockefeller Institute for Medical Research. In 1936, he gave the hospital its new (and present) site, a square city block which he had bought up for $3 million, and then had the General Education Board, of which he was chairman, contribute $3 million toward the building and equipping of the new twelve-story hospital. When it opened in 1939, it was the largest of all institutions devoted to cancer. It had the only cancer ward for children in the world. By the end of the war, it was poised for still more advances, as Alfred P. Sloan, Jr., the industrial genius of General Motors, founded the Sloan-Kettering Institute for Cancer Research as part of Memorial and took a leading hand in its affairs. Laurance was elected to the board of Sloan-Kettering in 1949, joining Sloan on both governing boards and beginning what he later described as an "exceptional relationship" with the elderly Sloan, who had no children.

For Laurance it became a rare opportunity to see one of the few great intellectuals of American industry at work devoting his business and organizational acumen to the fight against cancer. For Sloan, it was an opportunity to groom as an heir apparent at Memorial a young Rockefeller trained in the business world as well as in the cancer cause. Despite their father-son rapport, however, a fundamental difference of opinion separated the two men on how best to conduct cancer research. Sloan, who had successfully kept automotive research apart and independent from production, marketing and sales at General Motors, believed with equal firmness that cancer research should be kept pure and screened off from the exigencies of hospital and clinical treatments. The relatively high costs of hospital and clinical care were considered by Sloan to be a drain upon limited resources better used for basic research. Laurance, on the other hand, sought to convince Sloan and other board members of his father's "faith and vision" in donating the hospital site so as to create an environment of cross-pollenization of ideas among the professional staffs and programs of Memorial, Sloan-Kettering, New York Hospital, the Cornell Medical School and the Rockefeller Institute. In the realities of those days, however, there were more cross-rivalries than pollenization in the diverse theories and practices in cancer research and treatment, as well as the normal amount of personality differences among the scientists, doctors and administrators involved in all those institutions. The president of Memorial Hospital, for instance, was said to be allergic to the pungent odor of formaldehyde and never once set foot in the laboratories of Sloan-Kettering. Nor did the president of the Institute, guarding his domain, ever invite him. In any event, Alfred Sloan, as the chief benefactor at Memorial, prevailed and in 1959 the new Donald S. Walker Laboratory for cancer research was opened in Rye, New York, a good twenty-five miles away from Memorial. Nevertheless, Laurance continued to advocate his own concept of a single synergistic environment in which the various facilities for cancer research and treatment in and around Memorial Hospital would combine to find the cure or cures for the most dreaded disease in America. No one, of course, could predict where or when or how new advances would be made in the fight against cancer. Lay members of boards of directors could strive only to provide the needed money, facilities and support for the scientific community—and hope for the best.

Among the five brothers, Laurance became his father's lieutenant and alter ego in almost all matters of conservation. All of the boys had been raised to know and to love the beauty of nature around them in Pocantico Hills, Mount Desert Island in Maine, and on field trips across the Hudson to the Palisades of New Jersey. The trips to the Far West, starting when Laurance was sixteen, enlarged his horizons. He beheld the grandeurs of the Grand Canyon, the Grand Tetons, Yellowstone Park and Yosemite in 1924 and made his lifelong commitment to conservation then, hardly knowing it at the time. The grandest mountains in the nation, the deepest valleys, the raging swift rivers and powerful waterfalls he observed as a boy had made upon him an impression he would neither forget nor forsake. From his teen-age years on, he absorbed an intimate knowledge, understanding, love and concern for the preservation of the natural beauty of America. His mentors were his father and two of the nation's most prominent conservationists who were often associated with his father: Fairfield Osborn, president of the New York Zoological Society, and Horace Albright, superintendent of Yellowstone National Park in 1926 and later director of the whole National Park Service.

It was only natural and expected within the family for Laurance, upon finishing his schooling, to become a trustee of the New York Zoological Society in 1935. His grandfather had been a founder in 1909, followed by his father, and then Laurance had been elected a founder and second vice-president in 1940. His first public appointment was to the Palisades Interstate Park Commission in 1939, following his father's donation of seven hundred acres of land atop the Palisades, land that he had bought piece by piece since the 1920s in order to preserve the integrity of the magnificent New Jersey skyline facing New York. Then, in 1940, his father established the Jackson Hole Preserve as a non-profit conservationist and educational corporation. One of its chief functions was to manage the Rockefeller holdings in the valley of the Grand Tetons, and Laurance, at age thirty, became its first president.

Upon his return from World War II, he moved quickly into the forefront of conservation activities. By then, he had served his apprenticeship in conservation over some twenty years in the American Geographical Society, the American Museum of National History, the New York Botanical Garden and a host of other organizations. His father, now in his seventies, was easing himself out of his commitments and Laurance was stepping into the gap. The two deans of conservation, Fairfield Osborn and Horace Albright, had become his close friends, advisers and sources of inspiration. There was not a man in the United States who knew more about national parks, forests and the preservation of the wilderness than Albright, who had retired as director of the National Park Service. Osborn shone in Laurance's eyes as an ideal: as a young man Osborn had planned his life and stuck to the plan. First he became a classics scholar at Princeton and Cambridge, then he earned a fortune on Wall Street, married and raised a family. At age forty-eight he quit the business world and devoted the rest of his long life to conservation and wildlife management. In 1948, Osborn wrote a trail-blazing book on ecology, *Our Plundered Planet*, which set forth the manifold dangers of man's incursions upon nature. In that year, he and Laurance co-founded the Conservation Foundation as an educational organization designed to research and publish factual data on conservation. It was the first of its kind. At the same time, both men worked tirelessly to expand the activities and influence of the N. Y. Zoological Society from a purely local organization overseeing the Bronx Zoo into one which would conduct conservation and research activities on a national and international scale. As a trustee of the Zoological Society and the Geographical Society, Laurance helped organize and joined in an African safari to bring new wild animals to the Bronx Zoo. As President of Jackson Hole Preserve, he turned over one thousand acres of Rockefeller land in Wyoming for research and conservation of endangered species of elk, moose and buffalo. Thus the Jackson Hole Wildlife Park was born. Laurance was in a unique position of bridging almost all of the facets of conservation in America by simply joining and becoming active in almost all of them.

At the time there was scant public interest in wildlife, conservation or the quality of the environment. Ecology as an issue did not exist. In the postwar concern over immediate problems and issues, the long-range needs of conservation received a low priority and little attention. Laurance along with his father and his brothers understood this. It was nothing new. A small group of aware people always needed to lead the way before the government or the vast body of the public would make a new value judgment and change national policy. Private philanthropy's prime role was to serve as that forerunner and cutting edge where government would not tread out of political fear, ignorance or unconcern. When land was put up for sale north of the New Jersey Palisades, Laurance bid high and bought parcel after parcel, turning them over to the Palisades Park Commission in anticipation of the value and future need of park lands for the growing metropolitan New York area.

Patience and perseverance were Rockefeller bywords for three generations. Laurance's father from 1926 through 1929 had bought up piece by piece 33,562 acres of prime land in the Jackson Hole valley of the Grand Tetons to save them from commercial exploitation. He offered it all as a gift to the United States as an addition to the Grand Teton National Park and then he waited and waited and paid state taxes on the land for twenty years before his gift was accepted. Politics, emotions and local economic interests all played their part in preventing the thirty-mile strip of land, which afforded the most glorious views of the eleven peaks of the Grand Tetons, from becoming a national park. But patience and perseverance finally wore down the last of the opposition and in 1949 Congress acted affirmatively. Laurance signed the deeds over to the United States on behalf of his father and the Jackson Hole Preserve, creating one of the finest and best-loved parks in the Western Hemisphere.

When the thirty miles of valley, the "hole" between the Grand Teton and Gros Ventre mountains, became part of the national park system, their preservation was guaranteed into the foreseeable future. John D. Rockefeller, Jr.'s dream of 1926 had been fulfilled. But then the question arose: preserved for what?

The whole conservation movement from the turn of the century and Teddy Roosevelt's foresight had been predicated upon the wisdom of saving the great natural areas of beauty in America from predatory commercial exploitation and that had been the extent of virtually all conservation efforts up to the Second World War. Then, however, the advances in air travel, affluence and leisure time in the United States brought these usually remote national parks and forests, with their lakes, rivers and waterfalls, within the reach of an ever increasing number of campers, mountain climbers and tourists. Laurance Rockefeller hardly needed to think this through. Thousands upon thousands of visitors to Jackson Hole and the Grand Tetons slept in their cars scattered all over the area where the existing roads would take them. The Park Service had no funds to provide proper and adequate visitor facilities and the landscape was beginning to suffer from misuse. To realize his father's dream of sharing with his fellow Americans the glory and inspiration he received from the Grand Tetons, it would be necessary to provide some kind of suitable accommodations for those flocking to the area. Laurance and his associates embraced a new, advance philosophy of conservation: conservation and use. The magnificent natural environment of the Grand Tetons, and similar areas around the country, must be preserved for future generations, but they also must be used and enjoyed by the people living now. The process rather than the goal, however, was the real challenge. How to do that, how to manage a wilderness area so that people can use it and yet not destroy it, where to draw the line between proper use and exploitation—that was the challenge for postwar conservationists, as Laurance viewed it.

The Grand Tetons became a pilot project for the Rockefellers, with Laurance spearheading the effort to demonstrate what could be done and how it should be done. It was a task which received the utmost tender loving care from the family, for the Grand Tetons, since that first visit in 1926, had always been a special place in the West for the Rockefeller family. The Rockefellers set about their task when it became clear that no one else would do it: with a short summer season of three or four months a year, outside concessionaires could not be found to invest. The federal government balked at spending money for such purposes. So Laurance, in close consultation with his father, Horace Albright and others, set out upon his own exploration. Colonial Williamsburg provided Laurance's only point of reference. There the Rockefellers had restored and rebuilt a colonial city and set up a separate company to operate lodges and restaurants for the tourists. But the wilderness of the craggy Rocky Mountains posed far more difficult and complex problems. In order to satisfy the needs of all those who would come to Jackson Hole, Laurance decided to provide three separate and distinct types of accommodations and services, from bare campsites for the hardy hikers to luxury-in-the-woods for the well-to-do.

The main facility, in the medium price range, was the Jackson Lake Lodge with three hundred comfortable rooms, a dining room which could seat 525 persons and an expansive main lounge with its sixty-foot picture window framing a spectacular view of the three major Teton peaks. With its fireproof concrete construction, interior decoration and natural artifacts and relics found in the area, this single facility cost the Rockefellers $6 million.

Several miles to the south, a small dude ranch which dated back to 1923 was converted and enlarged into the luxury-price Jenny Lake Lodge. Its thirty rustic log cabins (accommodating at most seventy persons) offered privacy in an informal atmosphere with every comfort of home deep in the woods of Wyoming.

At the other extreme of budget prices, the Rockefellers built Colter Bay Village, named for the fur trapper John Colter who explored and discovered the area of Yellowstone National Park with the Lewis and Clark expeditions. In a cooperative venture, the National Park Service built the roads, water and sanitary facilities at a cost of $1 million, while the Rockefellers spent some $2.5 million to build the 205 log cabins, a cafeteria, general store, launderette, showers and boat marina. The village concept was so popular that the cabins later were augmented by a tent village, a new concept of cabins made of logs and canvas, at even cheaper rentals, and still later a trailer village of 112 sites was added to Colter Bay.

What made all of this possible was a combination of John D. Rockefeller, Jr.'s generosity, his faith and belief in conservation, and the tax laws of the United States. There was never any expectation or much possibility of profit in making the wilderness of the Grand Tetons accessible to the American people. Yet John D. Rockefeller, Jr., "invested" more than $13 million in the Grand Tetons operation. He could do this by giving the money to the Jackson Hole Preserve, a non-profit corporation, and making it a charitable tax deduction for himself. The Preserve gave the money to its wholly owned subsidiary, the Grand Teton Lodge Company, which built the facilities, the access roads, the bus transportation system and operated all the hotels and services, paying local taxes on its holdings. Profits, if any, were to be returned to the Jackson Hole Preserve for its general conservation purposes.

The Rockefeller operation made the Grand Teton National Park a success from the start—not from a financial point of view but rather as a demonstration of what could be done with love and care and proper planning to make one inaccessible wilderness into a unique and favorite spot in America for those who sought to commune with one of the wonders of nature upon earth. Upon the opening of Jackson Lake Lodge in 1955,

Laurance set forth his philosophy on the subject: "Conservation today means far more than just preserving our national resources. It means their wise use and protection so that more and more people may enjoy and benefit by them."

That year, more than a million people visited the Grand Tetons. In the years ahead the number would double and triple. People would come away from the Grand Tetons renewed in spirit and with an appreciation of this well-managed park, unequaled elsewhere. Laurance, his father and others involved would realize their reward in the satisfaction they derived from a pioneering effort in bringing man and nature together harmoniously. Laurance, who had put together the project through his own rare combination of business acumen and conservation philosophy, always paid tribute to those who helped him, particularly to Horace Albright. With his usual wry sense of a situation, he liked to remark: "Horace is to our projects what yeast is to bread." Then with a pause to allow the meaning to sink in, he would add: "Of course, Father provided the dough."

Laurance never became the "workaholic" that his brother Nelson was but somewhere along the way he discovered—along with all the other Rockefellers—that the best way to circumvent fatigue or boredom from one job was to do another one. There is seldom if ever only one kind of food on a Rockefeller's dish, one task to complete before beginning another. Thus, when the principal planning was begun in 1949 for bringing the human amenities to the winter wilderness of the Grand Tetons, Laurance took his first vacation to the tropical climes of the Caribbean. Island-hopping on his new boat *The Dauntless,* he and his wife "fell in love" with the special combination of white sandy beaches, clear blue water, green foliage and warm, beneficent climate of the Caribbean. Most men, wealthy or not, would have taken their pleasure and departed. But Laurance, being a Rockefeller, conjured another vision: how could he share this sublime experience with others?

It came to him that the thing to do, if possible, was to build a hotel on one of the virtually uninhabited islands and make of it a haven which harmonized with the natural environment, a place where those who shared his love of unspoiled nature could come to seek release from the tensions and turmoil of modern city living. That was the birth of an idea. For the next five years, Laurance and his wife cruised the Caribbean every winter, stopping off and inspecting the great variety of small islands. In all, he visited just about 80 per cent of the hundreds of islands in the Caribbean from Miami to Trinidad, seeking just that "right" place. He did not just stop, look around and leave. He walked and worked with camera in hand, snapping pictures to record the beaches, the tropical vegetation, the coral, the topography, and once back home, he inspected his photographs, his notes, his research, comparing one island against the next, studying the advantages and disadvantages of this place against the next, until gradually in his mind's eye he knew what he wanted. Again, it was a labor of love. Others might say, and they did, that building a small hotel on a remote island would be particularly expensive, impractical and even foolhardy. But by the time Laurance was ready to make his move, he was confident that the joy and pleasure he had found in the Caribbean would attract many other people seeking what he had sought, and they would find their way to his hotel. He meant this to be a profit-making project, not a giveaway. Thus it would have all the attributes of a demonstration of what others could do, if he showed the way. It also uniquely combined what he cared for most, a venture capital enterprise and conservation of a national resource. But equally important, this would be solely a Laurance S. Rockefeller venture, initiated, planned, built and operated by himself with his own money, his own efforts, his own vision. It would be his coming of age.

14

Winthrop

"Carefree, pleasant and meaningless days."

Winthrop was, like Peck's, Rockefeller's bad boy. If there was trouble to get into, he managed to get into it. Through all the years of his growing up, it seemed that getting into trouble was the best way Winthrop could command the attention of his parents. For him, sibling competition always appeared particularly fierce.

Upon his return from the war—World War II, of course—Winthrop went back into the oil business. It seemed appropriate that at least one of the five Rockefeller brothers should carry on in the business so associated with the family name. Winthrop was the logical choice. He had started in at the bottom, working on the digging and drilling crews in the oil fields of Texas, he had worked in the industrial relations department of Standard Oil of New Jersey in Bayonne, and then briefly in sales for the Beacon Oil Company in Massachusetts and then for Socony-Vacuum in New York. And he had been the only one of the five brothers ever to have been actually employed, on a payroll, in the oil business.

In the magazine articles of the day, John D. Rockefeller, Jr., was portrayed as the white-haired, soft-spoken patriarch who had so cleverly divided the great Rockefeller empire, inherited from his father, among his five sons: John 3rd would be the philanthropist, Nelson would go into government, Laurance into the business world of investments, David would be the banker, and Winthrop would inherit the choicest cut of the pie—the Rockefeller oil business. It all seemed so appropriate, so logical. Not only was the Socony-Vacuum Oil Company a direct descendant of his grandfather's original Standard Oil Company, but Winthrop would report to work every day at the old famous address, 26 Broadway, where his father and his grandfather had worked before him. His career future seemed assured and bright—another Rockefeller in the oil business.

That was on the surface. Beneath it all, Winthrop was bitter, unsure of what he himself personally wanted to do with his life. He was bored with the office routine which confronted him on the steps up the executive ladder of the oil business. He had survived a different war than his brothers knew, six long years in the Army infantry, foxholes, mud, deprivation and combat in the Pacific theater. He had a great deal of living to catch up with, he thought. Life in and around the family enclaves at home or in the office seemed a world apart from Winthrop's life away from home. That he was thirty-four and a bachelor made him and his situation different from that of his brothers, all of them so well-married, settled, and raising families of their own. From the outside it might look as though all five Rockefeller brothers were cast in the same mold of heredity and environment, but to Winthrop's mind it often seemed as though there were four Rockefeller brothers and himself. Those pivotal experiences in life, recognized or not at the time, made Winthrop Rockefeller seem like a spare cog on the well-oiled Rockefeller machine. No less love and concern had been lavished upon Winthrop by his parents than upon any of the others. Yet he had never been able to toe the line of his parent's strict Baptist, puritanical upbringing; not as his brothers could, anyway.

At Yale, free for the first time of the strictures of his father and his prep school, Winthrop had fallen in with a group of young men that did, according to his standards at the time, "a fair amount of drinking." It amused them to get Winthrop Rockefeller drunk. It took only three drinks. Then there was one fun-seeking friend who taught Winthrop Rockefeller the pleasures of playing knock rummy. They played for hours and hours. That left little time for studying. At the very start, Winthrop fell so far behind in his studies that he never was able to catch up. Winthrop realized finally that he was just not suited for the academic life, either by desire, temperament or ability. It seemed to him that he was getting very little out of his college studies in proportion to the amount of work he had to put in. It was much more fun dating girls or driving through the back roads of New England with a college buddy and a fat, Falstaffian cab driver who told wild jokes. "They were carefree, pleasant and meaningless days but I knew they could not last," he would say later in retrospect, "and it began to be a question of what would happen first: whether I would quit or flunk out."

But the summer vacations away from Yale were altogether different. At the end of his sophomore year, he went to work as a trainee for Standard Oil of New Jersey, moving from one department to another. When he reached the producing end of the business in the oil fields of Texas, Winthrop found what he had been looking for: men at work with their

John D. Rockefeller 3rd.

With Babs.

Studying at home.

Young man.

With Blanchette, on their honeymoon in Bermuda.

The brothers in 1958, at 5600.

Blanchette Hooker Rockefeller.

John 3rd in his office, with portrait of his grandfather behind him.

Abby Rockefeller Mauzé.

With Brother Winthrop in Little Rock, for his second inauguration as governor of Arkansas, January 14, 1969.

Presenting a population and family planning report to President Johnson on January 7, 1969, with Wilbur J. Cohen, Secretary of Health, Education and Welfare, in the background.

Mr. and Mrs. John 3rd, welcoming Emperor Hirohito and Empress Nagako of Japan to Fieldcrest, their Pocantico Hills home, on October 5, 1975. An interpreter in the middle.

hands and their minds, producing something real, something of value that you could see. He was fascinated. He returned for his junior year at Yale with reluctance. Student life now seemed insignificant and make-believe. He fell hopelessly behind in his studies. Finally, during the Christmas vacation, Winthrop decided he had had it with school. Strangely enough, when he announced his decision, his father was pleased. He said it was good to have one of his sons in the oil business. Winthrop's smoking, drinking and spending of money were left uncommented upon. One young lady's parents in New Haven were obliged to deny vehemently to the press that their daughter had been engaged to Winthrop Rockefeller, who was leaving Yale.

Texas and the oil fields suited this big strapping young man of twenty-two, six-foot-three, with broad heavy shoulders, an open face and a ready smile. His training followed a logical course. Beginning with a geophysics crew and learning something of the preliminary exploration for oil, what to look for, how to test a site, how to use dynamite, he then joined the roustabouts, the day laborers of the oil fields, the men who dig ditches, do the dirty work, repair pipelines. Here Winthrop toughened up, physically and mentally. He soon learned that the roustabouts were a tough, independent crew who took pride in themselves and in their work. Winthrop learned how to lift heavy equipment, how to bend at the knees and get his back into it. More importantly, he learned about the working world outside of the Rockefeller orbit. No one made anything easier for him because of his name. Instead, they tested him and questioned him. What was he doing down there? Was he a company spy? How much money did he have? How many cars? How many brothers? Winthrop explained as best he could and working five days a week in Texas summer heat which often topped 100° he gradually proved himself and was accepted for the man he was. During the week he lived the life of an oil field hand, slept in a boardinghouse, ate with the men, drank beer with them, and after a while he was invited into their homes, little shacks on lease. This was in the depression days of 1935–37 and a new world to Winthrop Rockefeller, one in which a family usually owned only enough knives and forks for their own use; when a guest shared a meal, one member of the family would have to wait until another one finished with his utensils.

On weekends, however, Winthrop would drive into Houston to visit Humble executives and to go to parties or he would take off for a long weekend of hunting or partying at the King Ranch. The men he worked with understood this. In their straightforward manner, they would tell him, "You'd be a damn fool and a hypocrite if you didn't get away when you could." Winthrop grew up in a hurry. He learned about people who were so different from the guests his mother and father invited to their home. From roustabout, he graduated to a "boll weevil," an apprentice driller or roughneck. Here he learned how to take care in handling heavy drilling equipment, how to wield a thirty-pound wrench or a fourteen-pound sledge, how to mix surface mud with foaming mud from beneath the ground. When he was about to leave that crew, the foreman took him aside and said, "You are one of the best goddamn hands I ever had." Winthrop never forgot it, a simple and priceless compliment from one man to another. He became a roughneck, a full-fledged member of a drilling team and still he dug ditches for the foundations for drilling rigs, and he found that he could keep up with the other men, earn their respect and still be Winthrop Rockefeller. In Houston, Texas, he also learned at first hand the difficulties involved in bringing together the black and white races, which would prepare the way for a lifelong interest in the Urban League and civil rights.

Three years in the Texas oil fields passed swiftly and happily. When the time came, however, he returned to New York to spend a year as a trainee in the Chase Manhattan Bank. The idea was for him to learn the financial aspects of the oil business. He moved from department to department within the bank. But after the oil fields, Winthrop felt "bored to death." Halfway through that year, he quit the bank to work full time as the vice-chairman of the Greater New York Fund, one of the first united charity appeals. He helped raise $4 million. After that he went to work for Socony-Vacuum in its Foreign Trade Department. That was more like banking than working in oil production and Winthrop, looking around, decided he had better join the Army and do his part. He was twenty-five and it was January 1941, almost eleven months before Pearl Harbor, but the United States was preparing for war. Winthrop Rockefeller went off with considerable fanfare. Ten reporters walked with him to Pennsylvania Station where he reported for processing. Basic training at Fort Dix was awful, sleeping in pitched tents in freezing cold, mud up to the ankles, and then assignment to a great, old outfit, the 26th Infantry of the 1st Division of the First Army at Fort Devens, Massachusetts. Winthrop Rockefeller was the first draftee accepted into the division and, of course, he was a celebrity. The men there looked him over, questioned him, tested him and finally accepted him for the man he was. This was more like the life he liked in the oil fields. His best friends bore names like Tony Pugliese, Manny Lopresto, Frankie LaScala and Lou Caffaro. Winthrop worked hard at the rigorous training and he played hard too. He treated his new friends to the Stork Club and El Morocco and they met some of Winthrop's other friends with names like Joe E. Brown and Arthur Treacher of the entertainment world. His mother visited him at one of the training camps and, appalled at the lack of entertainment provided for the off hours, arranged to have at her expense automatic phonographs sent anonymously to the Army training camps throughout the United States.

Winthrop fared well in the Army. The discipline was not nearly as severe as his father's, and the physical hardships of training barely rivaled the sweat and strain of working in Texas oil fields. His size and strength made him an equal of any man. He was one of the few privates selected for non-commissioned officers training school and there he excelled as a machine gunner (thanks to his hunting experiences in Texas) and soon after he was made a sergeant he applied and was accepted for officers candidate school. Thus in January 1942, a year after he had enlisted, he emerged as Second Lieutenant Winthrop Rockefeller in Fort Benning, Georgia. He became a machine gun instructor and six months later he was promoted to first lieutenant and transferred to the 305th Infantry Regiment of the famous 77th Division, in Fort Jackson, South Carolina. One of his good friends at Fort Benning, Frank Newell, an insurance broker from Little Rock, Arkansas, was transferred with him to the 77th and they began a close friendship which would last all their lives. Newell, an all-around man of medium build, was an easygoing, savvy and compassionate friend with whom Winthrop could exchange thoughts on all kinds of subjects from women, family and pastimes to the meaning of life, personal values and hopes for the future. The 77th Division was one of the most decorated in the whole Army since it had won fame and glory on the battlefields of the First World War. Now the three thousand men of the 77th were in training for island assaults in the Pacific and it was, in the words of that day, a gung-ho outfit. Winthrop was the commander of H Company; Frank Newell, a second lieutenant then, was his executive officer. Abby Aldrich Rockefeller knitted socks and scarves for her son's company and his men wrote nice thank-you letters in return. Unbeknown to Winthrop, the commanding general of the First Army, Lieutenant General H. A. Drum, was keeping Win's father informed of his progress in the Army. The main point of interest seemed to be, as the general said in one of his letters, that Winthrop Rockefeller "neither asks for nor receives any special consideration or favors."

Winthrop did take a forty-eight-hour pass in August of 1943 to stand by his sister when she set up residence in Reno, Nevada, to divorce her husband of eighteen years, David Milton. Babs, although she was approaching forty years of age, never before had traveled anywhere alone, away from the family's protection. When she had arrived in Reno at three o'clock in the morning, she had been shocked and distressed to have been met at the train station by a swarm of inquiring newspapermen. Winthrop had committed himself to driving more than a thousand miles just to be with her for less than twenty-four hours. It was a crazy, illogical and wasteful thing to do, and she loved him, her kid brother, for it. They reminisced over the family and old times and the hard times involved in being a Rockefeller. Babs recalled the demands and expectations of the family and said she personally was "delighted not to carry the name of Rockefeller." All she ever had wanted was a good home life and her own friends and while she was perfectly happy to help people on a personal basis, she had no ambitions to go out and try to save the world. In explaining the reasons behind this, the first divorce in the immediate family, Babs confided that her husband had always been kind and good and considerate. But, she said, he had become an addicted traveler, a compulsive gambler, not in cards but in investments and buying and selling companies. He seemed determined to prove that he could make as much money as the Rockefellers, but he never stayed long enough with any one investment. Babs complained that not only were there times she would not see him for weeks on end but she just never knew when he would be home or away. "It had nothing to do with another woman," she told Winthrop.

It was a warm, good, family visit, long remembered by both of them. Babs recalled a lonely childhood, surrounded by walls and high gates and watchmen everywhere, and so few friends. Winthrop reminded her how she used to kid her younger brothers for not being big enough to take her out when she needed an escort. They marveled at how the war had dispersed them all. Winthrop also offered now to pay her back for a "lifesaving" loan she had made to him when he was desperately short of money at Yale. He did not quite remember the amount. "Oh, the money is not the important thing, Win," she said. "Why don't you give me a present instead, when you can get around to it?" Winthrop had a cigarette case made for her, bearing emblems of the armed services.

Winthrop left for overseas a few months later, promoted to the rank of major, the senior supply officer of his regiment, the 305th Infantry Regiment of the 77th Division, First Army. His first assault landing was at Guam, where he was credited with saving the life of a drowning soldier. Later, in the Battle of Leyte, in the Philippines, the 77th landed behind enemy lines and fought in a three-month-long struggle to win back the island from the Japanese. Living and surviving those three months along with the men of his regiment in the mud of the Philippine jungles under combat conditions, sleeping in a foxhole, eating K rations, itched by jungle rot brought about the low point in Winthrop's morale. All the bitterness of the G.I. Joe of the infantry beset him: the men of the Navy and of the Air Force seemed to have it so much easier; the Seabees (or construction battalions of the Navy) worked alongside the infantrymen only to build beach installations and then the Seabees went back to their clean ships and good food while the infantrymen had to slough on through the jungle, tearing down and building and fighting all the way. Winthrop also had time for bitter feelings toward his brothers' war efforts: Nelson had a desk job in Washington and was making a name for himself as a bureaucrat; John 3rd and Laurance were in the Navy but had less time at sea than Winthrop; David was in North Africa in intelligence, away from combat, and, according to a recent letter, was complaining about a house boy who deserted him and left his billet dirty, while Winthrop was half covered with mud and bugs in a God-forsaken Philippine jungle. The old sibling rivalry and bitterness rose like bile in his thoughts and then, when his morale was low, the chance to leave all this behind him arrived in the mail.

A friend at Socony-Vacuum wrote that a position was open which Winthrop could easily fill. Would he be interested in becoming the assistant coordinator of petroleum distribution, stationed in London? It was severely tempting, a quasi-civilian administrator position with enough priority to pull him out of the Army and back into the oil business. Winthrop pondered the question, confided in no one around him and then wrote to his father for advice. His father himself surveyed at least ten advisers and responded with a long, detailed letter on the pros and cons and, as usual, left the decision to his son. Winthrop was sorely tempted. A long list of arguments could substantiate reasons enough for taking the oil job. He was now Major Rock, well-known and well-liked throughout the division, but he was not indispensable. Then there was the potential for the making of his future career in the oil business. But the old puritan code, the old family sense of duty, dictated that a Rockefeller does not capitalize on his name, does not take the easy way out. Winthrop stayed.

Ironically, if the Rockefeller family puritanism had been as strong in Winthrop as it was in some of his brothers, he probably would have lost his life in the next engagement of the 77th during the invasion of Okinawa. The division was fighting on Kerama Retto Island immediately south of Okinawa, using the troop transport ship *Henrico* as its command post. On April 2, 1945, a meeting was called for 7 P.M. for the command of the 305th Combat Group in the ship's dining room. But Major Rockefeller did not attend; he was involved in a poker game in the officer's ward room, one deck down. That saved his life. At seven-fifteen a Japanese kamikaze crashed his plane into the ship's bridge. One of its two five-hundred-pound bombs fell through to the dining room and exploded. Every one of the senior officers of the regiment was killed, the commander, the executive officer, the adjutant, the intelligence officer and the plans and operations officer. Seventy-five men aboard the ship were killed, 150 wounded. Winthrop Rockefeller survived at the poker table, with flash burns of the hands and face. He became, in fact, the senior staff Army officer left alive aboard the ship, one month short of his thirty-third birthday. After six weeks' hospitalization at Guam, he returned to duty with his division, this time in the intelligence unit behind the front lines and this time without the sweeping, handle-bar mustache he had cultivated overseas. Not long afterward, Winthrop came down with a severe case of infectious hepatitis and at the war's end he was flown back to a hospital in San Francisco, where there were some fears for his survival.

Three months recuperating, most of them flat on his back, gave Winthrop ample time to take bearings and to think of what he wanted to do next. At the same time he became intrigued with the problems of all veterans readjusting to civilian life after the long war. When his own doctor advised that he should not try to undertake a full-time job himself for at least a year because of the hepatitis, Winthrop decided he could best use that time to help other returning veterans. He proposed to an old family friend, Anna Rosenberg, who was then Under Secretary of War, that he would like to survey veterans' readjustment problems, at his own expense. Approval came while he was still in the hospital from Secretary of War Robert P. Patterson. Winthrop recruited an old prewar sidekick and friend, Jimmy Hudson, who had been a private detective in Harlem, and together, after Winthrop was released from the hospital, they toured the United States, covering some seventeen thousand miles in six months, asking questions, seeking advice and conferring with civic leaders. Winthrop at the time was a lieutenant colonel still in uniform; Jimmy Hudson was a black man, slim and slight of build, who had served in the Coast Guard, soft-spoken and sophisticated. At the heart of Winthrop's survey report was the rather innovative recommendation that draft boards in reverse be established in cities and communities across the nation, staffed on a voluntary basis by civic leaders, and designed to help returning veterans find appropriate jobs, careers or educational outlets. The report reached the desk of the President and Harry Truman, immediately aware of the potential political windfalls, suggested that he would endorse the plan if he could appoint the director to implement it. Winthrop, who was asked to help set it up presumably at his own expense and then step aside, declined, and his report, never made public, died on the shelf along with so many other proposals on veterans' problems.

Leaving the Army in October 1946, with his Purple Heart and Bronze Star medals and his commission as a lieutenant colonel in the reserves, Winthrop still did not have a clear idea of what he really wanted to do next. Jimmy Hudson was on his payroll and he tried to persuade his friend Frank Newell to stay in New York and to become his associate in whatever Rockefeller activities he undertook. Winthrop explained to his friend the Rockefeller concept of multipliers, men who worked with rather than for one of the brothers, men who could help formulate policy and act for a Rockefeller, and thus spread the influence. On the more practical level, Winthrop pointed out that opportunities would be virtually limitless for Frank Newell: the family did not have an insurance man in its entourage but it did own a large share of the Merchants Fire Assurance Corporation of New York.

Newell heard him out and with a smile, drawled, "There's no way, Win. I'll see you living in Arkansas long before you ever see me working in New York." The two friends had long ago swapped life stories and intimacies and while Frank Newell had listened to the rich life of the Rockefellers, he had insisted that the easygoing, straightforward, close-to-the-earth life of Arkansas was far superior for a man than the smooth, sweet-talking, superficial life of city slickers you found in New York. When they had talked back in their Army days, Frank Newell had already sung the praise of his favorite spot on earth: the top of Petit Jean Mountain, some sixty miles northwest of Little Rock, where a man could be alone and happy, close to the earth, the cedar trees and the sky . . . That's what Frank Newell was going to do with his life, go back to Arkansas, work in Little Rock, take vacations on Petit Jean Mountain, maybe get married, maybe not, hunt, fish, enjoy life . . . But he would keep in touch always. They were friends . . .

Winthrop himself went back to work at Socony-Vacuum with less than burning enthusiasm. His future seemed to lie in finding some niche in the oil business and yet, while he had enjoyed learning about the actual production of oil, the upper echelons of business seemed to involve pushing papers, not disturbing the hierarchy and keeping nine-to-five hours. On the basis of his experience in dealing with men in the Army and oil fields, Winthrop was assigned to the industrial relations department of the foreign production division of Socony-Vacuum. He headed a task force on formulating employee relations policy. But here again he found himself working more with reports, memos and papers than with people. It was not inspiring. Winthrop involved himself in some of the family's activities. He became active once again in the National Urban League, which his father had supported since 1921 and which Winthrop had joined in 1940. He put in even more time in the family's efforts to help raise money for a new medical school for New York University which was planned to be merged with Bellevue Hospital, then be renovated and rebuilt by the city of New York. Winthrop's father and two brothers, John 3rd and Laurance, also worked and contributed in the highly successful campaign which established the NYU-Bellevue Medical Center, a teaching and research hospital considered one of the finest in the world. When a new board of trustees was selected for the medical center, Winthrop represented the Rockefeller family on it and soon afterward, in January 1949, was elected chairman.

Winthrop put in his eight hours a day at Socony-Vacuum but they were far overshadowed by the longer, or at least more exciting, hours he spent as a tall, dark, handsome and rich bachelor in the night spots of New York City. He was the prize catch of every gossip columnist as well as of every young lady for whom he bought dinner or a drink. In those years immediately after the end of World War II, Winthrop Rockefeller moved with ease into the whirl and maelstrom of what was known then as the "cafe society" crowd. They were the "beautiful people" of that era, the forerunners of the next generation's "jet set." They had the money, the time and the inclination to spend their evening, night and early morning hours with one another in New York's most famous and expensive night spots, El Morocco, 21, the Stork Club, Toots Shor, the Copacabana. Each of these establishments paid its own press agents to entice customers by publicizing the famous people who could be seen there. There was hardly a better name for that purpose than that of a Rockefeller. Winthrop thoroughly enjoyed the night life: he liked the conviviality of drinking, meeting people in the entertainment world, going to and giving cocktail and dinner parties. Nor did he much mind being mentioned in the press for winning a dance contest with Mary Martin or being seen with Ginger Rogers, Joan Blondell, Ginny Sims of the Kay Kaiser Band or a lesser-known movie starlet still aspiring to fame. When his name was linked in the gossip columns with one or another young lady, Winthrop would reassure his parents, particularly his mother, with a laugh and a caveat not to take such press notices seriously. Most of them were grossly exaggerated and others were complete fabrications. His mother, in her letters to him, put it down to "finding yourself" and wrote of her pleasure over her son's "having so many friends." His father said nothing, never mentioning Winthrop's night life in any of their correspondence. Winthrop was well aware of his father's strong antipathy toward liquor, smoking and, by Rockefeller family standards, profligate living. And his father knew that he knew. Obviously, Winthrop was too old now to be chastised or treated like a child. Both his mother and father accepted the situation and continued to give him support and affection, which apparently they believed he needed. As for Winthrop himself, he thought he was living no differently than a great number of other men and women in similar circumstances, albeit beyond the approved style of his puritanical family. "After all," he would explain in later years, "I was a bachelor in my thirties, with six years in the Army to make up, so what did they expect!" As the gossip column items continued to appear, reporting Winthrop Rockefeller at this night spot or that Broadway opening, or romantically involved with a Hollywood actress or a big-band singer, Winthrop secretly enjoyed the thought that his whole family, from his father down through his four married brothers, "all were living vicariously through Brother Win's exploits."

Winthrop also delighted in the knowledge that the gossip columnists, with all their snooping and speculation, never latched onto the object of his most serious romantic interest. She was a positively beautiful young woman, the prototype of classic American beauty, with light blond hair, a peaches and cream complexion and the look of fresh innocence. They had met, soon after Winthrop left the Army, at a dinner party given by Liz (Mary Elizabeth) Whitney, the former wife of John Hay (Jock) Whitney, publisher of the N.Y. *Herald Tribune* and scion of a communications conglomerate. Winthrop was soon stricken. She went by the name of Barbara Sears, although everyone called her Bobo, and, at the time, she was married, but estranged from her husband, a socially prominent Bostonian named Richard Sears, Jr., who was in the diplomatic service and stationed in Paris. She was perhaps more of a guest than a member in the cafe society crowd but she was always welcome and popular at the parties and goings-on of the rich: she had beauty, wit and savoir-faire. Winthrop began to date her casually and then more and more steadily. Bobo lived in a fourth-floor walk-up apartment on unfashionable Third Avenue, facing the ever rumbling Third Avenue El (elevated trains), but her apartment was lavishly furnished and rent-free, since her husband owned the building. Winthrop was often seen arriving at the building in a long black limousine, driven by a chauffeur (Jimmy Hudson), although no one on that block of antique and pawn shops and neighborhood saloons recognized a Rockefeller when he saw one. Winthrop and Bobo for the most part avoided the more popular night spots when out together in favor of quiet restaurants, the theater and private parties. Thus, beyond their own circle of friends their romance went largely unnoticed for a good eighteen months until February 1948, when Winthrop Rockefeller popped the question. Bobo had obtained her divorce, ending her seven-year marriage, two months earlier in Nevada and then had flown to Palm Springs, Florida, for a winter visit in the home of Winston Guest, the socialite whose name has become forever linked with polo ponies.

When they decided to marry, they also decided to do it right away. They set the wedding for one minute after midnight three days later, February 14, to comply with Florida's seventy-two-hour waiting period. Winthrop informed his parents, who were vacationing in Tucson, Arizona, and phoned his brother Laurance in New York, asking him to hurry down to stand in as his best man. Bobo's sister, Isabel, was already there, ready to be maid of honor. Nelson also arrived in time for the wedding. The Guests hurriedly telephoned invitations to fifty of Palm Beach's most noted winter residents, including the Duke and Duchess of Windsor, Woolworth Donahue, Mrs. Hudson Vanderbilt and society's restaurateur "Prince" Mike Romanoff. To accommodate the time schedule the reception was held before the ceremony so the couple could be married on the first minute of the third day. It was all very well planned. What they did not realize was that all marriage licenses were posted publicly in the local courthouse and the editor of the weekly Okeechobee News checked the list every day. His story on the AP wire reached across the country and made news. The press descended upon the scene. The tabloids headlined the story. The society editors loved it and the gossip columnists had a field day of inaccuracies. It was hailed as a modern Cinderella story: Winthrop Rockefeller was cast as the Prince Charming, heir to oil millions, and Barbara Sears was of course the Cinderella. The newsmen found out she was born Jievute Paulekiute of Lithuanian immigrants in a coal patch near Noblestown, Pennsylvania, and raised in near poverty close to the stockyards of Chicago. But then at the 1933 Chicago World's Fair, at seventeen, she had won a beauty contest and emerged as Miss Lithuania. She had become a model, posing for pictures in the Montgomery Ward catalogue, then an actress in summer stock, then a show girl; then marriage followed to a proper Bostonian, and then bit parts in movie Westerns, and then . . . marriage in Palm Beach to the most eligible, richest, most sought-after bachelor in America. Cinderella. The newspapers and presumably their readers loved it. It was not, of course, the kind of marriage or hoop-la the Rockefeller family cherished. Parents of the bride and groom, who did not attend the wedding, nevertheless expressed their pleasure over the marriage to the press. Julius Paulekiute, still a coal miner at sixty, divorced from Bobo's mother since Bobo was a small child, told reporters, "I am happy my little daughter is now a millionaire. I am poor, will be poor, and will die poor." The wedding made quite a story in its day.

In the more quiet aftermath, when the happy couple returned to New York from their honeymoon, Winthrop took his bride around the family circuit, introducing her to the more staid Rockefeller clan. His brothers and their wives made sincere efforts to welcome Bobo Rockefeller into their closed circle. In a way, they were also trying to welcome Brother Win back also; everyone was more or less aware that Winthrop, bitter over past sibling rivalry, had strayed from the flock. His father, still vacationing in Tucson, wrote him a month after the marriage, "I hope you are beginning to get back into a more unperturbed life and that the joy of your new relationship may in every way enhance the meaning and worthwhileness of each day."

Mr. and Mrs. Rockefeller returned from their annual winter vacation on April 2, a Friday, and immediately arranged for a weekend family reunion at Pocantico Hills. Five sons, one daughter, eighteen grandchildren plus the in-laws gathered for lunch that Saturday. The big house, inherited from John D. Rockefeller, Sr., was filled with spring flowers, good talk, reminiscences, future plans and activity. The young fourth generation of Rockefellers clearly predominated. It was a thoroughly happy weekend and driving back to New York Sunday evening, with David in the car and her youngest grandchild on her lap, Mrs. Rockefeller insisted upon stopping off to meet her newest daughter-in-law. Bobo, who had felt not well, had not joined the weekend family reunion, but she was pleased to be welcomed so warmly into the family by Mrs. Rockefeller and, of course, Mr. Rockefeller. It was a pleasant, gracious meeting of two women who loved Winthrop Rockefeller, and it was their last.

Mrs. Abby Aldrich Rockefeller died early the next morning of a heart attack. She was seventy-four and had suffered from high blood pressure but she had never been truly sick. The annual winter vacations in Tucson were designed over concern for John D. Rockefeller, Jr.'s precarious health. Of the same age as his wife, he suffered for years from asthma, emphysema and excruciating headaches. Her death, so unexpected, shocked and shook the family. Winthrop depended upon her, David and Nelson adored her, Laurance and John 3rd loved her as well, and John Jr., entered into a limbo of loneliness so intense that many feared for his own well-being. They had been married for forty-seven years. She had provided, all of her children came to realize, the adhesive of love, joy of life and optimism which bound that family together. As adults, the five sons and daughter recognized that it had been their mother who had leavened and enabled them to accept without outright rebellion the perfectionist and often rigid standards of their father. The same warmth, love and sentiment toward his family were within him but his own puritanical upbringing inhibited him from voicing aloud such sentiments. More often he took to writing. Mrs. Rockefeller was cremated on the day of her death and then virtually by demand, as more than two thousand letters and telegrams of sympathy reached the family, a memorial service was held a month later at Riverside Church. Her ashes were interred still another month later and that scene John D. Rockefeller, Jr., put down on paper in a private memorandum:

"On Sunday morning, June 20, 1948, with the early rays of the sun slanting through the surrounding forest and the dewdrops still sparkling on the ground, her ashes were mingled with the earth in the little, private burial place which is part of our Tarrytown home. There at least a half dozen years ago, Mrs. Rockefeller and I had caused to be designed and erected two simple headstones, complete except for the final date, set up side by side under great oak trees in the natural woods with hemlock, dogwood, rhododendron, laurel and all sorts of native things growing about, the ground in front of the headstones being carpeted with myrtle. Often Mrs. Rockefeller and I visited this spot during the war and not infrequently remarked how lovely a place it was in which to remain.

"Without disturbing the ground and the beautiful growth around the headstones, the boys and I ourselves mingled her ashes with the earth, with the children and grandchildren in goodly number standing about. A lifelong, minister friend of the family said a simple prayer and was the only one outside of the family present. There were no tears shed for we all felt that the dear wife, mother and grandmother, although invisible, was a member of the group that gathered there and we talked of her simply, frankly, naturally, as though she were present with us.

"Presents still go to the grandchildren from their grandmother as heretofore and they often say that they will thank her in their prayers."

Winthrop and Bobo's marriage simply was not a success. Cinderella marriages, however romantic and thrilling, seldom are. While his brothers and sister had chosen spouses of or nearly of the same background, upbringing and temperament as themselves, Winthrop and Bobo discovered they had none of those psychological foundations to their union. Winthrop, as a married man, learned of one incompatibility heaped upon another. Physical attraction was not enough for the long-term investment required of wedlock. They both tried. For a while, the birth of Winthrop Paul Rockefeller on September 17, 1948, helped smooth out the rough spots in their marriage, but soon afterward their differences, their verbal spats, their disputes over fundamentals caused them both despair. Winthrop took more frequent trips abroad on behalf of Socony-Vacuum, to Europe, to South America, and he did not take Bobo with him. The Rockefeller family tried to accept Bobo but she and the other wives seemed to be on different wave lengths, or at least she felt so. David and Peggy, who also had once won a dance contest, were the closest in trying to make Bobo feel part of the family. They at least enjoyed going dancing together. The Marcel Breuer model modern home, exhibited at the Museum of Modern Art garden to show Americans a type of home they could expect in the future, was disassembled after the exhibit and moved to the Pocantico Hills estate for Bobo and Winthrop. But in comparison with the other homes there, the Breuer house with its plain, squared-off rooms seemed so obviously temporary. It became increasingly obvious too as time went on that the marriage would not last.

While those close to the couple could see some signs of the disintegration of the marriage, within the privacy of their relationship things were even worse. Both Winthrop and Bobo had violent tempers and they and their tempers often clashed. Both sought relief in alcohol and their marital fights became even more tempestuous and emotionally wrenching. Finally, eighteen months after their Palm Beach wedding, Winthrop Rockefeller locked his wife out of their large Park Avenue duplex. It was his desperate manner of obtaining a separation. The gossip columnists had a field day.

Philosophically, their story was as old as history and as common as the perhaps one-third of all the marriages in America that ended in divorce. The single element which made it different and newsworthy was that one of the parties to this domestic malaise was Winthrop Rockefeller, still an heir to oil millions. The wife still loved the husband and he no longer loved her; he wanted out, a divorce, a chance to start over again; she wanted to keep him for herself and their son, and the more he wanted his freedom, the more possessive she became. He felt he was being torn apart by the fights, the squabbling, the tensions and the emotional drain. She felt hurt and was hurting back. From a bad situation it grew worse. Money was not involved, not at least in the beginning. But it dragged on for five torturous years, by which time Bobo Sears Rockefeller, the poor miner's daughter, let it be known that if her husband wanted a divorce he would have to pay for it: she wanted $10 million. The style in which the wife had been accustomed to live was at the time the legal yardstick for divorce settlements and the lawyers for both sides fought their battles. Ultimately, which covers a lot of ground, they reached a divorce settlement, said to be worth more than $6 million, the largest on record in any court.

Winthrop flew into Reno, Nevada, where Bobo had established legal residence for the divorce, and signed the settlement agreement without seeing his wife. She signed in one room of a hotel and he signed in another and left quickly. "I frankly don't believe in revealing marriage settlements," Bobo told reporters. "Mine is one of the few privacies I have left." Reporters nevertheless dug up the details: $2 million in cash; $3.5 million in two trust funds, one for Bobo and one for Winthrop Paul, then five years old; $100,000 to pay bills; and Bobo's choice of $500,000 outright or $70,000 a year for life. Bobo chose the lump sum. She also got the Park Avenue apartment and custody; he was given the right to have Winthrop Paul with him for holidays and vacations. And he had his freedom.

A full year before he had gained his legal freedom from Bobo, Winthrop also called it quits with New York City. It finally had dawned upon him that he was not a New Yorker in the sense that his brothers were. They had lived all their lives in and around New York City and they functioned well in that special environment. But Winthrop had spent his adult life away from New York: three years at Yale, three in the oil fields of Texas and six in the Army. The four years in New York after the Army, from ages thirty-seven to forty-one, had been a bust, in his own estimation, and he had little to show for it. The pace in New York had been too fast, too cosmopolitan, too artificial. The true friends he had made in New York he could always visit; the hangers-on, the borrowers, the sycophants he would be only too happy to cut off. And, at the time, he was still not free from Bobo. All these considerations flowed through Winthrop's thoughts as he made up his mind to start over, to take his friend Frank Newell at his promise and to lead a life close to the soil in Arkansas and more particularly atop Petit Jean Mountain, sixty miles northwest of Little Rock, where a man could commune with nature and with his God. Arkansas also offered more liberal divorce laws than New York, and that at the time was a special consideration not to be overlooked. Winthrop wanted distance between himself and his wife and the life they had led together.

The Rockefellers rallied around him. Despite the chagrin and embarrassment of the publicity over his marital difficulties, the tabloid stories and the gossip columns, each of his brothers and his father as well tried as best they could to convince Winthrop that they believed in him, loved him and would stand behind him. Perhaps the most overt gesture was their convincing Win that the family wanted him to take over the family's responsibility to Colonial Williamsburg. The reconstruction of the colonial city at a cost of $60 million had been the very first venture his father had undertaken on his own, not in the name of John D. Rockefeller, Sr., and it had been, perhaps sentimentally, his most cherished philanthropy. Then when he turned sixty-five, he had handed it over to John 3rd in 1939 and John 3rd had gradually changed Colonial Williamsburg from what had been essentially a city-sized museum into an educational force sending its messages across the country. John 3rd also had begun to breach the racial segregation of the reconstructed colonial city, which still was part of the state of Virginia. He did it in his own quiet way, without public announcement or argument, simply by having all the "Colored Only" signs removed from all drinking fountains, rest-room facilities and the like. Then in 1953, just before Win was to move to Arkansas, John 3rd, with his father's approval, turned over the chairmanship of Colonial Williamsburg to Winthrop. And that was duly announced in the newspapers, saying in effect that Winthrop Rockefeller was still a member in good standing in the Rockefeller family.

In Arkansas, Winthrop Rockefeller was welcomed wholeheartedly by the Establishment there. For the second poorest state in the union with average per capita income at $900 a year, Winthrop Rockefeller was an entirely new entity, a new natural resource. For Winthrop, personally, it was a chance to start all over again.

15

David

"I sometimes think he's got electricity in his head."

Of the five Rockefeller brothers, only David had brown eyes, a Ph.D. and a steady job. The brown eyes he inherited along with his name and wealth, but the Ph.D. in economics he *earned* from the University of Chicago after studying at Harvard and at the London School of Economics.

As for the job, he went to work for the Chase National Bank in 1946 upon his return from Army service in the Second World War. He was the first one in his family to do such a thing—enter the jungle of business competition—since his grandfather went to work for Hewitt & Tuttle ninety years earlier as an assistant bookkeeper. The circumstances, of course, were not quite the same. David's uncle, Winthrop Aldrich, was chairman of the board, the Rockefellers were one of America's wealthiest families and Chase was known in business circles as a Rockefeller bank. Nevertheless, David did start at the bottom of the executive ladder as one of many assistant managers. After two years in the European division, he was assigned to the Latin American section of the bank's Foreign Department because his brother Nelson was a well-known man south of the border.

At the bank's headquarters office in the financial section of lower Manhattan, David was generally accepted without much resentment. He appeared to be a genial young man of thirty, usually smiling and easy to get along with. He asked no favors and pulled no rank in the staid nine-to-five routine of a day's work. Besides, no one could guess how long he was likely to stay. The other Rockefeller boys—Nelson, Laurance and

Winthrop—had been in and out of Chase in fairly short order. It was understood that by working in the bank the young Rockefellers would gain the basic training in banking, finance and economics they needed as future millionaires. What outsiders did not know was that John D. Rockefeller, Jr., had truly hoped that at least one of his sons would take up banking as a career. Each of them, however, before David's turn came up, had reacted quite negatively to the staid and slow-moving atmosphere of banking in general and the Chase Bank in particular. Each of them coveted the freedom to do his own thing.

David saw things differently. In contemplating his own future, even while at Harvard, he decided that with his life he wanted to test himself in a discipline imposed by others and beyond his own control. He did not want to be taken as a dilettante. One reason he had gone on to the London School of Economics and then to the University of Chicago for his doctorate was precisely that: he wanted to test himself in the work required for a doctorate degree in economics and having earned the highest degree in the academic market place to prove that "there was something there besides a famous family name." His doctoral thesis, *Unused Resources and Economic Waste,* 260 pages of tightly written analyses of waste in business, industry, banking, monopolies, political institutions and natural resources, was published in 1941. The avoidance of waste became a dictum of conduct for him personally the rest of his life.

When the time came for wartime service, he decided to test himself in the United States Army. In May 1942, five months after Pearl Harbor, he enlisted as a buck private. He wanted to see what the hierarchy of the Army would do with him. By that time he had worked a year as an aide to New York's feisty Mayor Fiorello H. La Guardia and another year as assistant regional director of the U. S. Office of Defense, Health and Welfare Service in New York. Surely, he knew that he could have gone in as a commissioned officer or he could have had an office job in Washington for the asking. As a raw recruit, after some rigorous basic training under a memorably tough drill sergeant, David Rockefeller found himself shuffling papers as a clerk at First Army Headquarters on Governor's Island in New York, and for a while, when the Army discovered his boyhood training, he tended a general's horse. But finally, shortly before his company was to go overseas, he was posted to an officers training school in the engineers corps in Virginia, only to be plucked out of there and sent to the Army's intelligence corps school. When the Army discovered that David Rockefeller had been tutored in French as well as in handling horses, he was sent as a second lieutenant in intelligence to North Africa, where he worked with Free French forces. On the basis of that work and the valuable contacts he made, David was posted to Paris as the assistant military attaché to Major General Ralph S. Smith, a veteran officer with career ties to the French. Eight junior officers served under General Smith. The experience for young David Rockefeller was invaluable. It sparked a lifelong interest in foreign affairs. The military attaché's office in Paris, set up in a large rented mansion on the Boulevard St. Germain, served as a de facto American embassy in the critical interim between V-E Day and the arrival of an American ambassador to the new French postwar government. Many of the Free French officers whom David had met in North Africa were becoming key figures in the new French government and the military attaché's office became a sensitive listening post in France and for most of Western Europe. Most of the listening was done at breakfasts, lunches and dinners hosted by David Rockefeller at the tender age of thirty. But with that famous name, he flourished in the atmosphere of cordial diplomacy in which views and information were exchanged on politics, economics and military affairs. Thus, by the end of his two-year military career, he found himself more than competent and successful in a position which ordinarily would be held by a man far more experienced than he was at the time. He lacked no self-confidence as he returned home and turned his attention to family affairs and the Chase Bank.

The work load at the bank was well within the capabilities of this young, experienced, well-educated, well-fixed and efficiency-minded Rockefeller. The first six weeks at the bank he spent rotating around each section of the Foreign Department. It was supposed to be a get-acquainted orientation. But David made notes on what each section was supposed to do and later analyzed the work loads and the organizational structure within the department. He discovered there was virtually no such organizational chart in existence at Chase. The Foreign Department had far too many small units reporting directly to the head of the department. So David carefully wrote a short analysis of each section, drew up an organization chart which structured the department and presented his report to Sherrill Smith, the head of the department. That venerable gentleman took the report, politely thanked David Rockefeller for his efforts, put the report in the bottom drawer of his desk and never mentioned it again.

As an economist and as a Rockefeller trained by his father, David was punctilious in keeping his own accounts on all his activities, in measuring out the time he spent on each of the projects assigned to him by the bank and by his family and in writing out for himself projections of self-imposed goals. As soon as he settled in at the Latin American section of the bank, he vowed to himself to handle personally all the operating tasks assigned to him rather than delegate work. He also decided, after his experience with the organizational chart, never again to make recommendations beyond his own small sphere of responsibility. Knowing that many higher-ups in the bank were keeping their eyes upon him, he certainly did not want to appear to be a brash young man.

Because he was careful not to ask any special favors of anyone, his personal secretary, Eleanor Wilkerson, hired in 1947 to handle his family-connected work, did not have a desk, chair or typewriter to call her own at the bank. She carried work from 5600 at Rockefeller Center to the bank downtown and borrowed the desk and typewriter of any secretary who was absent that day. She wouldn't ask her boss for accommodations and he would not ask her. After a year of carrying David's personal stationery and other papers back and forth each day, she asked for a drawer to call her own. At David's request, the bank supplied an old desk and chair and an obsolete surplus typewriter for Miss Wilkerson. Promoted in 1948 to second vice-president, David was given a large desk near a window. Now he rated a bank secretary at a small desk facing him.

David got along remarkably well with his fellow junior executives. He was a calming influence in the department, where Latin tempers frequently flared. His soft-spoken arguments usually carried great weight with opposing forces. He had the quality of listening to the other fellow, hearing him out and then giving his own usually carefully considered opinion. His manner was the same in dealing with bankers and businessmen in Latin America. The underlying quality in this facet of his personality was that he liked people and was genuinely interested in what others could tell him. It was a quality he shared with his brother Nelson and one which served him well throughout his life. Others marveled at it. "David could listen to a bore go on and on explaining something which was obvious to everyone listening and still give that bore his whole undivided attention because he just might say something which David would not know," explained one business associate years later. "David has an all-encompassing sense of curiosity and interest in anything that might be new to him. I suppose you might say he is the eternal optimist."

In combination with liking people, David Rockefeller liked hard work. He was a fundamentalist in believing that work creates happiness. Long hours did not bother him, niggling details became fascinating if you delved deep enough, everything became personally interesting if you devoted enough time to it. Such were his beliefs. He also possessed the iron constitution and willingness to outwork anyone around him. His secret was that he enjoyed doing what others would consider beneath them, for he had discovered that the business of banking was simply fascinating in its detail. It caused little surprise and no apparent resentment when in February 1950, less than five years from when he started at the bank, David Rockefeller was promoted to vice-president in charge of the Latin American section of the bank's Foreign Department. It was sensed in his department that he had earned his promotion, that he had learned and mastered the intricacies of Latin American banking. More important, he had made many friends in the department and several men senior to him went out of their way to be helpful. There were indeed disputes over policies and programs, cross words were not unusual during the working day, but on many evenings the officers of the Latin Department went out for a convivial dinner with David Rockefeller. *Simpático* was an important asset in the banking business in Latin America and David worked at it then, as he did ever after. He was gifted, men around him found out, with a sensitivity to the moods and unspoken attitudes of those around him. It served him well.

He found he enjoyed the travel involved in supervising Chase's business in Latin America, he was fascinated with the business problems of American companies expanding to Latin America, he was intrigued with learning the Latin point of view on problems of that area, and the pace of everyday life quickened. Under his aegis and with his careful prodding, Chase opened three new branch banks in Latin America. Before each was approved, David had to demonstrate the need of a new bank, the projection of estimated new business for the bank and the value of aiding economic expansion south of the border. In the staid old bank, David Rockefeller began to make waves. They were, to be sure, moderate ripples in the over-all operations of the second largest bank in the nation. Nevertheless, they did not go unnoticed.

David also proposed a bank publication on business in Latin America and over considerable opposition his idea prevailed. He arranged for a friend, William Butler, an economist who worked for the family at 5600, to devote half-time at the bank and half-time at the Rockefeller office, to edit the Latin American monthly newsletter, called *Latin American Business Highlights*. While the publication was opposed as a non-money-making frill, David pushed the idea of the importance of good public relations for the bank overseas. By the end of its first year, David's innovation was a smashing success. The business community in Latin America looked forward to receiving it, talked about it and admired it. Eighteen months after it began, Chase established a domestic publication of the same sort called *Business in Brief*, and still later, it started up an international magazine, *World Business*, which lasted until 1970.

In late 1951, David took on the responsibility of heading a small group of low-echelon officers of the bank to work on planning and development. The Chase Bank, the largest "wholesale" or correspondent bank in the nation, at the time was in fact running downhill with a management which was fairly antiquated. Not only did its Foreign Department not have an organizational chart, the whole bank did not have a budget for its own internal operations. Uncle Winthrop, who had been chairman of the bank since 1933, was in fact not a banker, but a lawyer who had served as counsel and then president of Equitable Trust Company before it merged with Chase. His major efforts were in policy matters, leaving the actual business of banking to hired hands. The Chase Bank flourished from the depression years to the start of the Second World War, taking its deposits almost wholly from other banks and from large corporations. In turn, it had been second to none in handling lines of credit for other banks and issuing loans in the tens of millions of dollars to the nation's largest corporations. But in the business boom which followed the end of the war, with the tremendous expansion of U.S. business overseas, and with the dynamic upsurge in the American economy and more money in the pockets of wage earners, the Chase Bank found itself falling woefully behind the expansion efforts of other banks. Particularly, Chase's arch-rival, the National City Bank, had surged ahead in setting up branch offices all over Manhattan to attract the so-called "middle millions" of small depositors, and at the same time it was widening its lead in international banking.

While David's small group was working on structural and internal reorganization of Chase, Winthrop Aldrich tried to negotiate a merger in 1951 with the venerable Bank of Manhattan, which was established with the help of Aaron Burr in 1799 at 40 Wall Street. At the time, Chase was the third largest bank in the nation, specializing in wholesale banking, with twenty-seven domestic branches, only two of them outside of Manhattan. The Bank of Manhattan was the nation's sixteenth largest bank with a well-established network of fifty-five retail branches, most of them in the other boroughs. Each bank possessed the attributes the other lacked; together they would be stronger than their separate parts; they were ideal for marriage. When details were worked out and the merger plans announced to the press, the New York *Times* reported on August 21 that "the biggest consolidation in the history of American banking is being considered by two Wall Street banks." The next day, the *Times* headlined a page-one story: BANK MERGER OFF; TALKS ARE ENDED. Why? It seems someone at the Bank of Manhattan had thought to look up its original 1799 charter and found that under that charter the Bank of Manhattan could not be merged into another company without the unanimous approval of its stockholders. Of course, that was impossible to obtain.

There the matter rested—for four years—until a simple solution was found to the seemingly insurmountable obstacle by the man who succeeded Winthrop Aldrich as chairman of the board of Chase, John J. McCloy. It was indicative of the management of Chase that the bank could find no one on its own board of directors or within the organization to succeed Winthrop Aldrich. Nor was John J. McCloy a banker by profession. He was a lawyer, a brilliant one, who had been an Assistant Secretary of War, briefly the president of the World Bank and the U. S. High Commissioner for Germany at the end of the war. McCloy's solution was that if the Bank of Manhattan could not be merged into Chase, then perhaps Chase could be merged into the Bank of Manhattan. To that the directors of both banks agreed. On March 31, 1955, the Bank of Manhattan with $1.6 billion in assets absorbed the Chase Bank with its $6 billion in assets, or, as one magazine described it, "Jonah swallowed the whale." The new Chase Manhattan Bank immediately became the second largest bank in the country.

More important, the new bank in one swoop became a more rounded, all-encompassing institution, blending the Bank of Manhattan's retail banking strengths with the Chase National's predominance in corporate, correspondent and international banking. The new management, headed by McCloy as chairman and by J. Stewart Baker, former chairman of the Bank of Manhattan, as president, then launched into a massive reorganization and restructuring of the new bank and laid out plans for marked expansion in all departments and all markets of the world. David Rockefeller was appointed an executive vice-president in charge of the Bank Development Department.

In a real sense that promotion was a reward for David's past efforts. In 1952, he had been moved from the Latin American Department to customer relations in the New York branch offices. His big break came when John J. McCloy came in as chairman in 1953 and Uncle Winthrop departed the scene to become ambassador to the Court of St. James. David's small planning group was escalated up to a full-scale development-and-planning department with one of the bank's highest priorities, with David in charge. In this position, he came into his own as an economist, a management expert and an analyst capable of broad and innovative planning for the future. Up to that time, David and his small group had investigated the shortcomings, the gaps, the faults plaguing Chase management. But now he was given responsibility for proposing solutions to those problems and, in some cases, going further in advocating and implementing those recommendations. In unspoken banking parlance, he was entering the big leagues and it was tacitly understood he would rise or fall depending upon how he played the game.

Contrary to an opinion widely spread throughout financial circles, there was nothing foreordained that David Rockefeller would become head of the Chase Manhattan Bank. Neither his father nor his Uncle Winthrop had promised him that; it was not within their power. The Rockefeller family all together and with companies and foundations within their circle of influence at no time held more than 5 per cent of the bank's outstanding stock. They were major stockholders, to be sure, and Laurance sat on the board of directors as the representative of those holdings. But the other twenty-three members of the Chase board were, each in his own right, powerful entities in the business and banking world, each of them with a strongly held obligation to serve the bank and not the Rockefellers. The family's shares did not by a wide margin make the multi-billion-dollar Chase a family-controlled business. In the second largest bank in the country, the whim of one shareholder employee, no matter how important, cannot be catered to. A failure in operation would not and could not be tolerated in so large a publicly held corporation.

On the other hand, there was no doubt that as the years went on David Rockefeller moved into a very favored position in the race for the top. The board of directors had their eyes on him. He was tested in one department and then in another. And he was observed. His work product was inspected with extra care and attention, the assets and liabilities he brought to Chase were carefully measured and calibrated. The older men on the board of directors certainly were bright enough to grasp that this young man brought more than money and stock shares to the bank: he brought with him that famous name and the reputation in the business world that automatically accompanied that name. In short, the attitude on the board, at least during the first ten years that David worked at the bank, was one of watchful waiting. David could rise to the top. Or he could blunder or reveal shortcomings which would make it necessary to shunt him aside to a safe vice-presidency in which he could do no harm to Chase.

As for David himself, he had family responsibilities beyond those of the ordinary vice-president of a bank. While he was a junior executive at Chase, outside of the bank he was a Rockefeller. Soon after his return from the war, he took over his father's chairmanship of the International House in New York, which accommodated foreign students from all parts of the world, and a few years after that he was made chairman of the board of the Rockefeller Institute for Medical Research, his father's personal favorite. Those two were the major assignments of David in the division among his brothers for carrying on the philanthropic interests of their father. David also had his own personal commitments to his alma maters, Harvard and the University of Chicago, as well as his deep interest in the august and venerable Council on Foreign Relations, which he had joined just prior to his own wartime service. To each of these institutions, David felt deeply that inculcated Rockefeller concern to give more than money —to give also of his time and of his best efforts.

Characteristically, David believed in being thorough and acting only upon the basis of information and knowledge of the situation. Upon assuming responsibility for International House in 1946, when he was thirty-one, he hired a sociologist from the University of Chicago to make an independent study of the International House located near Columbia University in New York. And when he became chairman of the board of the Rockefeller Institute in 1950, he persuaded Dr. Detlev W. Bronk, then president of Johns Hopkins University, to head a committee to study that situation. Both institutions needed rejuvenation to meet the demands of the postwar world. What he wanted to know specifically on each of them was: where is it now and where is it going?

The prognosis report on International House was utterly bleak. Aside from some possible minor improvements, there was little that could be done for International House because, the report said, it was in a deteriorating area with a changing population, large apartments were being broken up into single-room occupancies and, in short, ghetto conditions were moving down into the neighborhood. Nothing which could be done for International House itself would help the situation in the long run if the area around it crumbled inexorably. So said the report.

But David had learned at his father's knee how to take an overview of a problem, undaunted by the possible magnitude of the solution. David took it upon himself to attempt to rejuvenate the entire area of Morningside Heights in uptown New York. The Lincoln School, which he had attended for twelve years, was part of Columbia University in that area, and David was appalled at the idea that this section of Manhattan, of which he was so fond, could be allowed to deteriorate. When he had been a boy, Morningside Heights had been the Acropolis of New York, standing high on a hill overlooking the Hudson River, housing such cultural giants as Columbia University, the Union Theological Seminary, the Jewish Theological Seminary, St. Luke's Hospital, Corpus Christi R. C. Church, the Juilliard School of Music, the Cathedral of St. John the Divine. Then, of course, the Riverside Church, an interdenominational church, was added by his father, as well as International House. Could the functioning and impact upon New York of all of these institutions be allowed to crumble with the neighborhood? Or could the spread of residential slums be reversed in time?

The simple answer, of course, was no. The difficult aspect of that simple answer was equally clear to David's mode of structured thinking: to find the right concept in the right place correctly executed. What Morningside Heights needed was the development of an environment which would support a neighborhood so heavily endowed with major non-profit institutions. What Morningside Heights needed first of all was large-scale middle-income housing to replace the growing slums. But how to accomplish that? For himself, David had formulated a method on how to break down and solve any given problem, such as Morningside Heights:

Develop a plan and a program determining the objective.

Develop a program to accomplish that objective.

Develop the organization to implement the program.

Determine the budget to support the organization and the program.

Devise the means of generating the funds to support that budget.

If that sounds simple, it isn't. It took David Rockefeller eight years before even demolition of the slums was begun in 1954. In the intervening years, he had surveys made of the entire area, he had to persuade the trustees of nine non-profit institutions to set up a central organization, called Morningside Heights, Inc., of which he was elected president, and then to agree on each and every step proposed by the new organization.

The major undertaking was the building of a $16 million complex of apartment buildings to house one thousand integrated middle-income families. That entailed the acquiring and demolition of ten acres of slums, the relocation of families dispossessed. That, in turn, required the approval of the city administration, a federal subsidy and a public fight against vociferous resistance by a militant group called the Save-Our-Home Committee. David worked diligently behind the scenes and out in front. To the surprise of many, he appeared personally to present his committee's plans to the city Board of Estimate, facing down the catcalls and usual aspersions cast in such situations where poor people are moved out of slums to make way for what later became known as urban renewal. Morningside Gardens, the name given the new houses, was opened to its first tenants in 1957 along with its new youth programs, cultural activities and its own private street patrol. It was the *first* integrated middle-income housing development in postwar New York. It presaged similar struggles between what the Establishment sees as necessary progress and the militant left sees as the usurpation of poor people's homes and sidewalks. The fight would be fought again and again all over New York and in the major cities of the country and the problem each time would be the same: how do institutions expand to fulfill their responsibilities to the community without encroaching on housing for the poor? But by the time that question arose in connection with deteriorating neighborhoods near the Rockefeller Institute for Medical Research in the east sixties of New York and in the downtown Wall Street section years later, David Rockefeller was something of an authority on the subject.

By the time those first tenants moved into Morningside Gardens, David Rockefeller had also completely revamped the internal structure of the governing body of the Rockefeller Institute for Medical Research, expanded the scope of its research and installed a new president. At the same time, having been elected by the alumni to the board of overseers of Harvard University, David headed a study group which recommended the expansion of facilities at that august institution and he became instrumental in helping Harvard raise $82.5 million for that purpose. It was at the time the most ambitious fund-raising campaign ever launched by a private institution. David gave the largest individual contribution—$2.6 million—and personally helped corral other Harvard alumni in the million-dollar class.

David had won the undying admiration of Harvard's then president, Nathan Pusey, even before the fund-raising drive, for Pusey had been invited by John D. Rockefeller, Jr., to spend his summers at Mount Desert Island, where he, his wife and children became fast friends with David, his wife and his children. "I just marvel at his industry and his energy and the way he keeps going," the Harvard president told an interviewer some years later. "He has a powerful mind. I sometimes think he's got electricity in his head."

Most of the men who know all of the Rockefeller brothers choose David as the "most integrated personality" of the brothers. He seems to have the rare ability to work diligently and intelligently at multiple projects at the same time, displaying not only sheer animal energy but also the capacity to compartmentalize. That is, he can delve deep into Harvard affairs and then turn to the Council on Foreign Relations, to Rockefeller University and then to the Chase Bank, all with equal energy, giving his complete attention to the project at hand, and still, at the end of each day, turn off his racing mental processes and give himself wholly to his family at home. And he smiles and enjoys it tirelessly—the work, the problem solving, the people he meets in business, his philanthropic efforts, his personal social life and the antics of his children at home.

To those who know David Rockefeller less well, who see him occasionally or who deal with him at only one level, he appears rather bland, open-faced, smiling and overpolite. The reason is that he deliberately prefers to listen than to talk, to take in the opinions of others rather than to express his own. He seldom puts out a random idea. His proposals are prepared beforehand and reinforced with information and data gathered by others. He is in a position to have others—either those at the bank or men he has hired for his own staff—search out the answers and the details he seeks and needs to use. What does not show is the retentiveness of his mind. Input is carefully catalogued and computerized in his mind, ready for recall months and years afterward, often to the amazement of his secretaries, staff and business associates. But David Rockefeller would no more flaunt his erudition, his opinions or biases than he would his wealth or his power. Neither does he hide them, however, nor make apologies for his status in life. He takes it all—so it seems—in stride.

By inclination as well as upbringing, David was always a rather reticent man. He carefully compartmentalized his private life and his emotional ties away from his business and public life. Few who knew him were aware of the one man whom David considered "the greatest influence upon my life, other than my father." That man was Richard Gilder, David's "best friend" at Harvard, an all-around brilliant student, mature beyond his years, who possessed a scholar's mind and a rare poise with dealing with people and everyday events. David, who had come to Harvard a shy, uncertain young man, blossomed under the unwitting tutelage of this best friend, who helped shape and broaden this young Rockefeller's attitudes toward life, people and the world around him. An ardent and idealistic Anglophile, Gilder left Harvard in his senior year to join in the battle to save England from the Nazi blitzkrieg and imminent invasion. Before shipping overseas as an air force fighter pilot, Gilder asked David to be his new son's godfather and to care for his family "just in case . . ." Both young men recognized the probabilities involved. Richard Gilder was shot down and killed, as he himself had expected, and David took in

young George Gilder and made him part of his family while he helped his
friend's wife until she remarried. Richard Gilder was never forgotten by
David Rockefeller, though he seldom spoke of him. But when a son was
born to David and his wife after the war, in 1949, he was named Richard
Gilder Rockefeller.

While all his brothers sought the anonymity of apartment living in
New York City, upon his return from the war David purchased a four-
story town house on Manhattan's fashionable East Side and, with Peggy,
set out to furnish it in English traditional and nineteenth-century art. At
Pocantico Hills, ever mindful of the specter of unnecessary waste, David
purchased the home of his sister Abby, who, having divorced her husband
during the war, had decided against living on the family estate. Large and
commodious, Georgian in style and built of the red bricks saved from
their parents' town house on West Fifty-fourth Street, the house is off
by itself to the west of the 3,500-acre family estate, out of sight of the
main house. David installed his own stable and horses, separate from the
family's stable and corrals, and later he bought a small herd of cattle
and sheep to graze the rolling meadows of green land around the house.

When David and Peggy moved into their New York town house in
1949, they furnished it mostly with fine old English furniture and a variety
of family artifacts they already owned. For the paneled walls, with economy ever in mind, they began buying eighteenth-century paintings of
landscapes and hunting scenes, which to David were "excellent buys" precisely because they were not in vogue. But when Margaret Barr, the wife
of the curator of the Museum of Modern Art, saw those paintings, she
shuddered. "If you really want to buy this sort of thing, at least try to get
something more exciting," she advised them.

She and her husband, Alfred Barr, decided to take David in hand and
gently expose him to "more suitable" works of art for a man in his position. David had recently become a trustee of MOMA, replacing his
mother, who had died, on the board. It had been a commitment made out
of love for his mother, one of the museum's founders, rather than any personal interest in modern art. When David attended his first exhibit at
MOMA as a new trustee, he had been "shocked" at the works of Miró,
Dali, Arp and other surrealists. He thought the artists were mocking the
viewer, for he could make no sense of what he saw. He was a realist. But
in time, the knowledgeable Barrs guided their neophyte into a new world,
the realm of modern and contemporary art.

David opened his mind to new knowledge and in 1951 he made his
first significant art purchase, *Gabriel* by Renoir, a semi-nude in a negligee
with bosom exposed. It was for David Rockefeller a leap forward not only
in the mode of painting he would purchase but also in the price he would
pay. After considerable hesitation and soul-searching, he paid $50,000 for

the Renoir. That was five times as much as he had ever paid before for a painting. But it opened the floodgates. As he became more and more interested and knowledgeable in modern art, he purchased important paintings by Cézanne, Seurat, Manet and others. He then found the collector's joy in discovering works by living, contemporary artists. Four years later from the time of that first Renoir, David Rockefeller was trying to convince the Chase Manhattan Bank directors that they too should open their minds and the bank's pocketbook to modern painting and sculpture.

Alongside of his career in banking and economics, and, of course, his own family, David's keenest interest in life through the years had been in foreign affairs. Nothing less than the world was his oyster, and at the start, natural curiosity was his clam knife. He joined the Council on Foreign Relations in May 1941, before enlisting in the Army, but it was not until his return from France after the war that he became active in the organization. By 1950, he was elected a vice-president of the Council. The Council on Foreign Relations, a private, non-partisan and non-profit organization, was founded in 1921 by several of Woodrow Wilson's advisers who had been involved in the Versailles Treaty and the establishment of the League of Nations. The Council's purpose was to study problems of foreign policy, particularly long-range problems, and then to make its study findings available first to the leaders of the United States and then to the public on important issues involving U.S. foreign policy. Its influence derives from the caliber of its membership, limited by invitation only to sixteen hundred, which includes ranking members of the government, past and present, and leaders in banking, business, journalism and academia. Every Secretary of State since Charles Evan Hughes, with only two exceptions, has been a member of the Council, and those exceptions have been General George Marshall under President Truman and William Rogers, who had had no previous experience in foreign affairs until his appointment by President Nixon. So august has been the membership of the Council that it has been seen in some quarters as the heart of the eastern Establishment. When it comes to foreign affairs, it *is* the eastern Establishment. In fact, it is difficult to point to a single major policy in U.S. foreign affairs that has been established since Wilson which was diametrically opposed to then current thinking in the Council on Foreign Relations.

The influence of the Council is most indirect. It makes no specific recommendations at all as a body. It never lobbies in the halls of Congress. It has never twisted the arm of a President. What it provides, more than anything else, is a meeting place in which experts exchange ideas on foreign affairs at the expertise level. Its quarterly publication *Foreign Affairs* is pre-eminent in its field as a professional journal and is read in capitals throughout the world. The Council works its wonders in two distinct ways. At regular luncheon or dinner meetings, American or foreign guests are invited to address Council members. Some of the most important U.S. policies have been unveiled at the Council at these functions and virtually every important foreign statesman to visit the United States has addressed its members at the Council's handsome five-story town house on Park Avenue at Sixty-eighth Street. But even more important than these addresses are the Council's own study groups, formed to help one expert prepare a paper or a book on a given subject with the help of Council members who have specialized knowledge on the subject. These papers and books are often most influential in the halls of government because of what they say rather than because of the mere imprimatur of the Council. One of the better-known such books was *Nuclear Weapons and Foreign Policy*, written in the 1950s by Henry Kissinger. To help him in that particular study group there were two former chairmen of the Atomic Energy Commission, two former civilian heads of the armed services branches, ranking officers from each of the three armed services and the Central Intelligence Agency, and two ranking men from the State Department.

From 1948 on David Rockefeller participated every year in at least one Council study group, including studies on Western Europe, France, European labor, the tariff, NATO, nuclear weapons, trade policy, the Alliance for Progress, China and the United Nations and an *ad hoc* discussion group on Vietnam in 1968. David headed one study group which continued for two years on European and American capitalism. More often, he was involved in the ceremonial aspects of the Council, and as vice-president of the organization in 1950 he presided at luncheons and dinners and served as host to foreign dignitaries. After all, his name was well-known and with his own travels abroad he was usually acquainted on a personal or business basis with those guests invited to speak. His financial contributions to the Council were strictly limited by himself to $25,000 a year, which was no more than 1 per cent of the Council's annual budget. But then again, his influence, directly or indirectly, did no harm when it came to applications to the Rockefeller Foundation or to the Rockefeller Brothers Fund for the financing of special projects. On an over-all basis, however, David Rockefeller tried to pull his own weight as an individual member of the Council rather than as a Rockefeller source of money.

To the extent that the Council was also a gentleman's club as well as a specialized group to study foreign relations, he was accepted as a working member whose genuine interest in foreign affairs was never in doubt. At the Council, the "school for statesmen," David Rockefeller became known as a thoroughly well-liked, easy-to-work-with, committed member whose instincts were intensely warm and human rather than organizational. In the interchange of ideas among peers at the Council, David soon established himself on the liberal wing of the organization, among the younger members, and yet he was careful in not throwing around the weight of his family name or that of the Chase Manhattan Bank. Of course, in David's early days on the Council, he was one of the younger members himself, outranked by men senior to him in international relations as well as in the business and banking communities, including John J. McCloy, who after his election as chairman of the Chase Manhattan Bank was also elected chairman of the board of the Council.

David's fascination with international relations, necessitating intimate knowledge of the governmental, social and economic policies of nations throughout the world, on both sides of the Iron Curtain, dovetailed uniquely with his interest and concern in expanding Chase Manhattan's business in the international banking market. One could not become expert in one without the other. From an initial interest in the affairs of Western Europe and of Latin America, one could not neglect the influence upon those areas of the Soviet Union. David soon found himself studying the available information in the West on the internal affairs of the Soviet Union and her satellite hegemony.

As a vice-president under McCloy at the bank, David led a movement to expand the international side of its business. In the early 1950s, Chase had only a few international branches around the world to serve its big U.S. corporate customers doing business overseas. But with the postwar demand for consumer goods, the nations of Western Europe and Latin America were experiencing a business boom in which national companies had great need of bank loans for expansions and for new business. To cash in on this business as quickly as possible, David and his planning group proposed that Chase, rather than trying to open new branches in country after country, should buy into existing banks in the Netherlands, Belgium, London and South America. It was a bold stroke. By purchasing 49 or 51 percent of a bank in Brussels, Hong Kong or Honduras, Chase would be able to introduce modern U.S. banking know-how into the local situation and reap the benefits of the local good will, experience and influence of the local affiliate bank. Where U.S. businesses might be attracted to the Chase name, local industries would be reassured by the national management of the bank. This expansion into the international market caused a major upheaval at the home office, involving a great many studies in the bank's overseas operations as well as the hiring of considerably more personnel. There was the usual foot dragging, a natural reluctance to change, among several groups at the bank. The opposition, however, was beaten down, not overtly but with the gentle persistence of study reports which answered the concern over the risks involved. David Rockefeller, more than anyone else, was credited with steering the program through the Chase board of directors. It was the start of an expansion which would make Chase Manhattan a worldwide banking facility with more than two thousand overseas locations in ninety-eight countries.

At the same time, the merger with the Bank of Manhattan in 1955 brought about an immediate expansion in local or retail banking for the new Chase Manhattan Bank. In one stroke of the pen, the Bank of Manhattan gave the new Chase Manhattan a total of sixty-seven branch banks serving the everyday depositor or borrower throughout New York City. The internal reorganization, the new policies and plans, the personnel changes needed for the operation of the newly merged bank were tremendous and important for the success or failure of the venture. Planning and development for these changes began, of course, before the merger even went through. The Chase management had to start from square one, for there were no precedents, no other banks of similar size or operation to copy. Chase was the first "wholesale" bank, specializing in corporate and correspondent banking, to go "retail" in the new postwar economy. Others, like the Bankers Trust Company, or Irving Trust, would follow in time; Morgan Guaranty would eschew that road; and Bank of America and First National City Bank were predominantly retail before the war.

David Rockefeller, now the undisputed protégé of McCloy, was put at the head of the planning and development committee with the task of reviewing the entire Chase operation and then overhauling it. The diagnosis and recommended surgery took years. The management structure of this huge bank, with its billions in assets, was found to be antiquated and slipshod; its pay scale was below the going rate; its fringe benefits were skimpy; its promotion policy was virtually non-existent; its reputation in the banking community was that of a staid, conservative giant unable to maneuver with rapidly changing times: even its own building was inadequate for the bank's size and scope. The surgery recommended and eventually performed involved the complete overhaul of the internal management structure of the bank. Separate committees were established to work out plans for management development, organizational structure, marketing and corporate planning. In effect, the design was to bring modern managerial practices into a staid old institution. Most well-managed companies already had these managerial functions, even though they were unknown at Chase. Personnel practices at the bank were completely overhauled. New people, new training programs, a new pay scale and fringe benefits were introduced. Chase not only went out looking for new customers, it went out and sought new economists, marketing experts and other specialists fresh out of colleges and graduate schools. An employee thrift and incentive program offered matched funds so that a young man with a career at Chase who retired as a vice-president at age sixty-five could amass a retirement fund of a quarter of a million dollars *plus* his ordinary pension from the bank. Despite all the expansion, bringing in new young people with promises of rapid promotion to match their ability meant getting rid of old dead wood by attrition or early retirement. The shake-up in personnel and structure was pronounced and the old-timers did not like it at all. But John J. McCloy, as chairman of the board, was in the driver's seat, with David Rockefeller alongside him, and with the board of directors behind him. As a result, Chase Manhattan, a goliath of banking, moved out into modern times and geared up to the tumultuous 1960s ahead.

Even for David Rockefeller, all this was pretty heady material. He was there on the ground floor, intimately involved in what in effect was the birth of a new modern bank bearing the names of two venerable but outdated institutions. As insiders viewed it, a new entity was being molded. On a personal basis, after a decade at the bank, David could feel a true sense of accomplishment: having submitted himself to a cause and a hierarchy much larger than himself personally, he succeeded in establishing himself as a member of the top management of the Chase Manhattan Bank. Two years after the merger, in 1957, he was appointed vice-chairman of the board of directors. His area of responsibility then became the administrative and planning functions of the bank as a whole. And, as anyone could then see, he was on his way up.

An integral part of the reorganization of the merged Chase Manhattan, and the most visible one to the outside world, was the obvious need for a new headquarters large enough to house the expanded enterprise and to pull together the scattered management of the bank. David undertook the leadership of that project with a special fervor at the time, years before his brother Nelson became governor of New York and the Rockefeller "edifice complex" became public knowledge. All of the Rockefeller boys had learned at their father's knee the delight of building something beautiful as well as functional with that "5 per cent extra" at the end to ensure superior quality. What the Chase board of directors discovered too was that the Rockefellers are accustomed to "thinking big." The youngest Rockefeller brother was no slouch. Working with one of the leading architectural firms in the city, Skidmore, Owings & Merrill, David came up with a concept of a sixty-story building, a giant shaft of glass and aluminum, without any setbacks or ornamentation, rising 813 feet straight from the ground, located only one block away from the then main office of Chase, with more than 2 million square feet of office space. The reaction came in gasps of disbelief and horror. Opposition came from all directions and from many sources.

First of all, they said, the project was far too grandiose, the bank had no need for so large a building now or in the foreseeable future. Secondly, it was too expensive at the projected price of $100 million. Thirdly, the building itself was too modern, too glassy-looking, and did not even resemble what a bank should look like. And finally and most important, it was positively myopic even to consider locating the new building in the old Wall Street district when all the other banks and large corporations were moving their headquarters to the fashionable midtown area of New York, near Rockefeller Center. Even the New York Stock Exchange was threatening to abandon Wall Street.

David argued that the threatened exodus by most if not all of its famous tenants was precisely why Chase Manhattan, as the second largest bank in the nation, should lead the way in an urban renewal of a kind of Wall Street. To him it was a matter of social responsibility. The world-famous financial district, the geographical heartland of American capitalism, was being threatened with extinction. It could become a depressed area. If, on the other hand, Chase Manhattan put up a modern, even futuristic skyscraper, symbolic of its faith, it would induce others to re-examine their decisions to move away. But, it was true, he had to admit, that no one had built a new building in the financial district since the depression days of the 1930s. In fact, as it was pointed out to him, no one had put up a sixty-story building anywhere in New York in more than twenty-five years. The last commercial building of that size built in New York was none other than the RCA Building, started in 1931 by his father as the centerpiece of Rockefeller Center.

It was a difficult and complex decision facing the Chase board of directors. The pros and cons were argued almost interminably. Despite all the studies and fact-gathering reports, the problem of where to locate the bank, how large to build it, what style to adopt—all rested on subjective considerations of what the future would hold for banking and the Wall Street area in general and for the new Chase Manhattan Bank in particular. In the new age of committee control and negotiated settlements, the Chase board of directors finally agreed on a compromise: they would build the new bank in the financial district if David Rockefeller would take it upon himself to convince others to remain in the area. They would hedge that decision by building a new main branch of the bank, handling the largest corporate accounts, in the Park Avenue midtown area. And they would agree to build a $100 million bank sixty stories high if twenty-five of those floors were rented out to other firms. It was a compromise—a sort of negotiated settlement—between the conservatives and the optimists on the Chase board. Nevertheless, it was seen at the time as an endorsement of the planning and development endeavors of David Rockefeller, who had pushed and persuaded for that course of action. It also put the onus of prime responsibility upon him for the move.

David went to work on his new assignment immediately. Within months of the public announcement in December 1955 that Chase would build its new headquarters in the financial district, David invited fifty-five business, banking and financial leaders to a luncheon, out of which evolved a Committee on Lower Manhattan. What he had in mind, he told this group, was an urban renewal project which would transform the one-mile area from the tip of lower Manhattan to Canal Street, an area in which 400,000 people worked and virtually no one lived. That area was often described as the heart pump of American capitalism. It contained the nation's two principal stock exchanges, a major portion of the over-the-counter securities market, five commodity exchanges, the headquarters of five of the nation's six largest banks and many of the nation's leading insurance companies. The transformation relied not upon any single enterprise but rather on a planned development of the area as a whole. He envisioned the building of apartment houses and complexes where people could live and walk to work. He foresaw development of the magnificent waterfront property then largely being allowed to deteriorate. He saw changes in transportation facilities, the possibility of building schools and colleges. But the most important facet was the opportunity of tearing down marginal property, the one- and two-story buildings of the nineteenth century, to make way for new skyscrapers housing the offices of new and expanded business firms facing the challenges of the second half of the twentieth century. The key to the project was integrated planning and development, of which David Rockefeller was becoming a master. The initial architectural plans for this over-all project, when first presented, appeared grandiose and, to some, beyond practicability.

Today, many years after that first luncheon and the consolidation of the Committee on Lower Manhattan with the existing businessmen's Downtown Manhattan Association, those original plans look meager. Even the planners themselves did not envisage the tremendous success and impetus of their early efforts. Success bred success. Planning and development for that one-square-mile area have now stretched to the year 1980 with more than $5 billion already spent or committed on new construction and on planned developments. To date, the area's office capacity already has been doubled with 47 million square feet of new office space built. It includes the world's largest office complex, the World Trade Center, two towers on the Hudson River which are the tallest buildings in the world, containing 10 million square feet of space. On another street, twelve new buildings have gone up with a combined total of another 10 million square feet, which is more office space than exists in all of downtown St. Louis or Kansas City. By 1980, more than 14,000 apartments, three office towers, stores and shops will be built on landfill along the Hudson River waterfront. Another 6,500 apartments, a new hotel and a new home for the New York Stock Exchange are proposed to be built on platforms above the East River. Wall Street will be turned into a residential area as well as the greatest complex of corporate and banking offices in the world. The concept and the accomplishment dwarf the miracle of Rockefeller Center, wrought by John D. Rockefeller, Jr.

The credit for the rejuvenation of New York's financial district goes largely to David Rockefeller by general acknowledgment. He was the originator and mainspring of the effort. Yet he did not do it alone, as his father had built Rockefeller Center, for times had changed and the social and business environment had changed. What David Rockefeller accomplished he did by exerting leverage, by talking to and persuading others to follow a course of action because it was right both for the individual corporation and for society as a whole. For coordinating all his efforts he used one of his "multipliers," a young man of his own age, Warren Lindquist, whom he had met as a captain in the military attaché's office in Paris during the war. Lindquist, whom he had brought into the Chase Bank after the war, became the executive vice-president of the Downtown-Lower Manhattan Association from the very beginning in 1958, working full time on planning and development and reporting to the Association's chairman of the board, David Rockefeller.

The lever and the prototype for this $5 billion in reconstruction was, of course, the new Chase Manhattan Bank headquarters at an ultimate cost of $140 million which included land, furnishings and equipment. It was the first new building in the area. Rising above the dirt-grimed stone buildings around it, it stood as a beacon of the future, with its shiny aluminum and its 8,800 oversized windows reflecting the sun, upon a 2.5-acre site, of which 1.7 acres was the first public plaza ever built in the area, adorned by young trees, a terrazzo terrace, benches for the weary visitors, modern sculpture and a sunken Japanese pool, designed by Isamu Noguchi, which sprouted water at the push of a button. It was at the time the seventh tallest building in the world and certainly the tallest bank building. The bank itself occupied thirty-five of its sixty floors as well as its six underground levels. Deep and secure beneath ground level, it also boasted the largest bank vault in the world, longer than a football field, weighing no less than 985 tons.

Then there was that something extra. Having convinced the Chase board of directors to go ahead with a $100 million modern bank building, David persuaded them to invest $510,000 in a program to buy works of art, most of them to be from living contemporary artists, to adorn the walls of the public rooms of the bank and of some of the executive offices. And this too was to be a first of its kind, a resounding success and stimulus for corporations throughout the country to do likewise, to buy art for art's sake in order to make their places of business more attractive to the public and to the men and women who worked there. For the lucky artists involved, it was the greatest boom in selling paintings, graphics and sculpture since the days of the Medicis.

By the time the 7,500 employees of Chase Manhattan moved into the new headquarters at 1 Chase Manhattan Plaza in April 1961, it was no surprise to anyone that the bank had a new president: David Rockefeller, age forty-five, of Pocantico Hills, New York.

Part Three

"*Ambition most of the time is not in terms of money. Nor for power. It is deeper—unconsciously an ambition for usefulness, for greatness.*"

—Georges Simenon

16

David

"The social responsibility of the
capitalistic system . . ."

The 1960s proved to be the most dynamic years of change in all the history of American banking. They also demonstrated that David Rockefeller as an economist and a banker was something of a visionary in his planning and development recommendations in the 1950s to the Chase Manhattan Bank. Expansion in every phase of banking—depositors, corporate and individual loans, new branches here and abroad, new services, new advertising and the new look—was the key tactic to success, and Chase Manhattan emerged as a leader in setting new trends. In financial circles around the world, David Rockefeller became the man of the hour.

The new Chase Manhattan Building itself was seen as a towering symbol of banking's new look. What other bank building in the world had 8,800 shiny clean windows, as if to say, "Come look and see what we are doing . . . We have nothing to hide." Modern and contemporary art was everywhere, inside and out, the interior furnishings all were stylish and new, integrated and contemporary, so pleasing to the eye that even the most Philistine visitor could not help but notice the aura of his surroundings. In fact, the building became one of New York City's listed tourist attractions. David also had persuaded his board of directors to change the symbol of the bank, heralding in its new era, from its stodgy globe superimposed upon a map of the United States to a simple abstract geometric shape somewhere between a circle and an octagon. The symbol would be used on all of the bank checks, letterheads, bank branch façades, ashtrays and whatever. It took two years and the consideration of several hundred possibilities before the bank's management agreed to David's choice abstract. The old-timers at the bank called it "the beveled bagel" but they went along. To attract new customers and new depositors, the bank went heavily into the latest methods of merchandising and advertising on the theme: "You have a friend at Chase Manhattan." Thus, Chase, which had disdained any business under $5,000 per transaction and spent only $320,000 a year on advertising when David Rockefeller joined the bank in 1946, spent $3.4 million in 1962 to advertise its readiness to give a $200 personal loan to anyone in need. Through the booming, go-go, inflationary years of the 1960s, banking throughout the country expanded and Chase Manhattan was among the top and most visible leaders. Always a leader in the large corporate loans, Chase thrived on financing loans to expanding American business. Its loan commitments at the time of its merger, for example, came to $3.7 billion; by the end of the 1960s, Chase loans grew to $12.5 billion. Its deposits for those years kept pace, growing from almost $7 billion in 1956 to more than $21 billion in 1970. Its branch banks in and around New York City increased to 119 in 1962 and then to more than 200 by the end of 1973. To keep pace with this growth, the number of Chase employees spiraled up from 7,900 in 1946 to 14,600 in 1956 to more than 25,000 by the end of 1973.

The new look in banking and particularly at Chase was planned and deliberate. Into an ocean of white shirts, David Rockefeller, the new president, began coming to work in a blue shirt and brightly striped tie; others followed suit. Tellers, loan officers and executives were advised to smile at customers, to welcome them, to help them and to serve them. "To be competitive today a bank has to serve its customers in ways it never did before," said David. The Chase management came up with innovations: the long-term, high-interest saving certificates for individuals as well as corporations; special student loans to finance education; and the automatic line of credit for special checking accounts.

Less visible but no less important was the introduction of new specialists in particular fields—oil, automobiles, textiles, mergers—men who were expert advisers ready to serve corporations with more than mere money. There were other ways for banks to make money, too. Chase, with the largest complex of computers in the banking business, began in its headquarters building processing 2 million checks a day—its own checks and checks of other banks—and then steadily increased that business to an average of 4 million checks a day by the end of the decade. Chase computers took over—for a fee—the vast paperwork of many institutions, including various tax and rent billings for NewYork City itself.

The bank's growth outpaced even its own most optimistic projections. Six busy years after moving into its new sixty-story skyscraper (and renting out twenty-five of its floors to others) Chase Manhattan ran short of space. With some embarrassment the bank was obliged to take a long-

term $200 million lease on twenty-five floors in another building in the
Wall Street area.

By no means was David Rockefeller responsible for all of this growth.
Nevertheless, he garnered the credit. He was there, visible to the public,
the new president of the Chase Manhattan Bank with its new look, its
new headquarters building and its spectacular new success. Besides, he had
that magic name. His speeches were reported almost without fail in the
daily press; his portrait appeared on the cover of the popular news-
magazines, accompanying long stories on him. He was the banker of the
hour, banker of the year. Competitors were quoted, singing his praises:
"David is an effective, able, all-round banker who makes keener competition for us because of his ability," said the chairman of a rival New York
City bank. "A lot of people think he is a success only because of family,
but bankers hold him in high esteem in his own right," said a Midwestern
banker. "Rockefeller is the most important and capable banker in New
York, therefore in the world," opined a Venezuelan banker.

Actually, David was only the co-chief executive officer of the bank.
He shared on an even par the over-all responsibility for running the bank
with the chairman of the board, George Champion, who was eleven years
his senior in age and who had thirty solid years of experience at the bank.
As John J. McCloy's retirement as chairman of the board became imminent, both men had vied to replace him as the bank's chief executive
officer. That was where the power to direct the bank lay. Titles were
merely titles. It was obvious at the time that Champion, who had been
president of the bank under McCloy since 1957, would be elevated to
chairman of the board, and David to president of the bank. But when it
came to defining the responsibilities and duties of each position, both
David Rockefeller and George Champion insisted upon becoming the
chief operating officer of the bank. As the bank's directors wavered over
the decision, each of the men threatened to resign if the other got the
nod. Each threat was sincere: David asserted he would leave rather than
devote another eight or nine years to working under the orders of the
chairman of the board, and Champion refused to continue at the bank
even as chairman if he retained no power to direct the bank. The board of
directors compromised and split the difference between the two men.
They made them co-chief executive officers of the bank, each of them
with different and separate responsibilities and each of them reporting
straight to the board of directors. As such, perched together on the top of
the executive ladder, they combined between them all the talents of a su-
perbly equipped chief executive of a major banking institution.

George Champion, who grew up on a farm in Illinois, and went on to
become a football star at Dartmouth College in 1925, was a direct, forceful, table-thumping bank officer who had worked his way up through the
ranks. His advancement came through the domestic side of the bank, par-

ticularly in the important corporated lending division, which handled some of America's largest businesses. Upon John J. McCloy's retirement in 1961 he was assigned responsibility for the bank's domestic business and its day-to-day activities. David was given the ultimate supervision of the bank's international affairs and, in addition, was made chairman of the bank's powerful executive committee of the board of directors, where policy and planning were formulated. One bank executive explained it all more simply: "Champion worries about where the bank will be ten minutes from now and Rockefeller about where it will be ten years from now."

The word load for the two men was split also along another diagonal. Champion became the inside man and Rockefeller the outside man for the bank. This played to the strengths of each man. While George Champion was truly a "banker's banker," familiar with the bank's personnel and the intricacies of every department and division, David Rockefeller possessed the cachet of the most famous and familiar name in American business. The value of that name was not lost upon the bank's board of directors. It was David Rockefeller whom heads of some of the largest corporations in America wanted to meet and to know as their friend at Chase Manhattan. It was David Rockefeller whom businessmen all over the country flocked to hear speak, more so than for any other bank president. When Chase Manhattan opened a new branch, it was David Rockefeller cutting the ribbon who brought that extra percentage of good publicity to the bank. The Rockefeller name was a valuable asset to Chase Manhattan: everyone who could, wanted to meet the man who carried the name. As president of the bank, David was superlative in bringing in new business, in going about speaking of the new, modern image of Chase Manhattan in the 1960s. Businessmen were in awe of him or perhaps of his name. The deference shown him was highly visible. Presidents of giant corporations sent word to the bank that they would like to meet the new president. David, a thoughtful and practical man, was careful never to take advantage of his name, his position or his family's business connections, but he was not loath to use them. He recognized his opportunities. As outside man of the highest rank for the bank, his job, or at least part of his job, was to pull in more customers and more business, just like any other salesman. Of course, there was a difference. When David Rockefeller pulled in new business, it most often involved anywhere from six to nine or ten figures, and that, even for Chase Manhattan, is big business. David was a natural salesman, convivial, gracious, a good conversationalist and genuinely interested in whatever you had to say. He spoke slowly, choosing his words, in a rather high-pitched voice with the broad *a* of Harvard origins, and, more important, what he said made sense. He prepared for his meetings, business or social, and the impression he gave forth was one of quiet, low-keyed confidence and knowledge. Oftentimes this came as something of a surprise to those who met him for the first time. Most businessmen have come to expect arrogance, either plain or disguised, in men of power, but in David Rockefeller they found a smile and obvious good will.

While he enjoyed meeting and exchanging ideas with people, David preferred one-on-one relationships. He could handle small groups with ease, but speaking formally before a large audience, he was often overcome with nervous stiffness. No matter how friendly the group, he found he just did not have a natural flair for public speaking. Soon after he became president of the bank, when formal speeches became an important part of his job, David submitted himself to weekly private speech lessons. They were painful for him, subjectively, like visiting a dentist. Even faint praise, given to encourage him, would be enough of an excuse for him to quit further lessons. But he went back as faithfully as one keeps his dentist appointments because he must. In time he became an adequate if not a good performer on a speaker's platform, almost always reading a prepared text rather than trusting himself to the ease of extemporaneous remarks.

One theme predominated in David Rockefeller's speeches through the years, reflecting a long-held, deep-seated faith he had learned from his father, a belief and faith which transcended even the words he used to describe it: "the social responsibility of the capitalistic system." The words changed to fit the topics discussed but again and again David Rockefeller would tell audiences of businessmen, bankers, financiers and governmental leaders that the capitalistic system was broad and viable enough to fulfill the needs of the individual people within the system as well as return profits to the entrepreneurs. Time and again he would say that the success of capitalism was not to be measured solely in profits or in gross national product but in services and products needed by the people.

Addressing a convention in New York of business managers from all over the world in 1963, he declared: "Though we are citizens of almost one hundred different countries, we nevertheless share a common goal, a common commitment, a common belief. The goal is human progress. The commitment is to increase the well-being of all mankind . . . The belief is that each of us, in his own way, can contribute to this objective through better management."

In that speech, he proposed a Managerial Task Force of Free Enterprise, which would have private corporations in Western Europe, North America, Japan and elsewhere send their own managerial personnel on full salary to the developing countries of the world, where upon invitation they would help plan and organize specific projects deemed essential to national economic development.

Ten years later, in 1973, David Rockefeller was still stressing the need of social responsibility among the corporate giants of America and this time on a much broader, sophisticated scale and with a new sense of urgency. "Capitalism today, as frequently in the past, is the object of strident criticism," he would say in an essay on the Op-Ed page of the New York *Times*. And, in order to respond to such criticism and to accusations of inequitable wealth, pollution and consumer deception, David Rockefeller, a personal symbol of capitalism himself, offered three suggestions:

"First, corporations must develop more effective tools for measuring the social, as well as economic, costs and benefits of their actions . . . Social objectives can be formally incorporated into regular business planning. Managers can be evaluated in part on their social productivity . . . Whatever the methods, it is vital that social accountability become an integral part of corporate conduct, rather than a philanthropic add-on . . .

"Second, businessmen must take the initiative to spell out more clearly and positively the longer-range economic and technical implications of current proposals for social problem solving . . . The enormous talents of the business community [must be] brought to bear on the problems of our society . . . Unless business takes a leadership role in creating workable solutions, it will only suffer with its environment.

"Finally, we must press forward on the national level to create broader and more viable long-range goals, to assess what business can and cannot do to meet these goals and to set more comprehensive strategies to combine the strength of public and private resources . . . Problem solving in America has a tendency to be short-lived—yesterday civil rights and education, today pollution, tomorrow crime, and so on . . . Rarely do we carefully examine the complex interactions of our society, calculate the necessary trade-offs and assign the required resources on a sustained basis."

David Rockefeller, of course, was not a lone, solitary man crying out for social responsibility on the part of American corporations. But the significant point for the business community, as he repeatedly emphasized social responsibility, was that it was David Rockefeller saying it, not some college professor—David Rockefeller, the scion of wealth and power, the successful head of one of the largest and most powerful corporations in the United States. As such, he was influential. Executives of other corporations listened and many, not all, heeded his words. The business community knew that David Rockefeller did not speak idly; action of some sort lay behind his words, action contemplated and planned or already begun.

Out of the 1963 speech came the formation of the International Executive Service Corps, popularly known as the "Paunch Corps" as a counterpart to the Peace Corps which recruited youngsters. The Paunch Corps, sponsored by 126 U.S. corporations with David Rockefeller as chairman, recruited American business executives, most of them retired (with or without a potbelly), to serve as volunteer unpaid advisers to local businesses in Latin America, Africa, the Mideast or wherever invited.

Concomitant with his speeches, David was the prime moving force inside Chase Manhattan all during the 1960s in the training, recruiting and hiring of blacks, Spanish-Americans and other minorities. Temporary branch offices were set up in New York's ghetto areas to find workers with certain specific skills. Chase Manhattan underwrote a "Great Teachers" program, conducted by the United Negro College Fund, which brought economics professors from leading universities to seventeen Negro colleges in the United States to stimulate interest there in banking careers. David also urged Chase Manhattan officers to look more favorably on making riskier loans in the ghetto areas involving housing, new businesses and services. Through the tumultuous 1960s, with the rise of the black liberation movement, student revolts and the radical New Left, David Rockefeller kept abreast of what he considered to be changing times. He tried to tell his peers what he was learning. In the background, not only did he and other bank officials meet with minority representatives, but Dana Creel, who headed the Rockefeller Brothers Fund and the family philanthropic activities, met quietly without fanfare but upon a steady basis with representatives of all the radical factions, asking time and again, "What do you really want?" and "Which of your problems can we realistically hope to solve and how?" They were serious meetings of give-and-take involving sober discussions with men and women, black and white, from all walks of life. The information was relayed to David as well as to each of his brothers.

Thus in the beginning of 1968 David could appear before the federal Equal Employment Opportunity Commission in New York and say: "Five years ago, if you had asked some businessmen to participate in a public service venture, you might have gotten the response: 'What will the stockholders say?' Today, there is a growing realization that management is not doing the job it should for the stockholders simply by earning as large a profit as it can this year, unless at the same time it is helping to shape an environment in which the business can continue earning a profit four or five or ten years from now."

David's view in this instance and in many others was appraised in most quarters as enlightened liberalism, the position of a responsible businessman at a time when business and the entire Establishment were under attack. Nevertheless, there were stockholder questions, challenges and even revolts at Chase Manhattan as well as in other large corporations. What right had management to "give away" profits which rightfully and lawfully belonged to the owners of the corporation, the stockholders? The ills and shortcomings of society were not the concern of individual companies, said the traditionalists. The business of business is profits, the bottom line of the income and expenditures columns—but this turned out to be a minority view of stockholders whenever the question was brought to a proxy vote. And yet, there remained a hard-core resentment among some toward David Rockefeller, the multi-millionaire who, in their view, was spending their money, not his own, for what appeared to be nebulous, insoluble problems.

There is no evidence that David Rockefeller was ever daunted by such criticisms. As an economist, more than a traditional banker, with a broad view of economic and political history, he was convinced of and personally committed to the proposition that *over the long haul* the entire free enterprise system depended upon its sensitivity to the needs of all the people within the system. When he traveled to the Soviet Union and to the People's Republic of China, he would return each time with a reinforced commitment that modern times demanded social responsibility upon the part of private, free enterprise. Over and over again he would make the point: the Chase Manhattan Bank, other banks, and corporations large and small could survive in America and in the free world only if they fulfilled the needs of the people. And yet his personal manner was so mild, his voice so soft and his recommendations for change so pragmatic that the full impact of his message was seldom fully realized or appreciated. Certainly, he did not shout from the rooftops. His speeches and more private talks were made before other bankers and businessmen, in government councils and at academic meetings.

His actions and his business decisions kept pace with his words. He sincerely wished to influence his fellow businessmen in following what he himself believed prudent and he knew full well that hardheaded businessmen paid far more attention to actions than to mere words. When he became chairman of the board of directors of Chase Manhattan and the sole chief executive officer of the bank, he could and would initiate far-ranging programs to mesh the concept of social responsibility and profits throughout each and every department of the bank. One entire division of the bank would be given over to community economic development, special criteria would be formally established to grant loans to minority-owned businesses which could not meet conventional credit standards of the bank. Acknowledging that a troubled New York City was the bank's home environment, Chase Manhattan would enter a variety of community programs: helping the city's Board of Education in finding and selecting the best school principals and leaders, developing a special course in which high school students in the ghetto areas would work and be trained every other week at the bank, establishing a Chase Volunteers for Community Action in which bank employees would join volunteer activities in the ghetto neighborhoods. Year after year, the bank's role as a concerned citizen of its home-town community would grow larger and more sophisticated. By 1972 the bank would be spending somewhat over $2 million in a broad range of activities covering some fifty smaller neighborhood action groups. "Key to all these efforts," the bank would declare frankly in its 1972 report to stockholders, "is the integration of social responsibility into the mainstream of the corporation . . . It is our firm conviction that a corporation such as ours depends absolutely upon its environment, and that we cannot survive unless we contribute significantly to both the social and economic vitality of that environment."

Through the years, David moved gingerly and with pragmatic care in advocating his philosophy on social responsibility. Even if the outside world believed David and his brothers Rockefeller controlled the Chase Manhattan Bank and that Chase Manhattan controlled American industry, David knew better. The Chase Bank had become thought of as the Rockefeller bank in 1930 when it merged with the Equitable Trust Company, in which David's father held a substantial (minority) interest ranging around 30 per cent, and John D. Rockefeller, Jr.'s brother-in-law, Winthrop W. Aldrich, who had been president of Equitable, became president of Chase National. At the same time, however, John Jr.'s percentage of holdings in the merged company was substantially reduced. It was continually and gradually reduced as the years went on, although the Rockefellers always did have a representative on the Chase board of directors. When David joined the bank in 1946, he personally invested $500,000 in Chase National stock. At the time, it was strictly an investment on his part. He was less sure that he himself would stay at the bank than he was that his investment would prosper. As time went on and David rose in the bank's management, he continued to buy more stock for what he considered obvious reasons: he had confidence in the bank; it made sense for him to "have a stake" in the company in which he was working; and, finally, it seemed simply "appropriate" for a man in his position as he rose in management. If he did not invest his own money in the bank, he reasoned, other shareholders would have a right to wonder why he did not. Consequently, as his father's and family's percentage of shares in the bank steadily declined to something less than 3 per cent (even including shares given to foundations, which cannot vote their stock), David's holdings grew to 337,500 shares, which was slightly more than 1 per cent of the 31,920,385 outstanding shares of Chase Manhattan stock at the end of 1972. Clearly, his personally held stock or even the shares owned by other Rockefellers, presuming they would be controlled by him any more than any other shares, which is a risky presumption in the Rockefeller family, do not in themselves spell control of an institution with more than $35 billion in assets and a board of directors of twenty-three powerful men, including the board chairmen or presidents of such institutions as American Smelting & Refining, Allied Chemical, General Foods, Squibb Corporation, Metropolitan Life, Exxon, Standard Oil of Indiana, AT&T, Burlington Industries and the University of Notre Dame.

On a practical day-to-day basis, David was well aware of the limits imposed upon his responsibilities and influence at the bank. His influence never even approached the realm of control. The matter never came up. Clearly, when he served as a vice-president under John J. McCloy, and later when he was president and co-chief executive officer with George Champion, his word, his advice and his recommendations carried weight, but the weight was measured by its wisdom rather than the number of shares of stock he carried in his portfolio. "In those days, we often disagreed and I by no means always won," David explained. Even after 1969, when he himself was chairman of the board and the sole chief executive officer of the bank, his influence at the bank was due to his position in management and not his family name, wealth or shareholdings. The power of representing the management's and bank operating officers' points of view was certainly immense, but David Rockefeller still was answerable to the bank's board of directors, and ultimately, in the actions they took, the powerful men on that board of directors knew they were responsible and answerable to the 800,000 stockholders who, by law, owned the corporation.

The Chase Manhattan, of course, is a vast enterprise spread around the world and run by an intricate bureaucracy of more than thirty thousand employees and five hundred vice-presidents. In reality, it is quite beyond the personal control of any one man. Whether a teller smiles at a depositor or a vice-president rejects a loan application or an officer in the trust department invests in one industry more than the next is beyond the real control of the man on the top. Does the President of the United States control the country? Does he even control the federal government? Or does federal bureaucracy control him? A little of each, perhaps? Or is it a matter of semantics and philosophy? The Chase Manhattan Bank as a corporation is a personal entity itself, in law as well as in reality, with its own history, tradition, momentum and vitality. It is, in a sense, greater than its parts; certainly, more than any one of its parts.

From the first day in 1961 when David Rockefeller became president of the Chase Manhattan Bank, it was clear to everyone who had an interest in the matter that, barring some terrible pratfall in public, David Rockefeller was slated to become chairman of the board and the sole chief executive officer. A pratfall was hardly expected. Throughout his career at the bank, David had always assumed full responsibility and accountability for the job he held. In each position as he climbed the executive ladder at the bank, David proved himself capable or more than capable of the tasks at hand. But, ever a man with long-range perspective, he devoted considerable time during the years as president of the bank in cultivating the respect, admiration and following of his fellow officers at the bank. He knew that the most important and delicate task of an executive is to motivate the men who work for you to give freely the full measure of their capabilities. That, in short, is the secret formula for moving a bureaucracy in business, government or the sundry affairs of men. More than mere job promotions, salary raises or incentive plans is involved. It is the art of good management, an ineffable quality or ambiance, which persuades subordinates to seek with equal fervor the same goals sought by the man at the top. Part of the formula is, of course, choosing your subordinates carefully and skillfully, being absolutely clear in defining the expected goals and then trusting those men to work on their own, to make their own decisions and to gain for themselves the gratification of a job well done. David seemed to have gained through years of self-cultivation that rare judgmental quality of seeking and taking counsel of experts in their field at the bank or in any of the other areas of his activity and then applying his own broad perspective to the advice given to him. In fact, one close associate of all five Rockefeller brothers, a man who had worked for the family activities for more than twenty years, had once defined the extraordinary rate of success which seems to greet almost all of their enterprises: "The Rockefeller brothers know how to make people do what they want them to, without those people feeling like pawns." Thus, each of the Rockefeller brothers called the men who worked closely with them their "multipliers" or "associates," never assistants, as if to say they were all working cooperatively in the same cause toward the same goals which engrossed them equally and from which they would each benefit. Within the hierarchy of a bank, however, the labeling was different, but David conducted himself there as he did with the men who worked for him on his interests and activities outside the bank. He has a way of inspiring confidence in those who worked for him and at the same time letting it be known that he has confidence in them. Rather than inspire fear in his subordinates, he goes out of his way to set at ease those who do not know him too well. Somehow, he lets it be known that he himself is putting out 100 per cent of his effort and that he expects the same effort from men working with him. No one ever remembers David raising his voice in anger. Some who have failed at an assignment are told, "I'm disappointed." They seldom forget it. For it also goes without saying that anyone who fails to measure up to expectations does not stay around David Rockefeller (or any of his brothers) very long.

The delicate balance maintained through these years with David as president and George Champion as chairman of the bank was due largely to the sophistication of both men. Each man recognized the supremacy of the welfare of the bank itself over his personal interest. Whatever differences, disputes or piques rose between the two chief executives were contained within the confines of the seventeenth-floor executive suites. The abrasion between two men who do not see eye to eye on many matters was held to the minimum. Each had his own sphere of responsibility which the other respected with the fidelity of a gentleman. Never a harsh or detrimental opinion was voiced by either which could be heard outside, and, of course, bankers do not gossip. Still, while the two men presented a united front to the outside world, the hierarchy within the bank was split between "David's men" and "George's men." The dichotomy was philosophical and basic between the banker's bankers—men whose hearts were given to the financial aspects of banking—and the economists, like David, who took the longer view of banking operating within its environment. Their goals, of course, were the same, however, different their means: expansion and profits for Chase Manhattan Bank.

In the normal course of events, George Champion turned sixty-five and retired. As expected, David was elected chairman of the board of directors and chief executive officer of Chase Manhattan on March 1, 1969. He was fifty-three years old and in the prime of his life. Responsibility now was his for the over-all operations of the bank here and around the world. Having prepared for this moment for almost ten years, David rapidly moved to do two things: to restructure the internal organization of the bank to conform more closely to his own vision of the future needs in banking; and to reorganize his own schedules and priorities, which already had filled almost every waking hour, so that he could handle double the banking responsibilities as he had before.

For the bank, David engaged the management consulting firm of McKinsey & Company, to make an independent appraisal of the bank's operations. David had long had in mind the restructuring of Chase Manhattan internally from traditional banking operations to a complete financial services corporation of which banking would be only one part.

Since Chase Manhattan had already spread its branches to more than ninety countries and about as far as federal and state banking laws would allow it within the United States, David reasoned, it now would have to expand horizontally in the *kinds* of financial services it offered.

On the personal level, David sought the advice of an old friend, Eugene Black, the former president of the World Bank and a director of Chase Manhattan. Black, one of the most respected men in banking, offered David not only advice but his own special assistant, Joseph Verner Reed, Jr., to serve as David's aide-de-camp. Reed, a tall, thin, active young man with a steel-trap mind and a ready smile, was the product of a background similar to that of David. While not nearly as wealthy, he came from a socially prominent New York-Greenwich family whose fortune still was in the millions and he worked as a banker not for the money but for the challenge of the job. He came to David Rockefeller's office as an efficiency expert, taking over tasks David previously had handled himself, such as keeping the expense accounts, making appointments and answering letters. Together the two men reviewed David Rockefeller's commitments to non-banking organizations, particularly those in the philanthropic field, and they agree that David just had too many demands upon his time. They began cutting back on his vice-chairmanships first, and then on the committee assignments where David was not the head, and finally upon memberships in certain other committees. It was a task of measuring priorities and it was not easy for David. It took a considerable

Nelson Aldrich Rockefeller, Vice-President of the United States.

At age twelve.

Soccer at Dartmouth.

Nelson and Mary Todhunter Clark on their honeymoon.

Speaking as Coordinator of Inter-American Affairs at age thirty-two, with his father listening and contemplating, in 1941.

CAMPAIGNING

Nelson and Happy on their wedding day.

Michael Rockefeller on the New Guinea expedition, 1961.

Abby and Nelson, 1973.

Happy and David.

Being sworn in as Vice-President of the United States, December 19, 1974.

The President and the Vice-President.

amount of time and persuasion for Joseph Reed to convince David that his railroad-subway commute to the bank did not make the best use of the chairman's time. But he finally talked David into investing in a Bell helicopter, an eight-seat executive craft which cut David's commuting time from an hour and a half to eighteen minutes. The bank's limousine whisked the chairman of the board the short distance from the Wall Street heliport to the bank. Once David had decided upon the helicopter, brother Nelson came in as a partner, so that he could be dropped en route at New York's midtown heliport. There were even occasions when the two Rockefeller brothers, flying over the Hudson River, could look down and see their brother Laurance cruising down to work in his forty-foot launch. To conserve his time and provide for his convenience on longer trips, David bought part-ownership in the ultimate in corporate jet aircraft, a $4 million Grumman II, which allowed him to go country-hopping around the world as the "outside man" of Chase Manhattan. As such he was irreplaceable and without parallel. Country-hopping for more than ten years, by 1969 he was personally acquainted, if not friendly, with the heads of state, the foreign ministers, the finance ministers and the bankers of every major nation of the world. No other banker anywhere approached the recognition and reputation of David Rockefeller in international banking. As chairman of Chase Manhattan, he would log more than 200,000 miles a year, visiting all parts of the world, on behalf of the bank. In his Grumman II, David Rockefeller would meet with leaders of fourteen countries in twenty-three days, covering more than 56,000 miles on a single trip. Several rapid swings through twenty-three American cities would easily eat up another 53,000 air miles.

David's work schedule as chairman of the bank rapidly became more highly organized and structured than ever before. Weeks of preparation would precede his arrival in Egypt or Israel or in cities like Detroit, San Francisco or Los Angeles so that he could conduct his business and fly out again in the shortest time possible. The bank's staff work behind these flying tours made it all possible and the preparations involved were not too different from those made for the President of the United States when visiting the same countries as David Rockefeller.

When foreign dignitaries visited the United States, almost all of them found it worthwhile to accept an invitation to lunch or dinner from David Rockefeller. A separate and distinct department at Chase Manhattan was established to handle the details of such entertainment and hospitality, right down to the menus, the wines and the floral arrangements at the table. All these niceties had their rewards, for business at the highest levels of governments, corporations and banks is influenced to a great degree by the personalities involved. The large commercial banks in the United States are highly competitive and their rates, services and charges do not differ as much as the men offering those commodities, and there

David Rockefeller has a unique edge. It was no accident that Chase Manhattan became the key banking institution at the United Nations or that King Faisal of Saudi Arabia would become one of Chase Manhattan's largest single depositors even though the same bank handled bonds for Israel. Years of work and good will were behind David Rockefeller's acceptance equally in the nations of Europe as in Japan and the Far East. Ten years of international conferences with economists of the Soviet Union and satellite nations made David Rockefeller, even though his name epitomized Wall Street capitalism, the most welcomed capitalistic banker behind the Iron Curtain.

To mark his twenty-five years at Chase Manhattan and in the Wall Street financial district in 1971, David made available to the bank a work of modern art which in a way symbolized his progressive influence in the business world. It was a monumental, forty-two-foot-high sculpture called "Group of Four Trees" by the renowned French artist Jean Dubuffet. The twenty-five-ton sculpture—four stark trunks with huge curvy leaves, made of heavy steel covered with layers of fiber glass, aluminum and plastic and painted with polyurethane in black and white—was installed to one side of the bank's main entrance on Chase Manhattan Plaza. When unveiled in October 1972, it drew comments of shock and surprise from the Wall Street community, including many inside Chase Manhattan. It was quickly nicknamed "Snoopy" by some and "The Mushrooms" by others. But in time, as with reactions to much of modern art, people in the bank and those in the area grew familiar with and came to appreciate those huge, cartoon-like trees standing alongside the sleek straight lines of the bank building. In making the presentation, David spoke of it as a "source of enjoyment and fun to all" and as "one more element in the broad cultural and architectural renaissance of lower Manhattan."

Indeed, that free-flowing, exuberant piece of sculpture stands as an unmistakable symbol of youthful freedom alongside a bank which itself so long had stood as the pillar of the Establishment. It seems to say to the beholder: this is the way of the future. It also symbolizes the place of the arts, as David Rockefeller sees it, in the business community of America. What started as an art program for Chase Manhattan under the aegis of David Rockefeller in 1959 with an appropriation of $510,000 for art works of contemporary painters, sculptors and graphic artists spread to the establishment, again under David's spearhead, of a Business Committee on the Arts in 1966 in which virtually every major company in America building a new headquarters or branch office decorated its new buildings and some of its old with art works. Chase Manhattan, with the most prestigious private art-collecting program in the country, spends on the average of $200,000 a year in art for its new branch offices. The selection of art works is made by secret ballot of the bank's art committee, comprised of men and women experts who purchase art for some of the finest museums in the nation. Thus, it is not only the money involved, it is the recognition also given which sustains and encourages so many young American artists. The success of this art program, aside from its aesthetic value and its benefits to the artists, has been accepted throughout the business community as simply good business. The Chase collection of 2,648 pieces purchased at $1.8 million, was appraised at the end of 1973 in excess of $3.5 million. That is a capital gain of almost 100 per cent since 1957, far better than the stock of Chase Manhattan did itself. Good business does not go unnoticed. Corporate art buying has increased over the years to an astounding level of $10 million a year.

David Rockefeller, as much as if not more so than any of the members of the third generation of Rockefellers, makes no bones or excuses about profits or the profit motive: profits are the heart and bloodstream of the free enterprise system and that, in David's view, is the only economic system compatible with freedom of the individual. The alternative can only be a form of totalitarian government which controls the economy and everything else around it. Committed intellectually and philosophically to the free enterprise system, in contrast to a controlled economy, David and his brothers manage their financial resources with as much acumen as they can muster and with all the expert help they can hire. Their money is fully invested and working for them in stocks, bonds and real estate or in cash poised for action. They consider it an obligation imposed upon them, part of their father's concept of the stewardship of the family fortune. David's concern with profits, for instance, is not focused on increased wealth he can pass on to his children. Trust funds established by his father and by himself provide more than his children and his children's children can possibly spend in their lifetimes. His own income from the Chase Manhattan Bank, in salary and stock dividends, averages more than $1 million a year; but that is only a fraction of the income he derives from the original trust his father set up for him in 1934. Over and above that money are the profits which flow in from his own investments. The more money he makes, the higher his salary at the bank only means, as he says, the more money he must give away each year. Nevertheless, profits and capital gains on investments are important to him as a measure of his own stewardship of his wealth and of the healthy functioning of the free enterprise system.

So it was that in the early 1960s, when he became president of the bank, David decided to move into a major new area of investment. A full and careful investigation of the prospects, to be sure, preceded the launching. It started with a suggestion from David's close friend and associate Warren Lindquist, who had handled the detail work in David's efforts to save the character of Morningside Heights and the financial district in lower Manhattan. It was the beginning of the go-go years of a risky spiraling stock market and Lindquist suggested that David might consider diversifying his investments from the market to real estate or land development.

The idea intrigued David Rockefeller. The Rockefeller "edifice complex" was as much as a part of him as it was with his brothers. He believed in growth as a necessary and creative part of the free enterprise system. The question, however, was how you handled that growth in relation to quality, the environment, the economy and other matters. In evaluating the real estate and stock markets with J. Richardson Dilworth, the family's chief investment adviser, David could recognize certain advantages in land development. In the stock market, one must choose not only the industry which will grow but the right company within that industry; and then the situation must be followed closely ever after because actions of the management of the company beyond the investor's control can rapidly alter the prospects of the investment. In real estate, one has only to choose the right type of development in the right place according to one's view of anticipated future growth, and that investment will be profitable. In short, if the country grows economically and you have real estate in the right place, you cannot help but share in that growth. From an evaluation and critique far more complex than this, David evolved a concept of what he sought: he wanted a large-scale real estate development which would yield long-term growth on his investment. He wanted the enterprise to have the extra dimension of social significance, something that would benefit all concerned, be environmentally feasible and at the same time be profitable, something that might set an example for other entrepreneurs.

What he had in mind was close at hand: Rockefeller Center. The complex of office buildings his father had developed a generation before had been erected on a most unlikely site of slums far from the then business center of New York, but its tremendous impact had raised the value of the surrounding area and in turn more than quadrupled the value of Rockefeller Center itself. As a land development project, Rockefeller Center had been well conceived, well executed and administered, and as a result increased enormously in value over a thirty-and-more-year stretch of time.

David sent Lindquist out on a quest to search the United States for such an opportunity in land development: a project in an economically depressed area which would benefit from the impact of a long-term development, be socially significant and profitable over the long haul. He added only two provisos. He was not interested in land speculation for quick profits, for it was understood that he already had all the money he needed. He also told Lindquist to steer clear of New York. He wanted no potential conflict of interest with his position at the bank or with his brother Nelson, who at the time happened to be governor of the state.

Lindquist did indeed search the country for the right opportunity. The proposed package he put together on David's behalf, with the help of

Dilworth and others, set the pattern for virtually all of David's future land development ventures. It involved setting up a separate corporation, David Rockefeller and Associates, which in turn would go into partnership with a local developer and whatever other local interests were needed for a specific project.

The first venture into land development by David Rockefeller and Associates was prodigious by any standard in terms of money, land, concept and risk involved. It took two full years to put together. By 1963, David's group had formed a partnership with the investment brokerage house of Lazard Frères and Company and the California concerns of the Croker Land Company and the Ideal Basic Industries, and together the partners had bought up a strip of waterfront and tidelands property stretching twenty-seven miles from the San Francisco Airport to the Santa Clara Country line. Altogether, it comprised more than ten thousand acres along San Francisco Bay. The partners, calling themselves the Westbay Community Associates, proposed to build no less than a satellite city to San Francisco at a projected cost of more than $1 billion. The plan called for the filling in of some two thousand acres of tidelands and constructing upon the reclaimed land residential, industrial and commercial buildings on 32 per cent of the land. Sixty-eight per cent would be left available for parks, shoreline promenades and wildlife preserves.

The idea behind the Rockefeller plan was the balanced development of the shoreline, providing public access to waterfront where marshes existed before, and to make the whole new integrated community economically self-sustaining at the same time. To David's surprise the public announcement of the plan was met with a fury of opposition. First, almost all of the small roadside restaurant, gas station and motel owners protested that they were being cut off from the waterfront and indeed they were being bypassed by the plan to build directly at the water's edge. Then the powerful Sierra Club entered its objections to any plan which would alter the natural environment of San Francisco Bay. But the greatest stumbling block was the length and breadth of the development plan. The Rockefeller venture required the approval of the San Francisco Bay Conservation and Development Commission, the county of San Mateo, and also the approval of seventeen towns and small cities holding some jurisdiction over those twenty-seven miles of shoreline.

On its first major test before the San Francisco Bay Commission, it failed. The development plan was rejected. Then the county of San Mateo came out with its own plan for the development of its share of the bay front. The Rockefeller group revised their initial plan to meet the objections. Five years later, in June 1968, another plan was submitted. It too was rejected. At this writing, more than ten years after the first plan was conceived, the billion-dollar development of that twenty-seven-mile strip of waterfront property hangs in limbo. David Rockefeller admits defeat;

he can or will do no more to foster what he believes is a bold, innovative and beneficial plan upon people who do not or seem not to want it.

However, even while the San Francisco Bay plan was in the process of failing, David Rockefeller was immersing himself in other land projects which attracted his interest. In 1964, David entered into an equal partnership with Benno C. Schmidt, a managing partner of J. H. Whitney & Company, to buy a sheep farm in Western Australia—15,250 acres of virgin brushland which sustained some sixty thousand sheep and nothing more. It was wild country of small bushes, weeds and topical growth on sand, gravel and clay. The initial investment was $3 million for both men. But they had bold ideas of developing that land. The exciting aspect of this project was using modern agricultural techniques to convert this low-value brushland to fertile pastures capable of sustaining one cow to every two acres and at least four sheep to every one acre. Fertilizers, dams, water storage, grass, clover, eighty miles of fencing and finally a small herd of Santa Gertrudis cattle from the King Ranch in Texas, all were brought to the Rockefeller-Schmidt spread called Orleans Farms. Ten years later, in 1974, Orleans Farms turned a profit for the first time. It was the leading breeding center of Santa Gertrudis cattle in that part of Western Australia, and all around it there grew an increasing number of other farms using the same cultivating techniques to transform the brushland into land capable of sustaining a variety of livestock and crops.

While David's new fascination with real estate investments was not generally known to the public, his brothers were aware of this interest. So when Elwood R. (Pete) Quesada, the dynamic air force general who had served after his retirement as the chairman of the Federal Aviation Agency, approached his old friend Laurance Rockefeller in late 1964 with an intriguing investment proposition, Laurance heard him out and then referred him to his brother David. He advised him to see first David's man in real estate, Lindy, as Lindquist is known to friends. Quesada met with Lindquist and then with David and others in David's entourage. Two days later they shook hands as partners. The venture was a natural for David, although Pete Quesada did not know that at the time. The proposition Quesada brought to David Rockefeller was the building of a small Rockefeller Center in the urban renewal area of the southwest section of Washington, D.C. The blueprints and plans were already drawn and approved by governmental agencies. Called L'Enfant Plaza in honor of the planner of the original Federal City, it was to be an office and shopping complex consisting of four office buildings (one of them in part a 378-room luxury hotel) framing a park-like plaza which, in fact, was the roof of a fifth underground building housing a shopping promenade, a theater, a service station and a parking garage. Cost: $90 million. More than ten years of work had already gone into this project. It had been the very first urban renewal project in the United States in which slums were condemned to make way for office buildings and its legality had been tested right up to the Supreme Court. William Zeckendorf, president of Webb and Knapp, one of the largest real estate firms in the nation, had piloted the project through governmental agencies and the courts. But in 1964, he found himself overextended in real estate and in severe financial difficulties. Quesada, who had originally sought to invest in one of the buildings, found himself offered the entire project by Zeckendorf. With David Rockefeller as his co-partner in a new corporation, it took Quesada more than a year to negotiate the purchase of Webb and Knapp's equity in the project for $8,450,000. By that time, in August 1965, Zeckendorf and his firm had filed for bankruptcy.

But from then on, it was smooth sailing for the investors. L'Enfant Plaza, an architectural gem, was constructed on schedule and its 2 million square feet of interior space was rented virtually as fast as it became available. Since then, one building has been bought by the U. S. Postal Service and another has been optioned by its major tenant, the Communications Satellite Corporation (Comat), each at a substantial profit to the original investors. Fulfilling all of David's expectations, the success of L'Enfant Plaza was secure well into the future.

Not long after David became involved with L'Enfant Plaza, a much larger real estate venture was referred to him through his brother Winthrop. Along the same conceptual lines as L'Enfant Plaza although twice its size, this one called for the construction of four high-rise office towers, an eighty-four-room luxury hotel, shopping, cultural, dining and entertainment facilities—all on eight and a half acres of urban renewal land in the heart of San Francisco, facing the bay not far from the city's famous old Ferry Building. With Rockefeller Center in mind, it was called the Embarcadero Center and it too upon completion would change the skyline and become a landmark in its home city. The estimated cost upon completion sometime in 1977 was $200 million.

The cleared slum land, which had lain dormant for almost nine years, had been bought at a bid in excess of $11 million by a highly individualistic and successful Texas land developer, Trammell Crow, and the project had been preliminarily planned by a relatively unknown architect named John Portman. The hotel alone was to make John Portman one of the most famous architects in America. Trammel Crow had approached Winthrop with the proposal because Winthrop had joined Crow in several ventures over the years, including apartment houses, warehouses and individual office buildings. But on a complex of this size, Winthrop demurred. "See my brother David," Winthrop advised. "He's doing that sort of thing these days."

Soon after David entered into a partnership with Trammell Crow and John Portman in the summer of 1966 and the Embarcadero Center project was announced, tremendous opposition arose in the city by the bay. David, the man with the most famous name, was singled out as the object of antagonism and scurrilous attacks. San Franciscans objected to skyscrapers in their city, recalling vivid images of the 1906 earthquake and the geological fault upon which the city was built. Residents of the famed Nob Hill complained the office towers would block their beloved view of the bay. The Alcoa-Perini real estate consortium, which owned the rest of the thirty-five-acre Title I site, feared the Embarcadero Center would dwarf its buildings. It was not easy. David's group defended its concept before the U. S. Development Agency, and the city's Planning Board and its Board of Supervisors. New technology had provided the know-how for building quake-proof high-rise buildings. Embarcadero Center would build on only 25 per cent of its land, allowing for a large public plaza, trees and assorted greenery. Although building up is far more expensive than spreading out, in the long run it is more advantageous to the public and more profitable to the investors. This time David Rockefeller won.

The first of the sleek towers, the forty-five story Security Pacific Bank Building, was fully rented in short order. By itself, it established the prestige address. But the second building was the Center's tour de force. John Portman's seven-sided Hyatt Regency Hotel astonished San Franciscans with its dramatic atrium court eighteen stories high, surrounded by rooms and balconies, with five sleek glass elevators to carry people up to the lobby on the eighteenth floor and to a revolving Equinox lounge, with its panoramic view of the city and the bay. It was hailed as an architectural masterpiece. The hotel, opened in 1973, drew expressions of approval and even delight from the public and professional critics alike. It became the number-one tourist attraction in San Francisco. At luxury prices, it soon was the hardest hotel in the city in which to book a room (and to ride one of those elevators, you must show your room key). Its convention facilities were booked solid right through to 1980. A veritable success. And then, even before the third building, the Levi Strauss Building, was opened for leasing in 1974, the happy owners Rockefeller, Crow and Portman had sold a 50 per cent interest in the $200 million project to a realty subsidiary of the Prudential Insurance Company of America for a $150 million financing package which included not only permanent mortgage commitments but a substantial cash profit to the initial partners in the happy venture.

David's major contribution to these ventures as well as in all his real estate undertakings was, of course, in the financial area. He put up the seed money to get the project started and then he arranged for the necessary building loans, secured by his personal guarantees (to make good if the project failed). As each building in the complex was completed, a regular long-term mortgage was taken out from a bank or an insurance company based upon (usually 75 per cent) the appraised evaluation. The buildings, with their square footage of rental space carefully calculated, were designed to pay for themselves. In short, David Rockefeller went through the normal real estate financing as anyone else did. The difference between David Rockefeller and the next fellow approaching a bank or insurance company for a loan was not so much the Rockefeller wealth (although that helped) but the reputation of David Rockefeller as a successful entrepreneur, a careful businessman who chooses his ventures and his venture partners with consummate concern for all the proprieties involved. For long-term loans, his guarantees were as good as his money. Actually David almost always chose to invest more equity money than the bank demanded so as to achieve what he considered a satisfactory proportion of equity to debt. Even David Rockefeller had to pay the going rate of interest on his borrowings. At the other end of the financial spectrum, the mere linking of the Rockefeller name with L'Enfant Plaza, Embarcadero or other projects went a long way in attracting quality tenants to the new buildings. David and David's men often played a key role in luring new customers.

Then there was the extra dividend which directly but significantly sweetened the pot. His investments in land and office complexes gave David Rockefeller an added presence and acceptance as a businessman in San Francisco, Washington, Atlanta—where he built a shopping center and a residential community—and other places as well. This acceptance and the natural contacts it brought in the business community allowed David Rockefeller to engender new business in loans, deposits and services for the Chase Manhattan Bank back in New York. Banking and its financial services were an integral part of all business. Virtually all of the outside activities in which David engaged increased his potential in bringing in new business for Chase Manhattan. His love and fascination for banking rested largely in what he describes as "the unque opportunity" banking affords him to do so many other things, all of which can serve to bring new business to the bank. It is an interrelationship difficult to measure in dollars and cents but it is there. On the other hand, David was scrupulous in separating his position at the bank with his multiple personal activities. Never did he apply to Chase Manhattan for his own financing of land development or other investments. Other than have his attorney notify the bank's board of directors of the indebtedness he incurs in these ventures, a requirement of the Federal Reserve Board, David did not need or seek the advice or consent of the bank's board for his outside activities, business or philanthropic.

On the other hand, to accommodate the interests of one of Chase Manhattan's important depositors, David took in on an equal partnership with himself Stavros Niarchos, the Greek millionaire shipbuilder, in the development of a 248-acre commercial/residential complex known as Interstate North on the outskirts of Atlanta, Georgia. Together they bought 50 per cent of the long-term development of 1.6 million square feet of commercial office space and 1,100 garden apartment rental units, about one quarter of which is now completed. The other 50 per cent was owned by a local Atlanta builder, Tom Cousins. The impact of David Rockefeller's reputation was such that upon public announcement of this project the price of the local builder's stock, Cousins Properties, Inc., soared from $15 to well over $100 a share.

How does he do it, this participation in more than $400 million worth of land and real estate development, while holding down the position of president of the then second largest bank in America? Simply through his trusted "multipliers," who act for him with his complete authorization, handling policy negotiations and details with the knowledge of what David would do in each given situation. They report to him in memos, telephone calls or personally and receive his replies usually within a day or two. "David never needs to be briefed twice on a given situation," explained one aide. "His mind is so retentive that you can pick up the gist of a situation where you left off six months ago. He remembers everything that went before." Warren Lindquist served as David's regent in real estate from the 1950s on until the burden became too great for one multiplier, and then Leslie H. Larsen, a young but highly trained man in real estate, was hired in 1964 as a second multiplier. Frank Musselman, of the venerable Rockefeller law firm of Milbank, Tweed, handles the legal work involved, as well as serving on the board of directors of the various projects. David's alter ego in non-banking, non-business activities is a young man, still in his twenties at this writing, Richard Salomon, who does David's detail work at the Rockefeller University, the Council on Foreign Relations, the Museum of Modern Art, Harvard or the Center for Inter-American Relations. Thus, while David Rockefeller might be touring Europe or the Near East, Lindquist would act as David Rockefeller at a meeting of the Downtown-Lower Manhattan Association or out in San Francisco, Larsen could be in Atlanta or Washington, D.C., and Rick Salomon could be at the Rockefeller University or the Museum of Modern Art's Development Committee or at both—all of them David Rockefeller at the same time in the same day. No matter where he himself is— in the United States or abroad, in his limousine or private airplane— David Rockefeller can be reached when needed by any of his senior staff or by others through any one of his three offices. The telephone, that marvelous invention so taken for granted, makes him instantly available to them.

On the personal level, David Rockefeller thoroughly and genuinely enjoys his full daily schedule. The wide variety of his activities and the range of men, women and committees he meets with on any given day safeguard him not only from boredom but also from fatigue. From nine in the morning to midnight or later, five and sometimes six days a week, David Rockefeller is at work, whether in an office, on the road or at a social business-connected affair. If tired working on one set of papers, he needs only to turn to another to renew fresh interest. Formulating a policy for the Rockefeller University's development fund can serve as a relaxation from a staff policy decision needed at the bank. David, like his brother Nelson, is an optimist, indefatigable and fascinated in seeking new information each and every day. What others consider problems, David regards as puzzles to solve, challenges to meet, opportunities to grasp—not problems to worry about.

He is so smooth, level headed and unflappable, very few outsiders and not too many insiders ever get the chance to observe how David handles the enormous workload and the necessary preparation for the meetings he attends or chairs. He works at home whether he is in the city, at Pocantico Hills, in Maine or on vacation in the Caribbean. A trip in the bank's maroon Cadillac limousine or a flight in David's private plane is not merely transportation from one meeting to another, it is an opportunity to read and sign the fifty to eighty letters that go out almost every day over his signature. Of course, the letters are prepared for him, as is the briefing book for each company or country he visits. Each Chase Manhattan branch serves as an ambassadorial post for the visiting bank president. The way is prepared for him. Every request or whim receives top priority, not for the fanfare involved but to conserve the time and energy of David Rockefeller. Every one of the more than twenty thousand men and women with whom David has come in contact through his banking, business, philanthropic and personal interests is listed by name, address and personal particulars in a name file at the bank. One or another of his three secretaries there sees to it that wherever David is going on a particular day, whether it be Oshkosh, Cairo or Budapest, he is never or seldom at a loss for a name.

David Rockefeller functions first and foremost as a banker and economist with his field of speciality in international banking. Through the years he has participated in virtually every important domestic and international banking conference. He himself spearheaded the annual convening of economists from the east and west sides of the old Iron Curtain, which led to the détente of the 1970s. He has been appointed by three Presidents of the United States to serve on commissions recommending monetary and banking policies of the nation. He need only pick up the telephone to reach the President, no matter who is the occupant of the White House at the time. He knows and deals with the men in governmental power from the top on down through the Cabinet. His advice is listened to and treated in high regard, even if his opinion does not carry. The remarkable aspect of the man is not that he is the best-known and one of the foremost bankers of the world. It is his range.

He is accepted as a peer by professionals in so many different fields. He is a land developer, an expert on the stock market, an expert in foreign affairs who can address with complete relaxation and confidence the Council on Foreign Relations. In fact, he is one of the very few men who is received as expert in both Europe and Japan. (Another is a close personal friend, Henry Kissinger, who, as Secretary of State, used David's town house in New York City on occasion for private meetings with visiting foreign dignitaries.) David, through more than twenty years of association with the Rockefeller University, is up-to-date on the latest research in various sciences. He is also a philanthropist who personally gives away as much if not more money every year than any other man in the nation. As a vice-president and director of the Urban Coalition, for a time he was among the white leaders of the civil rights movement during the 1960s, although he worked largely behind the scenes. His involvement with the urban problems of New York City goes so deep that he has been approached at least twice to run for mayor of the city. He has been sounded out time and again, twice during the Nixon administration, about accepting the appointment to Secretary of the Treasury. At least once, he considered a preliminary offer to become Secretary of Defense. He has politely rejected all such offers on grounds that he can be of greater service and maintain greater personal freedom to pursue what he sees as the greater good by remaining with the Chase Manhattan Bank. David Rockefeller knows a considerable amount about art from the nineteenth century through the latest abstract expressionism, and is recognized as one of the leading art patrons in the country. At the helm of his forty-foot sailboat, *Jack Tarr II*, he is an adept competitor in sailing regattas off the coast of Maine, although he prefers cruising to racing (Peggy Rockefeller is a more enthusiatic racing sailor than her husband). David can speak with the enthusiasm and knowledge of a collector on French wines, English fine porcelain, the horticulture his wife pursues as a hobby and a multitude of other subjects. Though his is not a scholar's mastery of entomology, he has retained his interest and skill in that area over the years. His curiosity is seemingly insatiable. For each new subject which attracts him, he devotes the necessary hours of study and research in an attempt to satisfy that insatiability. He is a collector of knowledge and of skills, all of them useful and fascinating to him. Not all of these skills came particularly easy to David Rockefeller. Rather awkward and ungainly physically, he has had to work hard for competence in golf, swimming or other sports. In camp as a young boy, he practiced for hours to win the only competition he had a chance in: floating on his back longer than any other camper. But David's philosophy is not to work at only the things you enjoy, but rather that anything you work hard at, you will come to enjoy.

    If one were, like a security analyst, to chart the personal progress of David Rockefeller over the years in banking, business, investments, foreign relations, civil rights, community participation, education, philanthropy and the arts, the graph line would show a steady upswing proportionately greater year after year. Looking back at the time he became chief executive officer of Chase, David himself would be able to recognize "only some tactical setbacks but no strategic defeats." His career as well as his personal life was marked with one success after another. He seemed to have it all and all of it well put together. A lovely quick-witted wife, six healthy and independent children, friends who remained friends since college days, a career crowned with success, and recognition of his accomplishments by his peers. So when the biggest setback of his career, tactical or strategic, struck rather suddenly despite its gradualism, David was taken somewhat unaware.

The fiscal year 1971–72, give or take a few months on either side, turned out to be what one Chase Manhattan executive described as "the darkest year in this bank's history." Everything seemed to go wrong at once. The all-important bottom line, showing profits and losses by which the bank's efficiency is measured, revealed decline in one department after another. It seemed as if the whole bank, in all its important operations, was slipping seriously.

First, Chase Manhattan lost its coveted position as the largest bank in New York in over-all assets. It was overtaken by its arch-rival, the First National City Bank, which then became the second largest bank in the United States behind the giant Bank of America, which enjoyed statewide banking in California (which was illegal in New York State). Chase Manhattan slipped to third place. The difference in assets was not stark but the loss was one of image: Citibank was on the way up and Chase was on the way down, or so it seemed to those on the outside. The shift in positions was attributed largely to the increase in international banking business and in that area Citibank traditionally had more branches and thus a wider base for profits overseas. But then First National City overtook Chase in domestic banking, in loans and deposits to and from large corporations. That was a bitter pill. To make matters worse, the bottom seemed to fall out of correspondent banking, in which Chase Manhattan for years and years had held the commanding position. By the end of 1971 it was seen that Manufacturers Hanover Trust Company, half the size of Chase, had gained the number-one position among all banks in the volume of correspondent banking. Chase had slipped to second. Wall Street could hardly not take notice. First National City's stock began to rise; Chase's began to fall. It was not that Chase Manhattan Corporation was losing money or that it was not growing every year. No. A securities analysis showed that from 1966 to 1971, Chase had a compound annual growth rate of 7.7 per cent; but during the same time Citibank grew at a rate of 10 per cent, and its chairman was predicting a future annual growth rate of 15 to 20 per cent.

The wagging finger was pointed at David Rockefeller. The banking community in New York, as elsewhere, is a kind of gentleman's club: one does not speak ill of a fellow member. Nevertheless, David Rockefeller was the personification of Chase Manhattan. As he reaped the benefits of Chase's expansion during the booming 1960s, all of his old critics heaped scorn upon his leadership in the lean years of the early 1970s. Almost all of the criticism was kept within the Wall Street confines, although the New York *Times* in a major article wrote of "The Chase at Ebb Tide?" Whispering on the Street renewed the old charges: that David was a figurehead at the bank, that he was an absentee landlord, the largest single stockholder who did not spend enough time at his job. One security analyst was quoted anonymously as explaining, "David is an abstracted man of enormous wealth who moves in a limousine from one global concern to another." At the root of much of this criticism was the pique of a large segment of the business community who resented David Rockefeller, with his vast personal fortune and family name, going about the country lecturing others on their lack of social responsibility, the gap between the rich and the poor in America and the need for the capitalist system to solve the age-old problems of poverty amid plenty. Now these critics could and did imply that David Rockefeller was in trouble because he had been paying too much attention to social responsibility and not enough to that all-important bottom line of profits. There was some talk, some conjecturing, that perhaps David Rockefeller would have to go.

Inside the bank, David himself was unflappable. He moved with the patience and care of his famous grandfather in accounting for the situation to Chase Manhattan's board of directors. Despite all his vaunted power, David was well aware of the limitations upon his position. While outsiders might go on believing the Rockefellers, and David in particular, controlled the Chase Manhattan Bank, David knew full well that he and his actions were accountable to the bank's board of directors, and they, in turn, were answerable to the bank's stockholders. Ultimately, the stockholders owned and controlled the bank. Where mismanagement or mere failure was serious enough, the chairman, the president or a director or all of them were dispensable. That was inherent not only in the system but also in the law of the jungle of competition: survival of the fittest still applied.

David's accounting took in three major reasons for First National City Bank's racing ahead of Chase Manhattan; two of them were largely beyond his or Chase Manhattan's control. First, Chase's traditional competitor was now headed by a dynamic, adept and forceful chairman, Walter B. Wriston, who had reorganized the First National City Bank three years before Chase had been revamped, and who then had launched a brilliant public relations campaign to capitalize on its own good management. In short, the competition was very good and there was nothing much David Rockefeller could do about it except compete.

Second, by chance, the market place in banking changed to favor Citibank's traditional strength in retail banking and in overseas branch banking. At the same time, Chase's traditional strength in correspondent banking was hurt by the recent growth of regional banking, which cut into the need for smaller banks to turn to Chase's services. And that same year the temporary tight squeeze on credit and the high level in the prime rate reduced the level of borrowing by big corporations, which had been one of Chase's most profitable sources of income.

The third and most important factor in Chase Manhattan's slippage was due to David's own overhaul and reorganization of the bank, instigated when he became chairman in 1969. Studied and planned for two years, the reorganization was put into operation on February 1, 1971, and its first year had been rocky indeed. Confusion took over, morale within the bank dipped to an all-time low, the bank's services suffered, customers were distraught. And yet David explained that in the long run, the reorganization had been absolutely necessary for Chase Manhattan's future expansion and well-being. From top to bottom the whole structure of the bank had been changed from the traditional concept of geographical banking to departmentalization on a functional basis. Thus, departments were shifted around, all major corporate accounts were moved to the headquarters bank and consolidated, small business accounts were separated from large corporate accounts, the emphasis was changed from banking loan officers to financial experts who could not only handle a loan but could advise a Chase customer on the esoteric financial needs of his particular business. Management personnel were shifted around so often that many could not tell whether they were being promoted or demoted. A good number of executives left the bank for positions elsewhere, including a vice-chairman, several executive vice-presidents and a number of senior vice-presidents.

After all the reshuffling it was found that of the bank's twelve executive vice-presidents and forty-seven senior vice-presidents—the top of the executive suite—more than 70 per cent of them had been shifted from one job to another. But those who survived were David Rockefeller's type of men—young executives whose average age was forty-six. They were given broad powers and responsibilities in their new positions and under a new organizational chart each one was held accountable for the bottom line in his own department. The tone of leadership in the bank had been fundamentally changed.

David succeeded in convincing his board of directors that the worst was over. The bank had been reorganized along functional lines in anticipation of future needs, much as had the First National City Bank three years earlier. David admitted Citibank's three-year lead, but insisted that Chase would now be competitive.

One major problem remained for David and it involved what was probably the most difficult and vexing executive decision of his banking career. After consultations with many members of the board, David reached the conclusion that the man he chose in 1969 to be president of the bank, Herbert P. Patterson, was not the best man for the job of implementing the day-to-day bank operations under the new reorganization. Patterson, the product of a socially prominent and wealthy family and a long-time friend of David's, had contributed importantly to the planning of the bank reorganization. But he was a rather shy, quiet man who seemed to lack either the drive or the know-how to inspire the bank officers working under him. There were several interrelated factors involved. Rather reluctantly, David concluded that his second-in-command just did not seem aggressive enough for the new thrust contemplated at the bank over the important next five years. David labored over that decision. Patterson was a friend, he had devoted most of his working life to Chase Manhattan, but he was not the man the bank needed now. Once the decision was reached, David acted promptly. On a Wednesday evening, October 11, 1972, David explained "the facts of life" to Herb Patterson and came away with the impression that his old friend was "relieved" at the decision. The very next morning, David called a press conference at the bank and announced that Patterson had resigned, effective that day, and would leave the bank. The announcement hit Wall Street with surprise and shock. Bank presidents were not ordinarily "fired" with such precipitousness. There was some criticism on David's timing. But it gave pause to those on Wall Street who ever had doubted that the mild-mannered David Rockefeller could make a tough and rough decision when one was needed.

Willard C. Butcher, former executive vice-president in charge of the International Department and vice-chairman for planning, expansion and diversification, was elevated to the presidency.

Butcher, an energetic, outgoing man, promptly defined his new role as one in which he would implement the policy decisions of David Rockefeller. "David writes the tune and I see to it that the bank dances to it." On David's part, it was a unilateral decision and he would bear the responsibility for it.

If 1971–72 marked the ebb tide in the affairs of the giant Chase Manhattan Bank and its famed chairman, then the tide flooded in the following year. In image alone, Chase Manhattan Bank could hardly have appeared any more aggressive. In a whirlwind tour of Hungary, Yugoslavia, Romania and Poland, David conferred with the heads of state and national banks there on foreign trade and related topics and then returned home to write a "diary" of the trip for the New York *Times*. Later he learned that he had been the first "live capitalist" that the head of the Polish Communist Party, Edward Gierek, had ever met, and as a result of their talks the socialist leader would propose new laws in Poland which would allow American corporations to share in the profits in joint ventures there.

In March of that year, Chase Manhattan announced that it was making the largest private loan in history to the Soviet Union, $86 million, matching a similar amount from the World Bank, for the construction of the largest truck factory in the world on the Kama River five hundred miles east of Moscow. Aside from the obvious advantages to the Soviet Union, the giant loan dramatically signaled the potential scope of increased trade between East and West, ending the twenty-year frost of the cold war. Virtually all of that money would be spent by the Soviet Union in buying American technology, helping America's balance of trade and making jobs for thousands of American workers. For Chase Manhattan it augured well for the future. While it was a large chunk of new business in itself, Chase lent the $86 million at a relatively low but yet profitable rate of interest. The important dividend lay in the future potential, for the Soviets let it be known that they had in mind some other loans in the $100 million class.

In May of that year, Chase Manhattan opened a representative office in Moscow, the first of its kind since 1929, beating out its competition, who were allowed in later, the First National City Bank and the Bank of America. There was no question in the minds of international economists that with the portents of increased East-West trade, the first banks on the scene would reap the harvest in the financing of that increased trade. Nor could this move help but increase the influence of David Rockefeller in advising American corporate heads how and in what areas it would be best to do business with the Soviets and the Soviet-bloc nations. And, of course, all these American corporate executives seeking David's counsel could demonstrate their own appreciation by doing business with Chase Manhattan, as David himself was not loath to point out.

The very next month, June, David Rockefeller was in Peking, conferring with Premier Chou En-lai and other Chinese officials on what he called "a large number of subjects." Following close on the heels of President Nixon's historic visit, which opened relations with the People's Republic of China for the first time since 1949, David was the first capitalistic banker to be welcomed behind the Bamboo Curtain. In a sense, it was the culmination of his twenty-seven-year career, synthesizing all his interests in banking, foreign affairs, education and the arts. For the new aggressive image of Chase Manhattan, it was a veritable coup. At the end of the ten-day visit, it was announced that Chase Manhattan would act as the correspondent bank for the Bank of China in the United States, handling the transfer of funds. The true significance of this agreement, to David's mind, was that the leaders of mainland China, who had deliberately cut their country off from the rest of the world in order to develop its own unique structure of society, now were confident enough of their own success to re-establish outside contacts and to seek the technology, capital and goods of the Western world. The potential for trade between China and the United States was enormous but still in the future. Chase Manhattan would be on the scene for the necessary transition, helping to work out the mechanics of exports and imports with the United States.

Because he was who he was and had done what he had done, David was able to offer the leaders of the most populous nation in the world more than the services of the Chase Manhattan Bank. He initiated proposals for future ties between the Council on Foreign Relations, of which he was chairman, and the People's Institute for Foreign Relations in Peking. Let the knowledgeable men in foreign affairs of both nations come together and discuss mutual areas of conflict and cooperation, he proposed. Then, as chairman of the board of Rockefeller University, he proposed the mutual interchange of ideas and men in the pure sciences between China and what had been the Rockefeller Institute for Medical Research. In all, it was for David a coming together of his major interests in life at the dawning of a new era of international cooperation.

Then, in September of 1973, for the first time since he became chairman, David went before a large group of Wall Street security analysts and, aided by the bank's new president, Willard Butcher, presented his view of Chase Manhattan as "an aggressive, high-quality international financial services corporation." After explaining the bank's reorganization, he offered a glimpse of the future for Chase Manhattan (and commercial banking in general). Chase Manhattan already had drawn up plans for statewide banking throughout New York and to go into the personal small loan business by purchasing the ninth largest finance company in the United States, if and when the legal restrictions were removed, as expected. Its long-range strategy called for broad diversification into the financial aspects of real estate, retail service, small businesses and computerized finance-information services—all of them on a worldwide basis.

A week later, Chase Manhattan stock rose eight points on the Stock Exchange. At the year's end, the bottom line once again showed a healthy upward mobility, morale within the bank was high, David Rockefeller was as busy as ever, fulfilling a jam-packed schedule of activities. In the rush, David has been obliged rather reluctantly to give up or to forgo entirely some of the amenities he once shared with so many other men. His wife Peggy accompanied him on the trip to China because that trip was something special, even for the Rockefellers. But since he became chairman of the bank, there has been less free time on his business trips, less free time to make it worthwhile for Peggy to help David mix pleasure with business. He has given up one of his loves, that of walking in the streets of Manhattan. After he became chairman, those around him finally convinced him that one, he was more recognizable, and two, the streets of New York were too dangerous for the chairman of Chase Manhattan.

Now the limousine waits for him. And a bodyguard has been added to the entourage and two revolvers are kept handy in the limousine. Now David cannot go to Parke-Bernet art auctions, because he is too well-known. He must search the catalogues and send one of his men to do the bidding and derive the pleasure thereof.

The inescapable point is that David Rockefeller is now recognizable as one of the ten most influential or powerful men in the United States. In the financial community, he is one of a handful at the very pinnacle of influence and power. In a list of world leaders, he is there always. Some point to him as perhaps the most powerful or influential man in America outside of the man in the White House. Not only is he one of the wealthiest men in America, he is the top man of a bank with more than $35 billion in assets, more than is available to most chiefs of state, but, more important, he knows and does business in one form or another with the men of power throughout the world. Having conferred with Chou En-lai for two hours in Peking, he knows everybody; he can reach anyone and he or she will listen to what David Rockefeller has on his mind to say. He is by general consensus the most successful, influential and powerful of the five Rockefeller brothers.

Even when the new Democratic Administration of Jimmy Carter took office in 1977, the presence and influence of David Rockefeller were discernible. The new President had cut his eyeteeth in foreign policy affairs as a citizen member of the Trilateral Commission, founded by David in 1973 as a means of gathering eminent private citizens from North America, Europe and Japan in periodical meetings to recommend policies which would foster closer economic and political cooperation between those three key areas of the world. The Trilateral Commission, with sixty members from North America and Japan and another eighty-five from Europe, was influential from the very start because its policy recommendations represented a wide consensus of expert opinion and its members had access to heads of state. But when Jimmy Carter was elected President of the United States, the Trilateral Commission seemed to become a veritable supply depot for appointments to the highest ranks of his government. The new Secretaries of State, Treasury and Defense, his new national security adviser and his chief arms negotiator as well as a good many deputy secretaries and undersecretaries and ambassadors all came from the ranks of the Trilateral Commission, as had the new President and the new Vice-President.

Within the Rockefeller family, however, the old childhood sibling rivalry remains. No matter what his achievements, David will always be the youngest of the Rockefeller brothers. David's promotions in the bank did not stop his brother Nelson from needling him from time to time, calling him Little David, knowing full well the old childhood put-down made his brother furious and incapable of responding; or if Little David seemed a bit too much, Nelson could use a substitute: he would call him Dave or Davey and equally conjure up old memories of David as the baby of the family. While outside scorekeepers might rank David as the most influential of all the Rockefeller brothers, his brothers were always poised to give him his comeuppance when necessary. At one Rockefeller Brothers Fund meeting, for instance, David was arguing for RBF increased support for the New York Philharmonic Orchestra and he tried to highlight the need by saying: "Why, I'm giving the Philharmonic $500,000 myself." At that brother Laurance leaned over the table, cupped his chin in his hand, looked his brother in the eye and mockingly exclaimed, "Oh, David, I didn't know you had *that* kind of money!"

But David of course *does* have that kind of money, and, more important to him, he has that kind of influence and power to affect men and events in New York, in the United States and really throughout the world. That does not mean he controls every one or most or even many of the situations in which he participates. But what he does exert is leverage, based upon his personal know-how, his track record in achieving specific goals and his key managerial position in one of the largest banks in the world, leverage to motivate and move others in worthwhile causes which are part and parcel of the democratic, pluralistic, free enterprise system.

David Rockefeller is a happy man, committed to an enterprise far greater than himself. He works hard at each of his commitments and he enjoys his daily life. One of his associates summed it up: "David is happy as a clam, completely self-assured, and entirely convinced that he is the best man for the job he holds at the bank and that the bank is the very best job for him." He himself has often given that same reason for turning down offers of government jobs. He has told those who approach him that he is not interested in elective office. He is happy and free where he is now.

17

Winthrop

"A victory even in defeat . . ."

When Winthrop Rockefeller announced publicly on June 5, 1953, that henceforth he was making his legal residence in Arkansas, the people of that deprived, backwater state shook their collective head in sheer wonderment: "Why would anyone like that, coming from New York, want to live down here?" People in Arkansas who had a choice, particularly the young with any sort of education, were going the other way, leaving Arkansas, assured that they could make more money anywhere else. In the midst of the postwar baby boom, Arkansas still had been losing population every year since the end of the Second World War. The popular assumption was that Winthrop Rockefeller had come to Arkansas only to get an easy divorce and that he would not stay long.

For Winthrop personally, however, Arkansas was offering him, at forty-one, a great deal more, all of which added up to a new lease on life. From the feeling of being superfluous in the Rockefeller family entourage in New York, from hearing far too often "Oh, let Winnie do it" when a Rockefeller project arose that none of his brothers wanted to do, Winthrop sensed that Arkansas offered him open vistas of opportunities to express himself individually, far away from the influence and watchful eye of his family. In Arkansas, he could make an impact. Much would be expected of him and he was ready to give; he had had more than enough of his playboy days of frustration in New York. He liked the people here, too. They reminded him of his happy days in the Texas oil fields, people who were straightforward, proud, close to the earth, men who worked with their hands and brawn as much as with their brains. Yes, Arkansas had a more liberal divorce law than New York: his move here would convince

Bobo that he was serious about getting a divorce (separation was grounds for divorce in Arkansas). But that was only part of it. Winthrop had decided he wanted to make a new life, somewhat along the lines that his old Army buddy Frank Newell had visualized for him years before, and he wanted to make it here in Arkansas.

He had decided upon Arkansas three months earlier, after he had driven down from New York in March with Jimmy Hudson in his black Cadillac limousine. Frank Newell had promptly dubbed it "the Hearse," and they all, along with Frank's new young bride, Jo-Anne, had gone up to see the top of Petit Jean Mountain. It had been cold, misty, gray, damp and overcast. The trees were bare and Jo-Anne was certain that Winthrop Rockefeller would not like it. The homestead that Frank Newell had in mind for Winthrop was on the northwest brow of the Petit Jean mesa, almost inaccessible, the sagebrush was so thick and the dirt road so rutted. The house itself was small and made of flagstone, with a large living room, two small bedrooms and a primitive kitchen. The owner was Walter C. Hudson, a recluse known as Old Man Hudson, a former banker well up in his seventies, who had lived there year round for more than twenty years, since he had been accused of embezzlement back in the 1930s. When Winthrop met him, the old man agreed to sell but he trusted no one, not Winthrop Rockefeller, not any bank, and he did not want cash or a mortgage. The place was a mess, frightful, lonely, all two-hundred-odd acres of it. But the house was located at the very edge of the mountain with a sheer drop of some 850 feet and the view over the edge of the mountain was spectacular. The Arkansas River stretched its jagged, winding way below for as far as the eye could see. Frank Newell assured Winthrop that on an ordinary day you could see for sixty miles and on a particularly clear day for perhaps a hundred miles. The Rockefeller in Winthrop loved it. It reminded him of how his grandfather had probably looked upon the Pocantico Hills property more than fifty years before, the expansive landscape, the high hill where the main house would stand and the view of the Hudson River down below in the valley. It was all here on Petit Jean Mountain to do over again and in his own way. The view, the potential and the sheer challenge of it all seemed far better than Pocantico Hills in his grandfather's or even in his father's day. In a little more than two weeks Winthrop decided to buy this homestead and he worked out the details: $85,000 in United States Savings Bonds, which Old Man Hudson had insisted were the only tender he would accept.

He spent those two weeks atop the mountain, as a house guest along with Jimmy Hudson of George Reynolds, a Little Rock businessman who had the only house on the mountain with one room air-conditioned, and he made fast friends with another of Petit Jean's leading citizens, Henry Kamp, a retired university professor of Latin and Greek. These two men introduced him to other friends and neighbors on the mountain. "I'm

Win Rockefeller," he would say in introducing himself time and again. He was absolutely casual, natural and outgoing in his demeanor and conversation. He talked for hours on end with everyone who had views and information about Arkansas, Petit Jean Mountain or life in general. Winthrop fairly soon decided that he wanted to live on this mountain and commute when necessary to Little Rock, as opposed to most who used the mountain as a summer vacation retreat, and he knew what he wanted to do up there: raise cattle. It was not a new idea for Winthrop. Back in 1937 when he visited Argentina with his brother Nelson, they both had entertained the idea of starting a ranch in Texas and Win had spoken enthusiastically of his memories of the King Ranch, which he had visited while a roustabout in Texas. But nothing had come of that idea, except of course that Nelson subsequently bought a ranch of his own in Venezuela, and Winthrop had been sidetracked into the Army. Now, after buying the Hudson property, he made a trip to the King Ranch to see his old friend Robert Kleberg, Jr., grandson of the founder of the largest cattle spread in the country, and they talked long into the night on the vicissitudes of cattle raising.

By June, Winthrop was ready to announce publicly his move to Arkansas and, with a certain sense of relief and satisfaction, to cut his ties with New York. He resigned from the state Chamber of Commerce, from the New York State Society for Medical Research, from the New York City Public Education Association, from the board of the NYU-Bellevue Medical Center, from the council of the United Hospital Fund, from the Board of Hospitals of New York City, from the governing council of New York University, from the Historical Society of the Tarrytowns. He also resigned as chairman of IBEC Housing, in which he had been associated with Brother Nelson and Nelson's son Rodman. And, most significantly, he resigned from the executive committee of Hills Realty, the company in which he shared ownership with his brothers in the Pocantico Hills estate. Nothing could be clearer than that to indicate that Winthrop had no intention of ever returning to New York.

With research and help from advisers at the Chase Manhattan Bank in New York and the local know-how of Frank Newell, Winthrop chose an attorney and an accountant to help handle his financial and legal affairs in Little Rock and then with wholehearted abandon he threw himself into the work transforming his mountaintop homestead into what would be recognized as the finest, fanciest, most manicured ranch in the state. Frank Newell brought up a young, fairly inexperienced but well-trained architect named Edwin Cromwell to fix up one bathroom for the millionaire on the mountain and Ed Cromwell stayed on for the next three years with the biggest job of his career. G. W. Adkinson, who owned a small ranch near Little Rock, came up to advise on the building of barns and corrals and stayed on as manager for sixteen years. Benjamin Mitchell, a former Pullman porter and cook, joined the Petit Jean crew as chief cook and bottlewasher, and remained as a friend of the family for the rest of Winthrop Rockefeller's life. All of them became fast friends on a first-name basis, Win and Ed and G.W. and Ben and, of course, Frank (Newell) and Jimmy (Hudson).

They worked, played, drank and joked together from early morning to 5 P.M. and then they gathered around the large white ice chest for drinks while they planned what they would do the next day. Ed Cromwell, the architect, made drawings and models of what Win Rockefeller thought he wanted. What did not work out, they changed. It was not long before they all discovered that Win Rockefeller indeed knew what he wanted. A good deal of what he wanted was deemed impractical, but only by their standard, not his, and he was the only one paying the bills. Ed recommended first of all that they push the old house over the side of the mountain and build a new one. That would be practical and cheaper. But Win insisted on keeping the old house for its weather-softened flagstone and building onto it. What he wanted was a home with a low profile which looked simple and natural in its setting, made of local stone and wood, one which would seem to have just grown in its place, all on one floor, ranch style, with living room, dining room, kitchen and four bedrooms. Afterward, there would be a separate guesthouse for visitors, a playhouse for exercise and entertainment, and many other amenities as needed. But at the start the primary task was building a home he could live in and a farm he could work.

G.W., as the experienced rancher, advised the obvious: you don't ranch cattle on top of a mountain; you should build the ranch part of this estate at the foot of the mountain, where the Petit Jean River flows into the Arkansas River and where water and grazing land are plentiful. But Win Rockefeller wanted to live on top of the mountain and he wanted his cattle right up there with him. He called in soil conservationists and water experts from the State Department of Agriculture and he consulted with the local county agent and he hired private experts for the information and advice he needed. And after he had drilled deep for water three times, at $700 a hole, and had come up dry, and after much time, effort and thought, he embarked on a fantastically expensive plan, which astonished his Arkansas neighbors, of pumping water from the Petit Jean River up to the top of the mountain, 850 feet. Because the land at the edge of the river was inaccessible to large trucks, the giant pumps had to be lowered into place by cranes from the top of the mountain. Aluminum pipes carried the water, pumped at 1,320 gallons per minute, up the sheer mountainside to a sprinkler system which could "rain" almost three inches of water on 5 acres of pastureland in four and half hours. Later the sprinkler system would be extended to 189 acres and the water would be pumped to and stored in six man-made lakes, named for his mother and favorite aunts. Lake Abby was the one closest to the house, used for swimming, boating, picnics and the site of the usual Sunday night family barbecue.

But all that was still in the future. The work was begun in the summer of 1953, long remembered as the hottest, driest summer in Arkansas history. Winthrop hired men from a list he requested from Dr. Kamp of the men living on the mountain and in need of work. They were trained on the job. Winthrop worked along with them, wearing the faded Levi's and the battered leather boots he had saved from his prewar days in the Texas oil fields. He worked hard and with his hands and he loved it. He lost weight and toughened up once again, regaining the physique and health he enjoyed in his Army days. He walked miles every day pacing off his land, fencing it, deciding where each barn, each pasture, each road should be built. He delved into every decision which had to be made. No blueprints were ever drawn for the main house or any of the buildings. They planned and built and revised and rebuilt as they went along, almost on a daily basis. For Winthrop, it was a very personal undertaking. From the very start he had a vision of what he could do with this unused scrub land. For the Rockefeller in him, it was the sheer joy of making something out of nothing.

More than just a homestead, a ranch or a farm, he visualized how this project would change life for all those on top of Petit Jean Mountain. As he learned about Arkansas from his frequent conversations with the men he met, he would correlate that local information with what he had learned as a Rockefeller: that by doing something positive, you could demonstrate rather than preach to others what could be done. In one simple, subtle stroke, for instance, he demonstrated his attitude on segregation and civil rights in the South. He made Jimmy Hudson the superintendent-manager of his operation on Petit Jean. He introduced him as "my associate." Anyone who wanted to sell anything to Winthrop Rockefeller had to do business with his associate, who just happened to be black. The labor force quickly grew to more than one hundred men and blacks and whites worked alongside one another without rancor. After all, it was by far the best job available on Petit Jean Mountain.

In August, a bare two months after he had begun, Winthrop flew down to the King Ranch in Texas for its annual auction of Santa Gertrudis bulls and heifers. He had already decided upon raising this first all-American new breed of cattle, developed on the King Ranch in the 1920s, which combined the best features of the Brahman (hardiness) and the Shorthorn (meat production). He had been attracted to the breed because the Santa Gertrudis was a beautiful, magnificent beast, large in size, dark cherry red in color and sleek in appearance. While not a particularly popular breed of cattle at the time, the Santa Gertrudis did have certain commercial advantages. They had high tolerance for hot weather and insects, were able to flourish on grass alone and could take a lot of drought punishment. Thus they could be raised successfully in many areas of the world where other cattle could not. Equally important, their hereditary characteristics were dominant. Thus, crossbreeding them would uplift the quality of any stock and in four generations of breeding the new strain would become pure Santa Gertrudis. Winthrop's concept was to operate a breeding farm rather than an ordinary ranch. He intended to make Santa Gertrudis a breed widely known, nationally and internationally. He was aware naturally of the tax advantages of raising cattle but in his tax bracket and with his vast annual income those tax benefits were minimal. He wanted to contribute something to society by raising cattle scientifically and to learn himself and then to show what could be done, as it had been explained to him. Of course, Winthrop Rockefeller wanted to start with the very best breeding sire available, and being a Rockefeller, he got just that by bidding at auction the highest price ever paid up to that time for a Santa Gertrudis bull: $31,500. It was a two-year-old, weighing 1,600 pounds, which at maturity three years later would weigh about 2,400 pounds. Naturally, he named this champion Rock. Twenty-four heifers and another bull (named Feller) completed Winthrop's entree into the cattle business.

Back at Petit Jean Mountain, attired in well-worn Levi's, boots and ten-gallon Stetson, sweating heavily under the fierce Arkansas sun, Winthrop Rockefeller plunged into the building of his farm: fertilizing the land, fencing in the hundreds of acres of pastures, planning and building new roads and, of course, the construction of barns, corrals, silos and ancillary structures. He insisted on the best of everything; price seemed immaterial when he wanted something and wanted it fast; every barn and every building became a showpiece; the corrals and cattle pens were made of oil pipe instead of wood, far more expensive but then they would never rot. Arkansans were shocked at Winthrop Rockefeller's standards in farming and at the cost. Jimmy Hudson was the only one, at least at the beginning, who could joke about it in front of Winthrop. "Why don't you just put up the Empire State Building here for the money you're spending?" he would ask at the ice chest at the end of a workday. It was Jimmy Hudson who could and did label the place as "the Gold-Plated Farm." Winthrop took it all in good humor. He insisted it was money well spent. If his operation was to mean anything at all, he wanted it to represent the very best. In fact, Winthrop said that so often, it became later the official motto of his operation: "The WR brand must always mean 'the Best.'"

For the long road leading up to the residence and farm, Winthrop planted young cedar trees and strung chicken wire to catch the seeds blown by the wind so that in time it would be lined and shaded with cedars. One venerable and magnificent cedar tree caught Winthrop's eye and when his U-shaped home was completed, he decided to move that cedar to the center of the front courtyard. Others said it could not be done; the tree would die. But Winthrop had seen giant pines moved at Pocantico Hills. In due course the old cedar was carefully, almost surgically, lifted out of the ground, roots and all, and dragged by bulldozer and replanted in that center courtyard, lighted at night, where it flourishes today as though it had been there long before the house had been built around it. Since the original house was perched at the edge of the mountain, Winthrop had his "back yard" built by extending the mountain itself. Rocks, earth and nine feet of topsoil were carried and planted at the mountain's brow, giving the home a new one-hundred-foot back lawn, new trees and a gracefully small swimming pool, which few people ever used. Actually, he had reshaped the contour of the mountain. Upon several man-made ledges he planted pines and cedars in tubs, pruned and shaped so that only their tops landscaped the land Winthrop Rockefeller and his guests would see from the living room picture window. Beyond the brow of the mountain, of course, stretched a vista of rural Arkansas as far as the eye could see, a bird's-eye view of farmland, a river, sky, and on the horizon, the distant outline of another mountain 2,800 feet high. One of the finishing touches installed by Winthrop was a huge boulder, "borrowed" from Dr. Kamp and implanted on the edge of the mountain a short walk from the main house, facing the setting sun, bearing a small bronze plaque with his mother's favorite quotation from the Bible:

> What doth the Lord require of thee but to do justly, and to love mercy, and to walk humbly with thy God?
>
> MICAH 6:8

The farm was never "finished" in any sense of absolute completion. It just continued to grow and grow. Winthrop, in the eyes of those around him, seemed to grow and grow with it. The emotional tension he brought from New York dissipated itself as he threw himself into more and more physical labor. The Rockefeller sense of perfectionism came out in him too. "If you're going to do it at all, do it right," he would say over and over again, whether to a laborer driving in a fence post or to someone arranging a complex business deal. He worked long hours and expected those around him to work just as long. His rule was that you worked as long as a given task required and then you took compensating time off. He was demanding. But he paid well. Beyond that, he went out of his way to help those who worked for him, even to the point of guaranteeing funds to send the children of all employees to college. To answer the fears that once the farm was built he would seclude himself on the mountaintop, Winthrop invited everyone living on the mountain and all his employees to a Christmas party the week before the holiday. Each family was given a turkey and each child under eighteen was presented with an individual gift with his name on it. Dr. Kamp played Santa Claus in costume and

Winthrop by his side handed out the presents to the children. It became a tradition on the mountain, Win's Christmas party. Despite the disparity in wealth and position, on the mountain Winthrop Rockefeller wanted to be taken as a friend and neighbor.

It soon became clear to Winthrop that he could not confine his life to the top of a mountain in Arkansas. George Reynolds and Frank Newell, his closest friends and advisers, talked with him for hours, days and months about Arkansas, everything about Arkansas, its economics, its politics, its sociology, its history, its customs and above all, its people. Winthrop became more and more involved. Just as he had built his manicured, model farm out of nothing, in a manner not unlike what his father and grandfather had done in Pocantico Hills, he now turned his attention to philanthropy and business as the Rockefellers had before him, starting small and close to home. Yet there was a difference. What was small to Winthrop Rockefeller was astonishing in size to most Arkansans. Six months after settling in Arkansas, he gave $100,000 in Standard Oil of California stock to four Arkansas colleges, two white and two black, to establish student aid funds. He followed that with a $50,000 outright gift to nine denominational colleges to launch a joint fund-raising drive to raise more money. He gave $50,000 in matching funds for a hospital addition. Those contributions alone were greater than the sum total of all scholarships given by others in all of Arkansas's history. He then became involved in setting up a rural health clinic in nearby Perry County, one of the many counties which had no doctors. This was much more difficult than merely giving money. Winthrop toured the county in order to convince people that, first, they needed such a clinic, and second, that they must prove their interest by their own contributions. Perry County raised $17,000, a portion of it in collections of pennies from schoolchildren, and Winthrop journeyed back to the Rockefeller Brothers Fund in New York to raise more than $100,000 to set up the health clinic, designed as a model for other counties.

Arkansas as a poor state had every kind of problem imaginable, in education, health and a host of other areas, but its foremost problem was economic. From a southern cotton economy, it had shifted to soybean and rice farming and then, hit by the technological revolution in agriculture after the Second World War, farm laborers were laid off their jobs and found no place to go for work except outside of Arkansas. More than 400,000 residents had been forced to emigrate in search of work since the end of the war. Then, in November 1954, a new and dynamic young politician was elected governor on the promise of bringing new industry to the state. His name was Orval Faubus, who rose from the backwoods of the Ozarks to become Arkansas's most popular and most powerful governor, elected six times despite or because of his singular defiance of the Supreme Court of the United States, President Dwight Eisenhower and the soldiers of the National Guard in the integration of schools in Little Rock in 1957. But in March 1955, soon after taking office for the first time, Governor Faubus convinced the Arkansas legislature to declare a state of emergency on unemployment and to form the Arkansas Industrial Development Commission (AIDC) to industrialize the state. He asked Winthrop Rockefeller to run it.

Winthrop welcomed the opportunity. He had been in Arkansas only two years at the time but he had already met most of its leading businessmen and had been schooled by Frank Newell, Dr. Kamp and others. But, more than that, he had learned if only by proximity and osmosis some of the Rockefeller family methods in handling large-scale projects. Altogether, it seemed he did everything right, particularly at the beginning when he hired the right men for the right jobs. Ignoring the low salary scale set up by the legislature, he hired a top-flight man from Baltimore to administer the program at $20,000 a year instead of at $8,000 as provided by the legislature, and so on down the line for the eleven members of his staff. When he had spent the full $127,500 budget provided before any actual work had begun, he launched a fund-raising campaign. First he recruited a hundred men into an Arkansas Industrialization Panel, for which privilege each of them contributed $1,000, and then he sent those hundred men out all over the state to raise more money and took in another $200,000. Then the AIDC got to work on what turned out to be the most innovative, energetic program to bring new business to Arkansas.

On the one hand, every city, county and town was urged to survey what it had to offer to new business: available skilled and unskilled labor, sites for new factories, transportation facilities, availability of water and utilities. On the other hand, the AIDC launched a $100,000 advertising campaign in major U.S. magazines to combat the state's hillbilly reputation and to sell the state's advantages: a big labor pool and cheap plant sites. They sent personal letters to the heads of every large manufacturing company in the United States with a B rating or better. The letters were followed by telephone calls and then by personal visits by staff men and then, when prospects looked hot, by Winthrop Rockefeller himself. The Rockefeller name helped. Winthrop could get in to see anyone, or almost anyone, he chose to call upon. That would be followed by an invitation to dinner and some talk at Winrock Farms. Some of those old Rockefeller precepts learned as a child now served Winthrop well: "There are no problems, only challenges," or "There is nothing bad that does not have something good in it." In talking to out-of-staters, Winthrop would often broaden his vowels so that one would swear he came from Boston or Groton country. His selling pitch would invariably be linked to the people's willingness to work in Arkansas. Without emphasizing the state's massive unemployment he would ask prospective customers: "Do you know that men would drive thirty or forty miles here on the chance of getting six dollars for a day's work? Now, a state with people like that has a future!"

Where resistance arose in any discernible pattern, the AIDC fought to wipe out specific objections. For small companies willing to come to Arkansas but financially unable to build, private investors or the state itself would buy bonds to pay for the new plant, which the company would pay off in twenty years at low interest rates. When some northern firms objected to the lack of cultural attractions in the state, the AIDC scurried all over the state to start up local playhouses, symphony orchestras and concert halls. It even sponsored a "Concert Hall of the Air" to broadcast classical music. When the AIDC lost out on a $100 million plant for Glenn Martin guided missiles, it launched a campaign which persuaded the legislature to establish a Graduate Institute of Technology at the University of Arkansas to provide advanced training for workers. Again, Winthrop Rockefeller was the driving wedge. He invited a distinguished group of scientists and educators to the Winrock Farms to recommend the program needed for the purpose at hand.

In 1956, its first full year of operation, the AIDC attracted 194 new or expanded industries to Arkansas, creating 12,521 new jobs and $130 million in new capital investment. The state's per capita income went up 9.3 per cent to $1,062. Most important of all, the state's population rose for the first time since World War II, which meant that Arkansans were coming back to Arkansas.

To practice as well as preach, in December 1955, Winthrop launched Winrock Enterprises, a venture capital company concentrating upon land development and new local businesses in Arkansas. One of the first ventures which intrigued him was the possibility of putting up a high-rise office building in Little Rock. None had been built in all of Arkansas since the crash of 1929.

With hardly a surprise at all, in 1956 Winthrop Rockefeller was voted Arkansas Man of the Year by the readers of *The Arkansas Democrat*. In the eyes of almost all Arkansans it seemed perfectly clear that Winthrop Rockefeller was actually "doing something" for the state. He became perhaps the most talked-about man in the state, the most sought-after speaker at conventions, dinners, fairs and schools. "Everybody's curious about him, and when they see and hear him, they like him—he's down to earth," was a typical comment during the early years of the AIDC, when Winthrop flew around the state sometimes making three or four speeches a day. And yet there was still the prevailing opinion throughout the state that he would not remain in Arkansas very long. Arkansans wanted him to stay, of course, but most believed he would leave. No matter how many times he proclaimed himself an Arkansan for life, and he did that in almost every speech, people in Arkansas just did not believe him. Arkansas society did its best to entice him with introductions to suitable and available women and the news media speculated on his romantic inclinations, linking his name with more wealthy widows than he ever met in Arkansas. One young society matron explained the situation in late 1955 to an out-of-state newsman: "After all, we don't have Rockefellers moving in on us every day of the week and naturally we want to hold onto him. Before Winthrop got down here, we didn't have much to talk about except the weather—now its the weather and Winthrop.

"It's very disconcerting, since somehow, regardless of what he says, we have the idea he'll never become part of our state until he either brings a wife to his ranch or, better still, marries one of our girls. There is always the risk that an outsider might not like it down here, particularly one of those Park Avenue butterflies, and the first thing you know Winthrop would be spending less and less time here. So I suppose it's only natural for us to take to pairing Winthrop off speculatively, with the girls we think he might like, and the next thing you know the stories are all over town."

On matters concerning the heart and personal affairs, Winthrop had learned to be thoroughly Rockefeller in keeping his own counsel. He knew, even before he came to Arkansas, who his new wife would be. They both had agreed to wait, first for his divorce from Bobo to become final, then for the furor and pain to die down and then simply for time so that the divorce and his second marriage would not be linked together. Through a mutual friend they had met in 1951, not long after his separation and her third divorce, and Winthrop had become a surrogate father to her two young children, Bruce and Anne, and she had met and been welcomed by the Rockefeller clan at get-togethers in Pocantico Hills. Jeannette, four years younger than Winthrop, was the daughter of William Edris, a Seattle industrialist and millionaire who owned extensive theatrical, realty and food-packing interests on the West Coast. In her youth she had been every bit as wild and irrepressible as Winthrop. At seventeen, she had defied her father and eloped with an All-American football player at the University of Southern California. Within a year, they were divorced. Three years later, she married a Seattle attorney, Bruce Bartley and they had two children. When that marriage failed after almost ten years, she married a New York business executive. That marriage lasted two years. Jeannette Edris, when Winthrop met her in 1951, was a mature, earthy and independent young woman living with her two young children in a three-bedroom duplex on New York's fashionable East End Avenue, overlooking the East River. Her fling of growing up was behind her and to Winthrop she seemed like an oasis of honesty and western straight talk in a desert of New York sycophants, phonies and hangers-on, which was, of course, a desert of his own making. She was not as pretty as Bobo or as any of the Hollywood starlets Winthrop escorted from time to time. But because of her own wealth, her past rough personal life and experience, she and Winthrop were a pair of equals and her children gave Winthrop the unquestioning love he could not get from his own son denied him by Bobo.

So the people of Arkansas had reason finally to begin to believe that their own Point Four program, Winthrop Rockefeller, really meant for whatever reasons of his own to live out his life as an Arkansan. Winthrop and Jeannette Edris were married by a justice of the peace in her father's summer home in Hayden Lake, Idaho, on June 11, 1956. Nelson flew out there to represent the Rockefeller family. The next day, in Winthrop's private plane, they flew to Reno to be married again in the same state where he had received his divorce from Bobo, just to make legally sure, and then they flew to the Grand Tetons in Wyoming for their honeymoon. On their honeymoon night in the premier cottage of the Rockefeller resort (owned by Laurance), the newest Mrs. Rockefeller took a pratfall. She mistook a cellar door for a bathroom door and in the black of night, lest she disturb her husband by putting on a light, she tumbled headlong down a steep flight of stairs and then spent the remainder of her honeymoon week, bruised black and blue, playing penny-ante gin rummy with a man worth hundreds of millions of dollars inside the small cottage, too embarrassed to venture outside. And so she arrived as the new mistress of Winrock Farms, still bearing the marks on her bruised and battered body with a story to tell of her unlikely honeymoon with Winthrop.

Jeannette arrived at Winrock in time to help put the finishing touches on what was the most unusual feature of the main house, the new dining room, designed to accommodate one hundred guests at a sit-down dinner and yet not too large for an intimate gathering of four, six or eight. Winthrop himself chose the design, based upon the chapel of the First Presbyterian Church in Arkadelphia, which he liked: a cathedral-type room made with laminated wood arches with a low side aisle which made the room seem half its actual size. Ed Cromwell designed the furniture for the room and a local carpenter built it. They sent to New York for a fumed oak floor and Jeannette made phone calls around the country to find the special pewter lighting fixtures. In all, they did not want a dining room that looked too large or too new or too fancy. And so it was with the whole house. Jeannette became involved in finding comfortable contemporary furniture that was the best money could buy and yet not in any way ostentatious. At the same time, Ben Mitchell's domain, the kitchen, was redesigned and enlarged for the first of two times to provide hotel-sized equipment large enough to feed the Rockefeller guest lists. It had become obvious by this time that Winthrop Rockefeller intended to do extensive entertaining in Arkansas. At the start, Ben Mitchell would cook hamburgers and a tasty recipe of beans, molasses and bacon for twelve to fifteen guests on a Saturday night but now as Winthrop became more involved with the AIDC it was not unusual to have one hundred guests for dinner. For the employees, a cafeteria was built under the new dining room. Then a new studio building was put up for Jeannette where she could work on enamel ceramics. The building turned out so well that Winthrop moved his private office there. The main barn was enlarged to a show barn and reception center for visitors, who were welcomed at all times in an effort to make Petit Jean Mountain a tourist attraction, with its four-thousand-acre state park. Winthrop opened Lake Abby on weekdays for various groups, merely for the asking, for swimming, boating and picnics. Two more barns were built for the animals. To service the establishment, he put up separate shops for auto repairs, painting, plumbing and carpentry work. By the time they were finished, Ed Cromwell, the architect who came to Winrock to "fix up" one bathroom, stayed on to design twenty-four separate buildings and ninety-seven toilets.

Rock, the bull, also performed well by Rockefeller standards. He lived to the age of twelve and sired a scientifically cultivated herd of Santa Gertrudis cattle which was stabilized at one thousand head of breeding cattle. Careful records were kept on each bull and heifer, bred for the best physical and temperament characteristics. The rest were culled out and sold for meat. As the herd grew beyond the pasture capacity on top of the mountain, Winthrop bought 2,700 acres at the base of the mountain and called that the Rockwin Division of Winrock Farms. When that overflowed, Winthrop purchased another 3,500 acres of pasture and farm land about eighty-five miles east of Petit Jean and called that the Carlisle Division. But still, in 1957, he had to face up to dire warnings of his accountant: his operation had lost money each year for four years and in one more year it would run afoul of the Internal Revenue Service's "hobby rule." That is, any business which loses more than $50,000 a year for five years is considered for tax purposes no longer a viable business but a hobby. As such, the losses would not be deductible. The cost of building Winrock Farms and the cost of running it every year were astronomical. So, to show a profit of some kind in the fifth year of operation, Winthrop in 1957 purchased an ongoing, very profitable thirty-thousand-acre rice farm in Oklahoma as part of his operation.

Winthrop was inordinately proud of what he had accomplished on Petit Jean Mountain. He had turned useless, silty brushland into a paradise of Coastal Bermuda grass upon which he raised one of the finest breed of cattle in the nation. It was the best of its kind, a showplace, and he insisted it was a model of what others could do for far less money if they were willing to devote far more time than he did in putting together this kind of operation. His friends in Arkansas and visitors from outside the state took one look and called it Shangri-La.

But the one man Winthrop wanted to impress declined his repeated invitations to visit Winrock Farms. He longed to show his father what he had done on Petit Jean Mountain and throughout the state, to see that at long last he, the "black sheep" of the family, had returned to the fold and was now indeed living a useful life, even by his father's standards. But Mr. Jr. in 1957 was eighty-three years old and in frail health, suffering from emphysema, a slight heart condition and his old migraine headaches. The trip would be too much for him, he said, for he still refused to fly in an airplane, a lifelong aversion. Although Winthrop understood the reasons given, he was bitterly disappointed. Acknowledging that his father would never see Winrock Farms, Winthrop brought Winrock to his father by way of film. At considerable expense, he hired a Hollywood crew and director to film professionally the operation of Winrock Farms. The sole purpose was to show Winrock to John D. Rockefeller, Jr., and it did accomplish that. Later that film would be used widely for political and educational purposes.

Politics too entered Winthrop's Arkansas life. It was a logical step, particularly after he became chairman of the Arkansas Industrial Development Commission and had to deal with the governor and the legislature. Political considerations came into play in almost any venture undertaken for the benefit of Arkansas. It was also a popular topic of conversation. Frank Newell, George Reynolds and other lifelong and important Democrats in the state urged Winthrop to declare himself a Democrat so that he could extend his influence and concern for Arkansas politically through the party which controlled the state. But Winthrop demurred. Personally he was non-political and not interested per se in politics, he told them. For the sake of his family and the family name and the association of Rockefellers with the Republican Party going back to the days of his grandfather, he, Winthrop, just never could become a Democrat. And if anyone asked, he was a Republican. George Reynolds and Frank Newell responded with a simple argument: there were no Republicans in Arkansas, certainly none that counted, and if Winthrop insisted on being a Republican, then he was cutting himself off from a huge area of influence in the state. They suggested that if he could not declare himself a Democrat, he could run for office—even governor—as an independent.

But Winthrop was not interested. Actually, no Rockefeller had ever run for public office until that year, 1958, when Brother Nelson had declared himself a candidate for governor of New York. And 1958 was a gala year for Winthrop in another respect: the first cattle sale of Winrock Farms was set for the second Saturday in May, with an offering of twenty-one Santa Gertrudis purebred bulls and twenty-three heifers, all of them two-year-olds and "guaranteed breeders" on a money-back basis. More than one hundred buyers and their wives were invited for a sit-down dinner the night before the sale and more than one thousand showed up for the roast beef buffet luncheon which preceded the 1:30 P.M. auction. The entire farm was polished and bedecked with flowers, food, liquor and entertainment on the eve of the sale; the day of the auction was the gala occasion of the year; and the Sunday after the sale was the happy, relaxed denouement of the weekend. As the years progressed, the numbers increased, 250 guests at the Friday night dinner, more than 1,000 for the luncheon and auction; more and more buyers were put up for the weekend in guesthouses on the farm, and in guest rooms all over the mesa of Petit Jean Mountain. Without doubt, anyone interested in cattle at all in the United States and abroad tried to make it his business to attend just one of the cattle auctions at Winrock Farms. It became also a year-round attraction for anyone visiting Arkansas. In time, the number of tourists visiting Winrock Farms just for a look around reached 150,000 a year.

The Winrock herd of purebred Santa Gertrudis cattle grew until it was deliberately leveled out at about one thousand bulls, cows and heifers, producing a progeny which were sold for more than $317,000 before he died in 1973. As the herd grew, the breeding became more and more scientific and sophisticated at Winrock Farms, even to the extent of following each animal's breeding, weight and personality characteristics by IBM computer. A program of artificial insemination was tested and used extensively at Winrock to prove that a single productive bull could be used to fertilize up to ten thousand cows a year. In time, a good portion of Winrock's business was selling and shipping semen, frozen with liquid nitrogen to 320° F. below zero, to all parts of the world. As the 1960s rolled around, Winrock Farms became big business, one of the nation's outstanding cattle operations. In 1963, Winthrop expanded Winrock Farms still further. He bought the ten-thousand-acre Turner Ranch at Sulphur, Oklahoma, from ex-Governor Roy J. Turner, adding some two thousand head of purebred Herefords, one of the finest Hereford cattle operations in the country.

As a result, the operation of Winrock Farms became more and more institutionalized. Experts were needed and hired, the labor force was increased, the bookkeeping, accounting and legal aspects became more involved. The carefree days of fun and work, trial and error, became fewer and fewer. The demands on Winthrop's time became fierce; to satisfy them all, impossible. Winrock Enterprises was gaining momentum, outside real estate investments were growing; the new Tower Building in downtown Little Rock was opened to tenants in 1960 and Winthrop moved his Winrock Enterprises offices into the seventeenth floor. He became through a series of circumstances the founder and chief benefactor of the million-dollar Arkansas Arts Center in Little Rock's MacArthur Park, conceived in 1957 and opened to the public in 1962. It was a gem of its kind, perhaps a decade ahead of its time, combining five exhibition galleries, a 389-seat acoustically marvelous theater, five studio-classrooms for instruction in painting, sculpture, graphic arts, dance and stage designing. Then to extend the art world to more Arkansans, Winthrop and others (Jeannette, his brother David and the Barton Foundation of El

Dorado, Arkansas) donated a $75,000 Artmobile—an art gallery installed in a forty-foot highway trailer—to bring a rotating show of paintings and a lending library of graphic arts to communities and towns throughout the state. Jeannette, as president of the Arts Center, traveled extensively through the state, organizing local chapters of the Arts Center.

Both Winthrop and Jeannette also became heavily involved in local school problems when her children, Bruce and Anne, chose to live at Winrock and attend the local public school in Morrilton rather than be away at New England boarding schools. Donating money to build a new elementary school and helping to expand the local high school was the easier part of the task. Persuading local people to invest in higher teacher salaries, to upgrade the curriculum, to institute college preparatory courses, to encourage families to allow farm children to go on to college—all that was far more difficult and time-consuming. But it was done. Years later, standard test results showed the Morrilton school system had improved and more than 50 per cent of the graduating class went on to college. The percentage held true for the Rockefeller home also: Bruce graduated and went on to the University of Arkansas; Anne eloped at age seventeen as her mother did before her. Both children, however, did make Arkansas their home when they grew up and left Winrock Farms. They had been happy there; it was a happy place.

Winthrop was happy at Winrock Farms. What he liked to do best, of all his activities, was to dress in old work clothes and mosey about his land, pruning trees and weeding the manicured lawn which separated his home from the edge of Petit Jean Mountain. He carried a chain saw in the trunk of his personal automobile and whenever his eye spotted an overgrown tree, he would stop and do a bit of pruning, reshaping the tree with the artistry of a plastic surgeon working on a hooked nose. He could alternately sit on his haunches or kneel on the ground for hours, carefully plucking weeds or crab grass from his lawn. Working with his hands was a form of relaxation. "If there is such a thing as reincarnation," his wife would remark, "I am sure Win will come back to this earth as a landscape gardener."

Winthrop himself had a favorite remark he enjoyed trying on new-comers to Winrock Farms. "I guess I need something to wash the dust out of my throat," he would say as he came in from a day's work and headed for the liquor table set up a corner of the living room. Scotch, gin and vodka were laid out in old-fashioned apothecary quart bottles, labeled only by silver medallions. Winthrop had been a social drinker, at times a heavy social drinker, when he came to Arkansas; a cocktail or mixed drink was a social routine, a lubricant not only for a dry throat but also for the flow of conversation. Gradually, as time went on, demands upon his time and his mind grew, frustrations became more frequent and his need for relaxation through alcohol became greater. He became a cyclical drinker.

He would drink increasingly more each day until he reached a limit which he alone recognized somewhere perhaps in his subconscious and then he would cut his consumption back to a minimum or he would go on the wagon altogether. Then slowly once again, the cycle would repeat itself; he would drink more liquor and more frequently each day until once again he reached his limit. He disguised from others the stages of his drinking cycle by mixing his own drinks, varying the proportion of vodka to tonic or scotch to water that he would pour into his double-bottom old-fashioned glass. Those who knew him well could recognize the state of his inebriation by the extent to which he slurred his words and became down-right garrulous. He was neither a happy drinker nor a mean one. But it was a problem. He could not fully control it and he was aware of it. "If I could only solve a problem or two which I have, I could cut out this stuff completely," he would tell his friends. But he never could. He could and did by sheer will power cut out drinking entirely for protracted periods when absolutely necessary for a particular project he was handling, but once over a hurdle, he would revert. Yet, physically, despite two bouts with hepatitis and dire doctor's warnings, drinking apparently did not harm him. He put on weight and went soft around the middle, but physically he had the constitution of an ox.

If there are, as some say, two kinds of people in this world, the day people and the night people, then Winthrop Rockefeller without doubt was a night person all of his life. On the farm, his daily routine was to sleep till ten o'clock, have breakfast and read the newspapers until noon, work in his office until two and then return to the main house for lunch until four. At four o'clock, his day would really begin. With incoming phone calls stopping at 5 P.M., he could work unbothered to eight, nine or ten o'clock at night. This might prove hard on the farm personnel who worked with him, such as G. W. Adkinson, the farm manager, who rose at 6:30 A.M., but that was the way "the boss" wanted it and they accommodated their hours to his. Dinner for Winthrop and for whoever was working with him on a given night would be served when he was ready for it, at any time from ten to midnight. Not infrequently he went back to work, sometimes till three o'clock in the morning.

Those first two hours of the day with coffee and the newspapers were the only time that Winthrop liked to be alone. Otherwise, he always preferred to have people around him. He genuinely liked people from all walks of life and their conversation. Never much of a reader, he conducted his business, farm and philanthropic affairs orally for the most part. He could listen to an explanation on a complex subject, remember it and repeat it accurately months later, and retain it even longer. Members of his staff reported to him verbally; he was adept at conducting the frequent meetings and seminars held at Winrock; he could delve into complicated situations, listen to conflicting advice, analyze alternate proposals and

reach justified conclusions, but he preferred to leave the fine print and details largely to his lawyers and to his aides. At times, this led to trouble. At
times those working for him did not understand fully what he wanted
them to do; sometimes he did not make himself clear. On occasion, there
were misunderstandings on business deals, almost always to the benefit of
the other man. On more than one occasion, a trusted friend would make a
small fortune at Winthrop's cost and it was never fully clear whether the
friend was taking deliberate advantage of him or whether Winthrop had
agreed to something to his own disadvantage or whether it was an honest
misunderstanding. Winthrop often would pass over the first such affair
and keep silent; he might say nothing about the second; but then, on the
third occasion, no matter how small, he would write that "friend" off and
let it be known he never wanted to see him again. Oftentimes, that
"friend" never knew what caused the break; others could see only that
Winthrop was dropping this friend or that, never knowing way.

Winthrop was quite aware that some people did try to take advantage of his generosity and open nature. He considered that part of the
price paid for being wealthy, for being a Rockefeller. He knew he was considered a "soft touch," that he lent money to people who neglected to pay
him back on the simplistic grounds that he didn't need the money, that
some men used his name or their association with him to foster an outside
scheme of their own, that there were innumerable different ways of taking
advantage of him and that the temptations were always there. He realized
that he was—to use his own word—"suckered" more often in Arkansas
than he ever had been in his early days in New York. And it hurt each
time he felt his friendship betrayed. But then, when enough time had
passed, he turned philosophical about such incidents. He helped people
with money because he wanted to, because he remembered how painful it
was to be in need of money and not have it. He never forgot how his father had kept him on short financial rein during his school years. And he
would often quote his mother's advice that although there may be some
bad in some people, there is also some good in everyone, if one would but
search it out.

On an over-all view, those were happy years in Arkansas, years which
showed visible accomplishments, a good mixture of work and play and, for
Winthrop, an inner sense of satisfaction. Winrock Enterprises was thriv-
ing, the Industrial Commission was succeeding in bringing in new industry beyond original expectations. Winthrop's high-rise office building in
Little Rock had become a city landmark and Winrock Farms had become everything Winthrop wished for it. His marriage was good, his two
stepchildren obviously loved him, Winthrop Paul (called Winnie) was
drawing closer and closer to his father during his vacations on the farm.
Jeannette and he had many friends whom they considered their peers
among Arkansas businessmen and cattle breeders. People from all walks of

life and from all over the world were invited and came as weekend guests to
Winrock Farms. Hospitality there was extensive and oftentimes lavish.
Winthrop thoroughly enjoyed having people around him. As chairman of
Colonial Williamsburg, he served as host at least once a year there to visit-
ing royalty and heads of state: King Hussein of Jordan, King Baudouin of
Belgium, the president of Peru, the president of India and others. Then
there were the trips abroad, usually one each year, to Central and South
America, to the Philippines, Tokyo and the Far East, and most often to
Paris and other points of interest in Europe. With his small private air
force on Petit Jean Mountain, which had grown to five airplanes and six
pilots, all parts of the United States were easily accessible to Winthrop
and Jeannette, together or on separate trips. Either or both of them could
get off their mountaintop any time he or she so desired. In 1963,
Winthrop decided upon his favorite vacation spot in the United States—
Palm Springs, California—and bought a second home there. It was the
good life. People around him began saying Winthrop Rockefeller had
found himself, found the useful, fulfilling kind of life that the Rockefeller
family stood for.

And then politics intruded, nudging its way into Winrock Farms and
into Winthrop Rockefeller. Probably there was no escaping it, given the
circumstances of Winthrop's unique position in Arkansas, his acceptance
by the public, his recognition and popularity and given his own compul-
sion to live up to his family name and to do what was appropriate and expected of him. By 1960, he had completed the seven-year residency requirement for running for governor. Even before that he had been
beseeched, cajoled and urged to consider running for that office—by men
of both parties. The reasoning was the same: if he really wanted to change
and help Arkansas, he could do it best by becoming governor and revamping the old, traditional political boss system which dominated every aspect
of the state. Of course, if he really wanted to be elected, he had better
switch to the Democratic Party. Arkansas, when all was said and done,
was a southern, Confederate state: no Republican had been elected governor since the Civil War; there were no Republicans in the legislature;
there were no Republicans of any importance even at the local county
level. Winthrop had been approached when he first came to Arkansas by
Republican leaders urging him to become more involved in party affairs
and they never let up. But he had resisted them, fully aware that the Republican Party in Arkansas was a kept party, a small patronage group
which was paid off with minor patronage by the Democrats in power.

Personally he did not want to get involved in politics. He was fundamentally a very shy man. He could be friendly and outgoing with those he
knew and yet embarrassed meeting strangers, shaking hands, smiling when
he did not mean it, making the gestures so important for a politician. Nor
did he really enjoy making speeches, standing in front of large crowds and

trying to please them. He had done much of this as chairman of the Industrial Commission, but he did not enjoy it. And yet, he felt it was incumbent on him to do something. Neither wanting to desert the family political position and become a Democrat nor willing to become an overt Republican activist, Winthrop joined a small group to form a "Committee for the Two Parties" in early 1960. During that campaigning year, he toured Arkansas urging upon his fellow citizens the benefits of the two-party system and a choice at the polls which would serve as a check on the party in power. It was a position under the circumstances of Arkansas politics with which he could live. He sincerely believed what he said. And yet it was for all political purposes the first grand effort to build up the Republican Party in Arkansas. He appeared on radio and television, he spoke at dinners and outdoor barbecues, and two weeks before the election he threw a gala "Party for Two Parties" at Winrock Farms, attended by some 850 Republicans and Democrats, where the liquor flowed and entertainment was imported from Hollywood. That "Party for Two Parties" was a memorable event for bringing the political activists to Winrock Farms and for plunging Winthrop Rockefeller into Arkansas politics.

In May of 1961, he was elected Republican National Committeeman from Arkansas, an honor he could hardly decline. The political bug had bitten. He began traveling through the state, encouraging the growth of the local GOP organizations. He began to contribute money where financial help was needed, which was almost everywhere. Republican politicians flocked to him; some of his old Democratic friends began to drift away. In 1962, speculation was rampant that Rockefeller would run for governor against Orval Faubus. He was sorely tempted. But reality prevailed and in a statewide television broadcast amid much fanfare, he announced that he was not a candidate. He thought he could serve the state and the Republican Party best, he declared, by working to build a strong Republican organization in the state. The people, he implored, should have a choice at the polls. Governor Faubus was elected handily to his fifth term in office. But that year 140 Republicans filed their candidacy for various offices and that in itself in Arkansas was claimed as a Republican victory of sorts.

Immediately after the 1962 election, with the glow of unabated political fever, Winthrop set out to help organize a grass-roots movement behind the Republican Party. As the Republican National Committeeman from Arkansas and a powerful member of the Republican State Executive Committee, he traveled across the state, visiting each and every county, urging Republicans and independents and dissatisfied Democrats that the time was ripe for putting an end to the stranglehold of the Faubus machine upon Arkansas. The Faubus image nationally, particularly since desegregation of the Little Rock schools at gunpoint, was holding back progress in the state, hurting the people economically, politically and socially, Winthrop argued. He worked at this with such determination and such obvious sincerity that those around him at Winrock Farms concluded that Winthrop had discovered a new mission in life: politics. To most others, though, he seemed still a political amateur, straightforward and naïve, a Don Quixote on a hopeless quest, tilting against an entrenched, sharp political professional like Orval Faubus, who, as governor, could do more for Republican politicians in Arkansas than could Winthrop or any other Rockefeller.

Winthrop's political efforts even became suspect among Republicans. The conservatives on the Republican State Executive Committee accused him publicly in 1963 of campaigning on behalf of his brother Nelson's presidential ambitions. Winthrop, of course, denied it, denied it vehemently, but he could not publicly reveal the sibling rivalry which had separated the two brothers all of their lives. His friends on the committee urged him to prove his sincerity by running for governor himself. That Winthrop did not want to do. Personally, he did not want to campaign for or to hold public office, to be up front and on public display; it ran counter to his fundamental shyness. He preferred to be the power behind the throne, a guiding and helping hand in political reform. But the pressure on him mounted inexorably. The arguments were sound. If he truly intended to establish the Republican Party in Arkansas, he himself would have to run for governor in 1964. His was the only name popular enough in the state to rally Arkansans to the Republican Party. He was the only Republican known and accepted widely enough to stand even a minimal chance of unseating Orval Faubus. And the final Arkansan argument was: "Put your mouth where your money is!"

While the grass-roots recruitment drive for the Republican Party met with little success, an honest ground swell of sentiment for Winthrop Rockefeller became apparent as he wavered in his personal decision. Friends formed a Draft Rockefeller for Governor Committee and hundreds of letters and petitions poured into Winrock Farms. The Republican State Committee unanimously passed a resolution urging him to run. So Winthrop Rockefeller put his mouth where his money was. On April 4, 1964, he announced he was a candidate for governor.

On the campaign trail, he stumbled and bumbled as an amateur would, and yet the honesty and sincerity of his convictions came through. He campaigned for the reality of a two-party system in Arkansas, for bringing the state out of the dark ages, for economic and social advancement, for an end to one-party political corruption. He stumbled over his words, he mixed metaphors, he could not read a written speech at all well and he appeared embarrassed delivering memorized spiels. He was best in the give-and-take of the question-and-answer period. Challenged on his wealth, he responded with stories of his Baptist upbringing, thrift and sense of responsibility. Heckled about the number of airplanes he owned, he replied, "If you were in the chips and you wanted an airplane, wouldn't you buy one? What's wrong with that?"

Called a carpetbagger, he responded with what he had already accomplished for Arkansas as a private citizen. In the ten years he had headed the Arkansas Industrial Development Commission, more than six hundred new industrial plants had come to Arkansas, providing some ninety thousand new jobs with an annual payroll of $270 million; per capita income had risen from $960 in 1955 to $1,500 in 1963; Arkansas led the South in new factory jobs per capita since 1955 and the state treasury revenues, as a result, had increased by 50 per cent.

He traveled more than twelve thousand miles campaigning. He walked down the main street of almost every Arkansas town. He shook hands with an estimated 300,000 citizens, white and black. He gave away thousands of Polaroid snapshots of himself alongside individual voters, some of whom never before owned a photograph. He financed most of the campaign himself. He talked and talked and talked. And he lost the election.

But in that defeat, he won 43.7 per cent of the vote, more than double that of any Republican candidate before him. Three Republicans were elected to the previously all-Democratic legislature. In Arkansas, it was considered a near-miracle. "We sincerely believe we won a victory, even in defeat," Winthrop announced the day after the election.

It was a clear signal of his intentions: he was running again. Some say he hardly stopped campaigning. In that old but apt cliché, he had got his feet wet and discovered that the muddy political water was not so bad after all. The next year was almost entirely devoted to politics: convincing Republicans that he truly meant to nurture a viable Republican Party in Arkansas, not a Rockefeller patronage organization, one which would outlast him, one which truly had a chance of winning. He wooed everyone in sight and he traveled to see as many people as possible. When the Supreme Court of the United States declared the poll tax unconstitutional, he spearheaded court fights for voter registration. He enlarged his own political staff and set to work correcting mistakes that cost him votes in the last election. And he filed early. On January 11, 1966, he announced he was a candidate for governor on a platform of a two-party system in Arkansas, an end to machine rule, efficiency and thrift in government, better education, better jobs and better highways. "My roots are deep in Arkansas and I have dedicated myself to its continued growth and development," he declared. "I am running again because I am not a quitter. And I believe I can serve Arkansas more as governor than in any other way."

After all, he needed only 7 or 8 per cent more of the vote than he had received in 1964 to be elected. He went after that vote this time with a hard political professionalism he had lacked before. The "secret weapon" of the campaign was a giant and sophisticated IBM 1401 computer with all the attachments, installed in Room 440 of the Tower Building in Little Rock. It cost him $7,000 a month to rent it, plus twelve employees to run it. But it gave him what he did not have before: a list of people and potential voters, their political views and their inclinations to vote. Before, all this information was kept by the Democrats in the county courthouses, unavailable to Republicans. The Rockefeller organization worked from telephone books, house to house canvasses of the most heavily populated areas, especially around Little Rock. Once the information was fed into the computer, the computer could spew out names and addresses of those likely to vote for Rockefeller, it could print out personal letters from him to these voters, it could help in organizing a much needed massive registration drive. It could do lots of things.

Then too, Winthrop was helped immeasurably by fortuitous circumstances beyond his own control—sometimes called luck. Orval Faubus, the incumbent re-elected six times, cannily looked the scene over and decided not to run again in 1966. Faubus' hand-picked candidate was defeated in the Democratic primary by James D. "Justice Jim" Johnson, an arch-segregationist who had organized the White Citizens Council in Arkansas in the mid-1950s and had campaigned for Barry Goldwater for President in 1964 throughout the South. A large and powerful group of liberal Democrats, supporters of Arkansas's Senator William Fulbright, formed a Democrats for Rockefeller Committee in retaliation. They supported and campaigned hard for Winthrop Rockefeller. The underlying point of the campaign then became: would Arkansas face its future as a southern, segregationist state, like Mississippi, or as a western, growing state, like Texas? The rural areas voted southern for "Justice Jim," and the cities and 90 per cent of the Negro vote went to Win Rockefeller.

Winthrop won by 55,000 votes! He had become the first Republican governor of Arkansas in ninety-four years, the first since the days of Reconstruction. The impact and the significance of the event were felt throughout the state. His election was hailed as the birth of a new era in Arkansas. Winthrop himself called for a new "Era of Excellence" and then, exhausted from the rigor and tensions of the campaign, he retired to the privacy of Winrock and proceeded, after a long period of abstention, to drink himself into oblivion. He was torn then and all of his life between the high ideals and deep responsibilities of being a Rockefeller and a deep inner lack of confidence that he could measure up to those Rockefeller standards. The aftereffect of being elected governor, certainly the greatest accomplishment of his life up to then, hit him like an awful hangover. He welcomed the stupendous challenge facing him, and feared it. He was a very human human being, a sensitive man thoroughly benevolent, who hurt easily, who lacked the tough hide required of politicians.

His wife Jeannette and his close associates understood Win's weakness for liquor and they could live with it. He never lost complete control of himself, nor became too boisterous or too depressed, nor did he become ill. It seemed he kept himself on a string and when the string was played out, his limit reached, he himself would reduce his intake and return to his normal routine. At the worst times, he would have to be put to bed to sleep it off, more from sheer exhaustion than inebriation. Unfortunately, the privacy of Winrock was a luxury that largely disappeared after he was elected governor. Meetings and conferences were scheduled at Winrock with important groups and the new governor-elect sometimes appeared somewhat less than sober and sometimes did not appear at all because he could not. Word got around. Then, in the first address to the legislature, he apparently sloshed some of his words. His defenders attributed it to his usual ineptness in reading a prepared text. The Democrats insisted he had been drunk or at least half-drunk. And in the joint legislature there were 3 Republicans and 132 Democrats. From then on, his drinking became public knowledge, openly discussed, a good deal exaggerated, and a political albatross. Some of the legislators, who could and did outdrink him and not infrequently within the chambers of the legislature, feigned a mock horror at the idea that the governor of dry, Baptist Arkansas was a drinking man. Hypocrisy was a way of political life in Arkansas.

Arkansas was a dry state and everyone who so desired drank. The lawmakers themselves were well known to do more legislative wheeling and dealing at the Gar Hole, the bar at the nearby Marion Hotel, than at the state capitol. Gambling was illegal and Hot Springs, the second largest city, was a tourist attraction with its wide-open gambling casinos fashioned after The Strip in Las Vegas. Every elected official and many if not most appointed ones were paid a pittance as a legal salary because they were expected traditionally to take graft, bribes or whatever they could in any way they could—of course, within reason. When the mayor of a suburban town near Little Rock complained that he could not live on his mayor's salary, a politician retorted and in the press: "Why, there's money all around him and if he's too dumb to take some of it, then he ought to be made to live on what he gets." The salary of the governor of Arkansas was $10,000 a year, and no one really expected him to live on that. When Orval Faubus left office, he retired to Huntsville in a remote woodland region of north Arkansas where he had grown up as a poor boy and built himself a rather lavish home there estimated to have cost anywhere from $150,000 to $300,000, depending upon whom you believed. When asked how he could do it, he replied he had always been "frugal" and saved the money. The man on the street's reaction to ex-Governor Faubus' new home was a mere shrug of acceptance. "Why, that ain't so bad," he said. "If you figure there's some two million people in Arkansas, it cost us less than twenty-five cents a head."

Governor Rockefeller, whose take-home pay was about $387 every two weeks, dipped into his private resources to pay supplementary salaries to those he wooed into governmental service, many of them from the academic community. The state attorney general denounced such private salary implements as illegal. Rockefeller said, in effect, "Sue me." He astounded Arkansans by sending in his newly appointed State Police director to lead a raid in Hot Springs, smashing hundreds of slot machines and gambling equipment, and declared that so long as gambling was illegal in Arkansas, the casinos in Hot Springs would remain shut. He shut down fly-by-night insurance and securities sales outfits which were milking Arkansans of millions of dollars. He exposed and fought corrupt practices in several of the state departments and commissions, particularly the Highway Department and the Game and Fish Commission. But he soon learned that his hands were tied when it came to the quasi-independent boards and commissions, whose members were appointed by his predecessor. He asked the legislature for independent audits of the Highway Department and several commissions, and he lost that battle. He proposed competitive bidding on school building bonds, a potential saving of millions of dollars, and he was turned down. He fought hard and long to reform the chain-gang brutality, corruption and mentality of the Arkansas prison farm system, and he won some and lost some of those battles.

The two years of his first term in office were without doubt the most hectic, the most trying and the most stimulating of his life. Winthrop was not a natural politician, not a wheeler-dealer. Accustomed for so long to having his own way and to having his orders carried out, he found it difficult if not impossible, at least at the start, to compromise on what to him were clear-cut principles. Nor was he much good at the political art of arm-twisting. He relied on the simple and perhaps naïve principle of logic and persuasion and in the nineteenth-century politics of Arkansas, the principle failed more than it succeeded. Winthrop would call in experts to make recommendations and then he would push their reforms, threaten to take his programs to the people if they were rejected by the Democrats in the legislature. Sometimes that ploy worked, but only in extreme cases. As often as not, some Democrats would oppose a program just for the sheer enjoyment of being able to go around and say, "I stopped that s.o.b. Rockefeller cold, that's the kind of power I got."

Winthrop as governor pushed and prodded to reform the structure of the state government, to bring it into the twentieth century, to set up structures and procedures designed to safeguard the state treasury from corrupt practices. Independent audits played a big part, for even the threat of an audit went far in drying up many of the more outrageous practices of corruption. Other reforms were possible by executive order, without legislative approval. His administrators found hundreds of millions of dollars of state money on deposit in a few favored banks which paid no interest. This money simply was transferred to other banks which did pay interest. A careful check of the state tax rolls disclosed more than eighty thousand Arkansans who had not been paying state income taxes at all and they were added to the tax rolls. He did manage to push through the recalcitrant legislature the establishment of a new Department of Administration, which consolidated several overlapping, loosely run agencies and that was a beginning at streamlining the state government. But the legislature blocked his requests for any auditing of the 167-odd independent state commissions and boards which were run by appointees of his predecessor, Orval Faubus, and were therefore beyond the control of Governor Rockefeller.

In 1968 Winthrop won re-election against an old-guard Democrat in the legislature, Marion Crank, who was an executive on the payroll of one of the largest utilities in the state. This campaign was harder and more vicious than the first. But he retained the much needed support of so-called enlightened Democrats and liberals of the state. The state's most respected newspaper, the *Arkansas Gazette*, supported him, saying: "He offers continued reform administration and progressive programs in state services, with emphasis on the needs of education. Arkansas is now a better state for Rockefeller having become governor, and he deserves his opportunity to finish the work that he has begun." Winthrop also was honored nominally by a favorite-son nomination for President of the United States at the Republican convention in Miami, and that, perhaps meaningless to outsiders, warmed his heart and spurred him onto his second term as governor.

The full story of his years as governor of Arkansas is beyond the scope of this book, but despite the almost daily turmoil, bickering, struggling and hardships, Winthrop helped move the state of Arkansas into the future, economically, socially and politically. He pushed through the first minimum wage law in the state's history. He inaugurated a program for kindergartens in the public schools. He attracted a higher quality of officeholder to government. He fought hard for increased salaries for department heads in government. He appointed the first blacks to serve on Arkansas draft boards and he hired more blacks to serve in positions of responsibility within the government than ever had been considered before. And he promoted throughout the state the concept that Arkansas was not an inferior state, that with good government it could become a land of opportunity for all.

Winthrop himself had never worked harder in his life. He worked hard and he drank hard. Still a night person, he struggled manfully to get himself out of bed at seven-thirty in the morning and begin his daily chores as governor. He and Jeannette lived in the Governor's Mansion in Little Rock four or five days a week and spent weekends at the farm. There he would hold staff conferences out on the lawn, plucking crab grass by hand as a means of relaxing while talking over state problems. As a former playboy and a mature man who dearly loved the relaxed give-and-take of social intercourse, Winthrop found less and less time to enjoy himself. His time almost never was his own. While he could delegate administrative authority, the demands upon his time for meetings, conferences and decisions were near overwhelming. He was constantly over-scheduled, consistently late for meetings. Personally he had not the heart to cut anyone short, so that a fifteen-minute appointment might stretch to half an hour. By the end of the day, the governor might well be one, two or even three hours behind his schedule.

At times, he felt himself alone, alone on a pinnacle of power, with no one to turn to in the Republican Party, facing the combined and powerful opposition and attacks of Democrats in and out of office. Politics came hard to him. His only retreat when he wanted a full day or two away from such demands was to fly off to his vacation home in Palm Springs, away from Arkansas, away from the telephone, away from everyone. There were the times of doubt, too, occasions when he wondered aloud whether he was really accomplishing very much in Arkansas, whether those accomplishments, for whatever they were worth, would outlast his own years in office. Ordinarily, he was proud of what he was doing in Arkansas. He felt that in serving the 2 million people of Arkansas he was doing as well or as much with his life as any of his brothers were back in New York. But there were times of depression and doubt. He worried too about Winrock Farms. Would anyone want to carry on Winrock Farms after he died? Should anyone? He considered alternatives. Should Winrock Farms be turned into a retreat of some sort, a think tank, or a luxury hotel, or a state tourist attraction, or what? He consulted others—his brother David, who had grown close to Win over the years, his nephew Jay, who visited him often, his son Winthrop Paul—but he could come to no firm conclusion.

Fatigued and harried, when 1970 rolled around, Winthrop faced the same kind of problem he had when he first ran for governor in 1964: he would have preferred someone else out front with himself as a guiding hand in the background, but there was no Republican other than himself with a chance of being elected governor. He wanted and felt he needed two more years to consolidate the reforms he had started. He needed the time to replace some more of the old holdover Faubus appointees still in the government. He wanted to finish what he had started. The 1969 U. S. Supreme Court reapportionment decision meant that the Arkansas legislature would lose a good deal of its rural domination. The court ruling that state legislators must represent approximately the same number of constituents would mean that a new breed of lawmakers would come in from the heavily populated cities of Arkansas. The Republicans in the party he helped put together urged Winthrop to run one more time. His personal friends urged him to quit while he was ahead. Winthrop decided to run; he was not a quitter. His wife Jeannette told him she had had it; she wanted a divorce.

They had drifted apart over the years, especially during the years of politics. It was the familiar story of men so involved in their careers, in their businesses or in politics that they had little time and little of themselves left over to give to their families. His being away so much on speaking tours, conferences and meetings was only the small physical part of the trouble. More than that, Winthrop was away mentally almost all of the time, thinking and living the problems of government, politics and Arkansas. Jeannette complained that she often found herself alone in her bedroom with a book when Winthrop was either across the state on business or in the next room talking politics with his cronies. She complained that since he had entered politics they had lost most of their old friends, their peer group among the businessmen and cattlemen who used to visit Winrock Farms. Now, she complained, Winthrop was surrounded by yes men, men who were on his payroll, men whose careers and livelihoods depended upon Winthrop Rockefeller and his every whim. "There's no one around here who dares to say no to you, Win," she told him, "except me."

There were hardly ever any major fights between them, only the off-and-on bickering which gnaws away at the fiber of love and trust. The differences in their personalities, which hardly seemed to matter before, now rose to the surface. Jeannette always had been a forthright, outspoken, independent woman, raised by a father who had taught her to speak out her troubles each day so that she went to bed with a clear, untroubled conscience. Winthrop understood this in her. But he told her that he had had such squabbles with his first wife that he had resolved never to have a domestic quarrel again. He would sooner flee to another room, trusting to time to soothe over domestic wounds. They had had only three major domestic squabbles in the fourteen years of their marriage, as Jeannette remembered them. But they had drifted apart. When Win's political friends and associates came to the farm, Jeannette retired to her room or to her ceramics studio. When her friends or guests from the mental health field visited, Winthrop would greet them politely and disappear from view. They began to take separate vacations, separate trips off the mountaintop.

Jeannette agreed to stay on for the 1970 campaign, but after that, she said, she would leave. She wanted to part while they were still friends. Winthrop agreed.

Fortunately for Winthrop, at the same time his second wife was deciding to leave, his son Winthrop Paul, now twenty-one years old, decided he wanted to get married and to come and live with his bride at Winrock Farms. Jeannette's two grown children had already left. Winthrop Paul, not unlike his father, had lived a gay, carefree life. A member of the jet

Laurance Spelman Rockefeller.

AROUND THE TIME OF THEIR MARRIAGE.

Laurance.

Mary French.

AVIATION

Laurance and Mary with Captain Eddie Rickenbacker of Eastern Air Lines.

In a Piasecki helicopter.

With James McDonnell, of McDonnell Aircraft.

With Nelson in the Adirondack Mountains.

All five brothers being honored with the Gold Medal Award of the National Institute of Social Sciences, 1967.

CONSERVATION

Nelson, as governor, and Laurance, as state parks commissioner, at the opening of Hudson Highlands State Park, N.Y., 1970.

With Lady Bird Johnson at the White House Conference on Natural Beauty, May 1965.

RESORTS

Mauna Kea Beach Hotel, Hawaii.

Caneel Bay in the Caribbean.

Grand Tetons, Wyoming.

Mary and Laurance on their fortieth anniversary, August 15, 1974, at Woodstock, Vt.

set, he shuttled between Switzerland, Paris, Athens, London until he flunked out of Oxford University after his first year. His fiancée was Deborah Cluett Sage, the pretty twenty-year-old daughter of Louis Davidson Sage of New Canaan, Connecticut, and Mrs. Nicholas Chryssicopoulos of London and Athens. They had met in London and had visited Winrock. Winthrop Paul considered it his true home. He felt there the same kind of peace and contentment his father had found there almost twenty years earlier. As the young couple went "house hunting" on the grounds, Winthrop was positively delighted that his son had chosen to live at Winrock. His love for his only son was tender, sentimental and soul-satisfying. In contrast to his second marriage, which had slowly unraveled, the father-son relationship had grown closer and more intertwined as the years went by. Winthrop Paul, handsome and young with a small mustache and shoulder-length hair, joined his father on the 1970 campaign trail.

Winthrop started out with the high hopes in a campaign against his old foe, Orval Faubus, who had re-entered politics. His major problem, as he saw it, was to explain away a pledge he had made two years before: that he would not run for a third term. He marshaled his arguments for his need of two more years to consolidate his reforms. But he and most of the state were in for a surprise. Faubus was upset in the Democratic primary by a young, utterly unknown attorney named Dale Bumpers out of the tiny town of Charleston in the foothills of the Ouachita Mountains in western Arkansas. His only elective office had been town attorney, but then he was the only attorney in town.

Nevertheless, Dale Bumpers was an eminently likable, plain-speaking man with a populist philosophy more western than southern, untainted by machine politics. He had great appeal to low-income groups. "He speaks a language that factory workers and hardscrabble farmers can understand," said one newspaper. He explained his platform not in statistics or high rhetoric but in simple anecdotes. Through it all, his message was clear: Dale Bumpers was for reform government and a new Arkansas and he, as a Democrat, could accomplish more with the Democratic legislature than Winthrop Rockefeller or any Republican. Of course, that was true. The appeal of Dale Bumpers reached a wide swath of Arkansans, farmers, the working class, blacks and the liberal Fulbright Democrats who had once supported Rockefeller against the segregationists.

Winthrop's defeat on election day was devastating. He lost by a two-to-one margin. Even his home county on Petit Jean Mountain went against him. Afterward, the political analysts would say that the people were tired after four years of wrangling and conflict between Rockefeller and the Democratic legislature and that they welcomed a man of Bumpers' character and political philosophy. They would also say that it was Rockefeller's reforms and his flailing of the Arkansans' consciences for a better life that made a man like Dale Bumpers possible.* But the truth was that Winthrop Rockefeller had not expected to lose. His own pollsters had predicted victory by a close margin, but victory. The resounding defeat, a rejection, left a bitter taste to the ending of Winthrop Rockefeller's public career.

In a bittersweet address of farewell to the legislature, Winthrop reviewed his past accomplishments and his hopes for the future of Arkansas, saying he was now looking forward to more leisure time at his "typical little Arkansas hilltop farm known as Winrock.

"As I take my leave, I wish you well," he said. "Today I look back over almost two decades, to the year in which I first moved to Arkansas . . . I see a different place . . .

"When the history of the past four years is written, I hope the historian may think of me as something more than a political phenomenon; but as a catalyst who hopefully had served to excite in the hearts and minds of people a desire to shape our own destiny."

Melancholy days, weeks and months followed at Winrock. One of his last acts as governor had been to pay a surprise visit to Death Row at the Arkansas State Prison and to commute the sentence of each and every one of the fifteen men there. He did it by executive edict, simply on humanitarian grounds; he did not believe in the death penalty. Before leaving office he estimated at a press conference that he had spent more than $35 million of his own money in Arkansas on business, philanthropy and "good government" over the past ten or fifteen years. He broke down the figures as "in excess" of $10 million on Winrock Farms, "well in excess" of $5 million for school, hospital and educational programs, and "in excess" of $10 million on Winrock Enterprises and the Tower Building in Little Rock. But once out of office, there was so little for him to do and so much time to reflect on past mistakes, real or imaginary, that a sense of gloom and quiet desperation set in. Winrock Farms itself was well managed and seemed to run itself; Winrock Enterprises and all its business aspects held little real interest for him; there seemed very little incentive to continue his usual social whirlwind of activities. What he still liked to do best was to pluck weeds from his back lawn, to prune trees, to reshape shrubs and bushes, to work with his hands outdoors and watch the calluses on his hands grow hard.

Jeannette left Winrock in February to set up residence in Reno, Nevada, for the divorce, and Winthrop Paul and Debbie chose a house for themselves around the brow of the mountain, not far from the main house but out of its sight. They were married on March 22, 1971, at Colonial Williamsburg in the venerable old Bruton Parish Church, which had been attended in colonial days by the Washingtons, Jeffersons, Monroes,

---

* Bumpers served two terms as governor, seemingly a new time limit to that office, and then in 1974 upset his old supporter, U. S. Senator J. W. Fulbright, in the Democratic primary and was elected to the U. S. Senate.

Tylers and Lees. For this wedding, most of the Rockefellers were there, Uncle Nelson, Uncle Laurance and Uncle John, and the aunts and the cousins. Uncle David was away in Europe on business. Winthrop Paul's mother, Bobo, and his stepmother, Jeannette, were there and his father conversed with each of them, separately and quietly.

When the young couple, after their honeymoon, had settled in at Winrock, Winthrop sat up late into the night with associates worrying whether or not his son would adapt to the quiet life at Winrock and decide to spend his life there. He worried too what he should do with Winrock. He loved the place but realized its heavy expenses might make it a burden upon his son after his death.

Rather than sink into sheer despondency, Winthrop took hold of himself and by sheer will power put a smile on his face, went on a diet, dropped twenty pounds very rapidly and also severely limited his drinking. Six months after leaving the governorship, he had retrieved much his old muscle tone, was bronzed by the sun and outdoor living, and looked better than he had in years. He invited five other Republican governors to Winrock for a conference and then announced to the press that in his considered opinion the United States wasted its former governors. "It's really damn foolishness for you taxpayers to train a man like me four years for something, and then, poof . . ." It was the old trouble: not enough to do for a Rockefeller not willing to retire. After all, he was only fifty-nine.

Winthrop did finally find a new cause: rural America. The urgent need of making rural America attractive to young people, to stop or stem the flow of population into already overcrowded cities, to bring the economic and social benefits of a modern industrial nation to its outlying areas—all this fascinated him and he threw himself and his energies and his money into this new enterprise. He gathered a staff to design a planned, independent, self-sufficient new city in a rural area for fifty thousand to eighty thousand people. It was to be called Murroc, located on the south brow of Petit Jean Mountain.

Then, in September 1972, on a routine visit to his family doctor in Morrilton, Winthrop complained of a small, sometimes painful cyst on his back near his left armpit. The doctor did a routine biopsy. The laboratory report was positive: it was a tumor and it was malignant. Winthrop received the bad news alone and stoically. Cancer, said the doctor, and most probably it had already spread through his body by way of the lymph glands. Winthrop so advised his brothers through a third party, rather than speak to them personally. He told no one else. Instead he flew to New York and checked into New York Hospital, avoiding the Memorial Sloan-Kettering Cancer Center, of which his brother Laurance was chairman: admission into Memorial would have been a public announcement of his affliction. At New York Hospital, a further biopsy and then exploratory surgery confirmed the original diagnosis of his Arkansas doctor. He asked his brother David to take over a speaking engagement for which he was scheduled. It was the first such request he had ever made of David and his brother canceled his own schedule to accommodate him. Winthrop went over his last will and testament with the family's lawyer, Donal O'Brien, never once mentioning his illness. He tried to put up a good front, but word got around. He discouraged talk of cancer, terminal illnesses and dying. Instead he sent reassuring memos to his own staff and he joked with his associates and friends that the pain-killing drugs prescribed for him were better than drink. "We're old friends, these little pills and me," he would say.

He carried on as before. But he lost weight and strength week after week. He had attended the Republican National Convention, where he had heard his brother Nelson nominate the incumbent President, Richard M. Nixon, for four more years. He went to Washington in January to attend the inauguration, but at the last moment he felt too weak to leave his hotel room. He returned to Winrock Farms but refused to become bedridden. Nor would he let on what was becoming to others painfully obvious.

Then, late one night in early February, he himself felt his time had come. He telephoned his chief pilot and said he wanted to be flown to Palm Springs, immediately.

He went alone, wanting to be by himself, wanting no crowd of well-wishers making a fuss over him, wanting to escape from the world around him. Carrying a bulging briefcase of work with him, he set up home in his Palm Springs residence, seeking sunshine and warmth. Winthrop Paul and his wife and a close aide flew out the next day, once the news reached them. He told them he really did not want to see anyone. But they stayed. Finally, he gave in to their requests and checked into a private room at the Palm Springs Hospital. Doctors were summoned but Winthrop already knew the prognosis: he was a terminal case.

An aide took it upon himself to inform the family in New York. The brothers conferred by phone and despite Winthrop's expressed wishes, David flew cross-country to represent the family. He pleaded with Winthrop to allow himself to be moved back to New York, where the best care in the world would be his. "It's too late for that," he replied. It was clear he was beyond further help. The brothers, as well as friends and associates, telephoned daily. Messages were conveyed back and forth. But Winthrop pleaded that he was too weak to speak with anyone. He sank into a coma and not long afterward, on the morning of Washington's Birthday, February 22, 1973, with his son at his bedside, he died, two months short of his sixty-first birthday.

18

Laurance

"The people of the United States want
a better environment and . . . they are
ready to work for it."

Caneel Bay is a tiny quiet alcove on the northwest tip of St. John Island,
the smallest of the three main Virgin Islands which belong to the United
States, out in the middle of nowhere in the Caribbean, some 1,400 miles
southeast of New York City. With its white sand beach, pale blue water,
green jungle foliage and azure sky, it is similar to hundreds of other
remote coves and beaches on the tiny islands which spot the Caribbean
from Miami to the coast of Venezuela. Yet to the keen and experienced
eye of Laurance Rockefeller, similarity is not sameness. He "discovered"
Caneel Bay in 1952 after a four-year exploration of the Caribbean and it
marked for him the culmination of thirty years of photographing, studying
and evaluating what nature had to offer man.

On his first trip to the Caribbean, in 1949 to test the attributes of his
new motor cruiser, *The Dauntless*, he had been struck with the unexpected serenity and beauty of the south seas of America. The contrast not
only from the city life of New York but also from the craggy and rugged
terrain of Maine, New England and the Rockies came as a revelation. The
idea was born in his mind that if he could build a hotel somewhere *here*
in the Caribbean, as he was then involved in at Jackson Hole, he could
bring the unspoiled beauty of this area to the attention of others. Instinctively, he felt that what he enjoyed here others would also enjoy. It started
merely as a germ of an idea, not a commitment, but it gave another dimension to his vacation cruise aboard *The Dauntless*. The Rockefeller in
Laurance disturbed him whenever he devoted himself full time to pleas-

ure. He had developed the habit over the years, almost subconsciously, that at least half of every day ought to be given over to work of some sort. Time was in short supply for a Rockefeller and, more importantly than money, should never be wasted, at least not deliberately.

So he began to study the islands of the Caribbean. In the back of his mind was the picture of a kind of hotel which he himself would seek out for a vacation from the frenzy of everyday life in modern, urban America. He knew what he wanted; he did not know where he would find the ideal location. So, with camera in hand, over the next four years, he inspected hundreds of islands between Miami and Trinidad, until he sailed into Caneel Bay on St. John Island. There he came upon the dilapidated remains of the old Caneel Bay Sugar Plantation, a small, old-fashioned hotel at the edge of the water in an area of unsurpassed and virtually uninhabited natural beauty. Its beach was crescent-shaped, looking out upon a tranquil, contained bay of clear sparkling water with the wonder of a thousand-foot mountain on one side and the thick foliage of a tropical jungle in its background. For him, it was perfection. To others, it was nothing more than a quaint spot for an afternoon swim and departure. Its remoteness made the cove as well as the whole nineteen-square-mile island impractical for human habitation. Columbus had discovered St. John on his second voyage in 1493. The Dutch, the English, the French, the Spaniards and the Danes in succession tried to settle that island and gave up. The sugar estates built there had been abandoned and the island had gone back to the bush.

When Laurance Rockefeller discovered St. John in 1952, more than 85 per cent of the land area was jungle, the population no more than four hundred. There was no electricity, no roads, no automobiles, no docks, no fresh water supply, none of the conveniences of modern life. But Laurance found what he had been looking for. His eye and his instincts told him so. With his training and experience as a conservationist, he was not loath to the concept that man can improve upon nature where needed. His grandfather and father had continually moved trees and earth to improve upon the landscape wherever they had lived, Pocantico Hills, Mount Desert Island and elsewhere. But here, in Caneel Bay, Laurance found what appeared to be the right combination of land, sea, air and natural serenity. The challenge was to open this area for the use of man, without spoiling the very natural attributes which man would desire.

A thorough investigation and study of Caneel Bay, St. John Island and all the pertinent aspects involved in building a luxury quality hotel there satisfied Laurance Rockefeller that the project he had in mind was feasible, despite what some of his own financial advisers predicted. Whether or not it would succeed financially was purely a gamble based upon his own instincts that others would react to the serene beauty and remoteness of Caneel Bay as he had. There was no way to know before he went ahead and built his hotel. But that was the exciting, stimulating and challenging part of the venture, seeking out the unknown.

Then the work began. The old Caneel Bay Plantation, which had been opened in 1931 as a small resort and fallen into virtual disuse, was bought from an estate held in trust after the original owners had died. With six hundred acres of land, the purchase price was $350,000, or about $500 an acre. Subsequent land acquisition became more complicated and vastly more expensive as word got around that a Rockefeller was buying. The last two acres purchased to round out the protected property cost Laurance $40,000 an acre. Such expenditures hurt but he yielded. His rule of thumb was to spend what was needed to achieve his purpose, neither more nor less. If it cost more to build a quality hotel in a remote spot in the Caribbean than it would elsewhere, if quality construction and interior decoration cost more than ordinary buildings, even if the whole project was overcapitalized, it meant only that it would take a longer time to reach the break-even point and period of profits. Laurance Rockefeller could afford to wait: the success or failure of venture capital projects was figured in ten-year periods, not one or two or three.

The focal criterion he set for his new hotel-resort was that the serene environment of Caneel Bay would be the star attraction for guests, not the hotel itself. That was a new concept at the time. Where other resorts featured luxurious accommodations, entertainment, a variety of activities and things to do, Laurance wanted to offer his guests a place in which they could get away from the frenzy of doing too many things, too fast, where they could sit and do nothing or next to nothing, experiencing the exhilaration of being part of the natural environment. Instead of a main hotel building, he built inconspicuous cottages out of sight of one another, virtually unseen from the beach or bay. Guests walked to one pavilion for their meals and the evening's light social activities. Swimming, snorkeling, nature hikes were available and the hotel offered first-class quality in rooms, food and service, but all this was subordinate to the genteel atmosphere of living in the tropics. There were no telephones in the rooms, no locks on the doors, no tipping for service, no fancy parties, no ostentation. At Caneel Bay, one bought privacy, serenity and the opportunity of renewing and refreshing one's self by a return to nature, accompanied by all the necessities of life at the luxury level.

The cost of all this in money, time and effort was enormous and not at all obvious. The submarine power cable bringing electricity to the island was unseen; the million-gallon water catchment was out of sight; the power plant, the roads, the service facilities, the staff housing all had to be planned, provided and paid for. The cottages, their furnishings and the landscaping all reflected the taste of Laurance Rockefeller. He tried and tested every type of chair, sofa and bed, he consulted personally on the color, textures and fabrics of all the drapes, carpeting and upholstery, he selected the paintings on the walls, tested the glow, ambience and proper location of every lamp. As his father before him, Laurance believed that every detail, like a brush stroke on canvas, was significant to the picture. For three months in his home and in his office, Laurance tested a small amber-glass lamp before he approved it for the dining room tables at Caneel Bay. He had to satisfy himself that the amber glow of light was the most complimentary to women, that it did not distort the appearance of the food on the table, and that the lamp was easy to take apart and clean. As anyone who has ever conscientiously decorated a new home would know, the number of details and personal subjective decisions involved was beyond counting.

Four full years of work and several millions of dollars went into Laurance's new Caneel Bay Plantation before it opened to the public on December 1, 1956. It provided only forty first-class double rooms, but each had a tiled bath, dressing alcove, private entrance, open patio, pleasant decor and sense of privacy. A prestige clientele—predominantly business executives but sprinkled with heads of state, high government officials and celebrities from all over the world—came to see what this Rockefeller had wrought, and finding the serenity, beauty and sense of refreshment that Caneel Bay offered, they returned again and again. Over the years, the Plantation was enlarged to 140 rooms, with accommodations for 290 guests at a time. Almost from the start, Caneel Bay achieved and maintained a year-round occupancy rate of 93 per cent, the highest in the resort business. Its success bred imitation in the Caribbean and elsewhere. Laurance Rockefeller was delighted beyond his own expectations. His concept of man renewing himself by a retreat to nature was vindicated. There was also that personal satisfaction common to the successful innkeeper, of having one's own personal taste in accommodations, food and services appreciated by paying guests who come back again and again.

While engrossed in Caneel Bay, Laurance came across an old, forgotten 1930s government study of St. John Island which had recommended more than twenty years before that its primitive, unspoiled beauty be preserved as a national park. The idea appealed to Laurance.

He asked his friend Frank Stick, a sportsman and fellow conservationist, to sound out how much of the island could be bought from private owners. Stick, guarding the anonymity of the Rockefeller interest, had little trouble in buying options to some five thousand of the island's twelve thousand acres. With that in his pocket, Laurance approached the National Park Service and the wheels were set in motion. In contrast to the Rockefeller experience in the Grand Tetons, there was little opposition to Laurance's land purchases on St. John. In truth, there was little commercial interest in that small remote island. So, with the help of the Rockefeller Brothers Fund, Laurance donated $1,750,000 to the Jackson Hole Preserve so that it could purchase the five thousand acres already optioned and deed the land package to the National Park Service. The Virgin Islands National Park, the nation's twenty-ninth national park, was opened to the public on December 1, 1956, to coincide with the formal opening of the Caneel Bay Plantation. Laurance felt he had the best of both worlds. To avoid any semblance of a conflict of interest or profit motive, more than a year before the park and the hotel were opened, Laurance had given up his ownership in the hotel. He donated the Plantation to the Jackson Hole Preserve so that expected profits from the hotel could be utilized for additional conservation projects in the national park. The Preserve, as a non-profit, charitable organization, would be used through the years as a vehicle for Laurance to finance and support conservation activities on multiple levels, including research, publications and, most important, the purchase of land parcels around the country in anticipation of future national and state parks.

Provisions were made to enlarge the Virgin Islands National Park to 9,500 acres as privately owned land became available for purchase. With the blessing and cooperation of the National Park Service, the Caneel Bay Plantation set up and operated campgrounds, tent sites and service facilities in the park, making it a smaller version of Colter Bay in the Grand Tetons. Several years later, the park was extended another 5,600 acres to take in some seven square miles of the Caribbean itself around the island. It thus also became the nation's first underwater national park with clearly marked snorkeling trails through the multi-colored corals, sponges, sea fans and fish of the Caribbean.

Laurance Rockefeller's interest in the Caribbean area was in itself considered a natural resource. After he had purchased the Caneel Bay property, Teodoro Moscoso, who headed Puerto Rico's economic development program, approached Laurance with an appeal to build a hotel in Puerto Rico. He promised government cooperation through its "Operation Bootstrap," which was designed to attract industry and tourism to Puerto Rico in an effort to alleviate unemployment and poverty and to give the island a sustaining economic base. When Laurance visited the site of the proposed hotel, he found a mosquito-infested swamp in the midst of jungle on the far side of the island, a place called Dorado twenty miles west of San Juan, known only for its extreme poverty and its active banditos. But Dorado had beautiful beaches facing the Atlantic Ocean. Laurance, who knew as much about Caribbean beaches as any man, roamed the area with camera in hand, and then declared he was interested.

The proposal was to build a luxury hotel resort and a championship seaside golf course, laid out by Robert Trent Jones, as a means of attracting tourists and golfers to the area. But the site selected was such a jungle wasteland that financial advisers to Laurance strongly advised against participation. "But this is what I like to do, what I get enjoyment from,"

Laurance responded. "If I put my money into building a private playland for myself, it would be a waste; here I have a challenge." It took almost two years for surveyors to hack their way with machetes through trackless jungle growth to provide a survey of land and for the plans and financial arrangements to be worked out. Three more years went to dynamiting, hacking, dredging and moving a billion yards of earth to fill the swamps and to tame the jungle and then to build the initial 136-room resort and the first eighteen holes of the Trent Jones golf course. Once again and this time on a bigger scale, Laurance oversaw the design and building of a low-rise hotel, a scattering of two- and three-story buildings which would blend with the landscape on a 1,500-acre site adjoining two miles of ocean beach front.

The Dorado Beach Hotel opened December 1, 1958, and was immediately acclaimed as one of the finest luxury hotels in the Western Hemisphere. It offered guests a spectacular Spanish-flavored environment of gnarled mangroves and jungle orchards with trails for hiking and bicycling, a palm-studded golf course equal to any anywhere and the fine unspoiled crescent beaches which first attracted Laurance Rockefeller to the area. It became the newest attraction in the Caribbean. For Puerto Rico, it was one of the greatest successes of its Operation Bootstrap. It provided new jobs for hundreds and hundreds of natives. The hotel employed some nine hundred men and women directly while another nine hundred were employed in businesses which grew up around the hotel in Dorado. Laurance Rockefeller now was heavily invested financially and personally in the resort-hotel business.

With all its attributes, however, the Dorado Beach Hotel owed its outstanding success to an unanticipated event, far beyond the control or planning of any Rockefeller. A year after the Dorado Hotel opened, Fidel Castro led a revolution which turned Cuba into a Communist state, closed down its hotels and gambling casinos and forced American tourists to seek their winter sunshine and play in Puerto Rico. The Dorado Beach Hotel, as a result, filled to capacity. Over the next few years, the hotel was expanded to more than double its original size, a second eighteen-hole golf course was added, an airstrip was laid down bringing Dorado within ten minutes' flying time of San Juan. As for gambling, Laurance fought it for three seasons, but finally yielded to the reality of the overwhelming tourist demand to gamble outside the continental limits of the United States. A small gambling casino was added in 1961 to the attractions of the Dorado Hotel and the hotel has flourished ever since.

The accomplishment at Dorado so impressed William Quinn, the governor of the new state of Hawaii in 1959, that he subsequently invited Laurance to consider building a similar hotel-resort on one of the Hawaiian Islands. Governor Quinn visited Dorado Beach as a guest of another new governor, Nelson Rockefeller of New York, and Nelson was in the best position to explain in great detail what and how and why his favorite brother had built at Dorado. Governor Quinn responded that Hawaii, then just admitted to the Union as the fiftieth state, had a similar need for new hotels and new tourist industry to enhance its economic base. Tourism was Hawaii's second largest industry, after defense, and if the state were to prosper, it would have to do everything in its power to attract more tourists.

As a result of that visit to Dorado, Governor Quinn invited Laurance Rockefeller the following year to tour the Hawaiian Islands as a guest of the government in search of what was euphemistically called "new tourism destination areas."

Once again the "beachologist" went island hopping from beach to beach, taking photographs, going in for a swim here and there and mulling over in his mind the potential, the possibilities and the dangers of still another gamble in the hotel-resort business. The emotional response came on an afternoon in July 1960 when Laurance came upon the Kohala coast of the isle of Hawaii. This spot on the globe seemed to offer in one place *all* of the wonders of nature: ocean, desert, mountains, arid warmth, cool rain forests, lush tropical greens and even snow. Here was a combination of the balmy atmosphere of Caneel Bay and the Grand Tetons, for within view of the crescent beach was a 13,796-foot mountain, Mauna Kea, snowcapped with its foothills running right down to the Pacific Ocean.

To Laurance's well-honed instincts on nature, the place was right for development and on a grand scale. On the practical business level, however, it would be one of the greatest gambles of his career, a $20 million throw of the dice. Some day in the future, the isle of Hawaii, the largest in the chain of islands, with its airport at Hilo, could become a jet-age vacation stopover midway between the United States and the Far East. When that day would arrive, Laurance could not know. On the other hand, Hawaii Island was remote, sparsely populated and almost inaccessible, 150 miles from Honolulu, and thus subject to particularly high building costs as well as the expense of bringing fresh water to the island. With all the studies and surveys made, Laurance ultimately had to rely upon his own instincts. It was a gamble: if he converted this semi-arid wilderness in the middle of the Pacific into a luxury hotel-resort, would enough people come to enjoy it and spend their money there? To a man, every impartial banker and economist he consulted advised him against the venture. But Laurance Rockefeller by this time was an experienced entrepreneur in venture capital and he thought in terms of long-range goals. Unlike most others, he could afford to be patient for a return on his investment. Despite the advice to the contrary, Laurance felt that the potential for profit and for the economical impact on Hawaii outweighed the risk of failure.

So he went ahead, as he had at Caneel Bay and at Dorado but on a larger scale. He acquired the rights to more than twelve thousand acres of land and two miles of beach front, he engaged a small organization of men to represent him there, he set architects and landscapers to work on designing a hotel-resort which would meet his own conceptual standards of subordinating the buildings to the natural environment. He became involved in Hawaii itself, beyond the hotel. He underwrote studies on the historical, cultural and geophysical aspects of the area. He sponsored a museum and historical research facility on the island. He worked closely with state and county authorities on the transformation of the Kohala coast of the island.

Five years later, almost to the day when he had first visited the site, the Mauna Kea Beach Hotel was opened to the public (July 1965), overlooking that same white crescent beach where Laurance had taken an afternoon swim. Once again, it reflected the tastes of Laurance Rockefeller in big things and small. The showerheads were custom made of wood because teak blended better than metal with the surroundings. Laurance wanted it that way and was willing to pay the extra expense. Once again, a Laurance Rockefeller hotel was recognized as one of the finest luxury hotels in all the world. Laurance originally had wanted a different design for the Mauna Kea Hotel, decentralized cottages hidden in their own foliage settings and opening directly onto the beach, similar to his plan at Dorado and Caneel Bay. But the exorbitant costs of building on the remote island, the heat on the beach itself and the danger of flash floods forced Laurance to settle for one long, low hotel building atop a knoll overlooking the beach. The design was modeled after native Hawaiian religious platforms found in the area, but Laurance afterward delighted in describing it as a huge aircraft carrier stuck high and dry on the beach. Actually, from the air the hotel and its surroundings resembled an oasis of green in the midst of a desert. The greenery was man-made in one of the most extensive landscaping projects ever undertaken in the Hawaiian Islands. More than a half-million plants of some two hundred varieties were imported, the roof of the hotel was made into a tropical garden to blend with the terraces below, the eighteen-hole golf course adjacent to the hotel shone emerald green in the sun and, of course, in the midst of this balmy atmosphere there still stood the snowcapped peak of the mountain which gave the hotel its name.

The completion and opening of the Mauna Kea Beach Hotel in 1965 was not the end of Laurance's venture into Hawaii, it was the beginning. With bookings reaching 97 per cent of capacity, it was not long before plans were drawn for an unobtrusive new wing, which in 1968 added 102 more rooms to the original 154-room hotel. Work was begun to build a new village with all facilities near but out of sight of the hotel to house the five-hundred-odd hotel employees and their families. In 1973, another floor was added to the original building with 54 more guest rooms. At the same time, Laurance became intrigued with the idea of expanding his hotel project to the size of a city!

To Laurance, Hawaii represented a new frontier, opened by his own Mauna Kea Beach Hotel, offering the vast potential of open space in which to live and to play, made accessible by the new giant jet airliners. The success of his new hotel had spurred a new land development fever throughout the Hawaiian Islands and Laurance was obliged to step in and to help purchase a number of historical and cultural sites, like the Seven Pools area at Maui, to safeguard them from commercial development. In one instance, he led a fund-raising drive in the islands which provided some $400,000 to purchase 3,900 acres to extend the Haleakala National Park from its mountain range to the sea. Meanwhile, his plans for a model resort city on the leeward side of the island of Hawaii took shape. Seven years of planning, amalgamating the old traditions of Hawaiian folklore and the modern advances of technology, such as vertical take-off aircraft, went into the master plan for a model city, ten miles square, based economically upon seven large resort-hotels, of which Mauna Kea would be the first, each with its own golf course, tennis club, natural park, summer homes for vacationers and smaller houses for the thousands of islanders who would be working at the hotels. As envisioned, twenty thousand people would live or vacation there.

For a venture of this size, estimated to cost $250 million, Laurance recognized that not even he would have the resources necessary to go it alone. As with his venture capital companies in aerospace, the time had come to merge his hotel-resort interests into a larger entity to gain greater financial and productive leverage. In late 1967, he sold one third of his ownership of the Mauna Kea Beach Hotel to Eastern Air Lines, which hoped to win a new route to fly to the Far East, stopping at the halfway point on Hilo, the capital of Hawaii Island. Then Laurance and Eastern formed a joint venture company with the Dillingham Corporation of Honolulu, the largest and oldest building construction firm in the islands. The new company, called Dilrock-Eastern, combined the Rockefeller know-how on designing and operating resort-hotels, the Dillingham expertise in building and its familiarity with the Hawaiian Islands through three generations of the Dillingham family, and the transportation capabilities and interests of Eastern Air Lines: all of them poised to implement Laurance's master plan for the development of the Kohala coast resort region.

At the same time, Laurance sold an 80 per cent interest in his Dorado Beach Hotel to Eastern and agreed to take a 20 per cent ownership in another hotel, the five-hundred-room Cerromar, designed as a convention resort, next to the successful Dorado in Puerto Rico. Eastern Air Lines, already serving New York and Puerto Rico, wanted to diversify into the hotel business on the theory that "what's good for the tourist is good for the transportation business." As for Laurance, he felt that he had proved his original point: hotels which harmonized with the natural beauty of the environment could be commercially successful despite high cost. As a financial investment, he had put ten years and $9 million into the Dorado Beach Hotel and now could walk away from it with $23 million in Eastern stock for the 80 per cent interest sold to Eastern.

Actually, Laurance did not walk away from the Dorado or any of his other hotels. He retained 20 per cent interest in the hotels and he kept control of the management and operation through a new management company, called Rockresorts. He recruited Richard Holtzman, the experienced and personable president of the Sheraton hotels in Hawaii, to head Rockresorts. That left Laurance free once again to turn to new, more challenging endeavors. However, as Laurance's reputation in the hotel business spread throughout the industry he was frequently approached with proposals and propositions to build a hotel here or there. The time and effort involved, more than anything else, limited his availability.

But there were exceptions. In 1959, Laurance was approached in his office by Ward Bond, the actor who had become famous as the announcer for Lucky Strike. Bond, on the brink of tears, cried, "You see before you, Mr. Rockefeller, a man who has made the biggest mistake in his life." For his retirement, Bond explained, he had invested all his life's savings into buying and refurbishing the Estate Good Hope on St. Croix in the Virgin Islands. It was small but luxurious, with only fourteen bedroom-living room suites. His dream had been to be the genial host of this small and friendly hotel where for $100 a day a guest could live in quiet luxury close to nature and dine on caviar and French cuisine. But he had found himself ill-equipped to handle the details of running a hotel—the plumbing and maintenance, the help problem, the finances—and now he was facing bankruptcy and ruin.

"I think your organization, with its success on St. John, can take it over and you can have it for whatever you think its value is," Bond declared, adding frankly, "I'm at my wit's end and I'm at your mercy."

"I'll look into it and see what I can do," replied Laurance. When the ingenuous actor had left, Laurance turned to Allston Boyer, then his chief hotel aide, and commented, "I don't think we want a hotel on St. Croix but why don't you go down there and look at it."

Boyer returned with a bearish report. "It's a lovely place and we can operate it, but we won't ever make any money there," he said and itemized his reasons.

"I agree with everything you say," Laurance replied. "But this man had that rare quality of facing the truth squarely. He laid his soul bare to us. His whole approach to that hotel was so meaningful, I think we should help him. I would like to pay him what he has in it so he can get out whole." Laurance bought the Estate Good Hope from Bond and his partners for $360,000, invested even more in an attempt, albeit unsuccessful, to make it pay and then, six years later, sold it at a loss for use as a boys' school.

Laurance invested $12 million to build a small but more viable hotel at Little Dix Bay on the northwest tip of Virgin Gorda in the British Virgin Islands. It was designed as a restful beachcomber's haven with fifty rooms, later expanded to sixty-six, plus a hundred-boat marina and a landing strip for light aircraft.

On St. Croix, the largest of the U.S. Virgin Islands, Laurance invited his brother David into a partnership venture in building Fountain Valley, a spectacular championship golf course and club, which opened in January 1966. It was Laurance's way of making up for having refused David's request to invest in a land development project in the Hawaiian Islands. Because of the brothers' long-standing agreement never to encroach upon another's field of interest in order to avoid open conflict or competition within the family, David had asked his brother's permission. Laurance had turned him down. Now, because David maintained an ultra-modern vacation home on St. Barthélemy, Laurance invited him into this project. The golf club was to be the forerunner of a residential land development of three thousand acres. But in partnership, the brothers never did see eye to eye on the project and a downturn in the economy on St. Croix squelched the land development project altogether.

Of all Laurance's hotel projects, the most difficult and most opposed was his effort to help out his wife's own home town, where he had been well-known for years: Woodstock, a picturesque nineteenth-century Vermont town of well-kept old brick and clapboard homes, manicured lawns and neat gardens, expensive shops and beautiful, wealthy and well-educated people, all in the rolling hills near the Green Mountains. Mary French had grown up there, she and Laurance had been married in its Congregational Church, they and their children came back summer and winter for at least one weekend every month or two. The Billings Farm and the Billings Mansion were landmarks, named for Mary's grandfather, who settled there in 1869. The town's chief tourist attraction was the venerable Woodstock Inn, built of clapboard in 1892, pretty and well painted on the outside and rotting within. Its owner-manager David Beach approached Laurance for help in repairing and modernizing the seventy-five-year-old firetrap. Surveys indicated the cost would exceed $600,000 even for inadequate remodeling. After much planning and many consultations, Laurance agreed to buy out David Beach, tear down the old hotel and build a new Woodstock Inn in its place. It would be the first new hotel built in Vermont since the 1930s, but Laurance anticipated a new birth of tourism in New England because the popularity of skiing had made the area a year-round attraction.

Nevertheless, the announcement of plans to build a new hotel in

Woodstock was greeted with vociferous opposition by a good many, if not a majority, of the townspeople and summer residents. It was certainly more than Laurance had expected. When he had built the Caneel Bay Plantation, no one particularly cared; St. John had been virtually deserted at the time. In Puerto Rico and then in Hawaii, he had been invited and welcomed with open arms; his building and environmental plans had been sped through the necessary legislative process. But on mainland America, the dowagers and country gentlemen of Woodstock, Vermont, sometimes referred to locally as "the mink and manure set," objected strenuously to change in their environment. There were fears and cries that Rockefeller was moving to take over Woodstock, to convert it into another Colonial Williamsburg, a captive community, something unreal, where the residents would be on display for the tourists. The townspeople knew Laurance had bought the Mount Tom ski area in 1960 and later had added Suicide Six to it; then he had bought the Woodstock Country Club, built a new clubhouse and rebuilt its eighteen-hole golf course and changed the location of the tennis courts; then he had bought the old White Cupboard Inn and converted it into the headquarters for the town's Historical Society. He had taken it upon himself to pay for putting underground all the electric and telephone lines which ran through the town's center. What the townspeople did not know, for it was not advertised, was that Laurance Rockefeller had not sought to do these things. The hotel and country club owners had come to him for help and he had first tried to persuade the town's council to get rid of the unsightly overhead wires. He had moved as he did because he thought he had to; no one else would or could do it. He held a special love for Woodstock. It was a second home for him and the childhood home of his wife. He felt an obligation.

In time, it had worked itself out and most of the townspeople recognized that Laurance Rockefeller's new Woodstock Inn, opened in 1971, contributed significantly to the economy of the whole town. It became the "in place" to hold a convention in Vermont, attracted new visitors each year and became in fact the town's largest single "industry."

Laurance, ever with his eye on the over-all, long-range view, buttressed his new undertaking by financing a broad study of the ecology and recreational potential of the entire region surrounding Woodstock. The study pointed the way into the future. It showed where a state park and several smaller parks could be built, where several scenic corridors of the area could be created by simple zoning. It proposed the building of an open-air museum and it recommended the steps by which the local river could be cleaned up and improved.

All of these hotel-resorts from Vermont to Hawaii were for Laurance pilot projects in microcosm of his deep-seated beliefs and faith in the cause of conservation. He wanted to demonstrate that the natural beauty of an area can be preserved and used and even enhanced, and at the same time be made commercially viable. He built the hotels not for profit *per se* but to show the way to what is possible. Partly as a result of this, the Dilrock-Eastern partnership in Hawaii collapsed at the end of 1971, barely three years after it had begun. Eastern's long-sought air route to Hawaii was awarded to American Airlines and to Braniff, and Eastern thereupon lost its prime interest in any hotel business in Hawaii. Dillingham, a profit-oriented business, found it could not shake Laurance Rockefeller from his socially oriented way of moving slowly toward long-range goals and they amicably parted ways. Laurance bought out Dillingham and traded with Eastern Air Lines his 20 per cent ownership in the Dorado and Cerromar hotels in Puerto Rico for Eastern's 33 per cent interest in the Mauna Kea Hotel in Hawaii.

By this time, Laurance's seven hotel-resorts, from the Caribbean to the Grand Tetons, from Hawaii to Vermont, were well-established. Bookings in each of them were the highest in the industry. With over-all policy set, Laurance began in 1967 to relegate the day-to-day operations and management to the professionals of Rockresorts, headed by Richard Holtzman, who, of course, reported to him. As chairman of the board of the multi-million-dollar hotel operation, Laurance remained the final arbiter, and as the whole operation ran rather smoothly, he personally gave less and less time to it, freeing himself for his host of other activities.

He followed that same practice on his venture capital investments. At the end of his first ten years of personal involvement, Laurance began to give less and less of his time to picking and choosing his investments. Instead, he delegated a good deal of the authority to a small group of trusted advisers, headed by Harper Woodward. They sought out the opportunities, investigated them and reported with recommendations to him for the final decisions. The only significant change in policy for the next decade would be the shift out of the aviation-transportation field into aerospace, electronics and nuclear energy. That was where the new cutting edge of technology was to be explored and discovered. And it was a fact now that Laurance and his three or four principal advisers were experienced and knowledgeable explorers in the wilds of venture capital enterprises.

So, in the summer of 1957, a few months *before* the Russians launched *Sputnik I*, Laurance and his associates decided to help form a new company to do research and development work on instruments and equipment needed in the exploration of space. The Geophysics Corporation of America, headed by Milton Greenberg, who had been director of the Air Force's Geophysics Research Directorate, went into business late in 1958. It was the right time and place. Laurance's initial investment of $250,000 for one fourth of the outstanding stock was worth $1.5 million three years later.

The most dramatically successful of all his investments was his backing of a small one-year-old Boston company called Itek, short for Information Technology, headed by a small group of scientists who were developing an electronic scanner which could classify and sort out information automatically. It was an instrument which, if successful, could be used widely in conjunction with computers by the Post Office and by large corporations. Laurance's initial investment in Itek was augmented to $875,000 before this new company went public. But then it soared into space. It took over another company, Vectron, and expanded into aerial and long-range space photography. Within two years, Itek, which went on the market at $2 a share, reached the astronomical high of $345 in the winter of 1958, split five for one, and then went even higher to $82 a new share ($410 for the old $2 share) in 1960. These were the go-go years for the glamour stocks on the over-the-counter market when investors and speculators became rich on the stock market and were willing to take a plunge. The plunge and the bath came in due course. By 1963, Itek had come back down to earth at $16 a share. Laurance did not sell out at the top. His investment was in the company itself and what it was doing, on a long-term basis. But he did sell a significant number of Itek shares along the way at go-go profits in the millions, and that gave him wide leeway to reinvest in still more esoteric ventures.

Laurance's money, reputation and men went into such enterprises as Scientific Atlanta, National Astro Laboratories, New England Nuclear Corporation, Cryonetics Corporation, Thermokinetic Fibers—all of them small, new research and development companies headed usually by one or a few men who were geniuses in their fields, but knew little or nothing of how to finance, staff and run a business organization. But these men, in Laurance's estimation, were on to something good, something important, something exciting. Cryonetics Corporation was working on what could be done under conditions of extreme cold (−459° F., which is absolute zero), such as developing special refrigerators for space travel or for developing an ultra-low temperature environment in which electricity could be transmitted ad infinitum without loss of energy. Thermokinetic Fibers, a company starting out with two engineers and a five-man board of directors, was working at the other extreme of temperatures. This R&D company was trying to develop a use for metallic "whiskers" derived from aluminum oxide vapors produced in an ultra-high temperature furnace. If successful, these "whiskers," smaller than human hair, could revolutionize the computer industry with their strength and extraordinary magnetic and optical properties.

The problems involved with venture capital are manifold. If you are in the risk capital business and you are reasonably successful, you get to a point where you might take fewer risks for fear of ruining your good record. On the other hand, if you experience a few disasters, you could tend to become overcautious. The idea, of course, was to try not to miss those few good ventures which come your way. If you get them at an early attractive stage, they tend to have a lot of risk, but the rewards can be fabulous. Laurance was well aware of the treacherous shoals on either side of the channel of too much caution and too little. He had also learned that the problems involved with venture capital multiply dramatically after and not before an investment and a commitment are made. Most often the problems in high-risk, speculative research and development companies are not with the venture itself or the product but with the people involved. Most creative people tend to be difficult. But they are always interesting. For Laurance that was part of the fascination in the business. He found he had to learn to live with their idiosyncrasies or to try to change the environment around them by adding skilled men to the management. He would constantly remind his associates, with a wry grin, that if these men were not so creative and difficult, they would be plodding at some job with General Electric.

More than a thousand business propositions and appeals for financial backing flowed into Laurance's office during this period. In the early days, someone in the office would take a look at everything that came along. Banks referred inventors to Laurance, friends sent him their friends, word of mouth brought others in. Then in the summer of 1959, the *Wall Street Journal* published an article depicting Laurance as the largest single investor in venture capital and the mail and personal appeals poured in like an avalanche. It seemed as though every inventor of a new can opener, gadget or machine wanted to demonstrate his product personally. The newest man in Laurance's office usually handled this flow. He encountered all types, from a talkative old man who presented childlike pencil drawings of a flying saucer to a self-made multi-millionaire who admitted that "despite all my money, I'm stricken with absolute awe every time I step into this office." The Rockefeller name held that magic in matters concerning money. Of the thousand or so unsolicited propositions which came into the office each year, perhaps two hundred warranted further investigation, and of those, about fifty received full field inquiries with visits to plants and consultations with the owners. Of those fifty, perhaps one or two or three a year received Laurance Rockefeller's financial backing.

Most of Laurance's investment opportunities were found by his own staff attending scientific conventions or reading scientific trade journals. He still preferred to invest in small new companies with good management rather than in single inventors. His initial commitment usually was in the neighborhood of $250,000. But added to that figure was also whatever his brothers wanted to invest in the venture, and beginning in 1969 Laurance offered each investment opportunity to the "cousins," the fourth generation of Rockefellers. It also became understood in the office that those who advised Laurance to invest in a particular venture were expected to back up their recommendation by joining him in that same venture. On the other hand, there was absolutely no pressure to recommend anything. During one lean period, the six men on his venture capital staff went for two years drawing full salary without proposing a single investment. They worked well together, smoothly and fully understanding of one another as associates, and perhaps this above all was the reason for their success.

In 1975, upon the retirement of Harper Woodward, his principal adviser, Laurance asked a member of his staff to do a complete recapitulation of his venture capital investments back to 1946, when he had started out with $1.3 million, invested primarily in Eastern Air Lines, McDonnell and Piasecki. Despite daily record keeping and year-end reports, he was curious about his over-all record. This is, in summary, what he found:

He had invested in a total of seventy-eight companies, including the original three, all of them high-risk ventures on the frontier of scientific technology, and on the basis of his original intent, he had been enormously successful: sixty-seven of those companies succeeded in developing, producing and selling new products for the market place. Generally, well more than half of all such high-risk businesses fail for one reason or another: bad management, insoluble technological problems, no market for the product or wrong timing. Against that average, 86 per cent of the companies in which Laurance invested grew from virtually nothing more than an idea to companies which produced credible products which fulfilled a need. Some of these companies made huge profits, some made less, some made no profits at all.

On a financial profit and loss basis, of the seventy-eight companies, thirty-eight were winners, thirty-two losers and eight broke even—although at least some of those losers had their future potential still ahead of them. Fifty-four per cent of the companies in which Laurance Rockefeller had invested had made money. But even that statistic can be misleading. By the very nature of venture capital investments, when this type of experimental company makes money, it usually makes a lot of money. When such a company fails the investors' losses are limited to the amounts of their investments. On that scoreboard, Laurance's thirty-eight profitable companies produced for him gains of $52 million. The thirty-two companies which lost money cost him $3.5 million. Thus, his over-all profit since 1946 on his original $1.3 million invested and reinvested over the years in venture capital, came to a total of $48.5 million. But there was a steady turnover of this money. Virtually all of the profits were invested in Laurance's expanding hotel-resort ventures, combined with his conservation activities.

With the exception of Winthrop, who had moved to Arkansas, Laurance's brothers and sister invested along with him, each according to his or her own penchant for taking high investment risks. Nelson was a keen and eager investor who most often followed Laurance's lead, up until 1958 when he was elected governor of New York and thereupon ceased to participate. Of the seventy-eight companies in Laurance's portfolio, David invested in fifty, John 3rd in thirty-five, and Abby Mauzé in thirty-five. However, the amount of cash each put into a particular company differed considerably, reflecting their individual personalities more than the amount of money they had on hand.

The final computation, the bottom line on the scoreboard for Laurance Rockefeller personally as he approached the age of sixty-five, revealed that he had accomplished what he set out to do upon his return from the Second World War: he had proved to his own satisfaction his personal business acumen, he had contributed to changing the face of America through advanced techology, he had enjoyed the stimulation of the process and, finally, he had made more money—much more money— investing in venture capital than he would have if he had sat back and put his money safely into oil stocks. His $1.3 million invested in blue-chip oil stocks in 1946 would have grown to approximately $10 million in 1975; in venture capital, it had grown to just under $50 million.

Computing and analyzing how Laurance Rockefeller "invested" his time, rather than his money, was a far more complex undertaking. Always, as far back as he could remember, there were more calls on his time than he had time available. He picked and chose as carefully as possible and still felt overextended. He knew of the dangers of spreading himself too thin, decreasing his effectiveness and leaving himself open to mistakes and errors in judgment. One such quick decision in 1970, for instance, caused him the most acute embarrassment of his career. During Nelson's fourth gubernatorial campaign, an aide relayed his brother's request for help in financing the publication of a book on his brother's opponent in the race, Arthur Goldberg, who had served on the Supreme Court of the United States and at the United Nations. So accustomed to accommodating his favorite brother, Laurance listened to the request for a mere five minutes, without realizing the implications. He agreed to give $60,000 for the venture, a fraction of what he usually contributed to his brother's campaign, and promptly forgot about it. Five years later when the facts came out— that the Rockefellers had financed a derogatory book against an opponent, a prima-facie case of a political dirty trick—an embarrassed Laurance Rockefeller apologized profusely at the nationally televised hearings on Nelson's nomination as Vice-President.

Laurance's time, aside from his personal life with his family, was devoted in the main to the three big C's of his life: Capitalism, Conservation and Cancer. Philosophy was a close fourth, a personal addiction for reading whatever others had to say on values, ethics and the meaning of life. He made a lifetime habit of collecting aphorisms in a small notebook he carried with him. His interest in philosophy had led him in 1942 to the Advisory Council of Princeton's Department of Philosophy, of which he later became chairman. He became active in his alma mater's Graduate Council and in 1967, he was elected to Princeton's board of trustees. In everything he joined, he became active, and he soon found himself leading the fight among the trustees to admit women undergraduates to the all-men's school. In the emerging struggle for equal rights for women of the late 1960s, Laurance argued loud and long at Princeton (and at the Massachusetts Institute of Technology, where he also was a trustee) for co-educational equality. The clincher in the argument for Laurance was that civil rights alone demanded equal opportunity at education for women. It was long overdue, he thought. Even his grandfather, old John D., had believed in that as far back as 1903, when he and John D., Jr., had established the General Education Board with a charter calling for "the promotion of education within the United States without distinction of race, sex or creed." How could Princeton University, sixty-five years later, deny education to a portion of the population because of sex? As for the practical argument that Princeton had no living quarters available for women, Laurance came up with an answer for that: he pledged $4 million for a dormitory for women on campus, and Princeton University announced it was going co-ed.

On the seventy-fifth anniversary of Memorial Hospital in 1960, thirteen years after he joined that board, Laurance was elected chairman of a thoroughly revamped institution renamed the Memorial Sloan-Kettering Cancer Center with a combined board of directors replacing the three separate boards of directors which had governed the hospital, the research institute and Ewing (Municipal) Hospital. To appease Alfred Sloan, who had donated more than $50 million to the research institute which bore his name, and to demonstrate a continuing faith in the importance of cancer research itself, the Sloan-Kettering name was retained in the Cancer Center. But now with Laurance's both hands on the helm, a major program was begun to integrate and upgrade the tripartite thrust of the Center in cancer patient care, cancer research and cancer education. It was a long-haul, many-faceted, step-by-step endeavor. Staff morale, personalities, traditions and professional rivalries were as much involved as policy decisions, finances and the setting of specific goals. In time, more and more of a feeling of "oneness" found its way into the vast institution. Cornell Medical School students worked at Memorial Hospital for school credits, Memorial physicians taught at the Medical School with professorial status, research scientists worked alongside cancer specialists at the hospital, information flowed more freely, elaborate and expensive equipment was shared instead of duplicated. At the same time, a new building program was launched in which Laurance, as chairman of the center, headed a drive which raised more than $100 million from private sources. Memorial

Sloan-Kettering Cancer Center in 1973 became the largest privately operated non-profit institution in the country dedicated to the conquest of
cancer. The new hospital—with its 565 beds, 15 operating rooms and a
whole floor devoted to clinical research and evaluating new forms of cancer treatment—provided in-patient care for more than 9,500 cancer victims during its first year of operation. Research facilities were thoroughly
upgraded. In all, the Center increased its staff to 4,500, including about
200 scientists, 300 physicians, 200 doctors-in-training and 550 registered
nurses. Its operating budget increased fourfold over a ten-year period, from
$25 million in 1965 to $108 million in 1975.

Great strides in cancer research, treatment and care were being made
during these years at Memorial and across the country. To cut the Gor-
dian knot of the cancer mystery, research scientists were attacking the
problem from all conceivable angles: basic research into the cell, molecular biology, the role of viruses, the possibilities of immunology, animal
experimentation, and with therapy itself on humans. Basic research, diag-
nostic technology and treatment procedures were becoming more sophisticated, more rewarding and much more expensive. It came to be felt
that cancer scientists were on the threshold of at least the possibility
of winning the long, long struggle against cancer. To give them a push
across that threshold, some of the lay leaders in the field agreed to try to
persuade the government, the only source of the amounts of money
needed, to elevate cancer research to the high-priority status of a national
goal. If John F. Kennedy could make a national goal of placing an American as the first man on the moon in ten years, Richard M. Nixon could
rally the nation behind the goal of conquering cancer in ten years, even if
the cost were the same. Laurance joined with Mary Lasker, Elmer H.
Bobst, early pioneers of the American Cancer Society, and with Benno C.
Schmidt, of the National Institute of Health, to form a prestigious committee of four to lobby for the concept. The four topped off their efforts
with a luncheon for the whole U. S. Senate at which they explained what
was involved; Bobst talked persuasively with President Nixon, a close
friend, and the outcome was a cooperative effort between the Republican
Administration and Democratic Senators Edward (Ted) Kennedy and
Ralph Yarborough to produce a National Cancer Advisory Board to disburse and administer more than $600 million *a year* of government funds
for cancer research. It was a shot in the arm the likes of which had never
been seen before in the scientific community. It was also a gamble, a tremendous act of faith in man. Laurance could well recall Alfred P. Sloan's
act of faith in founding the Sloan-Kettering Institute for Cancer Research
a quarter of a century before when Sloan announced: "I am convinced
that given time, facilities and talent, there is no problem that is beyond
the reach of aggressive scientific attack." Sloan had died of heart failure in
Memorial Hospital in February 1966, at the age of ninety, and he had ex-

pressed his own faith in Laurance's concept of an integrated cancer center by bequeathing $10 million to the cancer research facility which bore his name and $10 million to Memorial Hospital. For Laurance, the fight against cancer goes on. He has seen at first hand Memorial Hospital turned from a place of despair to an environment of hope. He looks forward to the day when long-term remissions achieved in cancers of the breast, prostrate and blood will be lifted to long-range cures, to the further day when all types of cancers will be eliminated from the ranks of major causes of death in America.

Laurance's concern with cancer was shared down through the years by his sister Babs, although her own interest focused more upon the personal aspects of patient care than upon impersonal research. Were there enough lamps in a patient's room for reading, enough coat racks for guests, enough staff to help make patients comfortable? These were the questions which concerned her when she became an advisory member of Memorial's board of trustees. As a contributor to the medical center, she gave generously in the millions, matching Laurance's own contributions almost dollar for dollar. And that made her one of the chief benefactors of the hospital. She also supported New York Hospital and Presbyterian Hospital in New York City. But she insisted upon anonymity in her giving. She wanted no thank-you dinners, no speeches, no awards and certainly no publicity. Instead, in 1962 Laurance and the Rockefeller Brothers Fund jointly endowed in her honor the Abby Rockefeller Mauzé professorship at the Massachusetts Institute of Technology for a distinguished woman scholar.

When in 1968 Mrs. Mauzé became enchanted with the concept of a new "vest pocket" park built by William S. Paley, the board chairman of the Columbia Broadcasting System, just off Fifth Avenue in Manhattan's East Fifties, Laurance assured his sister that he would be delighted to help her build a similar park. It was, after all, the first time Babs had said she wanted to do something publicly. Her interest in people surfaced and the idea of a tiny park where New Yorkers could sit down and rest seemed so simple. From the start she envisioned a tiny park with some green and some flowing water and some seats and benches which would in her words give New Yorkers "some moments of serenity in this busy world." Laurance, assisted by his aide Allston Boyer, undertook the task for his sister. It took one year and $1 million to find and to purchase the appropriate site for Greenacre Park with a frontage of sixty feet on East Fifty-first Street between Second and Third avenues. Laurance negotiated with three different parties, each owning twenty feet of frontage, before the package was put together. It took another two years and $5 million more to construct the park and establish the Greenacre Foundation, which would maintain and operate the park in perpetuity. But the park itself, when opened in 1971, was a gem in midtown Manhattan with a twenty-

five-foot-high waterfall over huge granite blocks and a small brook of
recycled water running from the sidewalk entrance to the waterfall. Landscaped in a variety of evergreens and honey locust trees, the park provided
small tables and chairs and a snack bar and, above all, a place in which to
sit down and rest. The Rockefeller brothers were so delighted with their
shy sister's "coming out" that they all attended the park's opening
ceremonies, one of the rare occasions upon which all five brothers and
their sister appeared in public together. Mrs. Mauzé dedicated the park in
gratitude to her brother Laurance and to Allston Boyer.

In March 1975, not long after Happy Rockefeller's successful operations for breast cancer at Memorial, Mrs. Mauzé joined her brothers
Laurance and Nelson in pledging $5.95 million to the Cancer Center over
the next five years. She did not live for five more years—a victim of cancer
—but she made good on her pledge.

The fight against cancer, a multi-million-dollar portfolio of high-risk
business investments, an empire of hotel-resorts from New England to Hawaii, Rockefeller Center, the Rockefeller Brothers Fund and sundry other
commitments occupied only about *half* of Laurance Rockefeller's working
time. The other half went to conservation. For him, it was a consuming
passion which transcended almost everything he did. It occupied a part if
not most of every one of his days since his early apprenticeship to his father on nature walks and camping trips out West. If he was not doing
something related to conservation and man's relationship to nature, then
he was thinking about it.

"Fitness and outdoor recreation go hand in hand," he explained to
one interviewer. "Tension and stress are the causes of many ailments. If
you can restore peace of mind and recreate a person, you've given him a
new lease on life." He more than believed this; he practiced it with care
and deliberation. His own working day often was sedentary and often
stressful, conferring with people at his office, reading reports, making high-
risk decisions, but he rejuvenated himself by balancing his mental work
with physical activity. On weekends at Pocantico Hills or in Woodstock
or on vacations at the Grand Tetons, Laurance chopped wood, split logs
or went hiking, camping or horseback riding, and he returned to his
tightly filled schedule of city work renewed and ready to go. He worked
seven days a week. When he visited his own resort-hotels, where others
rested and relaxed, he carried with him a briefcase bulging with papers on
which he would work alone several hours a day in his room. In the city
Saturdays were excellent days for gathering busy men together for meetings. Two to four hours on Sundays and holidays always could be found for
"homework" on the next week's activities. According to one close associate,
Laurance's impossible vision of perfection was to commune with nature
alone in a canoe on a remote lake somewhere—with a radio-telephone at
his side for direct communication with his office in New York. A day

without some work was for Laurance a day wasted and waste was the ultimate sin in the Rockefeller lexicon. What he sought was a balance between mental and physical activities, between the stressful demands of work and the spiritual renewal of nature. Beyond that, he sought a personal inner peace of mind by being in harmony with nature, his environment, his work and, most important and most difficult, his fellow man.

All this was part of conservation, as Laurance Rockefeller came to understand the broad implications of the term. Man was an integral part of his environment and if he were to survive in a modern, complex society with its multiple demands and stresses, then his natural environment had to be preserved and utilized as man himself in the best of good health. Conservation for Laurance included the philosophical realization of the importance of man's self-renewal by physical activity in the great out-of-doors. It was his own personal love for working with his hands, hiking, camping, swimming, boating which he wanted to impart to others. So modern man living in smog-filled cities and especially those fat, indolent Americans who were ruining their health under the guise of affluence had to be retaught somehow what they had forgotten about physical activity and their environment. And the environment itself had to be saved for the proper use of man. It was one thing for a small band of conservationists to attempt to buy up land and preserve it from commercial exploitation. But it was another and far more difficult task to persuade America and its people of the proper use of its open space and out-of-doors.

There were no short cuts, no simple answers to complex problems presented by man's use of his environment. There were no quick, ready solutions to long-range goals. Nor could the task of persuasion be wholly delegated to his subordinates. Laurance could and did help establish conservation-minded organizations of private citizens. But it was his name, his reputation and his influence, and at times his money, which put him in the best position to persuade others. He spent countless hours, days and months—more than half his time, as best as could be estimated—in conducting or attending conferences to advance the cause of conservation. He financed research projects, he lobbied in the halls of Congress, he spoke to Presidents.

Years of patient and unrelenting effort were invested in the attempt to persuade the federal government that the environment should be recognized as an important social value. But conservation *per se* had always been a politically controversial subject, opposed violently by special-interest groups, whether in the Grand Tetons, the Appalachians of New York or the Redwood forests of California. When it came to parks and outdoor recreation, the subject met with apathy or a lack of understanding. Conservation and outdoor recreation almost always were last in the list of priorities of things to be done for America. As one congressman put it to Laurance Rockefeller: "It's the frosting on the cake . . . and why should I get involved in putting frosting on the cake when we don't have the cake as yet in America?"

The baffling difficulty of answering that question, which went to the heart of the priority assigned to conservation and the environment, led Laurance Rockefeller to a new and significant concept. He asked himself how the cost of conservation measures could be justified in dollars and cents. The answer was to compute the cost-benefit ratio of each and every specific measure advocated and to show as much as possible the material benefits which outweighed the costs of conservation measures. The costs were clear but the return on the investment were not particularly visible. Hence the idea of researching and reporting the costs of pollution in the Hudson River, in Lake Erie and throughout America. The fish were dying, fishermen were losing their jobs, even towns were dying along the river as people moved away. The cost of all this far exceeded the cost of cleaning up the river. A cost-benefit analysis along these lines was something that people in business and the Congress could understand. It would make sense to the public at large.

It made sense particularly to the business-oriented administration of President Eisenhower. Sympathetic but still politically wary of the idea, the Eisenhower administration agreed to propose an outside, private study of the recreation and conservation needs of the country, one which would not be binding upon the government. It was a case in which a private citizens group, free of the political implications involved, could inform the nation better than its own government of what should be done to conserve and to use its great natural heritage. Thus, Laurance Rockefeller, clearly the most outstanding citizen involved in conservation, was given the task and the challenge by President Eisenhower to develop and promote ideas on the environment which would test public opinion on the subject without embarrassing his administration politically. In short, the message was: "Do your damnedest. I sympathize with your views and what you are trying to do. But I'll stay out of this one." The political realities of the mid-1950s were such that Laurance's project group was set up to report not to President Eisenhower but to whoever his successor might be.

Nevertheless, that was the major breakthrough for modern conservation efforts. In 1958, President Eisenhower appointed the Outdoor Recreation Resources Review Commission, headed by Laurance Rockefeller, and asked it to make an independent survey of the outdoor recreation and conservation resources and needs of the American people to the year 2000. For the first time in the nation's history, the President and Congress commissioned a program of basic research on the facts and figures of the American out-doors, its forests, parks, rivers and streams, and then asked the Commission (ORRRC) to make recommendations on how best to conserve and to use those resources.

It took a year to organize and staff the project and another three years to carry out what became the most comprehensive fact-finding survey ever made in the interrelated fields of natural resources, the environment, the outdoor recreation possibilities involved and conservation in general. Twenty-seven volumes of study reports were issued, covering virtually every river, lake, forest, park and shoreline in America. The major findings and more than fifty recommendations were presented in ORRRC's final report, called *Outdoor Recreation for America*. Specific programs were designed for increasing and improving the recreation use of both public and private land and water resources. The final report proposed a new national recreation policy, a new classification system for all outdoor recreation resources, a new Federal Bureau of Outdoor Recreation and a new program of federal grants-in-aid for state-sponsored projects.

The acceptance of these ORRRC recommendations was extraordinary. Within months, the Kennedy administration established a Cabinet-level Federal Recreation Council to advise the President and a Bureau of Outdoor Recreation in the Department of the Interior to administer many of the specific programs recommended. Even more significant, however, the ORRRC report sparked a new enthusiasm and awareness for conservation and outdoor recreation through the United States. State and local governments initiated programs based upon the commission's recommendations and private conservation groups clamored for more.

In fact, Laurance and the key people on the commission, aware of how other commission reports were so often filed and forgotten in Washington, formed a citizens committee to work with local citizen groups toward achieving the goals set forth in the ORRRC report. Laurance traveled across the country making speeches. He addressed conventions of state garden clubs, landscape gardeners, civic groups and businessmen's associations. He explained why open space and conservation should be an integral part of all urban planning, how a local community could set up a basic park system, how to defend existing parks and open space from encroachment from private developers or superhighways, how to change zoning laws to foster more green space in cities, how to set up a nature center in a town or city, how to educate and inform people of all ages on the multiple benefits of enjoying the outdoors. He helped spread the word.

People came to see a Rockefeller in the flesh and many stayed to be enlisted in the cause. Ever a shy man and loath to make public speeches, he could not deny the obvious impact of his own activities upon others, nor could he deny the satisfaction he derived from involving himself in the excitement of a cause on the move. The isolation of being a Rockefeller gave way to the pleasurable sense of being part of the community of conservationists. With a keen awareness of the inability of anyone to lead where no one would follow, Laurance involved himself with one group after another in the effort to help convince the nation of the significance of the environment.

The cause was advanced to national prominence with the advent of the Johnson administration. President Johnson and his wife, Lady Bird, who made their home on a vast ranch in Texas, loved and understood the land. For the focal interest of the First Lady, the President's wife chose the beautification of Washington, D.C. Her predecessor, Jacqueline Kennedy, had redecorated the inside of the White House; Lady Bird, who loved gardening and nature, decided to decorate the outside. As the scope of her activities grew, it led to the widely heralded first White House Conference on Natural Beauty in 1965, in which one thousand people from all sections of the nation met to draw up a new list of priorities on conservation and natural beauty of the environment. Laurance Rockefeller was chairman.

In summing up the purpose of the conference, Laurance explained to the National Press Club: "What we are really talking about is quality of environment—the health of the land and water and air on which man depends for life, as do all living things . . . We believe that natural beauty—or whatever term one chooses to use for it—is an idea whose time has arrived . . . We believe the people of the United States want a better environment and that they are ready to work for it."

The conference proposed a long list of what should be done to enhance beauty in the cities, in the countryside and upon the highway system. Task forces were set up to get rid of highway billboard signs, to persuade utility companies to put their wires underground instead of overhead, to make better use of open spaces, to build parks and swimming pools in inner cities, to fight the ugliness of city slums. The recommendations were drawn largely upon the findings of the ORRRC report, but the difference now was that the President of the United States and the First Lady were leading the cause. Thus, conservation was lifted to one of the top priorities of governmental action. At the conference and afterward, Laurance envisioned the time when natural beauty would come to be regarded as an integral part of the nation's life, no longer a frill or a luxury.

The White House Conference was followed with the creation of the Citizens' Advisory Committee on Recreation and Natural Beauty. President Johnson again chose Laurance Rockefeller to be chairman. Laurance worked closely with Lady Bird Johnson, for they hit it off beautifully from the start, found their thinking remarkably alike on many subjects, met often and with pleasure, exchanged visits to one another's ranches and became friends. The impact of their activities significantly affected public opinion and citizen action on environment across the land. The environment became a national concern.

By the time Richard Nixon became President in 1968, the band wagon was rolling, the euphemism "natural beauty" was elevated to "environmental quality" and everyone knew and understood what was meant. Laurance Rockefeller was named chairman for the new Citizens' Advisory Committee on Environmental Quality, and the emphasis was now focused on the protection and improvement of *all* aspects of the environment from air and water and open space to the appearance of industrial plants and the noise level permitted in neighborhoods. The federal government established an Environmental Protection Agency and business was put on notice that the government intended to investigate the environmetal impact of all its activities. The conservationists and environmentalists in America gained new clout. New airports, highways, factories, housing developments and nuclear plants now needed to satisfy environmental quality standards before construction could go ahead. The environmentalists, with vast public support, were instrumental in persuading Congress to stop Boeing from building a supersonic airliner because of its potential negative impact upon the environment. For the first time in its history the most industrialized nation of the world decided not to go ahead with a technological advance within its capabilities because of its side effects. That kind of "progress" was not worth its adverse impact on people, according to public opinion.

The future of the SST, nuclear energy and industrial pollution had not been decided or solved for all time. Where and how to strike a balance between needed technological improvements and their adverse infringement upon the environment will ever remain a dilemma, in Laurance Rockefeller's view. The nation will continue to need automobiles and highways, airplanes and airports, factories and industrial power, but it will also need clean air, unpolluted water, tillable land and open space in which people can live and breathe and see the stars. Thus, conservation and the protection of the environment will ever be an ongoing, complex struggle against the natural erosion of time, the mistakes of well-intentioned reformers and the needs and demands of a technological society.

But at long last, Laurance felt, the problem was at least recognized for what it was. The American public was aroused. Ecology had become a household word, a political issue and a national movement. More than fifty groups dedicated to improving the environment had been organized in the first six years since the National Environmental Act was passed in 1970. The production of pollution-control equipment has become a multi-million-dollar industry. In 1975 alone, some $15 billion was spent on such anti-pollution equipment—$5 billion by federal, state and local governments and $10 billion by industry. Fish life was thriving once again in Lake Erie, Atlantic salmon had returned to the Connecticut River after an absence of one hundred years. Shrimp and oysters were returning to Escambia Bay in northwest Florida, a clear indication that the natural ecology of the bay was being restored. Despite some tactical, temporary setbacks and some disputes over the pace of improving the environment, the accomplishments in recent years of the ecology movement have been significant beyond doubt. In fact, the rapid rise and gusto of the movement throughout the United States had left Laurance Rockefeller, one of its pioneers, "in absolute awe." The EPA, the citizen groups and even the general electorate have gone far beyond what Laurance had dared to expect when he began his quest.

Having devoted so much of his life to conservation, having organized some of the most prestigious conservation groups in the nation and having served as an intimate and influential adviser on conservation to five American Presidents, Laurance Rockefeller, as he rounded the retirement marker of age sixty-five, was rewarded above all accolades with a rare sense of personal fulfillment and a certain philosophical inner peace of mind which could well be the envy of any of his brothers or his peers. He was, to those who recognized his accomplishments, "Mr. Conservation" in America.

19

Nelson

"I am not standby equipment."

For his first foray into the raw and risky business of politics, Nelson Rockefeller chose to start as near to the top as possible. He decided on the governorship of New York, the most prestigious state office in the nation, a traditional steppingstone to the presidency.

Those with whom he consulted advised him against the move. The reasons were manifold. It was a wild and doomed venture. He had never campaigned for elective office before. He had served no apprenticeship in politics or in state office. The name Rockefeller, to put it discreetly, was untested with the public in the voting booth. Besides, he stood little chance of winning the Republican nomination. Two veteran state leaders —Walter J. Mahoney, majority leader of the senate, and Oswald Heck, speaker of the assembly—were vying for the nomination, and they were being challenged by Len Hall, the former Republican National Chairman. Moreover, the Democratic incumbent, W. Averell Harriman, a well-respected senior statesman who had presidential ambitions of his own, was expected to win a second term. No incumbent governor of New York ever had been defeated for a second term.

Thomas E. Dewey, three-time governor and two-time presidential nominee, the most experienced and politically powerful Republican in the state, personally advised Nelson against it. "Nobody knows your name in New York," Dewey explained in somber tones of fatherly advice at a private luncheon. "I might be able to get you appointed postmaster here, then you could try for Congress and then later, maybe then, you could run for governor." Nelson bridled at the idea that the Rockefeller name was unknown in New York. But he thanked Tom Dewey politely for his advice. He held his own counsel. Nelson understood the arguments and the risks involved. Yet the decision itself evolved over a two-year period. To Nelson, intuitively, it just seemed the "right thing to do."

Strangely enough, the man who did as much as anyone else to launch the political career of Nelson Rockefeller was the man he would defeat as governor of New York. Averell Harriman, astute in international negotiations, possessed little understanding of politics. First, in 1956, he agreed to appoint Nelson Rockefeller as the non-partisan chairman of a commission to study the need for rewriting New York's ancient and outmoded state constitution. Nelson was acceptable to Harriman and Republican legislative leaders because he was regarded as no political threat to anyone in either party. After leaving Washington he had sponsored the highly successful, publicized and erudite Rockefeller Panel Reports. These were seminar reports of expert opinion on the problems facing mid-century America in foreign policy, military preparedness, education and economic and social affairs. Financed by the Rockefellers, the project had been directed by that Harvard history professor who had so impressed Nelson at the Quantico seminars, Henry Kissinger. Nelson in turn persuaded him to take a six-month leave of absence to coordinate the work of all the specialists—and the work kept him in the Rockefeller employ for a good three years. Then his ties had become so close to Nelson, Kissinger agreed to accept a retainer to advise Nelson on foreign policy through the years on a part-time basis. Little did Henry Kissinger realize at the time that their association would continue for twenty years and more.

Nelson Rockefeller had a talent for attracting and keeping capable and knowledgeable men on his staff or within his ken. As chairman of the Temporary State Commission on a Constitutional Convention, Nelson traveled throughout the state, holding public hearings and learning firsthand the details of state problems and politics, and gathering new aides who were outstandingly capable in New York government, men who would serve him for many years to come. Two newcomers to the Rockefeller entourage were William J. Ronan, professor of government and Dean of Administration at New York University, hired as director of the commission, and George L. Hinman, an upstate attorney and local political figure, hired as counsel. They joined the Rockefeller old-timers, such as Roswell (Rod) Perkins, who had worked with Nelson on Social Security improvements at HEW, and of course, Nelson's personal advisers, Wally Harrison and Frank Jamieson, forming the nucleus of his key staff before he even decided to run for governor of New York. It was contingency planning. Then Averell Harriman provided another service for Nelson: he announced Nelson's availability in politics.

In a whimsical quip at the Albany Legislative Correspondents Association fun fest annual dinner in March 1957, Harriman declared: "I want to make a prediction. The man who will run against me in 1958 is right here in this room." After a pause for effect, Harriman peered into the crowd and cried, "Nelson, where are you, Nelson?" Whether Harriman was serious, fooling or making a Freudian slip, no one could tell. But the observers of the political scene agreed he had made one major political mistake. It was the first public announcement by anyone that Nelson Rockefeller might run for office.

Fifteen months later, on the last day of June 1958, just four months before election day, Nelson announced his candidacy in the small, elegant library adjacent to his office at 5600. The William Couper bronze bust of Nelson's grandfather stood in the background. Old John D. would have been pleased with the two years of diligent study and skillful maneuvering of his grandson Nelson. The key campaign staff was poised for action and the basic campaign strategy had been set, the party leaders had been sounded out and the private polls showed that Rockefeller was ahead of other Republican aspirants, although far behind incumbent Harriman. Afterward, Nelson would say that that latter poll helped him win the nomination. The political thinking at the time was that if the Republicans were going to lose, their candidate might as well be a man rich enough to pay campaign costs himself.

Within an hour of announcing his candidacy, he took off on an upstate tour to convince the conservative Republicans of the party that he, Nelson Rockefeller, was a budget-minded, knowledgeable Republican despite all suspicions to the contrary during his service under Franklin Roosevelt and the New Deal. The key element in his campaign for the nomination was the support of Malcolm Wilson, a hard-working, conservative assemblyman from Yonkers (in Westchester County, where Nelson made his home). Wilson had twenty years' political experience and know-how in the state. They traveled together in Wilson's old Buick, with Nelson's son Steven driving, covering a thousand miles a week, meeting and persuading Republicans who never before thought they would vote for this New Deal Republican with liberal leanings. Nelson Rockefeller displayed a charisma, charm and zest which could not be denied. When the August Republican convention was held, his nomination came on the first ballot.

"My fellow Republicans, you have placed your trust in me and I stand before you with a deep sense of humility," he declared. "I thank you from the bottom of my heart. You have offered me the greatest challenge of my life and the highest opportunity to serve the people of our Empire State. I proudly accept your nomination."

What is there in one political candidate and not in another which can spark and electrify a crowd of people? No one truly knows. But Nelson Rockefeller had the quality that night. As he pronounced the simple political clichés of a nomination acceptance speech, ten thousand Republican delegates came alive, applauded, cheered and stamped their feet in delight. The old political professionals shook their heads in amazement and reconsidered the prospects in the campaign ahead. They discovered, in the vernacular, that they had a "live candidate."

Malcolm Wilson was nominated for lieutenant governor at Nelson's insistence, even though both men were from the same county. Louis Lefkowitz of New York was chosen for attorney general, and after considerable arm-twisting, Kenneth Keating, an upstate congressman, was persuaded to give up a safe seat in Congress to run for the U. S. Senate and to help balance the Rockefeller ticket geographically, even though he was expected to lose.

But once again, Lady Luck smiled benignly at Nelson Rockefeller: at the Democratic State Convention, Governor Harriman became embroiled in a public fight with Carmine de Sapio, the political boss of New York City, over the choice of the Democratic candidate for U.S. senator. It was a stand-off situation until De Sapio demonstrated he had more power and more votes than the governor. Harriman conceded, suffering public humiliation. Frank Jamieson seized the situation as the first campaign issue. From then on it seemed that Harriman was never able to get off the defensive. Nelson, his old friend, ran with it and attacked and attacked and attacked throughout the sixty-two counties of New York State. The issue was not just "bossism" and Tammany Hall, but that Averell Harriman was a weak governor, unable to stand up to the bosses as old Al Smith had done in years gone by, when he had locked himself in a room for three days, swearing he would not run with a boss-picked candidate on his ticket.

However, that was a mere tactic. The over-all strategy of the Rockefeller campaign was carefully planned. Its prototype was the brilliant, successful campaign of an unknown Democrat in a Republican state—that of Edmund Muskie of Maine. Nelson had been impressed. The theme, hammered at again and again, was that New York was falling behind other states in economic and social progress. Rockefeller promised to create a climate for expansion of jobs, industry, business and agriculture, and he pledged to meet the state's increased needs in educational, health and welfare benefits. He appealed to upstate Republicans as a Rockefeller who was fiscally responsible and to the Democratic stronghold of New York City as a Republican who had served under President Roosevelt. Behind the scenes, labor leaders, particularly those in the powerful building trades unions, pledged neutrality and in some cases, support. They had not forgotten the Rockefeller family record in building Rockefeller Center, which provided jobs at union wages to more than 75,000 during the depression. Nor did they forget that the Rockefellers had initiated the first pension plan in the building trades at the time. The candidate himself was the single most important element in the campaign. He loved campaigning. In each of the state's sixty-two counties, he spoke in factories, on street corners, at rallies and at meetings big and small. Although not an accomplished or polished orator, his ardor and sincerity came across. As one upstate politician described the phenomenon at the time: "They come out to see whether he's for real, and then, bang, he's got 'em. I don't know what's doing it, that grin or the winks he throws around or just that he looks so goddamn regular, they believe in him. I guess he surprises them. Whatever it is, it's dynamite."

It was simply that Nelson Rockfeller enjoyed people and making contact with them. From the days of his first visits to South America, Nelson Rockefeller's natural manner was to touch people, to grasp an arm, to hold a shoulder, to look a person straight in the eye. He possessed an innate curiosity. He ate knishes in the Jewish Lower East Side, pizzas in Little Italy in lower Manhattan, hot dogs in Coney Island. He had a cast-iron stomach. He campaigned twelve and more hours a day, and got up ready to go the next day. He was indefatigable.

Averell Harriman, despite all his good intentions, was patrician in speech and demeanor. He was out of place on a street corner—when he tried to kiss a baby, the baby cried. He stumbled through lengthy, prepared speeches and lost his crowd. When he spoke of the common man, he did not have the touch of the common man. His own wealth and privileged background prevented the Democrats from trying to make political capital of Nelson Rockefeller's ancestry. No one asked Nelson Rockefeller if he had to work for a living or ride in a jam-packed New York City subway. The answer would have been no, and yet he sounded and seemed like a man you could know and trust and understand. By the time November 5 rolled around, Nelson Rockefeller looked and acted like a winner. The New York *Post*, the most liberal and ardent supporter of Harriman, switched to Rockefeller at the last minute.

Even the weather was right on election day, clear and bright. After voting in Pocantico Hills, the Rockefellers traveled down to Republican campaign headquarters in the Roosevelt Hotel in New York City. The ballroom was jammed in anticipation, the band blared, the packed-in people shouted and cheered and the vote tabulations showed a landslide for Rockefeller. When Harriman's telegram of concession reached him at ten forty-five that night, Nelson thanked Republican leaders in his hotel room, walked next door to shake hands privately with Frank Jamieson, who had helped him to win, and then led his wife and five children through the wild ballroom, proceeding single file, hand upon one another's shoulder, to the podium. There he summoned up his inexhaustible ebullience to promise: "We'll give it everything we've got." In his Park Avenue apartment, John D. Rockefeller, Jr., at eighty-four too frail to attend the celebration, danced a private jig of his own. A Rockefeller had been elected to office by the people! Ah, if Nelson's grandfather had only lived to see the day . . .

The very next day, Nelson Aldrich Rockefeller was a viable prospect for President of the United States. When the election results came in from all over the country, Nelson's victory would be described as "a Republican oasis in a desert of defeat." The Democrats had swept the congressional and senatorial contest across the country and had won almost every contested gubernatorial race as well. The exceptions were Mark O. Hatfield in far-off Oregon and Nelson Rockefeller in New York. The Rockefeller plurality of 573,034 certified the man with the well-known name as a genuine vote-getter. He also had long political coattails, pulling into office with him seven legislators with margins of a few hundred votes or less. With the country in an economic recession, the Eisenhower administration at its nadir of popularity, the Republican heir apparent, Richard Nixon, intensely disliked in the East, political writers in New York and Washington, the communications centers of the country, began to focus the nation's attention on this new, home-grown product of the eastern Establishment, this exemplar of new leadership in the Republican Party. The very first question put to him by the press after his election was: are you a candidate for President in 1960? Despite his expected disclaimers, the media heralded him, Nelson Aldrich Rockefeller, across the nation as very possibly the next President of the United States. His background, his personality, his political clout, his wealth and what he could bring to the presidency were recounted again and again.

Personally, it was very heady wine, indeed. And it did go to his head. Against the advice of the astute Frank Jamieson and others who presumably knew better than he did, Nelson had put his reputation and career on the line, exposed himself to public scrutiny, and he had won. The office of governor gave him the challenge of his lifetime, the opportunity to demonstrate what he could do as the *chief executive* of the greatest, most complex state in the Union. At fifty years of age, with one quick stroke, he was one step from the presidency of the United States. The question now was when and how to take that one step.

If anyone told Nelson Rockefeller at this time and in the months ahead to go slowly, to proceed with caution, to watch out, then that person's advice was relegated to a back niche of past cautions given by his father, his friends and his brothers which he, Nelson, had so seldom heeded. He believed in his own intuitions. So, while he began to set up his own state administration, he also organized a small, special group to *explore* the possibilities of his winning the Republican nomination for President. The heir apparent was obviously Richard Milhous Nixon, the Vice-President, but Nelson believed simply that he was the better man for the job.

Having observed Nixon closely within the Eisenhower administration, Nelson considered Nixon lacking in the breadth and depth of political philosophy needed by a President. Nixon's vituperation in the 1958 campaign, his virulent anti-Communist aura, his association with the extreme element of reactionaries within the party, his lack of administrative ability disturbed Nelson Rockefeller. In short, he personally did not like the man. It was all part of a pattern of his life, that abiding faith and confidence in himself. Genuinely, he harbored no doubt that he would make an excellent governor of New York, that through the years he had learned how to be a good administrator, knew how to get things done in government. He recognized and welcomed the challenge of being governor. In fact, he could hardly wait to get started. He looked forward to the grandest opportunity of all, the possibility of becoming President of the United States. Of course, he could not be sure that he would succeed, but neither did he have reason to believe he would fail. He had never failed before and all the vibrations seemed so right. Nelson was a happy man. Besides, during his gubernatorial campaign, he had begun to believe that he was falling in love once again.

His marriage to Mary Todhunter Clark had deteriorated long ago. She had campaigned at his side, the dutiful wife, because it was politically necessary, but she hated having to respond to silly or impertinent questions of reporters and smiling for photographers and at the wives of politicians. She was a quiet, regal woman who placed high value on her privacy and her way of life; still true to the old canons of the wealthy, she differed fundamentally from her extroverted husband. Their marriage gradually came asunder sometime after the birth of their last children, the twins Mary and Michael, in May 1938. Nelson's wartime years in Washington, when families throughout the nation were torn apart, made their own separation all the easier. For the sake of their five children, they agreed to remain together as father and mother, if not as man and wife, and they lived their separate lives with respect if not love toward one another. It was a way of life not unfamiliar in their circles and was no secret to their own intimate friends. In fact, when Winthrop's shaky first marriage hit the rocks, Nelson tried to persuade his brother to maintain the marriage as he himself was doing, but Winthrop would have none of it. For Nelson, as the years went on, the arrangement became more difficult.

In the Governor's Mansion in Albany, they set up separate bedroom suites, but at public functions—the inaugural ball and the reception at the Mansion—they stood side by side, smiling, clasping hands with their guests, saying what had to be said in public. With his left hand upon his grandmother's personal Bible, Nelson was officially sworn into office at 10:30 P.M. on New Year's Eve at the Executive Mansion in a private ceremony to comply with the law which ended his predecessor's term in office at midnight. At 1:45 P.M. the next day, he took the oath publicly at the state capitol and launched into an inauguration address which dealt as much with national and international affairs as it did with the state of New York. And that was duly noted as an indication of his future intentions. That afternoon, in his shirtsleeves, Nelson hung a sampling of his collection of modern art—Mirós, Picassos, Légers and others—in the downstairs rooms of the Governor's Mansion so that his first dinner guests that evening would see the outmoded Victorian Mansion—which had served as home to New York governors going back to Samuel J. Tilden in 1874—now looked like the home of Nelson A. Rockefeller. The inaugural ball that night was said to be the grandest and fanciest in the state's history. Nelson hired the entire company of the New York City Ballet for a performance at the State Armory. It was a broad hint, for those prescient enough to see, that this governor intended to bring an appreciation of the arts, all the arts, to the Empire State.

One large compartment in the labyrinth of this man's life had been art, the appreciation of and the collection of paintings and sculpture. Inherited from and nurtured by his mother, an avid collector, his affinity to art had begun in college and remained with him throughout his life. He became a voracious collector of all that struck his eye, from the primitive sculptures he first found on his round-the-world honeymoon with Tod in 1931 to the latest modern painting of an unknown artist he might have met yesterday. All of his homes—at Pocantico Hills, in Seal Harbor (Maine), at his ranch in the Venezuelan Andes, in his apartment on Fifth Avenue in New York—were filled with the superb art work of the masters, the near masters and the not so masterful.

The collection today is considered to be one of the finest and, of course, one of the largest held by any one individual in the United States. It is an ever changing collection which Nelson Rockefeller lives with day to day. In 1974, when it was appraised at $33,561,325, it contained 3,600 pieces, 2,300 of them modern or contemporary and 1,300 of past periods dating back to pre-Columbian and ancient Oriental periods. Nelson himself did not set out to collect what he collected. There had been no plan. As his mother and his father did, Nelson bought what he liked. His mother gave him his first significant modern painting, Henri Matisse's *Odalisque*, a voluptuous semi-nude in striped tight pants, when he became a trustee of the Museum of Modern Art, soon after he graduated from college. Several years afterward, in 1937, he commissioned Matisse to paint a mural over his fireplace in his New York apartment, a lovely sensuous painting of four women which flows from ceiling to floor in reds, blacks, blues, and lavender against a mahogany paneled wall. Canvases by Picasso, Braque and Léger are scattered through the apartment. The dining room is a work of art itself, the ceiling and four walls covered with a geometric modern abstract mural in bright primary colors by the Swiss artist Fritz Glarner. Throughout the apartment as in his different homes and various offices, Nelson kept small sculptures, either modern or primitive, on tables, shelves, bureaus and desks, which he constantly rearranged to gain new perspectives. When he took over the main house in the Pocantico Hills estate, after the death of his father, he built an underground gallery to handle the canvases which overflowed the walls and he placed some sixty-eight large sculptures on the grounds, around the house, the swimming pools, the rose garden, the tennis courts and at the edge of the golf course. And he constantly rearranged them, though some weighed a ton and more, just so he, his family and his friends could see the same works of art from different perspectives.

Most of his modern and contemporary American art was bought soon after it was painted, particularly the abstract impressionistic work done in New York in the 1940s and 1950s, works by De Kooning, Gorky, Jackson Pollock and others. He also began acquiring sculpture done by artists whose names later would become famous: Lehmbruck, Lachaise, Nadelman, and long before most other collectors did, Nelson Rockefeller placed those sculptures out-of-doors, where they belonged. In 1969, and afterward, he became more and more interested in Chinese porcelains and Oriental art, which had occupied so much of his father's life. He became so fascinated with the style that he and his second wife decided to build a Japanese house near the main house at Pocantico, a comfortable seven-bedroom home around a central garden, where the art of the ancient Orient fits in so well.

In the beginning, Nelson made the rounds of the art galleries and the studios of the artists. But after becoming governor of New York, when his free time was severely limited, he hired a personal curator, Mrs. Carol Uht, and made most of his purchases by first examining gallery catalogues and then sending Mrs. Uht or another representative to make his purchases. Nelson always bought what he liked and often called in expert opinion afterward. But he had developed a fine eye for art and especially for space and perspective in art. His tastes were eclectic. Like most collectors, he regretted only those pieces that got away, the ones he wanted and failed to buy. Not long after he became interested in Chinese porcelains, he sent a representative to buy a T'ang Dynasty (A.D. 618–907) porcelain horse, twenty inches tall, which was up at auction at Christie's in London. Nelson's man bid up to $150,000 for the piece and then stopped. Nelson was furious at having lost. He was even more so when he learned that the T'ang horse turned up on a shelf outside his brother John 3rd's office in Rockefeller Center: the two brothers had been bidding against one another and not knowing it, driving the price up to almost twice its market value. But not many such pieces get away from Nelson Rockefeller. He is as fierce a collector as he is generous in lending out parts of his collection and in giving away pieces which are admired by friends and visitors.

Like most addicted collectors, Nelson is acquisitive in buying more and more works of art. However, he collects not so much to build up a collection of any given period but rather for the sheer joy and pleasure of living with a unique work of art which moves him. Art is Nelson Rockefeller's primary hobby. It serves him well: it revitalizes him deeply. And he would agree wholeheartedly with the art critic Monroe Wheeler, who wrote of the role of art: "It is the greatest recreation ever devised by the ingenious mind of man. It gives relief from the pressures, frustrations and compromises of everyday life."

Nelson learned to collect art by collecting it. On the job too, as governor of the most complex, cosmopolitan state in the Union, Nelson learned by doing. Starting out as a novice to state government, he brought to the job his experience of applying businesslike, well-organized methods to problem solving.

One of his first moves was to convene a meeting of his high command, the men with the expertise, and set them to work analyzing the problems facing the state of New York. They ranged from finance and budget to education, health and welfare, to juvenile delinquency, narcotics, crime, the court system, transportation, highways and housing. Next, the problems were defined in detail, solutions recommended and priorities established. Talented men were recruited and lured into thirty-one specific study groups or commissions during the first months of his administration. He firmly believed, as he often repeated to those close to him, "There's nothing in God's world that cannot be solved—if you define the problem correctly and mobilize the talent required to do the job."

He was, of course, in the eyes of the cynic, the optimum optimist. His saving grace, however, was his practicability and pragmatism in attacking any given problem. His mind thrived on facts and figures, not theories. His basic political assumption was simple: the voters wanted good government, one which was responsive and responsible in meeting the people's needs. To that end, it was necessary to make New York State an attractive place in which business could invest and grow, creating new job opportunities, all of which, in turn, would support the improvement of the general welfare of the people. As he delved more and more deeply into the functioning of the state government and its relationship to the need of the people, he ultimately put his finger on the source of the trouble. The traditional role of the state had been limited largely to housekeeping: building roads, operating the prisons and mental hospitals, collecting taxes and distributing funds to localities for their operations. What he wanted to do and ultimately succeeded in doing, was to put the state directly into the business of seeking solutions to social problems, especially those problems which were overwhelming local governments. On a personal level, he felt that he as Nelson Rockefeller was in a unique position to accomplish this. He was at the start of a new administration; he had financed most of his campaign himself, he was beholden to no man or group or pressure, and his own wealth made him independent of the need of the job. In short, if he, Nelson Rockefeller, could not do the job that needed to be done, then no one could.

With that in mind and surrounded with experts in state matters recruited far and wide, he forged a series of programs to revitalize the state's economy, to expand educational facilities, to broaden civil rights procedures, to aid mass transit and commuter travel in and about New York City, to increase agricultural research, to increase middle-income housing, to attack juvenile delinquency, to improve various social insurance and pension programs and on and on. The bill to pay for these new programs came as something of a shock—the state's first $2 billion budget, some $240 million more than that of his predecessor. Even worse, politically, the state's constitution mandated a balanced budget: if he wanted all his programs, Nelson Rockefeller would have to ask for an increase in state taxes of a whopping $277 million, the largest in the state's history!

He was counseled strongly against taking such a course, especially by his more politically minded advisers. Most of those taxes would hit the voters in the pocketbook with a 35 per cent increase in personal income taxes, and at a time of economic recession. The more prudent route, he was advised, was to introduce the new programs and the new taxes piecemeal and less visibly. Nelson thought that would not be honest. He wanted to present the whole package intact to the legislature. Having accused the Democrats during the campaign of fiscal irresponsibility, he now wanted to put the state on a "pay as you go" basis of operations. Idealistically, he intended to set a pattern for the future years of his administration. He was practical enough to know he would have a tremendous fight on his hands. But then he enjoyed a good fight. So he did what he wanted to do.

The state legislature was taken by surprise, both by the scope of the new programs and the new taxes, and just as much by the man himself. Whether or not the veteran lawmakers expected the stereotyped dilettantism of a rich man's son or the fumbling beginning of a new governor, they discovered within the first month that Nelson Rockefeller was a "take-charge guy" who could persuade, wheel and deal, threaten, twist arms, offer the carrot or the stick and do whatever was necessary to get what he wanted. Not yet understanding that the art of politics is compromise, he was blunt, fearless and forthright, a fighter who seemed to relish wielding the considerable powers of the Empire State's chief executive.

His manner of working was unlike that of his predecessors. Governors Harriman and Dewey before him reigned from the governor's domain on the second floor of the capitol. They sent for the men they wanted to see. Nelson saw no reason to confine himself. He wandered through the halls, he bounded up and down the grand staircase separating the executive and legislative branches of the state government; he dropped into the offices of various lawmakers for chats or serious talks; when interested in particular debates, he took a seat in the back of legislative chambers. All the while, he talked up his state programs like a supersalesman of vacuum cleaners. He set a pattern and pace in those early days which had not been seen before, but which would continue for all his years in Albany. The day started with an 8 A.M. breakfast at the Governor's Mansion. Legislative leaders, party leaders, top staff or anyone needed for a particular purpose were invited to breakfast. Charts, memos, fact sheets were served with coffee and scrambled eggs. Lunch was almost always a business meeting in the governor's office at the capitol. Sandwiches and coffee were sent over from the Mansion. Dinner, too, served as an excellent opportunity for special pleadings and persuasion. The inherited Rockefeller stamina served Nelson well. He seemed indefatigable. He could and did work without surcease until ten or eleven at night and then, after milk and cookies, he slept easily and untroubled, waking early for a new day's activities. He thrived on it. He enjoyed working. He was goal-oriented. If he wanted a bill passed or a new program approved, he worked full out for that particular goal. Even those who voted against him on political or philosophical or economic grounds did not doubt his sincerity.

His nature was to be smiling, gracious and personally warm. But he could be equally stubborn and ruthless when necessary. Either way, he was a tough man to refuse. As time went on, he established good personal relations with most of the state legislators. Even in the years the legislature was controlled by a Democratic majority, Governor Rockefeller could achieve his usual better-than-90-per-cent record in administration bills passed by the legislature. Usually he worked intimately with the leaders of both houses of the legislature, but when necessary he met one on one with recalcitrant lawmakers to work his wonders of persuasion.

Of all the many political and legislative battles, none was so bitter, so hard fought as Nelson Rockefeller's first battle over the state budget and his unprecedented $277 million tax increase. He had gone headlong and full out, as usual, for what he wanted, staking his own reputation and prestige as well as his concept of state government upon getting the full tax increase he requested along with a state withholding income tax. Two months were put into that battle. It bore lasting scars. But Nelson Rockefeller won, by a mere two votes in the state assembly, and then he was hailed within and beyond the state borders for his political leadership, his fiscal courage, his resiliency, his toughness, his boldness . . . Washington reporters and columnists rushed into Albany to inform the nation of this Republican alternative to Richard Nixon in 1960. Nelson himself was jubilant in public. Privately, he was more serious. "Now we can go ahead with our state program," he told an aide that night. Publicly, he disclaimed any intention of running for President. "I have my hands full as governor," he told the press. Privately, he followed the political speculations with a keen eye on the White House.

There was nothing underhand or sneaky about his calculations. He hoped to prove his ability as a governor well enough to win election to the highest office of the land. Malcolm Wilson's support in the 1958 campaign had been based upon that tacit understanding: when Nelson stepped up or down from the governorship, he would return Malcolm's support for that office. Neither man envisioned for a moment that Nelson Rockefeller would remain in that office for fifteen years, longer than any man before him in modern times, elected and re-elected for four terms, changing from a political maverick to the senior governor in the United States. Even the wisest men have trouble forecasting the future.

A full accounting of the manipulations, accomplishments and failures of those fifteen years is beyond the scope of this book, except where they reveal the man himself in action. Neal R. Peirce in his erudite book *The Megastates of America* summed it up as well as any man when he wrote: "Nelson Rockefeller took the instrument [of state government], experimented with it and reshaped it, added on appendages (some of dubious constitutionality) to make money available to accomplish what he willed, and in the process built the most complex, fascinating, and socially advanced state government in U.S. history."

His greatest long-range accomplishment as governor, in the estimation of virtually all impartial observers, was the building of a state university system of the highest academic standing, accommodating more than 260,000 students, within the short span of ten years. He did it by what he liked to call "creative capitalism," based upon the prototype he used as coordinator in funding special projects in Latin America. In his first year as governor, he was astonished to discover that the Empire State, the richest in the nation, was the only state without a bona fide state university. The state ran just eleven institutions of higher learning: teachers' colleges, plus agriculture and technical two-year colleges, with a combined student body of 38,000. In his first budget, he asked for $20 million to build gymnasiums at these bleak schools, thinking the measure uncontroversial. But the legislature rejected ten of them. The only exception was the gymnasium designated for the school in the district of the chairman of the senate finance committee. The message was painfully obvious.

Nevertheless, he appointed a blue ribbon commission of educators to report on the future higher educational needs of the state. At the same time, he went to work on figuring out a way to build a state university without having to play politics every time he wanted to build a new college or university. He knew what he wanted and with the help of a noted Wall Street lawyer named John Mitchell, an expert in municipal bond issues, he devised a State University Construction Fund. This was a separate corporation authorized by the legislature to float its own construction bonds, secured by a $400 tuition fee charged each student. John Mitchell later became a law partner of Richard M. Nixon, the U. S. Attorney General in the Nixon administration and finally one of the key figures convicted in the notorious Watergate scandals following the 1972 election campaign. But in early 1960, John Mitchell was responsible for the innovative concept of "moral obligation" bonds, backed by revenues accruing from the project being built and the "moral" rather than legal obligation of the state to pay the bondholders in the event the project failed to produce the necessary revenue.

The concept was a smashing success. In less than twelve years, New York State built four university centers, twelve four-year colleges of arts and sciences and thirty-eight community colleges. Without the quasi-independent University Construction Fund issuing the construction bonds, the state would have been constitutionally restricted to asking the public to approve by referendum only one school construction project per year. Politically, it would have been impossible to gain statewide approval for colleges or universities benefiting only certain sections of the state. Once the construction was underway, the governor was in a better position to wheel and deal for legislative approval for operating funds for each new school. State appropriations for higher education rose more than six times over, from $95 million in 1959-60 to $591 million in 1970-71. Paying top-scale faculty salaries helped lure high-caliber professors to New York from all over the country, particularly from the riot-torn California campuses during the 1960s.

The single most controversial project of the Rockefeller administration was the construction of the Albany Mall, a Rockefeller Center of state office buildings: a forty-four-story office tower, four identical twenty-three-story agency buildings, a legislative office building, a judiciary building, a central headquarters for the Motor Vehicles Department and a cultural center containing a library and a state museum. The concept of the Mall originated from a multitude of needs. First of all, the state government was severely short of office space. The Motor Vehicles Department, for instance, had spread out into sixteen different buildings. The state was uneconomically renting office space wherever it could find it. Second, the city of Albany itself was appallingly dingy. The center of the city, directly in front of the capitol, had become one of the worst slums in the entire state with its run-down tenements, sleazy saloons and the city's red-light district. It cried out for urban redevelopment. The capital of the richest state in the Union was a disgrace and an embarrassment. The embarrassment became personal to Nelson Rockefeller and sparked the concept of the Mall, when the new governor and the mayor of Albany, Erastus Corning II, sat down to plan the motorcade route to carry Princess Beatrix of the Netherlands from the airport to the Governor's Mansion and discovered that there was no route through Albany by which Beatrix would not see the slums the Americans had made of the city her Dutch forebears had settled two hundred years ago. The fundamental problem in eradicating slums, true everywhere, is the lack of money. The mayor came up with the idea: if the state itself would not float the bonds necessary, why could not the county of Albany issue construction bonds, finance the urban redevelopment and then lease office space to the state on a forty-year lease-buy arrangement so that after forty years the state would own the buildings. Nelson went for the idea, according to the mayor, "like a trout for a fly."

The Mall became Nelson Rockefeller's personal pet project. The over-all architectural design was conceived by Nelson's old friend from Rockefeller Center days, Wallace Harrison. Nelson gave a disproportionate amount of his time, considering all the other concerns of a governor, to the design of the Mall. He went over every line in every architectural drawing and blueprint. He was consulted on building materials, the color of the marble of the buildings, the location of each building and every tree on the ninety-six-acre site. His own personal concept, as that of his father, was that for an extra 5 per cent of the cost, one could build something excellent and of superior beauty. The 5 per cent grew larger and larger, however, as he joined in designing what he envisioned as "the most spectacularly beautiful seat of government in the world." It certainly became the single most expensive state government project in the United States. Originally conceived as a $440 million project, the final estimated costs rose to $850 million by 1975.

Construction did not begin until 1964, and then, because Nelson had grave doubts about his chances of winning a third term in 1966, he accelerated the time schedule by contracting for simultaneous construction of most of the buildings. Then, when workers hit sliding Albany mud in excavating for the central platform of the Mall, which was to serve as the roof of an underground building, all other construction was held up. The state had to pay penalties for the delays. Critics harped at Nelson Rockefeller's "edifice complex," claimed he was building a monument to himself and decried the enormous cost of the grandiose project. Yet the Albany Mall has turned out to be spectacularly beautiful and aesthetically pleasing, its office space fully occupied and utilized, the people of Albany itself delighted with the urban renewal it provided. It remains to be seen, however, whether the state museum when completed will attract tourists in the numbers projected and whether or not the Mall itself will spin off an economic revival for all of Albany, as Rockefeller Center did for midtown Manhattan. Only time will tell if the Albany Mall goes down in history as "Rockefeller's Folly," as his critics predict, or, as he puts it, becomes "the greatest thing that has happened in this country in a hundred years."

When in the mid-1960s the New York City subway system verged on the brink of financial collapse, the bankrupt Long Island Rail Road was

near extinction and the Westchester commuter lines of the Penn Central
and the New Haven were sliding downhill rapidly, the Rockefeller administration moved in, bought out the private stockholders where necessary
and established a single agency called the Metropolitan Transportation
Authority, an independent corporation with broad, tax-exempt powers to
operate and to improve the whole mass transit system of that part of the
New York metropolitan area which lies within New York State. With one
stroke of legislation, Nelson Rockefeller created a giant holding company,
the largest in the field of transportation. Its task was to succeed where private enterprise had failed in moving 7 to 8 million people a day from their
homes to their places of work. Two billion dollars was invested in buying
new, modern equipment. To head the MTA, he appointed his close
confidant and chief aide in Albany, William Ronan, at a salary of $75,000
a year. It was a high-risk job. No one before him had ever figured out a
way to run the New York City subway system or the commuter railroads
out of fares the common man could afford to pay. And yet the bold stroke
succeeded to a degree. New equipment replaced outworn trains and tracks
on all the suburban lines as well as within the city. Fares went up, but the
new air-conditioned trains arrived on time, suburbanites returned to the
commuter lines and overall, it was generally agreed, the MTA rescued
commuter transportation throughout the New York metropolitan area.

Nelson Rockefeller relished the challenge to his own ability of trying
to solve the complex problems of government and society, especially those
which stymied the efforts of others. In him was the happy combination of
the idealist and the pragmatist. He could envision perfect solutions and
the way things should be, but he also was enough of a political realist to
know that he had to take one step at a time. Where to draw the line often
was the problem: how far short of the ideal solution should a man settle
at the risk of losing it all? Nelson's usual method was to define what
should be done; then what could be done; and then how best to accomplish the most possible, one step at a time.

The thorniest, most complex, nearest-to-insoluble problem faced by
New York's governor—as well as by other governors across the nation—
was to provide adequate housing for those too poor to pay adequate rents.
The state's Housing Finance Agency, created in 1960 to help with low-
cost mortgages, had helped—but more than 1 million New Yorkers still
lived in dilapidated housing which needed replacement. Studies showed
that by 1990, 6 million people would need new homes, and yet private
builders were doing less and less building each year. Sites cleared for low-
rent housing lay vacant for as much as fifteen years; private builders did
not want to touch them, not even with state help. The wave of riots in
the ghettos of Watts, Detroit, Newark and elsewhere, the assassination of
Martin Luther King in 1968 all threatened to touch off the burning down
of substandard housing in black ghettos across the country, of which New

York had its share. Using the urgency of that threat to persuade the New York legislature, Governor Rockefeller won approval of his project to create one more gargantuan independent public corporation, called the Urban Development Corporation, with unprecedented, broad powers to condemn property, raze old buildings, supersede local zoning and building codes, issue its own "moral commitment" bonds, and do whatever else was necessary to complete the job. Its task was to develop housing or other projects on its own or in conjunction with private builders and then, once the project was underway or even completed, to sell or lease back the projects to private enterprise, and reinvest the money in more housing. In order to make the UDC acceptable to upstate legislators, the UDC was empowered to develop not only housing for the poor but also factories, industrial centers, commercial buildings and the like. It was a complex package solution to a complex problem.

The search team seeking the best man for the job of heading the UDC recommended Edward J. Logue, who had won a national reputation for his pioneering and outstanding urban redevelopment work in New Haven and Boston. Logue was intrigued with the challenge of the job but declined. He felt he could not leave Boston while he still owed people money from his previous year's losing campaign for mayor of Boston—which, he explained, he could only pay off by working for private enterprise. Furthermore, he was broke; he could not afford housing even for himself and his family in New York. Nelson understood. It was the age-old problem of capable men who could not afford to work for the government. The solution for Nelson Rockefeller was clear. He persuaded Logue to take the UDC job because Nelson Rockefeller wanted him. And because he wanted him, he offered Logue a gift of $31,389 to pay off his campaign debts and a loan of $145,000 so he could buy a cooperative apartment on Manhattan's East Side. He thought nothing more of it. He had the money and he was using it as a tool. He had made similar loans to persuade other men so that they could afford to work in his administration: his Superintendent of Banks, his Commissioner of Housing, his closest aide, Bill Ronan, and others. Some of the loans were fully or partially paid back, some were fully or partially forgiven by Nelson. Sometimes money was given as gifts to friends or associates who were stricken with illness, financial setbacks or extraordinary and unforeseen expenses in their families. The loans or gifts were made on a personal and private basis, not as a matter of policy. No one spoke of such loans or gifts, not the recipient nor Nelson Rockefeller.

Edward Logue, during the next seven years, oversaw the building of 34,000 housing units and 69 non-residential projects in New York at a cost of $1.5 billion. But more than that, he set a new standard of architecture for public housing throughout the nation with the UDC projects. In 1974, he was given an honorary membership in the American Institute of Archi-

Winthrop Rockefeller.

Marrying Barbara (Bobo) Sears, at Winston Guest's estate in Palm Beach, Florida, 1948.

Building Winrock Farms in Arkansas, with Jerry Bailey, G. W. Adkinson and Jimmy Hudson.

Winrock Farms.

With a Santa Gertrudis bull, "the Cadillac of livestock."

At the ledge of Petit Jean Mountain with his mother's favorite Bible quotation.

The big event: the annual bull sale.

With Jeannette Edris Rockefeller shortly after their marriage, 1964.

In his office at Winrock Farms.

Campaigning.

Governor of Arkansas.

His son, Winthrop Paul, comes to Winrock.

tecture, a rare honor for a man who is a lawyer by profession. The UDC concept of financing low-rent projects was copied by some thirty states, which faced the same problems as New York.

Through the years, Nelson Rockefeller's administration set a standard for the nation of what state government could do in virtually all areas of citizen concern. Not everyone agreed with all of these programs and the cost involved. Many of them were new, pioneering and controversial. There was his 1965 Pure Waters Program, designed to satisfy needs as far ahead as 1990, launched with a $1 billion bond issue and expected to rise to a cost of $4 billion. There was a ten-year program for outdoor recreation development and a pioneering conservation program which added 375,000 acres to the state's parks. There were ambitious programs for nursing homes for the aged, new hospitals, a tenfold increase in mental health and retardation treatment community centers, a program to coordinate efforts to combat juvenile delinquency, a billion-dollar effort which failed to cope with drug addiction by treatment of addicts. There was the nation's first Council on the Arts, which sponsored some five thousand cultural events a year in seven hundred communities throughout the state. There were new agencies to help small businesses to train unskilled workers. The state's first minimum wage was established and increased through the years—consistently the highest in the land.

For every problem that faced him, Nelson Rockefeller sought the most apt solution. It earned him the reputation of a *doer*. Not all the Rockefeller solutions solved the problems. Heroin addiction did not yield to hospitalization or to a widely heralded methadone drug program. In response, the governor reverted to harsh mandatory prison penalties for drug pushers as the best practical deterrent; and the success of that program remains a subject of debate. The rapid and massive state aid to finance much-needed nursing homes greatly increased the supply of these facilities, but also opened the gates for scoundrels who sought the fast buck at the expense of the state and the elderly patients—and this led to a major scandal in 1975. In that same year, after Nelson Rockefeller had left office, the UDC ran into financial trouble as a result of the nation's economic woes. When the federal government cut back on its 90 per cent financing of low-rent housing, the UDC borrowed from the banks to carry on its building program and then found itself unable to pay off a $100 million loan. Facing bankruptcy, it focused national attention on the whole Rockefeller concept of financing through "moral obligation" bonds. The question, blunt and realistic, became: if the UDC could not pay off its loans or bonds, who would pay? The state? The commercial banks? Who? And that led to the fundamental question faced by Nelson Rockefeller in the first place: how does a capitalistic society, based upon private enterprise and profit, provide adequate housing (or other services) to the needy who cannot afford the price involved? The commercial banks balked (with the exception of David Rockefeller's Chase Manhattan Bank), the legislature balked at paying for something for which the state was not legally obligated. At the last moment, the private savings bank came to the financial rescue. But the aid was a temporary measure. The fundamental question remained unanswered. As a Morgan Guaranty banker put it: "Social goals are funded one way in this country and economic goals another way." Or, said differently: where is the dividing line between social responsibility and the bottom line of the profit and loss sheet?

Nelson Rockefeller, along with his brothers, favored social responsibility against the bottom line. His humanitarian programs all cost money. The harshest criticism plaguing him throughout his political life was that he was a *spender*. The New York State budget, under his four-term administration, rose from a record $2 billion for 1959–60 to more than $10 billion for 1973–74. The state's debt on its many building programs rose to an unprecedented $6 billion, mortgaging the future of the state to satisfy present and future needs. Taxes must pay for all this. And it is said in New York that taxes have gone up as far as they can go. New Yorkers pay more per capita in state and local taxes than any other state in the Union. Yet the people's needs still are there and continue to grow. Governor Hugh Carey, Democrat, in 1975 asked the legislature for $800 million more in state taxes, four times as much as Nelson Rockefeller requested in his first budget message.

One answer to the perennial fiscal crisis of state and local governments lies in another Rockefeller program, first proposed in 1970, and endorsed by President Nixon, that of revenue sharing with the federal government. The idea was for the federal government, which receives two thirds of all tax dollars collected, to share more of that money with the states and/or localities for use at the local level. Congress enacted the revenue-sharing idea in part, but the fiscal dilemma continues . . .

On the state level, Nelson Rockefeller gained a reputation for being the most powerful governor in New York's history and the most powerful in the nation. He learned through the years the art of politics, how to deal with political leaders and politicians, how to compromise, how to give and how to take. He acquired a finesse and sense of timing and, in short, got pretty much of what he wanted. Behind the ever smiling face, the broad wink, the wiggling of the eyebrows, there was the tough, determined mind, always clicking, aware of what was being said and left unsaid. He had the presence of a strong leader and he used it. With that success came the reaction of suspicion in many quarters that he was too powerful, that he held an iron grip on the political future of New York. That of course proved to be wrong one short year after he left office: Malcolm Wilson, his faithful and true lieutenant governor, served out Rockefeller's fourth term, ran for a full term himself in 1974 and was resoundingly defeated by Hugh Carey by more than 700,000 votes. Nevertheless, while he was governor, Nelson Rockefeller was considered all-powerful, a man who had mastered the art of state government.

On the national political level, it seemed he could do nothing right. He sought the Republican nomination for President in 1960, 1964 and 1968 and despite his popularity, his political power, his much vaunted wealth, he failed each time he tried for the golden ring.

Why? For many reasons. But underlying those practical and ostensible reasons was the character and personality of the man himself. The attributes which had served him so well all of his life and which most people admire in a leader—self-confidence, independence, integrity, toughness, doing the "right thing" at whatever personal risk—led him into making a disastrous political mistake during the presidential campaign of 1960.

Six months after he became governor, he put about seventy people to work on his behalf in exploring his chances of capturing the Republican nomination for President. The eastern press and the academic community looked favorably upon the possibility of Nelson Rockefeller's providing new dynamic leadership for the nation. But his closest political advisers told him he did not have much of a chance against Richard Nixon, then the Vice-President and heir apparent to President Eisenhower. But prudent advisers had always warned him to be more prudent. He had been advised not to do battle with Secretaries of State Hull, Stettinius, Dulles and others, but he had always fought hard and at personal risk for what he considered to be "right" and he had won. They had advised him against running for governor in 1958, and he did, and he had won. Now, in 1960, he sincerely believed President Eisenhower had allowed the nation to drift from crisis to crisis and that Nixon, whom he personally did not admire, was too ambivalent philosophically and personally to give the country the leadership it needed. From October to December 1959, he toured the country, speaking out as an undeclared candidate on foreign and domestic policy. He received a good press, a good audience reaction, but firm rejection from Republican Party leaders. They were committed to Richard Nixon, the Republican Party spokesman and warhorse over the past eight years who had campaigned for Republicans in almost every state of the Union. Nelson's team of delegate explorers returned to New York empty-handed. Even his brother David and the family's chief financial adviser, J. Richardson Dilworth, returned from their explorations with the sad news that the financial community of the Republican Party favored Nixon over Rockefeller. This last report came as something of a shock to Nelson, but he could understand the reason: Nixon was a known quantity. Nelson Rockefeller was unknown and untested and he had worked for *that man*, Franklin D. Roosevelt, and had supported his policies. He was considered *too* independent. He had been governor only a little more than one year. The kindest advice was that he wait his turn. So, upon the advice of his closest counselors, on the day after Christmas Day, with a "definite and final" statement, Nelson Rockefeller withdrew from the race.

That was the wisest course he could follow under the circumstances: Nixon was clearly the Republican Party's choice. But the decision just did not sit well with Nelson. His own intuitive feeling gnawed away at him that Richard Nixon was not the right man to lead the nation. Then, that May, America's U-2 spy plane, with Gary Powers aboard, was shot down over the Soviet Union, President Eisenhower was caught in a flagrant public lie, Premier Khrushchev angrily canceled a scheduled summit peace conference and America's international prestige sank to a new low. Nelson Rockefeller envisioned the possibility of his worst fears coming true.

So, once again, he explored the advisability of challenging Nixon for the nomination. Again his political advisers spelled out the only strategy open to him: wait and hope that Nixon would not be nominated on the first ballot, build up second- and third-ballot strength. But Nelson, still young and politically eager, could not reconcile himself to a wait-and-see policy. Disregarding the advice of his more prudent associates, he sat down at Pocantico Hills over the Memorial Day weekend with Emmet John Hughes, a highly skilled writer who had grown disillusioned as had Nelson with the Eisenhower administration, and together they drafted a blunt and straightforward message to America which came straight from Nelson Rockefeller's heart. It was a nine-point platform, calling for specific action on foreign, military and domestic affairs. In effect, it repudiated the lack of direction of the Eisenhower administration, attacked the Republican Party for its lack of new ideas or new actions and challenged Richard Nixon to declare immediately and precisely where he stood on the issues of the day.

George Hinman, his senior political adviser, warned Nelson of the explosive effect such a statement would bring. "The party will never forgive you if you make this attack on Nixon and on Ike and on the party itself," Hinman said.

"That is irrelevant!" Nelson snapped back. He had made his decision. The party needed a reawakening from its drifting somnambulance and he felt it was his duty to do the shaking. On June 8, he issued what has been described as one of the most politically straightforward and politically naïve statements in history. "I can no longer be silent on the fact. We cannot, as a nation or as a party, proceed . . . to march to meet the future with a banner aloft whose only emblem is a question mark . . ." And it went on from there.

From June to the Republican convention in mid-July, Nelson Rockefeller challenged the Republican Party leadership on the issues. He toured the country, appeared on television, spoke on radio, gave position papers on foreign affairs, national defense, social welfare and education. He brought his battle to the party's platform at the Republican National

Convention. He declared war and he was taken seriously. Citizens for Rockefeller committees sprang up in twenty-one states.

Richard Nixon let it be known he would be happy to have Nelson Rockefeller as his running mate. Nelson disdained the offer: there was no way and no circumstance under which he would run for Vice-President. "I am not standby equipment," he declared. The idea of working as a subordinate to anyone just ran against his grain.

Political strategists on both sides could see that Nelson Rockefeller was heading for a humiliating defeat at the party's Chicago convention. Nixon had the votes; Nelson had only a bulldog determination. And then Nixon "caved in," or so it seemed. Nixon secretly asked to meet with Rockefeller on neutral grounds and, upon Nelson's refusal, Nixon consented to meet at Nelson's apartment in New York in order to work out a party platform agreeable to Rockefeller, which would then bring the New York governor back into the fold.

For ninety minutes over dinner in Nelson Rockefeller's Fifth Avenue apartment, Richard Nixon tried to persuade him to run as his Vice-President. He cited the past and he envisioned the future. He gave reason after reason. Nelson was adamant. The answer was no. Then what did Nelson Rockefeller want for his support of the Republican candidate for President in 1960? The answer was a party platform with a stronger civil rights plank and a stronger statement upon national defense. This was the famous or—according to one's interpretation—the infamous secret meeting of Friday night, July 22, from 7:30 P.M. to 3:20 A.M. the next morning out of which was forged what became known as the Compact of Fifth Avenue. Nelson announced the fourteen points of agreement in the compact from his apartment and Richard Nixon proceeded to the Republican convention, where he rammed the new platform down the throats of the convention's platform committee.

The immediate press reaction was that this was a tremendous victory and show of strength for Nelson Rockefeller. The facts of the secret meeting came out: Rockefeller had set the terms for the meeting and Nixon had acquiesced to working out a joint agreement, to be announced by Rockefeller. It was Rockefeller's show all the way.

But the aftermath was something else again. Nixon, an astute politician, had gone to Rockefeller because he needed his support if he were to have any hope of carrying New York in the general election. He had the nomination, but to win the election he needed the support of liberal Republicans as well as independent Democrats. He had far more to gain than to lose in winning over Nelson Rockefeller and his supporters. His mistake—one which plagued him all his political life—was that he was so much of a loner that he failed to consult with his staff. Nixon's press secretary was denying the meeting even at the time it was going on.

The long-range effect of that single secret meeting was that it ruined the national political career of Nelson Rockefeller. He had gone too far in insisting that he was right about what was good for America while the rest of the Republican Party leadership was wrong. The conservatives in the party were outraged. What right had Nelson Rockefeller to dictate the terms of the party platform? He was labeled a "spoiler," and the kind of spoiled kid who wouldn't play the game unless you played it his way. Even the moderates shook their heads in wonderment over the arrogance of the man. In short, he poisoned his relationship with the Republican Party for the sake of a party platform which—as is traditional with all such political documents of intent—was promptly forgotten.

Nelson Rockefeller did support Richard Nixon. He campaigned for him throughout his state, but Nixon lost New York anyway. He lost Illinois and Texas, too, and went down to the narrowest of defeats in modern presidential elections, losing by less than 1 per cent of the vote. And Nelson Rockefeller forever afterward would be apportioned at least part of the blame. Then a bit of irony finished off the scenario. John F. Kennedy commented that if he, Nelson Rockefeller, had been the Republican candidate, he, Nelson Rockefeller, would have been elected President of the United States.

But the conservative wing of the Republican Party—the stalwarts ranging from moderates to ultra-conservatives along with some out-and-out reactionaries and John Birchers—remained furious with him. Not only did they disagree fundamentally with his liberal political philosophy and his concept of government action and spending, they disliked him personally: he was a "spoiler" when he did not get his way, and he epitomized in their minds the so-called eastern Establishment which had dominated national politics in the Republican Party since Alf Landon ran for President in 1936. Positively vengeful, the conservatives immediately went to work on the 1964 election. They put together a truly vast grass-roots movement across the nation, fighting for the leadership of every Republican county organization and for every delegate who would vote for a conservative candidate in 1964. For their standard-bearer, they chose Senator Barry Goldwater of Arizona, who had cried "treason" and "tyranny" at the platform changes wrought by Nelson Rockefeller in 1960.

The governor of New York had every intention of seeking the nomination of his party in 1964. President Kennedy believed he would be his opponent. But while Nelson Rockefeller and his large staff prepared by focusing on the issues of the day, the conservatives, with vengeance in their hearts, were quietly lining up party leaders and convention delegates. They eliminated Richard Nixon as a contender by opposing him in the primary and aiding in his defeat when he ran for governor of California in 1962. They faced little or no opposition in local fights. Many of the party moderates tacitly agreed to concede the 1964 nomination to the conservatives in order to assuage past hurts in a year when any chance of election of a Republican against the charismatic and increasingly popular Kennedy was considered hopeless. Then on that terrible day, November 22, 1963, John F. Kennedy was assassinated in Dallas, Texas, Lyndon Baines Johnson became President, the entire political picture changed suddenly and it was too late to stop the Republican surge for Barry Goldwater.

Nelson Rockefeller tried. He did battle with Barry Goldwater for the heart and soul of the Republican Party across the nation in the primaries from New Hampshire to California. Most impartial politicos considered his quest hopeless. He never considered it so. Straw polls indicated that he could win the election if he could get the nomination, and that he could not win the nomination. The ostensible, even flagrant issue against him was morality: the morality of his divorcing Mary Todhunter Clark, his wife of twenty-three years, mother of his five children, and his remarriage to Margaretta Fitler Murphy, who "forsook" her four children and her husband to marry him.

For Nelson, too, the decision to end one marriage and to begin another was a moral one: he loved one woman and not the other. Politics did not enter into it. He did not consult with his political advisers; he told them of his personal decision as their need to know became apparent. The two women involved, of course, were an intimate part of the decision. Mary Todhunter had agreed to the divorce. Their children were fully grown and out on their own. All of them were married, except for twenty-three-year-old Michael, who was far off on an archaeological and art exploration of New Guinea and the western Pacific islands. There was no further reason to maintain the legal formality of marriage. The increasingly known link between Nelson Rockefeller and Happy Murphy had become an acute embarrassment to his wife. The final embarrassment came when a late-night fire swept through sections of the Executive Mansion in Albany in early March, forcing the governor and first lady to flee in their night clothes from separate sections of the Mansion, disclosing in public that they had been occupying separate bedrooms. She never appeared with him in public after that.

For Happy Murphy, divorce was much more difficult. Her marriage to Dr. James S. Murphy (called Robin), a research microbiologist, had been much more difficult and stormy than had Nelson's. Differing temperaments, values and events had led to bitter jealousies and recriminations in their lives together. Both had come from broken homes. Happy, raised in the Main Line of Philadelphia in a wealthy family, had married Robin Murphy in 1948, and had been taken for summer vacations to Seal Harbor, Maine, where she had befriended a very lonely old man named John D. Rockefeller, Jr., who had lost his own beloved wife that year. He and Robin's father had been friends for years. So it was only natural that John Jr. wanted the Murphys to be near him. He helped Robin gain a position at the Rockefeller Institute for Medical Research (later the Rockefeller University) and invited the Murphys to build their winter home at Pocantico Hills. The Murphy family and the Rockefeller family saw more and more of each other. Nelson and Happy discovered one another and their needs for each other. When the time came, however, and they had decided to marry, Robin Murphy refused to give his wife a divorce. Then, reluctantly, he agreed to let her go only if he kept their four children. He was not about to lose both his wife and his children to Nelson Rockefeller. Faced with that ultimatum, she wavered indecisively and then sought psychiatric and medical help, which convinced her she must look after her own happiness and health first. After a long emotional struggle, she finally decided to seek her freedom. The matrimonial dispute, with lawyers fighting on both sides, continued for months, at times reaching peaks of ugliness, threats and anguish, and finally concluding (as so many such cases do) in a separation agreement distasteful to both husband and wife. Dr. Murphy retained legal custody of their four children, ranging in age from one to ten, but with the mother having the children at least half the time. Later, the custody agreement was amended to ease the visits of the children so that in fact they did spend more than half their time with their mother. But secrecy was part of the agreement. When the public learned later of the divorce, the impression given was that Happy Murphy had relinquished custody of her four children to marry Nelson Rockefeller.

The Rockefeller separation and agreement to divorce was announced to the public first, as quietly as possible. A family spokesman read a one-paragraph announcement at Room 5600 in Rockefeller Center late on a Friday afternoon, November 17, 1961, in time only for the slim and least-read Saturday morning newspapers. Both Nelson and Tod made themselves unavailable for comments.

But there was no hiding the fact. One of every four marriages in America at the time (the percentage is greater now) ended in divorce and the vast majority of those divorced do remarry. But Nelson was governor of New York—and a very possible candidate for President of the United States—and he was a Rockefeller, a celebrity, a colorful fish in a bowl whose life, or most of it, was open to the public gaze and curiosity. Yet, before the press could get at him, the whole matter was cast aside because tragedy, far beyond even the Rockefeller control, struck the family.

For the first time in the life of Nelson Rockefeller or in the lives of any of the Rockefellers it struck hard. On a Sunday, two days after the separation announcement, Nelson, while lunching with his brother David at Pocantico Hills, was called to the phone: Michael was missing and presumed lost at sea off the coast of New Guinea. Throughout the day, details flowed in piecemeal. With little or no hope held out, Nelson decided to fly out to be on hand, just in case. Michael's twin, Mary, flew with him. When they reached Hollandia, on the northern edge of New Guinea, the next day, the whole story was pieced together for them:

Michael and Rene Wassing, a Dutch anthropologist, had set out for a long stay in a primitive section of the Asmat jungle, rarely visited by white men, to trade for art objects with an aborigine tribe. They had lashed together two flat-bottom native canoes, planked over with rough boards, powered by a single outboard motor. Heavily laden with supplies, the makeshift catamaran began to ship water as the lashings became loose and strong currents swept the little craft out to sea. Two native guides dived overboard to swim back to shore. The motor quit. In the rough sea, the boat turned over. Michael and Rene clung to the plankings through the night. As they drifted farther and farther out to sea, Michael decided their only hope was for him to swim to shore. Rene Wassing, his guide and adviser, had to stay with the capsized boat: he was too weak a swimmer to try to make land. Michael tied two red empty gasoline cans to his waist for buoyancy and set out swimming strongly toward shore. He was never seen again. Wassing spent another day and night clinging to the boat until he was sighted by a rescue plane, twenty-four miles offshore. Later it was estimated that to have reached shore Michael would have had to swim from eleven to sixteen miles through rough, choppy, shark-infested waters. Extensive searches had been made over the past two and a half days, Nelson was told, and there had been not a sign of Michael: he must be presumed dead at sea. The air search continued, more for the missing red gasoline cans than for the slim twenty-three-year-old. The governor and his daughter went out on one four-hour search. They viewed the location at which Michael presumably left his boat and then flew over thick, fetid jungles along the shoreline. Finally convinced of what he had known in his heart before, Nelson set out westward for home.

At the airport in New York, he was met by his brother David, his sons Rodman and Steven and about two hundred reporters. The obligatory press conference in the glare of television lights was strained and subdued. Not a question was asked. No one knew what to say until Russell Porter, the respected and venerable reporter from the New York *Times*, expressed "the sympathy of the press." Then Nelson, obviously restraining his emotion, said in a low-pitched voice:

"I would just like to say a word about Michael himself. Ever since he was little, he had been very aware of people, their feelings, their thoughts. He is a person who has always loved people and has always been loved by people. He has a tremendous enthusiasm and drive, love of life. He has always loved beauty in people, beauty in nature and beauty in art, whether it is in painting or sculpture, and has been quite an artist himself . . . I think it is fair to say that he was never happier than he has been out there for some seven or eight months."

He drove home to Pocantico Hills and there he met his children and his estranged wife. With a map of the area spread out upon the floor, he explained in detail what must have happened to Michael.

Life went on, of course, for this busy, committed man. For the next year he scrupulously kept himself from speaking of Michael. This was a hurt he was not ready to share with outsiders. He had had a particular rapport with his youngest son, for they had many personal traits in common, based upon their high energy level. They had shared an avid interest in art, particularly in primitive art, and the father had envisioned a future when he would work in this field with his son. But with Michael gone, that was not to be; his death soured Nelson's interest in primitive art, and while he liked certain pieces personally, the "fun of it all" was gone. Michael's collection of 514 pieces of oceanic primitive arts—poles, shields, masks, canoes and paintings—one of the largest individual collections of its kind, was shown at the Museum of Primitive Art, then in a special exhibit at the Metropolitan Museum of Art and finally reproduced in book form. Nelson contributed handsomely to assure the building of a Michael C. Rockefeller Wing to the Metropolitan to house permanently his son's collection along with the 3,400 pieces of the Museum of Primitive Art, which Nelson had sponsored in New York in 1957. Gradually, after the tacit year of mourning ended, Nelson reminisced more and more often of Michael and of Michael's attributes as a Rockefeller. His became the only photograph standing on the governor's office desk at Fifty-fifth Street, where Nelson spent most of his time. In his country house at Pocantico Hills, at the head of the stairs leading to the underground art gallery (which Nelson passes every day he is there), there hangs a prominent photograph of Michael sitting in a boat. A painting by Michael hangs in his Foxhall Road home in Washington.

Not long after Michael's death and his parents' divorce, the gossip columnists printed the item that there was a Mrs. Murphy in Nelson Rockefeller's life. The political reporters took up the quest, for Nelson Rockfeller was an apparent candidate for President of the United States. He refused to comment. "I'm not going to answer rumors, and I'm not going to discuss my private life. There's nothing more to say," he insisted and he stuck to it through his divorce in March 1962 and Happy's divorce a year later. Then and only then did Nelson tell—he did not ask—his political intimates that he intended to marry the woman he loved, Happy Murphy. All of them, including George Hinman, Emmet Hughes, Bill Ronan and his press secretary Bob McManus, pointed out what was obvious: marriage at this time meant risking his chance to win the Republican presidential nomination and the election as well. But Nelson insisted that it would be less than honest to the electorate to run as an unmarried candidate when he fully intended to remarry if and when he got into the White House. "This is the reality of my life," he said of his love for Happy Murphy. "It's part of me and the people ought to know this. Then they can take me or not." (President Kennedy, upon hearing of the rumors of remarriage, commented privately, "He'll never do it!" Most political observers agreed.) The decision may have been politically wrong but it was morally right in Nelson Rockefeller's own estimation.

They were married at noon on a Saturday, May 4, 1963, which was as soon as possible after Happy's divorce and the adjournment of the New York legislature. It was a private and quiet ceremony at the home of his brother Laurance on the Pocantico Hills estate, performed by the pastor of Union Church of Pocantico Hills and announced later that day from Rockefeller offices at 5600. They spent their wedding night in the main house built for old John D., which Nelson had taken over after his divorce. The next morning they flew off for a month's honeymoon in the privacy of Nelson's Venezuelan ranch in the foothills of the Andes, "the most beautiful spot in the whole world," according to Nelson.

With his new wife smiling at his side and the "morality issue" ever present, Nelson Rockefeller sought the Republican nomination for President in 1964 in a fierce primary battle with Senator Barry Goldwater. In New Hampshire, they both lost to a write-in candidate, Henry Cabot Lodge, then U. S. Ambassador to South Vietnam, who did not campaign in the state; in Oregon, where Goldwater did not appear, Rockefeller won; and, finally, in California, the real primary battle of the campaign was waged furiously, bitterly, personally, fairly and unfairly. Down the line on virtually all the issues, it was black and white, the battle of the conservatives against the liberals for the heart of the Republican Party. Virtually all the stops were pulled in California, save one. The Rockefeller organization had put together a vitriolic half-hour television film, called "The Extremists," castigating Barry Goldwater and the right wing of the party. But at the last minute Nelson vetoed the project as "McCarthyism in reverse." He refused to use the tactics he saw being used against him. Some in his camp believe to this day that he then and there gratuitously threw away his best chance at the nomination. More realistically, outside observers feel he never had a chance to win California or the nomination. In California, where Rockefeller spent a fortune hiring workers, the Goldwater campaign had an army of passionate volunteers to ring doorbells and get out the vote. Then, on the Saturday before primary day, Happy Rockefeller gave birth to Nelson Aldrich Rockefeller, Jr., in New York, with the beaming happy father at her side. And that was his choice of priorities. He had campaigned exhaustingly in California for almost three weeks non-stop, but on weekends he flew home to be with Happy. That Tuesday, 1,120,403 California Republicans voted for Goldwater; 1,052,053 voted for Rockefeller. For Nelson, the 1964 campaign for President was all over but the shouting.

The shouting reached its peak on the second night of the Republican convention at the Cow Palace in San Francisco when Nelson Rockefeller was allotted five minutes to speak on a minority report on the party platform concerning extremism. Some say it was his finest moment in politics.

It was hardly that. But via television it showed to the nation a fighting, passionate Nelson Rockefeller, standing alone on a vast stage, facing down the frenzied boos, catcalls, insults and roars of the Goldwater extremists on the floor and in the galleries. In the primaries, he had called them kooks and denounced them and now they were proving his point, beyond the control of the Goldwater professional staff, booing, hissing, insulting and refusing to allow a fellow Republican his freedom of speech. The venom of fanaticism poured out. The convention chairman, Thruston B. Morton, tried to pull Rockefeller away from the microphones. The whole convention seemed likely to explode in a riot. But Nelson insisted upon his right to speak. Shrugging off Morton's efforts to pull him away, he shouted back at the roaring convention: "This is still a free country, ladies and gentlemen . . . These things have no place in America." Then he told of midnight calls, anonymous hate mail, goon tactics, bomb scares and threats of assassination. He spoke his five minutes, refusing to allow the interruptions from the galleries to count against his allotted time. Goldwater, offering the American people a "choice, not an echo," won the nomination and lost the election, one as handily as the other.

Nelson never expressed regrets about 1964. Some of those around him felt "it was a bum year all around," but Nelson himself believed he had fought hard for the nomination of his party, had defined the concept of the "mainstream" of American politics, and he had lost. Neither did he ever bear a grudge toward Barry Goldwater, whom he liked personally. Nelson possessed that rare quality of being able to think of himself and his actions in the third person. He did not take things personally, although there were exceptions. He could hold a grudge as well and as long as any man. The personal and the political decisions he made at this time of his life—to divorce, to marry again, to give no quarter and to seek no accommodation with the right-wing segment of his party—were choices based upon conscience and a highly valued code of ethics with which he had grown up. Given the circumstances and the alternatives, his mother and his father would have approved of those decisions. Nelson believed that.

He sought his vindication by running for a third term as governor of New York in 1966. On a personal level, he felt this would be the most important election of his career as he was putting everything on the line with the voters: his administration over the past eight years, his career, his way of life and his marriage. Things looked bleak. A statewide opinion poll, conducted privately for him, showed clearly that Nelson Rockefeller was at the rock bottom of his popularity in New York in May and December of 1965. He was stereotyped by most people as "a high tax man," "not for the people," "not helpful to the poor or the little man." In May, only 17 per cent of those polled believed he was doing a good or excellent job as governor; 78 per cent thought he was doing a fair or poor job. In December, only 12 per cent chose him as the man who would make the "best governor," in comparison with 37 per cent for U. S. Senator Jacob Javits and with 27 per cent for New York City Mayor John V. Lindsay. Three Democrats beat him by two-to-one margins, and one of them, Frank O'Connor, New York City Council president, won the nomination to oppose him in the election.

The bitter shock of that private poll opened Nelson's mind to what his senior staff had been trying to tell him for years: he would spend long hours, days and weeks working on complex state programs and then give hardly any time at all to explaining the problems, programs and projects to the people. He hardly prepared for press conferences; he spoke off the cuff, inexactly far too often and often to his own disadvantage; he paid far too little attention to the image he was projecting. Like Governor Harriman before him, the people did not know or understand what he was doing or attempting to do as governor. Out of that analysis grew a series of television films on state projects and a series of old-fashioned town hall meetings throughout the state at which the governor would answer questions from the citizens.

But more immediately, he launched an early, expensive, well-coordinated campaign for re-election which has since gone down in the books as the most nearly perfect state political campaign in history. The cost was in excess of $5 million, not counting half again as much for private studies, surveys and peripheral input for which he paid himself. Television screens were flooded with more than three thousand paid commercials, soft-selling Rockefeller programs and accomplishments in the first phase, then hard-selling Rockefeller as governor in the final weeks of the campaign. The voters were inundated with 27 million brochures, buttons, balloons, setting a new standard of expensive campaigning for the nation. Fortunately for Rockefeller, O'Connor turned out to be a limited, local candidate, unknown and without appeal to upstate voters, a political product of the New York City Democratic machine. His campaign was poorly organized and poorly financed. Nevertheless, starting out with an apparently insurmountable twenty-six-point percentage margin, he led Nelson Rockefeller in the straw polls all the way up to election day. Nelson, campaigning with his usual zest, privately geared himself up emotionally to losing. He warned his new wife, now pregnant with their second child, to prepare herself for a change in his career. On the state level, he tried to put his house in order. His two favorite projects—the Albany Mall and the State University building program—he pushed beyond the turnaround point so that neither could later be reversed or abandoned.

Nelson ran the gauntlet of 1966 alone, abandoned by most of the Republican leaders in the state. They had been too weak to deny him the nomination, although some tried, but they were secure enough to stand on the sidelines and watch him lose. When he won a third term in office by a plurality of 382,263, or 44 per cent of the vote, contrary to so many expectations and predictions, the effect was that of a baptism of new, mellowed self-confidence. He felt in his bones that he had now mastered the art of state government and he felt comfortable in tackling any problem of state government. He was beholden to no man, neither for finances nor for favors, because none had been given to him in the campaign.

Out of this flowed some of the more imaginative, innovative and politically risky programs of his administration: the Urban Development Corporation for housing, the massive bond issue financing for mass transit, the modernization of the state divorce laws, the legalization of abortion, the advancement of state Medicaid for the poor and Medicare for the elderly. His sense of timing and compromise, wooing and wheedling improved to such an extent that he became in effect a one-man government, whether the legislature was Republican or Democratic. He became a father figure in the state of New York, having grown to an elder statesman, the senior among all state governors, a man known nationally, and accorded even more credit for power than he actually possessed. He wielded his paternalistic control so deftly that he came under attack in some quarters for the very extent of his power. But he enjoyed it all, pushing through 95 per cent of his programs in a state where the Democrats outnumbered the Republicans by far. His second son of his second marriage, Mark Fitler Rockefeller, was born twenty-six days after the start of his third term in office. His wife was interested and involved in his work, his home life was happy, his schedule was full but running smoothly as he divided his time between Albany and New York City, his duplex city apartment and the big house at Pocantico Hills, with summers at Seal Harbor, Maine.

So when the presidential sweepstakes of 1968 rolled around, Nelson Rockefeller was surprised to find himself not emotionally committed to making a third try for the golden ring at the edge of the merry-go-round. His driving personal ambition and need to prove himself had silently slipped away. He felt he had redeemed himself in 1966 and that for now was enough. It was clear to him that the bitterness of the 1964 primary remained. The Republicans were polarized and the Goldwater conservatives could never be brought around to support him. So, while the opinion polls showed that among all voters he was the favored Republican candidate for President in 1968, Richard Nixon was the choice of the Republicans who would be going to the nominating convention in August. Nelson announced his support of George Romney, governor of Michigan, who, Nelson thought, might bring the party together again. He helped finance Romney's campaign, loaned him speech writers and staff, pledged his support, but political reporters still would not believe that Nelson Rockefeller did not want to be President. When Romney, after being an early front-runner, failed in his drive and withdrew before the

New Hampshire primary, everyone assumed Rockefeller would announce his own candidacy. Nelson, receiving advice from all quarters, wavered right up the last day before his announcement on March 21. Then he declared: he would not be a candidate for President because it was obvious his own party did not want him, although he would be available, if needed. His withdrawal came as a complete surprise.

But that was not the only surprise of the eventful presidential campaign of 1968. Ten days later, President Johnson astounded the nation when he announced: "I shall not seek and I will not accept the nomination of my party for another term as your President." The stakes in the game had been immediately changed. The liberal wing of the Republican Party pressed Nelson to run as its most prominent representative. Otherwise, it was said, the way was clear for Richard Nixon to capture the nomination. Nixon himself challenged Rockefeller to run against him in the remaining primaries. Both of them knew full well that aside from perhaps Oregon, Nixon would sweep all other primaries: the party faithful were on his side. But Nelson was pushed into this race by his obligation to the liberal and eastern wing of the party. So, on April 30, Nelson Rockefeller reversed himself: "Today I announced my active candidacy for the nomination by the Republican Party." He cited the growing unrest and anxiety in the nation over Vietnam and over civil rights. The campaign strategy was to win the Gallup, Harris and Roper polls, to demonstrate that Richard Nixon was a loser and that Nelson Rockefeller was needed by the Republican Party to win the election. The Rockefeller organization lined up second-ballot commitments as it sought to stop Nixon from a first-ballot nomination. But on the eve of the convention, the Nixon people leaked the results of a Gallup poll which showed that their candidate would beat either Hubert Humphrey or Eugene McCarthy on the Democratic ticket.

It was all over for Nelson Rockefeller. With 667 delegate votes needed to win the nomination, on the first ballot Nixon received 692; Rockefeller, 277; Ronald Reagan, 182. Nelson telephoned his congratulations to the winner.

At the end of his farewell press conference, the press rose to its feet and, in a rare gesture, applauded the hoarse, fatigued but still smiling loser. On the flight back to New York, there was hardly a dry eye on the plane. There would be no more tomorrows, everyone thought: Richard Nixon would win the presidency because of the Vietnam war, the black revolution, the riots in the streets, the rise in crime, the general dissatisfaction . . . And Nelson Rockefeller at sixty years of age would be too old in 1976 after two terms of Richard Nixon in office. Here was the man most qualified to be President of the United States . . . the man who could attract the best of the nation into the service of their country . . . But now it was too late. Among the faithful, there was reason for tears.

Nelson made his way along the center aisle of the plane, comforting and reassuring the weepy and the depressed. "I'm sorry I let you down . . ." he said, "I'm sorry, but I did the best I could."

And then he did not look back. He supported Nixon in his winning campaign. He urged his old friend Henry Kissinger to accept the key foreign affairs post in the Nixon administration of National Security Adviser. He offered advice and counsel to the new President and in time he came to believe that he had underestimated the ability of Richard Nixon. They would never become friends or establish a personal close rapport. They could not. Too much had gone on before to separate them; they were too different in temperament, background and personality. But they were also two professionals, and as time went on a mutual healthy respect grew between them. The President would phone, usually once a week, to discuss problems and Nelson would send him memos, mostly on domestic problems. They viewed issues from the long perspective of their experience and in reality Nixon was not as conservative as most people thought, nor was Rockefeller as liberal. Both were pragmatists. On foreign policy, Henry Kissinger was the link between the two men. He kept Nelson Rockefeller informed on foreign affairs because he knew Nelson was interested and concerned, even to the extent of telephoning him from Peking when he was on that historic mission to the People's Republic of China in 1972. Nelson, in effect, became an ex-officio member of the Nixon administration with greater access to the President than most of the members of his Cabinet. The relationship was kept private, since public knowledge of it would do neither any good politically.

Nelson believed he was achieving a significant degree of influence upon the President's thinking, particularly with domestic affairs such as revenue sharing, ecology and pollution control, health and education benefits and aid to the arts. In foreign policy, he generally supported the President's and Kissinger's broad strategy for world peace and in their efforts to extricate the United States from the Vietnam war. The price he paid was that when and where he disagreed, he felt it incumbent to remain silent. Thus, when the "White House horrors" of the Watergate scandal became public, the governor of New York felt bound to remain mute on that subject as well as on Vietnam. As he explained later, when Richard Nixon was out of office: "I was elected governor of New York and my responsibility was to the people of New York. You don't kick people in Washington in the shins if you expect them to do something for you." What they did for him and for New York, he explained, was to increase federal aid to New York during his administration from five to eighteen cents of every doller in federal taxes collected from New York. It was a statement he was to regret, for it expressed pragmatism over principle to a degree uncharacteristic of him.

At the Republican convention of 1972, Nelson Rockefeller, the perennial presidential candidate, was taken back into the Republican fold. He was chosen to nominate Richard Nixon for re-election. Happy Rockefeller appeared on the platform with him and Republicans in convention welcomed the couple with a warm, sustained ovation. The days of the maverick and the "spoiler" were over. The right-wingers of the party need not like the man or his political views, but they had to accept him. He had been re-elected in 1970 to a fourth term as governor of New York by a 730,000 plurality, the greatest in the state's history, and had served longer than anyone since George Clinton, New York's first governor. He was finally, at age sixty-four, an elder statesman. The Republican convention was keyed to the theme of "Four More Years" for Richard Nixon and, of course, for his running mate, Spiro Agnew. As for Nelson Rockefeller, Republicans were happy enough with the thought that he would remain in this niche: he could continue as governor of New York as long as he cared to.

But then there was Attica, that indelible black blot upon the kaleidoscope of Nelson Rockefeller's years as governor of New York. A singular, traumatic event, it captures the eye of the beholder, for, right or wrong, it was the bloodiest prison revolt in the nation's history: twenty-nine inmates and ten of their prison guard hostages were shot down and killed as New York State Police quashed a prisoners' rebellion. Criticism focused upon the governor, for he had refused the prisoners' demand to appear at the prison to negotiate personally with them. His critics could and did paint a picture in stereotypes of this wealthy man remaining secluded in his sumptuous estate at Pocantico Hills while poor men, black and white, were shot, gassed and manhandled. But the mistakes made, if any, were not those cited by the critics . . .

First word of the prison rebellion at Attica reached the governor shortly after it had begun on a Thursday morning, September 9, 1971. The news was relayed from Prison Commissioner Russell G. Oswald by the governor's personal secretary, Mrs. Ann Whitman, who interrupted him during a meeting of the Foreign Intelligence Advisory Board in Washington: the inmates (2,243 of them) had taken over Attica, were in virtually complete control and had taken 49 prison guards as hostages; standard operating procedure had been put into effect by the prison superintendent to regain control block by block; Commissioner Oswald was on his way there from Albany to supervise the operation.

Standard operating procedure called for a contingent of about one hundred State Police to enter a prison yard in a solid line, armed only with clubs, and then step by step force the prisoners back into their cells. The procedure also called for the prison commissioner, as the operations expert, to assume command of the situation, reporting to the governor as necessary.

The prison revolt did not come as a complete surprise to Nelson

Rockefeller. A month before, Commissioner Oswald had reported rumblings of an uprising to come somewhere in the state's four major prisons, instigated likely from the radical leftist and black movements which had recently moved their struggle against the Establishment from the streets of the ghettos to the prisons throughout the country holding large numbers of blacks and Puerto Ricans. Oswald had asked for more prison guards in anticipation; the governor had replied the state did not have the money.

The next word on Attica the governor received was that the State Police had succeeded in recapturing three of the four prison yards, had restored control over 962 prisoners and had freed 10 hostages. All well and good. Not a shot had been fired. The planned procedure had worked. Commissioner Oswald was on the scene: he had entered D Block, where some 1,200 rebellious prisoners were still gathered, in an attempt to negotiate the release of the remaining 39 hostages. That was not standard operating procedure.

The governor did not approve of negotiating under these circumstances. But he was not in a position to countermand his own commissioner at the scene. He felt he had to go along with him. He empathized with Oswald's concern for the prisoners. Three weeks earlier, Oswald had reported that many of the prisoners had legitimate complaints about the food (Black Muslims had religious scruples against eating pork, a staple prison diet) and other prison conditions.

What he did not know was that Commissioner Oswald felt he had little choice himself: he decided to negotiate because he had learned the prison militants had already brutalized some of the hostages, were threatening to kill all of them if attacked, and, moreover, he had too few State Police on hand to retake D Block without gunfire and massive bloodshed.

So, for the rest of the day and throughout the next day, Friday, Commissioner Oswald tried to negotiate. He agreed to rectify the prisoners' complaints and he promised no punitive reprisals for the uprising. The rebellion leaders did not believe him. He even sent someone by plane for a federal court order from a judge in Vermont, prohibiting the state of New York from making reprisals. The court order was torn up in the prison yard. The prisoners now demanded that observers be on hand to guarantee that there would be no reprisals. Observers poured into the melee, some named by the prisoners from the radical Black Panthers, the War Lords and more moderate organizations involved with prisoners' rights, while the state invited several black legislators and civic leaders; several attorneys who worked with minority groups came, including William Kunstler, known for his representation of radical defendants in historic trials. Then Tom Wicker of the New York *Times* joined the observers. In all, thirty-four outsiders comprised a Citizens Observer Committee at Attica, an unwieldy, divergent group of amateurs who never knew if they were there to observe or to mediate the conflict, or to protect the rights of the inmates, or to help negotiate the release of the hostages.

Whatever the true origins of the Attica revolt, whether it was a politicized radical uprising, as some say, or a spontaneous prison break, as others believe, with the advent of the more radical observers and the massive press and television coverage of the event, the Attica rebellion became truly politicized and polarized. The militant inmates now insisted that they were oppressed, political prisoners, not felons accused of homicides, armed robberies and the like, and they now added new demands. They wanted complete amnesty for any crimes committed during the rebellion and safe conduct out of the United States to a "non-imperialistic" country for those who wished to go.

All through the night and into the next day, Saturday, negotiations were conducted with the prisoners and within the observer group, and out of it all came a proposal for twenty-eight points of reform for Attica in exchange for the safe release of the hostages. They included a minimum $1.85 an hour wage for prison work, a prison ombudsman, political freedom and activity for prisoners, no censorship, no restrictions on outside communications, better food, medical treatment and more. Commissioner Oswald approved the twenty-eight points and upon his recommendation, Governor Rockefeller sent his approval.

The governor maintained contact with the authorities at the prison by telephone over the weekend from his home in Pocantico Hills. He received situation reports on the hour round the clock from 7 A.M. to midnight or 1 A.M. He never roamed more than a hundred feet from the telephone in his home office or on the terrace overlooking the Hudson River. This was his usual procedure down through the years. He went home for weekends and worked from there. Representing him personally at Attica were two of his closest personal advisers, T. Norman Hurd, his executive officer and second-in-command, and Robert Douglass, secretary to the Governor, who often served as his alter ego.

But Oswald and the governor rejected the prisoners' demands for amnesty and/or safe conduct out of the country. The prisoners rejected and jeered at the twenty-eight-point reform program. The deadlock was solid. The observers, the authorities and the prisoners, too, reached the threshold of nervous exhaustion. Then on that Saturday afternoon, Correction Officer William E. Quinn, who had been clubbed into submission at the outbreak of the uprising on Thursday and allowed to be carried out of the yard, died of a fractured skull at Rochester General Hospital. When word of his death reached the prisoners Saturday night, most of them realized that amnesty now was a forlorn hope: the governor could never forgive murder. The deadlock continued through the night. The thirty-eight remaining prison guards held hostage were blindfolded, with their hands tied behind their backs, and were guarded by Black Muslim prisoners against the threatened violence of other prisoners. But the other threat remained: unless the inmates were granted amnesty and safe conduct out of the United States, the hostages would be held; if the prisoners were attacked, all the hostages would be executed.

On Sunday, some members of the observer group, led by Tom Wicker, came up with a new idea: Governor Rockefeller could come to Attica, discuss the situation with the observers and perhaps break the deadlock. The proposal was thrashed out with Bob Douglass, who then relayed the proposal to the governor. The governor rejected it, saying there was nothing he could do at Attica that he could not do by telephone from Pocantico Hills. The key issue was amnesty and he could not and would not grant that. Further, he did not intend to undermine the position of the prison commissioner on the scene.

Later that afternoon, Tom Wicker telephoned the governor on his own and reviewed the situation. Other observers talked with the governor. He listened to all their arguments, but he was firm. What would be accomplished by his going to Attica that could not be accomplished otherwise? They could convince him of nothing—for they had no answers themselves. If they wanted more time to negotiate, they could have more time. But he would not yield to their demands. If he came to Attica, the prisoners would demand that he meet them in the prison yard, as they had done with Commissioner Oswald. Then what? He risked being taken hostage for no purpose. Suppose they demanded the President of the United States come to Attica? Then what?

He assured the citizens committee that he would give them all the time they needed to negotiate the freedom of the hostages and the restoration of order at the prison, but he was not about to bow to intemperate and intransigent demands of the rebel prisoners. Deeply concerned, he suffered increasing misgivings over Commissioner Oswald's attempts to persuade the prisoners to return to their cells in exchange for the state's promises of improved conditions at Attica. He was aware of the ramifications involved: any prison in the state or in the nation can be taken over by its inmates, the danger was always there; and if the Attica rebels succeeded, one could expect similar revolts at other prisons. Again, standard operating procedure called for the quashing of a prison revolt as swiftly and as forcibly as possible in order to discourage similar uprisings elsewhere. The state had sufficient force now at Attica to move swiftly on retaking the prison with the minimum loss of life. Waiting increased the risk to the hostages. But the decision on retaking the prison would have to be made at the scene by the state's prison expert, Commissioner Oswald.

The governor commiserated with the plight of Commissioner Oswald. He had spent his life in parole and prison rehabilitation work and had gained a reputation as one of the most humanitarian prison authorities in the nation. At Attica, he had done everything possible to avoid bloodshed. Three times he had entered the yard held by the prisoners at great personal risk. He had invited outsiders in, even allowing some radical leaders to talk with the prisoners. He had agreed to a long list of prison reforms. But nothing had worked. Only force remained, the course recommended from the start by the old-line prison authorities, who insisted that only force allowed a small number of correction officers to maintain control over a large number of confined and dangerous criminals.

Late that Sunday, Commissioner Oswald himself suggested that perhaps the governor should come to Attica, not because it would resolve the deadlock but rather for its public relations effect, proving to the public and television cameras that he, Nelson Rockefeller, had done everything in his power to resolve the deadlock without the use of force. Would it work? Did he think the prisoners would return to their cells? No. Then, said the governor, he would not come to Attica.

On Monday morning, the fifth day of the Attica rebellion, a last appeal to free the hostages was delivered to the inmates. They knew what was coming. In response, they paraded eight of their thirty-eight hostages on the roof of a tunnel in D Yard, each of them blindfolded, with hands tied behind his back, each escorted by an "executioner" with a knife at his throat. "Prepare for war!" the rebels yelled.

The war lasted fifteen minutes and the prison was retaken. The decisive weapon was CS gas dropped from a National Guard helicopter which began the battle at nine forty-five that Monday morning. CS gas, far more potent than ordinary tear gas, is a choking, disabling chemical which causes an unprotected person to double up with cramps almost immediately upon inhaling it. At the moment the gas was dispersed, eighteen police sharpshooters, armed with telescopic-sighted .270 rifles, opened fire on the "executioners." Three minutes later, 180 state troopers, wearing protective attire and armed with .12-gauge shotguns, entered into D Yard and fought their way through prisoners armed with makeshift knives, clubs and spears to reach the hostages, held in the farthest rear quadrant of the prison yard.

As the hostages were freed and led out of the yard, Bob Douglass counted them one by one for the governor on an open telephone line. The governor, at the phone in his New York City apartment, was initially delighted that twenty-eight of the thirty-eight hostages were rescued alive and well, although some of them had been slashed or cut. Then he learned that ten hostages had been killed and it was assumed and so reported to the newsmen on the scene that these ten had died at the hands of the rebels. Twenty-nine inmates had been killed in the retaking of the prison yard. Three other inmates had been knifed or clubbed to death by the rebels prior to the retaking of the prison, presumably for their opposition to the rebellion.

The immediate public reaction that first day was similar to that of the governor: it had turned out to be an unfortunate but successful venture, the best a reasonable person could expect from a basic "no win" situation; attempts to free the hostages and quell the rebellion by negotiation had failed; force as a last result had been used; men had died on both sides; but the lives of twenty-eight correction officers and employees had been saved; the rebellion of radicalized prison inmates had been put down.

The next day, however, autopsies revealed that each of the dead hostages had been killed not by the prisoners but by bullets of the State Police who had retaken the yard. Public opinion, to a large extent, turned around. Commissioner Oswald now was blamed for ordering the assault to retake the prison; Nelson Rockefeller was criticized by some and pilloried by the radical left for not having gone to Attica in person. The rights and wrongs involved may be argued for years to come. In the aftermath, Commissioner Oswald reflected that he entered the prison yard to negotiate, rather than use immediate force, because it never occurred to him that he might fail to persuade the prisoners to give up their hopeless quest for amnesty. Nelson Rockefeller, after scrutinizing the course of events at Attica, remained convinced that his own actions and decisions were appropriate for the situation. His only regret, as he expressed it later, was not having the opportunity of ordering the immediate effort to retake the prison. Once his prison commissioner had entered the prison yard and tried to negotiate with the rebels, it was too late for the governor to change direction. He would have been delighted if Oswald had succeeded, of course. On the other hand, as governor, he could not allow any small number of men, no matter how well organized, representing perhaps all shades of revolutionary ideology, to bring the established government to its knees by their threats to kill hostages. It would mean the start of the road to anarchy.

In 1973 Nelson chose not to seek a fifth term the following year. His decision had evolved just as slowly over a two-year period of time as did his first determination to run in 1958. Public speculation began soon after Richard Nixon's smashing re-election victory in 1972, which promised "a new majority" for the Republican Party, designed by the Nixon-Agnew administration, for years and years to come. No one could or did foresee the consequences of that "third-rate burglary" into the Democratic National Headquarters at an apartment complex called Watergate. For Nelson, the question was whether he could have more influence and impact in shaping the major events of the future by continuing as governor of New York or by branching out into something new.

The possibilities of something new were examined with care. A Cabinet post of stature in the new Nixon administration—Secretary of State, or Defense—would have been carefully considered and probably accepted.

Or perhaps an extraordinary post overseas—such as America's first envoy or ambassador to the People's Republic of China. But no such offer came. He was too strong, too popular and too independent a public figure for the Nixon administration. For the same reason, he did not really expect a call from the President when Spiro Agnew suddenly resigned in October 1973, having pleaded no contest to a charge of tax evasion involving alleged bribes in his home state of Maryland, and the nation was in need of a new Vice-President. Nelson would have liked such a call, but it never came. Realistically, he understood that Nixon, himself under fire over the Watergate scandals, needed a Vice-President who was influential with the House of Representatives. Representative Gerald Ford of Michigan was the man who fitted the need and he got the invitation. As for Nelson at the time, he was sixty-five years old, mellowed by age and by a happy home life with two young, beloved sons. Political warfare at the state level in Albany held less allure for him now that he had served almost four terms. He had already begun in 1972 to think of forming expert study commissions on the long-range problems of the nation. On a personal level, he felt he owed Malcolm Wilson, his lieutenant governor for so many years, a crack at the governorship. It had been promised at the start of Nelson's political career so long ago. But even more important to him than the personal aspects of the decision, Nelson had the deep feeling that the nation, with its attention focused on the Watergate scandals, was drifting once again at the mercy of events, without the benefit of long-range planning. Thus, he saw a special need which he, in his special position, could fill. And so he came around to the decision which he "felt" was the right one for him.

"I have decided not to seek a fifth term as governor of New York," he announced from Albany on December 11, 1973. "I will resign next Tuesday, after fifteen years of service to the people of New York. At that time, Lieutenant Governor Malcolm Wilson will be sworn in as governor.

"We live in critical times. I have great faith in our country and I'm optimistic about the future."

That was his theme throughout the day and he held to it steadfastly in the days, weeks and months which were to follow: at a time when the people of the United States were torn, bewildered and skeptical as they never had been before over the most disastrous war in the nation's history, the worst scandals involving unethical and illegal behavior—tape-recorded in the Oval Office of the President—and an economic situation of inflation and recession which hurt almost everyone's pocketbook, Nelson Rockefeller would proclaim his optimism about the future and his faith in the survival of the nation's way of life.

He announced that he intended to devote the next two years of his life to leading two national bipartisan study commissions: a forty-one-member Commission on Critical Choices for Americans, which would analyze alternatives in solving the long-range fundamental problems facing the United States in the fields of energy, ecology, economics, international relations, population, food supply, health and the over-all quality of life; and a fifteen-member National Commission on Water Quality, which would involve the study of every river and water basin in the country. To the skeptics at the press conference, he insisted the two commissions were not a "gimmick" or a "political trick" to advance himself in the 1976 presidential race. "Whether I will become a candidate in the future, I do not know," he declared. "I should like to keep my options open."

He meant what he said. He was not about to renounce his availability and the possibility of one day becoming President and thus lose the political power which flows to any man who might one day be President. Privately, however, he had decided that he could no longer seek the Republican nomination; his party would have to seek him, if and when the necessity arose. In fact, what he did do is what he had said he would: he immersed himself in the organization, the staffing and the work of his two commissions, especially Critical Choices, which in time produced volumes of studies, analyses and recommendations as a guide to actions upon a broad range of fundamentals affecting life in America. His preoccupation in national and international affairs was so complete and deliberate that, to the surprise of many, he maintained a hands-off attitude toward New York State politics and government, which he had dominated for fifteen years.

Along with the whole nation, Nelson witnessed the slow but steady disintegration of the Nixon administration over the Watergate scandals. Facing imminent impeachment in the House of Representatives, Richard M. Nixon announced his resignation as the thirty-seventh President of the United States. Vice-President Ford was sworn in as President the next day, and the nation suddenly faced once again the need of a new Vice-President.

Nelson, a private citizen for a mere eight months, suddenly found himself heading press speculations as to likely candidates. Virtually all political observers noted that he was the man eminently most qualified: he had thirty-four years' experience in government, had proven his ability as an administrator, had demonstrated his knowledge of state and local government as the senior governor in the country and had widespread influence with civic, business, labor and cultural leaders throughout the country. Moreover, a labeled "liberal Republican," he would give political balance to the Ford administration as it groped its way into the confidence of the American people. This time, the right-wing conservatives notwithstanding, the Republican Party had need of the man.

In the eleven days President Ford considered the question, Nelson remained virtually secluded with his family at his vacation home on Mount Desert Island in Maine. He worked each day on a bulging briefcase of memos, papers and problems of his two commissions. He taught his sons how to cook over a campfire. He swam and took long walks with his wife. And during it all, he considered all the aspects involved in the vice-presidency. Having known personally all the Vice-Presidents of the United States since Henry Wallace, who served under FDR, Nelson suffered no misconceptions about the job and the lack of power of the office. The power and influence of the Vice-President were what the President wanted them to be. No more, no less. Yet Nelson had worked with Gerry Ford on several occasions over the years and the two had liked and trusted one another. Ford was, indeed, still serving as a member of Nelson's Commission on Critical Choices. Nevertheless, despite all the speculation in the press how Nelson Rockefeller as Vice-President might overshadow President Ford because of their initial disparity in governmental experience, Nelson knew that as Vice-President his activities and influence in the new administration would be limited to what President Ford wanted them to be. He trusted that the President realized it too. His own job would be to serve the President. Fourteen years before, he had rejected the offer when Richard Nixon had virtually pleaded with him to be his running mate in 1960. Then he had felt and said he was not made to be "standby equipment." In 1968, he had been offered the vice-presidential nomination by Hubert Humphrey, to run against Richard Nixon. Nelson had replied that he was not about to switch political parties for any such reason. In 1974, however, the vice-presidency seemed to offer him the opportunity and the challenge to serve in a position and at a time when he was truly needed and could exert a positive influence upon the immediate course of events affecting the lives of 200 million people. Nelson concluded that if the offer came, he would accept. He was thoroughly relaxed about it. He put out the word that he wanted his friends to refrain from lifting a finger to help him get the nomination. The decision was that of the President to make.

The call came Thursday evening from Alexander M. Haig, chief of staff in the White House. "The President would like to talk with you sometime tomorrow. Will you be available?"

Nelson stared across his living room at the view of the Atlantic Ocean beyond after he had put down the phone. Then, snapping out of his reverie, he remarked to the one aide in the room, "That's it. I've got to tell Happy."

The couple took a long walk through the woods familiar to Nelson since his childhood. He explained. Happy agreed that of course he had to accept. She and the boys understood. They might have preferred for selfish reasons that the offer never came. Hadn't Nelson Jr. told Arthur Goldberg that he hoped he would win the governorship in 1970 so that "Daddy could stay home more." But Happy knew her husband well enough to know his own happiness depended upon his being in the thick of things all the time. Nelson sympathized with the sacrifices they made for him. Before the walk was over, he promised that as best he could he would reserve weekends for her and the boys. They would have to live in Washington, but they could fly home to Pocantico Hills every weekend.

The President called early the next afternoon. "We are seriously thinking of asking you to accept the vice-presidency," was how the President put it. The offer was subject to what ordinarily would have been a routine check by the Federal Bureau of Investigation. That routine check now assumed vital importance in view of closet skeletons in the lives of Spiro Agnew and Senator Thomas Eagleton, of Missouri, who was dropped by Senator George McGovern in the midst of the 1972 presidential campaign. "Is there anything which could be a bar to it with you?" asked President Ford.

"Nothing I can think of," said Nelson.

The President went on to discuss his hopes of Nelson's playing a prominent part in his administration, particularly in overseeing the work of the Domestic Council, a key group advising the President on domestic issues, as the National Security Council does on international relations. Nelson was delighted. They set the date of the announcement: Tuesday at 10 A.M. in the Oval Office.

Nelson passed that first FBI check. On that Tuesday morning, August 20, 1974, he was nominated by President Ford to become the forty-first Vice-President of the United States. The President introduced him as "a good partner for me and I think a good partner for our country and the world."

The President's choice was generally greeted with approval and praise from all over, with only a scattering of grudging remarks from the conservatives, but what then ensued over the next four months was undoubtedly the most extensive investigation ever made into the life, career, finances and qualifications of any man to hold high office in the United States. More than five hundred FBI agents scoured the country and delved deep into Latin America, seeking anyone who could cite reasons why Nelson Rockefeller might not be qualified to be Vice-President of the United States. They spoke to his first wife, they interviewed political opponents, they traced his landholdings in the mountains of Venezuela. Nelson himself supplied the Rules Committee of the U. S. Senate and the Judiciary Committee of the House with a lengthy summary of his life. He produced a statement of his net worth, a list of all his assets, stocks and bonds, trusts, real estate holdings. He turned over all his tax records for the past ten years, listing his annual incomes and income taxes, his gifts and his gift taxes, his contributions to charity and to political campaigns.

For the members of the congressional committees and, indeed, for the country as a whole, it all provided a field day of fishing and exploring into the private financial affairs of perhaps the most prominent of all wealthy men in America. In a sense, it was a historic occasion, for never before has a man of such wealth given away so much in information. Certainly, old John D. and John D. Rockefeller, Jr., had been on witness stands before and had been questioned on their financial transactions, but in those days, they took prideful delight in answering questions without revealing too much information. To this day, the net worth of Nelson's grandfather has never been revealed, only estimated. But Nelson, being in public life, had long believed that if pertinent a man seeking public office had an obligation to reveal any and all information which would demonstrate no conflict of interest. He had been prepared in the California presidential primary campaign of 1964 to reveal his net wealth and tax returns. He had the data prepared, but no one asked.

He did not begrudge the information ten years later when he submitted his financial records to Congress, but he did bridle when bits and pieces were leaked to the press which tended to distort the over-all picture before his confirmation hearings had scarcely begun. In fact, he welcomed the chance to destroy what he called "the myth or misconception" of Rockefeller control or influence over large segments of the American economy.

The fundamental question before the Congress, in confirming or rejecting the nomination, was whether or not Nelson Rockefeller's stockholdings in American businesses were so great and widespread as to make his public duties an inevitable conflict of interest. So it should have created quite a surprise, but in fact caused hardly a ripple, when he revealed that his net worth was $62,581,225, of which more than half ($33,561,325) was the estimated market value of his art collection. His annual income averaged $4.6 million, and was derived from the two trust funds established by his father, then worth $116.5 million, of which he was a lifetime beneficiary but which he did not control. He also revealed that his wife, Happy, owned $3.8 million in securities and trust funds, while his six children held assets of $35.6 million and most of that in trust.

"I've got to tell you," he told Senate Rules Committee Chairman Howard W. Cannon of Nevada, "I don't wield economic power." He pointed out that he owned no more than two tenths of 1 per cent of the outstanding shares in any oil company; he owned no shares in Chase Manhattan Bank; and neither he nor any other Rockefeller sat on the board of any oil company.

Nelson Rockefeller's list of stocks and bonds, including those in his trust funds, appeared to outside analysts as an ordinary, conservative portfolio of blue chips, a representative slice of America, which had suffered drastically in the recent stock market plunge, perhaps to the extent of one third of its previous value. But more important for Nelson Rockefeller, his portfolio revealed no area whatsoever of a conflict of interest. Here his caution over the years prevailed: since first taking public office in 1958, he had instructed his money managers to "bend over backward" to avoid any stock purchases which had even a potential conflict of interest for him. Upon confirmation, all his assets would be placed in a blind trust, beyond his control and knowledge, he pledged.

The Rockefeller family concern for what is "appropriate" also had led them through the years to arrange their financial affairs so that each of them did pay "appropriate" income taxes, even when there were legal ways to avoid them. With Richard Nixon's tax troubles in the background, the congressional committees looked with care into Nelson Rockefeller's tax returns. They found that for the past ten years, from 1964 through 1973, with a total income of $46.8 million, this Rockefeller had paid $21.7 million in federal, state and local taxes and had given $14.6 million to philanthropic and charitable organizations. During his lifetime, he had paid $69 million in taxes, made charitable contributions of $33 million and pledged another $20.5 million of art and real estate to be given upon his death. Despite those sizable amounts, he apologized profusely for not having owed or paid any federal income taxes in one year, 1970, because of stock transactions in one of his trusts; instead, that year the trust paid $6,250,000 in capital gains taxes, and he paid a mere $814,701 in other assorted taxes. As it turned out later, when the routine audit of his 1970 taxes was completed, he did have federal income taxes to pay that year after all.

For five days he testified before the Senate Rules Committee and for another five days before the House Judiciary Committee, averaging more than five hours a day, and although both committees were dominated by the opposition party, Nelson Rockefeller turned in a virtuoso performance, perhaps the finest public appearance of his career. With aplomb, he displayed a wide-ranging, in-depth knowledge and judgment on every conceivable subject upon which he was questioned. A New York *Times* analysis of the first day's hearing in the Senate, by James M. Naughton, captured the general atmosphere of all the hearings: "Some had expected the proceedings to become a significant exploration of the extent to which one individual—or, at least, one American family—might influence the course of national policy through its wealth. But the Senate hearings seemed, at least on their opening day, more an opportunity for the 66-year-old Mr. Rockefeller to display his self-assurance and preparedness . . . This time it was the witness who seemed in charge."

With the sensitivity over unethical campaign practices which followed the Watergate scandals, two subjects did arise at the hearings to embarrass the nominee. One was his authorization of the financing of a critical biography on his 1970 gubernatorial opponent, former Supreme Court justice Arthur J. Goldberg, which was then distributed at the Rockefeller campaign headquarters. At a message from Nelson, his brother Laurance had invested $60,000 through a dummy Philadelphia corporation to finance the publication of the biography, by Victor Lasky. "Let's face it—I made a mistake," he told the Senate committee. "It was a hasty, ill-considered decision in the middle of a hectic campaign in 1970." Both he and his brother Laurance apologized publicly to Justice Goldberg.

On the other issue, which dominated a good portion of the hearings, Nelson made no apologies. Over the previous seventeen years, while in public office, he had given almost $2 million ($1,972,078) in cash gifts to twenty men and women who were either present or former public officials or staff assistants. In addition, he had made loans of $507,656 to friends, associates and family members—including his wife and some of his children—of which $147,733 had not then been repaid. The question posed in the minds of the committee and the public was whether these gifts were bribes, gratuities, pressures to influence or strictly gifts made by a man who could well afford them. Most of the gifts were given first as loans which were later forgiven. Then Nelson paid gift taxes on the amounts, so that the recipients could keep the whole of what had been given. The gift taxes totaled about $840,000.

"Throughout my life, I have made loans and gifts to friends and associates to assist them in meeting the kinds of pressing human needs which all people have from time to time—problems such as severe illness and medical expenses, marital problems, education of children, problems of adolescents, problems of relocation, problems of meeting one's obligations to aged parents, and problems that have to be faced after retirement," he explained. "In many cases there were special human circumstances that dictated urgency of action, and I responded simply out of friendship and affection."

He had given $50,000 outright to Henry Kissinger when the Harvard professor had left his employ to join the Nixon administration, so that he could set up an education trust fund for his two children. He had given $31,000 in gifts and $145,000 in loans, of which $45,000 had been repaid, to Edward J. Logue, chairman of the Urban Development Corporation, to help him relocate to New York and to pay off several personal loans in Massachusetts. But the largest and most controversial loan-gift was made to his long-time chief aide, William J. Ronan—a gift of $75,000 when he agreed in 1958 to become secretary to the governor, and then a series of six loans, ranging from $50,000 to $150,000 for a total of $510,000, all of which were forgiven when Dr. Ronan left his $75,000-a-year post as chairman of the Metropolitan Transit Authority to become the unsalaried chairman of the New York-New Jersey Port Authority. To cap it off, at the time, he made another $40,000 gift to Dr. Ronan, for a grand total over the seventeen years of $625,000.

"The gifts were made to Dr. Ronan in recognition of our long friendship, his pressing family responsibilities and problems, and to assist him in meeting continuing financial responsibilities after retirement," Nelson declared. Bill Ronan was, in effect, the most effective "brain trust" behind Nelson Rockefeller as governor, and he faced repeated temptations to quit government service for private industry, where he could not only earn more money but also could put more aside in pension and retirement benefits. Nelson, who had the money, lent him varying sums for investments to keep him by his side in government. The important point was that Dr. Ronan and all of the other recipients had all been in his employ and answerable to him, they all shared the same objectives in government service and there was not nor could there be any conflict of interest or bribery involved.

"What I must say to you now, and what I do say to you now," he told the Senate committee, "is that not one of the gifts or loans I have made, not one of the loans I have forgiven during my lifetime was designed to corrupt or did corrupt either the receiver or the giver."

He went to great pains in explaining the Rockefeller ethic of stewardship of the wealth in its possession and he quoted his father's creed that "Every right implies a responsibility; every opportunity, an obligation; every possession, a duty." Asserting that his own successes in life were due largely to the help given him by the men and women who worked with him in a sense of common purpose, he insisted: "What kind of human being would I be if, under the circumstances, I had not returned their confidence, affection and commitment, if I had not welcomed opportunities to be helpful to them in their needs . . . ?"

Acknowledging cynicism and suspicion of abuses of trust in high placcs in the minds of the public, he declared firmly: "But I do not believe the day has yet come in this great country of ours where the decencies of human relationships disqualify one for public office."

The United States Senate confirmed the nomination by a vote of 90 to 7; the House of Representatives confirmed 287 to 128, and Nelson Aldrich Rockefeller, grandson of the founder of Standard Oil, on December 19, 1974, was sworn in as the forty-first Vice-President of the United States. The ceremony and its underlying implications were awesome, televised to the nation for the first time from the chambers of the U. S. Senate. The elected leaders of the Congress were there, on view, as the Chief Justice of the United States administered the oath of office to the new Vice-President, marking the official and final end to the Nixon administration and the disgrace of corruption in high office. The nation now had a new President and Vice-President, free, clear and clean of the scandals which had forced the resignations of their predecessors. For the first time, a President and a Vice-President had not been elected by the people of the United States. But, on the other hand, both had been thoroughly investigated, approved and confirmed in office by the people's representatives in the Congress under the new Twenty-fifth Amendment to the Constitution. The transition had been smooth and solemn. The democratic organization of this government worked. Nelson Rockefeller, for all his sophistication and long experience in politics and in ceremonial functions, was clearly moved. Tears welled in his eyes after he took the oath of office. He blew a soft kiss to his wife and the two sons of their marriage, sitting in the visitors' gallery.

During those four long months of confirmation hearings, Happy Rockefeller had discovered a lump in her left breast, having given herself a self-examination prompted by President Ford's wife's mastectomy a week earlier. Three nodules were found to be cancerous and the breast was removed; five weeks later, she lost the other breast as well to surgery for cancer. She had also lost any claim to privacy. Nelson, being in the public eye at the time and sensitive to any possible charges of cover-up, felt it incumbent upon himself to announce the first operation while it was still going on, before anyone else would make it public. In that way, he could stifle any rumors and emphasize the positive: the doctors gave Happy a better than 90 per cent chance of full recovery.

"I feel great and I'm thankful," the forty-eight-year-old Mrs. Rockefeller said upon leaving Memorial Hospital for Cancer and Allied Diseases for the second time on Thanksgiving Day. "Take heart and don't be afraid," was her message to the women of America.

Those four tumultuous months in the life of Nelson Rockefeller came as close as could be to the old cliché of washing one's linen in public. They affected the whole Rockefeller family. To help Nelson, the family had agreed to submit an aggregate listing of all stocks and securities held by all the members of the family. Nelson's niece, Abby Milton O'Neill, serving as hostess at the family employees' Christmas party that year, summed it up in a single quip: "Never have so many known so much about so few."

In office as the Vice-President, Nelson set out deliberately to maintain a low profile, as much as was humanly possible for him. Such was his reputation at the time that there spread throughout Washington and into the country fervid speculation and gossip that President Ford intended to resign in favor of his new Vice-President. To counter such rumors, the President was obliged to insist repeatedly that indeed he fully intended to seek election to a full term in office in 1976, and to have Nelson Rockefeller as his running mate. Nelson, for his part, went even further: he announced his pleasure with the President's personal decision and declared that neither he nor his friends would put any pressure upon the President in selecting his running mate in 1976. His political posture was that of one who is a member of the Ford team, nothing more. With a tight rein upon his usually forceful personality, he fought back temptations to exceed the limits of his own office. This did not prevent him from working his usual sixteen-hour day, presiding over the U. S. Senate, heading the Domestic Council, serving on the National Security Council, recruiting competent

men and women to serve in the new administration, working behind the
scenes to devise new domestic legislative programs, taking on special assignments from the President, all in addition to the usual diet of ceremonial and touring duties of the Vice-President. Through it all, however,
Nelson kept his personal pledge to Happy: they returned home to Pocantico Hills for the weekends. When weekend duties intruded, he com-
muted by helicopter from his back lawn and by *Air Force II* from Westchester airport.

In Washington, the Nelson Rockefellers moved into the new official
home for Vice-Presidents, the Admiral's House, on the grounds of the
U. S. Naval Observatory. He helped renovate the old, rather dilapidated
Victorian home, hung some of his modern paintings, gave nine "opening"
dinner partes and then quietly moved back into his own more comfortable
Washington home on Foxhall Road, which he had kept ever since his first
days in Washington thirty-odd years before.

As he settled in on his new job, he came to realize that he had indeed
lost the bureaucratic battle for power within the Ford administration before he had even begun to fight. The four-month hiatus due to his long
confirmation hearings had been enough time for the new Ford White
House staff to solidify the organization and structure of the White House
day-to-day operations. By the time Nelson Rockefeller was sworn in, he
was a fifth wheel in a mechanism designed to ride on four. Like all Vice-
Presidents before him, he was an added appendage to the structure of government with no constitutional responsibilities within the Executive
Branch, and any reach for power would be bitterly resisted by members of
the White House staff who might lose that power.

His relationship with President Ford remained cordial and close. As
promised when he had first accepted the post, Nelson was given responsibility for the Domestic Council, which he thought would give him primary responsibility for recommending domestic policy in the Ford administration. But on the job, he found that President Ford had fully adopted
the staff system within the White House. He would hear Nelson out on
his proposals, puffing on his pipe, remaining noncommittal, and then assign the proposal to a member of his staff for further action. And that
would be the end of it. For a pragmatic activist like Nelson Rockefeller,
the process was a slow torture of frustration. One of the very few Rockefeller proposals which survived the Ford staff was Nelson's recommendation for the establishment of an Energy Independence Authority, a
quasi-public finance agency empowered to float up to $100 billion in
bonds for the development of new energy sources within the United
States, designed to free this country from dependence upon Arab oil. That
proposal was sent to Congress with President Ford's blessings, and there it
too gathered dust.

As head of a special commission to conduct the first investigation of the Central Intelligence Agency, Nelson Rockefeller did make an important if not lasting contribution in the effort to curtail the power of the CIA. As head of the Domestic Council, he conducted public hearings on domestic policy in key cities throughout the United States and his recommendations were included in President Ford's State of the Union address in 1976. But after that, he bowed out of the Domestic Council and faced the reality of his position in Washington.

The beginning of the end came unexpectedly with the appointment of Howard (Bo) Calloway as chairman of the Committee to Elect Ford to a full term as President. Nelson had not been consulted. Calloway, a conservative opponent from past political wars, lost little time in announcing to the press that Nelson Rockefeller was his "worst problem" politically in the effort to win the Republican nomination for Ford. The Calloway political strategy called for the President to pick a conservative for Vice-President and head off the challenge of Ronald Reagan, California's ex-governor and totem figure spearheading the conservatives' crusade of 1976. Rockefeller was seen as too liberal to satisfy the ever more powerful right wing of the Republican Party. So, in November of 1975, with the political pressures far outweighing the rewards of the office, Nelson carried his letter of future resignation into the Oval Office, while one of his aides released the text to the wire services. There would be no turning back. The letter asked the President not to consider him, Nelson Rockefeller, as a possible nominee for Vice-President in 1976. He was stepping aside, freeing the President to win over the conservatives who objected to Rockefeller. The President accepted his Vice-President's decision with a puff on his pipe, an expression of regret and an attitude of neutrality on what was seen then as the practicalities of politics. The strategy was short-lived and doomed to fail. Ronald Reagan battled the President through the primaries and right into the Kansas City convention in August. The irony of the whole situation could not be seen at the time. No one could have guessed that Ronald Reagan, in his own effort to broaden his appeal and to win the Republican nomination, would choose as his running mate Senator Richard S. Schweiker of Pennsylvania, the most liberal Republican in the U. S. Senate, whose voting record had won the complete approval of the AFL-CIO and almost as much from the Americans for Democratic Action. That had been Ford's original reason for choosing Nelson Rockefeller in 1974, to broaden his own support throughout the country with a liberal running mate, but that gamble, once won, had been allowed to fritter away. Overall, the talents, appeal and usefulness of Nelson Rockefeller had been wasted. When political speculation once again turned to Nelson Rockefeller on the eve of the Republican convention, Nelson informed the President that he wanted none of it, that he would campaign for Ford, but that he himself had family obligations back home that he could no longer neglect. He did not want to be considered as a possible nominee for Vice-President.

Emotionally and intellectually, he had already put Washington behind him. His mind once again was dwelling on the future. He still saw no point to looking backward. He began to tell before- and after-dinner jokes on his accomplishments as Vice-President of the United States. His real and lasting accomplishment in office, he related, was to have redesigned the seal of the Vice-President of the United States: "I lifted the wings of the Vice-President's eagle, that's what I did."

In a "last hurrah" as odd man out at the Republican National Convention of 1976, Nelson addressed his fellow Republicans in a spirit of levity, nostalgia over past political battles and a call for future harmony. He really was past caring. But he was determined to show no sign of bitterness. Cavorting later with the New York delegation on the convention floor, he grabbed a Ronald Reagan placard from a passing supporter and ripped it up. Another Reagan supporter retaliated by tearing out the New York delegation's telephone. Nelson Rockefeller, enjoying himself and grinning from ear to ear, held the useless white telephone aloft for all the television audience to see. Still later, while campaigning for President Ford in New York, the Vice-President of the United States responded to a persistent heckler with that classical gesture of the street, the raised middle finger, signifying: "Up yours!" The gesture, well publicized in the press, dismayed many of his fellow Republicans. It was unseemly for a man in his position to do such a thing. But it did demonstrate once again that Nelson Rockefeller was still his own man, beholden to no one, as irrepressible at age sixty-eight as he had been as a little boy in Pocantico Hills.

Back home in the Rockefeller family estate in Pocantico Hills, the American flag is raised alongside the private tennis courts every day that Nelson is in residence, and home is where his heart is as he looks forward still to the future. Nelson Rockefeller, love him or hate him, has enjoyed a full, active, stimulating life which has had a significant impact upon this nation—more than that of any of his brothers, more than that of most men anywhere—and he can look back, if ever he finds the time, to a personal history of accomplishment, of having overcome in his lifetime the obstacles of wealth and privilege, as others have the obstacles of poverty. It is more likely, however, that Nelson Rockefeller will be looking forward to whatever opportunities and to whatever doors open for him in the future.

20

John 3rd

"This is an exciting time to be alive."

"Let us in all our lands—including this land—face forthrightly the multiplying problems of our multiplying populations and seek the answers to this most profound challenge to the future of all the world."

Thus spoke Lyndon Baines Johnson, President of the United States, setting forth a new national policy to the world at the General Assembly of the United Nations on June 25, 1965. The man behind those words was John D. Rockefeller 3rd. For twelve years he had devoted much of his daily life to convincing America—and, in fact, the whole world—that family planning, birth control and the stabilization of population growth were of paramount importance toward the well-being of mankind.

He strove to have the United States government take the lead. But in the 1950s, President Eisenhower had rejected the idea outright, holding that government had no right to interfere in the private lives of people and there was nothing more private than the number of children a man and wife might decide to have. The Kennedy administration gave some aid to John 3rd's efforts to foster family planning abroad, but it did so quietly as part of its foreign aid program and without the resolution of a national policy. It was only when Lyndon Johnson took office, only when the concept had won considerable acceptance where it was most applicable, in the Far East, that the federal government became more amenable to the one-man lobby on population stabilization in the person of John D. Rockefeller 3rd. Perhaps it was that the time for this idea had finally arrived; perhaps it was that John 3rd was better connected than ever before with men of high rank in the government, men like Secretary of State Dean Rusk, who had been president of the Rockefeller Foundation, or

John Gardner, Secretary of Health, Education and Welfare, who had been president of the Carnegie Foundation, men who knew John 3rd personally, knew that this low-key, self-effacing, humble man with the famous name had the persistence of a bulldog with his grip on a concept few others seemed able to grasp.

The concept, considering its import, was relatively simple and unassailable: the rate of population growth around the world, and particularly in the underdeveloped nations, was consistently outstripping economic and agricultural growth. Furthermore, it was aided and abetted by the decline in the death rate due to improved public health and medical research. Consequently, the standards of living and the quality of life of people were not improving and would not improve as years went on. Hardly anyone could argue with that. But no one quite knew then how to go about reducing the birth rate significantly enough to make a difference. Furthermore, the rate of population growth was a long-range problem, politically sensitive and in conflict with age-old traditions in the farmlands of the world, in conflict with the teachings of the Catholic Church and, finally, not an immediate crisis warranting immediate action.

For twelve long years before President Johnson spoke out on the subject, John 3rd went about the country trying to prod the government, business and civic leaders, philanthropic organizations and individual leaders to take up this cause. As much as he cringed from public speaking, he addressed group after group, testified before congressional committees, sat down to talk with key men in government. His message, in one form or another, followed the same line of reasoning:

"No problem is more urgently important to the well-being of mankind than the fast-rising world population. The grim mathematics are often recited but, like the warning symptoms of cancer, are too often disregarded. It took all of recorded time until the 1840s for the world to achieve a population of 1 billion, but less than a century to add the second, and only thirty years to add the third. At today's rate of increase, the world population will reach 4 billion by 1975, and 7 billion by the year 2000.

"No area of human concern, from agriculture to zoology, can ignore this accelerating increase. As a challenge to our generation, I regard the stabilization of population growth as comparable to the control of nuclear weapons. The atomic bomb is sudden, an act of violence; overpopulation is more subtle, like a wasting illness. But both endanger human life, or perhaps more important, life as men would want to live it.

"Upon our response to this challenge depends the preservation of those fundamental values that give meaning to life and dignity to the individual. So rapid is the growth of population, and so serious are its consequences, that ours may be the last generation to have a chance to cope with the problem on the basis of free choice."

John 3rd never did like to make speeches; he was too self-conscious to feel comfortable addressing groups, large or small. He did not like to be up front, a spectacle to be stared at. In any group photograph, John D. Rockefeller 3rd will always be found standing inconspicuously in the rear. He much preferred the one-to-one situation. In the privacy of an office he could explain his position and the facts and figures pertaining to his favorite subject, population stabilization. In his personal aversion to ostentation, he himself was unaware of the trouble he would cause his staff in arranging transportation and accommodations for his various trips.

On one trip to Washington, for a meeting at the White House, John 3rd had not only disdained a limousine to carry him from the airport to the White House, but he had also rejected the idea of hiring a car for the short trip. Flying tourist class, with barely enough time to make his appointment on time, he discovered at National Airport that his secretary's warnings had been accurate: it was raining there, and he could not find a taxicab *or* a car to hire. So he rented the only vehicle available and was driven to the west gate of the White House as the solitary occupant of a sight-seeing bus.

At the reception desk, the appointment secretary asked his name.

"John Rockefeller," he replied. The middle initial, in his opinion, also smacked of ostentation.

"Whom are you with, sir?" asked the receptionist, checking his appointment list. The question stumped the bewildered grandson of Standard Oil for the moment. "Why, eh, eh, no one," he replied. "I'm alone."

In a certain, sad sense, John D. Rockefeller 3rd had always been alone. All who know him attest to his happy marriage, his loving and supportive wife, son and three daughters, all of whom have turned out well and given him pleasure. Yet, away from his family, he seems to have no friends who are merely friends, he spends little time in mere social pleasantries. His relaxing activities are solitary, horseback riding in Pocantico Hills, chopping wood or sailing in Maine, all of which have the salutary side effect of being healthful and therefore useful. On trips, he gives little if any time to pleasure or sight-seeing. If it is a fact-finding trip, he wants to search out the facts seven days a week; if a departure is delayed an hour or two, he wants to fit in another appointment. Back home, his social life is based upon one philanthropic activity or another. Whether or not he is actually lonely, however, is debatable. By nature, he likes to be alone, he likes to work alone, going over reports by himself in his office or at home or while on vacation. He reads and digests material slowly and, according to his associates, he has a remarkable, selective memory. He may seem to forget something you told him two days ago, but he will remember a particular point that interested him two years ago. His strength as a mover of people and ideas lies in his persistence and his never forgetting a point he wished to get across. At board of directors meetings at the Rockefeller Foundation, at a local hospital, in the Asia Society or in population-minded groups, he will make his point gently and if it is not picked up by others, he will let it go by, never trying to force his ideas on others. But the following month or the following year before the same group he will make the same point, sounding out usually the same directors until he has won a consensus. "He can bear defeat after defeat," said one close associate, "but he keeps coming back, indefatigably, until defeat is turned usually to victory."

John 3rd believes in action by committee, action by a group of citizens with common purpose banding together to try to solve a problem facing all of them. He considers it one of the major strengths in the political and social structure of American democracy and he likes to quote De Tocqueville's *Democracy in America* (written in the nineteenth century) to the effect that the Americans are a peculiar people in that when they have a problem they turn not to their government but to themselves as private citizens, they form a committee and go about solving that problem themselves. America is the only country that has such a tradition, says John 3rd.

So when John 3rd failed again and again and again in his attempts to persuade the Rockefeller Foundation, of which he was a senior trustee, to take on the population question, he decided finally to do it himself, to gather up a group of citizens in a committee focused on the world's population explosion. He himself was convinced of the need. Nevertheless, he was aware that few others agreed with him. At the time, in 1952, there was little concern among government or civic leaders here or abroad. There were no programs designed to limit population growth. There were precious few trained personnel in the field and certainly no central organization to coordinate activities. Nor was there any indication of any such activity in the future. In fact, population stabilization really boiled down to birth control, and in 1952 that was still such a sensitive subject it just was not discussed in polite Establishment circles. Family advisers on philanthropy cautioned John 3rd against taking any precipitous action on so delicate a subject, lest his activities and purposes be misinterpreted.

John 3rd, cautious as ever, knew of the drawbacks involved. He did not want to form a committee on population merely out of personal interest or whim. If there were no real need, his venture would fail for lack of sustaining support.

To allay his own misgivings, he consulted an old colleague, a man he had known and worked with for years, one of the most eminent and knowledgeable scientists in the country, Dr. Detlev W. Bronk, president of the Rockefeller Institute for Medical Research, a trustee of the Rockefeller Brothers Fund and, as it so happened at the time, president of the National Academy of Sciences. Dr. Bronk, shrewd in the ways of the world and understanding the concern involved, set up a conference under

the auspices of the National Academy in June in the beautiful spring setting of Colonial Williamsburg. Some thirty Academy members, men eminent in medicine, physics, public health, demography, biology, economics,
conservation, nutrition, psychology and public affairs, spent three days
considering the "available facts and conflicting views about the effects of
population growth on human welfare." The conference ended with the
adoption of a single resolution: there was a need for a private, unofficial
organization to focus its attention on population problems "at a high level
of professional competence and public esteem."

That was the mandate John D. Rockefeller 3rd wanted. These eminent men of science had examined the situation impartially and had concluded there was a *need*, and he, John D. 3rd, could *respond* to that need.

John 3rd moved with dispatch, setting his own staff to work and himself lining up an outstanding board of trustees, which of course included
Frank Notestein, the professor of demography at Princeton who had been
John's mentor on the subject for years. Dr. Bronk agreed to join, as did
Karl Compton, the physicist, and Lewis L. Strauss, the former chairman
of the Atomic Energy Commission. After some persuasion, John 3rd
agreed to serve as the organization's first president and chairman of the
board. For chief operating officer and vice-president, John found an old
friend, one of the most admired figures in the social sciences, Frederick
Osborn, a scholar-gentleman who had quit Wall Street in the 1930s before
the age of forty to devote the rest of his life to promoting the study of
man.

The new organization was called the Population Council and its objectives and scope of activities were quickly spelled out. These men knew
what was needed to attack the population problem: to advance knowledge
in the field, to train personnel, to provide technical assistance on family
planning, to develop contraceptive technology, to serve as a clearinghouse
for worldwide information, to clarify policy issues and, lastly, to promote
public awareness on the subject.

There was no cheering over John 3rd's decision in the higher echelons
of the Rockefeller organization. His father remained neutral on the subject but some of his senior advisers still were advising caution on so sensitive a subject for a Rockefeller. Remembering to touch base with his
brothers, in line with their agreement on all activities which might affect
the family name, John 3rd invited his brothers to an early breakfast meeting at the Knickerbocker Club in New York. Eight o'clock in the morning
is usually free time for busy men on short notice. John 3rd did not so
much ask his brothers' permission as inform them of his decision and ask
for their reactions. There were no objections. They were pleased that
Johnny had finally launched into a venture all his own. They wished him
well. But they also warned him not to expect any particular help from any

of them: not because they disagreed with his objectives but rather that they thought he really should do this all by himself.

The Population Council was incorporated in New York City as a private, charitable, research and educational institution in November 1952. Office space was rented in a new bank building at 245 Park Avenue, near Grand Central Station, because it was cheaper than comparable space offered at Rockefeller Center. John 3rd provided all of the initial financing: $200,000 for the first year's operations and $1,250,000 in a reserve fund to guarantee at least five years of life for the venture.

It is one thing to know what you want to do—and relatively easy to set up an organizational chart and to write a policy of purpose—and quite another thing to be able to accomplish what you hope and plan to do. John 3rd had served a long apprenticeship under the tutelage of his father and his father's advisers. By November 1952, at the age of forty-six, he knew how to guide an organization by selecting the best men available for the job and then trusting those men with the freedom to handle their jobs as they saw fit, within the guidelines established by the trustees.

The success of the Population Council and the rapid expansion of its activities and influence year after year may be attributable to the caliber of men brought into the organization by John 3rd and to their know-how or to the sagacity of the policies and practices they pursued, or to the simple fact that the time was right, the need was there for a focus of attention on the world's population problems, or perhaps to a combination of all these factors.

The Council began its work in a very modest, quiet manner, giving fellowships to students interested in population problems here and abroad for study in demography and biomedical work. As the years went on these fellows returned to their native lands in the Far East, India, the Middle East and South America to play leading roles in a worldwide effort to control the rise in population. Another early effort was to gather information on fertility, family planning and migrations of population, all for future use. As part of this program staff members and trustees of the Council traveled widely through Asia and the Far East to inform themselves at first hand of the problems they sought to solve. John 3rd began to make the first of his two or three trips a year to the Far East in order to talk with heads of state about birth control and family planning and to venture out to the rural areas to talk with village leaders about babies, food supplies and poverty. He learned at first hand what few people would believe then and some would not believe even now, and the conclusions reached upon those early trips were summarized by the Population Council in a 1964 report, as follows:

> —Everywhere, large proportions of the people themselves say they want to limit family size—husbands as well as wives, rural as well as urban, the poor as well as the better-off.

—People's information about the actual processes of human reproduction is everywhere sparse and often wrong.

—Contraception is practiced by a small proportion of the people, typically by the better-educated and in the cities.

—Substantial proportions of women in the developing countries have had induced abortions—whether medical or not, whether legal or not.

—The central reason for wishing to limit the number of children is everywhere the same; the economic welfare of the family and a better start in life for the children.

—In every country there is a large latent "market" for a well-organized program that would provide acceptable and effective means of contraception.

The Population Council was only into its second year of operation when the Indian government appealed to it for help. What was the best contraceptive available for use in India? How could the Indian government set up a practical, workable program of family planning? The appeal for help went to the Population Council because, simply, there was in 1954 nowhere else to go. The Council responded by sending a team of advisers, headed by Dr. Frank Notestein, to New Delhi in 1955, and a few years later, neighboring Pakistan asked the Population Council for similar advice on family planning. In the early 1960s, South Korea, Tunisia and Turkey each asked for technical assistance on birth control. Taiwan, Hong Kong, the Philippines, Chile, the United Arab Republic followed with their appeals and the Population Council sent more advisers. Each venture entailed considerable finesse. The experts and advisers from America had to make it carefully clear that the Council was espousing no particular program of birth control for any nation. It merely was serving as a conduit of available scientific information on the subject. Once that information was made available, it was up to government leaders themselves to decide which solutions were best for their own population growth problems.

The most significant break-through in the field came on the scientific level in 1959 with the discovery of the modern intra-uterine contraceptive device (IUD), a simple, inexpensive plastic loop or coil which, inserted into the uterus, provided excellent protection against pregnancy. The Council became closely involved in developing and testing the new device. It spent almost $2 million in the process before the IUD was found to be both effective and safe. For the underdeveloped countries, the IUD was precisely what they needed, a convenient, cheap, highly effective means of birth control.

By 1963, the Population Council had established a technical assistance division devoted solely to distributing the new IUDs to nations requesting them along with detailed advice on how to set up programs of family planning. Fully 25 per cent of its budget now was devoted to this kind of technical assistance. The need became so great that the Council turned to others for help.

Operating funds for these expanded activities grew on a parallel course, with John 3rd taking the lead in soliciting funds from men and organizations he could convince of the need. There were, as always, more failures than successes. John Paul Getty said no; Aristotle Onassis said no, thank you; but the Rockefeller Foundation now said yes, it would grant funds for population studies, for biomedical research, but not for family planning. The Ford Foundation, the wealthiest of all foundations, recognized the problem of population growth and also the political sensitivity of the subject and gave funds at first only for educational grants, then for medical research, and only after a number of years for family planning. Eventually, however, when the IUD became a proven success, the Ford Foundation took on the immense and expensive task of distributing the inter-uterine device by the millions around the world in a cooperative program with the Population Council. Ford Foundation grants to the Population Council for specific projects which the Council itself could handle better than anyone else rose rapidly to more than $2 million a year in 1970 and afterward. Finally, the United States government itself, through its Agency for International Development, began to use the Population Council as a channel for making millions of dollars available for population control programs. Even the United Nations, with international funds, joined the Population Council in certain of its programs—census taking, demographic studies and family planning.

The Council itself expanded through the years on all fronts, particularly in its leadership in pure and applied research on fertility. It appears only a matter of time now before the technology of birth control will become near perfect, affording the average woman or man the world over a safe, easy and effective means to control fertility. The growth and impact of the Council's activities over the past twenty years, a story which can be told adequately only at book length, can be measured summarily by the expansion of its annual operating budgets: from John 3rd's $200,000 in 1953 to $1 million in 1959, $3 million in 1962, $4.5 million in 1964, $17 million in 1971 and almost $20 million in 1972.

The growth in this nation's commitment to population stabilization here and abroad, measured merely in the amount of money given by the Population Council's donor agencies to population problems, rose steadily year by year from about $5 million in 1962 to a whopping $275 million in 1972.

It was only when the Population Council was acknowledged as preeminent in its field that the irony of its very existence was recognized. The Council had been founded by John 3rd only because he could not convince the stalwart Rockefeller Foundation to take on the population problem. As it turned out, according to all the experts, it was the best thing which could have happened all around. The Rockefeller Foundation could never have made population problems more than one of its many concerns. Because of its own wealth and fame, it never could have been a recipient of funds from the Ford Foundation, the U.S. government or other agencies. But the Population Council, as a small nucleus of experts in the field, could and did become a focus and funnel of various and sundry efforts in the field, even though its founder had not quite planned it that way at the start.

One thing John 3rd did learn from the experience was that when the Rockefeller Foundation and others turned a deaf ear to his pleas, he himself could launch an organization to do the job he thought should be done. With his interest in Asian affairs, it seemed quite clear to John 3rd that no one was paying sufficient attention to the need in Asian countries for competence in dealing with the economic and human problems of agricultural development. The Rockefeller Foundation's activities and expertise were focused on scientific or biological farming. But who was teaching Asians the economics of farming, farm management, credit and banking, marketing of products? The answer was no one. So in December 1953, just thirteen months after founding the Population Council, John 3rd established the Council on Economic and Cultural Affairs with an initial budget of $250,000 and a reserve fund of about $1.7 million.

Once again, with the aid of outstanding experts in their field, a staff of agricultural economists was recruited, a board of trustees consisting largely of university economists and agronomists was enlisted and the Council on Economic and Cultural Affairs, with headquarters in Rockefeller Center, chaired by John D. Rockefeller 3rd, got underway to fill a need in Asia and the Far East. Fellowships were awarded to deserving Asians to be trained at American universities in the intricacies of banking, marketing, planning and economics as these fields pertained to farming. In time, these Asians would return to their own countries and become leaders in their own government ministries. Once again, a new organization was found to be fulfilling a real need so that ten years later this Council would find financial support for its projects from the Ford Foundation, the Rockefeller Brothers Fund, the U. S. Agency for International Development and the International Development Center. Its operating budget for ever expanding activities in the 1970s would exceed $1 million a year, with John 3rd contributing only a modest percentage of that amount. This is in line with his philosophy that if any philanthropic organization is to become a viable and ongoing concern, it must gain support from many more than one individual.

John 3rd is certainly the family's professional philanthropist. While his brothers have made philanthropy a part of their lives, John 3rd likes to describe himself wryly as the only one of his brothers who is unemployed. Not since he served in the Navy during World War II has he held a job.

Nor has he personally involved himself in any venture to make money. The management of his fortune he leaves to a professional staff of investment counselors who serve him and his brothers on a full-time basis. Of all the brothers, he is the most cautious about making new investments. The subject seems hardly to interest him. He acts as though such decisions are an imposition on his time. When some of his philanthropic activities, particularly those in the Far East, involve financial acumen, he instinctively turns for advice to his youngest brother, David.

On the other hand, John 3rd is as emotionally committed to and knowledgeable about philanthropy as the most dedicated businessman is about the bottom line of his firm's balance sheet. Through the years, John 3rd has defended philanthropy before congressional investigations and elsewhere as a thoroughly American institution which provides much more than mere material benefits to the needy; it is the keystone of the pluralistic approach to problems in America. John 3rd argues with fervor, however concealed, that the government consists of men no wiser than men in private life in finding solutions to public problems and that the private citizen or group of individuals, free of political stress and strain, can be far more venturesome in undertaking new and perhaps riskier courses of action than the government, weighed down by political considerations and a cumbersome bureaucracy.

This, in turn, places a grave responsibility upon private philanthropy, he says. It must strive to be as wise as possible, as venturesome as possible, and to be totally open and reponsible to the public trust in all its projects. Because of the family name and fame, John 3rd has personally placed upon himself the most stringent criteria of what is right and what is wrong in a private philanthropist. Many of those closest to him despair that he takes life and his work so seriously that he seldom finds time or the inclination for just sheer fun or the relaxed wasting of time. "He has the most highly developed conscience, which is working all the time, of any of his brothers and of all the people I know anywhere," comments one of his associates, a man driven to work as hard as his boss on projects for which there is no profit-and-loss statement at year's end.

John 3rd became involved in the planning, financing and building of the Lincoln Center for the Performing Arts in New York City in 1955 simply because someone asked him to. His involvement went far beyond the giving of money. He contributed the Rockefeller name to the project and approximately one half of all his working hours for thirteen years to a cultural complex of six buildings: the Metropolitan Opera House, the New York Philharmonic Orchestra's Philharmonic Hall, the New York State Theater for dance and operetta companies, the Vivian Beaumont Theater for a new theatrical company, the Juilliard Building to house the renowned school of music of that name and various recital studios for budding performers, the Library and Museum of the Performing Arts to house the New York Public Library's collections in these arts. Also included in the plan was the adjoining Damrosch Park with its band shell for outdoor concerts.

It was to become the first cultural center of its kind in the United States, bringing together all of these performing arts on one site, a concept the success of which would inspire adaptations across the nation, in Los Angeles, Washington, D.C., Milwaukee, Houston, Austin, Indianapolis, Pittsburgh, Baltimore, Atlanta and Birmingham.

And it all started so simply. John 3rd was attending a conference of the Council on Foreign Relations at a resort in the Pocono Mountains in September 1955 when, during a recess, he was approached by Charles M. Spofford, a distinguished attorney who was a member of the board of the Metropolitan Opera Association. Spofford explained that the Met was on the verge of choosing a site for a new opera house. John 3rd hardly needed to be reminded of the fiasco of 1929 when his father had tried to help; that had led to the building of Rockefeller Center. But now, explained Spofford, the New York Philharmonic Orchestra also was looking for a new house; it had been given notice to vacate Carnegie Hall within the next three years. As a result, the boards of directors of both institutions were studying the possibility of finding a single site for both the Met and the Philharmonic. And, as a third coincidence, there was a city slum clearance site available at a place near Central Park called Lincoln Square. So, to help settle the matter, would John D. Rockefeller 3rd be willing to join a number of citizens connected with neither organization to represent the public interest in choosing a site so much needed at this time?

John 3rd was intrigued. He realized that with his preoccupation with Asian affairs, he had not done very much for his "home town" of New York. After thinking it over and with customary due caution, he agreed to join the group, which called itself, quite accurately, the Exploratory Committee for a Musical Arts Center. John 3rd also brought in with him several other public-spirited citizens. In the back of his mind was the conviction that this was not to become a "Rockefeller project"; he would simply join and do his part.

At the first meeting of the enlarged group—board members of the Metropolitan and of the Philharmonic and the buffer group of citizens—they decided to meet for lunch every two weeks at the Century Club and to ask John 3rd to serve as chairman. How could he refuse?

The very first, most important and most controversial exploration of the committee delved into the concept itself. Should the new opera house and orchestral hall be put on one site or should they be separated so as to bring the vitality of the arts to different parts of New York? Then the question arose: should it be just a music center? The eminent New York City Ballet needed a new home as much as the Met and the Philharmonic. And then hadn't New York, America's home for the legitimate stage, always wanted and needed a repertory theater for the classics and the non-commercial plays of new playwrights?

The concept of a federation of institutions including all of the "performing arts" emerged slowly and John 3rd found himself playing a substantive leadership role. He was adept at gaining the cooperation of the directors of the Metropolitan and the Philharmonic, whose self-interest originally was focused only upon the survival of those two old, proud institutions. John 3rd's approach was as ever oblique and persistent. But his Rockefeller eye consistently sought out the bigger and bigger potential of a center for the performing arts. Again and again he came back to the primary point in his mind: this should be more than just a real estate venture—it also must do something to contribute to the life of the city and to the vitality of the arts in New York and throughout the country! When the committee agreed to add the dance and the repertory theaters to Lincoln Center, John 3rd then broached the idea of adding certain educational institutions to the center. It would "bridge the gap" between professional performances in the arts and the students and young learners who would benefit by being on the site of Lincoln Center, he explained. The Juilliard School of Music, a venerable and outstanding institution, housed in an ancient building near Columbia University, would benefit tremendously by being near the top professionals at Lincoln Center, and the Center itself would benefit by having interested youth partaking of professional performances at the Met and the Philharmonic. This was met with scant interest when first broached, but John 3rd moved so gingerly on the subject over so many months that gradually, one by one, the committee eased into agreement. So slowly did he move on this subject, when he finally did bring the inclusion of Juilliard to a vote, one member of the committee, Irving Olds of the Met board, commented plaintively, "Of course we are going to have it; I thought we had settled that a long time ago." The vote was unanimous. It was then relatively simple to agree that the world's largest collection of books and documents on the performing arts, then housed at the New York Public Library, also should be given a home of its own at Lincoln Center.

Thus the concept of Lincoln Center as it stands today was not nearly fully visualized when the members of the Exploratory Committee, after receiving several feasibility reports, decided to go ahead with the single-site idea and in June 1956 duly incorporated the Lincoln Center for the Performing Arts. John D. Rockefeller 3rd was elected president of the non-profit, membership organization, which had no funds, no staff and, as yet, no place upon which to build.

It took almost two years of tortuous negotiations, public hearings, disputes and discussions to buy the three-block site at Lincoln Square from the city, and then to add another half block to the site, and then to relocate 1,647 families from the slum housing being torn down.

Problems overlapped problems, one solution dependent upon another —the architectural design of each building and each in relation to the others, the acoustics versus the box office, the financing and the fund raising, architectural elegance versus the money available, the wishes of one constituent as against those of another. John 3rd was called in again and again to mediate differences and disputes which arose in the normal course of such a complex undertaking. More important than his name or position, it was the common knowledge that this quiet, gracious, always poised grandson of the founder of Standard Oil could be relied on to give an impartial opinion, free of self-aggrandizement or personal bias, that brought the others to call upon him so often to help reach a disputed decision.

For example, the six renowned architects hired by each of the six boards of directors of the constituent organizations were given the assignment to design six distinctive buildings blending into one architectural whole. Naturally each considered his building a work of art, one of its kind, a unique showpiece for the world. The architects met once a month with their models and plans at the New York offices of Harrison and Abramovitz in Rockefeller Center, and one by one, the numerous working models were criticized, altered and discarded. Distinctiveness was there but the harmony—in size, massiveness, line and tone—was highly elusive. John 3rd was then invited to join the group, not because of the "edifice complex" in the Rockefeller family, but because John 3rd somehow, however obliquely, could persuade these individualistic architects to work together toward an over-all single grand design that was to become Lincoln Center. He did not have the expertise to be an arbitrator or even a mediator on architectural design. His role, according to one of the architects, was that of "a guide, philosopher and friend" to the group. Participating in these all-day once-a-month sessions of architects, where they sent out for sandwiches and coffee for lunch rather than interrupt their creative efforts, soon became the most challenging, fascinating aspect of John 3rd's work on Lincoln Center.

On the other hand, fund raising was old-hat to this Rockefeller. He was as professional as any man in the nation in preparing a proposal for a grant from a foundation or in extracting a contribution from an individual. While insisting that support for Lincoln Center should come from as wide a spectrum of the public as possible, it was obvious that most of the money must indeed come in large donations, and John 3rd took it upon himself to go after those large donors—those who could give a million dollars or more. As a fund raiser, he could be as devious, knowledgeable and persistent as the occasion warranted. He did his homework. He studied the best approach to each individual, how much each could give comfortably, and he was unrelenting in his telephone calls, his invitations to lunches and dinner parties. For Vivian Beaumont Allen, considered one of the most eccentric millionaires in America, John D. Rockefeller 3rd put in three years of pleadings before she contributed more than $3 million for the theater that bears her name in Lincoln Center.

Fund raising was an utter necessity. The day was long past, as he constantly pointed out, when men like his father (with the help of one single mortgage) could reach into his portfolio and pay for the building of Rockefeller Center. John 3rd was in no position to do that. He simply did not have that kind of money. Nor, if he did, would he want to. It was a battle for him to convince people that Lincoln Center had to be a community project and that the Rockefellers would not—repeat not—bail the center out if the fund raising failed.

Because it was well understood that the arts were not and could not be self-supporting, the directors of Lincoln Center had agreed that all the buildings, land, plazas, art work and designs would be paid in full through fund raising: the constituent institutions would not be burdened by mortgage or interest payments. As non-profit institutions, they would pay no taxes. The planners hoped to make everything as easy as possible for future operations. What they did not envision were the financial problems inherent in just paying the maintenance costs of such splendid, palatial homes for the Met, the Philharmonic, the repertory theater and the others.

At the start, in 1956, the directors estimated that space requirements for Lincoln Center would total about 20 million square feet at a cost of about $75 million. But as the concept of the center grew and more detailed planning was completed, a more realistic estimate of the center's requirements emerged: 34 million square feet, at a cost of about $129 million. To that, the directors added $10 million for a special fund to help support educational, artistic and operational functions at the center. Thus, the first fund-raising goal was established in 1960 at $139 million. When the buildings, garages and plazas of the center were completed in 1969, there were 35 million square feet of space provided and the cost was $161.5 million. Most of the increase was due to rising construction costs over that decade, and even then, as the directors pointed out with some pride, the cost of building Lincoln Center over the estimates was 23 per cent at a time when major construction costs in New York City rose by 38 per cent.

To help raise funds, the directors finally did turn to New York State and New York City for help. John 3rd did talk money with brother Nelson, governor of the state, and the governor agreed that the state would contribute—but only in matching funds with the city. But since the law forbade either the city or the state from contributing to a private enterprise, long and tortuous negotiations ensued before the city agreed to build city-owned garages for the center and the state agreed to build the New York State Theater as part of its exhibit in the New York World's

David Rockefeller.

Starting out with the Chase National Bank in 1946 at age thirty-one.

In his office at Rockefeller Center.

TOP MANAGEMENT AT
THE CHASE MANHATTAN BANK

George Champion, incoming chairman; John J. McCloy, retiring chairman; David Rocke-feller, incoming president, 1960.

Nelson, Laurance, John 3rd and David at Pocantico Hills, October 1950.

Golfing.

In his office in the new bank building.

Outside the new bank building with Jean Dubuffet, sculptor of "Group of Four Trees," 1972.

With President Ford and Zbigniew Brzezinski at a meeting of the Trilateral Commission Executive Committee, December 1974.

With Golda Meir.

With Anwar el-Sadat.

With Chou En-Lai.

Peggy Rockefeller.

At a London embassy reception, 1973.

1973.

Fair. In all, the city and state contributed $37.1 million in capital funds, or 20 per cent of the total amount of money raised. Eighty per cent of all money raised—$141.4 million—came from private sources. These funds generated another $6.2 million in investment income for a grand total of $184.7 million.

Lincoln Center was not a Rockefeller project *per se*. But the combined Rockefeller sources gave just about one quarter of all the money raised to build the center. The Rockefeller Foundation, of which John 3rd was chairman of the board, made four contributions totaling $15 million (which was exceeded only by the $25 million from the Ford Foundation). On the individual level, John 3rd's father, who had pledged $5 million to the Metropolitan years before, gave that and another $5 million to the center. John 3rd made his own contributions as strategically as possible, a million here, a million plus there, to match funds with other donors as the campaign progressed. For the final contribution of the campaign in June 1969, he matched funds with Lawrence A. Wien, a vice-president of the board of Lincoln Center. Together they gave $2.5 million. Keeping to his low profile throughout, John 3rd has consistently declined to disclose the total of all his contributions to Lincoln Center. However, according to reliable sources, his gifts totaled approximately $11 million, more than any other individual's.

His greatest satisfaction in all his activities associated with Lincoln Center was the success of the concept itself. Lincoln Center had, in fact, given the arts a tremendous visibility in New York City. Along with the United Nations and Rockefeller Center, it has become one of the city's three major tourist attractions. On the economic level, Lincoln Center succeeded in uplifting the real estate value of its neighborhood, stimulating more than $150 million of private investments in urban renewal in the immediate area, and that, in turn, has resulted in increased tax revenues to the city of some $20 million a year. When this became known, aside from the positive effect of stimulating similar cultural centers in other cities, a number of cynics began to suspect that John 3rd's ulterior motive in working so hard for Lincoln Center was to increase the value of Rockefeller-held real estate in the area. One magazine reported such rumors as fact, only to print a retraction later when John 3rd could prove that no Rockefeller owned property anywhere near Lincoln Center. In truth, anticipating such cynicism, John 3rd had carefully checked that out *before* he began to work on the project.

His motive, so pure that some people still find it hard to believe, was to help do something which he thought should be done: to build a center for the performing arts in the city he considered his home town. What he did conceal from the public during his thirteen or fourteen years with Lincoln Center was that personally he was not particularly a buff of the opera, the ballet, the symphony or the theater. And when Lincoln Center was completed, the six distinctive and harmonious buildings standing in splendid glory around the grand plaza, the $184.5 million campaign finished, then John 3rd began to wonder how soon with good grace he could give up his seat at the opera and at Philharmonic Hall. In fact, he began to think about how soon he could, again without raising eyebrows, resign as chairman of the board. The appropriate time came in March 1971, when he turned sixty-five. He tendered his resignation and cited his age as the sole reason.

Throughout these years with Lincoln Center, John 3rd did not neglect his self-imposed responsibilities to other causes and organizations. Part of virtually every day was devoted to one ongoing activity or another—the Japan Society, the building of the six-story Asia House in New York and the International House of Japan in Tokyo, the Population Council, the Agricultural Development Council. Then there were the Rockefeller Public Service Awards, founded and financed by John 3rd, at the height of the so-called McCarthy era, to recognize "these unsung heroes" in the civil ranks of federal government. The awards, administered by Princeton University, were given annually—five awards of $10,000 each—to career men and women with outstanding records of service in the federal government. These awards were so successful in raising morale in the federal government that the Rockefeller Brothers Fund, upon John 3rd's recommendation, created the Ramon Magasaysay Awards of $10,000 each for five men or women each year "in recognition of greatness of spirit shown in service to the people" of Asia. Given each year since 1958, they have become know as the "Nobel prizes of Asia." And in 1958, John 3rd took over from his father the chairmanship of the National Council of the United Negro College Fund, which supported thirty-three predominantly Negro colleges and universities in the South, a cause close to his father's heart since the early days of the General Education Board.

However, of all the philanthropies with which the Rockefeller family had been associated for generations, "home base" was always the Rockefeller Foundation. It was the greatest and culminating achievement in philanthropy of John D. Rockefeller, Sr. His son, John Jr., served as its first president and then its first chairman of the board, from 1913 to 1939, when he retired at age sixty-five, setting the principle there of mandatory retirement at sixty-five to make way for younger men. Still, he continued in emeritus status and was held in such awe that among the staff he was always called Mr. Chairman, never by name, as the men in the White House refer only to "Mr. President."

John 3rd's election in 1952 as chairman of the board, succeeding John Foster Dulles, who left to become Secretary of State under Dwight D. Eisenhower, was a natural selection and a natural progression, for John 3rd had by then served as a trustee for more than twenty years.

Nevertheless, at the outset, his position at the head of so illustrious and proud an organization was extremely delicate. The other twenty trustees of the Rockefeller Foundation, all of them men of accomplishment and vigor in their own fields, were acutely aware of the need of safeguarding the reputation of the Foundation as an independent and competently operated organization, free of the dominance of the founding family. John 3rd, keenly aware of this feeling, which was never alluded to in so many spoken words, became masterly in conducting the semi-annual meetings of the trustees. Never once could anyone on the board remember John 3rd saying, "I think the Rockefeller Foundation should do this." He encouraged the trustees to express their views and to espouse their causes with vigor, while he, often holding equally strong views, would keep himself in check and never do battle. His low-key, serious demeanor was disarming and, in the end, it was found that the trustees almost always came to the conclusion he himself supported. Part of the reason was the manner in which the Foundation operated. The twenty-one trustees of the Foundation, serving without pay, had complete authority and responsibility for setting and enforcing the Foundation's policies and its making of monetary grants. The trustees had to pass on each and every grant of $25,000 or more. Beneath that figure, the trustees had delegated the authority to the Foundation's president, who served as head of the staff of experts employed by the Foundation, and who himself served at the pleasure of the trustees. However, the trustees, to guard against whims and favorite causes, also made it a policy that no item could come before them unless it was approved and submitted by the staff. Over the years, the staff had become so adept in submitting such fully documented and supported proposals that a veto by the board of trustees was a rare occurrence. John 3rd's method of working was to meet frequently alone with the president of the Foundation, Dean Rusk starting in 1952, to hear justifications of what the staff was considering and to voice what he called the "concerns" of the trustees. Then, at the meetings, John 3rd could act as a catalyst, encouraging debate—almost to a fault in the view of some. Rather than call time, he would go on and on asking for the views of the negative side of any question under consideration until a consensus acceptable to all was reached. The trustees were not to feel that they were "rubber stamps" of the staff, nor the staff complain of undue pressure by the trustees—not under the leadership of John 3rd.

The history of the Rockefeller Foundation is long and replete with accomplishments the world over in virtually every serious field of endeavor. Most often, its initial grants-in-aid were surprisingly low, and only in cases where pilot projects proved successful, the grants increased to hundreds of thousands of dollars a year, even to millions in the areas of major focus. More than in just the tens of millions of dollars it disbursed each year, the Rockefeller Foundation over the years has earned its reputation as perhaps the most highly respected institution of its kind. It was beautifully managed with low overhead and skillfully administered with a clear set of operating principles and policies of long standing. It set such high standards of excellence that a Rockefeller grant was considered and accolade in itself. Its recognized accomplishments in medicine, public health, agriculture, the biological and physical sciences, and later in the social sciences and in art, became the standard by which other foundations could measure themselves. In fact, the Rockefeller Foundation had become in the minds of many the Establishment of the Establishment in all areas of social responsibility.

John 3rd's major and lasting contribution to this acme of philanthropic institutions was his gentle but persistent persuasion to keep the Rockefeller Foundation abreast of changing times and changing needs. This meant change for the Foundation, a staid organization with entrenched staff and rather venerable and conservative trustees. John 3rd was always at the cutting edge of change, reminding his colleagues that the Rockefeller Foundation was meant to be a pioneering instrument, venturing into untried projects where the government and others feared to go. Or, when a Foundation goal had been reached or the government with its vastly superior store of funds entered the field, that it was time for the Rockefeller Foundation to move out of that area and pioneer a new one. Again, this meant change. And again, change is seldom accepted lightly.

When John 3rd took over as head of the Foundation, it had a solid record of forty years' experience in working toward "the well-being of mankind throughout the world" by identifying and analyzing basic problems and attacking them with some assurance of positive results. The changes in the problems chosen by its board of trustees over the years can be broadly charted. First came the momentous attack on infectious diseases, those great public health years from 1913 to 1928, with worldwide campaigns against yellow fever, hookworm, malaria and the like, and the founding of twenty-six schools of public health in twenty-two countries. Then came the concentration up to World War II on basic research in the life sciences—research in genetics, biochemistry, molecular biology and nuclear physics. The Foundation supported the very best people in these fields, particularly in the United States and Western Europe. Nobel prizes for outstanding achievements in these fields were awarded to many scientists whose support came from the Rockefeller Foundation. In the reorientation following the end of World War II, the Foundation turned to a new, pressing need: applying existing knowledge for the practical benefits of mankind, particularly in the underdeveloped countries. And the first obvious focus here was upon nutrition: food for people living in countries which could not feed their own populations. The results here were stupendous. Ultimately, it was called the "green revolution," and it spread around the world.

Starting simply from a suggestion in 1941 by Vice-President Henry A.

Wallace, who had been Secretary of Agriculture, the Foundation sent three agricultural experts to Mexico to survey the problem of increasing Mexican corn, bean and wheat crops. The initial outlay was $30,000. Not since the 1906 program on rural farming in America had the Rockefeller Foundation gone into this field. Working with the Mexican government, the Foundation sent a one-man task force to Mexico to launch a program of scientific farming or plant biology; that is, crossbreeding plants to produce a hybrid strain of corn and wheat that would thrive in arid Mexican soil. That one man was J. George Harrar, a little-known professor of plant pathology at Washington State University. In a multi-faceted program of research, pilot projects and teaching techniques of scientific farming that suited Mexican mores, Dr. Harrar over a nine-year period helped Mexican farmers produce high-yield, high-quality crops of corn and wheat. Each year thereafter saw bigger and better crops so that Mexico became self-sufficient in its basic crops of wheat and corn. The achievement was widely recognized as being the most significant contribution "toward the conquest of hunger" in modern times in any single country. Other nations took notice. Mexican wheat and corn seeds were exported to Colombia, to Chile and then to other South American countries, to the Middle East and to India.

What worked so well with corn and wheat worked equally well with potatoes, beans and finally rice, the basic food crop of more than half the people of the world. Dr. Harrar started a rice research project in 1952, and in 1959, the Rockefeller Foundation in cooperation with the Ford Foundation and the Philippine government launched the International Rice Research Institute at Los Baños, forty miles south of Manila. The Ford Foundation gave approximately $7 million for the construction of the most complete center in the world for research on rice. The Philippine government provided the land, and the Rockefeller Foundation provided—and has been providing—the technical direction and administration as well as about $500,000 a year in operating expenses. In the years that followed more than six thousand varieties of rice, collected from seventy-three countries, have been field-tested at the Rice Institute, and out of this has come a germ plasm bank for the exchange of rice seed around the world.

The Foundation's experienced finesse in working with foreign governments, training farmers, giving advance study fellowships to outstanding students was every bit as important as the scientific farming and plant biology involved. The Foundation sent only small staffs to foreign lands—only twenty Americans at a maximum ever worked at one time in Mexico, for instance—and once a program succeeded, the Foundation staff men retired, leaving the entire program and full credit for its success in native hands.

At the same time in the headquarters of the Foundation, in the Time-Life Building of Rockefeller Center, beginning in 1955, Dean Rusk, as president of the Foundation, focused attention on an integrated program which he called "the revolution of rising expectations" among the underdeveloped nations of Asia. John 3rd, with his lifelong fascination with Asia, was always in the forefront of policy changes that turned the Foundation's primary thrust from Western Europe to the newly independent nations of the Far East.

The role ultimately played by the Rockefeller Foundation in the Far East was explained in a noteworthy memorandum prepared for the trustees by Dean Rusk, in which he explained how the Foundation could exert "key leverage" in providing Western know-how to solve problems in the have-not nations of the world.

"We have officers and staff with long experience in underdeveloped areas," he said. "We can recruit for such service somewhat more readily than other types of organizations. We have earned a reputation for political disinterestedness; we are not widely regarded as the tool of any particular foreign policy; we are usually welcomed in politically sensitive situations; we have cooperated intimately with foreign governments without becoming involved in partisan rivalries or changing regimes. We are capable of acting promptly, with flexible and simple procedures. We can persist over a period of time where time is required. We can bring advances in knowledge in one part of the world to bear upon practical problems in another, reinforcing this with special investigation and research at crucial points. We have gained considerable experience in training leadership, both for science and scholarship and for various types of public service . . ."

The Rusk program, inaugurated in 1956, spread successfully from the Far East to India to the Middle East and to Africa. Dr. Harrar served as Director for Agriculture in 1955, overseeing the food-production program or "green revolution" as it spread across the world. When Dean Rusk was tapped in 1961 to become Secretary of State under President John F. Kennedy, he was succeeded by George Harrar.

The selection of Harrar, an agronomist, to be president of the Rockefeller Foundation was due almost entirely to John 3rd, who headed the Foundation's Search Committee for a new president. It was at the time a bold move and also a rare instance when John 3rd campaigned actively for a man or a subject of his own choice. While the trustees admired Harrar's work in Mexico, his experience was limited to agriculture, his education and background was a far cry from the eastern Establishment's, his knowledge of the humanities and social sciences was unknown. In short, he did not fit the prevailing portrait of what a president of the Rockefeller Foundation was expected to be. Nevertheless, John 3rd knew the man and his work and his capabilities through their years of association on the Foundation. Such personal knowledge meant far more to John 3rd than mere academic credentials. The trustees viewed John 3rd's choice as risky and bold, but they went along with him. The choice paid off handsomely. With the advent of the Foundation's fiftieth anniversary in 1963, George Harrar led the Rockefeller Foundation in a major reorganization of policy. While not completely abandoning past areas of focus, the Foundation turned its major attention from health and adequate diet to intensive and long-range support of work in the social sciences, the humanities and the arts. As John 3rd viewed it at the time: "Once you have helped make people healthy and well-fed, you must then ask, 'What for? What is the objective?' And the answer is: their quality of life as a whole."

Quality of life was a long-time favorite concept of John D. Rockefeller 3rd. It was all-inclusive, obvious and yet in its particulars so difficult to define. To John 3rd, quality of life extends beyond good health and food to include the ambiance of all life around you: the natural environment, the society in which you live, the number of children in your family, your appreciation of the beauty around you, the balance of work and leisure, the quality rather than quantity of your material possessions, inner peace as well as full employment. The list goes on and on.

In 1963, the Rockefeller Foundation took on the task of trying to improve the "quality of life" of mankind, with attention focused naturally on the have-nots of the world. Its five-point priority program, which continues to this day, included continued efforts toward the conquest of hunger; strengthening universities and research centers in the developing nations in the training of qualified personnel in all intellectual fields; broad support for civil rights and equal opportunity in the United States; increased support in the humanities and in the creative and performing arts; and, finally, major support of research and action in birth control and population stabilization.

Intensely concerned, even preoccupied, with the problem of overpopulation, John 3rd began in the 1960s to devote more and more of his time to the problem of gaining popular support for his cause. The early years with the Population Council had been devoted for the most part to research, organization and education—all done without publicity or fanfare. But in the 1960s, he felt the need to popularize what had been learned by the experts. There was still disagreement on tactics and priorities among the experts, but almost all agreed that *something* had to be done to stabilize (rather than control) the growth of population, which inexorably held poorer nations in the grip of poverty. The first step obviously was to begin at home, to convince our own national leaders of the need to take action on the problem of rising population growth. That milestone was reached in June 1965 when President Johnson proclaimed before the United Nations: "Let us in all our lands—including this land—face forthrightly . . . and seek the answers to this most profound challenge to the future of the world." Only then did John 3rd set out himself to gain international public recognition of the population explosion.

A month later, he sat in private audience with Pope Paul VI in the Vatican. For forty-five minutes he tried to persuade the pontiff to lead the Catholic Church in amending its stand against artificial means of birth control. He was rebuffed, politely, but rebuffed. The Church's responsibility, said the Pope, was the morality of the issue, not the economic or social aspects. John 3rd left the meeting blaming himself for not getting the message across. Despite a sense of failure, he followed up his visit with a six-page, single-spaced letter the next week to the pontiff on the morality question: "Would it be possible to shift the focus of this concern from the method itself to the uses to which the method will be put? Would it be feasible to state that the Church will leave to the discretion of the individual family its choice as to the method it will use to determine the number of children provided the method is not harmful to the user and provided it does not interfere with the meaning and importance of sexual union in marriage? . . . To express the above more concisely, what I am suggesting is that specific methods be regarded as merely instruments, like knives, whose use is morally good or bad depending on the intentions of those who employ them." All to no avail. The Pope was not persuaded.

Four months later, on a cold rainy November night, John 3rd spoke at length on the population problem to a large group of America's leading businessmen at a dinner meeting of the prestigious Economic Club of New York in the Grand Ballroom of the Waldorf-Astoria Hotel. He gave them facts and figures and pleaded for their "concerned support," for their leadership in arousing their communities to the need for long-range planning. "The clock of history is running fast," he warned. The businessmen of America applauded John D. Rockefeller 3rd politely but sparsely. It was clear on that November 8, 1965, that they did not share his concern.

He walked home from the hotel alone, late that rainy night, his head down, shoulders hunched up. The scene was incised in the memory of one of the dinner guests, who spied him from a taxicab and said to himself: "There goes one of the wealthiest men in the world, walking all by himself, dejected like a traveling salesman who failed to make a sale."

But a few months later, John 3rd was again selling what he believed in. Such defeats did not dismay him. He regarded them merely as tactical. With his eye on the future, however distant, he began to distribute to heads of state around the world a statement of policy on population growth which he had composed. He asked for their endorsement to the proposition that unplanned population growth was a threat to world peace of equal importance to the danger of a nuclear holocaust.

The statement asked world leaders to go on record that the population problem deserved long-range, national planning, that the "great majority of parents desire to have the knowledge and the means to plan their families; that the opportunity to decide the number and spacing of children is a basic human right," and that "the objective of family planning is

the enrichment of human life, not its restriction; that family planning
. . . frees man to attain his individual dignity and reach his full potential."

Within weeks of sending out this declaration, it was signed by twelve
heads of state and endorsed by Secretary-General U Thant (an old friend)
at the United Nations. During the next year, another eighteen world
leaders, including President Johnson, signed it. The penultimate signature
arrived on December 11, 1967, the day the statement was presented formally to the United Nations in New York. It came from President
Suharto of Indonesia just moments before the presentation ceremony
began. John 3rd made no comment, publicly or privately. But a close associate did recall with pleasure that years before, when John 3rd first
presented his ideas on family planning to Suharto's predecessor, President
Sukarno of Indonesia dismissed it as "imperialistic horseshit!"

The New York *Times*, commenting editorially upon the signing of
the statement on population, said that John D. Rockefeller 3rd was probably the only individual in the whole world who could have brought together thirty heads of state, some of them of Catholic countries, to a joint
statement on population, leaders who represent more than one third of all
the people in the world. In reality, the statement represented a vote of
confidence in the man, John D. Rockefeller 3rd, as much as an endorsement of the principles involved. And the truth of the matter is that he did
not come by that confidence and trust so very easily. In his early trips to
the Far East in the 1950s, John D. 3rd was met with as much suspicion
and distrust by the Orientals as he would be by cynical Western businessmen. The question which came up, asked or unasked, always was,
"What's in it for him?" It took years for men of all political persuasions in
Asia, the Far East and around the world to come to the realization of the
uniqueness of this man. As one of them put it: "He is the only one I can
think of who has no vested interest!" As much or as far as anyone could
look, they could find no profit motive on the part of John 3rd, financially,
politically, commercially or even personally. His interest rested solely in
the objectives of the organization or of the venture involved. He was apolit-
ical in dealing with Republicans or Democrats in the United States as he
was in approaches to Communist and non-Communist leaders abroad. By
maintaining a low profile and eschewing any credit for successful programs, he gradually won the trust of national leaders of all stripes. Prince
Norodom Sihanouk, when he was the head of Cambodia, made little secret of his opinion that he considered "all Americans bastards"; nevertheless, in sending his son to the United States for his education, he declared: "The only two men I would trust to sponsor my son are Benny
Goodman and John D. Rockefeller 3rd." That, regardless of the source, is
high endorsement indeed, indicative of the trust in which John 3rd was
held. It followed, of course, that once having won the trust of national

leaders, even those with enmity in their hearts for the United States, John 3rd was able to persuade them of the merits of his own convictions on the value of family planning.

In July of 1969 President Nixon proposed and in March of 1970 Congress created the Commission on Population Growth and the American Future. John 3rd was the logical man to head the twenty-four-member commission, composed of a wide cross section of Americans according to age, vocation, race, religion and background. After two years of voluble and volatile monthly meetings, the commission issued its report, which exploded on the front pages of newspapers across the nation. John 3rd received more visibility than ever before in his life.

The commission proposed a deliberate national policy of population stabilization on the new premise that "no substantial benefits will result from the continued growth of our population . . ." Replete with studies and statistics, the report spelled out clearly that if the average American family had two children, the population of the United States in a hundred years would grow to 340 million persons; an average of three children per family would produce nearly 1 billion persons in a hundred years.

No one could readily argue with that. But the commission also was definite and clear in its recommendations of how to achieve zero population growth. In fact, its recommendations were underlined and italicized throughout its 350-page report, published as a paperback book. They included widespread sex education in all schools, a population education program for adults and children alike, child-care centers for working mothers, elimination of discrimination against children born out of wedlock, reform of adoption laws, improvements of all services relating to fertility, including contraceptive services, voluntary sterilization and abortion.

There were a considerable number of eyebrows raised at such bold recommendations as birth control information and services being made available to teen-agers (married or unmarried), but the real furor arose over the commission's recommendations on abortion. "The Commission recommends that present state laws restricting abortion be liberalized along the lines of New York State statutes, such abortions to be performed on request by duly licensed physicians under conditions of medical safety." The commission went even further than that. It proposed that the federal, state and local governments finance abortion services and also that abortion be specifically included in health insurance benefits.

President Nixon received the commission's report coldly, condemning it with faint praise and declaring his own personal opposition to abortion as a means of birth control. The four Catholic members of the commission wrote dissenting opinions on abortion. The Catholic Church certainly did not change its view on the subject.

Nevertheless, birth control and abortion were out in the open. The commission's report and policy recommendations received wide acclaim and support throughout the nation and in various parts of the world from organizations and individual leaders. Overall, it can be said that the views of the commission became the majority view here and abroad. What had been an unspoken, indelicate subject twenty years before now could be seen as the Establishment viewpoint on population stability, birth control, family planning and abortion. John D. Rockefeller 3rd had come a long way since founding the Population Council in 1952.

Today hundreds of millions of dollars are being spent annually by the U.S. government, agencies of the United Nations and private foundations and organizations on population. Extensive fertility research is being conducted in university laboratories around the world in the search for better contraceptives. Postpartum programs on teaching birth control methods are being established at hospitals around the world. And yet, the success or failure of the commission's recommendations may not be fully known for years and years. Perhaps at the turn of the century or perhaps a hundred years from now, demographers, sociologists and historians will compare and correlate population figures then with efforts being made today and be able to assess the success or failure of efforts made by John D. Rockefeller 3rd and others in behalf of population stabilization and the quality of life in America and throughout the world.

As well as any man, John 3rd was fully aware that in philanthropy there is no so-called bottom line. At the Chase Manhattan Bank or in any business, at the year's end there is always that bottom line to measure profits and losses, assets against liabilities. But there is no way to measure one man's efforts in giving aid to the arts and culture in America, guiding the Rockefeller Foundation, fostering good relations between the United States and the Far East or trying to change attitudes toward family planning or the birth rate around the world. Such considerations, however, did not deter a man like John 3rd from the intense concern he gave to his daily efforts. From the start, John 3rd has conditioned himself for the long pull in activities of his own choosing which transcend by their nature short and quick solutions. Faced with a supposedly insoluble problem, he enjoys joshing pessimists around him by saying, "That's not a problem— that's an opportunity." But he is only half joking.

That kind of "opportunity" presented itself to John 3rd in April 1968. His youngest daughter Alida had clashed with the radicals of Stanford University, returning home in tears. The student revolt at Columbia University was in full cry, police were swinging their night sticks, students were occupying buildings and, in effect, shutting down the university. Looking out of the north window of his corner office at 5600 across the green expanse of Central Park, John 3rd could imagine the turmoil at Columbia. He felt that part of the city was "burning" and he was baffled. Along with many others at the time, he could not grasp what would incite well-off university students to revolt so violently against the Establishment. A few weeks later, he had lunch with an old friend, Lord Caradon, the British representative to the United Nations; talking about population, Lord Caradon remarked how wonderful it might be if the new activism of the young could be directed toward the problem of the population explosion. That struck a chord. The high ideals and the activism of youth presented an opportunity, a meaningful opportunity in the lexicon of John 3rd.

Back at his office, he discussed it with his staff and with his friends and decided to go ahead. What was it that America's youth wanted? That was the primary question. In true Rockefeller fashion, he went about systematically studying the meandering tentacles of the situation. He hired an outside consultant to augment his own staff in making studies. He invited some of the leaders of the New Left to his office for a "rap session." Few of them would have guessed that the oil portrait they faced on the wall behind John D. Rockefeller 3rd was that of his grandfather at the age of about fifty, a robust man with full mustache, the symbol of robber baronism. John 3rd, in his inimitable gracious manner, made his guests comfortable and then asked the probing questions which concerned him. And he listened to the answers as long as they went on. He was receptive. Meeting with students in groups or singly, he arrived at the conclusion that most of the dissident youth wanted to change the inequities of "the system" but they did not want to destroy it. In fact, most were willing to work within the system for those changes, if that were possible. But, they felt, no one in the Establishment, no one in positions of power seemed willing to listen to their complaints. John 3rd listened and warmed to the high idealism of most of the youths he met. He found he could empathize with their points of view and it struck him that the activism of today's youth, their spirit, their commitment to trying to change America for the better was *qualitatively* of more import than the usual youthful idealism which was easily stifled in the past.

When the Society for the Family of Man, a part of the Protestant Council of Churches, offered John 3rd their Family of Man Award for 1968, John 3rd accepted the honor primarily in order to speak out on the youth revolution. He honed that speech phrase by phrase over eleven drafts, working months on it as he continued to meet with high school and college students representing a cross section of political and social views. The speech, delivered October 23, 1968, was the finest of his career. At the Americana Hotel dinner he received a thunderous, standing ovation. Newspapers and magazines reported and, in many cases, reprinted the speech across the nation. It was the first time someone of John 3rd's stature and Establishment credentials had spoken out on the troubling youth revolution.

"Every generation has had its gap. But it seems to me unmistakably

clear that we are experiencing something much more than the age-old re-
belliousness of youth. The ferment of today is deep and intense. Although
the activists are a minority of young people, it is a large and more vocal
minority than ever before . . . There is a tenacity that was lacking in the
past. Young people do not seem to be merely getting something out of
their systems. Perhaps it is too early to tell, but I do not believe they will
slip easily into the comforts of suburbia and the career, leaving behind
their idealism and impulse for change . . .

"In an age of affluence and potential Armageddon, they are less concerned about material security and more concerned about basic human
values. They feel that time is running out on the great problems—war, ra-
cial injustice, poverty. They dislike the impersonalization of large organizations and of rapid technological change. Because of the influence of the
mass media and the freedoms of our society young people today learn
faster and mature earlier. They become quickly aware—and deeply resent-
ful—of the differences between what older people say and what they do.

"In short, the very accomplishments of our generation—in technology, communications, affluence—have served to focus the attention of the
young on what we have failed to accomplish . . . Instead of worrying
about how to suppress the youth revolution, we of the older generation
should be worrying about how to sustain it. The student activists are in
many ways the elite of our young people. They perform a service in shaking us out of our complacency. We badly need their ability and fervor in
these troubled and difficult times."

That was strong talk indeed for Mr. Establishment himself. He called
upon the older generation to respond to youth's idealism by joining in a
new attempt to fight injustice and to solve the massive problems of society. "A unique opportunity is before us," he concluded, "to bring together
our age and experience and money and organization with the energy and
idealism and social consciousness of the young. Working together, almost
anything is possible." And he reminded his listeners of the VISTA slogan:
"If you're not part of the solution, you're part of the problem."

His son Jay applauded too, but asked pointedly, "But what are *you*
going to do about it?" The speech stopped short of how and on what the
older generation might work together with the under-thirty generation,
said John D. Rockefeller IV. How do you implement such a program?

John 3rd committed himself for the long pull; he hired more staff,
more outside consultants, a public opinion polling firm. He established
what he called a Task Force on Youth, he traveled across the country for
rap sessions with the dissatisfied in Harlem and the Haight-Ashbury flower
people of the West Coast, he drew in heads of corporations and community leaders for an exchange of views on goals and programs. He worked
more than a year on the idea of establishing a National Service Corps in
which young people would serve a year or two in anti-pollution projects,

helping the underprivileged or volunteering health services. The idea was finally abandoned as too bureaucratic and too regimented to fit the mood or aspirations of today's youth. It was much like the military.

John 3rd, undeterred, turned to other ideas. His polls showed that indeed Establishment figures and youth did agree on the need to solve certain problems facing America. Pollution was an obvious one. So John 3rd, in December 1970, proposed to five colleges* located in and around Amherst, Massachusetts, that he give $25,000 to finance a pilot project on cleaning up the nearby Connecticut River Valley. He went to Hampshire College, a new open, unstructured institution, to make his proposal, and there he encountered a guerrilla theater performance which depicted all five Rockefeller brothers as stereotyped robber barons playing Monopoly with the world. There he faced a hostile audience alone, answering in his soft, genteel voice the most outrageous questions the students could throw at him and, in the end, winning the respect if not the support of the majority in attendance. At first, the students demurred from accepting his $25,000 offer on grounds of general suspicion. A few months later, the grant was accepted. But nothing came of it. The youngsters did not hold up their end. There was no study of the pollution in the Connecticut River Valley and no attempt to clean it up.

Following the campus riots of 1970 and the shootings at Kent State University, John 3rd helped to set up programs at fifty colleges in which classes would be called off so that students could help get out the vote and participate positively in the presidential election of 1972. Results were minuscule. There was no great difference in the youth vote that anyone could measure.

A third program set up youth-Establishment dialogues on specific community problems in cities across the nation: Minneapolis, Louisville, Cleveland, San Francisco and Jackson, Mississippi. One- to three-day conferences were scheduled for these rap sessions, out of which it was hoped action programs would evolve. Were they successful? It is too early to tell. But at least there was a beginning: youthful, concerned activists were talking with their elders, the concerned business, government and civic leaders of their communities, and they were listening to one another. John 3rd hoped the counterculture could change the consciousness of the dominant culture, while at the same time the anti-Establishment contingent would come to recognize the practical difficulties involved in implementing change.

John 3rd's exposure to America's youth movement and its cult had a significant effect upon him personally. He went to see Broadway's first nudity hit *Hair* and learned something of the Age of Aquarius; he began to listen to rock music and ballads of protest on the radio; he observed the life-styles of radical youth and listened to their explanations of why it was

* Hampshire, Smith, Mount Holyoke, Amherst and the University of Massachusetts.

better to "let it all hang out." Above all, he was impressed with the concern and inner idealism of the youths he met and how close they were to what he and his brothers believed and yet how far from the outward manifestations of the way they were raised. Nor was it lost upon him how sheltered and tight his own early life had been in comparison to the youth of today. And yet, at the bottom of it was the shared concern for the human values over materialistic ones.

It led him, a shy man who so loved to remain in the background and literally out of sight, to venture to write his first book, which he called *The Second American Revolution*, in 1973, outlining what he viewed as a basic change in American values from the materialism of the industrial revolution of his grandfather's day to today's concern for humanism—a devotion to human welfare and concern for one's fellow man. All of his own concerns were brought into it and correlated—an open society, equal opportunity, civil rights, the arts and culture, ecology and the quality of individual life. As he saw it, American society, thanks to its youth, was now on the move and "in the early stages of the Second American Revolution." The book was received politely. But the message struck no chord of popularity, received no great public response. John D. Rockefeller 3rd apparently was ahead of his time once again.

Undaunted, he turned his attention to the American Bicentennial celebration, working behind the scenes in an attempt to establish a national organization of private citizens who would pledge themselves in 1976 to a series of agreed-upon humanistic goals to correct specific wrongs in American society by the year 1989. It took the founders of this nation thirteen years—from the signing of the Declaration of Independence in 1776 to the ratification of the United States Constitution in 1789—to frame the kind of government and society we have enjoyed for the past two hundred years. John 3rd would have the people now join together in a private endeavor to establish a second American revolution to prevail over the next two hundred years. America's two hundredth birthday came and went and neither its citizens nor its civic leaders banded together in any concerted effort to reframe the weaker aspects of their government, society or way of life.

John 3rd then bent his efforts to persuading the Congress to enact a National Endowment for the Bicentennial Era, which would provide grants-in-aid to help communities and regions of the country sponsor local self-improvement projects in the spirit of a new refounding of the American way of life. Legislation for such a thirteen-year program was introduced and is still pending at this writing.

At the same time, John 3rd never ceased in his efforts to broaden the base of charitable giving in the United States. Aside from helping sponsor several massive studies on the subject, he personally has sought to find some way of giving added incentives to private individual and corporate philanthropy without opening new tax loopholes for those who would abuse the privilege. More than half of all giving in America comes from households with incomes lower than $20,000 a year—and the recent introduction of the standard deductions tax return, designed for convenience, has had the side effect of reducing considerably the amount of charitable giving from the average American. Corporations, on the other hand, which are permitted by the tax laws to give up to 5 per cent of net profits to charity, gave only less than 1 per cent.

As an outgrowth of his lifelong interest in population stability and birth control, John 3rd in the 1970s launched into the whole field of human sexuality. As he had set up the Population Council years before to undertake basic research in population questions, so in the 1970s he persuaded various foundations to sponsor basic research at the university level into the whole question of human sexuality. How are sexual attitudes formed? What are the effects of such sexual attitudes upon human behavior? What is really known of sexual attitudes? What is mere theory? What is genetic and what environmental in sexual attitudes and behavior? This project too was a long-term venture, a quest for basic scientific knowledge upon which an enlightened society then can base its actions.

Such views may be shrugged off by pessimists and cynics alike as the impossible dreams of an impractical man. But John D. Rockefeller 3rd, well aware of such criticisms, works on day after day unheralded in the practical steps of persuading others to join him in his quest. When he passed the age of sixty-five, a close aide and friend suggested that he ought to think of retiring, taking life easy and getting more fun out of what was left to him. "Write me a memo on it," he replied. "Tell me what you think I ought to do, and I'll think about it."

When his seventieth birthday rolled around in March 1976, he paid little attention to it. A small family dinner party at home sufficed. He worked that day. When a scheduled staff meeting at the office was turned into a surprise birthday party for him, he was genuinely surprised and touched. It was a coffee and cake affair and upon the cake was printed his own favorite expression: "This is an exciting time to be alive."

His personal gratification comes from the work he does, from the causes he espouses, from the battles he has won, from the changes he has helped bring about in the American way of life, from the secure knowledge that he is living a useful life in challenging times. He is totally sincere and committed to working for causes larger than himself or his own self-interest. Those close to him also recognize that this man with the famous name, who is so often thought of as Mr. Establishment, is in truth in the forefront of the American avant-garde. Who knows but that someday his vision of a possible America may become reality? Who knows but that someday John D. Rockefeller 3rd may well be heralded as the father of the second American revolution?

21

Rockefeller Power

"The blanket of happiness seems too short."

Money was only one part of the extraordinary inheritance of the Rockefellers. The five brothers and their sister inherited far less wealth than
most people assumed. But for John 3rd, Nelson, Laurance, Winthrop,
David and Abby, the intangibles they inherited meant more personally to
them than the fabulous fortune associated with the family name. Their
birthright was the excellent health, strong bodies, extraordinary stamina
and longevity of the Rockefeller family. No chronic diseases or ailments
for them, no weak hearts or lungs, no ulcers, not even a weak joint or muscle to impede their march through life. It all came to them as a blessing of
their birth, unearned as their wealth, which each of them was careful not
to waste. Except Winthrop. Even he, smoking two and more packs of
harsh Picayune cigarettes every day, drinking uncounted scotches and gins,
eschewing regular exercise, driving his mammoth, overweight body beyond
the endurance of a normal man, even he enjoyed the remarkable Rockefeller good health right up to the end. His more rational brothers performed their regular exercises daily, took care to get their needed rest and
were properly cautious toward the temptations of spirits and tobacco.
None of them smoked cigarettes; Laurance and John puffed on a pipe
more occasionally than regularly; Nelson and David smoked not at all.
David indulged himself in the businessman's one or two cocktails, usually
martinis, before dinner and on occasion one before a large lunch. But the
others drank Dubonnet or sherry. John 3rd liked to sip a cold beer on a
hot summer's day, but for him one beer was a special treat. Compared to
most other men's, these personal indulgences were modest. Compared to
the habits of their non-smoking, teetotaling father and grandfather and

consequently to their own upbringing, any and all of their smoking and drinking represented a generational leap. For the brothers, it was a matter of keeping up with the times, finding their places in the mainstream of America's changing customs.

Their inherited good health was linked to an extraordinary stamina, which served as an important ingredient of the successes they won in their careers. Each of them physically could outwork, outlast and outwear their peers or competitors. They were seemingly indefatigable in working twelve or sixteen hours a day, day after day, year after year. They could outsit almost anyone at a negotiating table, or seem to; they could and did rush from one meeting to another, jump from one subject to another, jet beyond the time zones of the world and hardly feel the lag; they could eat stale banquet chickens and roasts three or four times a week and suffer no bellyaches. They had stamina and it carried them a long way in the affairs of man. More than that, they also did not have the ordinary man's need to hurry. They had inherited the promise of long life: their grandfather had lived to within two months of ninety-eight years of age; their father to eighty-six.

So, as a matter of inheritance, the five brothers of the third generation of Rockefellers were healthy, and they certainly were wealthy, and they had every reason to be wise. They grew up in the most salubrious surroundings available in America. They had governesses, tutors, riding masters, the best schools and, more than all that, two loving parents who cared about them. Religion, ethics and values were an integral and important part of their everyday lives. They were surrounded by beauty. It was supplied outdoors by nature and the family's helping hand, and indoors by some of the most gifted artists of ancient and modern times. At their dinner table, they met and listened to some of the great men of the day talk on the great issues of the day. Doctors, lawyers, judges, clergymen, scientists, writers, statesmen, politicians, royalty, industrialists—all of them eminent or knowledgeable or both in their specialized fields—came to visit the Rockefellers because they had something special to tell them. For the Rockefeller brothers in their early years this was an education in itself, an education that ordinary youngsters could not hope to share, and it was all part of their inheritance.

If all this smacks of royalty and *noblesse oblige* in the heart of a democratic republic, so be it. It was there, named or unnamed. There was something special, very special, about being a Rockefeller, a descendant of *the* John D. Rockefeller. And, of course, there was a price to pay.

Like the aristocracy of bygone years, one's upbringing was circumscribed and special, one's childhood more lonely than others', one's real or imagined responsibilities and burdens heavier than could be carried comfortably. The Rockefeller brothers were taught and trained to accept the responsibilities, duties and commitments expected of men in their special station in life. Their father made no secret of it. Long before they became aware of the size and scope of the Rockefeller fortune, they learned of the family responsibilities. Their father put the concept succinctly in his personal credo: "I believe that every right implies a responsibility; every opportunity, an obligation; every possession, a duty."

In ethical terms, it was their cross to bear. In practical terms, their father promised each of them that unless he individually demonstrated his acceptance of the responsibilities, obligations and duties incumbent upon a Rockefeller, he would not get the rights, the opportunities or the possessions which were within the power of John D. Rockefeller, Jr., to give him. They had their austere father looking over their shoulders. He stood in solemn judgment observing each of them grow into manhood. He held the purse strings to the Rockefeller wealth and power. As the brothers reached their maturity, they came to learn that they also had the whole nation looking over their shoulders, trying to see what they had and what they would do with what they had. Much of their lives would have to be lived in a fish bowl of fame, notoriety, adulation, sycophancy, envy, hatred, misunderstanding and a touch of unreality. What was seen in the fish bowl was more in the eye of the beholder than in the inhabitants of the fish bowl itself.

From the outside looking in, many observers attributed to the Rockefellers the motives presumed to move all too many men: greed and guilt. They averred the Rockefellers sought more power and more wealth because all men are afflicted with the sin of greed. Some charged that all or most of the family's philanthropic activities were based upon either an oblique grab for more power or a guilty need to atone for the sins of the famous founder of Standard Oil. Actually, the second and third generation of Rockefellers felt no personal need to amass more money or more power and they felt no guilt whatsoever over the family fortune or how it was acquired. Certainly old John D., a deeply religious Baptist, harbored no guilt. He regarded the money he earned as a by-product of the competitive game of business proficiency he played all of his life with glee and satisfaction for the sake of the game itself.

Attention had long been focused on that family fortune and the extent of power it gave to the Rockefellers. The fortune was estimated as the greatest single concentration of usable and available money in the nation. Consequently the Rockefellers were regarded as the most powerful family of the most powerful capitalistic nation in the world. But it was this wealth and this power that were most hidden from the eyes of the world. With the inherent American right of privacy, the Rockefellers were no more liable to reveal the extent of their assets and income than would any Smiths tell their nextdoor neighbors what they had in their savings account or safe deposit box. Old John D. never told. Allan Nevins, the historian with access to the Rockefeller papers, could only estimate the size of

John D. Rockefeller's fortune. He put the figure at $900 million, but gave no source or accounting. Others guessed that the wily founder of Standard Oil must have had another $100 million somehow or somewhere and declared him America's first billionaire. The important point, however, was that John D. Rockefeller had amassed the largest, by far, personal fortune in America, greater than that of J. P. Morgan, Harriman, Du Pont, Carnegie or any other mogul of the nineteenth century. Old John D. neither confirmed nor denied any of these published reports. To this day, his family has not revealed the size of the original family fortune.

The extent of Rockefeller power, ever intertwined with the amount of the family's wealth, has always been open to speculation and interpretation. The situation was not unlike that of the five blind philosophers trying to describe an elephant. The man feeling the tail said it was like a snake; the one grasping a leg was sure it was a trunk of a tree; to the blind man feeling the side of the elephant, it was a kind of solid wall; and so on . . . To the social philosophers of this day and of the recent past—historians, economists, journalists and critics—"the Rockefellers" as a family and a symbol of capitalism has loomed so large that descriptions and interpretations have reflected only that part of the whole which was touched upon. Modern-day interpreters were like blind men of old groping for an answer, unable to grasp the over-all reality.

Blind estimates of the family's wealth ranged far and wide. Starting with the $1 billion attributed to John D. Rockefeller, Sr., and his one-fourth ownership of the original Standard Oil Company, the geometric expansion of that wealth through the years of industrial growth and inflation led some interpreters to estimate the present-day wealth of the Rockefellers at $5 billion or $10 billion or perhaps close to $20 billion. The computations were arithmetically correct and even logical, except they were not based upon facts or economic reality. Writers in the 1930s and 1940s ticked off the companies and industries and aspects of American life the Rockefellers of the third generation were supposed to control. The Rockefellers were said to control the oil industry through their holdings in the Standard Oil companies. When the five grandsons of the founder of Standard Oil left college and entered the world of business affairs, writers had no trouble in describing how their father, John D. Rockefeller, Jr., "directed" his five sons to five different spheres of influence: John 3rd into philanthropy, Nelson into government, Laurance into business, Winthrop into oil, David into banking. It was only logical to assume that their mission was to gain control over each sphere, just as their grandfather had built a monopoly in the oil resources of this country. It was logical to assume the Rockefellers would plan it this way. It was logical and coherent to assume that the descendants of John D. Rockefeller would be similar to if not exact replicas of John D. Rockefeller. It was logical then to assume that the five Rockefeller brothers would conspire and work together to help each other in reaching the peaks of power, control and wealth within their grasp. This is the conspiratorial interpretation of history: if five men with similar interests meet in a room, it is logical to assume they are conspiring to do something for good or evil. It is logical and even possible. But it ain't necessarily so.

That same conspiratorial theory for interpreting events lies behind the belief that the Rockefellers somehow secretly control much of American industry through interlocking directorates. If one man sits on the board of directors of two or more companies, and if that man is a Rockefeller, a Rockefeller representative or someone beholden to the Rockefellers, then he is presumed somehow to control the two or more companies on behalf of the Rockefellers. In the massive study of who owned the two hundred largest industrial corporations in America, done by the Temporary National Economic Committee (TNEC) from 1937 to 1939, it was disclosed that the total Rockefeller family holdings (including trust funds, personal holdings and foundation holdings) included 13.5 per cent of the stock of Standard oil of New Jersey, 11 per cent of Standard Oil of Indiana, 12 per cent of Standard Oil of California, 16 per cent of Mobil Oil and 19.5 per cent of Marathon Oil (formerly the Ohio Oil Company). The TNEC study then went on to compile a cross reference of directors of these oil companies who served on the boards of other companies. Using these figures, other economists went a step further in interpreting the TNEC data, asserting that the Rockefellers thus had varying degrees of control of all these companies through these interlocking directorates. These esoteric and academic studies—based more on preconceived theories than upon facts—were in turn further diluted in the more popular and more political tracts which averred that the Rockefellers wielded an enormous and undemocratic power over the economy of the nation. The attacks came from the far left, from the Communist, Marxist and Maoist interpreters, as well as from the far right of the John Birch Society, the Liberty Lobby and similar organizations. The steady onslaught, no matter how egregious, gave an inflated currency to the idea of the huge, unimaginable power of the Rockefellers to dominate and control the economy, politics and culture of America. Even if one did not fully believe and accept the interpretations of the extremists, one could suspect and half-believe.

Ferdinand Lundberg in 1937 wrote *America's 60 Families*, a much heralded and much quoted book, in which he asserted that "the United States is owned and dominated today by a hierarchy of its sixty richest families, buttressed by no more than ninety families of lesser wealth." He placed the Rockefellers at the head of the list of the sixty richest families, who supposedly controlled the country simply through wealth and stockholdings. There was a spate of books on the subject in the 1970s. William Hoffman devoted his book *David: Report on a Rockefeller* to a single point: "For David Rockefeller, the presidency of the United States would be a demotion." Myer Kutz in his book *Rockefeller Power* attributed the family's power in American life to its philanthropic endeavors. "Philanthropy generates more power than wealth alone can provide," Kutz contended, citing every cause and every institution to which the Rockefellers gave their money or their time. The most "scholarly" study or attack upon the supposed wealth and power of the Rockefellers came in an academic monograph of sixty printed pages by James C. Knowles, an assistant professor of the University of Southern California, in 1973. Professor Knowles, one of a group of so-called "radical economists," argued that what he called "the Rockefeller Financial Group" represented "the greatest single concentration of power in our society." He set out to prove this by showing that the Rockefellers through family ties, ancestors and marriages, however remote, and through interlocking directorates were linked to the Chase Mahattan Bank, the First National City Bank, the Chemical Bank (New York), the First National Bank of Chicago and to the Metropolitan Life, Equitable Life and New York Life insurance companies. Blithely ignoring all well-known and recognized facts to the contrary—such as the arch-rivalry of the Chase Manhattan Bank and the First National City Bank—Professor Knowles treated the four large banks and three mutual life insurance companies as though they were a single entity under Rockefeller domination. After that leap, it is easy enough to go on to extend the domination of the Rockefellers to each and every corporation, foundation, cultural institution or political area in which a single director of any of the banks or insurance companies played part, no matter how small or large. If one then adds up the total assets of the four banks and three insurance companies, the impression is given that this huge hoard of money and power is at the beck and call of the Rockfellers and their "financial group." The theory is there, only the facts are lacking. Nowhere in such studies is any evidence ever cited that these men who sit on the boards of two or more companies actually interlock their activities or do anything involving an illegal conflict of interest. It is merely *assumed* that they are part of a conspiracy of some sort, and usually for the benefit of the Rockefellers.

If such extrapolations, scholarly or otherwise, appear patently ludicrous, they were no more so than the rumors heard in Washington and across the land when President Nixon set out to choose a new Vice-President in 1973 and then again when President Ford had the same task in the extraordinary aftermath of the Watergate scandals in 1974. Cynics whispered both times that surely Nelson Rockefeller would be the nominee, for he could "buy" the office. The price of the bribe varied from $1 million to $10 million. But the conspiratorial premise was the same. Nelson Rockefeller could afford to pay that much or more and he wanted the office (usually with a secret agreement that he would soon thereafter move up to the presidency) and both Richard Nixon and later Gerald Ford certainly could personally use the money for comfortable retirement. So all the ingredients were there for a deal. Therefore, a deal would be made. The only thing omitted was the fact that none of those three men would actually do such a thing. When the 1976 election year rolled around, it was President Ford running for re-election and Vice-President Rockefeller retiring from office, having displayed during his two years of incumbency no more political power or punch than any Vice-President before him.

When Nelson Rockefeller was nominated for Vice-President in August 1974 by President Ford under terms of the Twenty-fifth Amendment to the Constitution, which required ratification by both houses of Congress, the stage was set for the revelation of Rockefeller wealth and power. Ratification was *almost* a foregone conclusion. Nelson Rockfeller, having served in government for almost twenty-five years, including fifteen years as governor of New York, having aimed for the presidency three times, was generally recognized in 1974 as a powerful and still alluring force in the Republican Party and, like him or not, a respected elder statesman with enough personal energy and political clout to make him a future presidential possibility. However, it was the post-Watergate era: suspicion and cynicism were rampant, and the public had come to expect the unexpected. Certainly Nelson Rockefeller was qualified to be Vice-President. It was generally conceded that if a civil service examination were given to choose a President, Nelson Rockefeller would win the office on merit alone. But the one potential bar to his becoming Vice-President was the possibility of a conflict of interest between his holding office as Vice-President and his holding too large a slice of the American economy as his personal or his family's wealth. "Did you hear," asked the political wags in Washington, "that in order to avoid a conflict of interest, Rockefeller's going to have to divest himself of Venezuela and New York?" Behind the jest was the honest wonder of how a man of Rockefeller's wealth, with his stocks and bonds and ownership of large slices of American business, could possibly divest himself of enough to avoid a conflict of interest while serving as Vice-President of the United States.

To Nelson Rockefeller personally, the suppositions about his wealth and economic power were based upon a myth of long standing. He was eager to set the record straight. In pre-hearing conferences with members of the House, he readily agreed to provide a full accounting of his wealth, his trusts, his stocks and bonds, his real estate, his cash on hand, backed up by his income tax returns for the ten previous years. He believed the public, especially in the aftermath of Watergate, had a right to know. Even before Watergate, Nelson had felt that a man seeking public office should reveal all his sources of income to reassure the public of no possible conflict of interest. During the California primary of 1964, when public attention had been focused on the private wealth of President Johnson, Nelson had been prepared to make public his own assets and sources of income. His office had compiled a complete financial accounting and he had gone through that bitter primary campaign armed with the facts and figures on his wealth. But no one had asked him.

Ten years later he came with those facts and figures updated to August 23, 1974, before the Senate Rules Committee in public hearings on his confirmation as Vice-President. On the opening day, he asserted to the Congress, to the nation and to the world: "I hope that the myth or misconception about the extent of the family's control over the economy of this country will be totally brought out and exposed and dissipated . . . I've got to tell you, I don't wield economic power."

His accounting, in rounded-off figures, showed $2.9 million in cash on hand and accounts receivable and $12.8 million in stocks and bonds. That was the amount he could readily put his hands upon, hardly enough to wield economic power in the financial market place. The remainder of his and his wife's personal assets were invested in art ($33.5 million) real estate ($11,252,000), furnishings ($1,191,000), automobiles, boats and airplanes ($1,768,000) and jewelry and coins ($533,700).

"As of August 23, 1974, the total assets of my wife and myself were $64 million and our net worth $62.5 million," he declared. Later, an Internal Revenue Service audit placed a higher value on his real estate, lifting his total assets to $73 million.

The primary source of his wealth came to him as a life beneficiary (of the income) of two trusts, set up for him in 1934 and 1952 by his father with total assets of over $116 million as of August 30, 1974. The first trust, started with $20 million in 1934, a dark depressed year for oil stocks, had risen to $106,272,000 and that included Nelson's share in Rockefeller Center ($25.5 million), which he himself added to the trust in 1969. Thus, in forty years, that trust, administered by the Trust Department of the Chase Manhattan Bank, had increased in value only four times. The second trust, started in 1952 with about $12 million, had decreased in value to $10,231,000. However, Nelson Rockefeller's income over the past ten years from these trusts and his own securities had averaged $4.6 million a year.

While this is indeed a princely income, the figures also reveal that just about half of it each year went to federal, state and local taxes, another million went for his share of office and professional services at 5600 and another million or more went for the upkeep of his various homes. It left him very little with which to wield economic power. The truth was that Nelson Rockefeller over the years experienced every man's need to live within his income.

As for the much speculated-upon Rockefeller grip on the Standard Oil companies founded by his grandfather, Nelson revealed that the largest amount of stock he or his trusts held for him in any one of those companies was two tenths of 1 per cent of the outstanding shares of Standard Oil Company of California (353,154 shares). His and his trusts' share of ownership of Exxon (formerly Standard Oil of New Jersey) was .18 per cent; in Standard Oil of Indiana, .01 per cent; in Mobil, less than .01 per cent. The total holdings of the whole family told the same story: 2.06 per cent ownership of Standard Oil of California, 1.07 per cent of Exxon and lesser amounts in the other companies. "None of the descendants of my father serves on the board of any of the oil companies," Nelson declared, "and we have no control of any kind over the management or policies of any of them."

The delineation of the candidate's wealth, the list of his stocks and bonds, his trusts, real estate, art collection and personal possessions did not fully satisfy some of the Democrats on the House Judiciary Committee, which held its hearings after those of the Senate Rules Committee. They demanded disclosure of the entire family's fortune and economic interests, contending that only with that information could they and the nation be satisfied that there was no inherent conflict of interest in Nelson Rockefeller's becoming Vice-President. Nelson, after some consideration, agreed that there was some merit to the demand.* It would serve a useful purpose in the lingering cynicism that followed Watergate, Nelson thought, to reassure the public that the Rockefeller family did not wield any undue influence over the American economy. He agreed to ask all the adult members of his family (for he could not force them) to reveal in aggregate their major holdings in American industry.

J. Richardson Dilworth, the family senior financial adviser over the past sixteen years, appeared before the House Judiciary Committee for that purpose. He brought with him large charts which listed the Rockefeller family assets, including a list of each and every company in which a Rockefeller held an interest of $1 million or more. By way of preface, the tall, lean and soft-spoken financier emphasized that the occasion was a "unique experience." Never before had any such compilation of Rockefeller stockholdings been made, not by his office nor by anyone else. "They do not act in concert on financial or other matters," he declared. "Nor, out of respect for each other's personal privacy, would they consider prying into the personal or financial affairs of their respective relatives." In other words, not only did they not act in concert, as some people suspected, but the brothers did not even know the size, extent or make-up of each other's fortunes.

* The Rockefeller brothers, long troubled with the exaggerated estimates and extrapolations made of their wealth and economic power, had at one point, several years before these hearings, contemplated giving the author for this book a summary compilation of the family's wealth and stockholdings. Their purpose was to put an end to the speculation once and for all. After the hearings they felt that they had revealed enough for their own purpose and politely declined to divulge their individual holdings.

The current Rockefeller family fortune, according to Dilworth, was divided basically into three parts: the 1934 and the 1952 trusts established by John D. Rockefeller, Jr., and the investments owned outright by the living Rockefellers, which were managed by Dilworth and his staff at Room 5600.

The largest part was the 1934 trusts, managed at the Chase Manhattan Bank, with total assets of $640 million. The 1952 trusts, managed by the Fidelity Union Trust of Newark, New Jersey, were valued at $98.6 million. Stocks, bonds and real estate owned outright by the Rockefellers amounted to a total of $242.2 million, plus another $51 million in trusts set up by the third (Nelson's) generation of Rockefellers for its progeny.

So the grand total of the Rockefeller family wealth added up to just over that magic figure of a billion dollars ($1,031,988,000). Later adjustments of the various figures put the total at $1.3 billion. Of course, these figures were changing and would change every day with the fluctuations of the stock, bond and real estate markets. More important than that, however, was that the Rockefeller fortune was divided among all the living descendants and their spouses of John D. Rockefeller, Jr.—eighty-four in number. Even not counting wives and husbands, the number of Rockefellers sharing the fortune was considerable: there were Abby, John 3rd, Nelson, Laurance and David (Winthrop having died in 1973). Among them, they had twenty-two surviving offspring (Michael having died in 1968), and they, generally called the Cousins, had in turn forty-one children thus far, with more likely to come as the younger Cousins married. Thus, the Rockefellers by birth to date numbered sixty-eight.

In summarizing the history of the Rockefeller fortune, the family's financial adviser traced what had happened to John D. Rockefeller, Sr.'s original billion. The founder of Standard Oil in his lifetime gave $550 million to various foundations and philanthropic institutions and he gave $465 million to his only son. In turn, John D. Rockefeller, Jr., gave $552 million to charity and $240 million to his family. He also left upon his death $72 million to his second wife, most of which went to charity upon her death. And, finally, the living members of the family had given to date more than $235 million to charity, which was close to the amount given to them in the first place. So it can be seen that the Rockefeller family fortune has been perpetuated over three generations at about $1 billion. The third generation—John 3rd, Nelson, Laurance, Winthrop, David and Abby—has neither squandered the fortune nor greatly increased it. The growth of the American economy and the inflation factor account as much as anything else for the growth of the family fortune in the third generation.

Dilworth testified in detail on how he and his staff of seven security analysts—backed up by accountants, tax advisers, attorneys and others—advised family members on his or her own investments. He stressed the point that each Rockefeller was treated as an individual client and each one's portfolio was handled separately and in accordance with the client's guidelines. Dilworth explained that he and his staff operated much the same as any other investment counseling service would in serving the general public. His charts and testimony showed that the $244.2 million in major Rockefeller investments, handled by his office, was well diversified: $114.7 million (or 47 per cent) in major stockholdings of over $1 million each; $8.5 million in small stockholdings; $31 million in bonds; and $90 million in real estate and special holdings.

The Rockefellers, he declared firmly, were long-term investors. They were not traders in and out of the stock market seeking fractional or quick gains. Nor has any one of them ever sought to gain control over a particular company, or to corner a market, or to make a killing. "It should be stressed that both the family members and their investment advisers in the family office are totally uninterested in controlling anything," asserted Dilworth. "The family members are simply investors. The aim and hope of the advisers is—in a most difficult and uncertain world—over time to achieve a reasonable total return for our clients." How well over the years have the financial advisers served the Rockfellers? No better and no worse than the average in professionally managed portfolios anywhere else, according to Dilworth himself.

The lists of Rockefeller family holdings, in trust and wholly owned, contained no surprises. Most of their money was invested in well-known, staid and venerable stocks: the oil companies, Chase Manhattan Bank, Eastman Kodak, AT&T, General Electric, IBM, Texas Instruments, Xerox, Minnesota Mining and Manufacturing, Monsanto, Aluminum Company of America. Outside experts and investment specialists enjoyed a field day analyzing the Rockefeller portfolios. Generally they reached the same conclusions: "It's what you'd expect," said one. The Rockefellers had invested in oil and other blue chip stocks; the trusts managed by banks were very conservative and almost identical in stocks held by most bank trusts departments everywhere; and in the Rockefeller personal holdings there were some "cats and dogs" but their major holdings were long-term investments in the major corporations of the country.

Ironically, the two companies in which the Rockefellers admitted having a controlling interest were not doing well at all. IBEC, the company Nelson started after World War II to demonstrate U.S. business know-how south of the border and which his son, Rodman, was running now, was selling (or not selling) at a buck and a half a share. The Rockefellers owned 78 per cent of that company. They owned 100 per cent of Rockefeller Center, Inc., and that fabulous piece of real estate was operating at a loss, according to Dilworth, having slipped back into the red because of the over-all disastrous real estate market in New York City, as businesses fled that beleaguered city in the 1970s. Actually, whatever might have been normal profits were eaten up by the high cost of maintaining the Center to Rockefeller standards and by the exorbitant rent the Center must pay each year to Columbia University, which still owns the land upon which Rockefeller Center was built.

A strange quiescence descended upon the subject of Rockefeller wealth, power and control over the economy following all this testimony. Perhaps it was a stunned silence. No editorials or analyses appeared in the press. No one recalled the half-joking demands for Nelson Rockefeller to divest himself of Venezuela. (His landholdings in all of Latin America totaled $4.2 million.) Some members of the House Judiciary Committee complained that they hardly had time during the hearings to analyze all of the financial material presented to them. But two years went by as Nelson served as Vice-President and no one, inside Congress or out, brought up the subject of a conflict of interest due to Rockefeller wealth or economic power. Nothing had been heard from the radical left; nothing from the extreme right, other than they still cannot abide Nelson Rockefeller. Dick Dilworth may well have put the quietus on what his boss, Nelson Rockefeller, said in the first place was a "myth or misconception" about the Rockefeller family's wealth and economic power. The $1 billion fortune is no larger than it was originally. It is shared by eighty-four members of the family. And three fourths of that fortune is locked up for years in bank-managed trusts beyond the control of the Rockefellers now living.

What then is the power of the Rockefellers? Surely, the Rockefellers are powerful. They exert a force in the United States and even beyond the boundaries of their own country. A case can be made that outside of the White House and the highest echelons of the government, they are the most powerful men in the nation. But only because it is difficult if not impossible to think of any others who are more powerful. Is it their fabulous wealth? Other men who were and are contemporaries of Nelson and his brothers were far richer and far less powerful in the affairs of the nation. The late John Paul Getty, Howard Hughes and H. L. Hunt of Texas each owned and controlled fortunes estimated at between $2 billion and $4 billion; the Du Ponts and the Mellon family have been said to be worth between $3 billion and $5 billion each. Yet none of them were or are presumed to have but a fraction of the power of the Rockefellers. *Fortune* magazine in 1968 said, "We believe we can identify 153 individuals whose net worth, including wealth held by their spouses, minor children, trusts and foundations, makes them centi-millionaires." In 1973, *Fortune* added another dozen men to the list who had "risen from relative obscurity to become centi-millionaires in the past five years." So there would appear to be at least 165 men and women in the United States with fortunes of more than $100 million—and *Fortune* magazine estimates that there are more whose privately held enterprises simply defy detection—and most of them are unknown by name to the general public. Wealth alone does not

make power, not the kind of power which extends beyond a single enterprise or business or a confined locality, not the kind of power which can
sway a nation on the whim of a man in control of $100 million or of $3
billion.

The power of the Rockefellers is simply not the kind of power their
critics have accused them of possessing to excess. It is not the power of
control. They do not wield any such control or authority over any segment
of American industry or government or upon any large group of people.
Their power is of a different kind. When a Rockefeller speaks, others listen. When a Rockefeller brother picks up the telephone to say something
to the President of the United States (Republican or Democrat) or to a
member of the President's Cabinet, or to a leader of industry, or, in fact,
to anyone, the telephone call goes through or is returned promptly. That
is the power of the Rockefellers, the power to influence, to be in a position
in which one's words produce an effect and move others to action. It is
that kind of power, the power to influence, that the Rockefeller brothers
have extended across the land as far as or farther than any other men in
the nation.

How have they acquired such power? Money plays a part, of course,
but only a part. The best answer has been given by their associates and
subordinates who work with them every day as well as by others who observe them at first hand in the course of a business day. They use different
words but the descriptions add up to the same three ingredients: the
Rockefeller brothers have and use lucre, leverage and longevity.

They do have enough money on hand to back up almost any enterprise or cause they choose to embrace. There was one instance in which
Nelson as a young man thought he had found the man who could solve
the food problem of India, only to be told by the family's counsel that the
man proposed to irrigate all of India's desert land and even the Rockefellers did not have the money for that project. In time, though, the
brothers learned how to launch a project with seed money and then to
husband the land and help the plant grow. They learned how to use
money as a carrot to entice others to embrace their concept of a controversial project. They have that kind of money and are willing to spend it
for what they believe in. John 3rd would finance the early years of the
Population Council until that organization gained its own footing and
prestige to attract outside financing. Nelson had the money to finance
much of his own political campaigns without having to bargain away his
own beliefs in exchange for the financial support of others. Laurance
could put up the money to launch the American Conservation Association, convincing the leaders of five separate and disparate conservation organizations to join forces for the common good. His arguments were per-
suasive but his money served as the carrot. The stick in such cases is rarely
needed. Winthrop with his money as the forceps served as obstetrician to

the rebirth of the Republican Party in Arkansas. David could buy contemporary art from living, struggling artists and put such things in a staid old bank and prove a point; he could lecture and demonstrate to the business world that a sense of social responsibility to the community, to the poor, to the minorities should and could be an integral part of good business policy.

The amount of such money actually invested was large by the standards of the common man. But, examined closely, one finds the money the Rockefellers of the third generation invested in such projects was not beyond the means of a great number of other wealthy men in this country, and certainly not beyond the reach of various groups or organizations of men.

Not having the wealth of their father or their grandfather, and knowing it, the Rockefeller brothers learned to use leverage to get what they wanted. They learned to work within groups rather than alone. Their careers are replete with associations and councils and organizations, as they joined with others and exercised leadership in bringing a combined force to bear upon a project at hand. Their seed money for new projects was a form of leverage. They gave "matching funds" long before the federal government adopted the concept, and thus a million-dollar contribution from a Rockefeller could be stretched to $2 million or $4 million. Where John D. Rockefeller, Jr., built Rockefeller Center and paid for it himself, John D. Rockefeller 3rd helped build Lincoln Center, planted some $11 million himself seed by seed and managed to raise over $100 million from others.

Longevity has been the Rockefeller long suit in their power to influence others. They have been around, prominently, for a long, long time, and associated with success. For three generations, the name has been a household word. The reputation of the first John D. Rockefeller as a wily, shrewd old man who could see further ahead than anyone else and then around corners has served his son and his grandsons down to this day. A strong charisma has always been attached to the name Rockefeller, whether comprised of awe, fear, admiration, adoration or a combination of emotions, the reputation of the Rockefellers rested in the eye of the beholder. It was all part of the "myth" of which Nelson spoke at his vice-presidential confirmation hearings. But in addition to the myth, Nelson and his brothers had developed a good track record for success in their own undertakings. They had moved warily before lending the Rockefeller name or finances to any new endeavor or enterprise. But once committed, they stayed with their commitments for the long haul, giving generously of their money, their time and their efforts. It became known in various civic and social circles that if a Rockefeller was involved, the project most likely had merit and was expected to succeed. The Rockefeller reputation and name and past history of success attracted and influenced others to follow their lead. It gave to the Rockefeller brothers a sway and leadership over men and events that were the envy of less fortunate men.

But there were very real limitations to that kind of power, just as there are restrictions to all types of power. This is so obvious it hardly warrants comment. Nevertheless, the "myth" of Rockefeller power is so great in some quarters that some obvious points are in order: Nelson Rockefeller, with all of his vaunted wealth, power and reputation, was not able, despite all his efforts, to win the Republican nomination for President. He was not even able to win the endorsement and support of the eastern Establishment. David Rockefeller was not able to attract enough business in his Chase Manhattan Bank to rival the success of its chief competitor, the First National City Bank. Winthrop did not win a third term as governor of Arkansas. David and his brothers may be able to pick up the telephone and talk to the President of the United States (or of France or Egypt) but that does not mean that the Rockefeller message necessarily will be heeded.

The passing of the second generation in the person of John D. Rockefeller, Jr., in 1960 did not in any material way greatly enhance the power or wealth of the third generation. In fact, it left the brothers with the financial burden of the family office and various homes which had been supported by their father. John D. Rockefeller, Jr., had been weak and frail when he succumbed at age eighty-six to a combination of pneumonia and heart strain in the Tucson Medical Center at noon on May 11, 1960. Nelson and Laurance had flown down from New York that morning to be at his side. His last years had been happy as he followed the seasons, spending the spring at Colonial Williamsburg, the summer on Mount Desert Island in Maine, the autumn at Pocantico Hills and the winter in a cottage on the grounds of the Arizona Inn in Tucson. When his wife Abby died in 1948, after forty-seven years of marriage, he had found himself lonely and lost and wont to dwell upon memories of the past. But three years afterward, at the age of seventy-seven, he married Martha Baird Allen, the fifty-six-year-old widow of his old college friend, Arthur Allen. His second marriage acted as a tonic of rejuvenation which delighted not only him but also his children. They called their new stepmother Aunt Martha. A woman of stable and calm disposition and a former concert pianist of considerable talent, she got along well with all of her stepsons, particularly Nelson. In his will, their father left his property in Maine to Nelson and David, his Wyoming ranch to Laurance, his Park Avenue apartment and his home Kykuit in Pocantico Hills to his second wife. His art treasures and artifacts for the most part he left to be shared by his sons equally and they drew straws to determine the order of rotation in which they would choose the pieces each wanted for his own home. The residue of the estate was divided equally between Martha Baird Rockefeller and the Rockefeller Brothers Fund. The $72 million willed to the RBF transformed it into a major instrument of philanthropic giving. It was a final message of approbation from a father to his sons. As for his wife, who had made the later years of his life so happy, John Jr. had told her he wanted to provide her with what he had had all of his life: "the joy of giving." As a professional musician, she gave the largest chunks of her inherited wealth to enhancing the world of music and, secondly, gave in those areas in which she believed her husband would have wanted his money to go. One of those areas was politics. John Jr. had been stunned and delighted when Nelson was elected governor of New York in 1958 and had contributed generously to that campaign. His widow continued to contribute generously to Nelson's campaigns, as she followed his political career right up to the time of her death in 1971. Soon after John Jr.'s death, she chose a simpler style of living and arranged with Nelson to have a new home built for herself at Pocantico while Nelson took over the main house. None of his brothers wanted it.

As the most fitting memorial for their father, whose ashes were buried alongside those of their mother in the family cemetery in North Tarrytown near Pocantico, the brothers decided to have their father's credo engraved in granite and placed at the entrance to the Rockefeller Center skating rink. A magnificent block of Ubatuba granite, mottled emerald green in color, twelve feet long, five feet wide and three feet deep, weighing sixteen tons, was quarried in a jungle in Brazil and shipped to Proctor, Vermont, where it was carefully cut with a diamond-tooth saw into five slabs and then trucked to the Stevens Shop, founded in 1705, the oldest stonecutting works in the United States, where the 1,335 letters of the credo were incised upon the highly polished granite memorial. Only when the granite slabs were lowered into place, attached to a concrete foundation, at Rockefeller Center was it discovered to the chagrin of the Center staff that a mistake had been made on the granite stone commemorating the most punctilious of all the Rockefellers. The date of his birth was in error. A wood hut was hastily constructed to shield the stone while the embarrassed stonecutter worked for two days to change 1876 to 1874.

Their father's seventeenth-century office in Rockefeller Center was kept precisely as it had been during his lifetime, unused for ten years until 1970. Then, in order to make more room for additional staff, the oak-paneled walls, the Elizabethan mantlepiece, the fireplace and the Jacobean chairs and tables were all removed and stored away in a warehouse. Still later, in 1976, when a permanent Rockefeller Archive Center was set up at Pocantico, his antique office was reassembled there.

The death of John D. Rockefeller, Jr., forced upon his sons the necessity of making several important family decisions. Many of the men intimate with family affairs in the office believed the brothers were so individualistic and headstrong they would split apart and go their separate ways. It was their father in or out of the office who had held them together as a family, many believed. But the men in the office who often tried to second-guess the Rockefeller brothers were wrong again. Family ties still bound the brothers strongly together and they decided to continue the office arrangement at 5600 with family counsel, family financial advisers, a public relations staff and library to be shared and to be paid for by all of them. The management of the family offices was put under the direction of a committee comprised of the brothers, Dick Dilworth and Harper Woodward.

What to do with the family's summer "cottage" on Mount Desert Island was the easiest of the decisions. No one wanted to live in or to maintain the three-and-a-half-story eyrie with its eighty rooms. So, in the spring of 1963, the big concrete and stucco mansion was razed and the Rockefellers saved themselves some $10,000 a year in state and local taxes. The doors, window frames, mantles and elaborate fixtures were auctioned off to the public. Their mother's gardens, however, were maintained and opened to the public on a limited basis.

In putting their own estates in order, the brothers found it much more difficult to decide what was to become of Rockefeller Center, their homes and grounds at Pocantico Hills and the family's papers and archives. These were very personal matters and a great number of people were involved and affected, particularly the brothers and the next generation of Rockefellers. Several studies were made, proposals followed, family conferences ensued, arguments and debates rose to new and higher pitches, and a full fifteen years went by before matters were settled by a combination of attrition and a gradually evolved compromise and consensus.

It took the Rockefellers ten years to set up a permanent archive for the millions of documents relating to the history of the family and the various institutions, organizations and causes associated with it. In 1965, the brothers agreed to try to find one central place in which to put this unique collection. Family documents, dating back to those first ledgers of their grandfather as a boy of sixteen, had been kept, catalogued and filed in cardboard boxes, jam-packed in a warren of little offices at the rear of the mezzanine floor of the RCA Building in Rockefeller Center. Nelson's voluminous gubernatorial papers had been kept separately, scattered between Albany and New York City. The Rockefeller Foundation, with its own bulging archives, and the Rockefeller University, with its mass of scientific papers, agreed to join in and to share expenses, along with several other, smaller organizations associated with the Rockefeller family. Wanting to keep the new archive centrally located and accessible to scholars, the Rockefellers proposed plans to build a new library and archive building on the campus of the Rockefeller University in New York City. But the unexpected opposition to the idea from faculty and students at the university, plus the enormous cost of the proposed project, squelched that plan. Several other plans were drawn up and rejected until the Rockefellers settled on Hillcrest, the home their stepmother, Martha Baird Rockefeller, had built at Pocantico in 1962 at a cost of $3 million. It was standing there empty, never occupied by their stepmother and bequeathed to the Rockefeller Brothers Fund. Another $1.8 million went into converting the home to offices, conference rooms, study carrels and building vast air-conditioned vaults which would house some 12 million documents pertaining to the family and its activities, 10 million papers of the Rockefeller Foundation and some 200,000 of the Rockefeller University. It was opened to scholars in August 1975.

As for Rockefeller Center, the brothers readily agreed that they wanted it to remain as a family enterprise beyond their own lives. It was the symbolic keystone of the family's business life. But how to pass that landmark office building complex to their children presented problems. If each brother willed his share to his children, he would leave them with a debilitating inheritance tax to be paid on a piece of property which yielded little or no income. An even greater dilemma was how to ensure the continuity of Rockefeller Center if control was passed to such a large group of cousins of such varying ages, acumen, interests and points of view. The brothers solved both problems by selling at appraised values their full ownership of Rockefeller Center, Incorporated, stock to the open-ended 1934 trusts which were managed by the Trust Department of the Chase Manhattan Bank. Thus, Rockefeller Center, which was conceived, financed and built by their father, would eventually pass to his grandchildren and great-grandchildren, but for the foreseeable future upon the death of the brothers, the Center would continue to be managed and operated by competent professionals answerable to the conservative fiduciaries of the Chase Bank.

What to do and how to plan for the future of the family estate at Pocantico Hills presented the brothers with their most vexing problem of all. They tried to persuade their children to build their homes there and eventually to inherit the beautiful rolling hills, woodlands, streams and everything contained in the 3,487-acre estate. But the taxes would have been prohibitive. They had various plans drawn up to sell acreage from the northern portion of the estate so that the Cousins and their friends and eventually others could develop a new township with their own schools, recreational facilities and whatever. But that would mean breaking up what many in the family considered to be a special place of beauty, the personal loving work of three generations of Rockefellers.

Over the years, there were several plans and proposals and counterproposals and debates and heated arguments among the Rockefellers of the third and fourth generations. Emotions, personal rivalries, past irritants, the generation gap and honest differences of opinion all came into play to an extent never before witnessed at family conclaves. After all, the Pocantico Hills estate was "home" for the Rockefellers.

The crux of the problem was that the brothers wanted to preserve the estate or to change it as little as possible to conform with future times. But the Cousins did not want to live there, nor did they want to own and pay taxes on a place where they did not reside. Only Nelson's son Rodman among all the Cousins had built his primary residence there on twenty-nine acres he owned next to the town of Pocantico Hills, where he was actively involved in local affairs. Steven kept a simple little cabin off in the woods which he used as a hideaway for meditation and reading. Laurance's son Larry had maintained a weekend house on fifty acres far off in the northwestern section of the estate, totally separated from the other homes. The other Cousins lived elsewhere, scattered across the continent from Berkeley, California, to Cambridge, Massachusetts.

A compromise plan finally was worked out and agreed upon. Since the Cousins did not want to own and support so large an estate, the brothers decided to give 2,157 acres of open woodlands of which they were joint owners to New York State for public use. Nelson announced the brothers' pledge in 1970 but no date for the gift was set. Winthrop took no part in the decision, for he had by then sold his share in the estate to his brothers. The central manicured 250 acres containing the big house, known as the Park, would remain under the joint membership of John 3rd, Nelson, Laurance and David. Each of the brothers would also retain without change their individual homes and property on the estate: Nelson owned 150 acres just east of the Park containing a lodge he used for informal living; Laurance had 281 acres west of the Park overlooking the Hudson River; John 3rd owned 309 acres on the northwest corner of the estate, also overlooking the Hudson; and David lived on 177 acres just north of the Park.

The final disposition of these properties as well as the individual fortunes of John 3rd, Nelson, Laurance and David will become known only upon the passing of those members of the third generation of Rockefellers. Undoubtedly, each will depend upon the separate and individual circumstances pertaining to the benefactors as well as the beneficiaries.

Abby Rockefeller Mauzé died of cancer on the night of May 27, 1976, at the age of seventy-two. She succumbed quietly in bed in her apartment at 1 Beekman Place overlooking New York's East River. Ever a woman of independent opinion, she chose to remain at home and to allow the disease to take its course, rather than enter the Memorial Sloan-Kettering Cancer Center, to which she had contributed $8.8 million over the years. As one of the hospital's largest benefactors, she had received its Medal of Appreciation in 1965 and had served as an advisory member of its board of trustees (of which Laurance was chairman). In her will, she left bequests of $1 million each to Memorial, New York Hospital and the Rockefeller

University, as well as $1.5 million to Greenacre Park, which she had built and endowed on New York's East Side. The bulk of her personal fortune, estimated at $14 million, she left to a charitable trust, stipulating that the income from the trust would go to charity for thirty-five years, after which the principal would be distributed among her descendants. Her two daughters, of course, were provided for through the original 1934 family trust, becoming beneficiaries upon the death of Mrs. Mauzé.

Winthrop, who died in 1973, also willed his residue estate, appraised at $81,616,220, to a charitable trust. He named as trustees an equal number of his associates in Arkansas and New York, including his brother David, Dick Dilworth and the family's counsel Donal O'Brien, instructing them only "to be innovative and venturesome in supporting charitable projects." He made modest bequests of personal items, cash and land on Petit Jean Mountain to his only son, Winthrop Paul, and to his stepchildren Bruce and Anne Bartley. But he did not leave Winrock Farms, as many had expected him to do, to Winthrop Paul. He did not want to burden his son with a gift he might not want; neither did he want to endanger the well-being of the ranch itself. So he gave his son the option of buying Winrock Farms if he wanted it and at the fair market value; he also gave the trustees the option of selling it to Winthrop Paul only if he demonstrated the interest and capacity to run the elaborate ranch.

Winthrop Paul, who had led a carefree, swinging life up to the time of his marriage at twenty-three, accepted at the age of twenty-four his father's challenge. He enrolled for a one-year course at the Ranch Management School of Texas Christian University and attended to his books and classes as he had never done before. Returning to Winrock Farms, the young father of two girls, he took over the management if not the ownership of his father's pride and joy. It was a difficult time of transition. The young heir worked hard to cut away the most blatant luxuries and excesses at Winrock, including many old-time employees. He sought to run a leaner operation than his father had and to find out for himself as much as to demonstrate to the trustees whether or not he could run Winrock Farms and find happiness there. At the beginning, almost all those who knew "Young Winnie" could not conceive how that young man could adjust to the tedious pace of life or the responsibilities atop Petit Jean Mountain in Arkansas. But after his return from the ranch school, many changed their minds. Knowledgeable opinion on the tantalizing family subject became equally divided. Real responsibility and necessity were known to have raised men to new, unsuspected heights.

In November 1975, Winthrop Paul reached his decision: he bought Winrock Farms at its appraised fair market value of $8,162,700. The package included 2,300 acres on Petit Jean Mountain, another 27,000 acres in four other counties and some 2,100 head of purebred cattle. To raise that kind of money, he had to invade the 1934 trust, which had passed from his father to himself as a lifetime beneficiary. And to do that, Winthrop Paul had to appear before the trustees at Chase Manhattan and explain that he intended to make his career at Winrock Farms, raising cattle, rice, soybeans and seeds. He explained that the trustees of his father's estate and he had worked together to reduce the portion he was buying to a manageable, profit-making portion of what his father had built up. The following May, Winthrop Paul conducted his first livestock sale under the new management and it was deemed a tremendous success. It too was a leaner operation and less of a fun fest than his father had sponsored and to the family overseers it augured well for the future. Winthrop Paul was an indication if not yet a proof that the fourth generation of Rockefellers could take over and continue . . .

For most of the Cousins—the other six sons and fourteen daughters over the age of twenty-one of the five Rockefeller brothers and their sister Abby—it was still too early to tell what role, if any, each would play in the future of the family and of the nation. With the exception of some of the older ones beyond the age of forty, most of the Cousins were still in transition, still in the process of changing, of becoming what they would become. All of them were raised in a manner similar to the upbringing of the third generation. But the times and mores had changed dramatically and they had six sets of parents instead of one. There were the prayer sessions and church and Sunday school and the allowances and the fines for bad table manners. But the strictness and rigidity and puritanism were not there. They had faded away with changing manners and social customs of the entire country. Their parents tried to open up vistas of all society to the fourth generation of Rockefellers and to free them from the overprotective shelter they themselves had endured as children. Valiant efforts were made to forge a bond of family togetherness for the Cousins. There were Sunday picnics and parties at Pocantico Hills and family dinners, meetings and conferences. But for all that, the Cousins were cousins and, as a family, never could be as close as blood brothers and sisters.

In the favorite analogy of the family's long-time counsel, John Lockwood, the Rockefeller brothers were like a solar system of planets revolving around their father. Each might travel in a different direction and at a different rate of speed, making different ellipses, but each of them like a planet was tied inextricably to the central sun-like figure of their father. No such analogy can be made for the Cousins. They were scattered more like buckshot. They revolved around no one central figure in the family. In personality, politics, private life-style, they range almost the full gamut of American prototypes.

Some of them were politically on the fringes of the far left, one was an avowed Marxist, some were conservatives, some middle-of-the-roaders; some lived simply, others lavishly, most of them lived in a style indistinguishable from that of the upper middle class. The political, social and economic upheavals of the 1960s had touched and influenced most of them—the anti-Vietnam cause, the youth rebellion on college campuses, the feminist movement and the civil rights and black revolutions. Cousins' meetings were usually dominated by violent disagreements. A family brand of stubbornness and pugnaciousness arose whenever these young people attempted to act as a unified group on any issue. At the 1972 family Christmas party at Pocantico Hills Uncle Nelson was astonished to discover that more than half of the Cousins had voted for George McGovern. It was perhaps not so much how the Cousins had voted that had shook him, but rather how much of the generation gap was showing in the family.

The name Rockefeller was regarded as more of a burden than an advantage to many of the fourth generation. Imprisoned by stereotype opinion, instant recognition, suspicion and distrust, or, on the other hand, by the unwanted sycophancy that attaches to wealth and celebrity like a suction cup, the younger Rockefellers had come upon the same problems of celebrity their fathers faced before them. Finding one's own personal identity had been even more difficult for the Cousins because their five uncles had pre-empted so many fields of endeavor. Little room had been left for them. Like their uncles, the Cousins did not wish to follow in the shadow of their elders; they wanted to do something on their own. Unlike their uncles, who worked through groups and organizations and sought the leadership in their fields, the Cousins for the most part have chosen careers in which success or failure rests upon individual efforts. They have gone into the professions: medicine, law, music, writing, teaching. Success or failure in these fields does not depend upon one's family name.

Sandra Ferry Rockefeller, the eldest daughter of John 3rd, was the first to drop the Rockefeller from her name, in 1959, after which she moved alone to Cambridge, away from the family, seeking anonymity and privacy. Several of the other girl cousins sought to escape the name by early marriages. Five of seven of these early marriages from 1956 to 1964 ended in divorce. Some of the young Rockefellers fled to psychoanalysis as a means of coming to grips with their heritage. Out of this, at least two of them found their careers. Lucy, Laurance's youngest daughter, after divorcing her first husband, graduated from Columbia Medical School with an M.D. in psychiatry, and took up practice in a suburb of Washington, D.C., near where her second husband, Dr. Jeremy Peter Waletzky, also a psychiatrist, practiced. Lucy's oldest sister, Laura, after divorcing her first husband and leaving the radical atmosphere of Berkeley, California, in the 1960s, returned to school in Cambridge, Massachusetts, seeking a doctorate in psychology. John 3rd's youngest daughter, Alida, also dipped into the radical movement at Stanford University as an undergraduate, only to flee home in tears when she was ejected from a meeting of the radicals and told: "We don't want you here . . . You and people like you are the problem, so how can you be part of the solution?" After graduating from Stanford, Alida, who apparently inherited the stunning beauty of her mother, chose to live in California, pursuing a career in photography and television.

On the other hand, the two daughters of Abby Rockefeller Mauzé have enjoyed well-adjusted, well-to-do lives as the great-granddaughters of the founder of Standard Oil. Abby (Mitzi) Milton O'Neill married at the age of twenty-one in 1949, had six delightful children by George Dorr O'Neill, an investment banker, and, as far as one can tell, lived happily ever after. Her sister, Marilyn, the mother of two girls, married at twenty-two and will celebrate her silver anniversary in June 1978. Perhaps their adjustment was easier than it was for their cousins. As daughters of Abby, the only woman in the male-oriented third generation, they did not grow up with the name Rockefeller. Then too, they grew up before the youth rebellions of the 1960s.

Only one Cousin (thus far) has gone public and launched himself as a Rockefeller upon the rough seas of public affairs and national attention. That is John D. Rockefeller IV, Jay to his friends and associates. A puzzlement to the heredity theory of personality, Jay is the only son of the most shy and retiring of the brothers and yet he is by far the most outgoing, brash, personable and practical of all the Cousins. Six-foot-seven, lean, well proportioned and poised with a gift of smooth, flowing speech, he seems to possess naturally that personal magic of leadership. A product of Phillips Exeter Academy and Harvard, he spent three years on Oriental studies at the International Christian University in Tokyo (living there with a middle-income family), returned for post-graduate work in Chinese at Yale and then, at the age of twenty-five, changed his mind. In 1962, he joined the Peace Corps as a special assistant to the director, Sargent Shriver, switched to the Indonesian Desk of the State Department in 1963 and lived the life of the gay blade and most eligible bachelor in Washington, a familiar figure around town in his XKE Jaguar. In the process Jay Rockefeller became a Kennedy Democrat. Learning as did his Uncle Nelson before him that political power was derived from the ballot box, Jay looked over the country, chose West Virginia as his most promising bailiwick, and in 1964, he went to work in there as a member of the President's Commission on Juvenile Delinquency. Two years later, he proclaimed himself a Democrat, the first Rockefeller ever to do so, and was elected to the state's House of Delegates. In 1967 he married the pretty Sharon Percy, a celebrity in her own right, daughter of Senator Charles Percy of Illinois, and set up home in Charleston. In 1969, he was elected secretary of state. Rapidly gaining control of the Democratic Party in West Virginia, Jay then won national acclaim when his own slate of Democrats swept into state offices in 1970. Two years later, as expected, he ran for governor. By this time, with such a whirlwind of success and political astuteness behind him, political observers had no difficulty in describing the presidential gleam in the eye of John D. Rockefeller IV. Teddy Kennedy, turning away questions as to whether he would run for President in 1972, referred the press to Jay Rockefeller. But in 1972, declaring himself opposed to strip coal mining, the major industry of West Virginia, Jay Rockefeller lost the election to Arch A. Moore, Jr. It was considered an upset. He retired gracefully to the presidency of a small college, West Virginia Wesleyan, and bided his time. Then in 1976 at the age of thirty-nine he surged out again to seek and this time to win the governorship of West Virginia. The gleam in his eye positively glistened.

Sharon Percy Rockefeller since her marriage into the family had become one of the leading and most influential of the Cousins, the first inlaw ever to be elected president of the Cousins group. More than that, she held her own as an integral member of her husband's political war council. She was one of his most influential advisers as well as a fierce campaigner in her own right. Smart, savvy and down to earth, she helped establish the Mountain Artisans, which encouraged and marketed local West Virginia handicrafts in the smartest shops across the nation. She also served as a trustee of Stanford University, her alma mater, the Rockefeller Family Fund and a number of other organizations. While taking an active role in the Rockefeller family among the Cousins, she remained strongly attached to her own family and brought Jay into a close personal relationship with her father and the liberal wing of the Republican Party.

Jay became so much a political figure of the younger generation that he was not infrequently mistaken in press reports as the son of Nelson. Such errors invariably caused him to bristle. Nelson Rockefeller's name had so dominated the political arena that Jay sometimes despaired of his quest to make it on his own in politics, even as a Democrat and a West Virginian. When Uncle Nelson in 1968 offered him the slain Robert F. Kennedy's seat in the U. S. Senate, Jay declined with no hesitation whatever. The offer was made in complete sincerity. Nelson wanted to help in the career of his politically minded nephew and believed he would serve with credit and accomplishment. But Jay wanted no favors from his famous uncle.

Nelson's oldest son, Rodman, the senior male Cousin, five years older than Jay, was regarded by his peers as the family's conservative cousin. He was the only businessman among them and seldom saw eye to eye on issues with his more liberal and radical cousins. A graduate of Columbia University's School of Business, he moved into his father's company, IBEC, and moved just as smoothly up to its presidency. A tough-minded, tireless worker, he ran IBEC as a profit-making business which also followed a policy of social responsibility. A good father and family man who participates in local civic activities, he also headed the International

Council for Business Opportunity, which provides free, expert consultation for black businessmen. He was in a distinct minority, if not alone, among the Cousins in his belief that the Rockefeller generosity in philanthropy should soon be ended and that the family should return to the market place and try unashamedly to replenish the Rockefeller coffers.

Rodman's younger brother Steven struggled long and hard in his quest for a personally meaningful mission in life. Quiet, shy and somewhat introverted, he tried the political campaign trails as an aide to his father, turned down an offer to work in Albany, tried working in the management of Rockefeller Center and then in 1960 gave it all up to delve deeply into theology. For three years he struggled to find his way through the labyrinth of religion at the Union Theological Seminary in New York and then he turned to post-graduate work in philosophy at Columbia while at the same time submitting himself to psychoanalysis. That took him through five more arduous years. During this personal struggle, his so-called Cinderella marriage to his parents' Norwegian maid, Anne-Marie Rasmussen, disintegrated and was dissolved and Steven Rockefeller, a serious and committed Doctor of Philosophy, went off to teach religion at the small and prestigious Middlebury College in the Green Mountains of Vermont.

Laurance's only son and the youngest of his four children, Larry, put off his decision on what to do with the rest of his life until he was almost thirty. Emerging from Harvard, he treated himself to the dream of almost every young flier with a private pilot's license. He bought himself a twin-engine Beechcraft Baron, enlisted a college chum who had just earned his student flying license, and together they flew around the world, covering 33,000 miles in fifty-six days. It was a hair-raising, dangerous and maturing voyage, which need be done only once in a lifetime for full satisfaction. To his father, who gave his consent with considerable trepidation, Larry's adventure symbolized the dramatic changes in three generations of Rockefellers. Larry's grandfather, who lived to 1960, refused ever to go up in an airplane; his father had invested in aviation and had flown hundreds of hours as a passenger, but only Larry had learned to fly for himself. Having mastered that kind of high adventure, Larry committed himself at age twenty-five to VISTA, the domestic version of the Peace Corps, working as a volunteer among poor Puerto Ricans and blacks in New York's worst slum of East Harlem. He spent three years there, living in a $90-a-month tenement room working one-on-one with children in the street. Then came his own period of indecision and groping: what do you do that is meaningful with your life when you are a Rockefeller?

After leaving VISTA, still a shy, introspective and highly idealistic young man, Larry became involved in the ecology movement. An experienced outdoorsman and health buff, he joined various groups devoted to preserving the environment against unlimited growth. But in a short while, young Laurance Rockefeller came to realize he was wanted and he was being used not for what he personally could bring to the movement but because his name so often would be confused with that of his father. The truth was that he was not particularly well equipped personally to make much of a contribution to the cause of environmental protection. Recognizing this, he enrolled in Columbia University's Law School, thrived there, discovered a new sense of maturity and self-confidence and earned his law degree with high honors. Then, in 1976, at the age of thirty-two, he went to work as a lawyer for the Natural Resources Defense Council, an environmental law firm which specialized in bringing lawsuits against those endangering the quality of the environment.

David's oldest son and namesake at the age of thirty-five (at this writing) was still undecided on the course of his future, except that he did not want to follow his famous father into the Chase Manhattan Bank. A bright young man of considerable ability, he had behind him Phillips Exeter, a Harvard degree in economics, Harvard Law School and postgraduate work in economics at Cambridge. But his true loves seemed to be poetry and music. A good baritone, he did not sing well enough to pursue a professional singing career. Instead he spent six years as the assistant general manager of the Boston Symphony while trying his hand at various allied projects, still trying to find his appropriate niche in life. He headed the Council for the Arts and Education, which conducted a nationwide survey on how art education can be improved in public and private schools. At the same time, he bought a part ownership in *The Real Paper*, an underground tabloid newspaper of which he was executive vice-president in the Boston area. Within the family hierarchy, David Jr. was regarded as a good bridge between the Cousins and the brothers. He had those qualities of tact, diplomacy and leadership which enabled him to operate well at both generation levels of the family. Along with Jay and Steven, David was seen as one of the three key male cousins in the family leadership. Unlike Jay and Steven, however, David seemed to protect himself behind a veil of privacy which neither his cousins nor outsiders could penetrate. He expressed himself with such considered caution and delicacy, which was so characteristic of his father, that few people felt they knew the whole man. Great expectations still hover over David Rockefeller, Jr., and he knows it, but just how or when or where they will be fulfilled neither he nor others seem able to determine.

David Jr.'s younger brother, Dick—Richard Gilder Rockefeller—is the most versatile of all the Cousins. Blessed with the good looks and sinewy physique of his mother, Dick was an athlete—a soccer player, a sailor, a skin and scuba diver and an airplane pilot. He was also something of an artist, painting and sculpting, a fine musician who played the guitar with near-professional talent. "He seems to do everything well," according to one family confidant. "He has a wonderful sense of humor and a marvelously natural way of communicating with people, no hang-ups at all on the Rockefeller thing. In fact, of all the Cousins, Dick reminds you least of a Rockefeller." With all the doors open to him, Dick scrutinized and considered the wide range of career choices open to a young Rockefeller, and at the age of twenty-five, in 1974, he opted out of the family sphere of influence and chose to study medicine at Harvard. There he met Nancy Anderson, attending Harvard Law School, and they were married in 1976.

David's eldest daughter, Abby, whom he named after his mother, grew up to become the family's most iconoclastic rebel, a philosophical Marxist and an ardent and radical feminist with a black belt in karate. She disdained men as oppressors, as she did dresses as symbols of women's enslavement. An early admirer of Fidel Castro, she came upon Marxism at the staid and genteel New England Conservatory of Music, where she went to study cello and came under the influence of a freshman English teacher who was a Marxist. Living in Cambridge, away from her family, she joined and contributed to radical organizations of all stripes, from the Socialist Workers Party to the Boston Draft Resistance Group, finding eventually an affinity for the rising feminist movement among college students in the Boston-Cambridge area. When she was portrayed in a magazine article as a braless black belt karate expert and early convert to the feminist movement, her father telephoned a protest that she was bringing inappropriate notoriety to the family name, adding wistfully that, after all, he had named her after his own mother. The implication was clear: she had a responsibility to that special name in the family. Her response was immediate: "But, Daddy, I never asked you to do that." Abby Rockefeller of the fourth generation was determined to go her own way. When the environmental protection movement rose to full swing in the 1970s, she came upon a new Swedish design for a flushless toilet, the clivus, which composted human excrement and household garbage in the basement of each home, thus eliminating those sources of environmental pollution. She purchased the rights to manufacture and sell the expensive flushless toilet in America, setting up a corporation called Clivus Multrum, USA. In that one stroke she transformed herself ironically into the first Rockefeller Cousin to become a business entrepreneur, albeit a Marxist one.

Each of the Cousins, upon reaching the age of twenty-one, was taken on an extensive tour of the family offices in Rockefeller Center, introduced to the various associates, advisers and specialty experts. Explanations were made, inquiries were invited, services were extended, and implicit in all this was the invitation: come join in, learn how we do things, prepare to take over and to carry on the stewardship of Rockefeller activities. As the older Cousins came and went without staying, the pressure grew upon the younger ones, especially the males in the family. Nothing was ever forced or even urged. But each of the young men of the fourth generation knew full well he was being looked over as the potential heir to the leadership of the family, the family as a unit. The brothers had faced that same issue in their time and had resolved among themselves to try to do both: to remain individuals pursuing their own careers and at the same time continuing the major causes and institutions to which their father, John D., Jr., had devoted his life. Of all the brothers, Nelson was the most concerned with continuing the unity of the Rockefellers as a family unit: "The strength of us as individuals had been enhanced by family unity and loyalty." But the Cousins were twenty-one in number, not five or six, and they were a full generation removed from the concept of stewardship of the Rockefeller inheritance of wealth, power, responsibility and duty.

The Cousins went along with their elders' suggestion in 1967 to establish their own philanthropic arm in the form of the Rockefeller Family Fund, a small replica of the Rockefeller Brothers Fund. Jay acquiesced to his father's wishes in joining the board of trustees of the Rockefeller Foundation, as his father was about to retire as chairman. But Jay displayed no intention or inclination to devote a major portion of his life to that cornerstone of Rockefeller philanthropy. David Jr. went on the board of the Rockefeller University, but has left; Neva Keiser, another Cousin, has taken his place.

No Cousin has come forth to set up a desk in the family's own offices at 5600, no one has wanted to serve as the overseer of the Rockefeller family affairs of the future, or to manage the investments, or to run Rockefeller Center, or to serve on the Rockefeller Brothers Fund, or . . . and the list runs on and on.

To be fair, many of the Cousins were still deciding, still in transition. Some of them might come forth as a nucleus group to assume the mantle of the Rockefeller stewardship. In 1976, for the first time, the Cousins voted to endorse a study into the future operation of the family offices: what services and what staff will they need; how much will it cost; how will it be managed and operated? No decisions have yet been made. But it was clear that changes would be made. The members of the fourth generation of Rockefellers still want to go their separate ways as individual, private persons, not as institutions. They want to seek or not to seek, as they please, self-fulfillment through personal achievement, as divorced as humanly possible from the awesome responsibility of being a Rockefeller. Yet some if not all of them have come to realize that there is no escaping that famous name. There is still the need, however much they would want to limit it, of facing the world as a descendant of the founder of Standard Oil.

Their grandfather, of course, tried to consider the future when he made out his generation-skipping trusts of 1934, which contained the bulk of the Rockefeller Fortune. As a cautious and punctilious puritan at heart, he knew he wanted the Rockefeller fortune to remain in trust, guarded and secure, for as long as legally possible. So he provided that each of the trusts would remain in force, the capital not disbursed, until the death of his last surviving descendant alive at the time the trusts were established. At that time, the end of 1934, John D. Rockefeller, Jr., had four grandchildren, his daughter Abby's two girls, Mitzi and Marilyn, and Nelson's two oldest children, Rodman and Ann. The Cousins will become the lifetime beneficiaries of the income of the larger 1934 trusts upon the passing of the third generation, but the bulk of the fortune, now some $640 million, will not be distributed until the death of the last surviving of the four eldest Cousins. Given the normal life span in the family, that may well be in the year 2014 or later. By that time, today's Cousins will be well into their dotage. The big trusts will in effect skip not one but two generations before the whole fortune is available for full use. The only Cousins who might still be of age to wield the power of that inherited wealth would be Nelson's two young sons by his second marriage, Nelson Jr., born in 1964, and Mark, born in 1967. Then, of course, there will be the forty-one second cousins of the fifth generation of Rockefellers who also will come into their inheritance. What any of them will make of it remains to be seen. The only glimpse of a clue can be gleaned from reports that Nelson Jr. shows every sign of being "a chip off the old block." One visitor to his home, while awaiting the arrival of his father, picked up a small pre-Columbian sculpture to examine it more closely and was startled to hear the thin chirping command of Nelson Jr., then age seven. "Put that down," he shouted. "That's one of Daddy's toys and we're not allowed to play with it!"

So the pattern has been set and is there for all to see. John Davison Rockefeller, born on July 8, 1839, started out as a bookkeeper, founded the Standard Oil Company, innovated corporate business as we know it today, established corporate philanthropy with the same sharp efficiency and left the greatest inheritance of any man in the history of America. Then John Davison Rockefeller, Jr., his son, expanded the parameters and horizons of enlightened philanthropy to the modern world in the social sciences and humanities as well as in the pure sciences. His five sons carried on and further enlarged and enriched the scope of man's knowledge and well-being.

Any guided tour of New York can point out the visible living monuments and edifices with which the name Rockefeller is intimately associated: Rockefeller Center, the Rockefeller University, Memorial Sloan-Kettering Cancer Center, Lincoln Center, Riverside Church, the Cloisters, the Museum of Modern Art, the new façade of Wall Street and lower Manhattan, the Chase Manhattan Bank. But it is upon what the eye cannot readily see that the Rockefeller family has had its greatest impact. A Rockefeller hand has helped this nation tackle, if not yet solve, the problems and needs of conserving our great natural resources and protecting our environment, of population growth and family planning, of health and medical care, of basic science and pure medical research, of higher education, of civil rights for all minorities, and equal opportunities for all, of the arts and cultural activities in our everyday lives, of international cooperation throughout the world, of the proper role of government at all levels. In virtually all aspects of modern American life, the Rockefellers have not only participated but have played an active leadership role. There is not a conservative among the five brothers in terms of a man of wealth seeking to maintain the status quo. Each of the brothers in his own particular field of endeavor has long stood for change, for a striving to improve upon the present for the future. They are neither great scholars nor intellects, but they are pragmatic activists who have worked long and hard to gather about them men and women of superior capacities in joint ventures to help make this nation and this world a better and kinder place in which to live.

To a man the Rockefeller brothers absolutely deny any sense of elitism among them or any conscious thought of being a "do-gooder" in their actions. That would be condescending to others. Any "good" they achieved was a by-product of their own needs to play a creative role in their community and society. They wanted to involve themselves in something meaningful beyond their own personal lives. In a four-hour-long search into and about the family's meanings and motives with this author, Laurance Rockefeller, who probably thought and philosophized more on the subject than any other man, summed it all up this way:

"Every living things seeks to fulfill itself according to its own potential. Creative fulfillment is a basic need of all people. With my brothers and myself, there was a difference in scale but the problems we faced in seeking self-fulfillment were not so different than those encountered by every man.

"If you think of the artist in every man seeking creative fulfillment and his life given to him as a canvas, then you see that we were given more materials and a larger canvas to work with than other men. And more was expected of us. But the search for creative fulfillment was not so different from that of other men. How we painted on our canvases and what the final pictures came to be is for others to judge."

However one judges the canvases, three generations of Rockefellers have devoted a major portion of their lives to the constant struggle of trying to enhance the well-being of mankind. It may well be, as Laurance reflected, that the needs of man exceed man's ability to fulfill them. Solutions to problems seem to create new problems. Progress appears to ride a rising and ebbing tide rather than to make a steady climb up a mountain. One generation of men swims toward shore approaching a long-sought goal, only to be swept back again on an ebbing tide, leaving the struggle to the next generation. Laurance Rockefeller's reflections as he approached the age of retirement echoed the haunting sentiments of his grandfather's adviser, Frederick T. Gates, who back in 1910 wrote to John D. Rockefeller these words:

"The older I grow and the more carefully I study society, the more difficult to me seems the problem of how really to promote human happiness, that is to say—to make happy people happier; to make contented people more contented and generally to lift up the level of positive good cheer in the world. The trouble is that the blanket of happiness seems too short; if you pull it up at the head, you expose the feet; if you tuck it in on the one side you uncover the other side."

ACKNOWLEDGMENTS

I wish to acknowledge here with pleasure and appreciation the co-opera-
tion and hospitality of the five Rockefeller brothers—John 3rd, Nelson,
Laurance, Winthrop and David—and of Mrs. Abby Rockefeller Mauzé,
as well as that of Mrs. Jeannette Edris Rockefeller and Rodman C. Rockefeller. They allowed me to enter into the world of the Rockefellers, to
look around and ask questions. Each of them acceded to my requests for
interviews. While they did not, for privacy's sake, answer each and every
question put to them, they extended themselves far beyond what I believe
they had ever done before. I toured their offices at Rockefeller Center and
the estate at Pocantico Hills, visited some of their homes and spent five
days at Winrock Farms. Beyond this, they opened the doors for me to
their associates and friends, men and women who had known them for
many, many years.

I appreciated the opportunity to probe in depth the interrelationships
and affairs of the family with those who possessed firsthand knowledge,
including J. Richardson Dilworth, their financial adviser; John E. Lockwood and Donal C. O'Brien, Jr., family counsel; Dana S. Creel, adviser
on philanthropy; Harper Woodward, adviser to Laurance Rockefeller and
involved in the family management; Lindsley F. Kimball, adviser to
John D. Rockefeller, Jr., as well as to the brothers. Members past and present of the family's public relations and office staffs were of invaluable help
in many ways: Steven David, George D. Taylor, Jr., Saul Richman, Mrs.
Shirley Clurman, Mrs. Audrey Guthrie and Miss Martha Dalrymple. My
special appreciation also goes to Dr. Joseph W. Ernst, the family archivist,

whose special knowledge helped and guided me in and about Rockefeller letters, documents and memorabilia.

More than fifty other associates, aides and friends of one or more of the Rockefellers talked with me at length on one or more occasions, for each of them was part of the Rockefeller story. Only the limitations of space precluded my putting all of them into the body of this biography. To them, my thanks, my appreciation and my apologies:

Bernard Berelson, Joan M. Dunlop, John E. Harr, J. George Harrar, Porter McKeever, Frank W. Notestein, Henry Romney, Edward B. Young. Also, Alfred H. Barr, Jr., the late Louise A. Boyer, Robert R. Douglass, John French, Wallace K. Harrison, George L. Hinman, Hugh Morrow, Leslie Slote, Carol K. Uht and Ann C. Whitman.

Also the late Allston Boyer, Henry L. Diamond, Richard E. Holtzman, Gene W. Setzer and G. W. Adkinson, Charles Allbright, Jane Bartlett, Edwin B. Cromwell, Henry Kamp, Jo-Anne Newell, George R. Reynolds, Carl E. Siegesmund, Craig Smith and John Ward.

Also the late William Butler, Richard H. Dana, Eugene H. Kone, Mary Lanier, Leslie H. Larsen, Warren T. Lindquist, Joseph T. Nolan, Joseph Verner Reed, Jr., Victor E. Rockhill, Richard E. Salomon, Fraser P. Seitel, Frederick Seitz, John Temple Swing and Eleanor W. Wilkerson. Also Gustav S. Eyssell, Caroline Hood and Devereux Josephs.

I also want to acknowledge with my thanks the various amounts of help I received from those not listed above who stipulated anonymity in giving me their interpretations of events as well as facts to which they were privy. That great repository of daily history, the New York *Times*, was invaluable to me in writing this book, as it had been before. Two men deserve mention here because they gave me out of friendship the benefit of their professional knowledge and experience in checking, confirming and understanding difficult material. They are Joseph F. Gelband, attorney-at-law, and William A. Copeland, president of MacKay-Shields Economics.

My thanks and everlasting appreciation go out to Stewart Richardson, editor-in-chief of Doubleday & Company, who stood behind me with sage advice, solid support and good cheer; to Michael D. Ossias, editor at Doubleday, for his skill in editing this manuscript; and to Howard S. Cady, editor and friend, who also helped immeasurably. I would also like to thank the *Reader's Digest* and particularly its editors Fulton Oursler, Jr., and Michael Blow and researcher Elinor Bratton, for their editorial help and support. I will always have a particular sense of appreciation for the haven given to me by that great and good place called the MacDowell Colony, the retreat for artists, writers and composers in Peterborough, New Hampshire, where portions of this book were written.

A special final line of deep appreciation is expressed here for the stalwart aid and comfort given me over these past eighteen years by my literary agent, adviser and friend, Phyllis Jackson, who read the completed manuscript but did not live to see this book in print.

Last and still foremost, my good wife Deirdre stood by my side through the long struggle, which she shared, of writing this book the way I wanted to write it, and I can never adequately thank her for all she has done.

With all the help received, the views expressed in this book are still solely those of the author.

Alvin Moscow
Sarasota, Florida
April 1, 1977

BIBLIOGRAPHY

For a further exploration into the Rockefeller phenomenon, I would recommend three books in particular for their accuracy, interest and proximity to the subject matter: Allan Nevins' *Study in Power: John D. Rockefeller*; Raymond Fosdick's *John D. Rockefeller, Jr.: A Portrait*; and John D. Rockefeller's own *Random Reminiscences of Men and Events*. A selective bibliography follows:

Abels, Jules, *The Rockefeller Billions* (1965)
Alsop, Stewart, *Nixon and Rockefeller* (1960)
Chase, Mary Ellen, *Abby Aldrich Rockefeller* (1950)
Collier, Peter, and Horowitz, David, *The Rockefellers: An American Dynasty* (1976)
Corner, G. W., *History of the Rockefeller Institute* (1965)
Cuninggim, Merrimon, *Private Money and Public Service: The Role of Foundations in the American Society* (1972)
Dalrymple, Martha, *The AIA Story* (1968)
Desmond, James, *Nelson Rockefeller: A Political Biography* (1964)
Fosdick, Raymond, *John D. Rockefeller, Jr.: A Portrait* (1956)
———, *The Story of the Rockefeller Foundation* (1952)
Gervasi, Frank, *The Real Rockefeller* (1964)
Hoffman, William, *David: Report on a Rockefeller* (1971)
Josephson, Matthew, *The Robber Barons*, (1934)
Kutz, Myer, *Rockefeller Power* (1934)
Loth, David, *The City Within a City*, (1966)
Lundberg, Ferdinand, *America's 60 Families* (1946)
———, *The Rich and the Super Rich* (1968)
Machlin, Milt, *The Search for Michael Rockefeller* (1972)
Manchester, William R., *Rockefeller Family Portrait* (1959)
Mills, C. Wright, *The Power Elite* (1963)

Morris, Joe Alex, *Nelson Rockefeller: A Biography* (1960)
———, *Those Rockefeller Brothers* (1953)
Nevins, Allan, *Study in Power: John D. Rockefeller* (1953)
Newhall, N., *Contribution to the Heritage of Every American: The Conserva-
    tion Activities of John D. Rockefeller, Jr.* (1957)
Pierce, Neal R., *The Megastates of America* (1972)
Pyle, Thomas, *Pocantico* (1960)
Rockefeller, David, *Unused Resources and Economic Waste* (1941)
Rockefeller, John D., *Random Reminiscences of Men and Events* (1909)
Rockefeller, John D. 3rd, *The Second American Revolution* (1973)
Rockefeller, Nelson A., *The Future of Federalism* (1962)
———, *Rockefeller Report on the Americas* (1969)
———, *Unity, Freedom, and Peace* (1968)
Saarinen, Aline B., *The Proud Possessors*
Shaplen, R., *Toward the Well-being of Mankind* (10 year report—Rockefeller
    Foundation) (1964)
Tarbell, Ida M., *The History of the Standard Oil Company* (1904)
White, T. H., *The Making of the President, 1960, 1964, 1968*

Among the thousands of magazine articles written on the Rockefellers, I found the following of particular interest:

Fistere, John, "The Rockefeller Boys," *Saturday Evening Post*, July 16, 1938
Smith, Richard A., "The Rockefeller Brothers," *Fortune*, February and March
    1955
"The Rockefeller Boys," New York *Times Magazine*, April 9, 1939

INDEX

INDEX

Abortion, 400
Abstract impressionism, 334
Acadia National Park, 44, 102, 103
Act of Chapultepec, 162, 164
Adams, Henry, 79
Adams, Sherman, 174
Adkinson, G. W., 269, 270, 283
Admiral's House (Washington, D.C.),
  374
Advisory Council (Princeton University),
  316
Agency for International Development,
  384, 385
Agnew, Spiro, 359, 368
Air Affairs (quarterly), 126
Airborne Instruments Laboratories, 185
Aircraft Radio Corporation of New Jersey,
  185
Air Force II, 374
Air Youth of America, 126
Albany Legislative Correspondents
  Association, 327–28
Albany Mall, 355; construction of,
  339–40
Albright, Horace Marden, 103, 191, 193,
  195
Alcoa-Perini (real estate consortium), 254
Aldrich, Abby, see Rockefeller, Mrs. Abby
  Aldrich
Aldrich, Nelson W., 6, 26, 89, 92, 115
Aldrich, Winthrop, 53
Aldrich, Winthrop W., 121, 213, 217,
  218, 219, 243
Aldrich family, 6, 48
Allen, Arthur, 421
Allen, Martha Baird, see Rockefeller, Mrs.
  Martha Baird
Allen, Vivian Beaumont, 389–90
Alliance for Progress, 226
Allied Chemical Company, 243
Aluminum Company of America, 417
American Airlines, 311
American Birth Control League, 114
American Cancer Society, 317
American Conservation Association, 419
American Federation of Labor-Congress
  of Industrial Organizations
  (AFL-CIO), 375
American Geographical Society, 191, 192
American Institute of Architecture,
  342–43
American International Association for
  Economic and Social Development
  (AIA), 168–69
American Museum of National History,
  191
Americans for Democratic Action, 375
American Smelting & Refining
  Corporation, 243
American Telephone & Telegraph
  (AT&T), 243, 417
America's 60 Families (Lundberg), 411
Amherst College, 404
Anderson, Nancy, see Rockefeller, Mrs.
  Nancy Anderson
Andrews, Clark & Company, 66–67
Andrews, John, 67
Andrews, Sam, 66, 68–69, 73
Appropriations Committee (U. S.
  Senate), 156
Araki, Eikichi, 150
Archbold, John D., 21, 70, 74, 77–78, 79
Arkansas, 212, 267–97, 314; gambling
  casinos, 290; integration of schools in
  Little Rock (1957), 275; per capita
  income, 212, 276; population growth,
  276; see also Winrock Farms
Arkansas Arts Center, 281, 282
Arkansas Democrat, The (newspaper),
  276
Arkansas Department of Agriculture, 270
Arkansas Game and Fish Commission,
  291
Arkansas Gazette, 292
Arkansas Highway Department, 291
Arkansas Industrial Development
  Commission (AIDC), 275–77, 278–79,
  280, 284, 288
Arkansas River, 268, 270
Arkansas State Prison, 296
Arp, Jean, 224
Article 51 (United Nations Charter), 164
Artmobile (art gallery), 282

Arts at Dartmouth, The (organization),
  117
Asia House (New York), 392
Atlantic Refining Corporation, 82
Atomic Energy Commission, 226, 381
Attica prison revolt, 359–64
Augustino (caddy), 60

Bacteriology, 87
Balfour, Dr., 146
Bandelier National Monument National
  Park, 102
Bankers Trust Company, 228
Bank of America, 228, 259
Bank of China, 263
Bank of Manhattan, 218; merger, 227–28;
  see also Chase Manhattan Bank
Baptist Church, 9, 35–36, 62, 66, 72, 75,
  84, 198, 287, 409
Baptist Education Society, 84, 85
Baptist Home Mission Society, 89
Barnard, Chester, 144–45, 146
Barr, Alfred 224
Barr, Margaret, 224
Bartley, Ann, 277, 282, 426
Bartley, Bruce, 277, 282, 426
Barton Foundation, 281–82
Bassett Hall (Colonial Williamsburg
  home), 104
Baudouin, King of the Belgians, 285
Bayonne refinery, 128
Bayway Community House, 128
Beach, David, 309
Beacon Oil Company, 128, 197
Beatrix, Princess of the Netherlands,
  339–40
Bellevue Hospital (New York City), 205,
  269
Bell X-1 (experimental airplane), 185
Bible, 7, 9, 18, 35, 36, 40, 48, 49, 62, 73,
  120, 273, 332
Billings Farm and Mansion (Vermont),
  309
Birth control, 143, 145, 377–85, 392,
  397–401, 406; in the 1930s, 114;
  Rockefeller Foundation and, 143–47
Black, Eugene, 246
Black ghettos, 341–42
Black liberation movement, 241
Black Muslims, 361–62
Black Panthers, 360
Blondell, Joan, 206
Board of Hospitals of New York City,
  269
Bobst, Elmer H., 317
Bond, Ward, 308
Borella, Victor, 11
Boston Draft Resistance Group, 433
Boston Symphony Orchestra, 432
Bowers, L. M., 21–22, 23
Boyer, Allston, 308, 318, 319
Boyer, Louise, 11
Braniff Airlines, 311
Braque, Georges, 333
Briand, Aristide, 113
Bronk, Dr. Detlev W., 220, 380–81
Bronx Zoo, 125, 192
Brown, Joe E., 200
Browning School, 56, 112
Brown University, 16, 18, 26
Bryan, William Jennings, 82
Bumpers, Dale, 295–96
Bureau of Outdoor Recreation (U. S.
  Department of the Interior), 322
Burlington Industries, 243
Burr, Aaron, 218
Business Committee on the Arts, 248
Business in Brief (publication), 217
Butcher, Willard C., 262, 264
Butler, William, 217
Buttrick, Dr. Wallace, 89
Byrnes, James F., 152, 164

Caffaro, Lou, 200
California primary of 1964, 353, 413–14
Calloway, Howard (Bo), 375
Caneel Bay Sugar Plantation, 299–302,
  303, 305, 306
Cannon, Howard W., 369
Capitalism, 3, 121, 168, 226, 231, 248,
  315, 338, 410; laissez-faire, 68, 80;
  Rockefeller (David) on, 239–40
Caradon, Lord, 402
Carey, Hugh, 344
Carnegie, Andrew, 19, 20, 27, 35, 410
Carnegie Foundation, 378
Carrel, Dr. Alexis, 87
Carter, Jimmy, 265
Casements, The (home), 98, 99, 100
Castro, Fidel, 304, 433
Cathedral of St. John the Divine, 221
Catholic Archdiocese of New York, 146
Center for Inter-American Relations, 256
Central Intelligence Agency, 226;
  Rockefeller (Nelson) investigation,
  374–75

Century Club, 387
Certificate No. 1 (Standard Oil of
California), 101
Cézanne, Paul, 225
Champion, George, 237–38, 244, 245–46
Charles of London (antique dealer), 8
Chase, Mary Ellen, 46
Chase Manhattan Bank, 45, 55, 110, 130,
155, 181, 189, 200, 213–20, 223, 225,
227–32, 235–49, 255–64, 269, 344,
369, 401, 412, 414, 416, 417, 421, 424,
432, 435; advertising expenditures, 236;
art program, 248–49; branch banks
(New York City), 228; China and
(1970s), 263–64; expansion of, 235;
formed, 218–19; ghetto neighborhood
volunteers, 242; "Great Teachers"
program, 241; growth of, 235–37, 260;
headquarters, 229–32, 235; loan
commitments, 236; merger, 227–28,
243; Moscow office, 263; overseas
expansion, 227, 246, 263–64; personnel
practices, 228; reorganization of,
228–29; Soviet Union loan, 263; stock
and stockholders, 241, 243, 264
Chase Manhattan Building, 235
Chase Manhattan Corporation, 259
Chase Manhattan Plaza, 229–32, 248
Chase National Bank, 10, 14, 120, 121,
129, 182, 189, 243; merger, 218–19;
structural and internal reorganization
of, 218
Chase Volunteers for Community Action,
242
Chemical Bank (New York), 412
Chicago World's Fair (1933), 207–8
China, 74, 75, 114, 142, 145, 226, 242,
358; Chase Manhattan and (1970s),
263–64
China Medical Board, 113
Chorley, Kenneth, 10, 104
Chou En-lai, 263
Christie's (auction house), 334
Chryssicopoulos, Mrs. Nicholas, 295
Churchill, Winston S., x
Citizens' Advisory Committee on
Environmental Quality, 324
Citizens' Advisory Committee on
Recreation and Natural Beauty, 323
Citizens for Rockefeller committees, 347
Citizens Observer Committee at Attica,
360
Civil rights movement, 336, 347, 357

Civil War, 65
Clark, Mary Todhunter, *see* Rockefeller,
Mrs. Mary Todhunter Clark
Clark, Maurice, 64, 65, 66, 67
Clark & Rockefeller (commission
merchants), 64, 65–66
Clark family, 118–19
Clinical Research Bureau, 114
Clivus Multrum, USA corporation, 433
Cloisters, the, 435
Collective bargaining, 23
Colonial Williamsburg, 10, 28, 113, 120,
125, 193, 211–12, 285, 297, 310, 381,
421; cost of reconstruction, 211;
restoration of, 103–4, 106
Colorado Fuel and Iron Company, 21–23
Colorado State Militia, 22
Colter, John, 194
Colter Bay, 303
Colter Bay Village, 194
Columbia Broadcasting System, 318
Columbia University, 4, 56, 105, 106,
132, 150, 220, 221, 418, 430, 431, 432;
student revolt (1968), 401–2
Columbus, Christopher, 300
Commission on Critical Choices for
Americans, 365–66, 367
Commission on Population Growth and
the American Future, 400
Committee on Lower Manhattan, 230–31
Committee to Elect Ford, 375
Communications Satellite Corporation
(Comat), 253
Communism, 142, 155, 163, 168, 304,
399, 411
Communist Party (Poland), 262
Compact of Fifth Avenue, 347
Compton, Arthur, 93–94
Compton, Karl, 381
"Concert Hall of the Air" (radio
program), 276
Connecticut River Valley, 404
Conservation, 10, 44–45, 101–5, 125,
190–96, 302, 307, 310–11, 319–25;
New York State program (1965), 343;
Rockefeller (Laurance) philosophy on,
195
Conservation Foundation, 191–92
Consolidation Coal Company, 97
Continental Trading Company, 24–25
Copacabana (nightclub), 206
Cornell Medical School, 189, 190, 316
Cornell University, 141

Corning, Erastus, II, 339
Corpus Christi R. C. Church, 221
Council for the Arts and Education, 432
Council on Economic and Cultural
  Affairs, 385
Council on Foreign Economic Policy, 171
Council on Foreign Relations, 220, 223,
  225–27, 256, 258, 264, 387; founded,
  225; influence of, 225–26; Rockefeller
  financial contributions to, 226
Council on the Arts, 343
Couper, William, 328
Cousin Properties, Inc., 256
Cousins, Tom, 256
Crane, Jay, 155
Crank, Marion, 292
Creel, Dana, 241
Creole Oil Company, 153
Creole Petroleum Company of Venezuela,
  122
Croker Land Company, 251
Cromwell, Edwin, 269, 270, 278, 279
Crow, Trammel, 253–54
Cryonetics Corporation, 312
Cutler, Bertram P., 10, 122, 154

Dali, Salvador, 224
Dalrymple, Martha, 11
Dartmouth Alumni Magazine, 117–18
Dartmouth College, 116–19, 237
Dauntless, The (motor cruiser), 188, 195,
  299
David: Report on a Rockefeller
  (Hoffman), 411–12
David, Steven, xi
David Rockefeller and Associates
  Corporation, 251
Debevoise, Thomas M., 9–10
Declaration of Independence, 405
De Kooning, Willem, 334
Democracy in America (Tocqueville),
  380
Democrats for Rockefeller Committee
  (Arkansas), 289
Depression of 1929, 7, 15, 105, 106, 109,
  110, 166, 199
De Sapio, Carmine, 329
Détente of the 1970s, 257
Detroit race riots, 341
Dewey, John, 56, 57, 116
Dewey, Thomas E., 156, 326–27, 336
Dillingham Corporation, 307, 311
Dillingham family, 307

Dilworth, J. Richardson, 250–51, 345,
  415, 416–17, 423, 426
Division of Medical Sciences (Rockefeller
  Foundation), 146, 147–48
Dodds, Harold Willis, 144
Domestic Council, 373, 374, 375
Donahue, Woolworth, 207
Donald S. Walker Laboratory, 190
Doodlebug (monoplane), 180
Dorado Beach Hotel, 303–4, 305, 306,
  307
Douglas, Donald, 187
Douglas, Howard, 7
Douglass, Robert, 361, 362, 363
Douglas Skyrocket jet, 185
Downtown-Lower Manhattan Association,
  232, 256
Downtown Manhattan Association, 231
Draft Rockefeller for Governor
  Committee (Arkansas), 287
Drake, Edwin L., 65
Drum, Lt. General H. A., 201
Dubuffet, Jean, 248
Dulles, John Foster, 93, 146, 148–49,
  172, 173, 174, 345, 392
Du Pont family, 410, 418

Eagleton, Thomas, 368
Eastern Air Lines, 126, 127, 178, 179,
  181, 186–87, 307–8, 311, 314
Eastman Kodak Company, 417
Ecology, 192, 324–25; *see also*
  Conservation
Economic Club, 398
Edris, Jeannette, *see* Rockefeller, Mrs.
  Jeannette
Edris, William, 277
Eisenhower, Dwight D., 274–75, 302,
  321, 331, 345; administration, 169–75;
  election of, 169–70
Eisenhower, Milton, 170
Election of 1936, 348
Election of 1940, 156
Election of 1944, 156
Election of 1952, 169–70
Election of 1960, 348
Election of 1964, 289
Election of 1972, 364
Embarcadero Center (San Francisco),
  253–54, 255
Energy Independence Authority, 374
Environmental Protection Agency,
  324–25

Equal Employment Opportunity
Commission, 241
Equitable Life Insurance Company, 412
Equitable Trust Company, 217, 243
Eskimos, 119
Esso Building, 165
Estate Good Hope (St. Croix, Virgin
Islands), 308
Evans, Fanny, 100
Evans, Roger, 144
Ewing (Municipal) Hospital, 316
Excelsior refinery, 68
Exeter Academy, 429
Exploratory Committee for a Musical
Arts Center, 387, 388
Export Committee (Standard Oil
Company), 76
Exxon (Standard Oil Company of New
Jersey), 10, 81–82, 122, 128, 154, 155,
197, 198, 243, 411, 415

Faisal, King of Saudi Arabia, 248
Faubus, Orval, 274–75, 286, 287, 289,
290, 292, 293, 295
Federal Aviation Agency, 252
Federal Bureau of Investigation, 159, 368
Federal Bureau of Outdoor Recreation,
322
Federal Recreation Council, 322
Federal Reserve Board, 255
Fermi, Enrico, 93–94
Ferry, Charles, 115
Fidelity Union Trust of New Jersey, 416
Fifth Avenue Church (New York City),
35
First National Bank of Chicago, 412
First National City Bank (New York
City), 228, 259, 412, 421; Chase
Manhattan rivalry and, 259, 260–61
First Presbyterian Church (Arkadelphia,
Ark.), 278
1st U. S. Division, 200
Fisk University, 133–34
Fitler, Margaretta, *see* Rockefeller,
Mrs. Margaretta (Happy)
Flagler, Henry, 69, 73, 77
Fleming, Dr. Arthur, 170
Flexner, Dr. Simon, 87
Folsom's Commercial College, 63
Ford, Mrs. Betty, 373
Ford, Gerald, 365, 366, 367, 368, 374–
76, 412, 413
Ford, Henry, 82, 103

Ford, Henry, II, 55
Ford Foundation, 93, 384, 385, 395
Foreign Affairs (publication), 225
Foreign Intelligence Advisory Board, 359
Forrestal, James, 155–56
Fort Tryon Park, 103
Fortune (magazine), 418
Fosdick, Rev. Harry Emerson, 100
Fosdick, Raymond B., 4–5, 94, 106, 147
Fountain Oceanis (Pocantico Hills
estate), 30
Franklin, Benjamin, 27
Frasca, Lucille, 99
Frasch, Herman, 74
French, John, 116, 117, 125
French, Mary Billings, *see* Rockefeller,
Mrs. Mary French
French, Mrs. Mary M. Billings, 116
Frick, Henry C., 20, 27
Fulbright, J. William, 289, 296

Gabriel (Renoir), 224–25
Gardner, John, 378
Gary, Elbert, 23
Gates, Frederick T., 16, 18, 19, 84,
85–86, 87, 89–90, 92; advice to
Rockefeller, Sr., 90, 437
General Education Board, 89–92, 95,
101, 113, 189, 316, 392
General Electric Company, 313, 417
General Foods Corporation, 243
General Motors Corporation, 126, 179,
189, 190
Geneva summit conference, 172, 173, 174
Geophysics Corporation of America, 311
Geophysics Research Directorate (U. S.
Air Force), 311
Getty, John Paul, 384, 418
Gierek, Edward, 262
Gilder, George, 224
Gilder, Richard, 223–24
Glarner, Fritz, 333
Goldberg, Arthur J., 315, 367, 370–71
Goldstone, Harmon, 183
Goldwater, Barry, 289, 348, 349, 353,
356; Republican Convention (1964),
353–54
Goodman, Benny, 399
Goodwin, William A. R., 103
Gorky, Arshile, 334
Graduate Council (Princeton University),
316

Graduate Institute of Technology
  (University of Arkansas), 276
Grand Canyon National Park, 102, 191
Grand Teton Lodge Company, 194
Grand Teton National Park, 191, 192,
  194
Grand Tetons of Wyoming, 188, 193,
  278, 302–4, 319, 320
Greater New York Fund, 129, 200
"Great Teachers" program (Chase
  Manhattan Bank), 241
Greenacre Foundation, 318
Greenacre Park (New York City),
  318–19, 426
Greenberg, Milton, 311
Greene, Jerome D., 94
Greenrock Corporation, 38
Gregg, Dr. Alan, 146, 147–48
Grenfell, Sir Wilfred T., 119
"Group of Four Trees" (Dubuffet), 248
Guest, Winston, 207
Gumbel, Robert, 11

Haig, Alexander M., 367
Hair (musical), 494
Haleakala National Park, 307
Hall, Len, 326
Haloid Company, 187
Hampshire College, 404
Harding, William Barclay, 179
Harkness, Stephen V., 69, 73
Harmon Houses, 183
Harrar, J. George, 395, 396–97
Harriman, W. Averell, 326, 327–28, 329,
  330, 336, 355, 410
Harrison, Wallace K., 15, 155, 167, 183,
  327, 340
Harrison and Abramovitz (architects),
  389
Harvard Law School, 124–25
Harvard University, 7, 55, 57, 130, 131,
  173, 181, 213, 214, 220, 222, 223, 256,
  327, 429, 431, 433
Hatfield, Mark O., 331
Hawaiian Islands, 304–7, 309, 310, 311
Heck, Oswald, 326
Heckscher, August, 120
Henrico (transport ship), 203
Henry, Patrick, 103, 104
Hewitt & Tuttle Company, 63–64, 65,
  213
Hillcrest (home), 421
Hills Realty Company, 269

Hinman, George L., 327, 346, 352
Hiroshima University, 150
Historical Society of the Tarrytowns, 269
History of Standard Oil, The (Tarbell),
  80
Hitler, Adolf, 131
Hobby, Oveta Culp, 170, 171
Hoffman, William, 411–12
Holtzman, Richard, 308, 311
Hooker, Blanchette Ferry, *see* Rockefeller,
  Mrs. Blanchette Hooker
Hooker, Elon Hunting, 115
Hookworm (disease), 91–92, 153
Hoover, Herbert, 43
Hoover, Herbert, Jr., 172, 174
Hopkins, Harry, 159, 160
Horizons, Inc., 185
House Beautiful (magazine), 32
House of Burgesses (Virginia), 103
Hudson, Jimmy, 204, 207, 270, 272
Hudson, Walter C., 268
Hudson Pines (estate), 49
Hughes, Charles Evans, 25, 225
Hughes, Emmet John, 346, 352
Hughes, Howard, 418
Hughes, Rowland, 172, 174
Hull, Cordell, 157, 162, 345
Humble Oil and Refining Company, 128
Humphrey, George, 172, 174
Humphrey, Hubert, 357
Hunt, H. L., 418
Hurd, T. Norman, 361
Hussein, King of Jordan, 285
Hyatt Regency Hotel, 254

Ideal Basic Industries, 251
Indiana University, 147
Industrial Revolution, 80, 178
Industrial Workers of the World
  (IWW), 22
Information Technology (Itek), 312
Institute of Aeronautical Sciences, 126
Institute of Inter-American Affairs, 160
Institute of Pacific Relations, 113
Inter-American Escadrille, 126
Internal Revenue Service, 14, 279
International Basic Economy Corporation
  (IBEC), 168–69, 417, 430
International Business Machines
  Corporation (IBM), 417
International Christian University, 429
International Council for Business
  Opportunity, 430–31

International Development Center, 385

International Executive Service Corps ("Paunch Corps"), 240

International House (New York City), 132, 220–21

International House of Japan, 150, 392

International Houses, 150

International Rice Research Institute, 395

Interstate North commercial/residential complex (Atlanta), 255–56

Intra-uterine contraceptive device (IUD), 383–84

Irving Trust Company, 228

Island Packers, Inc., 184

Isolationist policies (U.S.), 156, 164

Israel bonds, 248

Jackson Hole Preserve, 103, 191, 192, 194, 299, 302–3

Jackson Hole Wildlife Park, 192, 193–94

Jackson Lake Lodge, 194–95

Jack Tarr II (sailboat), 258

James I, King, 8

Jamieson, Frank, 11, 167, 327, 329, 330, 331

Japan, 150, 239, 258, 265

Japan Society, 150, 392

Javits, Jacob, 355

Jefferson, Thomas, 104

Jenny Lake Lodge, 194

Jewish Theological Seminary, 221

John Birch Society, 411

Johns Hopkins University, 220

Johnson, James D. "Justice Jim," 289

Johnson, Mrs. Lady Bird, 323

Johnson, Lyndon B., 323, 349, 357, 377, 378, 397, 399, 414

Johnson Foundation, 93

Jones, Jesse, 158

Jones, Robert Trent, 303

Juilliard Building, 387

Juilliard School of Music, 221, 388

JY Ranch (Wyoming), 45

Kahn, Otto, 104–5

Kamp, Dr. Henry, 268, 271, 273–74, 275

Kay Kaiser Band, 206

Keating, Kenneth, 329

Keebler, Philip F., 10

Keiser, Neva, 434

Kennedy, Edward M. (Ted), 317, 430

Kennedy, Mrs. Jacqueline, 323

Kennedy, John F., 317, 322, 348, 349, 352, 377, 396, 429

Kennedy, Robert F., 430

Kent State University, 404

Kerama Retto Island, 203

Khrushchev, Nikita, 346

Kimball, Lindsley F., 45

King, Martin Luther, 341

King, W. L. Mackenzie, 22–23

King Ranch, 199, 252, 269, 271

Kinsey, Dr. Alfred C., 147–48

Kinsey Report, 147–48

Kissinger, Henry, 171, 172–73, 226, 258, 327, 358; Rockefeller cash gift to, 371

Kleberg, Robert, Jr., 269

Knapp, Seaman A., 91

Knickerbocker Club, 381

Knowles, James C., 412

Koch Institute, 86

Korean War, 181

Kunstler, William, 360

Kutz, Myer, 412

Kykuit, house at, 27–33, 39, 59, 100, 161, 166, 421; *see also* Pocantico Hills estate

Lachaise, Gaston, 334

La Guardia, Fiorello, 130, 131, 214

Laissez-faire capitalism, 68, 80

Lake Abby, 271, 279

Lakewood, New Jersey, 98

Lamps for the Light of Asia, 75

Landon, Alf, 348

Larsen, Leslie H., 256

LaScala, Frankie, 200

Lasker, Mary, 317

Laski, Harold, 130

Lasky, Victor, 371

Latin American Business Highlights (newsletter), 217

Laura Spelman Rockefeller Foundation, 93

Lawrence, Lovell, 184

Lazard Freres and Company, 251

League of Nations, 115, 225

Lee, Ivy, ix–x, 22

Lefkowitz, Louis, 329

Léger, Fernand, 333

Lehmbruck, Wilhelm, 334

L'Enfant Plaza (Washington, D.C.), 252–53, 255

Lenin, Nikolai, 121

Le Page helicopters, 181

Levi Strauss Building, 254

Levy, Lawrence, 11, 167

Leyte, Battle of, 202
Liberal Party (Canada), 22
Liberty Lobby, 411
Library and Museum of the Performing
Arts, 386–87
Lima oil field, 74
Lincoln, Abraham, 121
Lincoln Center for the Performing Arts,
420, 435; financing and building of,
386–92
Lincoln School, 56–58, 116, 124, 127,
183, 221
Lindquist, Warren, 232, 249, 250–51,
252, 256
Lindsay, John V., 355
Lloyd, Henry Demarest, 78–79, 80
Lockwood, John, 167, 427
Lodge, Henry Cabot, 353
Logue, Edward J., 342, 371
London School of Economics, 7, 130,
213, 214
Long Island Railroad, 340–41
Loomis School, 57, 112, 127, 128
Lopresto, Manny, 200
Lower Manhattan planning and
development project, 229–32, 249
Lubricating Committee (Standard Oil
Company), 76
Ludlow strike of 1913–14 (Colorado Fuel
and Iron Company), 21–23
Lufthansa (airline), 160
Lundberg, Ferdinand, 411
Lutz, Dr. Frank E., 55

MacArthur Park, 281
McCarthy, Eugene, 357
McCarthyism, 353, 392
McCloy, John J., 218, 219, 227, 228–29,
237, 239, 243
McClure's Magazine, 80
McCormick, Edith Rockefeller, 95
McDonnell, James S., Jr., 126–27,
180–81, 187
McDonnell Aircraft Corporation, 126,
180, 181, 187
McDonnell-Douglas Aircraft Corporation,
187, 314
McGovern, George, 368, 428
McGrath, Margaret, *see* Rockefeller, Mrs.
Margaret (Peggy)
McKellar, Kenneth D., 156
McKinsey & Company, 246
McManus, Bob, 352

Madison, James, 104
Madison, Ward, 99
Mahoney, Walter J., 326
Malone, Walter, 177
Managerial Task Force of Free
Enterprise, 239
Manet, Édouard, 225
Manufacturers Hanover Trust Company,
259
Manufactures Committee (Standard Oil
Company), 76
Marathon Oil Company, 411
Marcel Breuer (model modern home),
210
Margaret Sanger Birth Control Clinic
(New York), 114
Marine Corps School, 172
Marquardt Aircraft Company, 185
Marshall, George, 225
Marston, Randolph B., 181
Martin, Glenn, 276
Martin, Mary, 206
Marxism, 433
Massachusetts Institute of Technology
(MIT), 316; Abby Rockefeller Mauzé
professorship, 318
Matisse, Henri, 333
Matthews, "Red," 45
Mauna Kea Beach Hotel, 305–7, 311
Mauzé, Abby, *see* Rockefeller, Abby
"Babs"
Medicaid, 356
Medicare, 356
Megastates of America, The (Peirce),
338
Mellon family, 418
Memorial Hospital for Cancer and Allied
Diseases, 125, 189, 316, 317–18, 373
Memorial Sloan-Kettering Cancer Center,
297, 316–17, 425, 435
Merchants Fire Assurance Corporation,
10, 204
Merryday, Dr. Harry L., 99
Mesabi iron ore range, 19–20
Mesa Verde National Park, 102
Metropolitan Life Insurance Company,
106, 243, 412
Metropolitan Museum of Art, 121, 352
Metropolitan Opera Association, 387
Metropolitan Opera House (New York
City), 105, 386, 387, 388, 390, 391
Metropolitan Transportation Authority
(MTA), 341, 371

Mexico, scientific farming program in, 395, 396
Mexico City Conference (1944), 162–63
Middlebury College, 431
Midwest Refining Company, 24
Milbank, Tweed (law firm), 256
Milligan, Harold, 100
Milton, Abby (Mitzi), 110, 373, 429, 435
Milton, David, 49, 201
Milton, Mrs. David, *see* Rockefeller, Abby "Babs"
Milton, Ellen, 49
Milton, Marilyn, 110, 429, 435
Minnesota Mining and Manufacturing Company, 417
Miró, Joan, 224, 333
Mitchell, Benjamin, 269–70, 278
Mitchell, John, 338–39
Mobil Oil Corporation, 411
Monsanto Corporation, 417
Moore, Arch A., Jr., 430
Morgan, J. P., 19–20, 103, 410
Morgan Guaranty Trust Company, 228, 344
Morningside Gardens (houses), 222
Morningside Heights, Inc., 221–22
Morningside Heights middle income housing (New York City), 221–22, 249
Morton, Thruston B., 354
Moscoso, Teodoro, 303
Mountain Artisans (West Virginia), 430
Mount Desert Island, 44, 54, 58–59, 101–2, 118, 190, 222, 300, 366–67, 421, 423
Mount Holyoke College, 404
Mount Palomar, telescope at, 93
Mount Tom ski area, 310
Muckrakers, 78–79
Murphy, Dr. James S., 349–50
Murphy, Margaretta Fitler, *see* Rockefeller, Mrs. Margaretta (Happy)
Murphy, Starr J., 87
Museum of Modern Art, 11, 121, 150, 154, 210, 224, 256, 435
Museum of Natural History, 55
Museum of Primitive Art, 352
Muskie, Edmund, 329
Musselman, Frank, 256
Myers, Dean William I., 141

Nadelman, Elie, 334
National Academy of Sciences, 380, 381
National Astro Laboratories, 312

National Cancer Advisory Board, 317
National City Bank, 20, 218
National Commission on Water Quality, 366
National Committee on Mental Health, 114–15
National Council of the United Negro College Fund, 392
National Endowment for the Bicentennial Era, 405
National Environmental Act, 324
National Institute of Health, 317
National Park Service, 191, 193, 194, 302, 303
National Press Club, 323
National Security Council, 171, 368, 373
National Service Corps, 403–4
National Urban League, 205
Natural Resources Defense Council, 432
Nazi Party, 156, 157, 163
Neal, Mrs. Herbert, 55
Negroes, 153, 292, 392, 431; recruiting and hiring of, 241
Nevins, Allan, 19, 80, 409–10
Newark race riots, 341
New Deal, 161, 328
Newell, Frank, 201, 204–5, 211, 268, 269, 270, 274, 275, 280
Newell, Mrs. Jo-Anne, 268
New England Conservatory of Music, 433
New England Nuclear Corporation, 312
New Haven Railroad, 341
New Left, 241
New York Botanical Garden, 191
New York Chamber of Commerce, 107–8
New York City Airport Authority, 126
New York City Ballet, 333, 387
New York City Board of Education, 242
New York City Public Education Association, 269
New York City subway system, 340–41
New Yorker (magazine), 121
New York *Herald Tribune*, 206
New York Hospital, 189, 190, 297, 318, 425
New York Life Insurance Company, 412
New York-New Jersey Port Authority, 317
New York Philharmonic Orchestra, 266, 386, 387, 388, 390
New York *Post*, 330
New York Public Library, 388

New York State Housing Finance Agency, 341

New York State Motor Vehicles Department, 339

New York State Society for Medical Research, 269

New York State Theater, 386, 390

New York Stock Exchange, 6, 98, 105, 189, 230, 231

New York *Times*, x, 131, 218, 240, 260, 262, 351, 360, 399

New York University, 205, 269, 327

NYU-Bellevue Medical Center, 205, 269

New York *World*, 79

New York World's Fair, 390–91

New York Zoological Society, 191, 192

Niarchos, Stavros, 255–60

Nixon, Richard M., 52, 171, 174, 225, 263, 317, 324, 331–32, 337, 345, 346, 356, 357, 367, 371, 372, 400, 413; California gubernatorial campaign (1962), 348; election of 1972, 364; Fifth Avenue apartment meeting, 347–48; Rockefeller nomination of, 298, 359; tax troubles, 370; Watergate scandal, 339, 358, 364, 365, 366, 412, 415

Nobel brothers, 75

Noguchi, Dr. Hideyo, 87

Noguchi, Isamu, 232

Norris, Frank, 79

North Atlantic Treaty Organization (NATO), 164, 226

North Haven, Maine cottage, 139

Notestein, Frank W., 144, 381, 383

Nuclear Weapons and Foreign Policy (Kissinger), 226

Nusbaum, Jesse, 102

O'Brien, Donal, 298, 426

O'Connor, Frank, 355

Odalisque (Matisse), 333

Office of Population Research, 144

Office of the Coordinator of Commercial and Cultural Relations Between the American Republics, 156

Ogden, Robert C., 88

Ohio Oil Company, 411

Okeechobee *News*, 207

Okinawa, invasion of (World War II), 203

Olds, Irving, 388

Onassis, Aristotle, 384

O'Neill, Mrs. George, *see* Milton, Abby (Mitzi)

O'Neill, George Dorr, 429

Open doors of opportunity, theory of, 165

Operation Bootstrap (Puerto Rico), 303–4

Operations Coordinating Board, 171

Oppenheimer, J. Robert, 93–94

"Opportunity" (Malone), 177

Orleans Farms, 252

Osborn, Fairfield, 103, 191–92

Osborn, Frederick, 381

Osler, William, 86

Oswald, Russell G., 359, 360, 361, 362, 363, 364

Our Plundered Planet (Osborn), 191–92

Outdoor Recreation for America (Outdoor Recreation Resources Review Commission), 322

Outdoor Recreation Resources Review Commission (ORRRC), 321–23

Packard, Arthur W., 10, 141

Page, Walter Hines, 91–92

Paley, William S., 318

Palisades, the, 27, 103, 190, 192

Palisades Interstate Park Commission, 191

Palisades Park Commission, 192

Palm Springs Hospital, 298

Parke-Bernet art auctions, 265

Pasteur Institute, 86

Paternalism, 23

Patterson, Herbert P., 262

Patterson, Robert P., 129, 204

Paulekiute, Isabel, 207

Paulekiute, Jievute, *see* Rockefeller, Mrs. Barbara Sears (Bobo)

Paulekiute, Julius, 208

Paul VI, Pope, 398

Payne, Colonel, 73

Payne, Oliver H., 70

Peace Corps, 429, 431

Peirce, Neal R., 338

Peking (Peiping) Medical College, 114

Penn Central Railroad, 341

Pennsylvania oil rush of 1859, 65–66

Pennsylvania Railroad, 119

People's Institute for Foreign Relations (China), 264

Percy, Charles, 429

Percy, Sharon, *see* Rockefeller, Mrs. Sharon Percy

Perkins, Roswell (Rod), 327
Perón, Juan, 162
Perry County Health Clinic (Arkansas), 274
Petit Jean Mountain (Arkansas), 205, 211, 268, 269, 271, 272, 279, 282, 285, 295, 297, 426
Petit Jean River, 270
Philanthropy, x, 3, 8, 10, 14, 15, 16, 18, 20, 33, 83–98, 101, 109, 113, 114–15, 129, 139–51, 166, 168, 179, 181, 189–90, 205, 211–12, 226, 255, 258, 274, 285, 296, 319, 370, 379, 386–92, 405–6, 435; in education, 84–85, 88–92; Gates letter on, 90; in medicine, 86–88; Negro causes, 88–89; and tax loopholes, 406; *see also* names of institutions
Philharmonic Hall, 386, 390, 392
Piasecki, Frank, 181
Piasecki Helicopters Company, 181, 314
Picasso, Pablo, 333
Platt le Page Company, 181
Pocantico Hills, village of, 27
Pocantico Hills estate, 11, 18, 22, 26, 35, 37, 39–40, 44, 55, 56, 77, 79, 99, 100, 113, 119–20, 125, 165–66, 188, 190, 208, 210, 224, 257, 268, 269, 273, 274, 277, 300, 319, 333, 346, 350, 351, 353, 356, 368, 374, 376, 421–25, 427, 428; brothers' purchase of, 166; expense curtailing at, 33; Fountain Oceanis, 30; front terrace sculpture, 30; furnishings, 29, 30–31; grounds, 29, 31–32; Japanese house near, 334; location of, 4, 27; planning and construction of, 27–33; as a private enterprise, 38; size of, 4, 27; underground art gallery, 334, 352; victory gardens (World War I), 43, 49; view of New York from, 29, 31
Poland, American corporation investments in, 262–63
Pollock, Jackson, 334
Population Council, 381–85, 392, 397, 401, 406, 419; distribution of IUDs, 383–84; incorporated, 382; 1964 report, 382–83
Populism, 78, 80
Porter, Russell, 351
Portman, John, 253–54
Powers, Gary, 346
Prairie Oil and Gas Company, 24
Pratt, Charles, 70, 74

Prentice, Alta Rockefeller, 95
Presbyterian Hospital (New York City), 318
President's Advisory Committee on Governmental Organization, 170
Princeton University, 34, 50, 57, 112, 113, 116, 124, 144, 316, 381
Principles and Practice of Medicine (Osler), 86
Production Committee (Standard Oil Company), 76
Prohibition, 112, 124
Protestant Council of Churches, 402
Protestant Ethic, xi, 83, 177
Prudential Insurance Company of America, 254
Puerto Rico, 303–4, 310, 431
Pugliese, Tony, 200
Pulitzer, Joseph, 79
Pure Waters Program (1965), 343
Pusey, Nathan, 222

Quantico seminars, 327
Quesada, Elwood R. (Pete), 252, 253
Quinn, William E., 304–5, 361

Ramon Magasaysay Awards, 392
Random Reminiscences of Men and Events (Rockefeller), 27, 28, 29, 65, 67–68, 73, 83
Rasmussen, Anne-Marie, *see* Rockefeller, Mrs. Anne-Marie
RCA Building, 4, 8, 29, 62, 64, 105, 169, 230, 423; *see also* Rockefeller Center
Reaction Motors Company, 185–86
Reader's Digest, x
Reagan, Ronald, 357, 375, 376
Real Paper, The (newspaper), 432
Reconstruction Finance Corporation, 158
Redwood forests, 320
Reece Committee, 148
Reed, Joseph Verner, Jr., 246–47
Republican National Convention (1964), 353–54
Republican National Convention (1976), 376
Republican State Executive Committee (Arkansas), 287
Reynolds, George, 268, 274, 280
Rickenbacker, Capt. Eddie, 126, 178, 179, 180, 186, 187
Riesman, David, 150
Rivera, Diego, 121

Riverside Church, 28, 100, 106, 115, 209, 221, 435
Robber baronism, 71, 82, 402, 404
Rockefeller, Abby, 433
Rockefeller, Abby (Babs), 13, 110, 111, 129, 224, 315, 318, 407, 416–17, 427, 429; birth of, 33; childhood, 45, 49–50, 52, 53; death of, 425–26; divorced, 201–2; marriage of, 49, 109; philanthropic interests, 318–19; RBF meetings, 167; trust fund, 110, 111
Rockefeller, Mrs. Abby Aldrich, 8, 26, 29, 30, 33, 35–36, 37, 97, 102, 110, 118, 119, 139, 147, 148, 154, 165, 178, 201, 206, 214, 222, 409, 416–17, 421, 435; child rearing (role as a mother), 46–48, 50–51, 54, 55, 56; death of, 208–9; Red Cross bandage unit, 42; "tea time" with, 48; trust fund, 110, 167
Rockefeller, Alida, 401, 428–29
Rockefeller, Ann, 111, 435
Rockefeller, Mrs. Anne-Marie, 431
Rockefeller, Mrs. Barbara Sears (Bobo), 206–11, 277, 278, 297
Rockefeller, Mrs. Blanchette Hooker, 115
Rockefeller, David, 4, 12–15, 16, 42–43, 129–31, 137–38, 197, 209, 213–32, 235–66, 281, 293, 297, 298, 309, 350, 351, 386, 407–9, 410, 412, 416–17, 420, 421, 426; allowance (childhood), 40–42; art collection, 224–25, 248, 258; birth of, 33, 34; on capitalism, 239–40; Chase Bank and, 45, 55, 189, 213–20, 223, 225, 227–32, 235–49, 255–64, 344, 432; childhood of, 7, 34–45, 52, 53, 54–56, 59, 214; China trip, 263–64; and Council on Foreign Relations, 225–27; doctoral thesis, 213, 214; "edifice complex" of, 250; education of, 7, 55, 57–58, 109, 111–12, 124, 130, 213, 214, 223; entomology interests, 54–55, 130, 258; European business tour (1971–72), 262–63; identity crisis, 5; lower Manhattan planning and development project, 229–32, 249; Morningside Heights housing development, 221–22, 249; personality of, 216, 223; philanthropic interests, 226, 255, 258; philosophy of social responsibility, 239–43; Pocantico Hills and, 224, 257, 425; realty undertakings, 250–56; San Francisco Bay plan, 251–52; stock shares (Chase Bank),

243; trust fund, 110, 111, 249; venture capital investments, 315; Washington, D.C., project, 252–53; wealth of, 265–66; World War II, 131, 202, 213, 214, 225
Rockefeller, David, Jr., 432, 434
Rockefeller, Mrs. Deborah Sage, 295, 296–98, 298
Rockefeller, Mrs. Jeannette, 277–78, 281, 282, 284, 285, 286, 289, 292, 294, 297
Rockefeller, John D., ix, 3, 4, 5, 6, 16, 19–20, 31, 52, 59–86, 62–71, 107–8, 117, 118, 119, 125, 161, 208, 211, 316, 328, 369, 392, 408; birth of, 62, 435; childhood, 62; death of, 99–101, 107; early business ventures, 64–67; education of, 62–63; estimated wealth (1913), 82; first job, 63–64; fortune of, 410; Gates advice to, 90, 437; genius for finance, 68–69, 75–77; marriage of, 67; merger tactics, 69–70; muckrakers and, 78–79, 80; passion for golf, 38–39, 60–61, 98; penchant for efficiency, 69; philanthropy of, 83–98; Pocantico Hills estate, 27–33, 39–40, 77, 79; realty investments, 63, 75, 77, 98; resentment against, 71, 82; in retirement, 38–39, 50, 77–78, 79; single-mindedness of, 72–73; Standard Oil and, 67–86, 93, 97, 99, 101, 410, 416, 435; transfer of fortune to John, Jr., 95–97, 101
Rockefeller, John D., Jr., ix, xvii, 4–5, 8–11, 17, 18–33, 109–11, 118, 119, 125, 177, 193, 194, 197, 206, 243, 316, 330, 349, 353, 369, 392, 433; child rearing (role as a father), 34–45, 46, 51, 52, 56; conservation interests, 10, 44–45, 101–5; construction of Rockefeller Center, 7–8, 15, 105–7, 420; death of, 421, 422; dislike of dogs, 39–40; education of, 18; ethics of, 9, 25; formula of success, 9, 18, 40; "kinship of humanity," 24; labor-management relations, 23; Ludlow miners' strike and, 21–23; marriages of, 26, 421; Mesabi iron ore negotiations, 19–20; National City Bank resignation (1902), 20; 1924 tour of national parks, 102; office staff of, 9–11; personal credo, 132–34, 422; philanthropic interests, 3, 8, 10, 14, 15, 16, 18, 20, 33, 87, 88–89, 90, 92, 94, 101, 166, 181, 189, 211–12, 435;

Pocantico Hills estate, 27–33, 421, 425; proxy fight (1929), 25; religious beliefs, 35–36; responsibility as company director, 24–25; reward to children for not smoking, 49; sense of humility, 18; Standard Oil and, 18–19, 20–21, 37; stewardship (family), 99–108; tour of Colorado mines, 23; transfer of family fortune to, 95–97, 101; trust fund arrangements, 110–11, 167, 416; Tucson vacation, 208–9; U. S. Steel stock sale, 23; Washington industrial conference (1922), 23; will of, 14, 15–16, 421–22; "Wolf of Wall Street" fiasco, 94

Rockefeller, John D., III, 42–43, 102, 119, 124, 126, 128, 137–51, 197, 209, 297, 377–406, 407–9, 410, 416, 422, 425; allowance (childhood), 40–42; American youth revolution and, 401–5; art collection of, 334; Asian tour (1929), 113; audience with Pope Paul VI, 398; birth of, 33, 34, 49; childhood, 35–45, 49, 50, 52, 53, 59; demography project proposal, 143–47, 148; education of, 34, 50, 56, 57, 111–12, 113, 116; Europe and Asia trips (1946–47), 141–43; Family of Man Award (1968), 402–3; identity crisis, 5; involvement with Japanese culture, 148–51; letter to New York *Times* (1941), 131–32; Lincoln Center and, 386–92, 420; marriage of, 115; personal credo, 132; personality of, 5–6, 112; philanthropic interests, 109, 113, 114–15, 139–51, 212, 379, 386–92, 405–6; philosophy of, 139; Rockefeller Foundation and, 141–51, 391, 392–97; Rockefeller office of, 4, 12–14, 15, 16, 122, 137, 334; Standard Oil and, 113; style of life, 139; support of birth control, 114, 143, 377–85, 392, 397–401, 406; trustee duties, 113, 140; trust fund, 110, 111; venture capital investments, 315; wealth image, 138–39; World War II, 5, 131, 132, 137, 202, 385

Rockefeller, John D. (Jay), IV, 293, 403, 429–30, 432, 434
Rockefeller, Larry, 424, 431–32
Rockefeller, Laura, 428
Rockefeller, Laurance Spelman, 42–43, 102, 119, 123–27, 129, 130, 137–38, 153, 176–96, 207, 209, 247, 252, 266, 278, 297, 299–325, 353, 370–71, 407–9, 410, 416–17, 419, 421, 435–36; allowance (childhood), 40–42; aviation interests, 126–27, 178–81, 183, 186–87, 312; birth of, 33, 34; cancer research interests, 125, 189–90, 315–18, 319; Caribbean investments, 195–96, 299–304, 307–9; at Chase National, 189, 213; childhood, 34–45, 51, 52–53, 58, 61, 177; conservation interests, 125, 190–96, 302, 307, 310–11, 319–25; education of, 56–58, 111–12, 124–25; hotel projects, 299–311; identity crisis, 5; marriage of, 125; NYSE seat, 6, 126, 189; ORRRC chairmanship, 321–23; personal advisers, 181; philanthropic interests, 179, 189–90; philosophy of, 176–77, 178, 195; Pocantico Hills and, 125, 188, 190, 319, 425; Rockefeller Center office, 4, 12–14, 15, 16, 109, 187–88; shoeshining chore, 42, 51; style of life, 188; "three-legged-stool ownership" policy of, 186; trust fund, 110, 111, 181; venture capital interests, 179, 182–89, 196, 311, 312–14; Vermont project, 309–10; World War II, 176, 180, 191, 202, 315

Rockefeller, Mrs. Laura Spelman, 6, 20, 28, 29, 39, 52, 67, 83, 93, 101
Rockefeller, Lucy (dau. of Big Bill Rockefeller), 100
Rockefeller, Lucy (dau. of Laurance Rockefeller), 428
Rockefeller, Mrs. Margaret (Peggy), 131, 210, 224, 258, 259, 264
Rockefeller, Mrs. Margaretta (Happy), 349–50, 352–53, 356, 359, 367–68, 369, 373
Rockefeller, Mark Fitler, 356, 435
Rockefeller, Mrs. Martha Baird, 421, 422, 424
Rockefeller, Mary, 332, 350–51
Rockefeller, Mrs. Mary French, 125, 188, 309
Rockefeller, Mrs. Mary Todhunter Clark, 118–19, 120, 123, 332, 349, 350, 351
Rockefeller, Michael, 332, 349, 350–51, 352, 416
Rockefeller, Mrs. Nancy Anderson, 433
Rockefeller, Nelson Aldrich, 42–43, 44, 64, 100, 115–22, 123, 126, 129, 130, 137–38, 197, 207, 209, 213, 216, 247,

257, 265–66, 269, 278, 287, 297, 309,
326–76, 407–9, 412–18, 421, 430, 433;
as administrative assistant for
inter-American affairs, 155–56;
aggressiveness of, 6; allowance
(childhood), 40–42; art collection, 6,
120, 333–35, 369, 414; as Assistant
Secretary of State for American
Republic Affairs, 152, 156, 162–63,
164; Attica prison revolt, 359–64; birth
of, 33, 34; California primary (1964),
353, 413–14; campaign of 1964,
348–49, 353–54; cash gifts to
individuals, 371–72; childhood, 34–45,
49, 50–53, 54, 58, 59, 153, 174;
commitment to Latin America, 153–69,
338; as Coordinator for Inter-American
Affairs (IAA), 156–62, 169; Diego
Rivera fresco, 121; dislike of Nixon,
332; divorce of, 349, 352; education of,
56–58, 72–73, 111–12, 116–19, 124;
Eisenhower administration, 171–75;
election of 1958, 330–31; Fifth Avenue
meeting with Nixon, 347–48; Goldberg
book incident, 315, 370–71; as governor
of New York, 229, 315, 331–45, 350,
356, 358, 359–65; gubernatorial
campaigns, 280, 315, 326, 327, 328–30,
332, 354–56, 370–71, 422; identity
crisis, 5; Kissinger and, 172–73, 327,
358, 371; Logue loan, 342, 371;
marriages of, 123, 352–53; memo to
FDR, 154, 155–56; nomination of
Nixon, 298, 359; open-door policy, 122;
optimism of, 6; personal advisers, 327;
philanthropic interests, 168, 319, 370;
Pocantico Hills and, 30, 32, 119–20,
165–66, 333, 334, 346, 350, 351, 353,
356, 368, 374, 376, 422, 425, 428;
postwar era, 4, 6, 12–17, 164–75;
pragmatism of, 335, 358; presidential
ambitions, 153, 174, 298, 337–38,
345–59; Republican National
Convention (1964), 353–54;
Republican National Convention
(1976), 376; Rockefeller Center office,
4, 12–14, 15, 16–17, 109, 120–21, 153,
165; Roosevelt administration, 154,
155–56, 328, 329, 345; San Francisco
Conference, 163–64; Senate testimony,
369–72, 413, 414, 415; shoeshining
chore, 42, 51; as Special Assistant for
Foreign Affairs, 171–75; Standard Oil

and, 120; state convention
chairmanship, 327; tax returns
(1964–1973), 370, 413; trust fund,
110, 111, 122, 414; Venezuela trips,
122, 154; venture capital investments,
315; vice-presidency, 367–76, 412–13,
414; wealth of, 414–15, 418; World
War II, 152, 154, 158–59, 160, 202
Rockefeller, Nelson Aldrich, Jr., 353, 367,
435
Rockefeller, Richard Gilder, 224, 432–33
Rockefeller, Rodman, 110, 115, 169, 269,
351, 425, 430–31, 435
Rockefeller, Sandra Ferry, 428
Rockefeller, Mrs. Sharon Percy, 429, 430
Rockefeller, Steven, 328, 351, 425, 431,
432
Rockefeller, William, 64, 69, 73, 77, 79,
98
Rockefeller, William (Big Bill), 62, 64
Rockefeller, Winthrop, 4, 7, 12–13,
14–15, 16, 42–43, 100, 115, 130,
137–38, 197–212, 214, 253, 332,
407–9, 410, 416, 419–20, 421; AIDC
chairmanship, 275–77, 278–79, 280,
284, 288; allowance (childhood),
40–42; in Arkansas, 212, 267–97, 314;
birth of, 33, 34; childhood, 34–45, 50,
52–54, 55, 56, 58, 59, 60; Colonial
Williamsburg chairmanship, 212; death
of, 298, 426; divorces of, 210–11,
267–68, 277, 294; drinking problem,
282–83, 289–90; education of, 56–58,
109, 111–12, 127, 128, 198; elected
Republican National Committeeman
(1961), 286; election defeats, 288,
295–96; election of 1966, 289; identity
crisis, 5; marriages of, 207–8, 210;
mountain homestead, *see* Winrock
Farms; oil business, 197–200, 201, 205,
210; philanthropic interests, 129, 205,
212, 274, 285, 296; Pocantico Hills
and, 208, 210, 268, 269, 273, 274, 277;
political career, 280, 285–96; re-election
of 1968, 292; "soft touch" of, 128,
284; Texas oil apprenticeship, 128–29,
197, 198–200, 201, 211, 267, 271; trust
fund, 110, 111; voted Arkansas Man of
the Year, 276; World War II, 6–7,
129, 197, 198, 200–4
Rockefeller, Winthrop Paul (Winnie),
210, 211, 278, 284, 293, 294–98,
426–27

Rockefeller & Andrews, 67–69
Rockefeller Archive Center, 422
Rockefeller Brothers Fund (RBF), x,
  153, 166–67, 241, 266, 274, 302, 318,
  319, 385, 392, 421–22, 424, 434
Rockefeller Center, 4, 7–17, 28, 230, 253,
  340, 387, 414, 431, 435; board of
  directors, 15; Brothers' Meetings,
  13–14, 138; construction of, 7–8, 15,
  105–7, 231, 329, 420; Diego Rivera
  fresco, 121; management of, 424;
  ownership of, 4, 417–18; remodeling of
  (fifty-sixth floor), 15, 16; total building
  costs, 106
Rockefeller family: attacks and criticism
  of, 411–12; competitiveness, 12–13;
  conspiratorial theory and, 411–12;
  economy of 1970s and, 417–18; extent
  of wealth, 409–10, 416; new beginnings
  (post-World War II), 3–17; number of
  descendants, 416; power and wealth, 8,
  407–37; sense of perfectionism, 273;
  stock portfolio, 417; style of living, 4,
  427–28; TNEC data and, 411; type of
  power, 419–21
Rockefeller Family Archives, 64, 77, 423
Rockefeller Family Fund, 430, 434
Rockefeller Foundation, 10, 12, 22–23,
  45, 95, 101, 111, 113, 120, 141–51,
  377, 380, 384–85, 391, 392–97, 423;
  charter of, 5, 141; Division of Medical
  Sciences, 146, 147–48; endowment, 93;
  experimental school, 56; incorporated,
  92–93; Kinsey research, 147–48;
  medical research, 93; Mexican farm
  program, 395, 396; original concept of,
  147; Philippine program, 395; rejection
  of family planning, birth control and
  contraception programs, 143–47;
  reputation of, 393–94; Rusk program,
  395–96; stock owned by, 25; trustees of,
  393
Rockefeller Foundation, The (Fosdick),
  94
Rockefeller Institute for Medical Research
  (Rockefeller University), 15–16, 43,
  92, 95, 101, 113, 116, 189, 190, 220,
  223, 256, 258, 264, 349–50, 380,
  423–24, 425–26, 435; governing body
  of, 222; incorporated, 87; Nobel prizes,
  87–88
Rockefeller Memorial Chapel (University
  of Chicago), 85

Rockefeller Panel Reports, 327
Rockefeller Plaza (New York City), 4,
  139
Rockefeller Power (Kutz), 412
Rockefeller Sanitary Commission, 92, 93,
  95
Rogers, Ginger, 206
Rogers, Henry H., 70, 74, 77, 79
Rogers, Will, 59
Rogers, William, 225
Roman Catholic Church, 146, 378, 398,
  399
Romanoff, Mike, 207
Romney, George, 356–57
Ronan, Dr. William J., 327, 341, 342,
  352; Rockefeller cash gift to, 371–72
Roosevelt, Mrs. Eleanor, 150
Roosevelt, Franklin Delano, 131, 156,
  157, 158–59, 160, 161, 328, 329, 345,
  367; Rockefeller (Nelson) memo to,
  154, 155–56
Roosevelt, Theodore, 78, 82, 156, 193
Rosenberg, Anna, 204
Rothschild family, 75
Rovensky, Joseph, 155
Ruml, Beardsley, 155
Rusk, Dean, 93, 377, 393, 395–96

Sage, Deborah Cluett, *see* Rockefeller,
  Mrs. Deborah Sage
Sage, Louis Davidson, 295
St. Luke's Hospital, 221
Salomon, Richard, 256
San Francisco Bay Conservation and
  Development Commission, 251
San Francisco Board of Supervisors, 254
San Francisco Conference, 163–64
San Francisco Planning Board, 254
Sanger, Margaret, 114
Save-Our-Home Committee, 222
Save the Redwoods League, 103
Scales, Florence, 50–51
Schmidt, Benno C., 252, 317
Schweiker, Richard S., 375
Scientific Atlanta Company, 312
Seal Harbor, Maine, 31, 42, 43, 44, 54,
  56, 101–2, 333, 349, 356
Sears, Barbara, *see* Rockefeller, Mrs.
  Barbara Sears (Bobo)
Sears, Richard, Jr., 206–7
Second American Revolution, The
  (Rockefeller), 405
Security Pacific Bank Building, 254

Settler's New Home Association, 63
Seurat, Georges, 225
77th U. S. Division, 201, 202
Sexual Behavior in the Human Female
  (Kinsey), 148
Shenandoah National Park, 103
Sherman Antitrust Act of 1890, 33, 81
Shriver, Sargent, 429
Sierra Club, 251
Sihanouk, Prince Norodom, 399
Simenon, Georges, 234
Sims, Ginny, 206
Sinclair, H. F., 24
Sinclair, Upton, 79
Skidmore, Owings & Merrill, 229
Sloan, Alfred P., Jr., 189–90, 316, 317–18
Sloan-Kettering Institute for Cancer
  Research, 189–90, 317–18
Smathers, William, 157
Smith, Adam, 78, 80
Smith, Al, 329
Smith, Barney & Company, 180
Smith, Maj. Gen. Ralph S., 214–15
Smith, Sherrill, 215
Smith College, 404
Smyth, Henry, 93–94
Socialist Workers Party, 433
Social Security, 171
Society for the Family of Man, 402
Socony-Vacuum Oil Company, 109, 129,
  197–98, 200, 203, 205, 210
Spanish-Americans, recruiting and hiring
  of, 241
Spellman, Francis Cardinal, 146
Spelman, Laura Celestia, *see* Rockefeller,
  Mrs. Laura Spelman
Spelman Fund, 113
Sperry, Mr., 54
Spofford, Charles M., 387
Squibb Corporation, 243
Standard Oil Building, 8
Standard Oil Company, 3, 4, 10, 18–19,
  20–21, 23, 37, 60, 72–82, 109, 120,
  182, 372, 379, 389, 409; antitrust suit
  against, 92; capitalization (1870), 69;
  committees, 76; company growth,
  70–71, 74–78; "control" of, 74; crude
  petroleum costs (1861), 68;
  incorporation of, 69, 83; kerosene
  market, 75; Lima oil field, 74; move
  from Cleveland to New York, 75; New
  Jersey move, 81; overseas expansion,
  74–75; program of competition (1896),

79; railroad rebates to, 70–71;
  resentment against, 71, 78; resignation
  of John, Jr. (1910), 21; Rockefeller,
  Sr., and, 67–86, 93, 97, 99, 101, 410,
  416, 435; as Rockefeller & Andrews
  Company, 67–69; secret political
  contributions, 21; shares, 69, 82;
  Supreme Court on, 33, 81–82; vertical
  integration of, 68
Standard Oil Company of California,
  101, 274, 411, 415
Standard Oil Company of Indiana,
  24–25, 74, 82, 95, 243, 415
Standard Oil Company of New Jersey, *see*
  Exxon
Standard Oil Company of New York, 82
Standard refinery, 68
Stanford University, 401, 428–29, 430
Stassen, Harold, 173
State University building program (New
  York), 355
State University Construction Fund,
  338–39
Stavid Engineering of New Jersey, 185
Steffens, Lincoln, 79
Stettinius, Edward R., Jr., 162, 163, 345
Stewart, Col. Robert W., 24–25
Stewart, Walter W., 147
Stick, Frank, 302
Stiles, Dr. Charles Wardell, 91–92
Strauss, Lewis L., 381
Suharto, 399
Sukarno, 399

Taeuber, Dr. Irene, 144
Taft, William Howard, 92, 156
Taoism, 149
Tarbell, Ida, 80, 82
Task Force on Youth, 403
Teachers College, 56
Teapot Dome scandal, 24
Temporary National Economic
  Committee (TNEC), 411
Temporary State Commission on a
  Constitutional Convention, 327
Texas Christian University, 426
Texas Instruments Corporation, 417
Thant, U, 399
That Brotherhood May Prevail, 150
Thermokinetic Fibers Company, 312
305th Infantry Regiment, 201, 202
Tilden, Samuel J., 333
Tillich, Dr. Paul, 150

Titusville oil well, 65, 66
Tocqueville, Alexis de, 380
Tolstoy, Leo, 82, 136
Tower Building, 281, 289, 296
Treacher, Arthur, 200
Trilateral Commission, 265
Truman, Harry, 148, 152, 164, 204, 225
Tucker, George, 88–89
Tucson Medical Center, 421
Turnbull, Barton P., 10
Turner, Roy J., 281
Turner Ranch, 281
Twenty-fifth Amendment, 372, 413

Uht, Mrs. Carol, 334
Union of Soviet Socialist Republics
  (U.S.S.R.), 131, 163, 172, 173, 227,
  242, 263
Union Theological Seminary, 146, 221,
  431
United Hospital Fund, 269
United Mine Workers of America, 21, 22
United Nations, 152, 162, 163–64, 226,
  248, 315, 377, 384, 397, 399, 401, 402
United Nations Charter, 164
United Negro College Fund, 241
United Service Organizations (USO),
  133
U. S. Constitution, 405, 413
U. S. Defense Department, 170
U. S. Department of Commerce, 157
U. S. Department of Health, Education
  and Welfare, 170–71, 327
U. S. Department of State, 149, 152,
  157, 161, 162, 226
U. S. Department of the Interior, 322
U. S. Development Agency, 254
U. S. Office of Defense, Health and
  Welfare Service, 214
U. S. Postal Service, 253
U. S. Public Health Service, 91
U. S. Steel Corporation, 10, 19, 20, 21,
  23, 188
U. S. Supreme Court, 13, 33, 274, 315;
  on Standard Oil Company, 33, 81–82
University of Arkansas, 276, 282
University of California, 93
University of Chicago, 7, 130, 213, 214,
  220; founding of, 84–85
University of Massachusetts, 404
University of Notre Dame, 243
University of Southern California, 277
Unused Resources and Economic Waste

  (Rockefeller), 130, 214
Urban Coalition, 258
Urban Development Corporation
  (UDC), 342–43, 344, 356, 371
Urban League, 200
U-2 American spy plane, 173, 346

Vandenberg, Arthur, 164
Vanderbilt, Cornelius, 27
Vanderbilt, Mrs. Hudson, 207
Van Dusen, Henry, 146
Veblen, Thorstein, 72
Vectron Company, 312
Venezuela, 122, 154, 168, 269, 299, 333,
  368, 413, 418
Versailles Treaty, 148, 225
Vietnam War, 181, 226, 357, 358
Viking (liquid-fuel rocket), 184
Virgin Islands National Park, 303
Vivian Beaumont Theater, 386
Voltaire, 139
Volunteers in Service to America
  (VISTA), 403, 431

Waletzky, Dr. Jeremy Peter, 428
Walkowicz, T. F. (Ted), 181
Wallace, Henry A., 157, 367, 394–95
Wallace Aviation Company, 185
Wall Street Journal, 313
Wanamaker, John, 88
Warfield, Janet, 11
War Lords (organization), 360
Washington, George, 121
Washington and Lee University, 88
Wassing, Tene, 351
Watergate scandal, 339, 358, 364, 365,
  366, 412, 415
Watson, Gen. Edwin M. (Pa), 158
Watts race riots, 341
Wealth Against Commonwealth (Lloyd),
  78–79, 80
Webb and Knapp (real estate firm), 253
Welles, Sumner, 157
Wentworth, 27
Wentworth house, 26
Westbay Community Associates, 251
Wheeler, Monroe, 335
White, E. B., 121
White Citizens Council, 289
White House Conference on Natural
  Beauty (1965), 323
Whitman, Mrs. Ann, 359
Whitney, John Hay (Jock), 206

Whitney, Liz (Mary Elizabeth), 206
Whitney, William C., 27
Whitney & Company (J. H.), 252
Wicker, Tom, 360, 362
Wickersham, Gen. George, 92
Wien, Lawrence A., 391
Wilkerson, Eleanor, 215–16
Willkie, Wendell, 156
Wilson, Charles, 174
Wilson, Malcolm, 328–29, 338, 344, 365
Wilson, Woodrow, 23, 158–59, 225
Windsor, Duke and Duchess of, 207
Winrock Enterprises, 281, 284, 296
Winrock Farms (Arkansas), 269–74, 276, 278–82, 284–85, 286, 287, 290, 293, 294, 296, 297, 298, 426–27
"Wolf of Wall Street" fiasco, 94
Women's Army Auxiliary Corps (WACS), 170
Women's University (Japan), 150
Woodstock Inn (Vermont), 309–10
Woodward, Harper, 181, 186–87, 311, 314, 423
World Bank, 218, 246

World Business (magazine), 217
World Trade Center, 231
World War I, 42–43, 103, 126, 148, 156, 158–59, 179, 201
World War II, 5, 6–7, 23, 126, 132, 133, 137, 148, 152, 154, 158–59, 160, 176, 178, 180, 181, 191, 193, 202, 223–24, 315, 385
Worthley, Wallace, 42–43
Wriston, Walter B., 260

Xerox Corporation, 187, 417

Yale University, 109, 127, 128, 198, 199, 202, 211, 429
Yalta Conference, 163
Yarborough, Ralph, 317
Yellowstone National Park, 102, 191, 194
YMCA, 112, 128
Yordi, John, 99–100
Yosemite National Park, 103, 191
YWCA, 47, 116

Zeckendorf, William, 253